THIRD EDITION

ORGANIZATIONAL REALITY

REPORTS FROM THE FIRING LINE

PETER J. FROST
University of British Columbia

VANCE F. MITCHELL
University of British Columbia

WALTER R. NORD
Washington University

SCOTT, FORESMAN AND COMPANY   GLENVIEW, ILLINOIS   LONDON

To Nola, Fran, and Ann

Library of Congress Cataloging-in-Publication Data
Main entry under title:

Organizational Reality

   1. Organizational behavior—Addresses, essays, lectures. I. Frost, Peter J.
II. Mitchell, Vance F. III. Nord, Walter R.
HD58.7.074 1986   650   85-14570
ISBN 0-673-16663-5

PREFACE

The enthusiasm with which the previous editions of this book have been greeted by colleagues, students, and practicing managers far exceeded our initial expectations. The contrast between organizational life as presented in academic texts and the "reality" that emerges from the essentially non-academic literature from which so many of our selections are drawn has provided a rich and flexible basis for teaching. The regularity with which students read well beyond assigned material and draw on their additional reading for class discussions attests to their reception of the book. Practitioners have also responded enthusiastically; managers frequently tell us that many of the readings describe "their" organization.

Nearly 60 percent of the selections in this edition are new. Although a number of favorites (yours and ours) remain, the third edition is substantially different from the first. In a number of instances, the selections we dropped were dated and have been replaced by more contemporary material. Other substitutions seemed to us more representative of the organizational reality we seek to present. As in the second edition, we have included a number of news clippings to augment and to illustrate some of the larger selections. While these clippings are listed in the Table of Contents to make them easier to locate, they are not always commented on in the Introduction to the sections in which they appear.

The stimulation and enjoyment we have experienced from discovering and selecting the contents are as great as before. In some ways the task is more difficult because of the increasing attention that "real life" in organizations has received in the mainstream literature in our field and the popular management literature more generally. There is simply more to read and to choose from today than there was ten years ago when we compiled the first edition. On the other hand, the task is less difficult because this increased interest makes it easier to find good selections on topics that had been previously ignored. For example, when we did the first edition, it was very difficult to find selections relevant to secretaries. While secretaries are still given less attention in the organization literature than their numbers, power, and dilemmas warrant, there is considerably more written on them today than a decade ago.

Finally, the book is a product of the efforts of many people. Once again, our contributions have been distributed equally throughout the book, and the ordering of names on the title page is simply a carry-over of the random selection procedures followed in preparing the first edition. Of course, no book is solely attributable to those whose names appear on the title page, and this book is no exception. Thea Vakil did a great deal to make this revision possible by identifying and obtaining the numerous and often obscure permissions to reprint that were required. We also thank Merle Ace, David Cawood, Diana Cawood, Jill Graham, Bob Berra, Howard Blaustein, Linda Krefting, Kerstin Sonnerup, Elizabeth Doherty, Linda McDougal, and David McPhillips for material they sent our way that, in one form or another, found its way into this edition. We owe a debt of gratitude to the many university and professional students in our courses whose reaction to the first and second editions guided this revision and served as a prod to our endeavor. We also thank the many astute and articulate students of organization whose reports comprise this book.

Jim Sitlington and John Nolan, our editors, have been a continuing source of support and encouragement. Finally, our deep thanks to Ginny Guerrant, Project Editor, and Guy Huff, Permissions Coordinator, who shepherded this book through with grace, good humor, and skill.

Peter J. Frost

Vance F. Mitchell

Walter R. Nord

CONTENTS

INTRODUCTION

The introduction to the first edition of *Organizational Reality* began with the following four paragraphs.

"Suppose that you are a visitor to Earth from the distant planet Utopia. One of your assignments is to bring back printed materials to Utopian scholars who are attempting to understand what Earthlings call formal organizations. You have limited space so you must choose very carefully. One option you have is to bring back one or two of the leading textbooks on organizational behavior. Another option you have is to bring back selections from newspapers, business and general periodicals, and short stories and plays about life in organizations. Which would you choose to bring back?

"The picture that the Utopian scholars will develop from each of these sets of materials will most likely be very different. If you were to choose the textbooks, the scholars would most likely come to understand organizations as systems which are managed in a rational manner in pursuit of certain stated goals. They would be more than likely to conclude that organizations are staffed by people who are committed to achieve these objectives. Also, it is probable that the scholars would come to believe members of organizations are oriented towards cooperation and are sincerely concerned with each other's well being. Depending on the particular textbook you brought back, however, the scholars might conclude that organizations do not in fact operate in these ways, but that through the application of a certain set of procedures, techniques, philosophies, and so on, any organization which is not operating both rationally and cooperatively could be made to do so.

"By contrast, if you happened to take this book or some other collection of materials from periodicals, newspapers and other sources which have been less completely filtered by the academic mind, the picture of organizations the scholars derived would be quite different. They would be likely to decide that organizations are anything but rational, cooperative systems. They would conclude that members at all levels of the organization frequently pursue their own interests at the expense of others in the organization as well as at the expense of the achievement of the goals of a total organization. The scholars would see that organizations are frequently quite inhumane systems. Individuals experience intense stress from task demands as well as intense and often bitter conflict and rivalry with members of their own work group and with members of other work groups and organizations. One would also find that organizational participants often respond aggressively against these pressures and against whatever threatens their own interests. Furthermore, it is unlikely that the scholars would conclude that there is any discernible set of principles, techniques, and philosophies which seems capable of turning most organizations into rational, cooperative systems. It is more likely that they would discover that various strategies of power, manipulation, human relations and 'all out war' are used, all having varying degrees of success in giving different organizational participants different degrees of influence in organizations.

"Most students in organizational behavior, introductory business and even management policy courses are exposed only to the first set of sources. In this book, we plan to provide a ready collection of the second set. We do not offer this collection as evidence that the normative views presented in most academic textbooks are totally irrelevant. In fact, we believe that the normative views are very relevant. However, it is ineffective to present them to students without complementary information about how organizations are experienced. Students readily discover that organizations as described in the textbooks are not the same as organizations they actually experience. Consequently, students and managers reject the 'whole package' of organizational behavior as 'soft,' theoretical or irrelevant without examining the potentially relevant materials. Many students take their courses in management and organizational behavior because they are required, but turn to accounting, finance, economics, information systems, and even marketing when they seek to discover what organizations really are. Other students accept the text material while in school, but never find ways to translate it into action when they become managers."

These ideas provide a suitable introduction for this edition as well, since there appear to have been few changes either in the nature of organizations or in the description of organizations by academics. While a few anthologies similar to *Organizational Reality* have been published and more traditional anthologies on organizational behavior have begun to include a very few selections from non-traditional academic sources, for the most part textbooks in organizational behavior still fail to provide adequate descriptions of organizations as they are experienced by people. There have, however, been some changes in the general management literature. There are more systematic efforts to see the world from nonmanagerial perspectives. Still, these efforts are at most attachments to conventional treatments rather than integral parts of them.

Although the major thrust of this book remains the same, there are several reasons for publishing a revision at this time. First, many aspects of organizations are closely tied to current events; any book that attempts to deal with organizations as they are experienced will become dated very quickly. The dating does not seem to be due to the fact that old problems have disappeared but rather to either the appearance of new problems or the fact that old problems get discussed in somewhat different terms. The second, and most important, reason for this revision is that we continue to discover exciting new and insightful material. Moreover, we have become aware of several topics and a few excellent pieces that we wish we had included in the first two editions. Third, we feel that a bit more attention to some of the positive aspects of the reality of organizational life is useful for stimulating a fuller discussion of the issues. While these positive aspects are well represented in conventional texts, they often appear in abstract form. By including some of these ideas in a form that parallels the rest of the material in the book—i.e., more "in the words of the participants themselves"—we hope greater appreciation for the complexity of life in organizations can be derived from this edition. In short, our goal of providing a collection of materials that will introduce students to organizations as they are experienced has not changed. We do feel, however, that the updated edition provides a more stimulating, comprehensive collection for today's students.

Even though our basic purpose and approach remain the same, reactions of colleagues, students, and other readers to the first edition have influenced our current positions in several ways. First, the number and intensity of the positive reactions we have received have strengthened our belief in the value of the perspective portrayed in this book. While we were not surprised by the favorable reactions of students, we have been particularly impressed by the fact that many of the most positive reactions have come from experienced managers, who have reported seeing their organizations in a different and more informed way. In fact we are even more confident in what we are doing than we were before. Recently, one of our friends—a Jungian therapist—said, "What you have done is to portray the 'shadow side' of organizations." In Jungian terms the shadow is the part of one's personality that is so threatening that it is held out of normal awareness. This comment and our growing affinity for the work of scholars such as Ian Mitroff have given us "better words" to describe what we were attempting to do initially. With these "better words" came more self-awareness and feelings of legitimacy that have given us increased confidence in our approach. We are exploring the shadow side of organizations, and there is good reason to believe that such exploration is necessary to understand the whole.

Second, we are still cognizant of the somewhat arbitrary nature of our organization of the materials under the section headings we employ. This point was made quite well in Dr. Todd Jick's review of the first edition in the *Administrative Science Quarterly*, March 1979. He observed that many of the presentations in the book are really holistic by themselves. Consequently, they

" . . . do not subdivide into neat conceptual categories as textbooks and myopic journal articles would imply. Thus, it becomes an ill-fated effort to impose groupings among relatively holistic presentations." (p. 159)

Jick's criticism is a sound one. Many of the selections are rich; almost every one deals with at least several important issues. While we admit there is a certain arbitrariness in our grouping of the materials, we remain convinced that our message can be best communicated to students if the readings are organized in a framework that helps them to contrast these ideas with the ones they study in traditional textbooks and journals. The difficulty in organizing these materials that capture "holistic" experiences under either conventional headings or unconventional ones indicates how complex life in organizations is in comparison with our ability to talk about it.

One further change has taken place—in us. Our view of organizations is quite different from the one that resulted from our academic training. While we still feel that traditional academic approaches are worthwhile, we now see them merely as one set of perspectives on the reality of the social processes we call organizations that needs to be complemented by other perspectives.

We do not propose that this collection captures the "true" essence of organizations. We do suggest, however, that current management and organizational textbooks do not capture this essence either. Moreover, it may seem that the current collection provides a very distorted, biased picture of organizations. Undoubtedly there is some bias; we did not use a random selection procedure to determine which articles would be included. However, we did not systematically seek out muckrakers. We were amazed at how many articles we could find that make points very similar to almost all the ones we have included. Therefore, we remain convinced that the contents of the book give an accurate picture of many aspects of what people perceive to be the reality of organizations. Still, our own tastes and values are embodied in our selections in ways that we are unable to make fully explicit even to ourselves.

We ask the reader to pay careful attention to the sources of the articles included in this collection. Many of the selections come from what are normally considered mainstream business publications such as *Fortune*, the *Harvard Business Review*, and *The Wall Street Journal*. Other selections come from fictional works, academic texts and journals, publications of organized labor, and several best-selling books. Still, a number of selections were written by critics of organizations and individuals who are discontent with many elements of modern life. We believe these selections, taken together, provide a useful picture of a number of aspects of modern organizations.

Of course, the reader must ultimately determine how realistic the picture is. Unlike the interplanetary scholars, most readers of this book will have a number of alternative sources of information about organizations as they exist on the earth. In addition to academic textbooks, they will have access to personal experiences and to the reactions of others who, willingly or not, have the quality of their lives thoroughly affected by modern organizations.

1

STAFFING

Strip away the social properties and you are left with a primitive, ritualized confrontation, one which involves the mutual manipulation of firmly held self-interests.

—Landau and Bailey

During every working day, an intense struggle goes on in organizational settings. The focus of this struggle is the staffing decision—who gets into, moves in, and moves out of the organization. On one side is the organizational representative, typically a manager or administrator; on the other side is the individual, the job applicant or the candidate for promotion, transfer, or firing. The manager has at his or her disposal a wide range of tools, techniques, tactics, and devices, many of which have been revised and refined by behavioral scientists, and an insider's view of what the organization wants and intends from the staffing decision. These weapons provide the basis for the manager to probe and pry, to try to penetrate the protective armor of the individual on the other side of the decision equation. The weapons serve also to provide managers, if they wish, with protective cover so that they do not have to reveal a position unless by choice. A manager's tools include physical and psychological tests; tactics take the form of the panel interview, the business lunch, the appraisal interview, and the deep-end treatment. Devices managers use are the private secretary, as a buffer against intrusion, and the classification schemes themselves, which by defining people, jobs, roles, positions, and so forth, symbolize and shape what is within the organization's perspective and what is excluded.

The individual who wishes to gain entry to the organization, be promoted, move within, resign, or contest removal from the organization likewise has tools, techniques, tactics, and devices at his or her disposal. However, this protagonist in the struggle is not well served by behavioral scientists in any systematic sense. The applicants or contenders must make it on their own, drawing on personal resources, experience, a good deal of intuition, political savvy, and a smattering of survival or "how to" manuals written in the popular press. The objective for these individuals is to assess what the organization has to offer or has in store for them, while at the same time putting their best foot forward and protecting their self-esteem and self-interest.

We chose the articles in this section to display this battle and to point up and to dramatize certain features of the encounter. Taken as a whole, the articles provide an interesting spectrum of staffing issues. Getting past the receptionist to see the person who makes staffing decisions is a skill which Geoffrey Lalonde suggests requires firmness, a smile, and a certain amount of subterfuge. He recognizes the political nature of the struggle and identifies the role the receptionist plays in the process. In "What Every Woman Should Know," Landau and Bailey also recognize the politics of the staffing process. They identify several strategies imbedded in the selection interview at middle and senior levels of organizations and suggest ways to recognize and deal with these strategies. They note that the selection interview contains some traps to which women as job applicants are especially vulnerable.

Employers usually have quite definite ideas concerning just what type of new employee they wish to acquire. The selection "Building a Team" describes how the individuals charged with the design of a new computer reached their decision concerning just what type of employee they wished to hire. The recruiting practices that were followed, the interview tactics that were used to probe an applicant's motivation, and the reasons successful applicants responded to the challenge inherent in the job for which they were being considered are very typical of those practiced in the burgeoning high-tech industries.

Once hired, failure to accurately assess the situation with which the new employee is confronted can damage the individual, as Sally Quinn found to her cost in her brief career with CBS in "We're Going to Make You a Star." In this case the struggle took on Kafkaesque proportions as neither side appeared to know which reality they were inhabiting. The emotional, psychological, and physical costs to individuals and, at times, the financial and effectiveness costs to organizations seem high when the staffing decision is either too loose or too programmed and depersonalized.

The final selection in this section, "The Tricky Task of Picking an Heir Apparent" acquaints us with the variety of techniques that are used by giant corporations in picking a new chief executive. It is interesting to note that the processes by which the selection decision is made at this level are far more varied than those employed for lower level managerial positions. Indeed, the personalities of the present incumbent and members of the board seem to be the primary determinants of how and whom will be selected. The imperfections of this selection process are underscored by the number of instances in which newly selected chief executives are "tried in the balance and found wanting."

Getting Past the Receptionist on the Phone or in Person

Geoffrey Lalonde

WHAT SEEMS DIFFICULT IS REALLY VERY EASY

Now we are going to show you how to get past a secretary/receptionist or administrative assistant in order to get right through to the boss.

The job of the receptionist or assistant is to screen everyone wanting to see the boss (ensuring that the boss's time is not wasted), and direct traffic to the right people.

You, as the job hunter, must get past the receptionist to see the boss. You don't want to be interviewed by the receptionist.

WHAT TO SAY

The most important thing to remember when you go into the room and see that receptionist is *smile* and *keep smiling*. (Refer to "Telephone Technique" for smiling!)

Remember, the job of the receptionist is to direct you to somebody else. Your job is to get to see the man who will help you with your career. Be convinced of the special contribution you can make to the organization. Make sure you are always in command of the situation. Be polite, but firm. Don't take no for an answer. Smile and move foward, assuming, as a matter of course, that you're going to get in.

Stand quite close to the reception desk. When a person stands a distance from the desk, it conveys an automatic subconscious impression that you do not think your business is really important enough to see the boss and that there really isn't much of a chance you will get in anyway.

So stand quite close to the reception desk, *smile,* and say:

"Good morning, may I see Mr. Jones (President, Manager, Executive)?"

When you say this, you're going to get a reply from her, such as:

"Do you have an appointment?" or "I'm sorry, he's busy." or "Why do you want to see him?" or "I'm sorry, you have to have an appointment." or "Mr. Jones always insists on knowing the nature of the business before seeing anyone." or "I'm sorry, he's busy this week."

Your response is:

"No, I don't have an appointment." or "It's personal. May I see Mr. Jones now?" or "It's personal. Could you tell him Geoffrey Lalonde is here to see him?" or "It's a personal matter. Could you tell him Geoffrey Lalonde is here to see him?"

The receptionist must make sure her boss doesn't spend time with a visitor she judges would be a waste of time. She may feel it would not be in his interest because it might be more appropriate for you to see another person. In each of the preceding questions the receptionist is doing the job that she is paid to do. You are likely to be a complete stranger to her. Part of the receptionist's training is to determine what your business is (what you want) and then send you to the appropriate person.

Don't be nervous if the receptionist questions you. *But don't tell her the purpose of your visit.* As soon as you tell her, she will be on the offensive and will fall back on her training. She'll send you to the Personnel Department—and you're dead!

Under no circumstances should you let the receptionist know what you want to talk to her boss about.

What will happen next? She may let you in by first calling her boss and getting a clearance. Then you're in.

She may not let you in and may give you a standard stall, "I'll have him/her call you." Your reply: "Thank you, I'd be happy to have him call, but could I make an appointment now? Could I see Mr. Jones at 3:00 P.M. this afternoon, or would 9:00 A.M. tomorrow morning be more convenient?"

Remember, she can only go so far. As long as you don't spill the beans and tell her the nature of your business, she will eventually have to pass you through to her boss.

The good secretary or receptionist has usually developed a considerable number of sneaky replies designed to trap you into stating your business.

She may come back with a legitimate response: "I'm sorry, Mr. Jones is busy. Would you care to see his assistant?"

Your come-back: "No, thank you. It's a personal matter. Would you tell him Geoffrey Lalonde was in to see him. I'll call him. When would be a good time? This afternoon at 2:00 P.M., or would 3:00 P.M. be more convenient?"

She may say, "I'm sorry, he's away in Nova Scotia until the end of the week."

Your come-back: "When would it be possible to set up a short meeting with him for ten minutes? Could I see him next Monday at 10:00 A.M., or would 11:00 A.M. be more convenient?"

She may say, "Sure. 10 o'clock. Could I tell him what it's about?"

Don't fall into the trap! This is a subtle trap to get you to tell her your business.

Simply reply: "Could you tell him it's a personal matter?" Then thank her and leave.

Remember, she is only doing the specialized screening job she was trained for. If she is unable to get the answer she wants from you, she has no alternative but to pass you on to her boss. That is exactly what you want.

Again remember, simply reply: "Could you tell him it's a personal matter?" Then thank her and leave.

HOW COMPLETE STRANGERS GOT IN TO SEE THE MINISTER

In the three years I worked for C. M. Drury in Ottawa there were many strangers who got in to see him in spite of a large staff of assistants, executive secretaries, secretaries, and receptionists. These people called on the phone, or came in person without appointments. These people did not know him personally.

In our office on Parliament Hill, besides myself, there were two executive secretaries and the Minister's personal secretary. Among our many responsibilities was running interference on total strangers demanding to see the Minister. We were very successful in the vast majority of cases, giving prompt attention to the public by handling their problems personally, or referring them to other members of the staff of twenty-two, or to department officials. But regularly, week after week, strangers would get through us. How? By using the technique I have just outlined.

For example, a person would come in and ask to see the Minister. S/He would invariably run into the polite but formidable Edith Cornblatt, the Minister's personal secretary. If Edith didn't get to the bottom of the problem and was having trouble she would call me to help her or the visitor.

I would swing into high gear with "May I help you?" but, provided the visitor did not reveal his/her reason for wanting to see the Minister personally, there was absolutely nothing to be done but arrange an appointment.

Now, to put your mind at rest, let me tell you there were many other things which the visitor had in his/her favor. First of all, Edith might have felt the Minister could do with some public contact on that particular day. Second, sometimes Mr. Drury had a few free minutes because a meeting had finished early and would come through the door, speak to the visitor, ask if he could be of assistance, and invite the visitor in. Often the Minister would criticize our inability to spot a crank after a particularly onerous meeting—but still, week after week, we had to let through those who stuck to "It's personal."

What Every Woman Should Know

Here's how to cope with those tricky executive-level job interviews

Suzanne Landau and Geoffrey Bailey

Top job interviews are not often friendly. Neither are top-job interviewers, though they may appear to be on the surface. In fact, the higher up the business hierarchy you climb, the less likely you are to be interviewed (in the traditional sense of the word). You will engage in apparently genial and composed discussions whose outer informality disguises a scrupulous exercise in personal assessment. Strip away the social proprieties and you are left with a primitive, ritualized tribal confrontation, one which involved the mutual manipulation of firmly held self-interests. Be coldly realistic about this. Most men are. Keep in mind that the kind of person you have to persuade to hire you is a wily corporate pro. Competence will impress him, but not that much more than worldliness, self-assurance, and realism.

Think tough. At least during the last day or two before you start attending serious meetings. Have someone whose cynicism and business acumen you trust (you may even decide to use your genial neighborhood headhunter) go over your résumé and fire some hard questions at you. Get that person to play fast and loose with your accomplishments: attacking, probing, putting down. Keep in mind that somewhere out there, laying in wait for you, is a grizzled old pro who will rip your claims about yourself to shreds. Defend yourself against that possibility ahead of time, with a few dry runs.

Be prepared to:

- identify and discuss in detail the kinds of projects you worked on and what the precise consequences of your involvement were;
- justify your employment history, especially in terms of moving from one job to another, with carefully propounded reasons;
- express your career goals convincingly, preferably on the basis of a three-to-five-year timetable;

From the book *The Landau Strategy: How Working Women Win Top Jobs.* Published by Lester & Orpen Dennys Limited. Reproduced by permission.

- rebut impertinent (and illegal) questions about marriage plans, intention to procreate, and domestic arrangements while you work.

Questions along these lines represent an unnecessary intrusion into your private life and are irrelevant to your professional preoccupations. Say so.

Try to develop early insights about the person scheduled to interview you. Does your prospect receive you promptly? Lack of punctuality suggests one of four things: exceptional business (a good sign); a power-play mentality (a bad sign—power plays are for corporate infighting, not interviewing newcomers); disorganization or carelessness; or, finally, downright insecurity (disastrous). Observe the manner in which you are received: in person, or through a secretary. It's a surefire sign of a loser if an interviewer with an unprepossessing office feels the need to send a secretary out to fetch callers.

Bear in mind that an interview starts the moment your arrival is announced, not later when you cross the threshold of your prospect's office. It's astonishing (and more than a little frightening) to consider what some high-ranking people perceive as being significant personality indicators. One headhunter we interviewed talked at length about the pre-interview ploys he used to make early candidate assessments: the magazines people picked up (as an indication of their intellectual pro-clivities) and the chairs they chose.

Once inside your prospect's office, choose your seat carefully. Look for the second most powerful place to settle in (unless, of course, your choice is made for you) and slip into it gracefully.

Let your prospect lead. Especially during those vital early intuitive seconds of the meeting. Imagine that your prospect is a rather successful, professionally accomplished maiden aunt who, out of a distant interest in your personal development, has invited you for tea at her apartment. Behave towards your prospect as your aunt would almost certainly expect you to behave towards her: with a discreet mixture of controlled warmth and respect.

Pleasantries dealt with, go, urbanely, with the flow. That first transition, from the conversational to the professional, tells all. The range and variation of interview procedures women encounter are more complex and demanding than those met by men. Beyond having to deal with routine questions about background and technical ability, female candidates for particular job opportunities are frequently subjected to mild forms of harassment. Our research (and considerable personal experience) suggests that, broadly speaking, there are seven different kinds of interview, ranging from the routine fact-finding exercise right along to the business lunch. At least two of the interview formats we have isolated ("Big Daddy" and "Just a Gigolo") are, in our view, unique to women. The remainder are common to both sexes:

1. Down the line
2. Trick or treat
3. Big daddy
4. Just a gigolo
5. Menage à trois
6. Out to lunch
7. Only Cartesians need apply

Down the Line

The straightforward informational kind of interview, one that seemingly amounts to little more than a routine checking of your personal and professional background, is frequently misunderstood by women. Naively, they tend to believe that apparently honest, dispassionate-sounding questions deserve equally honest, dispassionate-sounding responses. But the politics of the recruitment process suggest that this kind of interview has to be treated not as an exercise in epistemology, but rather as an opportunity for some subtle showing-off.

"The secret with these routine interviews is to regard them as personality tests. Don't get bogged down with too much detail. Tell the interviewer accurately and snappily what he wants to hear—about yourself, your background, why you're interested in the job. Keep the delivery upbeat and fresh. The fact is that summarizing personal and career details in an interview is the easiest thing in the world to do. Okay. So recognize that. And put everything you've got into verbal presentation. But don't be cute."

Nancy Mayer knows what she's talking about. She works in the personnel department of a major Fifth Ave. retailer, interviewing hundreds of people a year in her job. She talks to women applying not only for secretarial and sales jobs but also for more senior positions in sales and general management. Many of her interviews are of the routine, fact-finding kind—exploring the when, what, and where of an employment history, prior to a candidate going forward to more detailed discussions with line managers.

"Very occasionally," Mayer told us, "I get to meet a young woman who turns me on during one of these exercises. Those that do turn me on—and remember I can do these interviews in my sleep—tend to have three characteristics in common. First, they're not afraid to be direct and warm. They look me in the eye and, believe it or not, they smile. Second, they're prepared to be humorous in the right places. I ask a routine question, they recognize it for what it is and respond with a sense of irony and fun about the thing. That's fine. It means they're alive, thinking. We don't hire people who appear to have just been lobotomized. Third, and this is very important, they take the trouble to give the impression that their job moves follow some kind of logic, that there's some kind of rhyme and reason to what they want to do. I can't stand it when women come to me and say, 'Gee, I just think it'll be a gas working here.' And some do say that, you know."

Think of the "Down the Line" interview as an opportunity to define and determine, quite apart from your basic occupational resources, a group of selling propositions about your character and personality that make you different from the competition. Since in the basic recruitment scheme of things women are still regarded as number twos, they have but one alternative: to try harder.

Trick or Treat

The principal difference between the "Down the Line" and the "Trick or Treat" interview is one of psychological and intellectual intensity. The former is, in principle anyway, "coastable." The latter is all sudden inclines, blind curves, and unexpected changes of pace. You are, at "Trick or Treat" time, on trial. The interviewer, though pleasant on the surface, will probe your background and experience with great resolution and incisiveness. If there is a chink in your armor he will pierce it and unless you maintain an impeccable facade, coolly watch you bleed.

During the "Trick or Treat" interview, your interviewer is quite likely to pick up on what you consider to be your finest and most clear-cut achievement, and belittle it. You may have been responsible for a $150,000 export deal or involved with a pivotal company economy or acquisition. No matter. "Trick or Treat" interviewers are more interested in personal or professional analysis than in any particular sense of self-worth their prey might have.

Your résumé is a thesis whose contents you are under an obligation to defend. The quality of your defense will determine, in the eyes of your questioner, the value of your professional achievements.

One woman we spoke to told us how the size of the budgets she was responsible for managing while working for a Canadian company operating out of Vancouver were ridiculed by a man interviewing her for a job in Los Angeles. Her response was cut and dried. She said, rightfully, that since markets in Canada were 10 times smaller than those in the United States, an intellectually honest appraisal of her performance by him would mean that every financial statement made in her résumé ought to be multiplied ten-fold.

Big Daddy

Big Daddy comes in two varieties: the paternalist and the soothsayer. Of interview encounters between the two, the latter is likely to be the most promising, for the soothsayer at least is capable of understanding you and your ambition on the only terms that count, those you have set for yourself. The paternalist sees you as an attractive stereotype, a fascinating version of the daughter he either has or has always wanted.

Much has been made of the role that certain kinds of sympathetic older men can play in the careers of young, ambitious women. The soothsayer (or rabbi, as he is sometimes referred to), identifiable by his honest enthusiasm for the energetic and intelligent efforts that you are evidently making to find yourself a job, is an interviewer whom it is least necessary for you to make a contrived effort to impress.

One woman we spoke to, working for a federal agency in Washington involved with developing financial aid programs for the Third World, observed that the secret with the soothsayer interview is that there is no secret. "Frankness and clarity of career intentions are what work in this kind of interview," she said. "Games, ploys, and stratagems are inappropriate. Just tell him what you've done and what you'd like to do. True to his nickname, he'll tell you whether your ambitions are realistic, and, if he takes to you, he'll also help you achieve them."

No such luck with the paternalist. In fact, of all the interview situations you encounter, the one involving him is least likely to bear fruit. It would be wonderful if we were able to recommend a list of stratagems that would enable a female interviewee to turn the tables on a dyed-in-the-wool male paternalist. But we can't—not quite. Paternalism, particularly towards women, is one of the most profoundly entrenched attitudes in corporate life. Like a debilitating disease, paternalism can only be treated by the sustained use of appropriate medication: first-class work presented unambiguously as your own. However, while this approach makes sense once you have a job, it is clearly irrelevant in a situation where you are trying to secure one.

One woman we interviewed (Elayne Bernay, research director of *Ms. Magazine)* was convinced that there is nothing you can do about overt paternalism in an interview situation. "We don't hire our children," she says bluntly. Another executive woman with whom we discussed the problem did have one recommendation. She advises that you unabashedly flatter your prospect into submission. "Tell him that the central reason why the job interests you is because of the opportunity to learn through the example and under the guidance of someone (namely him) whose reputation is of the highest order."

This statement puts your prospect in a double bind. He can only disagree with you at the risk of publicly diminishing his professional standing (and paternalists, rarely do that); or he can agree, in which case you have furnished him with a reason, over and above whatever hard qualifications support your candidacy, to take you more seriously than he did at the beginning of the meeting. Even if the paternalist sees through your soft soap, chances are that he will still be sufficiently impressed to offer you half-a-dozen referrals. If he doesn't, ask for them.

At this stage you have nothing to lose.

Just a Gigolo

The sexual harassment of women is extremely pervasive at all levels of working life. And there is no indication that it diminishes the higher up the socio-economic scale one goes. It becomes subtler perhaps but, according to at least two contemporary books on the subject (*The Secret Oppression: Sexual Harassment of Working Women* by Constance Backhouse and Leah Cohen, and *Sexual Shakedown: The Sexual Harassment of Women on the Job* by Lin Farley) no less prevalent.

While the male chauvinist is more likely to badger you once you've been hired—and you therefore have more to lose—he's by no means averse to pick-up attempts during job interviews. Since sexual harassment will probably take place in the privacy of an office, you have very fragile empirical grounds on which to lodge a complaint to the interviewer's superior, if you decide to do so. No Civil Rights Act can protect you from sexual innuendo expressed behind closed doors.

"Just a Gigolo" comes in all shapes and sizes. But if he has a single characteristic feature it is narcissism, a rabid self-love.

Any attempt at sexual harassment has to be handled sternly. The response, "My understanding is that this was intended to be a business meeting. I'm not prepared to respond to any questions or suggestions that bear on my personal life unless they are clearly relevant to the subject under discussion," is probably the most appropriate because:

- It serves notice that you take exception to his line of questioning;
- It is vague on the issue of whether or not the interviewer is deliberately testing you, therefore giving him an opportunity to backtrack;
- It gives the interviewer a chance to proceed on a civilized basis in a way that a straight "Listen, buster, this is a place of business not a singles' bar" does not;
- It works on men of all ages, from the pubescent stud to the middle-aged lecher.

A straightforward reprimand always beats moral indignation. It's more worldly, less ambiguous. Prissy people lack class. However, it's one thing to finesse a pass; it's another to work for the man who made it. Remember, you'll be seeing a lot of this man if he hires you.

Menage à Trois

It's two against one. Mr. X and Mr. Y. Mr. X asks the questions, Mr. Y sits there, watching, listening, and maybe taking notes. The atmosphere is formal, subdued, and almost alarmingly polite. It's like being back in the classroom.

The very artificiality of the situation is the reason why the "Menage à Trois" interview is the trickiest for a candidate to come through unscathed. The political chemistry of the meeting can very easily get confused, particularly if the relative status of your two interrogators has not been made plain. For some women, used to full-scale sales presentations that obliged them to address several people simultaneously, the "Menage à Trois" interview will present few problems. But for the rest it can be downright terrifying.

And a terrified candidate, like a terrified actress, stands a better than average chance of flubbing her lines.

We spoke to one uncharacteristically hopeful and conscientious head-hunter who spent a great deal of her time and energy preparing her candidates for interviews. We raised the issue of the two-against-one interview and asked if she had any advice to offer candidates, particularly women, confronted with such a situation.

"Absolutely," she says. "The two-on-one interview, as you call it, can be very unnerving and counterproductive, in my view. I have a couple of clients, though, who feel it to be a proper part of the recruitment procedure, and they do it frequently. They either double up a line manager with someone from personnel, or, if they have more than one opportunity available in different divisions, they may set the thing up between the two appropriate managers and cut out personnel altogether. I tell my candidate to try to do three things in these cases: (a) establish the relative seniority of the people doing the interview so you can at least have a crack at impressing the most powerful; (b) address your answer to both parties, switching your attention from one to the other, so that neither feels left out; and (c) try to create a discussion group atmosphere rather than that of a tribunal."

The headhunter went on to say that if the quieter of the two interviewers remains unresponsive, you have no alternative but to return to a straight question-and-answer session with the more talkative of the two. "But at least you've tried to get outside the straitjacket. And that shows determination, originality and strength of character, three very definite pluses."

Out to Lunch

There are three major tactical considerations for the job-related lunch: eat little, drink less, and stay alert to leading questions. An invitation to lunch is a further test, not a certificate of approval. While it suggests that your candidacy is being taken seriously (your prospects are prepared to invest some expenses in you), it certainly does not mean that you have been accepted and that further discussions are a formality.

In many ways the job-related lunch is the most demanding of all interview situations. Apart from being subjected to routine restaurant distractions (sudden outbursts of laughter, the clink of glasses), you are also obliged to juggle menus, cutlery, a napkin, the timing of your next mouthful.

The business lunch can be a trying affair, even for people who under-take it routinely. "Nevertheless," observed one former Hollywood agent we interviewed in Toronto, "there are rules. Believe me. I've breakfasted, brunched, and lunched my way into a zillion deals over the years and I know exactly what they are."

While our contact was not specifically concerned about discussing the problems associated with the job-related lunch, the observations she made are entirely appropriate to it:

- Order something simple or something you know. Don't use the lunch as a culinary experiment. Choose forkable food. An attempt to negotiate a bowl of spaghetti, for example, could be disastrous;
- Have no more than one drink. Order a white wine spritzer, something light anyway. Keep in mind, especially if you had no breakfast, that a drink unaccompanied by food will loosen your tongue faster than a drink consumed while eating;
- Don't equivocate when the time comes to order. Execute the task swiftly and surely. Stay away from the "shall I have this or shall I have that," syndrome;
- Don't forget that you're at a meeting where, coincidentally, food is being consumed. Your primary task is to concentrate on the conversation;
- Be as attentive to your smoking habits as you are to your drinking habits. Smoking is increasingly unfashionable these days. If you must smoke, at least ask the people with whom you are lunching whether or not they mind.

Only Cartesians Need Apply

We have all been subjected to the philosophical interview. Introduced towards the end of a series of preliminary discussions, or, perhaps, at the conclusion of a long, single conversation, the philosophical interview begins with the preamble: "Tell me. Now we've covered the basics about your job, let's talk about the future of (if it's your specialty) the synthetic rubber industry. Our problem is this. One of the major applications of our product is the prevention of soil erosion. But soil erosion is a topographical characteristic of Third World countries whose politics are, in general, erratic. What do you think our corporate policy should be?"

More than a few candidates have lost a job opportunity because they were unequal to the task of discussing long-term implications of their work. The response, "To be perfectly frank, I've never felt comfortable theorizing about the future of the synthetic rubber industry. Speculation is for academics or astrologers, not me," is rarely sufficient to turn the line of questioning away to more empirical ground. On the contrary, a declared reluctance to stargaze is the sign of a closed mind, of a parochial intellect.

Never go into a major job interview without being prepared for some tough exchanges about basic approaches, basic philosophies. And if you feel uncertain about your strengths in this area, bone up fast. Talk to colleagues, go to the library. Top job interviews rarely stop at technical qualifications. Being able to express a reasonably coherent overview of your subject can represent the difference between being passed over and being hired.

Concepts count.

In the Cartesian spirit of healthy skepticism and clarity of mind, we offer you a concluding checklist of five general questions you may be asked during your interviews. Since very few questions asked in interviews are entirely unambiguous, we have provided each one with a parenthetical translation:

Tell me a little about yourself. Translates to: How much trouble have you taken over your career? How well are you able to track your professional life?

Why do you want to leave your current employer? Translates to: What is the nature of your dissatisfactions and how rationally and coherently are you able to express them?

Tell me about your current job. Translates to: Give me a concisely expressed summary of your present responsibilities in a way that enables me to see how well your current work will have applications here.

What do you think of your current management? Translates to: To what extent are your present dissatisfactions likely to be duplicated here?

And finally, we list below working precepts to take with you to all your interviews:

- If there's a silence, don't fill it. Let the interviewer step in with a further question to which you can deliver a crisp, relevant answer;
- Never leave a weakness unqualified;
- Never leave a strength unsold.

The trouble with so many individuals involved in the recruitment process is that they have a natural, human aversion to rejecting people. This means that, unless brought firmly up against the issue, they will prefer prevarification to frankness. It's hard to look someone in the eye and tell her she is not going to make it. Far harder than a regretful telephone chat or, less upsetting still, than sending a tactful note.

The point of an interview is to proceed further. Better to provoke a turndown in a sequence of interviews by asking outright about your chances of success than to risk wasting time and energy pursuing the unpursuable.

One of your most formidable foes, at least during the interview stage of your campaign, is false hope. Your conviction that you have been outstandingly impressive in an interview is worthless without the interviewer's corresponding conviction that he wants to either continue the dialogue or make you an offer.

An offer closed is the job hunter's equivalent to a sale made.

Building a Team

Tracy Kidder

Convinced that Eagle would be a wart, a bag, a kludge—and suspicious that it would go the way of EGO and Victor—some of the brightest hardware engineers around expressed no interest in joining the project. Others went along, some reluctantly at first, and by the very early spring of 1978 West had gathered the makings of a team. He had Rosemarie and Alsing and about a dozen other experienced engineers, who had worked for him before. For a time West thought that their numbers would suffice, but really they were just a cadre. It became obvious, when they started designing the "logic" of the new machine, that such a tiny group would never be able to produce a computer like this in a year. "We need more bodies," said West to Alsing, and Alsing agreed.

North Carolina's leaders had assembled a large crew mainly by luring experienced engineers away from Westborough and other companies. But around this time videotape was circulating in the basement and it suggested another approach. In the movie, an engineer named Seymour Cray described how his little company, located in Chippewa Falls, Wisconsin, had come to build what are generally acknowledged to be the fastest computers in the world, the quintessential number-crunchers. Cray was a legend in computers, and in the movie Cray said that he liked to hire inexperienced engineers right out of school, because they do not usually know what's supposed to be impossible. West liked that idea. He also realized, of course, that new graduates command smaller salaries than experienced engineers. Moreover, using novices might be another way in which to disguise his team's real intentions. Who would believe that a bunch of completely inexperienced engineers could produce a major CPU to rival North Carolina's?

"Shall we hire kids, Alsing?" said West.

For a couple of weeks he and Alsing discussed the idea. To make it work they'd have to hire the very best new engineers they could find, ones who would know more about the state of the art in computers than they did. They told each other that they'd have to be sure not to turn away candidates just because the youngsters made them feel old and obsolete; on the contrary, those were the candidates they'd have to welcome. Smiling, West allowed that if they did this, they might be hiring their own replacements—their own assassins. Even if they did hire prodigies, of course, the scheme might not work. Maybe you couldn't build a major CPU with kids. It was awfully risky. It was a compelling idea.

Between the summer of 1978 and the fall of that year, West's team roughly doubled in size. To the dozen or so old hands—old in a relative sense—were added about a dozen neophytes, fresh from graduate schools of electrical engineering and computer science. These newcomers were known as "the kids." West was the boss, and he had a sort of adjutant—an architect of the electronic school—and two main lieutenants, each of whom had a sublieutenant or two. One lieutenant managed the crew that worked on the hardware, the machine's actual circuitry, and the members of this crew were called, and called themselves, "the Hardy Boys." The other main part of the team worked on micro code, a synaptic language that would fuse the physical machine with the programs that would tell it what to do. To join this part of the group, which Alsing ran, was to become one of "the Microkids." There were also a draftsman and some technicians. The group's numbers changed from time to time, generally diminishing, as people dropped out. But usually they totaled about thirty.

How was it to be one of "the kids"? You were in no danger of being fired, but you didn't know that, and besides, when you are brand-new in a job you want to make a good impression right from the start. So you set out to get to know your boss, as Hardy Boy Dave Epstein did. You walk into his office and say, "Hi, I'm Dave," and you begin to extend your hand. Epstein would never forget that experience: "West just sat there and stared at me. After a few seconds, I decided I'd better get out of there."

Going to work for the Eclipse Group could be a rough way to start out in your profession. You set out for your first real job with all the loneliness and fear that attend new beginnings, drive east from Purdue or Northwestern or Wisconsin, up from Missouri or west from MIT, and before you've learned to find your way to work without a road map, you're sitting in a tiny cubicle or, even worse, in an office like the one dubbed the Micropit, along with three other new recruits, your knees practically touching theirs; and though lacking all privacy and quiet, though it's a job you've never really done before, you are told that you have almost no time at all in which to master a virtual encyclopedia of

technical detail and to start producing crucial pieces of a crucial new
machine. And you want to make a good impression. So you don't have
any time to meet women, to help your wife buy furniture for your apartment, or to explore the unfamiliar countryside. You work. You're told,
"Don't even mention the name Eagle outside the group." "Don't talk outside the group," you're told. You're working at a place that looks like
something psychologists build for testing the fortitude of small animals,
and your boss won't even say hello to you.

New and old hands told the same story. Chuck Holland: "I can hardly
say I do anything else now. It takes about three days to get Eagle out of
my mind, so if you have a three-day weekend, you're just sorry to see
Monday come." Microkid Betty Shanahan, the group's lone female
engineer: "You can end up staying all night. You can forget to go home
and eat dinner. My husband complained that the last three times he's had
to do the laundry." Jon Blau: "I've had difficulty forming sentences lately. In the middle of a story my mind'll go blank. Pieces of your life get
dribbled away. I'm growing up, having all those experiences, and I don't
want to shut them out for the sake of Data General or this big project."
Jim Guyer, a Hardy Boy and an old hand at age twenty-six, said: "I like
my job, it's great, I enjoy it. But it's not what I do for recreation. Outside
of work, I do other things, like rock-climbing and hiking." Guyer
paused. A thought had just occurred to him. "I haven't done any of that
lately. Because I've been working too much."

But where did the relish in their voices come from?

At the start of the project, a newcomer could expect to earn something
like $20,000 a year, while a veteran such as Alsing might make a little
more than $30,000—and those figures grew enormously at Data General
and elsewhere over the next few years. But they received no extra pay for
working overtime. The old hands had also received some stock options,
but most seemed to view the prospect of stock as a mere sweetener, and
most agreed with Ken Holberger, sublieutenant of Hardy Boys, who
declared, "I don't work for money."

Some of the recruits said they liked the atmosphere. Microkid Dave
Keating, for instance, had looked at other companies, where de facto
dress codes were in force. He liked the "casual" look of the basement of
Westborough. "The jeans and so on." Several talked about their "flexible
hours." "No one keeps track of the hours we work," said Ken Holberger.
He grinned. "That's not altruism on Data General's part. If anybody kept
track, they'd have to pay us a hell of a lot more than they do." Yet it is a
fact, not entirely lost on management consultants, that some people
would rather work twelve hours a day of their own choosing than eight
that are prescribed. Provided, of course, that the work is interesting.
That was the main thing.

A couple of the Microkids were chatting. They talked about the jobs
they had turned down.

"At IBM we wouldn't have gotten on a project this good. They don't hand out projects like this to rookies."

"They don't hand out projects like this to rookies anywhere but Data General."

"I got an offer at IBM to work on a memory chip, to see what could be done about improving its performance. Here I got an offer to work on a major new machine, which was gonna be the backbone of company sales. I'd get to do *computer* design. It wasn't hard to make that choice."

Bob Beauchamp, another Microkid, had come from Missouri. He wore a small red beard. He was perhaps the most easygoing of the recruits. He had wider experience of the world than most, having taken a year off from school to play in a traveling rock band. Beauchamp seemed to be one of those fortunate souls: likable, modest, good-looking and smart. He had compiled an unblemished, straight-A average in graduate school. "I tended to enjoy takin' tests through school. I kinda like to measure myself," he said. "I'd spent five years in college learning, never really doing anything. When I got to Data General, I figured it was time to do something; and also I was new to this part of the world, and by myself, and even on weekends I didn't have a whole lot better to do. I might as well pass the time at work." But Beauchamp had opted to work on a part of the project that turned out to have a low priority. "There was no pressure. I felt out of the mainstream of things. There was intensity in the air. I kinda liked the fervor and I wanted to be part of it." Eventually, a suggestion came down that Beauchamp go to work on some of the machine's microcode. He was essentially offered the chance for some grueling work, and he accepted with alacrity. "I jumped on it, really," he said.

Talk about Tom Sawyer's fence.

There was, it appeared, a mysterious rite of initiation through which, in one way or another, almost every member of the team passed. The term that the old hands used for this rite—West invented the term, not the practice—was "signing up." By signing up for the project you agreed to do whatever was necessary for success. You agreed to forsake, if necessary, family, hobbies, and friends—if you had any of these left (and you might not if you had signed up too many times before). From a manager's point of view, the practical virtues of the ritual were manifold. Labor was no longer coerced. Labor volunteered. When you signed up you in effect declared, "I want to do this job and I'll give it my heart and soul." It cut another way. The vice president of engineering, Carl Carman, who knew the term, said much later on: "Sometimes I worry that I pushed too hard. I tried not to push any harder than I would on myself. That's why, by the way, you have to go through the sign-up. To be sure you're not conning anybody."

The rite was not accomplished with formal declarations, as a rule. Among the old hands, a statement such as "Yeah, I'll do that" could constitute the act of signing up, and often it was done tacitly—as when, without being ordered to do so, Alsing took on the role of chief recruiter.

The old hands knew the game and what they were getting into. The new recruits, however, presented some problems in this regard.

The demand for young computer engineers far exceeded the supply. The competition for them was fierce. What enticements could the Eclipse Group offer to the ones they wanted that companies such as IBM could not? Clearly, West and Alsing agreed, their strongest pitch would be the project itself. Alsing reasoned as follows: "Engineering school prepares you for big projects, and a lot of guys wind up as transformer designers. It's a terrible let-down, I think. They end up with some rote engineering job with some thoroughly known technology that's repetitive, where all you have to do is look up the answers in books." By contrast, Alsing knew, it was thought to be a fine thing in the fraternity of hardware engineers—in the local idiom, it was "the sexy job"—to be a builder of new computers, and the demand for opportunities to be a maker of new computers also exceeded the supply. West put it this way: "We had the best high-energy story to tell a college graduate. They'd all heard about VAX. Well, we were gonna build a thirty-two-bit machine less expensive, faster and so on. You can sign a guy up to that any day of the year. And we got the best there was."

But the new recruits were going to be asked to work at a feverish pace almost at once. They'd have no time to learn the true meaning of signing up on their own. They had to be carefully selected and they had to be warned. Common decency and the fear of having to feel lingering guilt demanded that this be done.

The Eclipse Group solicited applications. One candidate listed "family life" as his main avocation. Alsing and another of West's lieutenants felt wary when they saw this. Not that they wanted to exclude family men, being such themselves. But Alsing wondered: "He seems to be saying he doesn't want to sign up." The other lieutenant pondered the application. "I don't think he'd be happy here," he said to himself. The applicant's grades were nothing special, and they turned him away.

Grades mattered in this first winnowing of applications—not only as an indication of ability but also as a basis for guessing about a recruit's capacity for long, hard work—and with a few exceptions they turned down those whose grades were merely good.

Alsing hoped to recruit some female engineers, but in 1978 they were still quite scarce. Only a few young women applied, and Alsing hired one, who had fine credentials.

When they liked the looks of an application, they invited the young man—it was usually a young man—to Westborough, and the elders would interview him, one by one. If he was a potential Microkid, the recruit's interview with Alsing was often the crucial one. And a successful interview with Alsing constituted a signing up.

Alsing would ask the young engineer, "What do you want to do?"

Exactly what the candidate said—whether he was interested in one aspect of computers or another—didn't matter. Indeed, Alsing didn't care if a recruit showed no special fondness for computers; and the fact that an engineer had one of his own and liked to play with it did not argue for him.

If the recruit seemed to say in reply, "Well, I'm just out of grad school and I'm looking at a lot of possibilities and I'm not sure what field I want to get into yet," then Alsing would usually find a polite way to abbreviate the interview. But if the recruit said, for instance, "I'm really interested in computer design," then Alsing would prod. The ideal interview would proceed in this fashion:

"What interests you about that?"

"I want to build one," says the recruit.

("That's what I want to hear," thinks Alsing. "Now I want to find out if he means it.")

"What makes you think you can build a major computer?" asks Alsing.

"Hey," says the recruit, "no offense, but I've used some of the machines you guys have built. I think I can do a better job."

("West and I have a story that we tell about Eagle machine. But I want to hear this guy tell me part of that story first. If he does, if there's some fire in his eyes—I say 'in his eyes,' because I don't know where it is; if it's there, it's there—but if he's a little cocky and I think we probably want this person, then I tell him *our* story.")

"Well," says Alsing, "we're building this machine that's way out in front in technology. We're gonna design all new hardware and tools." ("I'm trying to give him a sense of 'Hey, you've finally found in a big company a place where people are really doing the next thing.' ") "Do you like the sound of that?" asks Alsing.

"Oh, yeah," says the recruit.

("Now I tell him the bad news.")

"It's gonna be tough," says Alsing. "If we hired you, you'd be working with a bunch of cynics and egotists and it'd be hard to keep up with them."

"That doesn't scare me," says the recruit.

"There's a lot of fast people in this group," Alsing goes on. "It's gonna be a real hard job with a lot of long hours. And I mean *long* hours."

"No," says the recruit, in words more or less like these. "That's what I want to do, get in on the ground floor of a new architecture. I want to do a big machine. I want to be where the action is."

"Well," says Alsing, pulling a long face. "We can only let in the best of this year's graduates. We've already let in some awfully fast people. We'll have to let you know."

("We tell him that we only let in the best. Then we let him in.")

"I don't know," said Alsing, after it was all done. "It was kind of like recruiting for a suicide mission. You're gonna die, but you're gonna die in glory."

We're Going to Make You a Star

Sally Quinn

The countdown: Dick Salant, president of CBS News, was beaming. Hughes Rudd was chuckling to himself and Sally Quinn was fending off questions about her sudden rise in TV news. The setting was a luncheon at "21" in New York and the guests included members of the press, who were given an opportunity to meet and chat with the CBS correspondents who will go on the air next Monday. Salant was saying he'd love to switch the time of the *CBS Morning News* show from 7 A.M. to 8 A.M. but he'd run into opposition from the fans of *Captain Kangaroo*. "I know because I raised all my children on *Captain Kangaroo*." If the new team is a success, Salant said naturally he'd take credit for the show, but if the show bombs he said he's going to find someone to point the finger at. Who dreamed up Rudd and Quinn? he was asked. "That was Lee Townsend." Townsend, the executive producer, however, modestly disclaimed credit. "It was a group effort," he told Eye, *Women's Wear Daily*, Tuesday, July 21, 1973 . . .

When Gordon and I first discussed the job I told him I had grave reservations about his choice. I reminded him that I was controversial, opinionated, flip, open and had no intention of changing. Was he sure this was what he wanted on television? Did they really want me to say what came to my mind during the ad libs, and would they not try to turn me into a bland, opinionless, dull-but-safe marshmallow? And I wondered aloud whether, if we were supposed to be journalists, we could maintain any kind of objectivity and still express controversial opinions—or any opinions, for that matter.

"Paley wants controversy," Gordon had said. "And so does Salant. You can get away with much, much more at that hour than you ever could on the *Evening News*."

I had doubts and so did a lot of people I talked to, but I figured CBS knew what it wanted.

I also pointed out to Gordon that I had a rather unconventional life style. I had been living on weekends with Warren, I explained, and if I moved to New York I would move in with him. I would also be talking about him openly and freely in interviews. I saw nothing wrong with it, and I had no intention of hiding the fact.

I think Gordon gulped a little at that one, but he gamely said that was just fine, I could say anything I wanted to. After all, CBS was not hiring me because or in spite of my personal life.

On Friday morning, June 22nd, the first piece about me appeared in *The Washington Post.* The head ran "SHOWDOWN AT SUNRISE," and it carried pictures of me and Barbara opposite each other. I wasn't too crazy about that. It created an atmosphere of rivalry I would have preferred to avoid. But my editors laughingly pointed out that I was now a public personality and had no say in the matter. They also pointed out that it was clearly the right angle for the story. They were right.

TV critic John Carmody had written, "Although a number of her candid interviews had attracted CBS's attention, it was, ironically enough, her appearance on Miss Walters' *Not for Women Only* TV program that whetted the network's interest." He quoted Salant as saying that the format of the revamped show would "have no relationship to the *Today* Show" and would "retain the integrity of the basic news show." But also as predicting that *"Today* is ripe to be taken."

Stuart Shulberg, the producer of the *Today* Show, was quoted: "We welcome fresh competition. *Today* has led the morning field for so long that we could run the risk of growing too fat, smug, and sassy. This will speed up the pace, sharpen our competitive spirit, and provide the kind of honest competition we need and relish. May the best program win."

Barbara Walters was quoted: "The only thing I can say as a woman in broadcasting is that I welcome any new member to the fold. . . . I have respect and friendship for Sally. I know her very well. And I applaud both her and CBS for a very smart choice."

And Sally Quinn said: "Barbara is a great friend of mine and one of the most professional people I've ever known. As far as competing with each other, we covered the Shah's celebration in the desert of Iran together last year and stayed in the same dormitory. That's like being in combat together, and I imagine this will be a somewhat similar situation."

And we were off. . . .

Monday, rehearsals began. Thank God. Now they were going to roll it all out for us, lay it on, let us in on all the fabulous plans for the first week of shows. And it was about time. I had begun to have doubts, but I knew that they would disappear as soon as we got to the studio and saw what they had for us.

We were to arrive at 6 A.M. to start getting the feel of getting up early. We would watch the *Morning News,* then go into a simulation of what our anchor booth was going to look like (it wasn't nearly ready) and tape a news broadcast. We were to write it from the same wires and newspapers that John Hart had used earlier.

Lee Townsend was jittery. Townsend, the most even-tempered man I know, was also as irritated as I had ever seen him. He had been against the promo tour (though he didn't object violently enough) because he felt we could have better used our time rehearsing. His objections had been overridden by Blackrock, which—who? I never got the pronoun straight—had insisted that it was necessary. So Townsend was nervous and angry because we had been away and virtually co-opted by the PR department, and because it was then clear to him that we didn't have a super-duper razzle-dazzle show to put on the air in a week's time. And no real studio to rehearse in.

He had reason to be more than nervous, and we did exactly what we had done for the pilot except at greater length. We wrote a little news and a few lead-ins to film pieces, and Hughes wrote an essay. I couldn't think of anything that morning, and besides, I'm not an essayist. I'm a reporter and interviewer. Hughes would do essays, which he did marvelously, and I would do what I did best.

In front of the camera, they outfitted me with an ear-piece on a wire, called a Telex, which enables them to talk to you from the control room. They handed us mikes, rolled our copy onto the TelePromTers, and away we went. It was a disaster. There were two cameras and I didn't know which one to look at. The stage manager waved his hands around, but I hadn't a clue what he was trying to tell me. I was fumbling my words and couldn't read the prompters. They were shouting in my ear through the Telex to do this and do that, and three minutes here and twenty seconds there, and ad lib here. The ad libs were always by surprise, and I would fumble around trying to think of something clever to say about a film piece we had just seen. It might have been a bloody plane crash or a dairy farm. It BOMBED, and I was shell-shocked by the time it was over. Suddenly I *knew* this was the way it was going to be. There was nothing I could do about it. It was too late to get out of it.

I was even more upset when everyone came out of the control booth and said it was just fine and all it needed was a little smoothing out and we would be just great by the end of the week. No mention of any guests for interviews, no mention of any special film pieces that would lend themselves to interesting, informative ad libs and, most frightening of all, no mention of anything I should do to improve myself. I realized fully for the first time that I didn't know anything, and I panicked.

As we were filing down the stairs to the *Morning News* section, Jim Ganser, one of the producers, caught up with me. He was to be the only one at CBS who really tried to help me.

"Try to punch your words a little more," he sort of whispered out of the side of his mouth, as though he didn't want anyone to hear.

I fell on him. "What? How? What do you mean?" I said desperately. "Tell me, for God's sake. Tell me what I'm doing wrong."

And he told me. "You're wrong to expect anyone to give any help or guidance of any kind. You're a big star now, and people figure if you're a big star you must know what you're doing. Nobody's going to stick his neck out to help you."

I went to the ladies' room and threw up. But I had to hurry. Hughes and I were the "big stars" of a large press luncheon at the "21" Club, and we were late. . . .

We finally got into our own studio on Friday, and we rehearsed there Friday and Saturday. Nothing went right. Friday morning after John Hart's last show someone came into the Cronkites, where we were working, and said that the staff of the *Morning News* was having a farewell party for John and the old producer. I hadn't really seen John to talk to him. I like and respect him a great deal, but we had been so busy working the lobster shift (that's the night shift in newspapers) that we just hadn't had a chance to see each other.

"Oh, great, I'll go up and tell John goodbye," I said, jumping up from my chair.

"I wouldn't if I were you," someone said. "There's a great deal of hostility up there toward the new team. And the atmosphere upstairs is more like a wake than a party. I think you had better forget it."

That was the first I had heard of resentment or hostility on the home team front. It worried me because, except for Townsend, Hughes and me, the "team" was the same. There had been no staff changes. I had found that curious. If they had really wanted a whole new format, with more entertainment and a lighter mood, I thought that they would surely have tried to bring in some people who were more in the show-biz line. The *Morning News* staff was very good. But they were hard-news oriented, and Gordon had said the idea was to take on the *Today* Show.

That morning when I went in to get my makeup done for the rehearsals my hair was a mess. While I was upstairs, the woman who was doing my makeup said her friend Edith, the hairdresser for *Edge of Night,* was right down the hall and maybe she would roll my hair up on the hot rollers for me. She called Edith, and a round-faced woman in her late fifties, with reddish hair, big, wide innocent eyes, a very strong New York accent, and dyed-to-match pants, vest, blouse, and shoes, came rushing in. Edith said she would be delighted. She had the lightest, most soothing touch, and the whole time she did my hair she told me how great I looked and how terrific I was going to be on the air and that she was honored to do my hair. Then she asked who my official hairdresser was.

"Hairdresser? I don't have a hairdresser." Both women were stunned. "You have to have a hairdresser," they chimed. "Every woman on television has one. You can't just go on with your hair like this every morning."

Edith asked me if she could be my hairdresser and said she was sure that if I asked they would let me have one. I told Lee and Sandy Socolow about it and they both went blank. Nobody had given my hair a thought. They okayed it right away, but it indicates how little thought went into the planning for the first woman network anchor. Edith was a godsend. She not only took care of my hair, she took care of my ego.

After the rehearsal on Saturday, I was about to leave. No interviews were lined up for me for the following week. The big interview for Monday was with Patrick Buchanan, the President's speech writer, and that would be out of Washington. I had no idea what film pieces were going to be used. They weren't sure.

I was so depressed and scared that I didn't really care. I wanted to go somewhere and hide. As we were leaving (Sunday was a free day) Lee Townsend gave me a big smile and said, in a way I couldn't decide was joking or not, "Let me know if you have any good ideas tomorrow for the show."

Sunday was the worst day of my life. I thought about ways to disappear where no one would hear from me for years and would think I had been kidnapped by some freak. I considered the possibility of having plastic surgery so I would never be recognized as Sally Quinn. I fantasized about going on the broadcast and saying, "Good morning, I'm Sally Quinn and we are not prepared to do this show and I don't know what I'm doing up here." I thought seriously about calling Salant and Manning and telling them. I came close to quitting.

The water pipes broke in our apartment and I had to go to a friend's place on West End Avenue to wash my hair.

When I got out of the shower, I put on a large white robe that was hanging on the door. I came out of the bathroom draped in that robe and I said to Warren, who had been babysitting me all day, "I really feel like one of those ancient Aztec virgins who has been chosen to be sacrificed on top of the temple of the gods. All the other virgins are wildly jealous of her because she has this fabulous honor bestowed on her. What they don't know is that she doesn't want her heart cut out with a knife anytime by anyone. It hurts."

I went to bed at 5 P.M. It was bright and sunny outside, and I could hear the children playing on Riverside Drive and happy couples walking and chatting and laughing as they strolled in Riverside Park.

"I will never be happy again," I thought. "My life is over."

I never went to sleep. We had been coming in around 4 or 5 in the morning that week, but it wasn't proper preparation for coming in at 1:30. The alarm went off at 1:00 A.M. Warren was waiting to walk me to my limousine, which arrived promptly at 1:30 A.M. It was like being escorted in a golden carriage to the guillotine.

I didn't feel too hot. I figured it must be because I hadn't slept. I slipped into the gloamings of the enormous black car and we glided over to Hughes' apartment, the Apthorpe, a few blocks away on West End

Avenue. He hadn't slept either. We didn't say a word. A few minutes later we arrived at the studio and went directly back to the *Morning News* area and into the Bullpen.

In front of each of us was a pile of news wire stories, the first edition of *The New York Times* and the *Daily News.* Bob Siller, the copy editor, was there and so was Dave Horowitz, one of the assistant producers. They would make up the "line-up." The line-up was a sheet on which the show was blocked out minute-by-minute. Taking all the film pieces and counting their time, they would, along with Hughes and me and Lee Townsend, decide what the top news stories were and allot a certain amount of time to each, from forty-five seconds to a minute, and then block out time for commericals (we had only network commercials for the first six weeks) and station breaks. They would leave about a minute and a half for Hughes' essay, and what was left—roughly five minutes—would be allotted for "ad libs."

While this was going on, Hughes and I read the papers and the wires to get an idea of what stories we wanted to use. When we had finished, about 3 or 3:30, Bob and Dave came back with the line-up designating which one of us would write which stories and which lead-ins to film pieces. If the film piece was ready, Hughes and I would try to take a look at it so that we could write a clearer lead-in; if not, there was generally some kind of script. Often the film piece wasn't ready. Horowitz and Siller, with our advice or without, would figure out which film piece seemed like the best topic for conversation and block in a certain amount of time for ad libs after those pieces. There was some freedom to move around, but not much. Everything we were to say we typed out on our enormous typewriters.

We had two writers who were to do the weather, sports and late-breaking news. Hughes was to read all the sports. We had tried to divide it, but I didn't understand sports and kept fumbling and breaking up in the middle of the report. Hughes hated it too, but it wasn't quite as ridiculous when he did it.

By the time Hughes and I would have read everything thoroughly, discussed camera angles with Bob Quinn, our director, who came in about 4, written all our news items, lead-ins and station and commercial breaks, had something to eat at our desks (it was called "lunch" and usually came from the CBS cafeteria, known appropriately and without affection as "the Bay of Pigs"), it would be about 6 A.M.—time for Edith and Rickey, the makeup person, to arrive and get us ready.

At around 3:30 I had started to break out in a cold sweat and I became weak and dizzy and slightly nauseated. I couldn't concentrate on what I was writing. Finally I went into Townsend's office and passed out. I tried to get up about 4 A.M. and write, but I stayed at my typewriter for about twenty minutes and then went back to Townsend's office and passed out again. I thought it was probably because I was tired and nervous, but by then my throat was so sore and I was coughing so badly that I could barely talk. I had shivers and had to be wrapped up in a blanket.

Everyone piled into Townsend's office and stared at me in horror. "Do you think you can do it?" Lee asked, terrified.

"I just don't know, Lee." I didn't.

I think at that point I was more scared not to go on than to go on.

"I'll try. I'll really try. But I can't talk. And I'm so dizzy. Is there any way I could get a vitamin B shot or something to give me quick energy?"

By then it was 5:30 in the morning and I was so sick I couldn't breathe. I kept trying to sit up and I would just fall right down. I couldn't tell whether the beads of perspiration on my head were from temperature or desperation. Finally Townsend said that they had to get me to a hospital. Somebody had a car and they carried me out to the front of the building, stuffed me in the car, and drove two blocks away to Roosevelt Hospital to the emergency room. A young doctor took me back to examine me and take my temperature. I had a temperature of 102 and he said he thought I might have pneumonia. I was coughing so badly that my body was racked. "You don't understand," I practically screamed. "I'm making my television debut in an hour."

"So I've heard," he smirked.

"Well, I can't possibly go on like this. Can't you give me a vitamin B shot or something? Anything."

He said that in my condition a vitamin B shot wouldn't do any good. The only thing he could do for me was to give me a throat spray that would stop me from coughing for a few hours. But he suggested that I get to a doctor immediately afterward for proper medication.

"Anything else I could give you now," he said, "would knock you out." Oh, how I wished . . .

He left the room and came back a few minutes later with the most enormous syringe I have ever seen, with a needle a mile long.

"Forget it," I said, backing away from him.

"Don't get hysterical," he said, laughing, "This is a throat spray. I'm not going to stick the needle in you."

He stuck the needle in my mouth and sprayed a gooey liquid, which coated the inside of my throat.

Lee grabbed me, back we went into the car, and we screeched off around the corner and back to CBS as though we were bank robbers getting away.

It was a little before 6:30. Edith and Rickey were frantic, and Hughes looked as though all his blood had drained out of him. Edith rolled my hair while Rickey sponged some makeup on me. I lay down while all this was going on. The hot rollers stayed in too long and I looked like Shirley Temple when my hair was combed out. There was nothing we could do about the frizz. At about ten minutes to seven they finished on me. I was still so weak and dizzy that I could barely move, and all I can remember is a large fuzz of Warren leaning over me asking me if I was all right, Townsend in a frenzy, and Hughes pulling himself together as he walked into my dressing room. "Hughes—" I tried to smile—"get me off this horse immediately." Hughes tried to smile, too, but he wasn't very convincing. "Don't worry," he growled, "you'll make it, kid."

I tried to say thank you, but the throat spray had a numbing effect, like Novocain, and I couldn't feel whether my tongue was touching the roof of my mouth or whether I was forming my words properly.

"You look beautiful, darling, just beautiful. You'll be wonderful, I know you will," Edith was murmuring.

I looked in the miror. I was hideous. My hair was frizzy, the granny glasses looked wrong, and the only thing I owned that wasn't blue (I hadn't had time to shop that week) was a yellow battle jacket that made me look like a dyke.

"Well," I thought, "there's no way anybody is going to accuse me of being a sex bomb this morning."

Somebody shoved a pile of telegrams in my face and I tried to read. They were all amiable, from close friends and family, but it was upsetting me. "Oh, God," I thought, "if only they knew how terrible I'm going to be."

They were screaming for me to get into the studio and I ran in, got behind the desk, had my mike adjusted, and somebody handed me my Telex, which I stuck in my ear.

"One minute," yelled the floor manager.

My mouth was dry. No possibility of talking. I looked at Hughes. He was looking at me as though we were copilots and I had just been shot. He tried to smile. I tried to smile back.

"Thirty seconds," said the floor manager.

I looked straight outside the glass partition to the newsroom and saw everyone staring.

"Five seconds," the floor manager said.

For a fleeting moment I thought maybe I would wake up and find out this wasn't happening.

An arm went out to me and a finger pointed. I gazed at the TelePromTer.

"Good morning," I read, "I'm Sally Quinn. . . ."

I don't remember much else about that hour. I was propped up with several pillows because I was so weak and dizzy that I couldn't sit up by myself.

I coughed a lot. I remember a swirl of sweltering bright lights, moving cameras, different noises and shouts in my ear through the Telex—"Turn to Camera 2, thirty seconds to ad-lib, five seconds till commercial, ten seconds more of interview"—hand signals, desperate and self-delirious mumblings . . . and then it was over. And when it was over I felt completely numb. Nothing. . . .

When I walked back into my office there were three bouquets. One was from Charlotte Curtis, then editor of *The New York Times'* Family, Food, Fashions and Furnishings, now editor of the op-ed page of *The Times* and probably the woman I admire most in journalism. One from Vic Gold, former press secretary of former Vice President Spiro T. Agnew and now a columnist. And one from Connie Tremulis of "Flowers by Connie," Rockford, Illinois.

I still have their cards.

Everybody was talking at once and saying what a great show it had been and how did I ever get through it, and, boy, what a terrific start we had gotten off to, and how terrible the *Today* Show was outdoors in front of Rockefeller Center. I don't remember seeing Hughes. I remember Lee Townsend taking me by the hand and leading me outside to a taxi. I put my head back on the seat and stared out the window as we went whizzing up Central Park West. It was a beautiful day. I thought about all the people walking along the street and bicycling in the park and about how happy they looked. I thought how odd it was that my work day was over and it was only 8, and that that was going to be my life from now on. And how depressing it was. I did not think about the show. It had not happened. Nor did Lee mention it. . . .

During the first week, I had not seen or heard from Gordon. I debated whether or not to call him or leave a message, but then I figured if he wanted to see me he would have come back or sent a note. I will never understand why, after the first show, he didn't come screaming back to the *Morning News* and fire everybody, or put Hughes on with straight news, tell the world I had terminal pneumonia, and send me away to some hideaway studio in Connecticut with his trustiest producers and cameramen to work me over.

As far as I knew, nobody had seen or heard from Gordon. I waited each day for him to ask me into his office and explain gently that I needed some kind of training; that they were going to change the format, get a new set and a jazzy producer, set me up with taped interviews, get me out of reading the news, get me voice lessons, make me put on contact lenses, and demand that I grow my hair longer and cut out the ad libs.

Nothing.

The broadcast Monday was uneventful, including my first live television interview. It was—I still have a hard time believing this was the best person CBS could think of for my TV interview debut—the designer Emilio Pucci. I discovered that he was branching out from lingerie into sheets and men's wear.

Hughes did not participate. He wasn't all that anxious to, didn't particularly like to do interviews, and I'm sure he didn't have all that much to talk to Pucci about anyway, except the fact that they were both World War II pilots.

I called Gordon and left a message after the show. I was told he was out. Gordon soon became for me a Major Major Major figure from *Catch-22*. Hard to reach. . . .

My health all along had not been good. I still felt dizzy and nauseated in the early mornings, and I was constantly exhausted though there wasn't anything wrong with me as far as anyone could see.

There was, however, a major cosmetic problem.

For the first time since I was seventeen years old, I was developing acne. And it was getting bad. Rickey switched to an allergenic makeup, but it didn't help. The makeup and the bright lights must be doing it, I decided. I should have my face cleaned.

I remembered that a classmate of mine from Smith had a mother who ran an Institute of Cosmetology on East 62nd Street, which I occasionally read about in *Vogue* or *Harper's Bazaar*. Her name was Vera Falvy, and she was a Hungarian with the most beautiful complexion I had ever seen.

Mme. Falvy examined my face carefully and asked about my eating habits, health, and life style. She knew I was on TV but had no idea of the hours or the pressure. She felt the breakout was caused by emotional tension. I would need regular treatment. We made another appointment and she gave me a special lotion which I was to use under, or preferably instead of, makeup.

Altogether I visited Madame six times, and the bills ran close to $300. She did her best, but the tensions kept building and my face got worse. My complexion has never been the same. I have scars on my face to show for those horrible months. . . .

That week I got a call from Barbara Howar. We chatted for a bit and Barbara, who had had her own TV shows, gave me a few pointers. She told me that I was coming along really well and shouldn't worry. Then she said, "Why don't you look at the right camera when the show is closing each day? Half the time the camera zooms out to the newsroom while you're looking straight ahead into the camera in the studio, and whenever the camera is in the studio you're looking across at the newsroom. You've got to keep your eye on the red light."

"Red light?"

"For God's sake," she screamed, "hasn't anyone told you about the red light?"

"No," I said. "What about it?"

"There's a light on the side of the camera," she said, "and when it goes on red it means that camera is on you and that's where you're supposed to look."

"Oh, no," I moaned. "No wonder. I saw that light flash on and off but I didn't know what it meant." . . .

Thanksgiving was the next day, and we never had holidays off. It was the tenth anniversary of Kennedy's assassination. When I looked at the line-up that morning, I saw that the only scheduled interview was one I had done several weeks earlier with a woman who had written a diabetic cookbook.

I couldn't believe it. Hughes complained to no avail. That seemed like the final straw. On the tenth anniversary of a president's death we were to do a mediocre (at best) taped interview with a diabetic-cookbook writer. There was no hope for any of us, or that broadcast.

Without staff meetings, there was still no coordination. Things hadn't gotten better. Usually, we didn't know who the guest was to be until we came on the program, and half the time it was someone neither of us was interested in or wanted to interview. We wrote lists of suggestions and notes, but nothing ever came of them. It is not that the people on the staff were incompetent, but just that there was zero direction, that morale was low, and that there was no coordination.

We had a rule about not accepting guests if they'd already been on the *Today* Show, and they had the same rule about our show. What that meant was that we hardly ever got any of the good people because the *Today* Show had a much larger audience and no publisher would allow his author on our show unless he couldn't get him or her on the *Today* Show.

I thought that was dumb. I thought we should take people who'd been on the other show, then try to do a better, or a different kind of interview. We were in a no-win situation.

Another problem I kept hearing about third-hand from my friends was that some of them had talked their publishers into letting them go on our program because they were friends, and then for some odd reason they were rejected. This happened to Art Buchwald and Teddy White. There would be some vague explanation; but usually there were about three people involved in setting up the interviews, and often they weren't there when I was, so I couldn't find out. It was a mini-example of the total method of functioning at CBS. It was exasperating and, in the end, useless to try to do anything about anything.

The broadcast was beginning to take on a slight death smell. I had to get out. . . .

I've often asked myself how CBS could have made so many mistakes, how they could have let me go on the air with no experience.

Part of my despair during that terrible time had stemmed from trying to fathom where I had gone wrong. The thing is, nobody really yet understands the medium. Television isn't even fifty years old. Shows go on and off every month, people are hired and fired ruthlessly, because nobody knows what will work and what won't. They don't know what terrible vibes a great-looking or -talking person may give out over the air or what good vibes a clod may transmit. So they don't want to make decisions—especially long-term ones. Therefore nobody does. It's what Sander Vanocur calls the "how-about?" school. Somebody said, "How-about-Sally-Quinn?" and there was a generalized mumble, and that was it. They hired me and nobody ever did anything about it again. Mainly because they didn't know what to do.

So much money is at stake—millions and millions of dollars in advertisements—that those who make mistakes cost their company a lot of money. If they do that too often they lose their jobs. On newspapers everything doesn't ride on one story or one series but on the long run. Everyone in television is basically motivated by fear.

And television news is run by the network. It is not really autonomous. Those in charge of entertainment have ultimate charge over the news programs. CBS News has a buffer between the management and the news division: Richard Salant. In fact, that is his primary function. He is a lawyer, not a newsman, and he is able to negotiate the vast differences of approach between the news side and Blackrock and to work out acceptable compromises. . . .

Thursday of the first week, Small asked me to come down to his office. Gordon was sitting there. I was surprised, to say the least. He hadn't told me he was coming down. He asked where I would be later in the day. He said he would call.

He called around 3:30 and asked if I could have a drink with him. I suggested he have a drink with Ben [Bradley, *Washington Post*] and me, since they were old friends.

He hedged. Then he said he could get a hotel room and stay over if I wanted him to. We could have dinner. I suggested we all have dinner. He hesitated. I couldn't figure out what he wanted. "Well, Gordon," I said finally, "what do you want?"

He mumbled something about dinner for the two of us and how he could get a hotel room. I said I thought it would be more fun with the three of us. He blew up. . . .

"Gordon," I said quietly, "I'm going to quit CBS. I'll try to be out in about six weeks. But I've got to find a job first. Just get Small to let me stay in Washington until then. I can't—won't go back to the anchor job. But I don't want to just quit and have it look like I was a total loss. I want to have a great job to go to. Will you do that much for me? Just hold them off for a while?"

He looked relieved. "I'll do it," he promised.

We walked in silence to the Watergate Terrace Restaurant and made polite conversation through dinner. Nobody ate anything. I ordered gaz-pacho but I couldn't swallow it. As we were leaving I asked Gordon what I had been longing to ask him since we went on the air.

"Gordon, why did you do it? Why did you hire me and then throw me on the air like that with no training? Why did you do it to me?"

"What if I had told you we wanted to make you the anchor on the *Morning News* but that you'd have to have about three to six months' training on one of our local stations first. Would you have done it?"

"Of course not."

"That's why.". . .

The morning after I quit, Hughes signed me off: "Sally Quinn is leaving CBS News for *The New York Times*—not necessarily sadder, but certainly wiser. And we hope she's happier there than she was here. For one thing, the help over there don't have to get up as early as they do here."

I thought it was touching and funny in Hughes' own gruff way.

Later that morning Richard called to say that Don Hamilton, Director of Business Affairs, wanted that day to be my last day. I pointed out that I had two film pieces to finish and that I intended to work two more weeks, that I had two further weeks of vacation coming to me, and that therefore they could count me on the payroll for another month. I wasn't to start at *The Times* until March 18.

Richard said Hamilton wouldn't buy that. I told Richard that I would call Salant or Bill Paley if I had to, and give interviews about what a cheap crumby outfit CBS was if I heard another word on the subject. Just get me the four weeks' pay. I didn't care how he did it.

Richard understood that I meant it. A half hour later he called back and said, "It's all set."

It still made me chuckle, though, that such a huge corporation would be so unbelievably cheap, especially under the circumstances. But I don't know why I was surprised, after what I had been through.

Saturday, I got a letter from Dick Salant.

> *Dear Sally,*
>
> In case you missed the AP story, I am attaching it. It quotes me absolutely correctly.
>
> I am terribly sorry that things did not work out as we all expected and hoped. The fault, I honestly believe, was ours—mine.
>
> In any event, best wishes for every sort of satisfaction and happiness. And if you can bear it, do drop in so I can say goodbye and good luck.
>
> All the best,
>
> *Dick Salant*

The AP story was enclosed. It said: "CBS News President Richard Salant said Thursday that CBS would not hold her to her contract. Asked if he considered Miss Quinn's move a slap at CBS, Salant said, 'No, not at all. She doesn't owe us a thing. We owe her a lot. And we damn near ruined her by making a mistake and pushing her too far too fast.' "

On February 7 Gordon Manning was fired from his job as news director. He was given a job as "vice president and assistant to the president of CBS News."

Gordon had been news director for nine years. His ten years were up in June and he was to receive a pension. That's why he was given that job, to hold him over so he could get his pension. He was fifty-seven in June, 1974. Somehow Gordon managed to redeem himself, partly by landing Solzhenitsyn for Walter Cronkite to interview. He stayed on after June and became a producer for the public affairs division of CBS News.

Bill Small was given Gordon's job. Sandy Socolow was given the Washington bureau. The day the change was announced Small was in Gordon's office.

Reached there, he said he was completely surprised by the promotion. "I've only been at this desk for six hours," he said. "I'm just trying to find out where the men's room is and where they keep the key to the liquor cabinet."

On February 28 Lee Townsend was fired. They had no ready title for him to assume. He was later assigned to the investigative unit. The new *Morning News* producer was the Rome bureau manager, Joseph Dembo.

The Tricky Task of Picking an Heir Apparent

Picking a successor, say chief executives, is the most important decision they and their directors will make. It also may be the toughest and one of the worst. "You see the wrong guy selected a lot," says J. Peter Grace, 69, the longest- reigning chief executive of a FORTUNE 500 company, who is reluctantly beginning to think about replacing himself at W. R. Grace & Co. Within the next three years, 35 of the 100 biggest corporations among the 500 are due to change leaders.

Roy Rowan

To explore the selection process, FORTUNE recently interviewed 25 reigning and former chief executives. Clearly it's a sensitive subject. The boss doesn't relish talking about that near or distant day when he will abdicate power, nor does he want to tip his hand. "Obviously I don't go around talking about who should succeed me," says Edward Jefferson, 61, chairman of Du Pont. And an ex-chief executive is loath to give away secrets about a company that he probably still serves in an advisory capacity.

Departing bosses and their boards will talk in general terms about the kind of replacement they want, and how this up-and-coming leader should be groomed. They identify the most sought-after qualities as integrity, self-confidence, physical and mental fitness, the ability to think strategically, and a facility for communicating ideas. They also expect the new chief to be homegrown—either cultivated in the headquarters greenhouse or farmed out to a major division until he's ripe. Directors stress the importance of an orderly transition, or "no surprises," as they say.

But surprises persist. This is a dangerous time for men at the top. Increasingly the freshly picked chief gets fired or quits in a huff, and a headhunter rushes to the rescue. RCA has become a revolving door for chairmen and presidents, having survived a total of eight in the past eight years. ITT stumbled dramatically trying to fill Chairman Harold Geneen's giant shoes. His first successor, Lyman C. Hamilton Jr., lasted a mere 17 months.

Sometimes it's the Job-patient heirs apparent who are passed over with stunning suddenness. Just this year two long-serving presidents, David Judelson of Gulf & Western and Ronald Pidler of Black & Decker, watched their executive vice presidents catapult into the chief's seat. Then there are those widely heralded hired-gun successors, who sometimes get sacked before they succeed—a not entirely unexpected happening if they've entered the employ of such hardy perennials as William Paley, 82, of CBS—who finally yielded up the chief executive's title to Thomas Wyman—or Armand Hammer, 84, of Occidental Petroleum.

"Not enough thought is given to the psychological fit of a chairman or president to his role," says Harry Levinson, publisher of a Cambridge, Massachusetts, management newsletter that frequently dwells on succession problems. He cites International Harvester's appointment of Archie McCardell as chief executive in 1978 as a flagrant case of a company "failing to put together a behavioral job description before bringing in a new chief." Though few blame Harvester's problems entirely on McCardell, he was fired four years later after a long and largely fruitless battle with the United Auto Workers and much criticism of his generous compensation arrangements.

A sagging economy can also alter the specs on chief executives. In boom times budget, production, and marketing miscalculations are easier to cover over. "Today the tightfisted bottom-line manager is the guy everybody's looking for," says David F. Smith, New York director of Korn/Ferry International, the largest executive search firm. But he claims companies know only what kind of chief executive they want at a particular moment. "Obviously it's a longer-reaching decision," he says. Smith believes that in a year or two the bottom-liners may be out of fashion and the "strong marketers" back in vogue.

In the best of times, selecting a new boss is an impressionistic process. Much of it is unspoken and intuitive. A glance or a nod at a board meeting may carry more weight than words when the choice is being made. So in many cases the deciding factors are never known. Headhunters believe that selection committees frequently feel frustrated because they are searching for a composite—a mythical executive who combines all the best traits of the candidates being considered. "Often they're looking for the impossible dream," says Russell S. Reynolds Jr., chairman of the search firm that bears his name.

Although his firm's computerized retrieval system keeps tabs on 15,000 executives, Reynolds concedes, "The best C.E.O.s tend to come from within." The inside appointment, he says, is better understood and less of a shock. "Companies do not respond well to shocks," he adds. "It takes a boat a long time to stop rocking."

E. Pendleton James, President Reagan's former White House personnel director and a headhunter who specializes in recruiting directors and chairmen, lays a lot of the blame for succession problems on cronyism among directors. "I'm negative on boards as they're now constituted," he says. "They're ossified and incestuous." Many directors, he feels, "stay too long at the fair" and serve on too many boards. "After reading this," he adds, "no one will want to retain me."

When a board is willing to look outside the company, James sees a new tendency to look outside the industry as well. He points to CBS's Wyman, recruited from Pillsbury; Burlington Northern's new chairman, Richard Bressler, brought in from Atlantic Richfield; and former Secretary of Transportation Drew Lewis, hired to head Warner Amex Cable Communications. "They came after Lewis because he was a man with great leadership and management skills, not because he was a transportation expert," observes James.

Only paltry statistics have been kept that bear on the success and failure of the chief executive selection process, and most of the figures are buried in headhunters' computers. Carl Menk, president of Boyden Associates, a search firm based in New York City, reports that during the three years beginning in 1976, 62 FORTUNE 500 companies changed chief executives, an average of 21 a year. During the four years starting with 1979, the average jumped to 36, an increase of 80%. During both periods slightly more than a quarter of the new bosses were recruited from outside the company.

Eugene Jennings, professor of business administration at Michigan State University, says that 22.5% of the two top officers of a sampling of major companies either resign or get fired before reaching retirement age, compared with 5% in 1969. His "mobility auditing program" lumps together the records of the No. 1 and No. 2 executives at 480 corporations—a list that he claims is roughly comparable to the FORTUNE 500. "Almost a third of those now leaving early have got caught up in some kind of palace revolt," reports Jennings, who spends more time advising chief executives than he does teaching. Conflict over the strategic direction of the enterprise can trigger early departure. "Disagreement over where the company is going and how it should get there takes its toll," Jennings says.

Big companies have no standard procedures for picking the people to run them. A standing nominating committee that the board uses to get new directors frequently takes on the task. If he's especially strong, the outgoing chief will take the lead. Lately, however, boards have become more independent. "More and more you see the selection committee of the board picking their own person and derailing the chief executive's candidate," says Jennings.

Some companies mark the finalists well before a winner is declared. General Electric named three vice chairmen in 1979 and a year later made one of them, John F. Welch Jr., chief executive. Many big firms use formal "leadership identification" programs. Some even color-code personnel records to indicate an executive's potential—red for "not promotable," yellow for "take another look," and green for "promotable."

But no fail-safe system prevents a candidate colored green throughout his company career from bombing as boss. On today's fast track the highest-octane performer "may be burned out by the time he sinks into the chief executive's chair," says Robert W. Lear, former chairman of the F.&M. Schaefer Corp. and a visiting professor at the Columbia University Graduate School of Business. Or he may have been judged too much on efficiency, rather than on less tangible character traits. "Chief executives can fail or succeed depending on whether they attract the trust of their colleagues," says Kenneth R. Andrews, editor of the *Harvard Business Review* and a director of Xerox. "It's a rather slippery thought, but it's important, especially with all the hoopla about the failure of the American manager because he's too short-term oriented and not concerned about the development of people."

From the chief executive's vantage, choosing a successor is a complex task that requires as much help as he can get. "I don't think any C.E.O. sits in his office and comes up with a name," says Du Pont's Jefferson. "I have an exchange of views with members of the board and former chief executives, including Irv Shapiro, Charles McCoy, and Crawford Greenwalt. The other thing I do is make sure that the senior members of management get plenty of exposure—reviewing plans at board meetings, and under more informal circumstances. That way all the directors have a pretty good understanding of the merits of the people who could be candidates when we finally get down to a replacement."

The $33-billion-a-year corporation has one executive committee for traditional Du Pont operations and another for Conoco, acquired in 1981. "Both report into the office of the chairman," Jefferson explains. "Three of us are there—myself, Dick Heckert, who's vice chairman for the traditional business, and Ralph Bailey, who's vice chairman for the Conoco division. In the course of the deliberations of those committees you get quite a reading on people, and what they accomplish."

Like many chief executives, Jefferson believes that new directions taken by the company will help determine who succeeds him. "Where you're trying to go," he says, "is part and parcel of the decisions on people. I've got to emphasize, though, that there are many ways of skinning a cat and many ways of running a business. Different people bring different things. But then you're asking me to comment on something I haven't done yet and will only do once."

Jefferson's mentor and predecessor, Irving Shapiro, 67, admits that in a big corporation with the executive depth of Du Pont there were several potential chief executives to pick from. "It's a close call," he says. "You're looking for that indefinable extra quality—wisdom in all its aspects. Besides, I think that fellow has fire in his belly."

Now a partner in the Wilmington office of the law firm Skadden Arps Slate Meagher & Flom, Shapiro began reviewing his thinking about a successor with the board a year before the vote. "It's like dealing with a family," he says. "You know whatever your successor does well is going to reflect on you. That feeling is part pro-enterprise and part selfish."

Another succession, just as carefully orchestrated, is about to occur. On May 1 James Evans, 62, will turn over the Union Pacific throttle to William Cook, who will be 61 in September. The two men have worked together for 14 years, and although their ages are close, Evans insists he "wants to give Cook the stripes for a few years." Evans, however, will retain the chairmanship and concentrate on long-range strategy for the diversified rail and energy company, whose assets swelled to $10 billion after a merger with Missouri Pacific last December.

"A guy burns himself out," admits Evans, who has been the boss since 1977. "It's better for the company if I turn over control to Bill. That'll give him four years." Evans sees several possible future chief executives in the 50- to 55-year-old age bracket. "We have a group of executives who are keen for the job," he says. "But I'd always go with the guy 55 over the guy 45. He's had ten more years' experience and has been roughed up in the fray. Also he's more willing to listen to others and not make too many unilateral decisions. People do get wiser, you know."

One corporation where the crown may not be lifted from its present head and placed on another without fuss is W. R. Grace. Chairman Peter Grace has been undisputed boss of the chemical and natural resources conglomerate (1982 sales: $6.1 billion) for 38 years. Has a succession plan been worked out? "Since I don't want to retire, I haven't addressed myself to that question." he replies crustily, though clearly he has given it considerable thought. Two years ago he picked Carl Graf, 57, as president and chief operating officer, and Charles Erhart Jr., 57, his cousin and a great-grandson of founder W. R. Grace, as vice chairman and chief administrative officer. "These are the only two in a position to succeed," says Peter, who quips: "Unless Graf changes the *f* to *c e*, the next chief executive won't be named Grace."

A member of the Grace family—by birth or marriage—has always run the company, which became publicly owned in 1953. In 1945 Peter's father suffered a stroke and telephoned orders from his sickbed to install his son in his place. "I got the job without any right to it," admits Peter, who says his selection caused "quite a bit of fighting, and things couldn't be worked out for two weeks."

Last month Peter again discussed succession plans with the board: "I said we think Graf and Erhart are the two best people to get the training, and the board agreed." Although Grace says he would be "appalled" if the board went outside for the next chief executive, he prefers to deal with outside directors. "When I first became president, the board was dominated by inside directors," he says. "I found out quickly how dangerous that situation is. Because the chief executive is superior to these people for 29 days a month, you find them sticking it to you on the 30th day. Two or three might even close ranks and say, 'We don't like the way he's pushing us around.' "

For filling lower-ranking slots, Grace holds a high regard for headhunters. "I used to dislike them intensely," he says. "They'd come in and start tampering with our team. They have unbelievable antennae." But Grace thinks chief executive pickings are slim on the outside. "I serve on ten boards, and I know exactly what's out there," he says. "Even when I'm not a director of a company in the process of picking a new chief executive, I think I know when they've picked a lemon. If the chief executive is imaginative and has good ideas, but isn't too well organized, his No. 2 man may be able to put the pieces together. But when No. 2 gets promoted, they discover he hasn't got the innovation or the drive, and his entire capability hinged on working alongside his old boss. I've seen this happen a number of times."

For 145 years Deere & Co. of Moline, Illinois, had similarly been run by a descendant of its founder, blacksmith John Deere, or by an in-law. Last September, when Chairman William A. Hewitt, 68 (husband of Deere's great-great-granddaughter), was named Ambassador to Jamaica, he broke the string by engineering the appointment of his No. 2, Robert Hanson, 49. "I talked only with the outside directors," says Hewitt, who was boss of the tractor company for 27 years. "It would have been futile to discuss this with the inside directors because they were all contenders."

A pothole-filled transition occurred at Greyhound Corp. By the time Gerald Trautman, 70, the curmudgeonly chairman for 16 years, retired to his tennis, golf, and stamp collecting, he had left a slew of No. 2's by the roadside. Just in the last five years the transportation and food conglomerate has tried out four heirs apparent. "We almost ended up suing Booz Allen because of the way they conducted the search," Trautman says. "They kept pushing five or six different candidates." Booz Allen declines comment.

The carnage started in 1978 when James Kerrigan, head of Greyhound Lines Inc. and Trautman's presumed successor, was fired. Now chairman of Trailways, Kerrigan told a reporter: "Nobody's going to have a different view on anything in the Greyhound Corp. than Gerry Trautman." In 1980 Robert Swanson, recruited from General Mills as heir apparent, resigned after eight months. Ralph Batastini was named president briefly and then kicked upstairs to vice chairman. Finally, in October 1981 John W. Teets, 49, who was back at Greyhound after a nine-year hiatus, was made chief executive. (He got the chairman's title from Trautman just eight months ago.) Says Teets: "It's interesting to see the failures in picking C.E.O.s, especially when the board goes outside. Generally, it's the chemistry that doesn't work. Or the rank and file may not accept the new leadership."

The close Teets-Trautman relationship was unusual, considering Teets's defection from Greyhound. "But he was a good learner and knew when to ask questions," says Trautman, who kept in touch with Teets all the time he was away. Adds Teets: "There was a feeling of camaraderie, and I knew he was interested in me as a person. He made it very easy for me to come back."

But in business the two men functioned very differently. "I knew my style of management was not a bit like his," says Teets, who was initially put in charge of the problem-plagued Armour division and thought it only remotely possible that he would end up as chief executive. "I was more meeting-oriented, and had more interaction with people. Gerry reviewed everything and didn't get personally involved. I asked if he'd like me to change my style. He said no. Instead he gave me a longer tether."

Trautman continues to serve as a consultant. "He's been very helpful," says Teets politely. "You don't always find that to be the case when a man's been as dominant as he has." But then the tireless Trautman is not relaxing his grip completely. "I will remain on the board of Greyhound, and on the boards of all major subsidiaries," he proudly declares.

Another old war-horse pushing 70 and still pulling hard is Ben W. Heineman, chairman of Northwest Industries. He's had four careers: attorney, railroader, conglomerator—and, for a spell three years ago, interim boss of the First National Bank of Chicago. As an outside director he stepped in to keep the bank running after A. Robert Abboud, the abrasive chairman who had cleaned out some 200 executives in the ranks below, was himself dismissed. "There was a vacuum from top to bottom," reports Heineman, whose hurry-up task was to find a new chief executive. He turned to headhunter Russell Reynolds. "Call me every hour if you have to," he told Reynolds. "It would be impossible for you to overcommunicate with me." By the time Barry Sullivan was brought in from Chase Manhattan, Reynolds says, "every member of my family knew Ben Heineman's voice."

Ben Heineman is adamant that a company should never hesitate to go outside for a new chief executive. He says, "At Northwest Industries we operate a number of large companies and I have not always taken the recommendation of the retiring chief executive. I thought I knew better. And I had to live with the decision. Besides, chief executives tend to replicate themselves and pick people in their own image. But what might have been right in the past may not be right for the future. The world changes. Business changes. On the other hand, if it turns out the board has to choose between two or three very fine inside candidates—well, that's a very high class problem."

To uncover those hot inside candidates, management consultants advocate switching the executives among difficult slots to see how they perform under pressure. Richard Beaumont, president of Organization Resources Counselors Inc., headquartered in New York City, calls this "playing the Parcheesi game." He says: "You have to make spaces available to move candidate X out and candidate Y in, if for no other reason than to provide experience and exposure."

One company trying that is Texaco. "We're so big," says Chairman and Chief Executive John K. McKinley, 63, "that four of our divisions would be in the top 100 companies. One way of developing new leadership is to give the best men the responsibility for those divisions. Texaco set up a succession contest. Last month the board elevated two division chiefs, James W. Kinnear, 55, and Alfred C. DeCrane Jr., 52, to vice chairman and president, making them the front-runners in the race for McKinley's job. "The board," he says, "expects me to make a recommendation. I would be surprised if it didn't give that recommendation a high priority."

But this is not the way Richard M. Furlaud, 60, chairman of Squibb Corp., is playing the succession game. "Even ten years from retirement," Furlaud says, "the chief executive should advise the board who is most likely to succeed him. That way rivalries won't consume the company." In 1978 he picked Dennis C. Fill, 53, the former executive vice president for operations, to be president and clear heir apparent. Like Teets of Greyhound, Fill had left the company; he was living in Asia, serving Squibb as a consultant. Furlaud lured him back. "We had worked closely together," says the chairman. "That's the real test of a protégé." However, Furlaud leaves himself an out. "If a mistake is made, it can be corrected," he says. "But it's a shame to go outside. Being chief executive is the ultimate prize."

Because executive talent windfalls are always possible, Chairman Forrest N. Shumway, 56, of the Signal Companies dislikes the idea of giving the board a succession plan years in advance. "All of a sudden some whiz-kid vice president comes along and your plan is shot," he says. Also, he claims the outside directors don't have enough contact with the candidates. "They meet them on a legal deal or on a financial deal," says Shumway, "but they don't know who can stand up at a stockholders' meeting and take the kind of pounding you get there, or if a candidate is going to blow up everytime he talks to the press."

Early this year when Signal, a builder of petrochemical plants, aircraft equipment, and trucks, acquired Wheelabrator-Frye, an environmental, energy, and engineering concern, Shumway felt that one of the biggest prizes he had won was his eventual successor, Michael D. Dingman, 51. But to make room for Dingman, who had been Wheelabrator-Frye's chairman, Shumway had to demote Signal's president. "We haven't changed our opinion of our guy one iota," says Shumway. "But obviously the head of Wheelabrator had a lot more experience and stature." As for setting up a horse race between them, Shumway adds: "That way you waste two years and lose two guys while you're wrecking the company."

What does it take to succeed at the top? Professor Jennings calls that "the biggest guessing game in business." As he says, it's always been a gamble and always will be, "because there's no rung on the way up the corporate ladder that prepares you for the last one." From one rule of thumb, however, occupants of the lower rungs may take comfort. Academicians, headhunters, and the men who have actually perched at the top agree that it helps to have been knocked down a couple of times during your upward climb.

2

MAKING IT

Winners are losers who never give up—Sign in the window of an automobile dealers showroom July 25, 1982—(in midst of a major slump of car sales).

"Making it" is a long-standing concern. Whereas in earlier times it seems that hard work was associated with making it (i.e., succeeding), more recently the notion of making it has taken on a somewhat different connotation. As Daniel Rodgers observed in his excellent book, *The History of the Work Ethic*, the notion that hard work leads to success appears increasingly to be more of a myth than a fact. As organizations have become larger and more impersonal it appears that more than hard work and competence at one's work is required to make it. While competence and diligence are still relevant, it seems that often the appearance of competence is less strongly correlated with actual performance than managers frequently assume. So many things combine to determine the results of one's efforts that attributions of success or failure to individual persons, while still made, seem tenuous. Moreover, given the fact that these attributions are often difficult to support with documentation, appearances (and the manipulation of appearances) often play an important role in determining an individual's success. Under these conditions success is a judgment call.

The contrast between this view of making it and the more traditional view is well illustrated by a story related by Karl Weick. It seems that three umpires were discussing their job of calling balls and strikes. One umpire said, "I calls them as they is." A second umpire said, "I calls them as I sees them." The third umpire observed, "They ain't nothin' till I calls them." In this view, "making it" is seen as having strong elements of subjectivity, arbitrariness, and even invention of facts.

Furthermore, our revised view of making it suggests that many of the elements which contribute to a person being judged successful involve social, political and personal attributes which may have little to do with the technical aspects of one's work, but in actuality contribute a great deal both to a person's ability to get things done and to being called successful. Finally, as the readings in this section suggest, making it for many people has a more basic component than being successful: making it often means merely surviving!

The selections in this section deal with how people make it in organizations. Doug Tindal argues in "Take Charge" that the first week on a new job can make you or break you. He offers a number of suggestions concerning the perils managers face on assuming a new job and hints on how to deal with them. "Managing Your Boss" by John J. Gabarro and John P. Kotter explores an issue which many managers confess has been a major key to their success or failure in organizations. Like Tindal, Gabarro and Kotter point out that often subordinates wait passively for their superiors to define their mutual relationship. Their article explains how subordinates can play more active roles.

The next four articles reveal a number of skills which people use both to survive and to succeed in organizations. Acquiring a base of power and influence to operate as a leader is not necessarily an assigned or a static event, as Doris Kearns in "Campus Politico" shows in her analysis of Lyndon Johnson as a student. Johnson created a position of leadership through intelligent definition and use of a very low level post in the college administrative hierarchy. Halberstam's account of the career of Walter Cronkite reveals how a combination of elements contributed to Cronkite's success. Some of these elements are clearly congruent with the traditional view of how to make it; however, much of Cronkite's success reflected his ability to manage power relationships within CBS. On the other hand, Daniel Seligman argues in "Luck and Careers" that the evidence he has uncovered offers considerable support for the notion that luck is an important determinant of success in almost any field. Judith Garwood takes still a different approach in "The Imaginary Manager."

Garwood maintains, and we agree that there is a clear need for creativity in the practice of management. She asks, "What would happen if we, as a society, started emphasizing the *creative* side of doing business?" Her argument that a whole generation of Americans has been raised to think of business as dull is underscored by Robert Schrank's views expressed in "Management." As a production manager with a background as a blue-collar worker and union organizer, Schrank finds managers and engineers much less interesting than blue-collar workers.

Our final selection, "Furniture Czarina," by Frank E. James is the delightful success story of a Russian immigrant who arrived in this country penniless and achieved such recognition as an entrepreneur that at age ninety she was awarded New York University's coveted honorary doctorate in Commercial Science, a prize "the school reserves for world-class captains of industry."

Take Charge

The first week on a new job can make you— or break you

Doug Tindal

It may not seem fair, but your first week in the new, executive job is going to make you or break you. Your first days will establish you as a strong performer who'll lead the company on to higher sales and wider profit margins than ever before. Or they'll mark you as a dud. Naturally, you won't head into the office on day one wearing your plaid sports jacket. You'll wear one of your navy blue suits—the one with the fine pinstripe would be a good choice—and, naturally, you'll wear the vest. So at least you'll look right, which certainly is a step in the right direction—but only a very, very small step, because there are so many pitfalls in a new job, so many envious skeptics waiting for you to slip, that your first days are downright perilous, to say the least.

What if you put your car in the president's parking spot? What if you get stuck in an elevator (sure, it could happen to anyone, but when it's your first day on the job . . .)? And what if Gladys from accounting is stuck in there with you? These are unlikely dangers, of course, but most of the perils of a new job are entirely real. And though they may be much more subtle, they're also much more serious.

Fortunately, there are things you can do and steps you can take (carefully) that will start you off on the right foot, as they say. There are correct moves to make—and a great many wrong ones to avoid—as you seek out the levers of power. And the key point to bear in mind, according to the experts, is that you should let the specifics of the job wait for a bit. Your first concern should be first impressions, and obviously this goes far beyond the appropriate suit or picking the right place to park.

You have to impress a lot of people. You have to impress upon your boss, and others at his level, that you're sharp and aggressive and on the move; you have to convince your peers that you're a team player, a trustworthy colleague. And the very first move, the experts say, is to make a good impression on your staff, to win their respect and trust—especially when it comes to the bright young fellow who may be all set to torpedo you because he wanted your job. The way you handle this situation will color the way the rest of the staff receives you. If you fire him, for example, you may risk a palace revolt—and lose his ex-

---

perience. If you let things slide, hoping that he'll soon grow to love you, you're probably deluding yourself.

Peter Frost is a consultant and professor of organizational behavior at the University of British Columbia, and he says it's probably a good idea to assume that someone in the company has a grudge against you, even if you have no direct evidence. "It's very rare, in my experience, that a senior position is awarded without there being an internal candidate, and normally this individual feels a bit bruised when he doesn't get the job."

So what should you do? Dave Urquhart is a partner in the management consulting firm of Urquhart & Preger, Inc., in Toronto, and he recommends a very neat solution: "Chances are your subordinate was passed over because senior management figured he wasn't quite ready. So you go to him and offer to groom him—when you're ready to move on, you point out, he'll know everything he needs to know to step right into your shoes. This way, you convert a potential enemy into a valuable ally; and, you clear the way for yourself to advance, because generally, you can't move up in a company until you've prepared someone to take your place."

Urquhart says, incidentally, that when you get to the final stage of the hiring process, just before you take the job, it's quite legitimate to ask if there's an internal candidate, and if so, who. In other words, know your enemy.

There's another thing you should establish at this early stage: who will be your secretary? You may have the option of keeping the same secretary your predecessor had, and the obvious advantage of this is that she'll know all the ropes. The disadvantage is that some of them won't be *your* ropes; and if your predecessor is still with the company, your secretary may have conflicting loyalties.

So you might be better off to hire someone new. Either way, you should realize that your secretary can be much, much more than someone to answer phones and type correspondence; she (or he) can be your link to the great secretarial intelligence grid, and her perceptions of other people can be a big help.

Whenever you start a new job, you face a great many important questions that can be answered only over a period of time. You have to find out, for example, how much of your success depends on meeting performance standards such as sales targets or production quotas, and how much depends on pleasing the boss in subjective ways. If your boss is the kind of guy who likes to be at his desk by 7:45 A.M., then chances are he likes to see other people at their desks by 7:45. If you don't come in until 8:30, this may affect the way your boss perceives the quality of your work—no matter how good it is.

Frank Musten, an industrial psychologist who practices in both Ottawa and Toronto, points out that each company has its own set of norms: Should you work through the noon hour or should you take a two-hour lunch? Do you have to go to company parties? Does your spouse have to go, too? Should you join your staff in the lunchroom occasionally, to be friendly—or would they consider it an intrusion? Well, Musten says, try it: carry your bowl of tomato soup over to join the staff one day and see what happens. Nobody is likely to tell you to shove off, but if you're not welcome, you'll know it—for one thing, the conversation will dry right up.

But you don't necessarily have to obey all the norms. "If you try to become totally a company man, you'll be useless to both the company and to yourself," Musten says. "So you should decide which norms you can live with."

Peter Frost adds that when you move into a company at a senior level, usually you're expected to stir things up a bit and make some changes: "In other words, there's a degree to which you have to make the company fit you, not the other way around."

Laird Mealiea is an associate professor of organizational development at Dalhousie University in Halifax, and he points out that your new company can provide a great deal of formal information about your job. "You should make an effort to get hold of all the company's policies and procedures manuals, job descriptions, personnel files—anything that describes your position and your relationship to others. These aren't gospel, of course; you have to weigh them against the information you pick up informally and find a balance."

Urquhart suggests a number of ways to pick up informal information: "You should take the initiative to go around and meet other managers throughout the firm," he says. "Try to get to know them a bit—not just what they do, but what they value.

"It helps you to build some bridges to these guys, so they'll be more receptive to cooperating with you when you need them and it gives you a line on what kinds of people get promoted in the company. It also gives you a chance to look for potential allies, people you can use to test your thoughts about the organization."

Urquhart suggests you should find out about any key people who've recently left the company: "Call them up, tell them you'd like to take them to lunch and pick their brains about where the company is at, who the key players are, all that stuff."

Finally, he suggests you meet with your predecessor and ask him about your new subordinates: which ones are top performers, which are marginal. Naturally, you won't necessarily be guided by his perceptions, but it's valuable to hear what he thinks; and it will probably tell you something about the way he ran the department.

Pamela Ennis, an industrial psychologist who has her own company, Pamela Ennis & Associates, Industrial Psychologists, says you should also speak with subordinates: "Find out about how independent they were under your predecessor, what controls there are on their actions, how they feel about their jobs, what kind of formal communications there are in the department—you want to do something like a miniature organizational survey."

Ennis has some interesting ideas about the world of power politics and the ways it can affect your first few days on the job. "Power politics is the informal world of management," she says. "It doesn't appear on any management chart and it's not studied in any of the texts, but unless you know how to play, any success you have will be short-lived. The first thing you have to understand about power is that it's not the same thing as authority. When you go into a job on day one, you have a certain amount of authority which comes to you automatically as a result of your position, but your power is almost nil—power is the ability to influence other people and this is something you must earn."

Ennis adds that the ways to power will vary from one company to the next because the sort of thing that influences the key people in one company may cut no ice at all somewhere else. In a company that's heavily dependent on information, you might have to learn to sweet-talk the computer—if you can figure out how to get a particularly lucid kind of monthly report from the maze of data stored in its memory, you may wind up with more clout than the president. In another company, one with a heavy marketing orientation, for instance, you may have to learn how to hustle and promote yourself.

Sometimes this means you'll have to learn a whole new language. Frost says you should be alert to casual conversation and notice if people tend to talk in the language of, say, finance. If your company is planning to expand its factory, do people say the expansion will cost $3.5 million, or do they say it will trim first quarter earnings by 17 cents a share? Naturally, you should copy the corporate style on things like this. "Also," he says, "try to pick out the corporate buzzwords. Do you hear people talking about LRC (linear responsibility charting) or MBO (management by objectives)? These things may be part of what makes your company tick."

In most companies, Frost says, there's a particular story that the old hands always tell the newcomers, and you should listen for it because it can reveal a lot about the way your new colleagues see themselves: "In one company I heard of from a colleague, there's a story about a nine-day fortnight. Years ago, the company had a serious drop in sales and they had to cut back. So everyone, from the president to the janitors, took off one day without pay every two weeks. They worked nine days, instead of 10, each fortnight, and they kept this up for several months until sales picked up."

New employees of this company soon hear about "the nine-day fortnight" and, if they're alert, they realize that it's a story about how these people pulled together, toughed it out through the lean times, and went on to win. So this company may place an unusually high value on cooperation and teamwork.

"In another company, the key people like to pretend that they don't take their jobs very seriously and that they never really work hard, so they're always talking about how they take four-hour lunches. In fact, they do often take four-hour lunches, but they never talk about what happens after the lunch—they go back to the office and work until midnight." Obviously, if you want to get anywhere in this company, you should take care to project an easy-going kind of image and make it look as though you're having a good time.

Arnold Minors is an in-house consultant specializing in organizational development for Imperial Oil Ltd., in Toronto, and he points out that most companies also have corporate myths. "The corporate myth is usually in the form of a prohibition," he says. "There's something—it could be anything—which, according to everybody else in the company, you *must not do*." For example: never make a presentation to the boss without using a flip chart. If you question this prohibition, Minors says, you'll probably find that it's not written down anywhere, that no one in living memory has tried to do it, and that, quite obviously, no one knows what will happen if you try. So the prohibition is a myth and the odds are that if you go ahead and do the thing— illustrate your presentation with an overhead projector instead of a flip chart, for instance—you may be able to pick up a reputation as a bold innovator.

Minors has just joined Imperial, and he says he spent nearly all his time during his first few days getting around to meet key people. This isn't always as easy as it sounds because, as Ennis points out, the real power points in your company may be far removed from the top positions on the organizational chart. You need to find out who actually gets things done, not who holds the title: The reason your secretary is sitting there with no typewriter could be that you sent the requisition to the head of supply services, when everybody knows nothing happens unless you send the requisition directly to Betty in the stockroom.

In your company, there are probably a couple dozen behind-the-scenes people just like Betty. These are the real movers and shakers, and it's so critically important for you to learn how to spot them that, with help from the experts—Frost, Urquhart, Mealiea, Musten, Ennis and Minors— we've put together a check list to help you:

- Whose names come up most often in conversation?
- Who do people turn to when they need information or advice?
- Who sits on the greatest number of key committees (the committees that allocate resources, money, staff, equipment, computer time and so on)?
- Who draws up the agenda for policy meetings?
- Who seems to give the most direction to these meetings (not necessarily who talks the most)?
- Who seems to have the easiest access to the president?
- Whose offices have the best view?

- Who has first call on staff time?
- When the president sends out a policy memo, who gets it?
- Whose departments got the largest budget increases last year?

The people whose names turn up most frequently on this list are the people with clout and, naturally, you should try to develop especially good relationships with them: as the experts point out, power rubs off. You can answer most of these questions by simple observation, and Laird Mealiea, the Dalhousie professor, says you should be able to complete all these observations within the first several weeks, depending on the size and complexity of both the job and the organization. But some questions, such as "Who gives the most direction to policy meetings?", require some judgment. You should check your judgments on these questions with other people and, in fact, Urquhart suggests you should try to find a mentor to help you.

Basically, he says, you should try to find someone in a senior position in the company who is willing to take you under his wing and point you in the right direction. Ideally, your boss should perform this role, but often he can't—especially at first: "Your boss has to watch you closely for the first few months to decide whether you can handle the job," Urquhart explains, "so it's often difficult for him to give you as much support as you may need. Because of this, at least one company I know of has begun to appoint a senior executive to act as a mentor for each new manager."

So you find a mentor, and you learn about all the power points and the company's language, and you hear its particular story and discover what its values are, is there anything else you ought to do? Says Mealiea: "Once you've gathered all this information, so that you know the environment, you can begin to become successful at the job. You can shove your concerns about politics more into the background and get on with doing the job."

Minors, the Imperial Oil consultant, offers a good example. On his first day on the job, Minors wore a navy blue, pinstriped suit, with vest. Minors was known as a fairly stylish dresser on his previous job, but he says he doesn't stand out at all now because everybody at Imperial seems to dress well. "I haven't seen polyester since I got here."

The surprising thing is that Minors thinks this may be a problem. "As a consultant in organizational development, my job is to help people adapt to change in the organization," he explains, "and to do this I think I have to be seen as a bit of an individual, someone who is able to question the corporate norms. So," he says, "I may be forced to buy a pair of jeans."

Managing Your Boss

John J. Gabarro and John P. Kotter

To many the phrase *managing your boss* may sound unusual or suspicious. Because of the traditional top-down emphasis in organizations, it is not obvious why you need to manage relationships upward—unless, of course, you would do so for personal or political reasons. But in using the expression *managing your boss,* we are not referring to political maneuvering or apple polishing. Rather we are using the term to mean the process of consciously working with your superior to obtain the best possible results for you, your boss, and the company.

Recent studies suggest that effective managers take time and effort to manage not only relationships with their subordinates but also those with their bosses.[1] These studies show as well that this aspect of management, essential though it is to survival and advancement, is sometimes ignored by otherwise talented and aggressive managers. Indeed, some managers who actively and effectively supervise subordinates, products, markets, and technologies, nevertheless assume an almost passively reactive stance vis-à-vis their bosses. Such a stance practically always hurts these managers and their companies.

If you doubt the importance of managing your relationship with your boss or how difficult it is to do so effectively, consider for a moment the following sad but telling story:

Frank Gibbons was an acknowledged manufacturing genius in his industry and, by any profitability standard, a very effective executive. In 1973, his strengths propelled him into the position of vice president of manufacturing for the second largest and most profitable company in its industry. Gibbons was not, however, a good manager of people. He knew this, as did others in his company and his industry. Recognizing this weakness, the president made sure that those who reported to Gibbons were good at working with people and could compensate for his limitations. The arrangement worked well.

In 1975, Philip Bonnevie was promoted into a position reporting to Gibbons. In keeping with the previous pattern, the president selected Bonnevie because he had an excellent track record and a reputation for being good with people. In making that selection, however, the president neglected to notice that, in his rapid rise through the organization,

---

Bonnevie himself had never reported to anyone who was poor at managing subordinates. Bonnevie had always had good-to-excellent bosses. He had never been forced to manage a relationship with a difficult boss. In retrospect, Bonnevie admits he had never thought that managing his boss was a part of his job.

Fourteen months after he started working for Gibbons, Bonnevie was fired. During that same quarter, the company reported a net loss for the first time in seven years. Many of those who were close to these events say that they don't really understand what happened. This much is known, however: while the company was bringing out a major new product—a process that required its sales, engineering, and manufacturing groups to coordinate their decisions very carefully—a whole series of misunderstandings and bad feelings developed between Gibbons and Bonnevie.

For example, Bonnevie claims Gibbons was aware of and had accepted Bonnevie's decision to use a new type of machinery to make the new product; Gibbons swears he did not. Furthermore, Gibbons claims he made it clear to Bonnevie that introduction of the product was too important to the company in the short run to take any major risks.

As a result of such misunderstandings, planning went awry: a new manufacturing plant was built that could not produce the new product designed by engineering, in the volume desired by sales, at a cost agreed on by the executive committee. Gibbons blamed Bonnevie for the mistake. Bonnevie blamed Gibbons.

Of course, one could argue that the problem here was caused by Gibbons's inability to manage his subordinates. But one can make just as strong a case that the problem was related to Bonnevie's inability to manage his boss. Remember, Gibbons was not having difficulty with any other subordinates. Moreover, given the personal price paid by Bonnevie (being fired and having his reputation within the industry severely tarnished), there was little consolation in saying the problem was that Gibbons was poor at managing subordinates. Everyone already knew that.

We believe that the situation could have turned out differently had Bonnevie been more adept at understanding Gibbons and at managing his relationship with him. In this case, an inability to manage upward was unusually costly. The company lost $2 to $5 million, and Bonnevie's career was, at least temporarily, disrupted. Many less costly cases like this probably occur regularly in all major corporations, and the cumulative effect can be very destructive.

MISREADING THE
BOSS-SUBORDINATE RELATIONSHIP

People often dismiss stories like the one we just related as being merely cases of personality conflict. Because two people can on occasion be psychologically or temperamentally incapable of working together, this can be an apt description. But more often, we have found, a personality conflict is only a part of the problem—sometimes a very small part.

Bonnevie did not just have a different personality from Gibbons, he also made or had unrealistic assumptions and expectations about the very nature of boss-subordinate relationships. Specifically, he did not recognize that his relationship to Gibbons involved *mutual dependence* between two *fallible* human beings. Failing to recognize this, a manager typically either avoids trying to manage his or her relationship with a boss or manages it ineffectively.

Some people behave as if their bosses were not very dependent on them. They fail to see how much the boss needs their help and cooperation to do his or her job effectively. These people refuse to acknowledge that the boss can be severely hurt by their actions and needs cooperation, dependability, and honesty from them.

Some see themselves as not very dependent on their bosses. They gloss over how much help and information they need from the boss in order to perform their own jobs well. This superficial view is particularly damaging when a manager's job and decisions affect other parts of the organization, as was the case in Bonnevie's situation. A manager's immediate boss can play a critical role in linking the manager to the rest of the organization, in making sure the manager's priorities are consistent with organizational needs, and in securing the resources the manager needs to perform well. Yet some managers need to see themselves as practically self-sufficient, as not needing the critical information and resources a boss can supply.

Many managers, like Bonnevie, assume that the boss will magically know what information or help their subordinates need and provide it to them. Certainly, some bosses do an excellent job of caring for their subordinates in this way, but for a manager to expect that from all bosses is dangerously unrealistic. A more reasonable expectation for managers to have is that modest help will be forthcoming. After all, bosses are only human. Most really effective managers accept this fact and assume primary responsibility for their own careers and development. They make a point of seeking the information and help they need to do a job instead of waiting for their bosses to provide it.

In light of the foregoing, it seems to us that managing a situation of mutual dependence among fallible human beings requires the following:

- That you have a good understanding of the other person and yourself, especially regarding strengths, weaknesses, work styles, and needs.
- That you use this information to develop and manage a healthy working relationship—one which is compatible with both persons' work styles and assets, is characterized by mutual expectations, and meets the most critical needs of the other person. And that is essentially what we have found highly effective managers doing.

UNDERSTANDING THE BOSS & YOURSELF

Managing your boss requires that you gain an understanding of both the boss and his context as well as your own situation and needs. All managers do this to some degree, but many are not thorough enough.

The Boss's World

At a minimum, you need to appreciate your boss's goals and pressures, his or her strengths and weaknesses. What are your boss's organizational and personal objectives, and what are the pressures on him, especially those from his boss and others at his level? What are your boss's long suits and blind spots? What is his or her preferred style of working? Does he or she like to get information through memos, formal meetings, or phone calls? Does your boss thrive on conflict or try to minimize it?

Without this information, a manager is flying blind when dealing with his boss, and unnecessary conflicts, misunderstandings, and problems are inevitable.

Goals and Pressures   In one situation we studied, a top-notch marketing manager with a superior performance record was hired into a company as a vice president "to straighten out the marketing and sales problems." The company, which was having financial difficulties, had been recently acquired by a larger corporation. The president was eager to turn it around and gave the new marketing vice president free rein—at least initially. Based on his previous experience, the new vice president correctly diagnosed that greater market share was needed and that strong product management was required to bring that about. As a result, he made a number of pricing decisions aimed at increasing high-volume business.

When margins declined and the financial situation did not improve, however, the president increased pressure on the new vice president. Believing that the situation would eventually correct itself as the company gained back market share, the vice president resisted the pressure.

When by the second quarter margins and profits had still failed to improve, the president took direct control over all pricing decisions and put all items on a set level of margin, regardless of volume. The new vice president began to find himself shut out by the president, and their relationship deteriorated. In fact, the vice president found the president's behavior bizarre. Unfortunately, the president's new pricing scheme also failed to increase margins, and by the fourth quarter both the president and the vice president were fired.

What the new vice president had not known until it was too late was that improving marketing and sales had been only *one* of the president's goals. His most immediate goal had been to make the company more profitable—quickly.

Nor had the new vice president known that his boss was invested in this short-term priority for personal as well as business reasons. The president had been a strong advocate of the acquisition within the parent company, and his personal credibility was at stake.

The vice president made three basic errors. He took information supplied to him at face value, he made assumptions in areas where he had no information, and—most damaging—he never actively tried to clarify what his boss's objectives were. As a result, he ended up taking actions that were actually at odds with the president's priorities and objectives.

Managers who work effectively with their bosses do not behave this way. They seek out information about the boss's goals and problems and pressures. They are alert for opportunities to question the boss and others around him to test their assumptions. They pay attention to clues in the boss's behavior. Although it is imperative they do this when they begin working with a new boss, effective managers also do this on an ongoing basis because they recognize that priorities and concerns change.

Strengths, Weaknesses and Work Style   Being sensitive to a boss's work style can be crucial, especially when the boss is new. For example, a new president who was organized and formal in his approach replaced a man who was informal and intuitive. The new president worked best when he had written reports. He also preferred formal meetings with set agendas.

One of his division managers realized this need and worked with the new president to identify the kinds and frequency of information and reports the president wanted. This manager also made a point of sending background information and brief agendas for their discussions. He found that with this type of preparation their meetings were very useful. Moreover, he found that with adequate preparation his new boss was even more effective at brainstorming problems than his more informal and intuitive predecessor had been.

In contrast, another division manager never fully understood how the new boss's work style differed from that of his predecessor. To the degree that he did sense it, he experienced it as too much control. As a result, he seldom sent the new president the background information he needed, and the president never felt fully prepared for meetings with the manager. In fact, the president spent much of his time when they met trying to get information that he felt he should have had before his arrival. The boss experienced these meetings as frustrating and inefficient, and the subordinate often found himself thrown off guard by the questions that the president asked. Ultimately, this division manager resigned.

The difference between the two division managers just described was not so much one of ability or even adaptability. Rather, the difference was that one of the men was more sensitive to his boss's work style than the other and to the implications of his boss's needs.

You and Your Needs

The boss is only one-half of the relationship. You are the other half, as well as the part over which you have more direct control. Developing an effective working relationship requires, then, that you know your own needs, strengths and weaknessess, and personal style.

Your Own Style   You are not going to change either your basic personality structure or that of your boss. But you can become aware of what it is about you that impedes or facilitates working with your boss and, with that awareness, take actions that make the relationship more effective.

For example, in one case we observed, a manager and his superior ran into problems whenever they disagreed. The boss's typical response was to harden his position and overstate it. The manager's reaction was then to raise the ante and intensify the forcefulness of his argument. In doing this, he channeled his anger into sharpening his attacks on the logical fallacies in his boss's assumptions. His boss in turn would become even more adamant about holding his original position. Predictably, this escalating cycle resulted in the subordinate avoiding whenever possible any topic of potential conflict with his boss.

In discussing this problem with his peers, the manager discovered that his reaction to the boss was typical of how he generally reacted to counterarguments—but with a difference. His response would overwhelm his peers, but not his boss. Because his attempts to discuss this problem with his boss were unsuccessful, he concluded that the only way to change the situation was to deal with his own instinctive reactions. Whenever the two reached an impasse, he would check his own impatience and suggest that they break up and think about it before getting together again. Usually when they renewed their discussion, they had digested their differences and were more able to work them through.

Gaining this level of self-awareness and acting on it are difficult but not impossible. For example, by reflecting over his past experiences, a young manager learned that he was not very good at dealing with difficult and emotional issues where people were involved. Because he disliked those issues and realized that his instinctive responses to them were seldom very good, he developed a habit of touching base with his boss whenever such a problem arose. Their discussions always surfaced ideas and approaches the manager had not considered. In many cases, they also identified specific actions the boss could take to help.

Dependence on Authority Figures   Although a superior-subordinate relationship is one of mutual dependence, it is also one in which the subordinate is typically more dependent on the boss than the other way around. This dependence inevitably results in the subordinate feeling a certain degree of frustration, sometimes anger, when his actions or options are constrained by his boss's decisions. This is a normal part of life and occurs in the best of relationships. The way in which a manager handles these frustrations largely depends on his or her predisposition toward dependence on authority figures.

Some people's instinctive reaction under these circumstances is to resent the boss's authority and to rebel against the boss's decisions. Sometimes a person will escalate a conflict beyond what is appropriate. Seeing the boss almost as an institutional enemy, this type of manager will often, without being conscious of it, fight with the boss just for the sake of fighting. His reactions to being constrained are usually strong and sometimes impulsive. He sees the boss as someone who, by virtue of his role, is a hindrance to progress, an obstacle to be circumvented or at best tolerated.

Psychologists call this pattern of reactions counterdependent behavior. Although a counterdependent person is difficult for most superiors to manage and usually has a history of strained relationships with superiors, this sort of manager is apt to have even more trouble with a boss who tends to be directive or authoritarian. When the manager acts on his or her negative feelings, often in subtle and nonverbal ways, the boss sometimes *does* become the enemy. Sensing the subordinate's latent hostility, the boss will lose trust in the subordinate or his judgment and behave less openly.

Paradoxically, a manager with this type of predisposition is often a good manager of his own people. He will often go out of his way to get support for them and will not hesitate to go to bat for them.

At the other extreme are managers who swallow their anger and behave in a very compliant fashion when the boss makes what they know to be a poor decision. These managers will agree with the boss even when a disagreement might be welcome or when the boss would easily alter his decision if given more information. Because they bear no relationship to the specific situation at hand, their responses are as much an overreaction as those of counterdependent managers. Instead of seeing the boss as an enemy, these people deny their anger—the other extreme—and tend to see the boss as if he or she were an all-wise parent who should know best, should take responsibility for their careers, train them in all they need to know, and protect them from overly ambitious peers.

Both counterdependence and overdependence lead managers to hold unrealistic views of what a boss is. Both views ignore that most bosses, like everyone else, are imperfect and fallible. They don't have unlimited time, encyclopedic knowledge, or extrasensory perception; nor are they evil enemies. They have their own pressures and concerns that are sometimes at odds with the wishes of the subordinate—and often for good reason.

Altering predispositions toward authority, especially at the extremes, is almost impossible without intensive psychotherapy (psychoanalytic theory and research suggest that such predispositions are deeply rooted in a person's personality and upbringing). However, an awareness of these extremes and the range between them can be very useful in understanding where your own predispositions fall and what the implications are for how you tend to behave in relation to your boss.

If you believe, on the one hand, that you have some tendencies toward counterdependence, you can understand and even predict what your reactions and overreactions are likely to be. If, on the other hand, you believe you have some tendencies toward overdependence, you might question the extent to which your overcompliance or inability to confront real differences may be making both you and your boss less effective.

DEVELOPING & MANAGING THE RELATIONSHIP

With a clear understanding of both your boss and yourself, you can—usually—establish a way of working together that fits both of you, that is characterized by unambiguous mutual expectations, and that helps both of you to be more productive and effective. We have already outlined a few things such a relationship consists of, which are itemized in the [accompanying table], and here are a few more.

Compatible Work Styles

Above all else, a good working relationship with a boss accommodates differences in work style. For example, in one situation we studied, a manager (who had a relatively good relationship with his superior) realized that during meetings his boss would often become inattentive and sometimes brusque. The subordinate's own style tended to be discursive and exploratory. He would often digress from the topic at hand to deal with background factors, alternative approaches, and so forth. His boss, instead, preferred to discuss problems with a minimum of background detail and became impatient and distracted whenever his subordinate digressed from the immediate issue.

Recognizing this difference in style, the manager became terser and more direct during meetings with his boss. To help himself do this, before meetings with the boss he would develop brief agendas that he used as a guide. Whenever he felt that a digression was needed, he explained why. This small shift in his own style made these meetings more effective and far less frustrating for them both.

Subordinates can adjust their styles in response to their bosses' preferred method for receiving information. Peter Drucker divides bosses into "listeners" and "readers." Some bosses like to get information in report form so that they can read and study it. Others work better with information and reports presented in person so that they can ask questions. As Drucker points out, the implications are obvious. If your boss is a listener, you brief him in person, *then* follow it up with a memo. If your boss is a reader, you cover important items or proposals in a memo or report, *then* discuss them with him.

Other adjustments can be made according to a boss's decision-making style. Some bosses prefer to be involved in decisions and problems as they arise. These are high-involvement managers who like to keep their hands on the pulse of the operation. Usually their needs (and your own) are best satisfied if you touch base with them on an ad hoc basis. A boss who has a need to be involved will become involved one way or another, so there are advantages to including him at your initiative. Other bosses prefer to delegate—they don't want to be involved. They expect you to come to them with major problems and inform them of important changes.

Creating a compatible relationship also involves drawing on each other's strengths and making up for each other's weaknesses. Because he knew that his boss—the vice president of engineering—was not very good at monitoring his employees' problems, one manager we studied made a point of doing it himself. The stakes were high: the engineers and technicians were all union members, the company worked on a customer-contract basis, and the company had recently experienced a serious strike.

The manager worked closely with his boss, the scheduling department, and the personnel office to ensure that potential problems were avoided. He also developed an informal arrangement through which his boss would review with him any proposed changes in personnel or assignment policies before taking action. The boss valued his advice and credited his subordinate for improving both the performance of the division and the labor-management climate.

Mutual Expectations

The subordinate who passively assumes that he or she knows what the boss expects is in for trouble. Of course, some superiors will spell out their expectations very explicitly and in great detail. But most do not.

And although many corporations have systems that provide a basis for communicating expectations (such as formal planning processes, career planning reviews, and performance appraisal reviews), these systems never work perfectly. Also, between these formal reviews expectations invariably change.

Ultimately, the burden falls on the subordinate to find out what the boss's expectations are. These expectations can be both broad (regarding, for example, what kinds of problems the boss wishes to be informed about and when) as well as very specific (regarding such things as when a particular project should be completed and what kinds of information the boss needs in the interim).

Getting a boss who tends to be vague or nonexplicit to express his expectations can be difficult. But effective managers find ways to get that information. Some will draft a detailed memo covering key aspects of their work and then send it to their bosses for approval. They then follow this up with a face-to-face discussion in which they go over each item in the memo. This discussion often surfaces virtually all of the boss's relevant expectations.

Other effective managers will deal with an inexplicit boss by initiating an ongoing series of informal discussions about "good management" and "our objectives." Still others find useful information more indirectly through those who used to work for the boss and through the formal planning systems in which the boss makes commitments to his superior. Which approach you choose, of course, should depend on your understanding of your boss's style.

Developing a workable set of mutual expectations also requires that you communicate your own expectations to the boss, find out if they are realistic, and influence the boss to accept the ones that are important to you. Being able to influence the boss to value your expectations can be particularly important if the boss is an overachiever. Such a boss will often set unrealistically high standards that need to be brought into line with reality.

Managing the Relationship with Your Boss

Make sure you understand your boss and his context, including:

His goals and objectives
The pressures on him
His strengths, weaknesses, blind spots
His preferred work style

Assess yourself and your needs, including:

Your own strengths and weaknesses
Your personal style
Your predisposition toward dependence on authority figures

Managing the Relationship with Your Boss

Develop and maintain a relationship that:

Fits both your needs and styles
Is characterized by mutual expectations
Keeps your boss informed
Is based on dependability and honesty
Selectively uses your boss's time and resources

A Flow of Information

How much information a boss needs about what a subordinate is doing will vary significantly depending on the boss's style, the situation he is in, and the confidence he has in the subordinate. But it is not uncommon for a boss to need more information than the subordinate would naturally supply or for the subordinate to think the boss knows more than he really does. Effective managers recognize that they probably underestimate what the boss needs to know and make sure they find ways to keep him informed through a process that fits his style.

Managing the flow of information upward is particularly difficult if the boss does not like to hear about problems. Although many would deny it, bosses often give off signals that they want to hear only good news. They show great displeasure—usually nonverbally—when someone tells them about a problem. Ignoring individual achievement, they may even evaluate more favorably subordinates who do not bring problems to them.

Nevertheless—for the good of the organization, boss, and subordinate—a superior needs to hear about failures as well as successes. Some subordinates deal with a good-news-only boss by finding indirect ways to get the necessary information to him, such as a management information system in which there is no messenger to be killed. Others see to it that potential problems, whether in the form of good surprises or bad news, are communicated immediately.

Dependability and Honesty

Few things are more disabling to a boss than a subordinate on whom he cannot depend, whose work he cannot trust. Almost no one is intentionally undependable, but many managers are inadvertently so because of oversight or uncertainty about the boss's priorities. A commitment to an optimistic delivery date may please a superior in the short term but be a source of displeasure if not honored. It's difficult for a boss to rely on a subordinate who repeatedly slips deadlines. As one president put it (describing a subordinate): "When he's great, he's terrific, but I can't depend on him. I'd rather he be more consistent even if he delivered fewer peak successes—at least I could rely on him."

Nor are many managers intentionally dishonest with their bosses. But it is so easy to shade the truth a bit and play down concerns. Current concerns often become future surprise problems. It's almost impossible for bosses to work effectively if they cannot rely on a fairly accurate reading from their subordinates. Because it undermines credibility, dishonesty is perhaps the most troubling trait a subordinate can have. Without a basic level of trust in a subordinate's word, a boss feels he has to check all of a subordinate's decisions, which makes it difficult to delegate.

Good Use of Time and Resources

Your boss is probably as limited in his store of time, energy, and influence as you are. Every request you make of him uses up some of these resources. For this reason, common sense suggests drawing on these resources with some selectivity. This may sound obvious, but it is surprising how many managers use up their boss's time (and some of their own credibility) over relatively trivial issues.

In one instance, a vice president went to great lengths to get his boss to fire a meddlesome secretary in another department. His boss had to use considerable effort and influence to do it. Understandably, the head of the other department was not pleased. Later, when the vice president wanted to tackle other more important problems that required changes in the scheduling and control practices of the other department, he ran into trouble. He had used up many of his own as well as his boss's blue chips on the relatively trivial issue of getting the secretary fired, thereby making it difficult for him and his boss to meet more important goals.

WHOSE JOB IS IT?

No doubt, some subordinates will resent that on top of all their other duties, they also need to take time and energy to manage their relationships with their bosses. Such managers fail to realize the importance of this activity and how it can simplify their jobs by eliminating potentially severe problems. Effective managers recognize that this part of their work is legitimate. Seeing themselves as ultimately responsible for what they achieve in an organization, they know they need to establish and manage relationships with everyone on whom they are dependent, and that includes the boss.

NOTE

1. See, for example, John J. Gabarro, "Socialization at the Top: How CEOs and Their Subordinates Develop Interpersonal Contracts," *Organizational Dynamics*, Winter 1979; and John P. Kotter, *Power in Management*, AMA-COM, 1979.

The Wall Street Journal, June 16, 1981.

> BIG DEAL: Being tall may help
> you get ahead. A survey of 156 chief
> executives at major companies found
> that 56% ranged from six feet to six
> feet, seven inches tall. Only 3% were
> under five feet, seven inches, says
> Howard-Sloan Legal Search, a
> recruiter. The executives' average
> weight was 184 pounds.

Campus Politico

Doris Kearns

From the beginning at San Marcos College (later Southwestern Texas State Teachers College), Johnson set out to win the friendship and respect of those people who would assist his rise within the community which composed San Marcos. Most obvious was the president of the college, Cecil Evans, whose favor would have a multiplier effect with the faculty and student body. But Johnson was not alone in the desire to have a special relationship with Evans. "I knew," Johnson later said, "there was only one way to get to know Evans and that was to work for him directly." He became special assistant to the president's personal secretary.

As special assistant, Johnson's assigned job was simply to carry messages from the president to the department heads and occasionally to other faculty members. Johnson saw that the rather limited function of messenger had possibilities for expansion; for example, encouraging recipients of the messages to transmit their own communications through him. He occupied a desk in the president's outer office, where he took it upon himself to announce the arrival of visitors. These added services evolved from a helpful convenience into an aspect of the normal process of presidential business. The messenger had become an appointments secretary, and, in time, faculty members came to think of Johnson as a

Abridged and adapted from "Lyndon Johnson and the American Dream" by Doris Kearns, as it appeared in *The Atlantic Monthly.* Copyright © 1976 by Doris Kearns. Reprinted by permission of Harper & Row, Publishers, Inc.

funnel to the president. Using a technique which was later to serve him in achieving mastery over the Congress, Johnson turned a rather insubstantial service into a process through which power was exercised. By redefining the process, he had given power to himself.

Evans eventually broadened Johnson's responsibilities to include handling his political correspondence and preparing his reports for the state agencies with jurisdiction over the college and its appropriations. The student was quick to explain that his father had been a member of the state legislature (from 1905 to 1909, and from 1918 to 1925), and Lyndon had often accompanied him to Austin where he had gained some familiarity with the workings of the legislature and the personalities of its leaders. This claim might have sounded almost ludicrous had it not come from someone who already must have seemed an inordinately political creature. Soon Johnson was accompanying Evans on his trips to the state capital in Austin, and, before long, Evans came to rely upon his young apprentice for political counsel. For Johnson was clearly at home in the state legislature; whether sitting in a committee room during hearings or standing on the floor talking with representatives, he could, in later reports to Evans, capture the mood of individual legislators and the legislative body with entertaining accuracy. The older man, on whose favor Johnson depended, now relied on him, or at least found him useful.

The world of San Marcos accommodated Lyndon Johnson's gifts. If some found him tiresome, and even his friends admitted that he was difficult, they were nonetheless bedazzled by his vitality, guile, and endurance, his powers of divination, and ability to appeal to the core interests of other people. In two years, he became a campus politician, a prizewinning debater, an honors student, and the editor of the college *Star*.

Walter Cronkite at CBS

David Halberstam

The 1952 Democratic convention was important in part because it brought a new face to the American people, a face that would be known in television history. The CBS team going to Chicago knew that it was going to be on the air live for endless hours and it needed someone to hold the broadcast together. The word for that in the trade, but not yet in the popular vernacular, was anchorman. Murrow himself, still at the

From *The Powers That Be*, by David Halberstam. Copyright © 1979 by David Halberstam. Reprinted by permission of Alfred A. Knopf, Inc.

peak of his influence, was not much interested. Nor were many of his colleagues. Walter Cronkite, however, was. Walter Cronkite was not one of the Murrow Boys. Cronkite in 1952 was perhaps the one rising star within the company who was outside the Murrow clique. There was a time in London during the war when he might have made the connection with Murrow. He was a United Press correspondent in London and a very good one. He was, in the eyes of Harrison Salisbury, the man then running the UP bureau and an exceptionally good judge of talent, the best on his beat. . . .

He finished the war with UP and there was no doubt of his excellence; the brass there thought highly of him and he was awarded, as a sign of his success, the Moscow bureau. Those were days of minimal creature comforts in Moscow, and he and his wife, Betsy, were warned that they had to bring everything to Moscow, which they did, and on the day they departed someone mentioned to Betsy Cronkite that she would do well to buy a lot of golf balls since there were none available in Moscow, which she immediately rushed out and did, buying hundreds and hundreds of them; an exceptional supply, considering that (a) Walter Cronkite did not play golf and (b) there were no golf coures at all in the Soviet Union. Moscow in 1946 was not very great fun, nor for that matter was United Press; the Russians were fast discontinuing their policy of limited friendship to brotherly Western correspondents, revoking the marginal privileges that had once existed; in addition, the financial generosity of United Press, which was always somewhat limited, seemed to diminish. The UP car was of antique proportions and did not run, and when, during one of the worst winters of recent Russian history, Cronkite asked for permission to buy a new car since even the Russians were complaining about the condition of his vehicle, his superiors suggested that he get a bicycle.

Things like that often undermine a correspondent's confidence and Cronkite quickly asked to be brought out of Moscow. He came home to America for a year with a promise that he would soon return to Europe as the number-one man on the entire Continent. His salary was then a hundred and twenty-five dollars a week, and, with family obligations growing, he asked for more. The UP executives assured him, probably accurately, that he was already the highest-paid man on the staff. Which was fine except he still wanted more; yes, he said, he loved United Press, which he truly did, he loved scooping people and getting the story straight and clean and fast with no frills—even years later, reminiscing, there is a kind of love in his voice talking about the old UP days, how much he loved UP, how he liked the feel of dirt in his hands, he was not at home with a lot of commentary—but love or no, there had to be some money. So Earl Johnson, his superior, said that he thought it was time that he and Walter had a little talk, since Cronkite apparently did not understand the economic basis of United Press, an economic attitude which was legendary among most journalists and secret only to Cronkite. "No, I guess I don't understand it," Cronkite said, and so Johnson explained: "We take the best and the most eager young men we can find and we train them and we pay them very little and we give them a lot of room and then when they get very good they go elsewhere."

"Are you asking me to go somewhere else?" Cronkite asked.

"No, no," said Johnson, though adding that a hundred and twenty-five dollars a week is a lot of money for us, though probably not for you.

So Cronkite returned to Kansas City, whence he came, on a kind of extended leave, and while he was there he saw an old friend named Karl Koerper, who was a big local civic booster and the head of KMBC, which was a CBS affiliate. And Cronkite, who was disturbed by what he had found in Kansas City, told Koerper at lunch that Kansas City seemed to have died, there was no spirit and excitement any more. What had happened? Then he answered his own question, it was the death of the Kansas City *Journal*. You get monopoly journalism, he said, and something goes out of a city, a sense of excitement and competition. When a newspaper competition dies, something dies with it. Kansas City is a duller town now, Cronkite said.

"What do you mean?" Koerper asked.

"It's your fault," Cronkite continued. "You radio guys cut the advertising dollars so much that you drove the newspapers out but you haven't replaced them. You have no news staff."

"We certainly do—we have eight men," said Koerper proudly.

"Do you know how many reporters the Kansas City *Star* has?" Cronkite asked.

"But that's their principal business," Koerper answered.

"There!" said Cronkite, seizing on it. "That's the answer!" So the upshot of the conversation was that Walter Cronkite was hired in 1948 by Karl Koerper to work as Washington correspondent for his station and a series of other Kansas and Missouri stations, which was the beginning of Walter Cronkite's career as a broadcaster. He was thirty-one years old, he was from the world of print, and more, he was from the highly specialized, fiercely competitive world of wire-service print. But he went to Washington; his salary was $250 a week and he was working for a string of midwestern radio stations. Somehow in the snobbery and pecking order of American journalism there was something slightly demeaning about seeing Walter Cronkite, who had been a big man during the war, hustling around Washington as a radio man for a bunch of small midwestern stations, although Cronkite did not find it demeaning since he liked the excitement of Washington and since he intended to return soon to Kansas City as general manager of the station.

He worked in Washington for about a year and a half, not entirely satisfied, but not all that restless, and then the Korean War broke out and he got a phone call from Ed Murrow asking whether he might be willing to go to Korea and cover the war for CBS. Would he? Well, Murrow better believe that he would, it was the kind of assignment he loved and wanted, it was exactly where he wanted to be. There was, Murrow said, no great problem with KMBC since it was a CBS affiliate and that type of thing would be easily straightened out. In the meantime, Cronkite should get himself ready to go overseas again. But there was some delay because one of his children was about to be born. Then in the middle of all this, the freeze on ownership of stations ended and CBS bought WTOP, which had been a locally owned Washington station, wanting it as a major outlet in the Washington area, a kind of political flagship. The station television news director asked Cronkite to do the Korean story every night, and inquired what he needed in the way of graphics, which turned out to be chalk and a blackboard. Everyone else was trying to make things more complicated and Cronkite, typically, was trying to make them more simple. He worked so hard in preparation for it, backgrounding himself, going to the Pentagon to develop independent sources, that his mastery and control of the subject were absolutely unique. He simply worked harder than everyone else, and in a profession as embryonic as television news, peopled as it frequently was in those days by pretty boys, he was an immediate success. He had that special quality that television demands, that audiences sense, and that is somehow intangible—he had *weight,* he projected a kind of authority. The people in the station knew that he was stronger and more professional than anyone else around and very soon he was asked to do the Korean War story twice a day, and then, very soon after that, the entire news show, and then two news shows a day. He was an immediate hit, a very good professional reporter on a new medium, and he soon began to do network feeds from Washington back to the network news show in New York. Korea began to slip away as an assignment.

Among those most aware of Cronkite's talents was Sig Mickelson, who was then in charge of television news at CBS. He was in effect the head of the stepchild section of CBS News, trying to build up television, but doing it very much against the grain, since in comparison with Murrow he had no bureaucratic muscle, and since all the stars of the News Department were in the Murrow group. Mickelson was quietly strengthening the rest of the News Department. He had known Cronkite in earlier incarnations and from the start he had seen Cronkite as the man around whom he could build the future television staff. As the 1952 convention approached, radio was still bigger than television, although the convention itself would help tip the balance in favor of television. The Mickelson group wanted a full-time correspondent who would sit there all day long and all night long and hold the coverage together, not get tired, and have great control over his material. Mickelson asked for Murrow, Sevareid, or Collingwood, the big radio stars. But the radio people told Mickelson to get lost. Instead, negotiating through Hubbell

Robinson, they offered a list of reporters who were ostensibly second-stringers. On the list was precisely the name that Mickelson wanted, that of Walter Cronkite.

The Murrow group had never really considered Cronkite one of them and there was a certain snobbery about it all; Cronkite was somehow different from the others; it was not just that they had been stars longer than he, they were of a different cast and a different type and it would be crucial in the difference between television news reporting and radio news reporting. Cronkite was then, and he remained some twenty-five years later, almost consciously a nonsophisticate, and he is even now, much as he was then, right out of the Midwest, and there was a touch of *The Front Page* to him, he was almost joyously what he had always been, a lot of gee whiz, it was all new and fresh even when surely he had seen much of it before, and it was as if he took delight in not having been changed externally by all that he had seen. He was above all *of* the wire services—get it fast and get it straight and make it understandable and do not agonize over the larger questions that it raises. The Murrow men—Sevareid, Howard Smith, Collingwood, Shirer, Schoenbrun—were notoriously cerebral and had been picked for that reason; they had been encouraged to think and analyze, not just to run as sprinters. They had dined with the great and mighty of Europe and they had entered the great salons and taken on the mannerisms of those salons; they were, whether they wanted to be or not (and most of them wanted to be), sophisticates. If they had once worked for organizations like UP, they were glad to have that behind them and they did not romanticize those years. Sevareid, for example, came from Velva, North Dakota, which was smaller than St. Joseph, Missouri, where Cronkite came from, but Sevareid had left Velva behind long ago and there was a part of Cronkite which had never left St. Joe, and which he quite consciously projected.

Cronkite had come to the 1952 convention knowing that it was his big chance. He had come thoroughly prepared, he knew the weight of each delegation and he was able to bind the coverage together at all times. He was, in a field very short on professionalism, incredibly professional, and in a job that required great durability, he was the ultimate durable man. By the end of the first day, in the early morning, the other people in the control booth just looked at each other, they knew they had a winner, and a new dimension of importance for television; they knew it even more the next day when some of the Murrow people began to drift around to let the television staff know they were, well, available for assignment. Cronkite himself had little immediate sense of it, he was so obsessed by the action in front of him that he had no awareness of the growing reaction to his performance. It was true that people kept coming up and congratulating him on his work and it was true that there seemed to be a new attitude on the part of his colleagues, but he still did not realize what had happened. On the last morning of the convention, when it was all over, he went for an early-morning walk with Sig Mickelson along Michigan Avenue. Mickelson said that his life was going to change, he was going to want to renegotiate his contract and he would need a lot more money.

"Do you have an agent?" Mickelson asked.

"No," said Cronkite.

"Well, you better get one," Mickelson said. "You're going to need one."

"No, I won't," Cronkite said.

"Yes, you will," Mickelson said. . . .

Sig Mickelson and some of the other news executives had been looking to replace Doug Edwards as the anchorman of the evening news as early as the mid-fifties. Edwards was the original CBS anchorman, he had been given the job during the embryonic days of television. He had been fine standing off the "Camel News Caravan" of NBC's John Cameron Swayze ("Let's hopscotch the world"), but the rise of Huntley-Brinkley was a serious challenge. Edwards did not project the kind of weight that Mickelson and the others wanted, he simply did not seem strong and solid enough a personality to anchor a new modern news show. Douglas Edwards might close the evening news by saying, "And that's the way it is," but people might not necessarily believe that that was the way it was. . . . The job was the most prestigious that CBS had, but it was also not a commentator's job, television was simply too powerful for that kind of personal freedom. For the correspondents in their regular nightly appearances were an interesting combination, part wire-service men (in terms of the narrow spectrum of personal expression and the brevity of their reports) and part superstar, known to the entire country, as recognizable on a presidential campaign and often as sought out by the public as many candidates themselves. But the power was so great and the time on camera so limited that the reporters themselves often seemed underemployed. They were often serious and intelligent and sophisticated, and they seemed more knowledgeable than their nightly reports. The difference between the insight of the CBS reporting team on a brief spot on the news program and its performance at a national convention or during a Watergate special seemed enormous. Even a half-hour show was like trying to put *The New York Times* on a postage stamp, and there was a standing insider's joke at CBS that if Moses came down from the mountain the evening news lead would be: "Moses today came down from the mountain with the Ten Commandments, the two most important of which are . . ."

Sevareid and Collingwood might be the disciples of Murrow, and Cronkite might be the outsider who had never crashed the insider's club, but his style was now more compatible with what the show needed. His roots were in the wire service, he was the embodiment of the wire-service man sprung to life, speed, simplicity, scoop, a ten-minute beat; Hildy Johnson with his shirt sleeves rolled up. He came through to his friends and to his listeners alike as straight, clear, and simple, more interesting in hard news than analysis; the viewers could more readily picture Walter Cronkite jumping into a car to cover a ten-alarm fire than they could visualize him doing cerebral commentary on a great summit meeting in Geneva. From his earliest days he was one of the hungriest reporters around, wildly competitive, no one was going to beat Walter Cronkite on a story, and as he grew older and more successful, the marvel of it was that he never changed, the wild fires still burned. . . .

In addition, he had enormous physical strength and durability. Iron pants, as they say in the trade. He could sit there all night under great stress and constant pressure and never wear down, never blow it. And he never seemed bored by it all, even when it was in fact boring. When both Blair Clark and Sig Mickelson recommended him for the job, the sheer durability, what they called the farm boy in him, was a key factor. He was the workhorse. After all, the qualities of an anchorman were not necessarily those of brilliance, he had to synthesize others. There were those who felt that Sevareid had simply priced himself out of the market intellectually. Eric was too interested in analysis and opinion and thus not an entirely believable transmission belt for straight information. He was an intellectual, he wrote serious articles in serious magazines, and yet he wanted to be an anchorman as well, and there were those who thought this a contradiction in terms. When he found out that Cronkite was getting the job he was furious. "After all I've done for the company," he protested to Blair Clark.

The casting of Cronkite was perfect. He looked like Middle America, there was nothing slick about his looks (he was the son of a dentist in St. Joe, Missouri, and his accent was midwestern). He was from the heartland, and people from the Midwest are considered trustworthy, they are of the soil rather than of the sidewalks, and in American mythology the soil teaches real values and the sidewalks teach shortcuts. Though he had been a foreign correspondent and a very good one, in his television incarnation he had been definitively American, in those less combative, less divisive days of the late fifties and early sixties; Good Guy American. He had covered conventions, which were very American, and space shots, which were big stories where no one became very angry. When there was an Eisenhower special to do, Walter did it; he was seen with Eisenhower, and that too was reassuring. Ike and Walter got along, shared values, it spoke well for both of them. (Among those not comforted was John F. Kennedy, who, shortly after his election to the presidency in 1960, took CBS producer Don Hewitt aside. "Walter Cronkite's a Republican, isn't he?" Kennedy asked. No, said Hewitt, he didn't think so. "He's a Republican," said Kennedy, "I know he's a Republican." Again Hewitt said he didn't think so, and indeed he suspected that Cronkite had voted for Eisenhower over Stevenson and Kennedy over Nixon. "He's always with Eisenhower," insisted Kennedy. "Always having his picture taken with Eisenhower and going somewhere with him.")

Cronkite was careful not to be controversial, disciplining himself severely against giving vent to his own personal opinion and prejudices, and this would be an asset for CBS in the decade to come. He represented in a real way the American center, and he was acutely aware when he went against it. To him editorializing was going against the government. He had little awareness, nor did his employers want him to, of the editorializing which he did automatically by unconsciously going along with the government's position. He was never precipitous. His wire-service background gave him a very strong innate sense of the limits to which a correspondent should go, a sense that blended perfectly with what management now deemed to be the role of the anchorman and the news show itself. He represented a certain breed and he was by far the best of the breed. He was wise and decent enough to be uneasy with his power, and the restraints the job required were built into him. And so he was chosen to anchor the half-hour news show—a mass figure who held centrist attitudes for a mass audience.

He became an institution. His influence, if not his power, rivaled that of Presidents. . . .

Robert Kintner had brought NBC News alive, and in doing so strengthened the entire network. He was a driving, difficult man with a great instinct for excellence and a great feel for what television was, for the excitement it could project, *and* he knew that the quickest and the cheapest way to create excitement was through an expanded news organization. The news organization could be the sinews of the network, could hold it together, and a great news organization would make a reputation for NBC and thus for Bob Kintner as well. He loved the sheer electricity of news, and he delighted in instant specials (in 1964 when Lyndon Johnson had a heavy cold there were constant bulletins throughout the day about Lyndon's health, interrupting the NBC programming schedule and blowing up the cold to massive proportions). In addition, he had come up with the Huntley-Brinkley team, which was an almost perfect anchor: Huntley, from Montana, Cronkitelike in his rock steadiness; David Brinkley, from North Carolina, the tart, slightly rebellious younger brother who could by deft tonal inflection imply a disbelief and an irreverence that the medium with its inherent overseriousness badly needed. Backing them was a team of fine floor reporters. In 1956 NBC had challenged CBS's supremacy for the first time; 1956 was the Huntley-Brinkley Democratic convention and as it went on, hour after hour, much too long, journalistic overkill, ultimately picking the same two candidates who had run in 1952, it had become a fine showcase for Brinkley's dry humor.

The sudden surge in the NBC ratings had subsequently scared CBS, indeed terrified the news executives, and Don Hewitt, the CBS producer, had panicked and had gone to Mickelson and suggested teaming Cronkite, who was then doing the anchor, with Murrow. The two big guns of CBS against the upstairs of NBC. A sure winner on paper. Ruth and Gehrig on the same team. It was a disaster. They were both the same man, playing the same role—two avunculars for the price of one. They did not play to each other or against each other as Huntley and Brinkley did. The chemistry was bad: Cronkite liked to work alone, and Murrow was not a good ad-libber.

By 1960 Huntley-Brinkley was number one in the ratings. For the first time, Paley, who loved to be number one, took notice and began to complain to his news executives—not about content but about ratings. Kintner loved it; he ordered the NBC people to close the nightly news with a statement saying that this news program had the largest audience in the world. Bill Paley was Number Two! It grated on him terribly, but not so terribly that he would change the schedules of the five CBS-owned and -operated—O and O—stations (the five stations the FCC allowed each network to own outright, and indeed the richest source of network income) and put the Cronkite news on at 7 P.M. instead of 6:30, when it was then showing. NBC, of course, was showing Huntley-Brinkley at 7 on its O and O stations. Seven was the better hour, more people were at home then. The pleas of the CBS News Division that they be allowed to broadcast at seven, too, fell on deaf ears. It was a galling problem for the news people, it taught them how little muscle and prestige they really had in the company. Paley was adamant. Somewhere deep in the bowels of CBS, the news people were sure, there was a very smart accountant who was beating them on this issue.

It was in general a bad time for CBS News. The reason was simple: the rest of CBS was so successful, so dominant under Aubrey, that any interference with entertainment by public affairs lost money, real money; NBC, by contrast, not only was fielding an excellent news team at the peak of its ability, it was weaker in programming and had less to lose by emphasizing news, by interrupting programs, by promoting its apparent love of public affairs. Every NBC program seemed to bear some reminder that the way to watch the 1964 conventions was with Huntley-Brinkley. . . .

In 1964 NBC's success was awesome. A debacle for CBS. At one point in San Francisco NBC seemed to have submerged the entire opposition. Kintner, of course, loved it. He had a booth of his own with a special telephone to call his surbordinates—it rang on their desks when he picked it up. Julian Goodman was in charge of listening on the phone, but at one point Goodman was out of the room and the job handling Kintner and his phone fell to a producer named Shad Northshield. The phone rang.

"Northshield," said Northshield.

"The news ratings we've got are eighty-six," said Kinter's gravelly voice.

"That's great," said Northshield.

Kinter hung up immediately. A second later the phone rang again.

"Did you get that straight—eighty-six percent?" Kintner said, and hung up.

Seconds later the phone rang again.

"It seems to me that you could give me more of a reaction," Kintner said.

"Well, what do you want, a hundred percent?" asked Northshield.

"Yes," said Kintner. Bang went the phone. . . .

The difference between the NBC and the CBS coverage of the convention was not great; NBC was in command with a good team, and CBS with a younger floor team and highly frenetic new level of executive leadership was less experienced. But there were not that many stories missed, because there were not that many stories to miss. The real difference was in the ratings, and it was an immense difference. Someone would have to pay. Long, long afterward, Walter Cronkite was still bothered, not just by the fact that he had been scapegoated, but because his superiors, in their discussion of what had gone wrong, never mentioned the coverage itself. He for one did not think that the coverage was very good, he thought that he hadn't done a particularly good job. But no one, when the crunch came, ever mentioned his weaknesses. And no one, certainly, thought of blaming the people who had failed to support the news program, Aubrey and Paley.

Paley had seemed irritable and restless at the Republican convention, and when Friendly and Bill Leonard, his deputy, returned to New York, that small media capital where everyone was talking only about NBC's triumph, they found his irritability had hardened. Paley now wanted drastic and immediate changes in the convention team, he was not about to remain number two. Friendly and Leonard tried to explain the performance in San Francisco, they pointed out that this was a young team, that time was now on their side, and that besides it was simply too late to change the team for the Democratic convention. They had compromised themselves slightly in their talks with Paley by mentioning innocently that Cronkite had talked a little too much during the convention. They realized their mistake immediately. Paley had seized on the comment: Yes, Cronkite was talking too much. Suddenly it was clear to them that Cronkite was going to be the fall guy, as far as Paley was concerned. Why was Cronkite on the air so much? Why did he dominate the others? Why did he talk too much? He had to go. There would be a new anchor. Paley and Stanton—usually it was Stanton who brought down the word from the corporate level but this time Paley was there as well—asked what changes the News Department was recommending.

This was an ominous word, *recommending*. Friendly and Leonard said they planned to do nothing. Do you recommend, said Paley, that we get rid of Cronkite? Absolutely not, said Friendly. Then Paley told them to come back with specific recommendations in a few days. The corporation, it seemed, was about to confront the News Department. Friendly and Leonard met with Ernie Leiser, who was Cronkite's producer, and after much soul searching they recommended that it was impractical to do anything about the convention team. NBC was going to dominate at Atlantic City as it had in San Francisco and there was nothing that could be done about it. The best thing was simply to take your lumps and plan for the future.

It was not what Paley wanted to hear. This time the suggestion was a little less of a suggestion, more of a command. Come back and bring with you the names of the correspondents with whom you intend to replace Cronkite. Now they were meeting almost every day. At the next session Friendly and Leonard were still trying to hold the line, but Paley now had his own suggesion. Mudd. This terrific young correspondent Roger Mudd. Mudd, he said, was a born anchorman. (Which was perhaps true, particularly for a team that had been beaten by David Brinkley, for there was a touch of Brinkley in Roger Mudd, he was intelligent and wry and slightly irreverent, he seemed not to be overwhelmed by the gravity of occasions which, as a matter of fact, were rarely grave.) And now Paley became enthusiastic, there was nothing like this young fellow Mudd, he was terrific. And, with Mudd, said Paley, how about Bob Trout? If Mudd was young and from the world of television, Trout was senior and a word man, Trout could really describe things. Trout, of course, was a famous radio man who could go on for hours with lingering descriptions of events. A Mudd-Trout anchor, that was Paley's idea. The great thing about being Bill Paley, thought one of his aides, was that he could put the hook to Cronkite for Mudd-Trout, and then a few months later, when Mudd-Trout had failed, he could wonder aloud why he had allowed Friendly and Leonard to force such a weak team upon him.

In all this there was no talk of substance, no talk of missed coverage or bad reporting, it was all of image and ratings. Friendly found himself caught between his ambition and his News Department, and what bothered friends of his in those days, as he talked his dilemma out, was that he seemed or at least half seemed to accept management's right to make nonnews judgments on new questions. A sacred line was being crossed without protest. Telling Dick Salant, his predecessor on the job, of the pressure and of the case Paley was building against Cronkite, Friendly said he did not know what to do. He just did not know which way to go. Salant answered: Fred, is it just ratings or is there a professional case against Cronkite? And Friendly answered, inadequately, that it was their candy store, that it all belonged to Paley. Knowing that he was being ordered to fire Cronkite, Friendly warned Paley that Cronkite would not stand for it and would quit if he lost his anchor, and Friendly was shocked by Paley's response: "Good, I hope he does." Finally Friendly gave in. It was a shocking failure, a classic example of what serious journalists had always feared about television, that the show-biz part would ultimately dominate the serious part. Among CBS working reporters Friendly's decision was not accepted; two years later, when Friendly resigned over the CBS failure to televise the Fulbright hearings, most members of his own staff thought he had chosen the wrong issue at the wrong time, that the real issue had been the yanking of Cronkite.

Friendly and Leonard flew out to California to break the news to Cronkite, who was vacationing. There was some talk of the possibility of a Mudd-Cronkite anchor, but Cronkite, a wildly proud man, wanted no part of it, he did not want to share his role with Mudd, and he knew CBS did not want him in the booth. Cronkite in his hour of crisis behaved very well. He did not dump on the company. He was properly loyal. Privately, talking with friends, he protected the company and the institution of television, saying that as a newspaper had a right to change editors if it wanted to, so too did a network have a right to change anchors. Then he held a public news conference and said yes, he thought the company had a right to change anchormen. No, he was not going to worry about it. He did not complain, nor did he agree to the suggestion of the CBS PR man who asked him to pose by a television set for an ad that was to say: *Even Walter Cronkite Listens to Mudd-Trout;* his loyalty to CBS did not extend to fatuousness. At Atlantic City he happened, by chance, to enter an elevator that contained Bob Kintner of NBC. Reporters spotted them coming out and thereupon wrote that Cronkite was going to NBC, a rumor that helped him in his next CBS contract negotiations. All in all it could have been worse for him; he was buttressed by an inner and quite valid suspicion that a Mudd-Trout was likely to be an endangered species.

When Friendly returned from his trip to California, he called Stanton to let him know that the preeminent figure of television had been separated from his most important job, and Stanton had said (it made Friendly feel like a sinister character in a Shakespeare play—yes, the deed has been done, sire), "Good, the chairman will be delighted." Mudd-Trout duly appeared. They were a total failure. NBC routed CBS even more dramatically at Atlantic City (some Cronkite fans going over to NBC in anger), and there was one moment during the convention (which, of course, was not a convention so much as it was a coronation) that remained engraved on the minds of the two news teams. It was the night that Johnson was to accept the nomination. Sander Vanocur of NBC had known Johnson and knew his style, and what he was likely to be feeling like, so he positioned himself near the entrance and waited and waited, guessing that Johnson at this moment might just be in an expansive mood, and then Johnson appeared and Vanocur popped up and had him. Yes, Johnson was in a marvelous, rich, anecdotal mood and—perhaps because Vanocur was regarded as a Kennedy man, what better way to vanquish the ghosts—he had gone on and on. With no one from CBS there at all. It was a marvelous exclusive and Kintner ran it and ran it all night, and when the CBS people saw it come over they were appalled. There was no one near at hand and so Bill Leonard, who was the head of the election unit and not a reporter at all, put on an electronic backpack and went rushing over, panting, and Vanocur, his exclusive done any by now running on the air for the third time, a great scoop in a scoopless convention, turned with a small smile of comfortable charity (which might later have cost him a job at CBS) and said to the President of the United States, "Mr. President, you know Bill Leonard of CBS—he's a good man." Victory at Atlantic City. The end of the Mudd-Trout.

Friendly had worked hard to keep Cronkite from quitting outright to persuade him to stay with the evening news. Cronkite did stay, and that fall CBS put together a magnificent election unit that ran far ahead of NBC up through election eve and that gave CBS the major share of the ratings. Cronkite was, of course, immediately rehabilitated; at the same time, the Huntley-Brinkley format was slipping, it had played for eight years and that was, given the insatiable greed of television, a very long time. The Cronkite show, aided by what was to be exceptional coverage of the Vietnam War by a team of talented young reporters, regained its prestige. But there are two footnotes to the tensions of the 1964 convention.

The first deals with the question of being number one. Paley had wanted to be number one without paying the price, while Friendly and the others had argued for the change in evening time slots that would allow Cronkite to come in at the better hour. But Paley had never listened. Then the dismal ratings of San Francisco stirred him, and one night during the convention, when all the indicators were absolutely terrible, Frank Stanton flew from New York to San Francisco and gathered Leiser, Friendly, and Leonard for dinner. He had, he said, some very good news. And so with that marvelous delicacy which marks the way things are done in corporations (no admission that perhaps the News Department was right and that Paley had changed his mind—chairmen do not change their minds), Stanton said that if Friendly called the people at the local stations in New York and Philadelphia he might be able to argue them into letting Cronkite come on at seven o'clock. So Friendly made the calls, and lo and behold, his marvelous persuasive powers worked and Cronkite got just enough of a boost from the time change to regain his rating.

The second footnote deals with the man himself. For the Walter Cronkite who came back to work was a somewhat different man from the one he had been before being humiliated in public. As the next few years passed and he became even more the dominant figure of the industry, his pride intensified. In 1968 during the Democratic convention the delegates were voting on the peace plank. And suddenly, as sometimes happens at conventions, Cronkite and everyone else started using—overusing—a single word to refer to a situation. The word this time was *erosion,* which had obviously replaced *slippage,* the last convention's word. The vote came to Alabama and Cronkite mentioned that there was an erosion of two votes. He was broadcasting live and suddenly someone passed him a scribbled note: "Tell Walter not to use the word 'erosion'!" Cronkite, without missing a beat in the commentary, answered with his own note: "Who says?" Back came another note: "Stanton." Suddenly it was as if there were fire coming out of Cronkite's nostrils, and even as he continued the delegate count he wrote one more note: "I quit." So someone handed a note to pass to the brass saying: "Walter quits." And this was passed back and even as it was being passed back Cronkite was standing up and taking off his headset and reaching for his jacket. It was an electric moment. And suddenly someone was yelling, "For God's sake tell him to get back down there, don't let him leave. They're not trying to censor him. They just don't like the word 'erosion.' " So he sat down, and continued his broadcast. They might mess with him once, but no one messed with Walter Cronkite a second time.

Luck and Careers

Daniel Seligman

A report in the *New York Times* several weeks ago detailed a piece of horrendous bad luck that had befallen Major Stanley Daugherty of the U.S. Army. He was marching his 200-member company past the tent of the major general in command of Fort Riley, Kansas. The men were chanting a marching cadence that closes with the words "We like it here!" Unfortunately for Major Daugherty, a few of the men elected to supplement the approved text with what the *Times* cautiously characterized as "a barnyard epithet." After the general heard this word, the major was relieved of his command and shipped off to Fort Bragg. Another officer, who discreetly declined to be identified, observed sympathetically: "It was the wrong word at the wrong place at the wrong time. Now 14 years of work is totally destroyed for that one word."

Luck, good and bad, plays an important role in many people's careers. But for a chance encounter on a train, one businessman might never have put together one of the largest companies in the U.S. Another executive can trace his career footsteps back to a movie he happened to attend soon after World War II; it's reasonable to suppose that if he hadn't gone to that movie he wouldn't now be running another of our largest companies. Another man was propelled into the presidency of the U.S. by a long string of chance happenings.

It is possible to find some such happenstance in many careers. Many of us are able to think of chance events—events that we didn't intend, didn't foresee, and perhaps didn't even recognize as significant at the time—that prompted us to seek out certain routes rather than others in our wanderings through the great career maze. However, there has been little systematic thinking about luck in careers. Among the great philosophers, Aristotle is exceptional in having given the subject some serious attention. He argued in the *Nichomachean Ethics* that "all manner of chances" may affect one's prospects in life, that material prosperity is especially chancy, and that such prosperity is helpful although not indispensable in attaining happiness. (What *is* indispensable to happiness is a virtuous life.)

OUTSIDE THE SYSTEM

Possibly philosophers have stayed away from luck because so many of them aspire to build "systems," and chance events are, almost by definition, outside systems. It is very difficult, although I shall essay the task a bit later, to devise a framework, or theoretical model, that might help us to make sense of the "ifs" in our lives.

You could argue, of course, that your good or bad luck begins with the good or bad genes your parents gave you, along with the good or bad environment you grew up in. You could argue that your career prospects have been materially enhanced by the fact that you (probably) happened to grow up in the U.S. rather than in Chad. You could still argue, as this article was going to press, that the late twentieth century has in general offered better career prospects than other periods in human history. Let us, however, look at luck in careers from a much less cosmic perspective. Let us simply consider the extent to which career outcomes are determined by career "inputs"—that is, by the particular skills, characteristics, and credentials we start out with. If the inputs don't determine the outcomes, then we have to tell ourselves that luck plays a role. And looking back at our careers, we can fairly speculate that they might have turned out quite differently.

Take my own case, which I have always found especially interesting. Three decades ago, I was an extremely junior person on a widely unread magazine, earning $69.50 per week after 3½ years on the staff. No amount of inflation-adjusting is going to convert that figure into a decent salary. I asked for a raise to $100, quit when I was unsympathetically turned down, and was then miraculously hired when I applied for a position on FORTUNE, a widely read magazine. I have been haunted for years by the thought that I might have got that raise, or at least a little sympathy.

Stories about setbacks and frustrations that turn out to be good luck in disguise are quite commonplace. In Harry Truman's amazing career, defeat regularly kept turning into victory. Daniel Bell, professor of sociology at Harvard, observed recently that among his own contemporaries—he graduated from the City College of New York in 1938—the lucky ones often turned out to be those who *hadn't* got a good job before the war. At least, this seems to have been the case among those with intellectual inclinations. Many who found security as high-school English teachers, say, or government employees were "locked in" after the war when career opportunities for intellectuals began exploding. (The extent to which a young man returning to civilian life might feel locked in as an English teacher would, of course, have been affected by whether he'd picked up a wife and kids along the way.) Bell himself managed to remain in reasonably threadbare circumstances during the pre-1945 years as a writer and editor for the *New Leader.* Irving Kristol, a close friend of Bell's (the two were the co-founders of *The Public Interest*) and now a widely quoted neoconservative intellectual, was a machinist in the Brooklyn Navy Yard until he was drafted. Melvin J. Lasky, a friend of both men and now co-editor of the distinguished British magazine *Encounter,* was an elevator operator at the Statue of Liberty.

DICE FOR THE ENGINEERS

As these examples suggest, the good or bad luck associated with many careers is often a matter of timing. It might be argued, in fact, that professional and technical careers involve a kind of inescapable dice roll. A young person contemplating any such career is, of course, looking at very long lead times: it can take four years or more between the time he makes the career decision and the time he's actually ready to go to work. But the forecasts about future demand for trained professionals have been notoriously wide of the mark. During the last year or so, it happens, engineering graduates have been in clover: the defense boom, the basically strong showing of technology-intensive industries in the U.S., and our failure to produce enough engineering graduates in the 1970s have combined to create an explosive demand for those who are now graduating. The supply-demand balance is extremely favorable to them because in the mid-1970s the job market for engineers was discouraging.

Let me now anticipate some objections. You are possibly saying to yourself that people make their own breaks. You are agreeing with the axiom, traceable to Heraclitus, that "character is destiny." You note that engineering students, for example, don't just make a onetime career commitment and then look around six years later to see whether they had bet on a winner. Which is, of course, true: transfers out of engineering programs rise sharply in periods when the job markets seem to be shifting away from engineers. You are possibly also telling yourself that the event some successful individual will identify as a major turning point in his life was actually not decisive at all—that it was the individual's own talent, education, and perseverance that led to his success. In short, you believe that career outcomes are determined by the individual's own qualities rather than by those supposedly critical chance events in his life.

You might even cite Sigmund Freud on the hidden logic of some supposedly accidental events. In *The Psychopathology of Everyday Life,* Freud mentions the case of the ambitious young dramatist who never forgot to attend the meetings of a literary society as long as there was a chance that this group might help to get his plays produced—but who invariably forgot the meeting dates after his first play was produced. Possibly you do not even need Freud to reach the insight that success-strivers work hard at finding the places and times at which they're most likely to have lucky accidents.

I am actually willing to go a certain distance with you in this determinist direction. The chance events we're talking about may be *necessary* to cause someone's success, but they're almost never sufficient. I'd agree that there is a fallacy we must guard against: we tend to look at the people around us and conclude that most have ended up about where they belong—while at the same time being often over-impressed by all the "ifs" in our own careers. We fall prey to this fallacy because in looking at those other people we're seeing accomplished facts, which ordinarily have a certain amount of logic behind them and often an aura of inevitability. But in thinking about our own cases, we are privy to other information. We can recall vividly how our interests were shaped by some incident, or teacher, and we find it easy to imagine that this catalyst might never have come along. What's harder for us to see is the hypothetical catalyst—the one that might have come along later if we were still looking for direction.

Without doubt, many people, including some without enormous talent, are still trying to find themselves long after adolescence. In Bertrand Russell's autobiography, there is an arresting story about the author's association with Ludwig Wittgenstein around 1912. It appears that Wittgenstein, now identified as the patron saint of logical positivism and one of the towering intellects of the twentieth century, wasn't sure if he had the brains to make a career in philosophy. He went to Russell, beseeching an opinion and mentioning that if he couldn't make it in philosophy he planned to become an "aeronaut." Russell said that he frankly wasn't sure about Wittgenstein's capacity, and proposed that they resolve the issue by having the young man—he was about 24—write a paper on some philosophical theme that interested him. Wittgenstein later turned in a paper, of which Russell comments in the autobiography: "As soon as I read the first sentence, I became persuaded that he was a man of genius." (Unfortunately, Russell doesn't tell us what the sentence was.)

Professor Robert Nozick of Harvard, author of the just-published and much-acclaimed *Philosophical Explanations*, which has plainly projected him into the first ranks of contemporary philosophers, had a somewhat less dramatic moment of truth. Or maybe it was more dramatic. Nozick says that about 12 years ago, when he was already a tenured professor of philosophy at Rockefeller University, he decided to abandon his field and become a stand-up comic. Then, listening to a Lenny Bruce record one day, it suddenly struck him that he couldn't possibly be that funny.

Or, to get back to the corporate sector, take the Felix Rohatyn story. Rohatyn, a partner of Lazard Freres and one of the stars of modern investment banking, believes that there was a real possibility of his having had a quite different kind of career. He was a physics major at Middlebury College and reflects today that, if things had gone as he'd intended them to, he would very likely have ended up in some middle-level job in some scientific bureaucracy at, say, Union Carbide.

ANOTHER ROAD TO LAZARD

Is that really plausible? Alan Greenspan, when told the Rohatyn story, argued strenuously that it wasn't. Greenspan, an eminent economist who served as chairman of the Council of Economic Advisers in 1974-77, suggested that a man with Rohatyn's talents and ambition would most likely have risen to the top wherever he was. If he had been a mediocre physicist, he would have abandoned physics for something like finance, and "I can even see him then leaving Union Carbide and getting to be a partner at Lazard."

Greenspan gave the impression that, in forming this judgment, he had possibly been influenced by some details of his own career history. An alumnus of the Juilliard School of Music, he found himself in 1946 playing the clarinet and saxophone in a dance band and paying dues to Local 802 of the American Federation of Musicians. But after about a year with the band, he realized that he wasn't good enough to have any kind of distinguished career in music. So he began trying to educate himself, reading extensively between sets, and eventually decided that he needed to invest several years in getting a serious education; he had his M.A. in economics by 1950. Also a saxophonist in that dance band, incidentally, was Leonard Garment, who made a somewhat similar calculation and went on to become a lawyer. Years later, Greenspan and Garment were both national figures in the Nixon and Ford Administrations—a sequence manifestly arguing that people with brains and ambition do not easily allow themselves to be deflected.

RETURNING FROM SIBERIA

The case might be pushed further. Business history, and for that matter non-business history, includes endless examples of people who found their ways to "the right job" despite false starts and bad breaks. Major Daugherty, the barnyard-epithet victim, can possibly take comfort from the precedent of George C. Marshall. The Army Chief of Staff during World War II, and later Secretary of State, Marshall at an earlier stage of his career was, like Daugherty, banished by a superior (Douglas MacArthur) to "Siberia." Many career catastrophes are reversible; indeed, they may lead an individual to call on reserve strengths and push on to higher levels than those originally contemplated. Eli Ginzberg, a Columbia-based economist who has advised nine Presidents on manpower problems, observed the other day that most truly successful careers show some setbacks along the way. "You have to learn how to encapsulate defeat," he told me." If you're going very far up toward the top, there's no such thing, by and large, as a smooth career." Among those whose greatest achievements came only after they had got themselves into ruinous financial situations: Fyodor Dostoevsky, Abraham Lincoln, John Maynard Keynes, H. J. Heinz, James Cash Penney, Conrad Hilton.

Nevertheless, we must plainly set some limits on the determinist view of the matter. Anyone, however talented and driven, may be brought down by a medical disaster or an automobile accident. And while people may override failures, there is plainly a limit here too; at some point a succession of bad breaks will make almost anyone feel like one of life's losers. In Ginzberg's words, "We all need some positive feedback."

One reason for believing that luck matters is that an avalanche of academic research on the determinants of career success has never come close to pinpointing all the determinants. This research has involved a broad range of academic disciplines, but the principal work has been done by sociologists, economists, and psychologists. The object: to identify and quantify the relationships between success (the principal criteria being income and occupational status) and certain attributes (the ones most closely studied being educational level, race and sex, parental socioeconomic status, intelligence as measured by I.Q. and other tests, and a variety of personality traits).

THE VIEW FROM HARVARD

In 1972 a volume called *Inequality*, written by a young sociologist named Christopher Jencks and seven of his colleagues at Harvard's Center for Educational Policy Research, appeared to have made a major breakthrough in our understanding of luck. For a volume whose findings were based largely on multivariate analysis—in which everything gets correlated with everything else—*Inequality* was wonderfully readable, and it made a considerable splash even in nonacademic circles. (Total sales of the Basic Books trade edition: over 40,000 copies.) A principal conclusion of the book was that luck matters a lot. Jencks and his colleagues came to the rather startling finding that income wasn't as closely tied as expected to the variables being examined. The finding: "Neither family background, cognitive skill, educational attainment, nor occupational status explains much of the variation in men's incomes. Indeed, when we compare men who are identical in all these respects, we find only 12% to 15% less inequality than among random individuals."

CARING ABOUT MONEY

How could this be? The authors examined three possibilities. One was simply that some people value money much more than others, and organize their lives so as to earn more—by taking a second job, for example, instead of relaxing in the evening. Jencks and his colleagues found this explanation intuitively plausible, but they never succeeded in finding any empirical evidence to support the view "that caring about money has a significant effect on income." They ended up concluding that caring about money might, in fact, be more widespread among those without it than with it.

A second possibility was that the kinds of skills and competence they were measuring by no means exhausted the qualities sought by employers. Said *Inequality:* "Incomes may also depend on . . . the ability to hit a ball thrown at high speed, the ability to type a letter quickly and accurately, the ability to persuade a customer that he wants a larger car than he thought he wanted, the ability to look a man in the eye without seeming to stare, and so forth. We have no way of saying how much of the variation in people's incomes depends on characteristics of this kind, but it could be substantial."

Finally, there was luck. *Inequality* observed that "income also depends on . . . chance acquaintances who steer you to one line of work rather than another, the range of jobs that happen to be available in a particular community when you are job hunting, the amount of overtime work in your particular plant, whether bad weather destroys your strawberry crop, whether the new superhighway has an exit near your restaurant, and a hundred other unpredictable accidents." Mulling over their data, Jencks and his colleagues reached an astonishing conclusion. They said they suspected "that luck has at least as much effect as competence on income."

This rendering of the evidence was viewed as a considerable overstatement by many academic critics of *Inequality*, some of whom argued that the authors had gone overboard on luck because they hadn't done a thorough enough job of measuring the personal attributes that affect income. In a successor volume called *Who Gets Ahead?*, Jencks and a different group of collaborators seem to have traveled part way toward the critics' view. The new volume was a condensed and somewhat revised version of an enormous study, funded by assorted public and private grants, that analyzed and contrasted the results of 11 prior surveys of the determinants of economic success. *Who Gets Ahead?* leaves you thinking that career outcomes are more predictable, and luck somewhat less important, than you'd earlier been led to believe. The revised finding is that men's personal characteristics at the time they enter the labor force might explain as much as half the variance in annual earnings and two-thirds of the variance in occupational status. The still-substantial unexplained variance is more or less synonymous with luck.

A THREE-LEGGED MODEL

So where does that leave us? Plainly still needing some kind of framework for thinking about the enigmatic role of luck in careers—some model of the problem. I hereby propose a crude model based on three propositions: (1) Luck matters plenty. (2) It matters more in the careers of people who start out with fewer advantages. (3) The big breaks, to the extent that they are really turning points, are apt to come early in careers.

(1) The academic research on the determinants of success plainly leave plenty of room for luck. You can think of the data as a kind of morning line in the career horse race. Given various data about an individual's characteristics at the time he enters the job market, you can express the probability of his getting certain kinds of jobs, earning certain levels of income, and attaining a certain status. Take, for example, the relationship between I.Q. and income. In its purest form—that is, after subtracting out the effects on income of such factors as age, region of the country, and the state of the economy at the time the data were collected—the "coefficient of correlation" is estimated to be quite high, around 0.6. That number signifies a strong and positive, although far from perfect, relationship between I.Q. and income. The square of the number, which is .36, is the so-called coefficient of determination —which tells us that 36% of the variation in income reflects I.Q. dif-

ferences. Other relationships between I.Q. and income are reported in the second Jencks study. It notes, for example, that among otherwise identical individuals, increasing I.Q. scores by about 15 I.Q. points increases expected lifetime earnings by 20% to 30%. A 15-point difference in brothers' scores is associated with a 13.8% difference in their earnings, assuming that they have the same amount of schooling. So you have to conclude that above-average I.Q.s mean you'll probably have above-average incomes, and vice versa.

Similar probabilistic statements might be made about your occupational status. The measurement of status, a major product of the sociology industry, is rooted in surveys in which respondents have ranked many different occupations by the prestige they felt was associated with each. For example, on the famous Duncan Index of Occupational Status, the rankings proceed from the zero given to laborers in tobacco plants to figures in the 90s for, say, judges. While I.Q. is probably the single best predictor of income, educational level is best for occupational status. *Who Gets Ahead?* estimates that high-school graduates outrank elementary-school graduates by 11.6 points and are in turn outranked by college graduates by 25.6 points.

(2) The proposition that luck is more important to people who've got less going for them might seem, at first blush, self-evident. Take the case of Charles Lachman, who had the great good fortune to be one of the founding partners of Revlon, an enterprise founded with $300 (no zeros omitted) in 1932 and expected to have $2.5 billion of sales this year. In consequence of his having been around at the beginning, Lachman years later had 30% of the stock and was immensely wealthy when he retired in 1965. By all accounts he was not brilliant or highly motivated, and it seems quite clear that, from the beginning, he was given essentially no managerial or other responsibility. In an entertaining book about Revlon called *Fire and Ice,* by Andrew Tobias, Lachman is quoted as having explained, when asked what he did at the company: "I've got a rake and I rake it in."

THE MAN WHO HAS EVERYTHING

However, the stray case of the individual who hits it big despite his seemingly limited potential is not particularly instructive. It is more fruitful, I would say, to ponder the quite different implications of luck in the careers of people who start out with many advantages and those whose case is more problematical. We all know, or know about, some people who have just about everything going for them as they approach the career maze. They're intelligent, creative, ambitious, energetic, well organized, and well connected and we have to assign an extremely high probability to their having successful careers. If they're in the corporate world they will almost certainly end up in some kind of senior-executive role. To be sure, nobody knows how to predict, early in careers, that such individuals will make it all the way to the chief-executive station. Eli Ginzberg of Columbia, and several experienced corporate directors with whom I've been talking recently, expressed the view that there are always large random factors in determining which of the various super-achievers near the top will make it to C.E.O., with the mysterious workings of personal chemistry often proving to be decisive.

Ginzberg observed that it is similarly difficult to predict who will move to the very top in intellectual careers. Back in the mid-1930s he was one of a group of elite students taking graduate economics courses under the guidance of Wesley Mitchell. The group included Milton Friedman and a half dozen others who went on to various forms of eminence as economists in the academic world, business, and government. "Of the group I was in, everyone I know of had a successful career," Ginzberg reminisced. "But if I'd had to guess who would end up as a Nobel laureate and a worldwide eminence, I'd never have picked Milton, even though he obviously had a lot on the ball. I'd have said that the strongest contender was"—at which point Ginzberg named an economist who had a modestly distinguished career as an insurance-company officer.

THE CASE OF THE DUMB SALESMAN

What about the problematical cases—those who have some but not all of the characteristics that predict success? The scientist who's brilliant but lazy? The life-insurance salesman who's energetic, well organized, and gregarious, but not very bright? The reporter who's talented but often misses deadlines? A wide range of outcomes seems possible for such people. A mediocre economist, with poor work habits, no particular creative capabilities, and no connections, might nevertheless end up having a decent career if, say, he has been lucky enought to earn his Ph.D. in the early 1960s and got tenured at some respectable university a few years later—a period when the demand for academics was peaking. Alternatively, he might have come along a decade later and found that his kind of skills weren't in demand anyplace. He might have ended up looking for work in a dance band.

In the course of my recent wanderings around the academic world, I mentioned to Professor Richard Hernstein of Harvard the view that luck is much more crucial to some people than others. Hernstein is a psychologist and a leading participant in the I.Q. debate. (His review of *The Intelligence Controversy*, by H. J. Eysenck and Leon Kamin, appeared in our August 10 issue.) "That's not an unreasonable hunch," he responded. "But let me try restating it a little differently. Obviously, there are observable relationships between getting ahead and certain personal traits. There's some slippage in the system, however, some disparity between what you'd expect from someone's traits and what he finally achieves. We find the slippage at every level, whether we're talking about someone with all the desirable traits or only a few of them. Suppose, to be specific, we're predicting socioeconomic standing from an individual's score on a test that somehow manages to measure everything—intelligence, personality, looks, drive, everything. People with a very high score are predicted to end up very high in life. Since there's some error in the predictions, those people might end up a fair amount below what's predicted, which leaves them still well off. But when you start out with a low score, then you're really at risk. The shape of the distribution curve is such that being off by a unit means you end up no place."

In other words, bad luck for the heavy favorite means that he ends up as merely a middle-level executive. Bad luck for a less-favored individual might involve much more, perhaps even a loss of middle-class status.

(3) The proposition that luck's influence is greatest early in careers seems intuitively compelling; it's also supported by a certain amount of academic research. Intuitively, we can reason somewhat as follows. At the beginning of your career, you have the broadest range of options. At age 16 a chance meeting, or a magazine article you pick up in the dentist's anteroom, might lead to your getting interested in astronomy or acting or selling cars, all of which have decidedly different implications for the kind of life you'll end up leading and probably for your income too. It's true, of course, that the earliest career decisions are also the most reversible, as the Greenspan example reminds us. But for most people, those first career decisions cast a long shadow.

BLUE-COLLAR LUCK

Indeed, some research suggests that early career situations and incomes are powerful predictors of status and income later on. Richard B. Freeman, a Harvard economist who specializes in the economics of education (and who has lately been arguing that the economic returns on education have been in a sharp decline), is in general more disposed to a determinist than a luck-emphasizing perspective on careers. In any given year, he notes, about two-thirds of the income differences among people are related to characteristics that are permanent and stable (even if not all of them can be measured). It's overwhelmingly likely that people around the top of the income distribution one year will also be on top in later years, and the same is true for those at the bottom. While anything is possible in a given case, the general rule is that the first serious job a young person gets after school says a lot about where he'll end up.

"So if there's much luck in the picture," Freeman concludes, "it comes in with that first job." His example: "A blue-collar worker gets out of school and shows up at General Motors when they happen to be hiring. He gets some kind of skilled job and he's set for life. But another young guy shows up when GM isn't hiring. He ends up working at Joe's Garage, which goes out of business three years later. The data say that the guy from Joe's Garage never catches up to the GM man."

INCHES AND BOUNCES

Luck tends to matter less later in careers, but it obviously never goes away. Like baseball, life can be a game of inches. Like football, to make an equally seasonal reference, it keeps getting affected by the way the ball bounces. Seeking to end this article on a lofty philosophical plane, I ask you to contemplate a certain famous bounce in the career of Louis XVI of France.

The writer Hilaire Belloc once produced an essay arguing that a certain Citizen Drouet, a modest French provincial, had altered the course of history. Drouet, it appears, had dragged a cart across a gateway near the bridge at Varennes, on the route by which Louis and Marie Antoinette were attempting to escape from the revolutionary mobs in Paris. The cart forced the royal coach to halt and led to the capture of the passengers.

It was Belloc's contention that if only Drouet's cart had got stuck, the history of Europe would have been different: the King would have escaped, his armies would have defeated the revolutionary forces, the rise of Napoleon would never have taken place, which in turn might have prevented the first stirrings of modern nationalism and perhaps even deflected the industrial revolution. In his endlessly readable *The Hero in History,* Sidney Hook demolishes these notions. He leaves you firmly persuaded that, with or without that cart, the broad outline of events would have been something like what we now read in the history books. However, it does seem clear that the cart significantly affected the careers of Louis and Marie Antoinette.

The Imaginary Manager

Judith Garwood

Sometime after World War II—probably during the Eisenhower years—somebody applied a dirty word to business. Now, a lot of dirty words have been applied to business in the course of several hundred years of history. But this four letter word is not only unfair, it also has had some unfortunate side effects. The word is *dull*.

If business were dull, it would only be reasonable to assume that business people—including managers—were unimaginative, uncreative plodders who made decisions by the numbers. What adolescent of intelligence and vision would want that for a future? A whole generation was thus brought up to believe that creative people did not go into business unless they failed at whatever it was that they really wanted to do. This happened, I believe, at least partly because of the movie and television image of businessmen, and partly because of the bum rap business got from school teachers and professors. But it was not only the *image* of American business that suffered as a result of the epithet. Throughout the sixties, as children of all ages dropped out to look for self-actualization, many creative, innovative people looked elsewhere than to business for careers, and productivity and innovation suffered as a result.

What would happen if we now went the other way and educated a generation of students to think of business as an outlet for creativity, the way they might think of science or art? What would happen if we started out by telling students that in business, just like in art, there isn't a narrowly correct way of doing things or a single right answer—and that getting good answers means, just like in science, that you have to start by asking the right questions—and that sometimes the whole process may border on the absurd? What would happen if we, as a society, started emphasizing the *creative* side of doing business?

The result might be innovation. The result might be a generation of managers who wanted to manufacture a product or provide a service in such a way that the pursuit itself was rewarding. The result might be the revitalization of American business.

But this would only work if it is true that the process of managerial decision making is, in fact, a creative one that requires vision and the ability to translate vision into product, just like any other creative job.

From *NEW MANAGEMENT*, Vol. I, No. 4, 1984, pp. 16–20. Reprinted by permission.

When I mentioned to a friend—an artist/actor/musician—that I planned to write about the link between the artist and the manager, and explained to him that the link between them is imagination, he immediately whipped out his sketch pad, drew a single chain link floating in space, and labeled it, "The link between them was imagination." His point was that the artist and the manager were unlinked. I told him he had made the link real by drawing it and asked him for the sketch, but he wouldn't give it to me. He crumpled it up and threw it out rather than have a real link to his imaginary adversary, the businessman. It was a dramatic gesture. This man has no moral reservations about making money from his talents; but he leaves the "unpleasant details" to his business manager. He thus *pretends* he has no link to business. But I suggest that there *is* a link between the artist and the manager, and that it should be labeled imagination. Without imagination, without creativity, neither one will be successful.

Imagination was used by Arthur Koestler in *The Act of Creation* to link the artist to the scientist and the comic. He stated that each of the three shares a place in a triptych (a work of art with three leaves hinged together). Each one, according to Koestler, does essentially the same thing, but from a different perspective, and with a different goal in mind. Each one is doing what Koestler calls "bisociating"—connecting two things that either would not go together at all under normal circumstances, or would at least not go together in the way that the comic/scientist/artist has suddenly seen. Bisociating is making a sudden turn in space from one plane of thought to another. The result of this process may be a joke, an invention, a philosophical/aesthetic insight—or a better way to run a business.

The triptych might be changed to a lucite cube containing photographs of the comic, the scientist, the artist, and the manager on four of its sides. The photographs usually face outward, but if they are turned inward and the cube placed on a flat surface, someone looking down from the top of the cube could see all four photographs facing one another. And the link of imagination would be evident.

Examples of imagination—and bisociation—exist in all four disciplines. The most obvious ones are humorous, such as the joke about the actor who fell in love with the NFL quarterback. At first his wife was worried, but then she realized that the quarterback was just a passing fancy.

The classic example of bisociation in science is that of Archimedes, the crown, and the bathtub. Archimedes was faced with a problem of determining whether an ornately carved crown was solid gold. To do that, he needed to find its density. We will never now how many baths he took, how many times he watched the water level rise and fall as he got in and out, before it occurred to him that if he displaced an amount of water with the same mass as his body, so would the crown.

Artists and mystics, of course, are expected to see things a little differently. Perhaps the farthest out example of this is art trouvé ("found art"), such as Picasso's "Steer," made from the seat and the handlebars of a bicycle.

It is the link of imagination that connects comic with scientist with artist. For example, there is the whimsy of the scientist who named subatomic particles quarks, and sub-subatomic particles charms, flavors, and colors. Very large numbers are called googols, and very, very large numbers are called googolplexes. These unseeable things are so called not only because a scientist or mathematician had a sense of humor, but because their very discovery was a creative, artistic act.

On their part, artists took the scientists' multicolored laser beams, made them dance to music, and created a new art form. And movies—particularly the special effects—are probably the most common examples of scientific technology used for art.

But how does all this connect to managers, the guys who reputedly do things by the numbers? Let's look at it from the other side—how does anyone decide what the numbers really are? How does anyone decide, for example, what a company is worth?

There are a number of ways of valuing a company, and there are even some ways of attempting to quantify the intangibles. But I have a picture of a bunch of guys (maybe one woman among them, but probably not) sitting around a conference table in their shirtsleeves, ties loosened, waiting for answers from the three men who are performing fugues on their calculators. The three come up with different figures. Then somebody says, "Oh, the hell with it, let's offer $48 per share."

There is a story illustrating how much can be done with numbers which is attributed to Elliott Estes, the former president of General Motors: Once upon a time, a CEO was looking for a new chief accountant. Three people interviewed for the job. When the first one walked into the office, the CEO asked, "How much is two and two?" "Four," replied the applicant. The CEO dismissed him and called for the second applicant. The CEO once again asked, "How much is two and two?" The reply once again was "Four." The CEO called for the third applicant. In response to the same question, the third applicant got up, shut the door, drew the drapes, leaned over the desk and whispered, "How much would you like it to be?"

Just because some decisions are not made according to the numbers doesn't mean all decisions are creative ones. But at least a few of them are. Ralph G. H. Siu, in *Management and the Art of Chinese Baseball,* speaks of business as if it were on an axis between science and art:

"Small executive decisions are weighted toward the scientific polarity; BIG executive decisions are weighted toward the artistic."

There are certain areas of business where we have no trouble thinking of the people involved as creative. In advertising agencies, we expect to find artists—but not making the business decisions. In the movie industry, the line between the artists and the businessmen (and the comics) is blurred.

But we are still uncomfortable with the idea that one can be an artist and have financial success. While Paul McCartney's talents seem to have found fairly widespread acceptance, there is still controversy over the extent to which a Mick Jagger or a Barry Manilow is a true artist. How many people want to believe that if Shakespeare were alive today, he would be writing and producing movies for television, and Ben Jonson would be writing commercials, because that is where the money is (and the mass audience)?

Even if there had never before been a link between the artist and the manager in terms of an approach to making decisions, one would be necessary now. The creative leap has probably always been necessary, in that when all the information was assembled and it was time to make a decision, someone could question whether all the facts were in. The problem today, however, is one of too much data. No single executive can possibly read and absorb all of the information that his/her subordinates can gather (computer assisted) about all of the problems faced by the company. A classic example of someone who tried is former President Carter. He made all the small decisions regarding the use of the White House tennis courts, but he couldn't pull the details together to form a cohesive, encompassing economic and political philosophy.

Such big decisions are complicated when corporations have a number of different divisions—marketing, production, engineering, accounting, and R&D. No matter what his/her background—sales, or finance, or whatever—the CEO must assimilate data from reports provided by each of those divisions. Or else—and this is much more likely—the CEO will look at the Executive Summary that accompanies every report, get the concept involved, make a leap of faith, and come to a decision. These so-called "hunch" decisions are, in fact, the creative packaging of a lot of information. The flip side of the "too much data" coin is "too much uncertainty." Today's numbers may not be tomorrow's numbers.

I have been focusing on the CEO, but what outlets for creativity can be found for the data-gathering subordinates? Clearly, there are different ways of being creative. Computer programming is a creative job that demands the same maddening attention to detail that one might find in a master woodcarver. Generally, however, the opportunity for creativity is lessened for those whose job requires specialization. (I imagine that the apprentices to the great artists of the Renaissance may have had this same complaint.)

But there are outlets for creativity to be found in almost any job. One of these is the memo, which is in some respects the art form of the bureaucracy.

The best examples of the memo—and everyone will immediately re-member his/her favorite—are certainly creative, a blending of vision and craft.

Anyone who has ever fought his/her way through a prospectus for a tax shelter will have encountered another kind of creativity, in this case a kind used to circumvent laws (or find the loopholes in them). This is probably a less productive kind of creativity than others one could name, but these prospectuses are, in their own way, works of art. I am reminded particularly of one for tank cars that came out in the early 1970's. It was a masterful prospectus, a brilliant tax shelter, but no one checked to see whether the company actually owned the tank cars. (If you happen to be thinking, "Well, of course, business people who dream up fraud are creative," you might like to know about the assistant operations officer of a small branch office of a large bank who said to me, "Anybody who isn't smart enough to figure out how to embezzle from this bank isn't smart enough to hold this job.")

But the really creative things are the ones that have to be done all the time in order for a business to be successful. How do you design a new compensation package? What kind of benefits do you provide for a workforce that doesn't want the same things their parents wanted? How do you develop a marketing plan for a new product? How do you start a new business—when every day you have to make decisions that nobody has ever made before, because nobody ever started *this* new business? How do you plan for the effects that changing technology is going to have on your company over the next five years when nobody knows for sure how the technology is going to change? How can you make *any* of these decisions or a dozen others without calling yourself creative?

The point of all this is that it is important that we think of managers as creative, and that they think of themselves that way. We are an affluent society, and we like it like that. That affluence was created by, and is dependent upon, business. Without business, we would be an agrarian society in which each of us had to aim for self-sufficiency or barter for the goods we could not make or grow ourselves.

It is important that we work to counteract the impression that going into business allows one to make money but stunts one's creative growth. No job that requires constant synthesizing of information and decision-making in the face of constant change is dull. Described proper-ly, business should attract bright, creative people who are looking for challenge, even for self-fulfillment through their work. The use of creative imagination should be encouraged as a way of approaching life, *on* as well as *off* the job.

It took the children of the sixties a long time to realize that it was pos-sible to become businesspersons without abandoning the search for self-actualization. If the children of the eighties are allowed to shorten that process, the result may be a healthier society for us all. The good news is that all the signs are pointing that way. It's the business classes that are full these days on college campuses, despite a general drop in enrollments. The bad news is that too many of them are still being taught by the numbers, and that too many business schools are still across the river from the arts and the humanities, where creative thinking is encouraged. But some bridge-building is being done, and some students are learning to swim, and perhaps our own children will find it easier to say, "I want to be an entrepreneur when I grow up."

Management

Robert Schrank

I went to a fancy Madison Avenue employment agency, and within a few days I was on a new job as a foreman in the machine-building and maintenance division of a small retail data-processing company. After spending so many years fighting the bosses and their managers, becoming part of management proved to be more traumatic than I had expected.

I began to relax into being the foreman by spending a lot of time talking to the employees, listening to their beefs and suggestions. In the main, their suggestions were strictly work-related—the grinders are inaccurate, the spindle on the Number 4 miller is off, the light over the jig borer is insufficient, and so on. Then I spent sleepless nights asking myself, What will I do if the company tells me to do something to the employees that I find I cannot do? I said to myself, You're part of management now. You have to learn to play the role. But what if that role turns out to be a bastard? I will just tell them they can shove the job they know where. On and on the paranoia grew until things proved not to be as bad as I had feared. Once again, the anticipation was far worse than the fact.

I began to remember the things workers beefed about when I was a union officer. Now I was determined to pay attention to the conditions of work. After all, I rationalized, even the socialist brotherhood in any form had to have some kind of supervision. I kept asking myself: Could I supervise others without myself becoming a mechanical robot?

There were about forty-five men, almost all skilled workers, in the department. There was no union. My first efforts were to become familiar with the work as well as to straighten out job order systems and establish

Reprinted from *Ten Thousand Working Days* by Robert Schrank by permission of The MIT Press, Cambridge, Massachusetts. Copyright © 1978 The MIT Press.

cost centers and parts inventory. The plant manager was pleased with what I was doing. "You're doing a great job, Bob, keep it up." Now, I thought, I can start paying attention to working conditions.

I started by improving the ventilation, cleaning up the toilets, building an eating area, getting the windows washed; generally making the physical surroundings more pleasant. The employees loved it; and with no urging on my part, production began to increase. I had become an instant success, yet I did not have to do anything as a foreman that I considered antithetical to the interest of the workers, whom I now called employees. My paranoia was decreasing. I was beginning to enjoy being in management. I would learn in time that as a supervisor I used McGregor's model Y, the humane, participative, open management style. What I had fought so hard as a union organizer was what McGregor called management X, the traditional, authoritarian style.

Most behavioral scientists concerned with workplace issues have so little understanding of the part that unions play in alleviating working conditions that it is no wonder union leaders become frustrated: They find practically no recognition in the behavioral science workplace literature of the role of the labor movement in humanizing work. Without the work of the unions, it is hard for me to see how American business and industry could even consider the next steps toward autonomy, participation, and codetermination.

My relations with the men in the department were easy-going. I would walk around checking on the work, doing quality control and at the same time kidding about the difficult jobs, sports, politics, and sex in about that order. Thinking back, second only to being competent as a toolmaker machinist, the most important management quality I would say I had was a good sense of humor. The work itself I sort of knew by rote, and I could get answers, too, by consulting others. That was never of any earth-shaking importance to me, so I would joke about what had to be done. The men would sort of laugh, yet they rushed to meet schedules. That turned out to make me look good.

I told each man when we finished a job how he had done in terms of both quality and time. We joked a lot about how long it takes to get things right. Humans seem to have an almost limitless ability to solve mechanical problems and at the same time show an enormous inability to understand how to live with themselves and each other. I began to see the function of humor as a way of acknowledging the absurdity of the human condition in the face of this apparent contradiction.

I began to attend engineering expositions and conventions, meeting many men whose lives revolve around the design and development of machines. I remember a dullness about them, as though the gray of the steel had entered their souls. Compared to plumbers or my old union friends, they seemed like a drab lot. An old saying suggests that "dull people find dumb work." Well, I don't think so, because I too felt a certain lifelessness growing in me. The machines themselves seemed to be making ceaseless demands for the improvement of their efficiency, and their demands were draining my life energy. I had started to carry a small pocket notebook with me to jot down little ideas for improving or redesigning machines. It was a constant challenge to keep them from wearing out and at the same time make them do more for less.

There was something new in that engineering experience that I only recently have come to understand. It involves the nature of conflict in work. Working with machines has conflicts and tasks that involve objects and materials, all of which are inanimate. People are used as the instruments of the objects or machines. Engineers deal in the main with these inanimate things, whose only resistance is in the limits of their physical nature. They lose the human, living, dynamic element in work. Over time I found engineering work comfortable and absorbing, but my only challenges were excessive friction, unstable raw materials, tighter machine tolerances. I was becoming a very neutral person whom I was gradually getting to dislike. For someone who had tasted the excitement of human conflict in the unions and national politics, there was not much romance in developing a better rack and pinion mechanism for a high-speed press.

In contrast, the issues in the labor movement almost never were concerned with objects. They were the problems of people, of their working conditions, pay, and benefits. Union work also required me to take a stand, one that might be unpopular with management, and at times with the members. In the very neutral, alienated world of engineers there is a sense of being above or beyond the conflict issues, a sort of technological person. I found engineers reserved, expressing little or no curiosity outside of their engineering specialty. Compared with the openness of the average shop worker, their interest in sex, for instance, was a hidden, secretive business.

I was attending an engineering convention in Chicago, and because my company did considerable business with a major electrical manufacturer, I was assigned a lovely female friend to keep me company, if not warm, in the windy city. Helene, who had been "Helen" back in Des Moines, was a model-type—tall, skinny, and shining from an endless round of soaps and lotions. She had been trained in charm. We went to dinner, and for most of the evening I plied her with questions about her job. "I am hired as a bridge to customers like you, in order to further expose the potential buyer to our product line." I fantasized: Helene and I go to my room. We get into bed. We are about to go to it when out comes the newest high-speed gear box sample. "You were saying . . ."

"We are hired to give understanding to the customer."

"Do you go to bed with all the customers?"

"The decision is up to us. Now you must understand we don't *have* to. After all, we're not just call girls, but if we desire to, we can."

"Is your pay scaled to going to bed with a customer?"

"No, we get a flat rate a day during the convention, but if you want to be called back, you have to build a reputation for being friendly."

"How many conventions do you do a year, and what kinds?"

"Oh, maybe fifteen or twenty of all kinds; pharmaceutical companies are great, with doctors; then there are engineers, dentists, printing companies, truckers, political meetings." Helene was really enjoying the interview. She laughed. "I draw the line on morticians. Darned if I am going to have some undertaker work me over. No siree. Every job has to have its limits."

"How do you like this engineering crowd?"

"They're OK. Most of them are not like you. They don't talk much, and they're very secretive, so you have to meet them in their rooms, and they don't want you to know their names. They seem to be scared. I don't know of what. Now you take truckers. They're tough, they could care less, and they are great spenders."

My efforts on behalf of the company were rewarded by promotions, first to chief plant engineer and then to division engineer responsible for three plants. As the demands of the job increased, I found myself increasingly committing more of my life to the company. To the envy of other managing engineers, I began to be consulted by the vice president in charge of production at the head office of the corporation. I was now mixing with the corporate executives, traveling first class, eating at 21 Club with three corporate vice presidents to discuss the Swedish operation. Good food, fine wine, the best cigars—I felt big, contented, and sure I had made it. After all, the labor movement didn't want me, so why should I feel guilty about sitting here in the 21 Club making it? I thought Bertolt Brecht was stupid. Am I supporting corporate oppression if I share in the power, or can I use my position to humanize existing institutions? An irresolvable contradiction, or a paradox. Why be a man when I can be a success? Listen, Bertolt, class status is so damned insidious. You think that a little socialist shit can affect the intoxication of being accepted into the higher reaches of the corporate world. You're nuts. I was moving up, and, by God, I liked it.

Though sometimes deeply buried in our unconscious, the drive upward is everlastingly present. Being summoned to an audience with king, pope, president, secretary general, or prime minister gives us a heightened sense of importance, power, status, no matter how cynical we feel toward an institution. Even if I did not actually hold the power, just being in its presence was heady stuff. Antiestablishment people (we used to call them "radicals") suffer a heavy ambivalence.

I was now working for corporate headquarters. I found myself becoming more involved, absorbed, single-minded, with an excitement for equipment deadlines and new ideas that created in me a general sense of euphoria. Yet there was a difference between this kind of work and the

labor movement. What was it? Slowly I was missing the old companion.
ship, the wonderful conversation of all my friends in screw machines,
turret lathes, and the machine shops. The management world was a cir-
cumspect one full of innuendo, nuance, correct dress, and carefully
choreographed behavior. The result was little or no spontaneity, no feelings, no physical contact. All this meant zero sensuality. I was beginning
to miss walking with my arm on another guy's shoulder at a union
meeting. Doubts began to take root about whether I could make it as a
corporate executive.

One winter night in a fine old Boston restaurant, the corporate boys
from Yale and Groton, having belted down a few too many martinis,
kept asking about life on the outside, the plant, the union, sex. I had a
growing feeling that I was being spied on by a bunch of Harvard Business
School voyeurs who seemed to sense something missing from their lives
but were not sure what. I was missing something too. A short time later
the vice president in charge of production, having learned that I was
"getting antsy," said to me, "Schrank, you are too smart to lose; if it is
the last thing I do, I am going to shoehorn you into this corporation."

I was going to college at night, having been urged to do so by the company, when they learned that I had no school beyond the eighth grade.
"You're corporate material, but you will have to get a degree." College
was a real growth experience, and it was reinforcing my distaste of corporate managing. I was on my way out.

Some doubts have grown in me about engineers and managers. The
first has to do with management's ability to manage, and the second has
to do with behavioral science notions about work, motivation, and job
satisfaction. In my days as a union official, there was a fantasy that corporations were homogeneous, single-headed, efficient monsters systematically exploiting workers. Talk about being convinced by one's own
propaganda! Institutions and professions now appear to me as tribal
groups defending their turf—territoriality: their secrets, sacred bundles,
and their leaders and tribal councils. When I moved from the union tribe
to the corporate tribe, I learned some of their secrets. They were fumbling around pretty much like the rest of us, yet they were better able to
conceal it through public relations, with its handouts, image building,
color slide and sound shows. Then there is always the secrecy that is
called up to "protect us from our competition" or from other tribes, but
this is usually baloney since it is more often used to hide mistakes from
the world at large.

The loss of perspective on their lives, the lack of joy in their work,
seemed so natural for the engineers. Yet I became very involved in what I
was doing, even though it made no social sense. It was so absorbing that
it caused me to lose interest in a world of feelings and sensuality. Was it
sublimation? I would doubt it. Maybe it happens because the work is
with metals or plastics, usually to close tolerances in measurement or

composition or both. The thing—the object, the task, the gear, cam, housing, nuts, bolts, timer—engulfs and dominates one's life until an obsession like building a better zipper takes over all thought and no one thinks to ask what was wrong with the button. The pressure of corporate life to come up with new products makes managers and engineers fearful if they do not constantly create and innovate. This makes for individual competition resulting in a lonely crowd. Productivity for engineers does not indicate the quantity of work produced but rather what new ideas or improvements they have generated. The pressure to come up with solutions to problems sends at least some competent engineers off into dealing or specializing.

I think that engineers and managers would rate considerably higher on the alienation scale than most unionized workers. The competition of managers vying for recognition and position creates little trust, and that means little human contact or concern. The corporation I worked for was liberal and easy-going, but even there the higher up the totem pole you climbed, the faster they went for your jugular. Life in the corporation tended to be isolated and cold, with some fucking, no love, and little sharing of sexual fantasies. It all reminded me of Wilhelm Reich's *Listen Little Man:* "Security is more important to you, even if it costs you your spine of life."

The gentility and civility of engineers and managers seemed to make them less sensuous, robust, and less aware of the organic qualities of life. They often struck me as being without affect because of their preoccupation with a large inanimate object or some minute, trivial part of it. It is the syndrome of overspecialization that Mumford talks about in *The Pentagon of Power,* when one becomes so highly specialized in the head of the pin that in time one no longer knows what the rest of the pin looks like, or worse, what it is used for. And there I was, totally involved in the feed mechanisms of continuous-web letterpresses.

Was this group of managers and engineers more satisfied with their jobs than plumbers or machinists? In general I would say yes, but I would add that most of these men were so completely and exclusively focused on the "head of the pin" that they had given very little thought to what they were doing, why they were doing it, and at what cost to themselves. In the recent NASA layoffs, some aerospace engineers had been forced into new careers. In an interview with one of them who opened a hot dog stand, he said he had suddenly discovered—guess what—that there was more to life than Wernher Von Braun's "bigger and better rockets." "I love owning my own business, but more important, I am my own boss."

Managers and engineers tend to lose their concern about people because of their total preoccupation with "the product." In my case, feed mechanisms, the product, took over most of my psychic energy. Such narrow frames of reference have an impact on how managers and engineers view other people. Preoccupied and obsessed with the product line, they can begin to view people, or the workers, as obstacles to reaching their objectives.

In the whole production matrix, people are probably the most frustrating for managers since they constitute the most difficult variable to control and predict. No matter how predictable society tries to make its members through its various socializing mechanisms, people continue to give managers the most trouble. Managers are always complaining about "those workers." "If only they would do what we tell them or learn to follow instructions, we would surpass all our quotas." It is this obsession with the product and the consequent neglect of human needs that could fill case-history books with stories of management's insensitivity to workers. This insensitivity is often turned around and explained as a "lack of worker motivation." Workers become strangers to many managers and are seen only as an extension of a piece of machinery in which a capital investment has been made. This leads to the engineering dream of eliminating the "human element" in production.

A good illustration of this phenomenon came up in a union negotiation. Sitting around the huge conference table in the mahogany-paneled conference room during an intensive collective bargaining session with the Republic Steel Corporation, the company was reciting a litany of how much production time is lost as a result of lateness, extended coffee breaks, lunch time beyond the bell, and early quitting. The whole discussion seemed kind of absurd, so I kept encouraging the industrial engineers to give us the data on what the lost-time factor added up to. Out came the slide rules as the figures multiplied upward. "The company has 5,000 employees in this division. Estimated loss on starting time seven minutes; on two coffee breaks, twelve minutes; and quitting ten minutes early. That makes a total of 2,400 hours a day." The company was very impressed with these figures. After all, they were clear evidence of the cost of malingering.

I said, "I would like to have a recess." It was agreed. The company representatives left the room, and the union committee remained. I asked the committee members how many times the average worker went to the toilet during the workday to pee or shit, and how long did each function take. After some bickering back and forth, we agreed on three times: two short and one long, the short about seven minutes, including travel and smoke, and the long about fourteen minutes. We calculated an average of twenty-eight or thirty mintues per employee lost a day in the toilet. I asked the committee if they would permit me to bargain away at least some of that time, or in other words, if we could reduce the toilet time in exchange, let's say, for a couple more holidays. Everyone appreciated the absurdity of this, but they were happy to join the dramatic fantasy that would reveal the production engineers' thought processes.

When the company representatives returned to the bargaining table, I put forth our propositions, in the course of which the absurdity of it all seemed to carry me away. "We are not only willing to reduce defecation time, but we have recently become aware of a pill that taken each morning, would assure the employer of no defecation on company time." Noticing on the other side of the table the industrial engineers all playing with their slide rules, the committee members almost blew it with their giggling.

Charles Hunsteter, chief of production engineering, a pudgy fellow with thin strands of hair plastered to his sweaty forehead, announced, "You thing it's funny. Well, 1,166 hours a day at $5.00 per hour labor and overhead cost, $5,830 a day times 250 workdays a year: $1.500 million a year." The figures so excited him that he said, "Schrank, I don't know if you're kidding or serious, or what. But the fact is this could change our entire competitive position, and I would hope you would give our company first crack at it." Well, the poor committee members thought they would bust. The company attorney, a little more reality-oriented, was embarrassed by the joke and changed the subject. On the way out the door at the end of the session, Charlie said, "Schrank, you may be kidding, but this could be an extremely useful tool in production scheduling."

That incident epitomizes a particular kind of industrial engineering management viewpoint that I am amazed to find still prevails in some manufacturing companies. How to perfect a completely programmed person to eliminate the human element from technology continues to influence the thinking of at least some behavioral scientists and industrial engineers concerned with productivity and worker motivation.

How fulfilling is engineering and managing in terms of Maslow's higher-order needs of autonomy, creativity, and self-actualization? Blue-collar malaise is explained by some social scientists as caused by an absence of opportunities for autonomy, decision making, creativity, and self-actualization. I have often wondered to what extent these elements were present in the work life of engineers and managers. And though it may be true in some cases that persons of this rank in organizations have more opportunity to be creative and make the decisions related to their work, nowhere in the literature is an even more important question raised, that of the *purpose* of their creativity. What is it used for? In its most extreme form, the question of how one's creative energies are used is what confronted the atomic physicists when asked to perfect the bomb. What tends to get lost from Maslow's schema and its application to the workplace is the moral issue that asks: What does my creativity create? What is the impact of my self-actualization beyond me?

When I was busy increasing the speed and feed accuracy of high-speed web presses, it caused an isolation from living things that tended to negate the human concerns at the workplace. Relationships were important to me in terms of how they complemented my machine. I became caught in the treadmill of making better widgets, forgetting what I had learned many times as a union official when workers would say, "Listen,

Schrank, I don't give a fuck for the junk we make here. I am here to make money so I can get my kicks outside of this dump." That often repeated basic philosophy of work stirred my subsconscious as I wondered, How much did I really care about increasing the speed and efficiency of high-speed dumbwaiters?

Compared to managers and engineers, blue-collar workers seem more able to shed their work concerns at the end of the day. Workers are more concerned with security and pay than the product. Managers and engineers are concerned with upmanship. To get there, they must efficiently deliver a product. Different jobs create very different kinds of anxieties. Workers' concerns have most to do with security, wages, hours, and working conditions, but these tend to be group concerns that create a common bond. Manager-engineers tend to be primarily preoccupied with their own performance as a way of getting ahead—getting ahead of someone else—and thus produce a highly competitive, individualistic, nongroup life.

I believe blue-collar workers are able to shed their workplace anxieties more easily than managers because of less responsibility as well as a deeper resignation to their situation. Since Karl Marx, much of the literature on work alienation has had to do with blue-collar workers, but I experienced them as far less alienated than managers or engineers. Workers at least had each other. I have a hunch that some of the literature on blue-collar alienation written by behavioral scientists is more often an expression of their own malaise and alienation than that of the workers. The longer I was in the world of managers, the more I missed my union buddies, their ribald spirit, our singing together, their sensuousness, their sexuality. By comparison, managers were a deadhead lot who had traded humor and sensuality for the role-playing Kabuki world of the corporate headquarters. I have met more people having fun as clowns on one plant floor than in all the very many corporate headquarters I have gone in and out of.

Engineers, managers, or behavioral scientists, with their compulsive, competitive preoccupation with "making it," tend to see this as a paradigm for all workers. But many workers are not interested in "making it" in a career of power and responsibility, or even in increasing their autonomy and creativity. Some blue-collar workers prefer to make bowling the center of their lives. That may be a greater demonstration of autonomy and creativity than building a better high-speed gear box.

Furniture Czarina

*Still a live wire at 90, a retail phenomenon
oversees her empire*

Frank E. James

Two salesmen with sample swatches from Karastan Rug Mills stand before 90-year-old Rose Blumkin in the carpeting department of her sprawling store, the Nebraska Furniture Mart. Sporting a bouffant hairdo and seated atop the motorized three-wheeled cart she drives around the store, she speaks in her Russian- and Yiddish-flavored broken English.

"How much?" she asks. They tell her. "Seven dollars?" she says skeptically. "We go bankruptcy tomorrow should we pay that." A live wire, she revs up her cart and zooms off.

Within minutes she is back. The younger of the two salesmen drops to his knees as though kowtowing and gives her a close-up of the $7 sample, already reduced from $19.50 a square yard, wholesale. "OK, I'm going to gamble," she says. "Give us up to 800 square yards of this pattern." She again steps on the accelerator.

Later, during a quiet moment, she says: "Here's Karastan who didn't sell me for 47 years, the big shots. I wasn't good enough. Today they beg me. If it's a bargain, I buy. Otherwise I don't need it. That was a bargain."

Mrs. Blumkin, also known as Mrs. B., is one of Nebraska's best-known rags-to-riches stories. She came to the Midwest from Russia in 1917 "with not a penny" but with a never-say-die attitude. In time she created a furniture-store empire by keeping long hours (she still works over 60 hours a week) and by following her simple motto: "Sell cheap, tell the truth, don't cheat nobody and don't take kickbacks. That's the world's worst."

Long a hit in the nation's heartland, the 4-foot-10-inch czarina of home furnishings will visit Greenwich Village's Washington Square Park tomorrow. There, during New York University's commencement exercises, she will become the first woman to receive the prize the school reserves for world-class captains of industry, an honorary doctorate in commercial science. (Last Saturday, in a warm-up, she received an honorary doctor of law degree from Omaha's Creighton University.)

'BORN WITH BRAINS'

But how is it that the illiterate daughter of a poor rabbi should get such awards? Simple, says Mrs. Blumkin. "I'm born, thank God, with brains. In Russia you don't have no adding machine or nothing, so you have to use your head. So I always used it." She has more than brains, says Laurence Tisch, chairman of NYU's trustee board and of Loews Corp. "She's more of a business leader than anyone we've ever honored before." He heard about her during a QE2 cruise last fall with Warren Buffett, chairman of Omaha-based Berkshire, Hathaway Inc., which bought Nebraska Furniture late last year.

Mr. Tisch's praise is high praise indeed. NYU's former business honorees include Walter Wriston and Clifton Garvin Jr., the chiefs of Citicorp and Exxon Corp., respectively, not to mention, Irving Shapiro, former head of Du Pont Co., and Thomas A. Murphy, former chairman of General Motors Corp. Big shots, as Mrs. Blumkin would say.

Those luminaries have nothing on her, though. How many of them could have taken a pawnshop basement and a borrowed $500 and transformed them into a retailing establishment that expects $120 million in sales this year? And that's with only one store, albeit a huge one: With its warehouse, parking lot and leased-out space, it spans 40 acres.

STARTED IN 1937

It wasn't until 1937 at age 43 that Mrs. B. found herself in the furniture business. Before that, she rented shotguns and peddled used clothing, jewelry, fur coats and anything else she could lay her hands on to help her husband, Isadore, a pawnshop owner who died in 1950. He had fled from Russia to the U.S. in 1914 with the outbreak of World War I; she followed after almost three years, later sending for her father, mother and seven other family members.

A Hollywood scriptwriter could barely improve on the emigration odyssey she describes. She boarded a train for Siberia the same day plotters murdered Grigori Rasputin, the mystic who wielded influence in Czar Nicholas II's court. At the Siberian-Chinese border a Russian border guard stopped her.

She did what any resourceful Russian peasant did at a moment like that—she fibbed. The guard let her pass after hearing that she was on a trip to buy leather for the army. The clincher, though, was the bottle of vodka she promised him on her return.

There were stopovers in China and Japan. And then the ocean voyage to Seattle. "I bought first class but they so damn crooked they put me in a peanut boat. Took me six weeks to get here. So many peanuts. I thought I'd never get here," Mrs. Blumkin recalled in a videotaped memoir broadcast on Omaha TV last year.

On rejoining her husband, putting down stakes in Omaha and getting into the furniture business, Mrs. Blumkin began the practice that is largely responsible for her success: She undercut the competition at every turn. Suppliers and banks scorned her either for selling too low or for being a small potato. She got around reluctant manufacturers by obtaining their goods through irregular channels or buying from other retailers.

Once she was hauled into court by another Omaha store that charged her with breaking Nebraska's fair-trade laws by selling below cost. Unable to afford a lawyer, she asked the judge what was wrong with giving her customers good deals, such as selling $7.95-a-square-yard carpeting for $3.95. The judge agreed with her to the chagrin of the three opposing attorneys. The next day, she says, the judge stopped by her store and bought $1,400 of carpeting. "He says, 'I never knew I could save that much,' " she recalls.

During an early, desperate point in her merchandising career, Mrs. Blumkin sold off the family furniture and appliances, emptying the house while her four children—three daughters and a son—were away from home. "When the kids came home," she says, "they cried like somebody would die." Nevertheless, she raised $800 to repay suppliers who had extended credit.

Frances Batt, 66, Mrs. Blumkin's oldest child, says she wasn't safe from having her mother sell furniture out from under her even after she married, moved from the family house and had her own child: "I get a call from Mrs. B. and she says, 'Empty the baby's storage chest, I got a customer.' Believe you me, I emptied the chest and the customer came and picked it up."

Even today, Mrs. Blumkin can't resist the urge. "She'll say, 'You know that dining room table you've got, I've got a customer . . .,' " Mrs. Batt says. "But she doesn't make me give it up now. She'll say, 'We don't have one in the store. Would you show it to him?' "

THE FRIENDLY BANKER

Nebraska Furniture has prospered ever since 1950 when business temporarily soured at the start of the Korean War. A friendly Omaha banker gave her a personal, 90-day note for $50,000 after she told him she couldn't pay her suppliers. She remembers worrying: "Oy, what he going to do if 90 days goes by and the war is still on, nobody walks in, and we don't sell nothing? Your own brother wouldn't give you $50,000."

She held a three-day sale in a rented hall and made $250,000 and repaid the banker and other creditors. Nebraska Furniture hasn't borrowed a cent since; the experience scared her into paying cash for everything. Even in 1970 when she bought a former insurance-company building for the store's new location, she paid $1.8 million in cash.

"Mother's taught us all about management. She's a one-woman business school," says Louis Blumkin, 64, Mrs. Blumkin's only son and the president of Nebraska Furniture. He actually runs the business except for the carpeting department, which is her baby. As chairman, however, she is still the ultimate authority in the store. "She's like God to us," he says.

Louis joined the store directly after leaving the service in World War II. His three sons—a former banker, a former Air Force officer and a one-time coffee farmer in Costa Rica—are all vice presidents at the store. Two of Mrs. B.'s sons-in-law also have worked as executives in the business, and each of her 12 grandchildren has worked there at some point.

PAYROLL OF $12 MILLION

The brightly lit store has 500 employees today and a $12 million annual payroll. Its display space, larger than most Sears stores', is a 250,000-square-foot forest of easy chairs, bedroom and dining-room sets and end tables. "If you can't find it there, nobody makes it. You'd better build it yourself," Mary Kay Rhodes, a writer for the Des Moines Register, says as she sits at home one morning waiting for her young daughter's new bedroom set to arrive from Nebraska Furniture.

The store's appeal is distinctly middle-class since it emphasizes moderately priced furniture, but $3,000 sofas and tables can be found there, too. Prices are generally 20% to 30% below those of other furniture retailers because overhead is lower; there are no rent or interest payments to make.

Its aggressive discounting has made Nebraska Furniture a powerful regional furniture store. Its delivery trucks regularly go to parts of Kansas, South Dakota and Iowa as well as more-western sections of Nebraska. Unmarked trucks are used for out-of-town deliveries to keep distant retailers in the dark about how much of their markets Nebraska Furniture is plundering.

There is virtually no major competition in Omaha left for Nebraska Furniture, according to Louis Blumkin. Numerous stores have gone under, some due to the latest recession, others no doubt due to Mrs. Blumkin. That doesn't keep his mother, who likens business to hand-to-hand combat, from one of her favorite pastimes: spying on the competition that remains.

A HOLIDAY ENCOUNTER

Howard Krantz, owner of Allen Furniture in Omaha, says he has seen Mrs. B. in action on a Jewish holiday when, he says, both he and she should have been in services. "It was very funny. I took a break. And who was looking in the window of our store but her and her daughter," he says. "They must have taken a break, too, or figured I wasn't going to be here, one of the two." His store has gone after Omaha's carriage trade to survive against Nebraska Furniture Mart. "We saw the handwriting on the wall," he says.

As Mrs. Blumkin would be the first to admit, she isn't getting any younger. That is why she sold Nebraska Furniture for $60 million to Mr. Buffett's company, which has interests in retailing, insurance, candy, publishing and textiles. By selling, she says, she was able to personally split the millions of dollars up among her children and ensure Nebraska Furniture's future.

Mr. Buffett, who trusts Mrs. Blumkin so much that he bought the store without an inventory or audit, has promised to be an absentee owner, allowing the family to continue minding the store. "Putting her up against the top graduates of the top business schools or chief executives of the Fortune 500 and, assuming an even start with the same resources, she'd run rings around them," he says.

What's left for Mrs. Blumkin to do? "Nothing," she says. Then, after a moment's reflection, she is inspired: "I could write a book and everybody would buy it. I'll have to find a publisher."

3

IMAGES

Like the shields carried by knights of legend, the modern corporate building reeks with symbolism.

— *Betty Harragan*

Whether people in organizations are consciously aware of it or not, they are constantly exposed to subtle and complex influences which play a part in determining what they think, feel, and do. Many of these images are intentionally created by organizational participants to bolster their positions and to maintain or enhance the power and control they have over others. Examples abound in the readings we have selected in this section.

In "To Trust, Perchance to Buy," Donald Moine draws parallels between the intuitive techniques and style of the successful sales person and those of clinical hypnotists. Moine observes that effective sellers match their customer's posture, body language, and mood. He also notes that their persuasive powers are enhanced by their ability and willingness to tell stories, anecdotes, and parables and to draw on metaphors to frame their messages. Loaded words are powerful images, as Frank Trippett points out in "Watching Out for Loaded Words." They reach the emotions of the listener in a very direct way, in effect bypassing the critical faculties of his or her mind. Several forms of vesting words with additional meaning, positive or negative, are discussed. Trippett argues that it is important for people to be aware of how often and in how many different ways words and phrases can be loaded. Such awareness increases chances of detecting bias that may distort our thinking and our choices.

The notion that colors and color preferences create images and have an impact on how we are seen and on how we see others is the focus of the brief excerpt "Color: A Guide to Human Response" by James Gray, Jr. While we have no information on the accuracy or validity of the predictions and prescriptions in the article, we think it is important to mention the thesis that color does play a significant role in the image of self as conveyed to others. Readers might reflect on their own color preferences and think about the relationship between such preferences and their interactions with significant others at work and at home.

Some influences pervade an organization by reflecting its culture, and are so taken for granted that it becomes necessary to challenge or to contradict the culture quite dramatically to reveal their elements and interconnections. Harragan's provocative description of the immobilizing and discriminating effects on females of women's attire in organizations is instructive ("Women's Apparel is a Badge of Servitude"), in "Games Mother Never Taught You". She also describes a variety of status symbols and images in organizations that are vested with a great deal of meaning for those who encounter them. In a similar vein, Korda's, "Symbols of Power," discusses the choice, positioning, and behavioral impacts of offices and office furniture.

Harragan and Korda each describe ways to read, manage, and respond to powerful symbols and images. Greenfield's, "The Trappings Trap," warns us of the dangers of treating symbols, especially those of power and control with too much respect. She reflects on an event in England in 1982, in which a young man penetrated the security system around Queen Elizabeth and appeared, unannounced, in her bedroom. "Things may not be what they seem to be" is in part, her message. In particular, she focuses on the illusion of invulnerability. The security system in and around Buckingham Palace, the power symbols of an organization, may not be as impenetrable as we assume them to be. We should not be seduced by the appearances of power we encounter in organizational settings. Our final piece in this section, "An Unmentionable Occasion," by Bob Greene, provides an illustration of how images are skillfully managed and manipulated to gain acceptance of a possibly sensitive idea. Greene describes a party of Undercover Wear Inc., "where sexy or saucy underwear is sold to housewives; where the sexual revolution and the Tupperware party meet." Many readers are most likely aware of the successful Tupperware organization, noted for its strong culture and use of a sales force comprised largely of housewives and the house party as the venue for selling their products. Greene describes how the president of Undercover Wear Inc., Tiffany James, sells negligees, nightgowns and other underwear to women at specially arranged house parties. It is apparent to us, that intuitively or by design, James has harnessed many of the ideas expressed in the articles in this section, and understands the subtlety and power of images and symbols.

The realities outlined in this section reflect a world more complex than it may seem on the surface. It is a combative world, it is not benign. The organization is an area in which it is wise to be wary. We think it is important for people to pay careful attention to the settings, languages, and trappings of their organizations. The precise nature of organization images and their character and impact remain to be carefully charted. Behavioral scientists are beginning to explore this perspective of organizational life.

The articles in this section also contain information that permits development of more humane organizations in which dignity and productivity can coexist. Examination and understanding of organizational images can assist managers to root out their more distinctive effects. An office layout can be prepared with the conscious attention of relaxing tension and encouraging communication and joint problem solving; dress codes need not be discriminatory; language need not be distinctive. While ignorance or its obverse, the self serving manipulation of images and symbols, may be common in organizations, they need not be inevitable characteristics of organizational life.

To Trust, Perchance to Buy

Maybe what Willy Loman needed was lessons from Dr. Mesmer. The best persuaders build trust by mirroring the thoughts, tone of voice, speech tempo, and mood of the customer— literally, the techniques of the clinical hypnotist.

Donald J. Moine

The real-estate agent, who normally speaks quickly and loudly, is responding in a slow, soft, rhythmic voice to her slow-speaking, quiet customer. The agent opened the sales interview with a series of bland and flatly accurate remarks about the cool weather and the lack of rain. Now she is explaining her hesitation in showing her customer a particular house: "I know you want to see that house, but I don't know whether I should show it to you. It is expensive, and "—and imperceptible pause—*"just looking at it will make you want to buy it."* A bit later she repeats something that, she says, a previous customer told her about a house he'd bought: "The house has been worth every penny. My wife and I just enjoy it so much"—another pause—*"we can't understand why we took so long to buy it."*

The agent, an extremely successful saleswoman, is instinctively using weapons from the arsenal of the skilled clinical hypnotist, whose initial aim is to create in a subject a state of intensified attention and receptiveness, leading to increased suggestibility. All successful persuaders produce such an effect, probably without understanding the exact nature of the techniques that accomplish it. Our real-estate woman is lulling her customer into a mood of trust and rapport by taking on his verbal and emotional coloring, and her techniques are almost identical to those that therapists like Herbert Spiegel use with patients who come to them to be hypnotized out of, say, their fear of cats.

The conclusion that a successful sales presentation is an intuitive form of indirect hypnosis is the most provocative finding of a psycholinguistic analysis that I performed in 1981. My initial study focused on eight life-insurance salesmen, four of whom were identified as "top producers" by the presidents of their companies, and four as only average. The two groups were closely matched on such characteristics as age and experience. Taking the role of the customer, I spoke with the eight men, recorded their comments, and analyzed those comments for the 30 techniques of persuasion that Richard Bandler and John Grinder had identified in the work of the master hypnotist Milton Erickson. I next examined the work of 14 top sellers of real estate, luxury automobiles,

Reprinted from *Psychology Today Magazine.*
Copyright © 1982 American Psychological Association.

stocks, commodities, and trust deeds. Since 1981, I have tested my findings with more than 50 other people, who sell, among other products, jets, computers, and oil and gas leases. My basic finding was confirmed: Superior sellers use the techniques of the clinical hypnotist; mediocre ones do not.

GETTING IN SYNC

The best sales people first establish a mood of trust and rapport by means of "hypnotic pacing"—statements and gestures that play back a customer's observations, experience, or behavior. Pacing is a kind of mirror-like matching, a way of suggesting: "I am like you. We are in sync. You can trust me."

The simplest form of pacing is "descriptive pacing," in which the seller formulates accurate, if banal, descriptions of the customer's experience. "It's been awfully hot these last few days, hasn't it?" "You said you were going to graduate in June." These statements serve the purpose of establishing agreement and developing an unconscious affinity between seller and customer. In clinical hypnosis, the hypnotist might make comparable pacing statements: "You are here today to see me for hypnosis." "You told me over the phone about a problem that concerns you." Sales agents with only average success tend to jump immediately into their memorized sales pitches or to hit the customer with a barrage of questions. Neglecting to pace the customer, the mediocre sales agent creates no common ground on which to build trust.

A second type of hypnotic pacing statement is the "objection pacing" comment. A customer objects or resists, and the sales agent agrees, matching his or her remarks to the remarks of the customer. A superior insurance agent might agree that "insurance is not the best investment out there," just as a clinical hypnotist might tell a difficult subject, "You are resisting going into trance. That's good. I encourage that." The customer, pushing against a wall, finds that the wall has disappeared. The agent, having confirmed the customer's objection, then leads the customer to a position that negates or undermines the objection. The insurance salesman who agreed that "insurance is not the best investment out there" went on to tell his customer, "but it does have a few uses." He then described all the benefits of life insurance. Mediocre sales people generally respond to resistance head-on, with arguments that presumably answer the customer's objection. This response often leads the customer to dig in his heels all the harder.

The most powerful forms of pacing have more to do with how something is said than with what is said. The good salesman or -woman has a chameleon-like ability to pace the language and thought of any customer. With hypnotic effect, the agent matches the voice tone, rhythm, volume, and speech rate of the customer. He matches the customer's posture, body language, and mood. He adopts the characteristic verbal language of the customer ("sound good," "rings a bell," "get a grip on"). If the customer is slightly depressed, the agent shares that feeling and acknowledges that he has been feeling "a little down" lately. In essence, the top sales producer becomes a sophisticated biofeedback mechanism, sharing and reflecting the customer's reality—even to the point of breathing in and out with the customer.

I have found only one area in which the top sales people do not regularly pace their customers' behavior and attitudes—the area of beliefs and values. For example, if a customer shows up on a car lot and explains that she is a Republican, a moderately successful salesman is likely to say that he is, too, even if he isn't. The best sales people, even if they are Republicans, are unlikely to say so, perhaps because they understand that "talk is cheap" and recognize intuitively that there are deeper, more binding ways of "getting in sync" with the customer.

THE SOFT SELL

Only after they have created a bond of trust and rapport do the top sales people begin to add the suggestions and indirect commands that they hope will lead the customer to buy. One such soft-sell technique is using their patently true pacing statements as bridges to introduce influencing statements that lead to a desired response or action. For example: "You are looking at this car and you can remember the joy of owning a new reliable car," or "You are 27 years old, and we figure that your need for life insurance is $50,000." These pacing-and-leading statements resemble the way a hypnotist leads a client into hypnosis: "You are sitting in this chair, and you are listening to my voice"—the unarguable pacing statements—"and your eyelids are getting heavy, and they are beginning to close. . . ."

There does not have to be any logical connection between the pacing statement and the leading statement. They can be totally unrelated, yet when they are connected linguistically, they form a "sales logic" that can be powerfully effective, even with such presumably analytic and thoughtful customers as doctors and college professors.

The power of these leading statements comes from the fact that they capitalize on the affirmative mental state built by the undeniably true pacing statements, with which the customer is now familiar. Customers who have agreed with sales people expect, unconsciously, further agreement, just as customers who have disagreed expect further disagreement. The "traditional" truth of these pacing statements rubs off on the leading statements, and, without knowing it, the customer begins to take more and more of what the sales agent says as both factual and personally significant. Using hypnotic language, the agent activates the customer's desire for the product.

Average sellers combine pacing and leading statements less frequently and with less skill than do their superior colleagues. They also speak in shorter, choppier sentences, and thus fail to create the emotional web of statements in which the truthful and the possible seem to merge.

One of the most subtle soft-sell techniques is to embed a command into a seemingly innocuous statement. "A smart investor knows how to *make a quick decision, Robert.*" "I'm going to show you a product that will help you, *Jim, save money.*"

Sales people insure that their embedded commands come across by changing the tone, rhythm, and volume of their speech. Typically, as they pronounce the commands, they intuitively slow their speech, look the customer directly in the eyes, and say each word forcefully. A clinical hypnotist does the same thing deliberately. "If you will *listen to the sound of my voice,* you will be able to relax."

The placement of an individual's name in a sentence seems like a trivial matter, yet the position of a name can make a significant difference in how strongly the sentence influences the listener. Placed before or after the command portion of a sentence, it gives the command an extra power.

By changing their speech rate, volume, and tone, the best sales agents are able to give certain phrases the effect of commands. "If you can *imagine yourself owning this beautiful car,* and *imagine how happy it will make you,* you will want to, *Mr. Benson, buy this car.*" The two phrases beginning with 'imagine' become commands for the customer to do just that. Owning the car is linked to the leading statement of how happy it will make the customer. Finally, the statement carries the embedded command: "*Mr. Benson, buy this car.*"

THE POWER OF PARABLES

A final soft-sell technique of the best sales people is the ability to tell anecdotes, parables, and stories, and to frame their comments in metaphors. For thousands of years, human beings have been influencing, guiding, and inspiring one another with stories and metaphors, so it should be no surprise that sales people routinely use them to influence customers. What is surprising is the frequency and skill with which they do so.

Some sales agents I have studied do almost nothing but tell stories. They tell them to get the customer's attention, to build trust and rapport, and even to deliver product information. A piece of information that in itself might be boring takes on a human dimension and stays in the customer's memory when placed in the context of a story. "I sold a receiver like this a week ago to a surfer from Torrance and what he liked best about it was its FM sensitivity of 1.7 microvolts."

Metaphors and stories are used to handle customers' resistance and to "close" on them without endangering rapport. A top insurance agent was attempting to close a deal for a policy with a young man who was considering signing with a smaller company. As part of his clinching argument, the salesman wove the following metaphor into his pitch: "It's like taking your family on a long voyage across the Atlantic Ocean, and you want to get from here to England, and you have the choice of either going on this tugboat or on the Queen Mary. Which one would you *feel safe* on?" Had the salesman tried to make his point with a litany of facts and figures, he might never have focused his customer's attention; the discussion could have descended into a dispute about numbers. Instead, his story spoke directly to the customer's concern about his family's safety and implied that it was now in the customer's power to decide between two choices that were clearly unequal.

Note, too, that the salesman used conjunctions to link the metaphor in one unbroken chain and give it a hypnotic cadence. Mediocre sales people who know such a story would probably tell it as several separate sentences. In addition, they probably would give no special emphasis to the phrase "feel safe" even if they had heard better sales people do so. The skill in telling it is more important than the material itself.

The same can be said about all the skills that constitute the intuitively hypnotic arsenal of the best sales agents. But obviously, these skills are not exclusive to sellers. They are common to others—politicians, lawyers, even preachers. No less than sales people, these persuaders try to influence their audiences. No less than sales people, they attempt to implant in their audiences a resolve to do something. And, like sales people, all of them use, to some extent, variations of the techniques of Mesmer, Cagliostro, and Rasputin.

Watching Out for Loaded Words

Frank Trippett

Via eye and ear, words beyond numbering zip into the mind and flash a dizzy variety of meaning into the mysterious circuits of knowing. A great many of them bring along not only their meanings but some extra freight—a load of judgment or bias that plays upon the emotions instead of lighting up the understanding. These words deserve careful handling—and minding. They are loaded.

Such words babble up in all corners of society, wherever anybody is ax-grinding, arm-twisting, back-scratching, sweet-talking. Political blather leans sharply to words *(peace, prosperity)* whose moving powers outweigh exact meanings. Merchandising depends on adjectives *(new, improved)* that must be continually recharged with notions that entice people to buy. In casual conversation, emotional stuffing is lent to words by inflection and gesture: the innocent phrase, "Thanks a lot," is frequently a vehicle for heaping servings of irritation. Traffic in opinion-heavy language is universal simply because most people, as C. S. Lewis puts it, are "more anxious to express their approval and disapproval of things than to describe them."

The trouble with loaded words is that they tend to short-circuit thought. While they may describe something, they simultaneously try to seduce the mind into accepting a prefabricated opinion about the something described. The effect of one laden term was incidentally measured in a recent survey of public attitudes by the Federal Advisory Commission on Intergovernmental Relations. The survey found that many more Americans favor governmental help for the poor when the programs are called "aid to the needy" than when they are labeled "public welfare." And that does not mean merely that some citizens prefer H_2O to water. In fact, the finding spotlights the direct influence of the antipathy that has accumulated around the benign word *welfare.*

Every word hauls some basic cargo or else can be shrugged aside as vacant sound. Indeed, almost any word can, in some use, take on that extra baggage of bias or sentiment that makes for the truly manipulative word. Even the pronoun *it* becomes one when employed to report, say, that somebody has what *it* takes. So does the preposition *in* when used to establish, perhaps, that zucchini quiche is *in* this year: used just so, *in* all but sweats with class bias. The emotion-heavy words that are easiest to spot are epithets and endearments: *blockheads, scumbum, heel, sweetheart, darling, great human being* and the like. All such terms are so full of prejudice and sentiment that S.I. Hayakawa, a semanticist before he became California's U.S. Senator, calls them "snarl-words and purr-words."

Not all artfully biased terms have been honored with formal labels. Word loading, after all, is not a recognized scholarly discipline, merely a folk art. Propagandists and advertising copy-writers may turn it into a polished low art, but it is usually practiced—and witnessed—without a great deal of deliberation. The typical person, as Hayakawa says in *Language in Thought and Action*, "takes words as much for granted as the air."

Actually, it does not take much special skill to add emotional baggage to a word. Almost any noun can be infused with skepticism and doubt through the use of the word *so-called.* Thus a friend in disfavor can become a *so-called friend,* and similarly the nation's leaders can become *so-called leaders.* Many other words can be handily tilted by shortening, by prefixes and suffixes, by the reduction of formal to familiar forms. The word *politician,* which may carry enough downbeat connotation for most tastes, can be given additional unsavoriness by truncation: *pol.* By prefacing liberal and conservative with *ultra* or *arch,* both labels can be saddled with suggestions of inflexible fanaticism. To speak of a pacifist or peacemaker as a *peacenik* is, through a single syllable, to smear someone with the suspicion that he has alien loyalties. The antifeminist who wishes for his (or her) prejudice to go piggyback on his (or her) language will tend to speak not of feminists but of *fem-libbers.* People with only limited commitments to environmental preservation will tend similarly to allude not to environmentalists but to *eco-freaks.*

Words can be impregnated with feeling by oversimplification. People who oppose all abortions distort the position of those favoring freedom of private choice by calling them *pro-abortion.* And many a progressive or idealist had experienced the perplexity of defending himself against one of the most peculiar of all disparaging terms, *do-gooder.* By usage in special contexts, the most improbable words can be infused with extraneous meaning. To speak of the "truly needy" as the Administration habitually does is gradually to plant the notion that the unmodified *needy* are falsely so. Movie Critic Vincent Canby has noticed that the word *film* has become imbued with a good deal of snootiness that is not to be found in the word *movie. Moderate* is highly susceptible to coloring in many different ways, always by the fervid partisans of some cause: Adlai Stevenson, once accused of being too *moderate* on civil rights, wondered whether anyone wished him to be, instead, immoderate.

The use of emotional vocabularies is not invariably a dubious practice. In the first place, words do not always get loaded by sinister design or even deliberately. In the second, that sort of language is not exploited only for mischievous ends. The American verities feature words—*liberty, equality*—that, on top of their formal definitions, are verily packed with the sentiments that cement U.S. society. The affectionate banalities of friendship and neighborliness similarly facilitate the human ties that bind and support. The moving vocabularies of patriotism and friendship are also subject to misuse, of course, but such derelictions are usually easy to recognize as demagoguery or hypocrisy.

The abuse and careless use of language have been going on for a long time: witness the stern biblical warnings such as the one in *Matthew 12:36:* "Every idle word that men shall speak, they shall give account thereof in the day of judgment." Yet the risks of biased words to the unwary must be greater today, in an epoch of propagandizing amplified by mass communications. "Never," Aldous Huxley said, "have misused words—those hideously efficient tools of all the tyrants, warmongers, persecutors and heresy hunters—been so widely and disastrously in-fluential." In the two decades since that warning, the practice of bam-boozlement has, if anything, increased. The appropriate response is not a hopeless effort to cleanse the world of seductive words. Simple awareness of how frequently and variously they are loaded reduces the chances that one will fall out of touch with so-called reality.

Color:
A Guide to Human Response

James Gray, Jr.

How does color affect the impression you make? Color preferences offer clues to personality and guide human response.

Most interesting and revealing research and theory come from color expert Faber Birren. In his book *Color and Human Response,* he looks at personal color preferences and describes how color relates to personality. The colors people select and wear consistently are a large part of their image. Look around your office. What colors do people wear? Who wears warm colors and who wears cool colors? Birren found that

> There is a major division between extroverts, who like warm colors and introverts who like cool colors. As to general response to color, it is wholly normal for human beings to like any and all colors. Rejection, skepticism, or outright denial of emotional content in color probably indicates a disturbed, frustrated or unhappy mortal. Undue exuberance over color, however, may be a sign of mental confusion, a flighty soul, the person who flits from one fancy or diversion to another and has poor direction and self-poise.*

The following commentaries, adapted from Birren's book, show how color and human response are connected.

Red. There are different red types. The first comes honestly to the col-or, with outwardly directed interests. He or she is impulsive, possibly athletic, sexy, quick to speak the mind—whether right or wrong. The complementary red type is the meek and timid person who may choose

---

*Faber Birren, Color and Human Response (New York: Van Nostrand Reinhold, 1978).

the color because it signifies the brave qualities that are lacking. Look in this person for more hidden desires, for more sublimation of wishes than usual. Where there is dislike of red, which is fairly common, look for a person who has been frustrated, defeated in some way, bitter and angry because of unfulfilled longings.

Pink. One of Birren's studies showed that many people who liked pink were dilettantes. They lived in fairly wealthy neighborhoods and were well educated, indulged, and protected. Birren found them to be "red souls who, because of their careful guardianship, hadn't the courage to choose the color in its full intensity." A preference for pink may also signify memories of youth, gentility, or affection.

Orange. Orange is the social color, cheerful, luminous, and warm rather than hot like red. Orange personalities are friendly, have a ready smile and quick wit, and are fluent if not profound in speech. They are good natured and gregarious and do not like to be left alone. In several instances, the dislike of orange has tuned out to indicate a person, once flighty, who has made a determined effort to give up superficial ways for more sober application and diligence.

Yellow. On the good side, yellow is often preferred by persons of above-average intelligence. It is, of course, associated with oriental philosophies. The yellow type likes innovation, originality, wisdom. This type tends to be introspective, discriminating, high minded, and serious about the world and the talented people in it.

Yellow in the Western world has symbolized cowardice, prejudice, persecution. Some may dislike the color for this reason.

Yellow-Green. From the few cases Birren encountered, he concluded that the yellow-green type is perceptive and leads a rich inner life but resents being looked upon as a recluse. There is desire to win admiration for a fine mind and demeanor but difficulty meeting others because of innate timidity and self-consciousness.

Green. Green is perhaps the most American of colors. It is symbolic of nature, balance, normality. Those who prefer green almost invariably are socially well adjusted, civilized, conventional. Green is perhaps an expression of Freud's oral character. Because the green types are constantly on the go and savor the good things of life, they are often overweight. The person who dislikes the green type may resist social involvement, and lack the balance that green itself suggests.

Blue-Green. Birren associated the type with narcissism, or self-love. Most people who prefer blue-green are sophisticated and discriminating, have excellent taste, are well dressed, charming, egocentric, sensitive, and refined. Where a rare dislike of blue-green is met, there is an ardent denunciation of conceit in others, the attitude: "I am as good as you are!" Or, "Who do you think you are!"

Blue. Blue is the color of conservatism, accomplishment, devotion, deliberation, introspection. It therefore goes with people who succeed through application, those who know how to earn money, make the right connections in life, and seldom do anything impulsive. They make able executives and golfers, and they usually dwell in neighborhoods where other lovers of blue are to be found. Blue types are cautious, steady, often admirable, and generally conscious of their virtues.

A dislike of blue signals revolt, guilt, a sense of failure, anger about the success of others, especially if they have not expended the effort of the hater of blue. Successful people are resented as having all the good breaks and the good luck.

Purple and Violet. Those whose favorite color is purple are usually sensitive and have above-average taste. Lovers of purple carefully avoid the more sordid, vulgar aspects of life and have high ideals for themselves and for everyone else.

Those who dislike purple are enemies of pretense, vanity, and conceit and readily disparage cultural activities which to them are artificial.

Brown. Brown is a color of the earth, preferred by people who have homespun qualities. They are sturdy, reliable, shrewd, parsimonious; they look old when they are young and young when they are old. They are conservatives in the extreme.

In a distaste for brown, there may be impatience with what is seen as dull and boring.

White, Gray, and Black. Virtually no one ever singles out white as a first choice; it is bleak, emotionless, sterile. White, gray, and black all figure largely in the responses of disturbed human beings. On the other hand, white is the color of innocence, virtue, truth and cleanliness. White is the preferred color for weddings and for formal social events.

Black-and-white contrasts also signal upper-class status. The famous Ascot races and other social events use white and black as primary theme colors.

A preference for gray, however, usually represents a deliberate and cultivated choice. Gray's sobriety indicates an effort to keep on an even keel, to be reasonable, agreeable, useful in a restrained way. To dislike gray is less likely than to be indifferent to it. It may be that a dislike is weariness of an uneventful life, or a feeling of mediocrity.

As to black, usually only the mentally troubled are fascinated by it, though there are exceptions. Some few persons may take to the color for its sophistication, but in this preference they may be hiding their truer natures.

People who dislike black are legion. Black is death, the color of despair. Such persons often avoid the subjects of illness and death, do not acknowledge birthdays, and never admit their age.

SELECTING COLORS THAT ARE RIGHT FOR YOU

1. Respect corporate or professional standards. If top level executives most often appear in navy and gray flannel, take the hint. It's a conservative environment and you will do well to follow the standard. Gray and navy are perhaps most readily associated with conservatism; bright or new tones are more liberal and may be de rigueur for fashion and design careers.
2. Don't be afraid of color. Respect professional and corporate standards, but let your personality shine through. The gray flannel suit or blazer comes to life with a scarf in the breast pocket, but to be safe, wear complementary colors.
3. Keep the season and climate in mind. White is generally considered bad taste in winter. Black absorbs heat on a humid, muggy day, but is comfortable in an air-conditioned office.
4. Complement skin and hair tones. Light skin and blond hair combined with white is a fade-out. Red hair and a ruddy complexion over violet and orange shocks. Cosmetic counselors in respected department stores conduct free color evaluations.
5. Select several colors that both complement your skin and hair color, and express your personality and buy clothes primarily in these colors. In addition it's difficult to own too many white shirts or blouses.
6. Consider the occasion. Delivering a speech at an after-six dinner meeting calls for dark, authoritative colors. Training a group of new employees might demand an authoritative, but less-threatening, gray flannel suit.
7. In choosing accessories, match and coordinate colors. Briefcases, shoes, and pocketbooks should not blatantly contrast suit or dress colors.

The previous chapter gave guidelines for selecting clothes according to body shape and size. The following guidelines tell how to use color to alleviate a problem with body shape and size. It's actually impossible to separate clothing and color guidelines, and you should consider both to create the most effective style.

The Tall, Muscular Male or Female. Choose softer, lighter shades in gray, beige or light blues. Avoid color contrasts and bright colors that draw attention. Choose subtle combinations of blue and gray.

The Tall, Thin Male or Female. Medium-dark tans and blues work well. Use subtle color contrasts to break a long, continuous look, a tan and cream combination, for example. Stick with solid colors; avoid bright colors and patterns.

The Small, or Short Male or Female. Stick with dark hues in blue or gray. Match colors rather than contrast them. Matched colors, especially dark colors, add power and authority. For example, a dark gray suit with a diagonally striped tie in medium to dark gray and navy is an authoritative color combination. For women, a medium-gray dress with a complementary, darker-gray jacket or blazer works well.

The Hefty Male or Female. Wear neutral, less attention-drawing colors, gray or tan hues. Wear lighter, cooler colors, even in winter. Avoid bright colors. Wear dark colors only on occasions that demand added authority.

Games Mother Never Taught You

Betty Lehan Harragan

To awestruck sightseers in the land of the business hierarchy, the architectural grandeur is overpowering and impressive. Stately edifices dominate landscaped vistas of suburbia and mighty skyscrapers silhouette the profiles of major cities. Flowering gardens, soaring plazas, ample parking, vaulted lobbies, air conditioning, musical elevators, carpeted lounges, spacious dining rooms, and hundreds upon hundreds of linear offices bathed relentlessly in fluorescent brilliance dutifully impress gaping tourists.

But all this structural munificence does not divert the expert gamester who looks beyond the steel and concrete public visor of the corporate persona to identify the heraldic markings painted on the battle armor. Like the shields carried by knights of legend, the modern corporate building reeks with symbolism. Far from being a mere architectural wonder, every pane of glass, slab of marble, and foot of carpet performs a dual function in identifying the tournament site. The buildings are impersonal monuments to the power and wealth contained therein. Space itself, in both the exterior and interior layout, is weighted with abstract significance. Just as a heraldic seal reveals a great deal about the one using it, so spatial divisions reveal important information about the modern-day knights.

Today's business building, especially the corporate headquarters, is a physical representation of the hierarchical pyramid. It is the tangible game board. A walk through a large office, from floor to floor, is like threading a course through the hierarchy. Trappings of rank, position, and power are spread around the place like icons in a cathedral. They identify the important players and signal their positions in the game. Neophytes must grasp the design of the game board and learn the initial placement of the pieces before making any irreversible move.

Very often businesswomen approach the game of corporate gamemanship as if it were a throw of the dice which pits their future against pure chance, or luck. The real game for women more nearly resembles chess, in which one of the sixteen playing pieces is a strong female (the Queen) and the object of the game is to "check" the adverse King. Chess is an intellectual military exercise based on a combative attack against equally matched opposing fighting units. The descriptive play language of chess is indistinguishable from that of war "games" or football or business—lines of attack, defensive systems, infiltration, onslaught, sacrifice, control (territory or foes), power, weakness, strength, strategy, tactics, maneuver, surrender, challenge, conquer, win. Each pawn, rook, knight, bishop, queen, and king in the chess set is endowed with specific agility to move only in certain directions and for stipulated distances. Each piece is made clearly identifiable so that players and observers can watch the game progress and know exactly what moves have been made. Unlike cards, chess is a public game spread out for all to see.

So is corporate politics a public game. In business the so-called status symbols serve to identify the playing pieces and reveal their positions on the board. The masculine pecking system, regardless of the all-male activity, is replete with emblems and shared identity signals, many of which speak louder than words and obviate the need for verbal communication. If you've ever wondered why your boss pays inordinate attention to "silly" objects or personal privileges, very likely these are crucial business status symbols. Few of the customs and practices of business life are meaningless. They only look that way to women who have not learned the fundamentals of the game.

HOW TO TELL THE PLAYERS APART

Status symbols are two-way communications. If you can interpret them, they tell you where a coworker stands in the ranking system, and they tell others where you stand. For that reason, women cannot afford to ignore these ubiquitous symbols because each tiny accumulation of visible status is an increase in power or advancement. Indeed, as the game plays out, a woman often needs her power emblems more than a title or salary increase to effectively use any authority she acquires. It is difficult if not impossible for a pawn to behave like a bishop or queen if she doesn't have the mitre or crown that differentiates the chess pieces.

Most of the common status differentials can be perceived at even the lowest levels. As employees move up the hierarchical ladder, the emblems are gradually emblazoned with additional symbols or sophisticated refinements of the basic seal. Here are some of the categories of rank insignia which help you tell the players apart and prevent you from being bluffed by someone at your own level who tries to "pull rank" on you without justification. Conversely, a familiarity with the status symbols protects you from being duped by management if you are offered an empty promotion or promise which carries no visible authority emblem.

How You Are Paid

Not how much, *how*. Cash in a brown envelope indicates the lowest rank. A check thus becomes a status symbol, a sign of progress. If the wage is figured on an hourly basis or a weekly basis (the nonexempt jobs which are subject to overtime beyond forty hours), it has a lower status than jobs which are exempt from overtime. I remember a junior writer who tried to lord it over her friends with a claim that she had been promoted to professional ranks. She lost all respect and admiration when it was discovered that she still filled out "the little green slips" which were required for weekly time sheets. She thought she was a "writer" because she was allowed to write; her shrewd coworkers knew she was still considered an hourly clerical worker by management because that's how she was paid. An annual salary paid out in the standard semimonthy equal installments is a symbol of the supervisory and professional ranks. Very high levels of management often have options to tailor payment methods to suit their own convenience. Many executives don't get a check at all; they have it sent directly to their banks and deposited to their personal accounts. Corporate officers almost all arrange to have big portions of their high salaries "deferred," that is, not paid to them until some later date or in some other form. It pays to keep an eye on how superiors receive and cash their salary checks. Incidentally, some executives send their secretaries to the bank with their checks; these secretaries are worth wooing if you're trying to collect salary data.

What Time You Report to Work

Flexibility in choosing one's own working hours is a clear mark of distinction. The lowest degree of status is reflected in punching a time clock or being "signed in" by an overseer, the sure tag of a manual or clerical job. The time-clock insignia also extends to lunch hours and coffee breaks which are strictly regimented to the prescribed minute. As one moves upward into supervisory and professional ranks, *it is taken for granted* that you have a degree of autonomy in fixing your work hours and lunch times or breaks. Women frequently don't seem to recognize that they have this status privilege, or else they are afraid to display it, and use it. I'm often jarred when I have lunch with an apparent "executive" woman who suddenly bolts her lunch and dashes away because she'll be "late" getting back to the office within an hour. This is the time-clock thinking, lowest-level clerical insignia. If her boss is what she's afraid of (as many have told me), she is being treated as a time-clock employee and allowing herself and her job to be thus degraded. No brownie points accrue to a game player who refuses to wear her status symbols. You establish privileges simply by taking advantage of work-hour freedom according to the local department pattern.

Freedom to determine your own working hours does not mean you work shorter hours or ignore the working timetable your boss adopts. Some women consider it wise to dovetail their hours with their boss's—so they are always in the office at the same time. Others work more independently and arrive at the hour most convenient to their personal schedule and vary lunch periods to suit personal or business commitments. One woman executive I know has remained at the same job level for twenty years although a more astute gamester with her options would have progressed several steps. Her problem is low-echelon thinking; she still acts like a time-clock secretary. Even though she travels on business regularly, she schedules her trips for one-day, eighteen-hour commutes and gets home after midnight to appear in the office before nine the next morning. Bedraggled and exhausted, she complains about her terrible schedule, but neither her subordinates nor her superiors have any sympathy; they've long since chalked her off as lacking management potential. Men who progressed from a duplicate position scheduled their trips over two or three days each time; they knew better than to ignore status symbols. If you're uncertain about your status entitlement in time flexibility, watch what male colleagues and bosses do. Then go out and do likewise! Don't, for heaven's sake, complain about men who proudly display their ranking privileges and wonder why your hard work isn't appreciated after you've thrown away your own equality symbol.

Where You Eat

Not only when but where one eats is a status distinction. The lowest indication is being restricted to the premises as are many plant and factory workers. Freedom to leave the work premises (whether you do or not) is a step upward. Voluntary on-site lunching in large corporations is usually stamped with clear status distinctions. Lower-echelon workers go to the general cafeteria; middle-management dines in the executive lunchroom; and top officers eat in the private dining room. Senior executives can always drop into the general cafeteria if they want, but it takes a symbolic ID card to get into the executive dining halls. Anyone who is eligible to eat in the executive dining room but eschews the privilege to continue lunching with friends in the general cafeteria is pretty sure to be knocked out of the game very soon. If, for example, you had a boss who did that, you'd know it was time to look for a transfer or new job because you're stuck with a dead-head. See how attention to visible status emblems can tip you off?

In some companies even eating at your desk can reveal status. Did you get the food yourself from the friendly mobile vendor? Did a secretary order it from a good delicatessen and have it delivered? Was a complete hot-plate sent from the executive dining room? Or did you bring a sandwich from home in a brown paper bag?

Are you beginning to think all this is silly, like who cares? That's just it; nobody cares—if you're a woman. All your male colleagues and coworkers will ignore your eating habits as long as it keeps you out of their favorite rendezvous. They've already decided you belong with the brown-baggers (low-paid secretaries and clerks who bring their lunch), so it won't surprise them one bit to see you ally yourself with lower-status lunch groups. As an ambitious woman you have to care. It will never do for you to exclude yourself from the semisocial lunch and cocktail gatherings where more business is conducted, more information exchanged, and more contacts made than during the regular working hours. If you can't worm your way into a suitable lunch group, go to a movie or go shopping for a couple of hours, but definitely exercise your status prerogative.

The Mail You Get

Mail sorters, if they were so minded, could diagram the organizational chart by noting the incoming mail for various individuals and the routing pattern on memos. One of the first status symbols is an in-box on your desk. The next improvement is denoted by an out-box. Increasing status is determined by the style of the containers, utilitarian metal being at the lower end and hand-woven straw, hand-painted wood, or other elaborate designs being better. Perhaps because this symbol is so widely distributed, some statusy types dispense with this common denominator and have incoming correspondence neatly piled on the center of an empty desk (they probably have little of significance to do and hope their status symbols will carry them through to retirement).

More important than the box is the incoming contents. Daily deliveries of the *Wall Street Journal* and *New York Times* or regular copies of *Business Week, Fortune, Barron's, Forbes, U.S. News and World Report,* or economic newsletters are distinctive emblems. Company-paid subscriptions are status symbols in general, but the more management-oriented the publication, the higher the status rating, *Harvard Business Review* outranking the Gizmo trade journal by far.

Outgoing mail also has status value if your name is imprinted on the corporate letterhead, either by itself or as one of the partners or officers of a firm.

Your Working Location

In a factory, the operator at the end of the assembly line has more prestige than one near the beginning because the product is more valuable in its finished state. The principle of increasing value of work follows through to the top of the hierarchy where the office of the chief executive is obviously the ultimate in status and power and the choicest in location. Proximity to the power generator exudes status, with the office adjacent to the CEO being the most prestigious but the entire floor sharing in shadings of top rank. In a suburban complex with several buildings, the one with the executive offices is the power generator and a poor location there is superior to choice space in any lesser building. In short, physical locale is a status symbol, so the location of your office is one of the most telling emblems in revealing your rank in the hierarchy and your favor with the boss. It's an important piece in the game.

HOW SPACE CONFERS STATUS

The "executive floor" is known to most employees by virtue of the fact that they have never set foot on it. This is the true inner sanctum, and the power emanations are so strong that minor employees are afraid to get near. I've seen adult men literally shake in their boots at the prospect of answering a call to the executive floor. For those who are physically located "in the boondocks," "over in the boneyard," or "out in the sticks," (i.e., distant buildings or branch offices), a move to the headquarters city or building signifies a boom in status long before anyone knows if the shift was accompanied by a change in title or a better salary. Geographic and internal physical office moves can track an executive's path through the hierarchical labyrinth more clearly than a title change. A company may have hundreds of vice-presidents or divisional managers but the really important ones are distinguished from titular peers by that prime emblem of status—the office location.

Within the physical boundaries of every corporate department or operation much the same pattern of office locale identifies the ranking of subordinates and superiors. Most department layouts are square or rectangular. The corner offices, which are larger, brighter, and most secluded, are choice spots and the highest ranking executives naturally choose them. The remainder of the outside walls are customarily divided into small offices so that each has a window or a portion of plate glass. These are known universally as the "window offices" and have much higher status value than nonwindowed offices. Size is also an emblematic factor, so a large window office is more valuable than a small window office, but a small window office is superior to a much larger "interior" office.

The internal space in a typical office floor layout can be left wide open and filled with rows upon rows of desks (generally populated with clerical women). Here employees work in the wide-open area with no privacy and where they can be easily observed by the supervisors.

Another solution is to partition the vast internal space with one or more rows of "interior" offices, each of which has walls to the ceiling and doors; these are real private offices but have no windows. The third alternative, and a highly favored one, is to erect movable partitions which enclose the desks of individuals in the interior sector. These tin or plastic partitions are waist- or shoulder-high; they block the view of a person sitting at the enclosed desk but allow any passer-by to look over the top and see the occupant at work. These constructions are well known to all working women as cubicles. Status-wise, they are a step up from the wide-open clerical or secretarial pool pattern (often referred to as "paper factories"), but not as prestigious as a fully enclosed office which carries more symbolic value even if it must be shared with another. A "window" office is generally considered an "executive" or supervisory symbol.

SYMBOLIC MEANINGS OF WINDOWS AND WALLS

Since window offices can be roughly defined as officers' quarters, the position of rooms "weights" their relative values. Proximity to the corner offices carries the most weight, then comes view. An unobstructed view of the skyline or gardens is far more prestigious than a window on the ventilating shaft or one overlooking the parking lot or delivery entrance. An office located on the traffic lanes, one in the center arena of business activity, represents higher status than one hidden away in an isolated nook or placed near the non-status "public" areas, such as cloakrooms, bathrooms, lounges, elevators, or storerooms.

Offices in the middle of the outside walls, that is, those that are equidistant from either corner office, are least desirable because the occupant's connection to either corner power generator is weak, tenuous, and not immediately identifiable. Michael Korda, the best-selling folk etymologist of sophisticated male business mores, attributes this midcenter office weakness to a power dead spot. In his book *Power: How to Get It, How to Use It,* he asserts that power flows in a X-shaped pattern from each corner office to the one diagonally opposite. The center of the space (where the X-lines bisect) represents the point at which the authority of the corner person peters out. Under his theory, the center of the floor layout is equivalent to a power blackout area and outer offices parallel with the center of the room are thus located in power dead-spots.

I've seen office setups where enclaves of competing executives use the X theory to amass power. With their cronies and subordinates flanking them, they set up hostile camps in each of the corners. Newcomers or nonaligned workers invariably float to the nondescript center offices. In firms where several executives have equal rank, for instance partners in auditing, law, or brokerage firms, they can apportion the corner offices by a coin toss and the power flow runs as easily down the sides as across a diagonal. Even so, the central offices are less prestigious because ranking executives like to have their closest allies physically near them. Proximity to a superior is undoubtedly the best gauge of status within a team group. Watch carefully when offices get switched around. It means that status symbols are changing hands and the rank of the movers is being visibly altered although their titles and salaries are unchanged.

A lot of women may think this game of musical chairs with office locations is also silly and unnecessary. It may be, but the accretion of status symbols is very serious business to ambitious businessmen. They know that a display of status symbols means as much in the corporate hierarchy as a chest full of medals does to an ambitious officer in the military hierarchy. If women are to function equally in the action arena of business they must be able to decipher the code and demand the proper rank insignia for themselves as they progress haltingly up the corporate ladder. To disregard the value of preferred office location is tantamount to selecting a rhinestone ring over a diamond because the first one looked "prettier." Refusing to wear epaulets which identify your business rank because you don't appreciate the genuine value is a disastrous mistake.

DON'T GARBLE THE LOCALITY MESSAGE

Judging from my personal observations during the past five years that women have begun moving ahead in corporate jobs en masse, it seems safe to say that many have ignored the status code. Which is to say that they get a better title but they seldom get the visible emblems of rank. If you believe you are making progress on your job, count the number of times you have changed offices. A meaningful promotion almost mandates an office change; a token title and slight salary increase does not give you the necessary authority to handle the new job unless subordinates and outsiders see that you were issued the appropriate rank insignia.

By and large, women are oblivious to rank symbols because so few working women have *any* office privacy that a room of one's own is—in comparative *women's* terms—the ultimate achievement. As long as it's private and "workable," women are inclined to "accept" any office offered them and make the best of the disadvantages that inevitably appear. I know women who have sat in the same office for the past twenty years. I don't know any men in that category. In the industry circles I travel, men who are that immobile were fired or quit years ago.

If you had trouble . . . in diagramming your department's organization chart or evaluating your own advancement potential, try a different tack. Make a floor plan of the office layout and see who's sitting where. This floor plan will guide you in determining which of several people on the same job level are the more favored or powerful—they will have offices very near the top-ranked superior, or they will have established a power enclave of their own in one of the opposite corners. Then locate your own office in relation to these authority areas. You should get a pretty good idea of what your superiors think of you and your potential according to the office they assigned you. It may be more than adequate by your personal comfort standards, but if it doesn't translate into appropriate status according to the male heraldic seal, you are being symbolically downgraded or dead-ended.

ALWAYS COLLECT YOUR EARNED MEDALLIONS

Reluctance on management's part to dispense money in the form of raises is understandable because of manifest business concern but unwillingness to issue women their status insignia is propelled by pure male chauvinism. A female corporate politician must be alert to this subtle form of sex discrimination and take steps to alleviate it. Specifically, *ask* for and fight for your office emblem. Before making a final decision on a new job offer, ask to see the office that goes with the job. If you get a promotion, inquire immediately about the new office that you'll get. If you discover you have a lesser status office than your job indicates, ask for the next vacant office in the area you decide you belong in. Keep your eye on possible office vacancies and ask for a more desirable location before they put a newcomer (usually a man) in a higher status office than you have. Keep asking.

One woman I know who was an analyst in the research department of a large investment firm reacted instinctively and volubly when her company moved to elegant new offices in a beatiful skyscraper. She was the only woman in an all-male group and the covey of expensive industrial designers, office planners, and management consultants had settled her in a noisy isolated corner next to the coat room and elevator banks and off-kilter from the rest of the section. "I didn't know anything about office sites," she told me, "but I felt like I'd been slapped in the face. My intuition told me there was something seriously wrong and I refused to take the office. A young guy who had just arrived was settled in an office I liked, so I demanded that one on the basis of seniority. I loved the job, but I refused to appear at the office until I got the right accommodations. They put up a terrible fight, until I was mentally prepared to quit over the issue." Her determination paid off and she got the office space she selected. Later that year, one of the firm's partners brought his wife in to meet her, saying proudly, "I'd like you to meet the only woman in our research department." My friend pointed out that there was now another woman in research but he brushed that aside, saying, "I forget about her. I consider you our only woman because you are the only one who fought for your office!"

By contrast, a lawyer I know got a very good job in the corporate counsel's office of a huge industrial corporation. She's the only woman on the executive floor and since her first day's pro forma expense-account lunch with a few of the senior attorneys she has been totally ostracized by her colleagues. That was easily accomplished because her office (with a spectacular view from the top floor of a Manhattan skyscraper) is on a corridor on the opposite side of the building from the legal department. For all intents and purposes, she is physically as well as psychologically isolated from the counsel's team! Asked why she accepted that office she exclaimed, "Oh, it's beautiful! Carpets six inches thick, anything I request in the way of furniture and equipment, and that astronomical view. They originally apologized for it, saying nothing better was available, but I told them this was perfect. How much better could you get?" But when visiting executives from divisional offices and subsidiaries regularly take her for a temporary secretary, it's partly because she has no rank insignia, no team identification.

WATCH OUT FOR FEMALE GHETTOES

The retailing industry and fashion merchandising are typical of businesses where women predominate at lower levels and have moved upward in restricted areas to executive levels (a handful are getting close to the top). These industries are nevertheless dominated by male status symbols, and clever corporate politicians must analyze the patterns and play the game by classic standards. Many women who have "made it" through the twisted paths of historic blatant discrimination have had no opportunity to learn the game rules in entirety. They are particularly blind to status emblems or, to be more precise, they were furnished garbled emblems intended to ghetto-ize them and they now have difficulty unscrambling the hodge-podge.

I will be watching the progress of an executive friend who just began playing the corporate game in the retailing field. Helena has been floating on a relatively high plateau in specialty fashion retailing for the past several years. She's spent her entire career—close to twenty years—working with women colleagues whom she likes and admires. But once she was alerted to the broad ramifications of the corporate politics game, she recognized that her advancement opportunities were nonexistent in the retail complex where she was employed. She found a new job with a national consulting firm, using her expertise in fashion retailing as the wedge to negotiate a 50-percent salary increase. In her new firm all the employees and executives are women except for the vice-president in charge of merchandising, who is a man.

"After doing the same job for years, this offers an exciting new opportunity," she told me. "The company is dynamic, the vice-president, my boss, sounds very progressive, and the other women executives are tops in their fields, stimulating people to work with. Everything about the job seemed perfect—until I evaluated the status symbols, especially office location. I drew diagrams of the layout to analyze where my office was situated. The picture prompted me to reopen negotiations although I had accepted the job. I realized I'd be stalemated again if I didn't insist on the right office locale. I got it changed before I started."

Helena's analysis was perceptive gaming. The male vice-president had the most prestigious corner office. She had been assigned a large office next to the corner in the diagonally opposite area. All the women in that area were fashion specialists, too. Each of the corners held clusters of women experienced in various retail specialties. Helena is cognizant of the categorizing which restricts women executives to food, fashion, home furnishings, fabrics, domestics, cosmetics, accessories or whatever gave them their start. "When men start in ties, they don't end up tie specialists—they branch out to merchandising executives. When women start in dresses, they don't end up dress specialists—they're catalogued as high fashion, budget, sports, evening, lounge, or boutique. They are constricted by experience, not broadened to becoming merchandising generalists." This was the pattern she saw duplicated in the office layout at her new firm—women segregated according to narrow specialties. Since her goal was to break out of overspecialization, she perceived correctly that an office located in the midst of fashion specialists would lock her into the very trap she was escaping.

"I didn't explain *why* I wanted the particular office I chose; after all I'll be working closely with the fashion group at the beginning. But my career plan demands some proximity to the vice-president and a door on the traffic lane to his office. I'll use it for visibility and getting to know the types of merchandising clients who visit the V-P. I intend to move toward merchandising management, and my first successful game move was getting myself dissociated from all the specialty enclaves."

Office location is invested with good and poor status insignia. Office positioning has a direct relationship to job advancement. Certain office locales have high status value precisely because ambitious, aggressive people fight for them in order to get close to the central action area. Once again, watch how progressing men move closer and closer to higher superiors with every promotion. Careers and office insignia move in tandem.

WHEN STATUS EMBLEMS AND STEREOTYPES COLLIDE, MOVE!

Not much is known yet about potential boomerang effects when classic male rank symbols are acquired by women. One danger area is already evident—the office adjacent to a male senior executive. Sex, sexism, and female stereotypes can rear up to cancel out all the job benefits and rank status that traditionally accrue to men who achieve this enviable geographic site, which frequently has the invisible logo "next in line for the top job." When a woman earns that status locale, the invisible logo shifts to "she's sleeping with her boss," or "she's a glorified secretary (who's sleeping with the guy)."

Over a lunch, a female officer of a subsidiary company of a financial corporation explained how her advancement was nearly jeopardized because she occupied the office adjacent to the president. "I'm not quite sure how I got assigned to the office since I was one of several vice-presidents who were eligible for it. Probably a misguided attempt to prove they didn't discriminate against women, a laugh considering I was the only woman executive in the entire firm at the time. Take it from me, token women are more to be pitied than censured; like the first child of nervous parents we suffer from the ignorance of our elders." At any rate, she occupied what male colleagues looked upon as the most enviable office in the company, but it slowly turned into nightmare alley for her. "I had an important and demanding job but I was interrupted constantly. Executives from our own company as well as all outside visitors marched straight into my office, left messages for me to relay to the president, explained their problems to me, or dropped in for idle chats if the president got an important private phone call during their appointment."

At first she tried directing the men to the private secretaries and assistants, but each day there were other strangers who made the same automatic assumption—that the woman closest to the top executive was naturally his private secretary or assistant. "I foresaw the end of the line in my career if I remained in that close proximity to the chief executive. I was becoming identified with him and his work, not my own operating responsibilities. My authority was rapidly eroding as I was stereotyped into an 'assistant' or 'helper' to the great man. I decided I *had* to get out of there and I'm absolutely positive I'd never be where I am today, a functioning administrator and top management, if I'd allowed the implied tie-up of superior male-subservient female to continue."

The educational aspect of her story was how she made her moves to solve the problem. She assayed all the male vice-presidents who were equally eligible for the office. From the group she picked the man she disliked the most and who returned the feeling with a vengeance. He was also the one most envious of her position and most blatant about his raw ambition and his disparagement of her qualifications. When she invited him to lunch with her, he was wary and hostile. "He almost choked to death on a piece of fish when I asked him if he'd like to trade offices. He couldn't believe anybody would be so stupid as to give up the ultimate status symbol, and it took a while to convince him I was serious. Once he saw that (swallowing my story that I really *liked* his office better for its afternoon sunshine!), he joined the conspiracy with me to get the trade approved without any flak." Between the two of them they arranged the transfer smoothly and she regained her independence as a line executive. Her male accomplice gained his most cherished desire. "He was in seventh heaven in that office and the superior rank symbol pushed him steadily ahead. My freedom from that office allowed me to grow and develop on my merits and demonstrated performance; we both benefited. Best of all, he turned from an enemy into an ally. He is one of my strongest supporters and advocates."

PORCELAIN INSIGNIA THAT WON'T FLUSH AWAY

Toilets seem to be the major obstacle to women's equality. If you don't think so, you haven't heard the nuttiest arguments against the Equal Rights Amendment (i.e., the ridiculous fear that public restrooms will be coed). Or you haven't been faced with employment problems which evolve from the superior status symbolism of urinals. The good news is that women aren't entirely alone trying to revamp this physical hallmark of sexual supremacy; management is a nervous wreck as working women demand equal facilities and senior executives in many institutions expend as much energy on the dilemma of bathrooms as they do on the next quarterly earnings' prediction. Porcelain status symbols are proving to be nonbiodegradable.

Some companies try to evade the entire subject. To this day, the J. Walter Thompson Company advertising agency refuses to recognize indelicate functions. Its dozens of bathrooms hide decorously behind plain unmarked doors and nary a disciminatory word such as "Men's" or "Women's" sullies its pristine halls or executive offices. Pity the new male client or supplier whose initial contact is a woman executive (if any); the prime executive-to-executive bond has evaporated into embarrased agony.

Some companies treat the subject like a huge, salacious joke. They are apt to be institutions that have given urinals the most visible priority status. One of the country's largest utilities (hardly the only offender in this category) left no doubt where its sympathies lay by installing men's urinals in spacious rooms off the well-lit hallways. Women's facilities (patronized by vast majorities of the working population) were jammed into dingy, cramped quarters on the unused stairway landings. Female complaints were dismissed cavalierly even though several women had been frightened or molested by rapacious public freaks who crept up the abandoned stairwell. The enraged women got together and organized a pee-in in the men's bathrooms until their class status was upgraded and the bathrooms were switched.

Some companies are just plain scared as women edge closer and closer to a highly prized male status symbol—"the key to the executive bathroom." One of the few women who arrived at this eminence insisted on her executive token and demanded her status key. She promptly ordered the sign changed from "Men" to "Executives." Every so often she pretends to use her key (of course she's the first and only woman to collect this rank emblem) just to see what male executive comes bounding out of his office to "check if it's clear." Privately she admits to gleeful friends that she'd never really use it. "I'll never give up my privilege to use the ladies' room. For one thing, I hear all the juicy gossip that doesn't get on the grapevine, or I hear things before any of the men at my level. But most of all because I'm in a position to help other women. I can get to know women from several departments and keep an eye on the progress of those I admire. Already I've pulled one promising young woman into my department simply from meetings in the bathroom. I'm anticipating the day when the women's bathroom becomes just as powerful a focal point as the men's urinals when it comes to internal political manipulation."

The Queen in the chess set (in case you don't know) can move any number of clear spaces in *any* direction, backward, forward, sideways, or diagonally. A lot of visible status symbols can be collected with that maneuverability.

WOMEN'S APPAREL IS A BADGE OF SERVITUDE

Men's clothing is not unique in assigning attributes to its wearers; women's clothing is historically symbolic, too. As far as I know, no contemporary feminist has researched the subject (no nonfeminist would care), but women who are moving into the male world of work must begin to pay attention to the symbolism of clothing.

Why are men's and women's clothes so different? Why, as a woman, do you wear what you wear? What is your conscious or subconscious motivation each morning as you dress for work? Why not just wear your bathrobe?

The phenomenon of sex differential in wearing apparel intrigued Lawrence Langner, a prodigiously successful businessman who was also an erudite scholar, a popular playwright, and a perceptive social observer. His many-faceted talents led him to the theater where he founded the Theater Guild and the Shakespeare Festival at Stratford, Connecticut. The importance of costumes to theatrical productions and the social significance of costumes impelled him to study the meaning and psychology of clothing throughout history. In 1959 he published his remarkable psycho-history of clothing through the ages, *The Importance of Wearing Clothes* (New York: Hastings House). Several years before the current wave of feminism erupted, his studies led him to the following conclusion about the marked dissimilarity between men's and women's clothes:

Contrary to established beliefs, the differentiation in clothing between men and women arose from the male's desire to assert superiority over the female and to hold her in his service. This he accomplished through the ages by means of special clothing which hampered or handicapped the female in her movements. Then men prohibited one sex from wearing the clothing of the other, in order to maintain this differentiation.

Langner traced his hypothesis as far back as Spanish Levant rock paintings, circa 10,000 B.C. and followed the evidence through subsequent ages, civilizations, and cultures. He found the primary purpose of women's dress throughout history was to prevent them from running away from their lords and masters. The ancient Chinese bound the feet of growing girls to hopelessly deform the adult woman's feet; African tribes weighted women's legs with up to fifty pounds of "beautifying" nonremovable brass coils or protruding metal disks; in Palestine women's ankles were connected with chains and tinkling bells; Moslems swathed women in heavy, opaque shrouds from head to toe; upper-class women in Venice and Spain had to be assisted by pages when they walked in their gorgeous gowns because of the fashionable chimpanies or stilts attached to their shoes—some as much as a yard high!

The only exception to foot crippling was found among nomadic tribes where women were forced to keep up with their men during the seasonal migrations. In these groups, the women were the beasts of burden, walking with the animals and loaded almost as heavily with household goods. They could walk but could not run far.

In Western societies the ubiquitous hobbling device for women has been skirts, usually accompanied by dysfunctional stilted shoes. Although skirt styles changed over time and in various societies, skirts of all kinds served to encumber women. Skirts that consisted of long robes reaching to or below the ankles hampered movement by entangling the legs in layers of heavy textiles. In more "modern" times straight fitted skirts effectively bound the knees or ankles together to impede free stride and enforce an awkward, staggering gait. Whatever the society, skirts for females were characterized by their impracticality, inefficiency, and uncomfortable designs. Not only walking but sitting, bending, stooping, and climbing were totally enjoined via "female" dress. Utility, comfort, ornamentation, or sexual attraction has nothing to do with why females wear skirts or other distinctively "female" articles of clothing. These garments were invented thousands of years ago by men to label females as dependents and to "keep them in their place." In consequence, "female" apparel carries a universal symbolism of servitude—the badge of subservience.

In contrast the exclusive male clothing in every society where women were constricted consisted of divided garments—trousers or knickerbockers—which permitted free, unrestricted movement while protecting the wearer's extremities. Men exerted superiority over women by laying exclusive claim to clothing which gives the greatest mobility, freedom for action, and self-protection.

At all times, from earliest societies, women were prohibited from wearing the clothing of males—and vice versa. The penalties for breaking the strict laws against transvestitism ("a morbid craving to dress in garments of the opposite sex") were (and are) severe. In Deuteronomy, the Old Testament thundered the "moral" imprecations which many women feel bound by even in the twentieth century. "A woman shall not wear that which pertaineth unto a man, neither shall a man put on a woman's garment."

Despite these savage laws and vicious punishments, women have periodically rebelled against their enforced clothing shackles, especially skirts. Early American feminists of the 1850s took up the issue of women's dress reform. Amelia Bloomer is the best known of the many who took to wearing short skirts or tunics over loose trousers gathered at the ankle. "Bloomers" became the derisive term for any divided skirt or knickerbocker dress. One optimistic feminist, Helen Marie Weber, told the Women's Rights Convention of 1850 in Worcester, Massachusetts that, "In ten years time male attire will be generally worn by women of most civilized countries." She was at least a hundred years off in her prediction; it has taken until the 1970s for women to dare to flout the age-old inventions of man to keep her inferior and immobile.

There are still corporations that issue edicts to keep women employees in their place by forbidding women to wear slacks or pants suits to work. Such a company policy is telling women employees that they are inferior beings whose only status in the corporate setup is to serve their male masters. The clothing symbolism says: "You have no mobility in this corporation." No woman who understands the significance of corporate status symbolism would be caught dead working for such a company. Displaying a blatant badge of servitude is no way to progress in the male corporate milieu, but that is exactly what "female" dress codes dictated by men set out to accomplish.

DRESSING FOR SUCCESS—FEMALE STYLE

Given all the historical, psychological, cultural, and social factors that impinge on the personal dress habits of women, there is, as yet, no clear-cut solution to the problem ambitious women must face in inventing a suitable costume for their business role. (Anything goes outside of business situations for both women and men; our concern is limited to work costumes.) Given my personal orientation in male business fashions, plus my lifelong abhorrence of "feminine" fashions, I am convinced that the most important consideration for women is the underlying symbolism of clothing. There is no question in my mind that many women are held back in their job progress because of their inattention to dress. Or rather, their introspective evaluation of what they wear. In business you are not dressing to express personal taste; you are dressing in a costume which should be designed to have an impact on your bosses and teammates. If your clothes don't convey the message that you are competent, able, ambitious, self-confident, reliable, and authorative, nothing you say or do will overcome the negative signals emanating from your apparel.

My personal observations of women at work, plus my own experiences over many years, plus the opinions of increasingly successful women at work today are all I have to go on when proposing the following suggestions for guiding women toward a female business uniform style. I pass them along not as definitive rules but as the genesis of a practical, symbolic movement toward revitalizing women's perspective on "proper" attire for management executives, female.

Be Aware of the Uniform Concept

An amazing number of women dress wholly at variance with the "uniform" of their male associates. Your first prerequisite is to study the attire of men in your department or company. For instance, if the important men wear dark, conservative suits with white shirts and rep ties, you do not "fit in" if you are partial to busy prints, exuberant colors, extravagant hats, mod fashions, or lacy, frilly blouses. You may be a genius at that business but I guarantee you will never make it far up that hierarchical ladder. On the other hand, if you work for a go-go company where hard-driving male executives have adopted high-style Italian jeans, expensive leather boots, and suede jackets as a trend-setting uniform, you are an eyesore if you appear in inconspicuous navy knits with sedate pumps and a string of pearls. You may have exceptional talent but you will be "hidden away" far from the male executives in a dead-end service job, kept away from the gaming tables.

Keep an eye on the costumes of *superiors* to ascertain the "tone" or "look" that is voluntarily adopted by upward-moving men. Be very careful not to dress in conformity with lower-echelon jobs. If your company has a written secretarial dress code, executive women must *never* obey it. They will instantly ally themselves with the clerical ranks rather than executive or supervisory ranks. One woman told me how the point was accidentally brought to her attention, although she was thoroughly confused when the incident occurred.

She had continued to wear what she described as "attractive, feminine dresses" when she was promoted to her first true executive-level job. She did a certain amount of traveling and decided she could be more casual and comfortable on airplanes. One day she joined her boss at the airport wearing a navy pants suit. When her boss came toward her, he too was wearing a navy suit that looked almost identical. "I blushed in embarrassment," she said. "We looked like the Bobbsey Twins and all I could think of was how angry women get if somebody else has on the same dress. I think I was afraid that he'd be mad at me." But her boss didn't react that way at all! Quite the reverse; he approved of the way she was dressed although he never said a word. "I could sense a change in his attitude toward me. For the first time in two years he was relaxed and comfortable traveling with me. It was as if he finally accepted me as an executive with the firm and not some secretary he was forced to accompany. The only thing different about me was the clothes."

Dresses versus Suits

Instinctively for most of my working life I preferred two-piece women's suits to one-piece dresses. For reasons I couldn't explain there was a feeling of defenselessness or nakedness about dresses when all the men in the room wore jackets. When you think in terms of symbolism, it seems quite obvious that a man's jacket is his "mantle of authority." The first thing a man does when preparing for a business meeting or visiting his boss is to don his suit jacket. Many women executives unconsciously adopt the idea in their favored work clothing. Some wear dress costumes with a matching or contrasting jacket. Some wear sleeveless tunics which seem to serve the same purpose. Others use sweaters by wearing twin-sweater outfits or merely carrying a jacket sweater over their shoulders. The current fashion in "layered looks" is possibly a recognition of this authority-mantle concept. At any rate, a separate jacket or shoulder mantle of some nature (a shirt over a T-shirt or turtle-neck sweater has somewhat the same connotation) gives a feeling of strength and control to women's appearance.

A women who hopes to manage affairs, control subordinates, and exert authority must avoid any kind of dresses which portray her as weak or indecisive. Any taint of the "little girl" look is anathema—pinafores, ruffles, bows, cute prints, flouncy skirts, clinging fabrics, or distinctively "feminine" frills will contradict any effort to be viewed as forceful.

Skirt Suits versus Pants Suits

As far as I can see, there doesn't seem to be any difference whether a woman chooses skirts or pants to go with her jacketed costume as long as the skirt is appropriate for her daily activities. That means the skirt must be pleated or flared enough to allow a free stride. Walk around in your skirt before buying it to make sure you can get into a car, mount the bus steps, climb stairs, or get on the commuter train without looking awkward, ungainly, or inept. A clumsy or mincing gait suggests that such a person may be clumsy or inept in other ways.

Pay particular attention to the skirt when you sit down. Test it in a mirror and see if it rides up above your knees or otherwise disturbs men, who all have an innate impulse to look between your legs. Assume that you will be seated on an open stage or head table at some point in your business rounds, so check that the skirt will not force you to concentrate on pressing your knees together or otherwise protecting your genitals from male peeks. If the shoeshine man comes around and you don't dare put your foot up to join in the ritual because of your "immodesty," that skirt is no good as a work uniform. On the other hand, voluminous skirts which get caught in doors or overhang chairs are equally inappropriate. In short, if your skirt distracts your own attention and observers' attention from the business matter under discussion, it is not acceptable as a work uniform.

Pants suits are booming in popularity with women for good reason. Once a woman starts wearing pants suits she finds it very difficult to go back to skirts and dresses. Pants serve the same function for women as they do for men. They give absolute freedom of motion, allow you to sit, stand, run, or bend over without worrying about how much "shows" or adopting all the female contortions that impede physical movement. But pants suits alone don't add up to a team uniform. There are many other details to watch when adopting this once forbidden male apparel.

Attention to Fit

Many women think they look terrible in pants (and many do) because they don't know how pants should fit. They must fit perfectly, just as men's do (or should). Relatively few women can buy a pants suit without having one or both the pieces altered. Women's pants should have a fitted waistband (not an elastic stretch which fits everybody and nobody), and the creases must fall straight to the floor. If you have acquired a lifelong habit of walking in a typically female knock-kneed position, pants will not hang right. Watch men in jobs above you to see what length they wear their trousers and lengthen or shorten yours to conform. A "high-water" look (i.e., so short your socks show) has always been the sign of a hayseed.

Suit jackets, too, must fit perfectly. Men notice those things even if you don't. I vividly remember my initial encounter with a clothing executive when I first entered the men's fashion promotion field. I was wearing a good-looking tailored woman's suit which I thought was very appropriate. The first thing he did was grab my jacket at the back of the neckline and say, "This thing doesn't fit you at all! What kind of a tailor do you have? The collar should lie flat with no bulges. Also, that shoulder seam hangs over a half-inch too far." I had never thought about such "minor details," but I immediately found myself a men's tailor, and that dear little old man gave me invaluable lessons in how clothes should fit, and can be easily altered by an expert, preferably one who tailors men's suits, until they feel as comfortable as a second skin.

Watch Your Fabrics and Finishing

A big part of achieving the "uniform" look is matching the fabric and quality of male colleagues' clothes. If your boss wears $400 wool suits, you are nowhere near the "uniform" concept in a $69.95 suit of polyester. One woman executive told me that the first thing she did when getting a promotion to a managerial position was go the the bank and make a $1,000 loan which she immediately spent on clothes. She recognized that her previous limitation on clothing expenses made her look dowdy and unsuccessful. An appropriately expensive wardrobe is likely to be a better investment in your future than a college course in some technical subject. Try to match the price and quality of your superior's uniforms, but don't surpass them. "It is not nice," one corporate wife was told, "to outdress the president's wife." The same holds true for bona fide team members. Men are inclined to understand immediately that they match but never overshadow their boss's clothes.

Remember the Function of Uniforms

Whatever else they represent, executive clothes are first and foremost appropriate to the demands of the job duties. By quasimilitary standards a uniform must appear as fresh, unwrinkled, and sharply creased at midnight as it did that morning although it was worn for a full day at the office, was drenched in a rain shower, traveled 5,000 miles by five modes of transportation, and had to be presentable for a late dinner and possibly a nightclub. Executive uniforms must be sturdy and versatile.

In this respect women executives' clothes must be equally versatile and adaptable to all business exigencies. If women travel with men, they must be able to take everything they need in hand luggage that can be carried on and off the plane, just as men do. The first truly great woman's commercial I've ever seen is one by United Airlines showing a woman executive deplaning in an efficient, self-confident manner, with the comment "The boss is on her way." To be so well organized and efficient she had to pay attention to the functionalism of her wardrobe. Fabrics that wrinke, rumple, sag, or wilt have no place in a woman executive's wardrobe.

Pay Attention to Coordination of Parts

One well-dressed woman executive who flatly says, "Most women dress terribly," confines her shopping to a single shop where she gets the full attention of the owner each year when she buys her standard $1,000 worth of replacement clothes. "By giving all my business to one shop I can be sure that everything matches and parts can coordinate with other things. The shop owner orders the right color blouses or accessories so that all of my clothes are quite interchangeable. The new outfits always go with the previous year's leftovers because we select compatible fabrics, styles, or colors."

Colors Are Ambivalent

Most successful corporate businessmen find that dark blues, grays, pinstripes, and subtle plaids convey the symbol of authority most effectively. With women I do not believe the same effect is achieved. Women executives can probably exert a stronger impression with distinctive colors or patterns that men cannot get away with. Navy, black (let's raze the "little basic black dress"), dull grays, or very subdued solids do not impress me as symbols of strength in women's clothes. They smack too much of "blending with the wallpaper" and taking a back seat to the powerful men. No man could wear a red suit, for instance, but a woman dressed in the red color spectrum has a definite air of confidence and assurance. Any such powerful color must be counteracted with blended and softening blouses or scarves, but strong colors may be the one male dress qualm which women can interpret to their purposes. Women by their very nature are not "conservative" in the business world. By their very presence they are breaking the establishment rule of no-females. Since women do have great fashion sense, the best way to judge is to examine yourself critically in the mirror and ask, "What impression does this outfit convey to others?" You are after a "strong" and "self-assured" look, not a mousy, timid, unassertive impression. Whatever costume creates that impact is probably right as a business uniform.

Never Wear a Man's Tie

Never, never, never. A man's tie is a penis symbol. No woman with any self-respect wants to walk around advertising "I'm pretending I have a penis." It was this article of men's clothing above all else that probably created the stereotype of the butch lesbian look. (No self-respecting lesbian would ever make such a mistake today, either, even in the gay bars.)

Wear Shoes You Can Walk In

As we have seen, foot-crippling shoes have been a favorite method to keep women in their place. The day is centuries off when "serious" business can be delayed because an executive's feet hurt. Urban businessmen do a lot of walking around the city streets, and women executives must be ready to join them and keep up with them.

Buy Clothes with Pockets

One manufacturing detail sets off women's clothes (even man-tailored clothes) from men's clothes—the lack of pockets. When I used to complain about this to buyers years ago, they insisted that women didn't want pockets because it would "spoil the fit" of their clothes, which presumably were supposed to be skintight over the torture-racks of girdles and padded bras. That's nonsense. Women's clothes don't have pockets because men like to reserve these essential and handy devices for themselves. I think women should insist that all their clothes have functional pockets, not cheap imitation flaps. No-pockets is an inferiority symbol.

Dump Your Burdensome Handbag

One favorite accessory of women deserves special mention—the ubiquitous carryall handbag. There's no denying that women need handbags to transport keys, money, checkbooks, glasses, makeup, cigarettes, credit cards, notebooks, and assorted sundries between home and office, but there are powerful reasons not to drag such an encumbrance all over a business office, especially to meetings. A purse or handbag is so uniquely a female article that it arouses a host of subconscious connotations among men. The typical male outfit contains an average of nine pockets, while women's clothes usually have none or no adequate ones, thereby forcing women to carry a hampering weight in the form of exterior hand baggage.

I once asked a woman track star if she practiced her running to beat traffic congestion during the day. "You can't," she said, "because of the handbag. It's impossible to run while carrying a purse in hand or on your shoulder—it slows your speed by half and throws you off balance." A woman vice-president in an all-male group says she's noticed that men "hate the sight of a woman settling a handbag under a conference table." Many bosses I've known in business consider it a sign of subservience to carry anything except vital business papers which they are entrusted to deliver to another executive. The image of messenger, errand boy, or beast of burden is avoided as much as possible by men. Symbolically, women are the burden carriers.

Both the physical and psychological handicaps of a handbag were exposed to a skeptical member of my Womanschool class when she tested the principle during a business luncheon with three male executives. "The difference was unbelievable," she reported. "I slipped a credit card and a few bills in my jacket pocket (and a comb and a lipstick, I must admit), but carried nothing in my hands or on my shoulder. We walked a couple of blocks to the restaurant and for the first time I kept apace with no trouble. I hadn't realized how often my big shoulder-bag bumped into people and forced me to zigzag or keep manipulating it. The men, whom I had lunched with a few times before, sensed something different but didn't know what it was. One said approvingly, 'You must have new shoes on today, I see you're keeping up with us.' At the restaurant I sat down freely and gracefully without shoving chairs or tables around to accommodate a spot for my usual luggage. I didn't have to warn waiters not to trip over it nor divert my attention repeatedly to check that my bag wasn't stolen or something. I can't explain the sense of freedom and equality I felt. And somehow it was communicated to my male companions—as if I really *belonged* in an expensive restaurant having a business luncheon with coequal executives."

Be Careful about Uniquely
Female Accessories

There's one cardinal rule: Don't wear anything that jingles, wiggles, clanks, or glitters. Executive insignia are silent, understated and unobtrusive—never sexy.

Jewelry—Dangling earrings, charm bracelets, metal bangles, chain collections, novelty pins, or garish, attention-getting items that distract listeners from what you are *saying* or *ordering* will dilute any woman's authority image. Take your cue from successful men in your organization. Their idea of jewelry will be reflected in their watches, possibly cufflinks, belt buckles, rings, and tie clasps. They seldom have a wardrobe of decorations; they stick to one or two favorites that look (and are) expensive, and wear them repeatedly. Never forget that money is the scorecard in this game so executive women's jewelry no longer acts as costume decoration but as a *symbol of success,* i.e. expensive and real, not junk. Women should probably limit themselves to one or two jewelry items at a time, such as a ring and a necklace. Neck jewelry indeed may become the female equivalent of men's ties so each piece should be selected with care and be what the jewelry trade calls an "important" design, one that stands alone as a distinctive, powerful emblem. The exception to expensive elegance is when you work for a company where the *men* wear extravagant jewelry; in that case your rule is probably "the funkier the better."

Perfume—Save it for after-work hours when it can perform its function of making you a desirable sex object. The lingering odor of the most expensive perfume is overpowering and headachey in the confines of a small office or closed conference room.

Makeup and Hairstyles—Women are no different than men in wanting to look their best when they are in the public eye, as they are at work. Just remember that your makeup and hairdo must hold up under all the exigencies of a business day without excessive attention. It goes without saying that all touch-ups, including lipstick, must be done in private. Naturalness, as opposed to painted artificiality, is the aim.

The development of a "superior" or "high status" uniform for female management executives must come from women themselves because men's reactions to female dress are highly suspect. Conscious and unconscious male attitudes toward women's dress will be skewed in the direction of reducing women to their traditional weak and dependent roles. A strong and authorative costume is apt to be criticized by men when a woman wears it. That may be the best sign you're on the right track—if you can scare a pewter-gray pinstripe into a worried comment about your bright green velvet blazer, you've accomplished something. Men will seldom tell women their clothes are inadequate to their job; they'll gladly let women make the wrong moves in the game. Some male comments can be tip-offs.

- "I see you're wearing a dress today—you look so pretty." If a man says that to you at the staff meeting, never wear that oufit again. Any time you look "sweet" and "pretty," you are in trouble; some fast-moving gamester has just captured your pawn.
- "I don't remember what she said, but she sure has great tits." When I heard this male summation of a brilliant woman's contribution to a prestigious government-business conference, I had visions of her in a neat brown-and-white print jersey V-neck dress which accentuated a generous bosom. I wasn't there; I don't know; but whatever she wore, it's obvious that her costume did more for her figure than it did for her career.
- "You have a good job. You ought to dress the part." If a man says that to you, adopt him as your mentor. He's the best business friend you've run across. It may sound like he's insulting your taste in clothes, but he's telling it like it is. He's trying to help you get ahead in business.

Maclean's, August 20, 1984.

Women and the Election

By CAROL GOAR

For 10 years Ursula Appolloni was one of the hardest-working members of the House of Commons. The 54-year-old mother of four was never a political star, but she served voters in her Toronto riding of York South-Weston well—and she was known in Ottawa as a tenacious fighter for immigrants and the elderly. Last September, tired of "scratching around like a hen in a barnyard to get money to help people," she decided to quit politics and subsequently turned down Pierre Trudeau's offer of a patronage appointment as a citizenship court judge. "Frankly, I felt I was being insulted," she recalls.

Then, in July Appolloni began to look for a job. She got in touch with Ottawa's Public Service Commission about the possibility of working in the federal bureaucracy. "Can you type?" the recruiter asked the flabbergasted Appolloni, who, after 10 years in Parliament, believed that she had other skills to offer. A few days later she received a call from the affirmative action branch of Canada Manpower. "I don't want to hurt you," the counsellor said, "but I should warn you straight away that women of a certain age who have been out of the labor market for a number of years can't get exactly what they want." Appolloni, who was finishing her duties as an MP, was crushed: "I thought that maybe I should be looking for my wheelchair."

From *Maclean's*, Vol. 97 No. 34, reprinted by permission of the author.

Symbols of Power

Michael Korda

Office furnishings have strong symbolic value. Take file cabinets—in themselves, they are meaningless. Most executives, in fact, place them out of sight, in their secretaries' offices or cubicles. Put a lock on the filing cabinet, however, and it becomes a power symbol, however unsightly and bulky. When you want to take a file out, you have to walk over to it and unlock it, the implication being that it contains material of great importance and confidentiality. Given a lock, the filing cabinet can become a central power symbol, well worth having in your own office, no matter how much space it takes up.

Furniture can tell one a great deal about the person. A *New York Times* reporter remarked to one tycoon that "Callers, supplicants and salesmen who make their way to [the chairman's] 42nd floor office get swallowed up and find themselves peering between their knees at him," helplessly sunk in deep, soft chairs. This is a fairly common power game, and can be observed in many offices. One young lady, job hunting, noted that almost every senior executive in the publishing business had a low sofa. "You go in," she said, "and they ask you to sit down on the sofa, which is about four feet lower than his desk chair, so he's looking down at you, and you're looking up from nowhere, with your ass practically on the floor and your knees up in the air. You couldn't arrange things better to make a person seem really unimportant."

This is not altogether true. There are more elaborate ways of making people feel unimportant. Harry Cohn, the tyrannical president of Columbia Pictures, designed his office in imitation of Mussolini's, a huge, elongated room with the desk at the far end, raised above floor level. "The portal to the position of power was a massive sound-proofed door which had no knob and no keyhole on the outside. It could only be opened by a buzzer operated from Cohn's or his secretary's desk . . . In later years Glenn Ford noted discoloration of the door jamb at mid-level; it had been soiled by the sweat of innumerable palms of those who had passed through to an audience with Harry Cohn."

This is a somewhat extreme example of power decoration, but even lesser power players will usually arrange their offices so that their visitors are obliged to sit in as much discomfort as possible. It is particularly helpful to make sure that all the ashtrays are just slightly out of reach so that visitors sitting in low chairs and unable to rise have to stretch awkwardly to dispose of their cigarette ash.

The disposition of furniture is a better indication of power than the furniture itself. Some offices run to luxurious decoration, others do not, but the scale of luxury is more likely to be dependent upon the management's whim than the occupant's status. At *Playboy's* Chicago headquarters, for instance, even the junior editors have "plush, cork-paneled hideaways, many equipped with soft chairs, stereo sets and stunning secretaries," an atmosphere of sybaritic luxury that emanates from Hugh Hefner's vision of himself, rather than from any power they may have.

Power lies in how you use what you have, not in the accouterments per se. All the leather and chrome in the world will not replace a truly well-thought-out power scheme. A large office is pointless unless it is arranged so that a visitor has to walk the length of it before getting to your desk, and it is valuable to put as many objects as possible in his path—coffee tables, chairs and sofas, for example—to hinder his progress. However small the office, it is important to have the visitor's chair facing toward you, so that you are separated by the width of your desk. This is a much better power position than one in which the visitor sits *next* to the desk, even though it may make access to your desk inconvenient for you. When a small office is very narrow (and most are) it is often useful to have the desk placed well forward in the room, thus minimizing the space available for the visitor, and increasing the area in which it is possible for you to retreat, at least psychologically. Thus, in a typical small office, the alternative desk/chair relationships would look like [those in the accompanying illustration.]

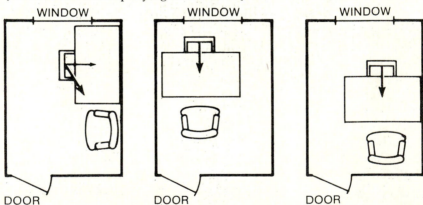

Of these possibilities, number three is by far the strongest power position for the occupant. Behind his desk, he has left himself plenty of room, so that he isn't likely to feel that his back is against the wall when arguing with a caller or a colleague, while his visitor is tightly enclosed, with little psychological space and breathing room. In drawing number two, the visitor is placed in an aggressive position, having more space than the occupant, and being further forward in the room. In drawing number one, the occupant has no power position at all, and is obliged to turn to his right at an uncomfortable angle to talk to the visitor. Power, let it be remembered, moves in direct lines. (Attempts to do without desks altogether, though popular in the recording and the broadcasting businesses, have never caught on. The desk performs a useful social function in power terms that is hard to eliminate.)

In larger offices, power arrangements are more varied. Most people prefer to divide their offices into two separate sections, one containing a couch, which can be used for informal, semisocial discussions, where decisions do not actually have to be made, and the other containing the usual desk and chair, for "pressure situations" and confrontations, in which the whole object is to reach a firm decision. In entering such an office, it is therefore very important to notice in what area the occupant wishes you to take a seat. If you have come to negotiate a deal, and he moves toward the sofa, you can be fairly sure that he has decided to stall you; if he asks you to sit at his desk, you can be equally sure that he is ready for serious negotiation. At the same time, you can influence *him*. By firmly seating yourself at the desk, you make it clear that you want an answer; by sitting on the sofa, you demonstrate that you are not eager to conclude the deal. A certain tug-of-war is often evident when the two parties have different goals in mind, the "host" trying to push the visitor toward the sofa, with the plea that he will be "more comfortable" there, the visitor obstinately making his way toward the desk, or vice versa, of course.

Some people are past masters at this game. When he comes to my office, a well-known lawyer of my acquaintance always manages to sit on the sofa between me and the telephone on the end table when he wants to persuade me to do something I would just as soon not do. In the first place, he has trapped me in a semisocial position, by getting us both on the sofa; in the second place, he has effectively cut me off from the telephone, so that I can't be interrupted by a call. In this position, he has me at his mercy—we are seated side by side, at the same level, both facing the window and away from desk and telephone. When he wants to *sell* me on something, he sits on the chair in front of my desk, then gradually works it around until it's beside mine, so that he's moved to my side of the barrier, so to speak. There are several ways in which he assures himself of this position, the first being to put his portfolio, hat and coat on the sofa, so that we *can't* sit on it, the second being to plead mild deafness, so that he has an excuse to come to my side of the desk, which implies an invasion of my territory. An attempt to prevent his moving closer by buying an armchair so massive and heavy as to be practically immovable failed; he pleads a bad back and asks the secretary to find him a simple, straight chair, which he then places exactly where he wants it.

This subtle use of space can be best understood by seeing how the two different areas, the semisocial and the pressure, relate to each other spatially [as in the accompanying illustration.]

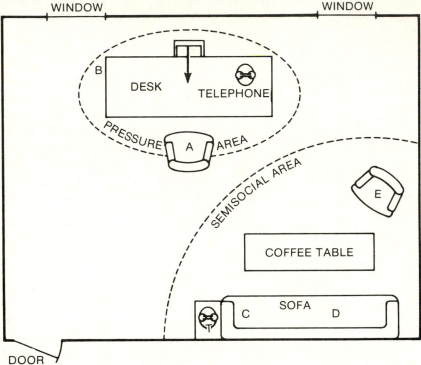

A typical office is divided into a "pressure area" and a "semisocial area." If the occupant is intent on serious business, he should try to place his visitor in position A, squarely facing the desk. If he wants to delay a decision or placate a visitor, he should try to place him in position D on sofa. An aggressive visitor will either move his chair to position B, or assume position C on sofa, forcing the occupant to sit at D, cut off by an intruder from his own telephone. Chair E is the weakest power position, and is reserved for unimportant third parties. Note that the coffee table separates one area from the other, and that the sofa should be as low as possible.

Still larger offices are sometimes divided into *three* areas, one end being set aside for a large conference table, with chairs around it. This is frequently the case with the offices of chairmen of the board, and is usually a sign that they want to maintain control over the board by holding its meetings on their own territory, rather than having them in a separate board room. As a general rule, boards that meet in an office a corner of which is used as a board meeting area have less power and autonomy than those that meet in a separate board room, and are to that extent less valuable to be on.

Boardroom tables, it should be noted, are almost never round, since it is necessary to have a very precise gradation of power, and above all, imperative that the most important person, usually the chairman, should sit at the end next to the window, with his back to it, while the second most important person, usually the president or chief executive officer, should sit to his right. If the latter sits at the opposite end of the table (playing "mother," so to speak, in dining-table terms) he not only has the sun in his eyes, but is almost always placing himself in an adversary position vis-à-vis the chairman, a sign that there is either a power struggle going on between them, or the likelihood that one will develop. If the chairman has an armchair and all the rest have straight chairs, it is an indication that the company is run along firm, authoritarian lines. If all the chairs are the same, the prospects for acquiring power are probably much better.

Even bathrooms can matter. It is obviously best to have a private bathroom in your office, second best to be close to a bathroom, and worst to be miles away from one. As one literary agent said, in explaining why he wanted a best-selling author moved from his present publisher to another, "He should have a nice office to come and visit, you know, someplace where he can sit down in a social way when he wants without feeling he's in an *office*. The bathroom should be in the same office, you know? If it's in the hall, it's a little less good. Where he is now, he has to go down the hall to wash his hands when he visits, it's not so nice."

Desks can tell us a great deal about people's power quotient. The objects most people place on their desks are not there by accident, after all, and usually give some clue to the power status of the occupant. One successful conglomerator was described as having "his desk peculiarly arranged—with a window at the back—so that outdoor light all but blinds the visitor while striking two polished glass paperweights on his desk, giving an impression that you have come under the scrutiny of two translucent orbs, that your thoughts are being read and your capabilities assayed in a second or two."

Desk sets—usually a pen and pencil set in a marble or onyx base—used to be potent power symbols, perhaps because of their phallic appearance, but they have been eclipsed, partly because of the popularity of the ubiquitous felt-tip marker pen, and mostly because too many people finally acquired a set. Framed diplomas are definitely out as power symbols, and so are stuffed fish, family photographs, children's paintings, mezotint engravings of Harvard Yard in 1889, all posters, Audubon prints (unless they're originals), 37mm. cannon shells converted into paperweights, anything made of plastic or lucite and ashtrays stolen from famous restaurants or hotels. Simplicity is the best way of suggesting power. It's also useful to maintain a certain amount of clutter, just enough to make it clear that you're busy, but not so much as to suggest you're a slob. A nice touch is to leave out two or three red folders marked "Confidential" and to push them out of sight once any visitor has noticed them. Stacks of magazines give a good impression, particularly if they have slips of paper inserted in them, as if for future reference. Care should be taken, however, to ensure that they aren't such magazines as *Playboy* or *Penthouse*—*Foreign Affairs* carries considerable prestige, *Psychology Today* suggests an interest in alternative life-styles, a large stack of *Fortunes* look very good, and *Forbes* gives the impression of a serious interest in money, never a bad thing. Television sets have become popular as power symbols, perhaps because the late Lyndon B. Johnson had three of them in his office (so he could see himself on all three channels at once). A television set in the office is supposed to connote a burning interest in current events and world affairs (nobody assumes the owner is watching reruns of *I Love Lucy* during office hours), and also implies that the occupant of the office works at odd and irregular hours, always a sign of power.

Indeed, semidomestic furnishings are very good power symbols, since they suggest the office is a kind of home away from home, not just a place in which one comes to work from nine to five on weekdays. Even people who go home religiously at five-thirty like to give the impression that they often stay to eight or nine at night, which explains the popularity of radios, clock radios, bars, small refrigerators, blenders, heating pads, exercise poles and Health-O-Matic scales, all of which I have seen in people's offices. Electric hot plates, on the other hand, are out, since they imply you haven't enough authority to send your secretary out for coffee.

A special category of office furnishing would have to be established for my friend Tim Hennessey, a successful sales executive who had a convertible sofa bed installed in his office. This was a doubly potent power symbol, since it suggested at once that he had to work late enough to spend the night in the office, and that his sexual successes with the office staff justified his having a sofa bed handy. To the best of my knowledge, it was never opened, but he acquired a valuable reputation as a hard worker and a daring cocksman, and became, overnight as it were, a legendary figure. Hennessey also had a lock fitted to his private telephone, a nice, small touch which certainly impressed many people, and a rheostat switch under his desk so that he could dim the lights, partly because he believed it would make it easier to carry out a seduction, partly because he liked to think he could persuade the more elderly executives that they were going blind by alternately dimming and brightening the lights during a meeting. He was also the first person in publishing to have three wall clocks, one for New York time, one for California time, and one for London time, suggesting an international scope to his job which was purely imaginary.

TIME POWER

Clocks and watches are in fact the ultimate power symbols; for time, in a very real sense, *is* power.

For people who make an hourly wage, time is money in a direct sense. Analysts, for example, inevitably see the day as being divided into so many hourly sessions (fifty-five minutes actually) at so much an hour. Freudian analysts tend to maintain a certain power over their patients by not having a clock visible—the patient knows when his hour is up when the analyst tells him it is, thus intensifying the analyst's control over the patient, who can hardly look at his watch and is therefore kept in suspense, unsure of how much time he has left to drag out a boring dream or compress a whole, rich life experience into a few minutes.

The greatest compliment a busy executive can pay to a visitor is to take off his watch ostentatiously and place it—face down—on the desk. It's a way of saying, "My time belongs to you, for as long as you need me." Alternatively, taking off your watch and placing it face *up* on your desk is a way of announcing that you're a busy man and can't spare much time for your visitor's business, that he'd better damn well state his case in a hurry and get out. I personally am such a taker-off and a putter-on of wrists watches that I have to go into Cartier's at regular intervals to have my watchstrap retightened, and often manage to leave it behind on my desk, or even on someone else's (leaving it in somebody else's bed is, generally speaking, a dangerous thing to do and leads to bad scenes and divorces).

One executive I know has a huge outdoor pool clock with numbers 2 inches high on the wall, and a second hand that clicks to signify passing time. It is arranged so that it faces his visitor squarely, thus announcing that his time is more important than yours, and has the same effect on most people as the writing on the wall at Belshazzar's unfortunate feast ("God hath numbered thy kingdom, and finished it"). This somewhat oppressive effect can be reinforced by arranging to have his secretary come in at regular intervals to announce that he's running behind schedule, or that Edward Bennett Williams is waiting outside to see him, but the consummate time player shouldn't need anything so obvious as this to fluster a visitor and give him the terrible guilt of wasting a busy person's precious time.

Lawyers, who usually charge on the basis of time, have their own ways of establishing their importance. At the lowest level, they have clocks that face toward them, status being set by the kind of clock it is. A round, wedge-topped battery-operated clock that sits flat on the desk and is only visible to the lawyer himself seems to be this year's favorite, though I greatly admire one lawyer who has a complicated Swiss "Atmos" clock in a glass case on his desk with the dial facing him, leaving the client to become mesmerized by the restless swing of the brass pendulum and the endless clicking of the gears and wheels—without ever being able to see what time it is. At this stage of power, the lawyer wants to know how long the client has been there, but would just as soon the client didn't know. More important lawyers announce that their time is expensive by having the clock face the client, digital clocks being favored by corporation lawyers and ancient, noisy grandfather and railroad clocks by the more traditional old-line lawyers. The *most* important lawyers have no clocks at all, the implication being that everyone they see is on a retainer basis anyway, and if they're not, there's a secretary outside to keep the log. Divorce lawyers, who have to listen to endless personal *Angst* from their clients, like analysts, seem to have no clocks and often no watches either, though one lawyer I know wears a Mickey Mouse watch which he never winds, on the grounds that it makes him seem like a simple, unthreatening figure, rather than a symbol of authority or a husband.

Just as there are fashions in clocks, there are fashions in watches, which can tell you a good deal about the people who wear them. The West Coast watchpower symbol is to have the letters of your name painted on the dial instead of numbers though this only works when your name has twelve letters, like Ernest Lehman, the producer, unless you can abbreviate your first name, like Irving Mansfield, the late Jacqueline Susann's protean husband, whose watch reads "Irv Mansfield." This fashion does not seem to have made it to New York, where the status is still the old Cartier tank watch, with one of those Cartier hinged gold buckles that is almost invisible except to the connoisseur, who *knows*. On the whole though, watch wearers are divided into two basic categories: those who like watches that are impossible to read, either having no numbers or four almost invisible dots, and those who like the kind of watches astronauts, pilots and skindivers wear, with enormous luminous dials and bezel rings that allow you to compute how much air you have left or what GMT is, in case you need to know. One executive I know wears a watch that actually tells the time in London and New York simultaneously at the push of a button, but my own experience is that the less powerful the executive, the more intricate the watch. The lowest power rating goes to those who wear little miniature calendars on their watchbands, thus indicating both that they can't afford an automatic date-adjusting watch and that they need to be reminded what day it is. A complicated watch like a Rolex "Submariner" usually shows the wearer is prey to extreme time anxiety, and thus fairly far down the scale of power. More powerful executives wear watches that hardly even show the time, so thin are the hands and so obscure the marks on the face. People who are really secure in their power sometimes show it by not wearing watches at all, relying on the fact that nothing important can happen without them anyway.

Styles of wearing wristwatches are pretty limited—after all, we only have two wrists—but I have noticed that a good many men now wear their wrist watch on the *inside* of the left wrist, an affectation that puzzled me for some time. In my youth it was one of those mysterious British military customs, like a rolled-up handkerchief in one's right coat sleeve, and indicated membership in the professional officer caste. I think officers wore their watches on the inside wrist so that the luminous dial wouldn't be visible to the enemy at night, or possibly so that you could look at the time while keeping the reins of your horse in the left hand (most military affectations are cavalry inspired). None of these reasons seemed to me to apply to modern businessmen, who could hardly have been inculcated in the sartorial traditions of Sandhurst and Cranwell, but close observation has shown that this habit has its purpose in the modern world. A man with a watch on the inside of his left wrist can put his arm around a woman and kiss her while looking at his watch, which will then be facing him at about the level of her left ear, invisible to her. This custom can be observed in a great many midtown bars and restaurants at lunchtime, when men are making the difficult decision of whether to stay and suggest an afternoon in bed or go back to the office and answer their telephone calls. It is obviously callow to look at one's watch openly; still, at a certain point, say, one forty-five, or just about the time one is thinking of ordering coffee, it's necessary to know what time it is and move accordingly. An arm around the shoulder and a kiss will quickly establish whether a proposition is likely to succeed and simultaneously, if one's watch is in the correct position, whether one has time to follow through.

Time has its own rules, its own victories and defeats, its own symbols. In a city like New York, Chicago, or Los Angeles, you can see the losers every day at lunchtime, if you care to, sitting at restaurant tables (usually too near the entrance—winners sit as far away from the door as possible), glancing at their watches and trying to look as if they had all the time in the world or intended to eat alone. They are the people who arrived on time for a luncheon and are going to be kept waiting for at least half an hour because their guest or host is still on the telephone in his office while they're already on their fourth Rye-Krisp, and wishing they had brought a magazine along.

Lunches, of course, and meals in general, are very much connected to time concepts. The late M. Lincoln Schuster, for example, used to fit as many as four lunch dates into one day's lunch, arranging to meet several different people at the same restaurant, taking soup at one table, main course at the next, dessert at the third and coffee at the last. Had he been a drinker, he could no doubt have managed a cocktail at the beginning of the meal with a fifth person. To get through this kind of gastronomic relay race takes an iron digestive system or a total indifference to food. Still, it can be done, and allows one to have as many as twenty lunch dates in a five-day work week.

The power trick in lunch dates, apart from making sure that you're never kept waiting (even if this involves lurking in a telephone booth to watch the doorway of the restaurant), is winning the preliminary battle to fix the meeting at a time of your choosing, and in many businesses, particularly those in large cities, a great deal of the morning is spent in determining whether to meet at 12:30, 12:45 or 1:00; the point being that the person who proposes to win must not only establish the time but arrange to arrive last.

Whether in a restaurant or elsewhere, the most important aspect of the time game is making people wait, the most familiar example being the old one of not speaking on the telephone until the other person is already on the line, a power struggle which can occupy many otherwise unproductive minutes in a busy executive's day. "Buzz me when X is on the line," says the power player, while X is naturally telling *his* secretary to buzz him when Y is on the line. Some people play another form of this game by answering all their telephone calls themselves, asking the caller to wait "just one second," then putting everyone on hold, until they have three or four people backed up waiting to speak to them.

Those who play the power game seriously can never be free from the tyranny of time, and don't even want to be, since a tightly packed schedule not only gives them a sense of importance, but is a perfect excuse for not doing whatever it is they don't want to do. A full calendar is proof of power, and for this reason, the most powerful people prefer small calendars, which are easily filled up, and which give the impression of frenetic activity, particularly if one's writing is fairly large. One of the best power symbols is a desk diary that shows the whole week at a glance, with every available square inch of space filled in or crossed out. It provides visible evidence that one is busy—too busy to see someone who is anxious to discuss a complaint or a burdensome request. At the same time, one can confer a favor by crossing out an existing appointment and, in the current phrase, "penciling in" the name of someone who has requested an appointment. A close inspection of such diaries often reveals that a good many of the entries read "Gray suit at cleaners" or "Betsy's birthday—present?," but the effect from a distance is awe-inspiring.

Many executives stroll to work in a leisurely fashion, stopping to look in shop windows and pausing to glance at pretty girls, then, as soon as they pass through the revolving doors of their office buildings, gather themselves up in a kind of Groucho Marx crouch, as if they wanted to run but felt constrained to hold themselves down to a fast, breathless walk. By the time they reach their offices, they are moving at top speed, already giving dictation while they're struggling out of their topcoats. Men who could quite easily allow themselves a good hour to get to the airport for a flight will happily waste time until they have to leave in a dramatic rush, shouting out last-minute instructions as they run down the hall and pursued to the elevator by people with telephone messages and letters to be signed.

STANDING BY

Another excellent tactic is to allow half an hour for meetings that are sure to last at least an hour long, so that the people who have to see you afterward are obliged to wait without knowing quite when they'll be called for. This is the familiar "stand by" game, in which people are warned to "stand by" for a meeting that was supposed to take place at 10 A.M. and probably won't begin until noon, or may even be postponed until next week. In the meantime, of course, they are more or less obliged to stay close to their phones, and may even have to cancel their lunch dates. The busier you can make yourself, the more you can impose your schedule on other people; the more you impose your schedule on other people, the more power you have. The definition of power, in fact, is that more people inconvenience themselves on your behalf than those on whose behalf you would inconvenience yourself. At the very summit of power—the President of the United States, for example—almost everybody will wait, go without lunch, "stand by" or give up dinner with a beautiful woman on your behalf. One doubts, for example, that everyone in the White House necessarily *wants* to rush through lunch in order to fly to Camp David in the Presidential helicopter at the last minute, canceling their weekend plans and their golf dates. But when power beckons, most people follow, at whatever cost to their comfort and private lives. The important thing is to keep moving and drag as many people along in your wake as possible.

A tight schedule is a guarantee of power, as anyone can tell from the description of David Rockefeller's departure from his office. "The man who runs the garage at the Chase Manhattan Bank Building has been keeping watch. When he saw David Rockefeller leave the Federal Reserve Bank of New York . . . he shouted, 'O.K., Chester!' No sooner has Chester pulled up the maroon Cadillac limousine than Mr. Rockefeller is into it (his aides are already waiting in the car, presumably having been sitting there for hours in the underground garage to be ready for the moment), and opening his scarlet folder marked 'For Immediate Action,' he proceeds to give his orders for the afternoon on the way to a waiting helicopter, its roter blades already turning, which will carry him to a cocktail party in Albany."

One might well ask whether a cocktail party in Albany is worth this kind of mobilized effort, but worth it or not, the elements of time power are perfectly illustrated in Mr. Rockefeller's breathless rush to the helicopter, involving the time of the pilot, Chester, the chauffeur, the aides who have been waiting in the car, the garageman who gives Chester the warning, and presumably a host of other people at both ends of the journey, all of whom are at "stand by" for hours in order to convey one man to a party. David Rockefeller's power would hardly be emphasized if he had strolled out of his office with time to spare, whistled at a passing girl, bought himself a Hershey bar and a copy of *Penthouse* and left himself plenty of time to walk to the Wall Street heliport. The higher up one goes, the more valuable one's time must appear to be.

Closely allied with time is the ability to make other people perform the small demeaning tasks of life for you. Men do not necessarily ask their secretaries to get a cup of coffee for them because they are lazy, or because they are male chauvinists, or even because they don't know where the coffee machine is. Getting one's own coffee is a sign that one's time is not all that important, that it can be wasted on inconsequential personal chores. People who are power-conscious would rather sit at their desks with their eyes closed "thinking" than get up and go for their own coffee, or collect their own dry cleaning, or fetch their own mail. In extreme cases, they insulate themselves from *any* trivial task; as John Z. DeLorean, the flamboyant former general manager of General Motors' car and truck division, put it, "I don't think the heads of state of many countries come close. You travel like an oil sheik." G. M.'s senior executives travel in private jet aircraft, limousines carry them to and fro, teams of PR men fly in a day or two before their visits to ensure that everything is in order, and check the hotel suites "to make certain, among other things, that flowers are in place." One PR man, *Fortune* reported, found what seemed suspiciously like semen stains on a sofa in the suite reserved for the president of G. M., and spent the afternoon before the great man's arrival cleaning the furniture off with his handkerchief.

Not everyone can aspire to this kind of insulation from everyday life, but it represents the ultimate symbol of power in our culture, the notion that one has no time for mundane details and that one's comfort and convenience are the responsibility of other people.

In the words of one executive, "I've always somehow associated power with cleanliness, maybe because at heart we're all afraid of falling back into manual labor, of having to get our hands dirty, like our fathers or grandfathers. Right from the beginning, I've always noticed that powerful people *never seem to get dirty.* You take a rainy day in the city, when everyone arrives with wrinkled, wet trousers and wet shoes, powerful people appear magically with knife-edged creases and shiny, dry shoes. How do they do it? I don't know. I can't even imagine it, which is the reason, I suppose, that I'm down here on this floor, and they're up there. Do they change when they arrive at the office? Do they walk around sealed in plastic Baggies? Is it just that they don't have to take the subway or stand waiting for the Fifth Avenue bus in the rain? Who knows? But it's true—they have this magic gloss to them, they don't sweat, you don't see them coming in after a taxi has splashed muddy water all over them. I know, deep down in my rational mind, that it isn't altogether true, and that a lot of it has to do with limos and company planes and things like that, but for me, powerful people are forever defined as those who can walk to work without stepping in a puddle. When all is said and done it's like the old vaudeville routine about sex appeal—'Some people got it, some people don't got it. I got it.' "

The Trappings Trap

Meg Greenfield

The more I ponder it, the less surprised I think any of us should be that the determined intruder made it up the drainpipe and into the royal bedchamber. Startled, yes—in particular, the Queen of England was surely entitled to have been somewhat taken aback at the sight of the uninvited Mr. Fagan standing by her bed at dawn. But surprised that it could have happened? No. The episode is just one more in an ever enlarging array of examples of the vast distance between myth and reality where the competence of organizations is concerned. The organization in this case was nothing less formidable than the security apparatus designed to protect the Queen of England—which turned out to have been, as it seems, on a several-years-long tea break. What a perfect metaphor for the characteristic revelation of our time.

There is, of course, something universally and eternally appealing to people in the idea of a single determined individual's confounding a formidable official barrier and making it to the other side, provided no harm is done to anything but the dignity and vanity of the officials who were trying to keep him out. Folks always cheer the lone protesting figure who manages to outwit the forces of exclusion and end up on the VIP side of the wrought-iron gate or velvet rope or whatever. And I think, too, that there is often at least a little mixed feeling, if not an actual whisper of reassurance, in confirmation of the truth that the guys with the guns—the police, the soldiers, the investigators and operatives and guards—are not 100 percent efficient, not supermen who can do whatever they want.

LORE AND NONSENSE

But I don't think the caption to this story is the daring and enterprise of a lone, romantic scaler of walls. And I don't think the major message is: thank God the authorities aren't too good (for our own good) at what they do. I think the Buckingham Palace caper is just another element in the crash of our assumptions about power and the trappings of power and the look of power. "Assumptions" is the key word here. We keep learning, though not necessarily believing, that daddy is not all power-ful, that the most masterful-seeming and authoritative-looking protec-tors of the general well-being are often neither masterful nor authoritative, that what seems safe or certain isn't.

Clearly we are using wrong standards of judgment, entranced by a veritable bouquet of romantic lore and nonsense. I mean: all those red-coats and the bearskin hats and the changing of the guard and the aura of invincibility and timelessness—it all transmits a powerful, if subliminal, signal that things are under control here, however chaotic they may be somewhere else. I don't know about you, but I fell for it, and I don't mind saying that I am getting a little embarrassed at the number of times this has happened over the past two decades.

For me, it began with the Bay of Pigs, right after the rumors of an im-pending American-supported action had been confirmed. I well remember sitting around with a bunch of young friends arguing pas-sionately among ourselves as to whether this was a justified military ac-tion, whether we as a country should do what John F. Kennedy had authorized. We assumed and did not even bother to stipulate an American victory. It simply did not occur to us that all those confident-looking government people with their much vaunted access to secret information and all those spiffy-looking military types could have it ab-solutely wrong, could blow it. Certain things one learned about the frail-ty and jerry-built enterprises of the security people during the Watergate years had the same capacity to astonish. And so, of course, did the infor-mation that came out in the aftermath of the failed hostage-rescue mis-sion at Desert One. The quality of the Queen's protection fits in nicely with all of this; it gives it a touch of class, puts a diamond crown on its head.

It is true that we all know that our own organizations—the clubs, businesses and bureaucracies within which we work—are not nearly so deliberate or controlled as they tend to look when the fruit of a series of accidents, confusions and general dishevelments is revealed to the out-side world as "policy." The wry, self-disparaging oneliners that adorn our office-hours coffee mugs and desk calendars attest to this. So it isn't just the security people. And I suppose it is also true that the press has played some part in reinforcing these illusions of omnipotence on the part of uniformed authority, even though we are more often charged with "tearing it down." We are, after all, blessed with the ability to characterize our own misapprehensions as universal, calling something a "surprise development" and thus sharing the burden of having been surprised with others. Still, I think that we are talking here about something distinctively to do with military and security forces and that people's widespread illusions on the subject are something more than merely what the press has encouraged us to believe over the years.

MYSTIQUE

It is the "trappings trap" we have all fallen into; we are suckers for the apparatus and appurtenances of power. After Watergate there was a lot of discussion about whether our presidents were enjoying such things too much, and Jimmy Carter declined to make use of many of them. But no one thought to ask whether the all-seeing, all-knowing machinery we have created, the thing with the siren on top and the scowling, chevroned personnel inside, knew what in the hell it was doing. Our perception of life abroad is susceptible to the same confusions: everyone knew the Iraqis would beat the Iranians because they were well-armed and -trained martial-looking third-worlders against a bunch of uluating weirdos carrying pictures of the Ayatollah Khomeini. Everyone knew the Cambodian hadn't been invented who had anything mean or military to him: they all wore pale, loose cotton clothes and smiled a lot and ate squooshy fruit—what kind of soldier is that?

We fall for a uniform, for an air of occidental-style proficiency, for a tough, mean look, for a shako headdress, for the mystique of regimental or magisterial tradition. We better look out. The calculations we base on all this concern a great deal more than drainpipes and people who fantasize about the Queen.

An Unmentionable Occasion

Bob Greene

To understand this, we must set the scene precisely. We are in the living room of Kristine Costello, in Methuen, Massachusetts, a suburb of Boston. Color photographs of her two children, Lea and Michael, adorn

---

Bob Greene, "An Unmentionable Occasion," from *American Beat*. Copyright © 1983 John Deadline Enterprises. Reprinted with the permission of Atheneum Publishers, Inc.

the walls. Fourteen other women, all invited here by Mrs. Costello, sit in chairs, on couches, and on the floor, drinking rosé wine.

With the exception of the reporter, there are no men in the house. Mrs. Costello's husband, Michael, had run a sweeper over the carpeting before the guests arrived, but he understood that once the party began he was expected to depart.

The women here range in age from their twenties to their fifties. Some of them are housewives; some of them hold outside jobs. The suburb is essentially mainstream American middle class, and so, by appearances, are the women.

Up a short step in the dining room, directly next to Mrs. Costello's supper table, is a metal clothing rack. Right now the rack is covered with a white satin drape, but soon, when unveiled, it will reveal the garments that have apparently drawn the women to the party. There will be filmy, see-through negligees; there will be nightgowns with names like French Connection and Flowing Passion, all gauzy and cut low in the chest and high up the legs; there will be crotchless panties; there will be lacy brassieres with the nipples snipped out.

At the moment, though, Tiffany James is addressing the group. Mrs. James is running the party tonight, and she invites the women to have another glass of wine. She thanks them for coming and assures them that their husbands won't be disappointed when they get home.

"Relax, sit back, and have the time of your life," Mrs. James says. She hands each woman in the room a scorecard and a pencil, and begins to deliver something called the Sensuality Test:

"If you're wearing a bra and panties of the same color, give yourself ten points.

"If you've ever finger-painted with a member of the opposite sex, give yourself ten points.

"If I say 'whipped cream' and anybody blushes, give yourself twenty points."

When the test is over, Mrs. James has everyone in the room read off her score. There is much giggling. She says she is just about ready to show the clothing, but first she wants the women to be even more comfortable. Once more, wine is poured.

"I want us all to know each other," Mrs. James says, "so I'm going to go around the room, and I'd like each of you to say your first name, and then to say something sensuous about yourself that begins with the first letter of your first name. I'll start: My name is Tiffany, and I like touching."

There is a momentary silence. These women would look at home in a Betty Crocker ad or in a corporate secretarial pool. But within thirty seconds, they have begun.

"My name is Carol, and I like caressing."

"My name is Linda, and I like luscious lip service."

"My name is Karen, and I like kinky men."

What we have here is a phenomenon so startling and yet so obvious that, had one pondered the factors that led to it, one could have almost predicted it. This is the natural outgrowth of free and open sexuality reaching into the heartland; it is the place where the sexual revolution and the Tupperware party meet.

Tiffany James, the woman directing tonight's party, is executive vice-president of UndercoverWear Inc.; along with her husband, Walter, she runs the company. Since this party is so close to the firm's headquarters, in Woburn, Massachusetts, she is acting as the party agent. But there are more than eight hundred UndercoverWear agents in thirty-five states; virtually every weeknight of the year, there is an UndercoverWear party going on somewhere in the country.

The premise of these parties is a simple one: American housewives have been titillated and aroused by the sexual openness that has spread across the nation. Most of them are not swingers or cheaters; they may feel a few twinges of raciness, but basically they love their husbands, their children, and their homes. They want to sample some of the exotic new pleasures they know are out there, but they do not want to feel dirty about it, and they certainly do not want to feel guilty.

Enter UndercoverWear Inc. By 1977 Walter and Tiffany James had realized that there was money to be made if they could find a way to offer these women tame, unthreatening thrills; to let them feel vaguely naughty without being unfaithful; to give them some quiet sin for a few hours, and then to deliver them safely home to their families again.

So UndercoverWear built up a line of bedroom attire that ranged from the risqué to the lewd. Instead of advertising it in the backs of true-confessions magazines like the old Frederick's of Hollywood merchandise, however, they arranged to bring it right into the women's own living rooms. There was to be none of the furtiveness of ordering from a magazine coupon. The Tupperware imitation was calculated and intentional; Mr. and Mrs. James realized that a great many women would find it more exciting to purchase nighties that bared their breasts than to watch demonstrations of burping bowls. And yet this was all to be done in the name of pleasing their husbands. This was to be done out in the open with friends; this was to be done with a sense of humor; this was to be a party.

"The party plan eliminates any feeling of embarrassment about purchasing these kinds of products," Mrs. James says. "If a woman wants to wear a garter belt and nylons for her husband, she might hesitate before going into a store. The feeling is, 'This salesclerk is going to think there's something wrong with me; I'm not as sweet and demure as I look, and what's she going to think of me?"

At an UndercoverWear party, however, the emphasis is on making the women feel they're all in it together. Although, as Mrs. James says, "It's our firm belief that what happens between a husband and a wife in the bedroom is private," the UndercoverWear parties are designed to assure the women that they are not having their bedroom fantasies alone.

The UndercoverWear theory of success is based on the assumption that these are not women who usually purchase revealing lingerie— "Maybe the husband would buy the wife one black nightie a year, at Christmas," Mrs. James says—and the whole idea of the parties is to persuade the women that what they are doing is socially acceptable. "We want the women to tell themselves: 'Just because I choose to wear something sensuous in my bedroom, that's no negative reflection on me.' Women today have a desire to be feminine and still think they're normal.

"We're not just selling them a piece of lingerie. We're selling them an UndercoverWear night. Not the night of the party, but the night they get to show the garments to their husbands. That's what the agents tell them at the parties: 'When you get your UndercoverWear, schedule your UndercoverWear night.' "

So, as darkness falls, the parties begin. No men are allowed. As each piece of lingerie is removed from the rack for display, the women are encouraged to talk about it. There is more a tingle of teenage romance in the room than a feeling of lust; the women *ooooh* at the items as if what they are looking at are tiny puppies instead of fringe-covered bras. The phrase most commonly spoken in the room is, "Isn't that pretty?"

The UndercoverWear agent realizes, though, that her commission depends on getting the partygoers to order the products, and that the most effective sales pitch is not based on aesthetics. So when a woman across the room asks, "Does that one come with pants, Tiffany?" Mrs. James looks her in the eye and says, "Yes, but we can't guarantee how long they stay on."

There is an odd combination of forces in play as the party progresses into the evening. On the one hand, the women are indulging their fantasies, feverishly marking down the names of the garments they hope to purchase at the end of the night. On the other hand . . . there is no real flavor of wickedness or raw sexuality here. This is definitely not a female version of a stag party. Times may have changed, and the items the women order may be of the variety that must be hidden from the children, but this *does* feel the way a Tupperware party must feel. The attraction for the women seems to be social; the party is like a gathering of sorority sisters, and the merchandise is, in a way, incidental. Sexy clothing may be the excuse that has brought them here, but simply being together away from men is clearly as important to them as the nightgowns they are buying.

"It's nice to be in someone else's home shopping," says Chris Canto, a social worker, who will purchase $50 worth of merchandise at the end of the evening. "I don't think there's anything dirty in the show; it's all very pretty." And Kristine Costello, in whose home the party is taking place—and who will receive free merchandise for being the hostess—says, "I like shopping at home with my friends. It's like a night out with the girls."

The reasons the women give for being in the room are traditional and almost wholesome. "I'm not one to order from a catalog," says one. "You can't really be sure of the quality and sizes in a catalog." And the youngest woman at the party—Carol Medeiros, eighteen, a salesclerk who plans to be married within the next year and who will spend $150 tonight—says she is planning to save the garments for her marriage. "They're for my hope chest," she says.

It is as if the world has changed, yet nothing has changed at all. Twenty years ago many of the fashions being sold here would have been too revealing to be featured in a girlie magazine; but here the women are, writing down their choices, talking quietly with one another, making new friends even as they select Fringe Benefits or Jungle Fever.

Perhaps it is best that the men are not allowed to see this; it would deflate the very fantasies that the UndercoverWear phenomenon is designed to inspire. In the male imagination, the idea of a party like this probably conjures up the dark emotional muskiness of a gang bang. But that's not it; if the truth be told, this is one part orgy, nine parts sewing circle, and the amazing thing about the women here is that they seem able to juggle both elements yet somehow keep them separate.

And now Tiffany James has finished the presentation. The last nightgown and pair of panties have been displayed; now the women are descending on the metal rack, grabbing Softly Sensuous and Double Trouble and the rest.

It is time to try them on. The women take their favorites and head for Mr. and Mrs. Costello's bedroom, for the children's rooms, for the bathrooms. Three or four of them go into each room at the same time, taking their own clothes off, putting the UndercoverWear fashions on.

In a matter of minutes, they are back in the living room. The effect is stunning. Earlier they had been in housedresses or slacks and sweaters. Now they are standing around together like so many hookers, all cleavage and belly and leg, telling one another how cute they look and how pleased their husbands will be. The voices are a jumble:

"Tiffany, does this one have bottoms?"

"Tiffany, does this one come with snaps?"

Tiffany James is busy accepting orders, telling each buyer that the items will be delivered in approximately three weeks. Some of the women are standing in front of a mirror staring at themselves. "Well, Eddie," says one, "you'd better be prepared."

"That looks so pretty on you," Mrs. James says to one customer, even as she is moving to the next and asking, "Did you want to try on Little Bo Peep?" It is 9:45 on a Wednesday evening in northern Massachusetts. In an hour these women will be back at home, ready to tuck the children in and turn on the coffeepot for the morning and drift to sleep. Perchance to dream.

4

BEING DIFFERENT

In the name of team play, there is no time or place for individual virtuosity . . .

—Ken Dryden

People and the organizations they create often act as if they are threatened by sources of uncertainty. Consequently, they often find it difficult to cope with stimuli that differ in salient ways from the stimuli they assume to be normal. Some of the symptoms of these difficulties take the form of perceptual errors such as stereotypes and perceptual defenses.

Of course perceptual activity is only one way people and organizations use to attempt to restore certainty when confronted by stimuli that are "different." Often they attempt to create environments that are free of difference. In organizations these attempts can be seen for example in selection processes which screen out people, who, because they are different, are not fully trusted. The article "Hidden Handicap," by Daniel Machalaba describes how some people, who cannot read, have slipped through the selection net and have gone on to careers that are successful for them and their organizations. Included in this category are a department manager, an executive, and a company chairman. Each has had to go to great lengths to cover up his or her difference. To each, this lack of skill has been a source of great anxiety and shame. Despite this difference, this handicap, they have contributed in important ways to their organizations.

This is not to say of course, that reading skills should be overlooked in a selection process. Knowing how to read and to write are much needed skills in a society such as ours that emphasizes so extensively, information flow and exchange. Machalaba's article does convey the sense of loss that arises when the organizational response to the handicap is to discard the whole person as a possible contributor to organizational excellence. Clearly, some people can and do make adjustments so that their strengths are utilized. Some companies seem to be trying to deal with the problem, at least among those they have already selected. Yet, the stigma is great. As one worker points out in the article, he is more acceptable as an acknowledged alcoholic than as an identified illiterate.

Some limitations on differences in behavior can be justified as necessary for efficient operation of an organization—after all, one of the major advantages of formal organizations is their ability to make the behavior of individuals highly predictable. However, it is well known that often the reduction of differences among organization members can cause the organization to stagnate by eliminating the diversity needed to cope with complex and changing environments. In short, many of the tactics that people and organizations employ to cope with people and other stimuli that are "different" can be described as neurotic—they are motivated to reduce anxiety and lead to dysfunctional outcomes.

In this vein, we observe that training and reward systems in organizations often emphasize conformity rather than difference. In "Lafleur," an excerpt from Ken Dryden's book on hockey, *The Game,* the author describes the training and development of Lafleur, a virtuoso hockey player. He contrasts his career path and the way he has been coached and rewarded with that of most players of team sports. We think Dryden's insights apply to organizations in other settings. Dryden's comments on the attitudes of administrators and coaches to the use of *time,* especially *free time,* are interesting and provocative. Free time, in his view, has become misunderstood, feared, and distrusted. For the gifts of individuals to emerge and mature and for individual differences to make a meaningful change in organizations, people need to be nurtured and to have unhurried time to practice, repeat, and experiment in their own way with the things they are trying to do. Given the use of time in this way, individuals can develop a store of physical and mental memories so rich and varied that when faced with the unexpected in their work, they will *invent* something new.

The rational design of organizations would provide for optimal levels of being different. However, the treatment of differences in organizations is seldom that rational. Often valuable human resources are underutilized. The costs of this underutilization are borne by the organization and the individuals who are "different." "The Deep Discontent of the Working Woman" article provides graphic evidence of the costs many women in organizations incur because of their differences from the norms in our organizations and in our society where the male worker is the primary candidate for job enrichment and career enhancement. The strains of working as well as managing homes and raising children are identified in the article as disproportionately the lot of women workers. There is also evidence that changes are occurring such that the potential and the contribution of women in organizations are being recognized in some organizations. This trend will no doubt continue to occur. Nevertheless, the feelings of boredom and of being exploited which the female office employees cited in the article attest to, likely still exist in many organizations.

Some organizations do recognize and harness the difference inherent in their membership. One such organization is the Los Angeles Raiders, a football team described in "Raiders Slightly, ah Different," by Gary Myers. Their experience is instructive. Considered by their peer organizations to be unorthodox, to say the least, they are at the same time highly successful. They appear to have a philosophy that encourages individuality, playfulness, and the opportunity for "characters" to emerge. Their approach allows personal alignments that enable individual self-interests and an organizational goal (to win) to be innovatively worked out (See a discussion of alignments in Culbert and McDonough's "The Invisible War:

Pursuing Self-Interest at Work," section 5). The Raiders organization is known for its policy of selecting talented players with blemished performance records who are allowed to find their way back to peak performance in a supportive setting. (The Raiders are referred to as a "second-chance" organization in the NFL.)

In "Mistakes Murder Redskins," Ron Rapoport provides a glimpse of the spontaneity and inventiveness (as well as luck) of the team in its record breaking 38-9 victory over the favored Washington Redskins in the January 1984 Superbowl championship game. He points out their capacity to overcome their own errors and to capitalize on those of their opponents. The inventiveness of their actions is perhaps best captured in the comments of one of their star players, Marcus Allen, who turned a potential mistake on his part into the longest touchdown run in the history of the Superbowl. "I tried to make something out of nothing." (Echoes of Dryden's statement about invention noted earlier.)

What is so startling and ironic about people who are "different" is how many of them there are! People who are different include those at the bottom of the socioeconomic ladder, blacks and other minorities, women, the aged, and homosexuals. In "Life at the Bottom," Lieberman and Goolrick describe the experiences of three workers to reveal a side of organizational life which, although real to a large number of people, is seldom found in modern textbooks.

"Institutional Bigotry" raises yet another discussion along which people are different—sexual preference. While the policy of the Air Force may be an extreme one, Leonard Matlovich's experience of being discriminated against because he was known to be a homosexual is by no means uncommon.

The final selection, "Two Women, Three Men on a Raft," by Robert Schrank, provides a stimulating capstone to this section. What subtle domination occurred on the river and with what consequence? Why did the raft flip over? The feedback processes he describes could apply equally well to many of the situations raised in this section, as well as to many situations that are not covered (e.g. employment of the physically handicapped). Overall, the experience of being "different" and of dealing with people who are "different" presents troublesome problems that have a major impact on how people experience life in organizations.

Hidden Handicap

For Americans unable to read well,
life is a series of small crises

Daniel Machalaba

Charles Wieben, who earns $40,000 a year managing the meat department of a suburban supermarket, has an unusual work habit: He doesn't read or write in his office.

If handed something to read, he feigns a headache. When he has to produce memos and sales reports, he takes the information home and dictates to his wife. The practices are part of an elaborate subterfuge that the 43-year-old Mr. Wieben has developed to keep people from discovering that he can barely read or write.

Although Mr. Wieben graduated from high school, he reads at a third-grade level. Reading—particularly reading aloud—is a "really scary experience," he says. Recently, he took himself out of the running for a promotion after learning that a written test was required. "I feel very crippled," Mr. Wieben says.

Illiteracy often goes unnoticed in a society that takes reading and writing for granted. But the International Reading Association in Newark, Del., estimates that some 20 million English-speaking, native-born American adults read or write so poorly that they "have trouble holding jobs or suffer loss of self-esteem."

LOST PRODUCTIVITY

Some companies are beginning to realize that reading problems can contribute to high accident rates and low productivity, and a few firms are trying to help illiterate workers. For example, Vimasco Corp., a small producer of Industrial coatings, estimates that the low reading and writing skills of some of its workers cost the Nitro, W. Va., firm about $25,000 annually, or 15% of its hourly payroll, in lost productivity.

William Pugh Jr., Vimasco's president, says he began to suspect that reading and writing were difficult for some of his employees after noticing that a foreman always gave everybody the same evaluation: "good worker, slow." An ouside testing service confirmed his fears. Ten out of 27 workers tested, including the foreman, weren't competent readers. Now Mr. Pugh requires tutoring for any worker who can't read or write at or above an eighth-grade level. "Adults who are illiterate have problems with their pride, and we want a more productive work force," he explains.

Carolyn Schworer, the executive director of the Minnesota Literacy Council, says illiterates live "a daily crisis, fearful that someone will stick something in their face to read. So much shame is put on people who can't read."

CALLED 'BIRD BRAIN'

Michael White, a 28-year old Minneapolis welder, knows that shame first hand. An undetected hearing defect kept him from learning to read as a child. When asked to read aloud in school, "I'd pretend to have something wrong with my eyes and I'd cry," he recalls. One of his classmates called him "bird brain."

As an adult he couldn't read well enough to decipher street signs. "I was like a dog," he says. "I knew my way home and how to get food." When lost, "I asked a lot of questions." He says he cheated his way through welding school because he couldn't understand the technical reading matter. The frustration, the burden of deception and fear of being caught, all hurt. "A lot of times I'd just go off and cry," he remembers. "I used to want to kill myself."

His inability to read caused him to make mistakes as a welder. He recalls installing an industrial blower incorrectly because he couldn't read the word "clockwise" in the instructions. The mistake cost thousands of dollars, he says.

Mr. White's problems started to evaporate two years ago when he began using a hearing aid and a girlfriend encouraged him to get reading help. Since then, his reading has improved to the fourth- or fifth-grade level. "I have a lot more confidence in myself now," he says. "I don't have to run around the shop looking for people to tell me what things mean."

BAD SCHOOLING

Some poor readers suffer from learning disorders, but the vast majority failed to acquire basic skills in elementary school. The reasons range from bad schooling to family and health problems. "If you're out for six months in the second grade with rheumatic fever, you may fall behind for life," says a reading specialist.

Thanks to compulsory public education, adults who can't read at all now are rare. But educators have coined the term "functional illiterates" to describe people who lack the reading or writing skills necessary to function smoothly—usually taken as a seventh-grade level. (Not everyone accepts that standard: Says Jonathan Kozol, author of "Prisoners of Silence," a book about illiteracy, "To read antidotes an a bottle of lye, you need to read at a 10th-grade level.")

Both public and private organizations are trying to combat functional illiteracy. The Army is currently putting about 60,000 soldiers through a basic reading program for those with skills below the ninth-grade level. About $300 million is spent each year by public schools, corporations and volunteer groups to teach a million adults reading and writing, estimates Sven Borel, the president of the Literacy Institute, in Signal Mountain, Tenn. Polaroid Corp. and the Pratt & Whitney unit of United Technologies Corp. have launched programs to teach basic skills to workers who can't read.

But current efforts fall far short of the challenge, says Peter Waite, the executive director of Laubach Literacy Action, a national volunteer group based in Syracuse, N.Y. "We're just bailing to keep ourselves from sinking any more," he believes. Although President Reagan has recognized the problem and called for an "adult literacy initiative," he hasn't proposed spending additional money to combat illiteracy. Mr. Reagan wants to spur voluntary programs to improve reading and writing skills.

Persuading people to face up to their handicap and present themselves for remedial instruction is a major problem. Mr. Wieben says he "was embarrassed as hell" when he first started tutoring. Even now, he refuses to attend classes at the public library, where friends might see him, and goes to his tutor's apartment instead.

Many poor readers resort to costly and time-consuming ruses to hide their handicap. They frequently blame nonexistent eye trouble for their inability to read in public and rely on friends or spouses to read to them at home.

TRYING HARDER

An executive for a computer company in New Jersey who makes $75,000 a year and supervises four staffers says he read at only the fourth-grade level until he recently started tutoring. He has been able to hide his inability because, he says, "I'm very good with people and numbers and have a logical mind." His wife gives him reading and writing help when it comes time for him to prepare sales reports. He ran up a $200 phone bill a year ago when he called her from Brussels and needed help to prepare a speech.

The 45-year-old executive says he has compensated for "feelings of inadequacy" by working longer hours. "People just thought I was a workaholic," he says. He figures he owes his business success partly to timing, because he entered the computer business in its infancy. "Almost everyone knew how to read," he says, "but the scarcity of individuals who understood computers put a premium on me."

The executive, who now is being tutored once a week, has hidden his illiteracy from his employer. If it were discovered, he says, "They'd pass me over for the next promotion; if there was a cutback, I'd be the first to go."

Oather McKee, the founder and chairman of McKee Baking Co., a Collegedale, Tenn., company with annual sales of $170 million, also succeeded in spite of illiteracy. "I was so humiliated over what I couldn't do that I worked harder," he says. Throughout his life the 79-year-old businessman has relied on others—his brother, his wife or his secretary—to do his reading for him. His secretary also stays on the line during business calls to take notes of his telephone conversations.

But it may get more difficult for illiterates to make it. One reason is the trend away from assembly-line jobs toward ones requiring more written work. "The jobs that don't require literacy are disappearing," says Nancy Oakley, the director of Project Learn in Cleveland, a remedial-reading program in which adult enrollment has increased 43% to 325 during the past four years. "You could get a job on the line and not be able to read, but now robots are doing those jobs," she says.

Any meaningful attack on illiteracy depends on the willingness of the afflicted to seek help. Daniel Murdoch, an electrician in Minneapolis, says, "I had a million ways of covering it up," including carrying a newspaper under his arm.

But his cover-up ended when Mr. Murdoch, 39, sought help for a drinking problem at Alcoholics Anonymous and couldn't read "Living Sober." With the help of a tutor, he has since partly overcome his reading problem, though not the stigma. "I'm accepted more if I say I'm an alcoholic than if I say I can't read," he says.

Lafleur

Ken Dryden

The Forum is disturbingly empty: just a few players sit quietly cocooned away in a dressing room; twenty-five or thirty staff work in distant upstairs offices; throughout the rest of its vast insides a few dozen men are busy washing, painting, fixing, tidying things up. There is one other person. Entering the corridor to the dressing room, I hear muffled,

---

From *THE GAME*, by Ken Dryden. Copyright © 1983 by Ken Dryden. Reprinted by permission of Times Books, a Division of Random House, Inc.

reverberating sounds from the ice, and before I can see who it is, I know it's Lafleur. Like a kid on a backyard rink, he skates by himself many minutes before anyone joins him, shooting pucks easily off the boards, watching them rebound, moving skates and gloved hands wherever his inventive instincts direct them to go. Here, far from the expedience of a game, away from defenders and linemates who shackle him to their banal predictability, alone with his virtuoso skills, it is his time to create.

The Italians have a phrase, *inventa la partita.* Translated, it means to "invent the game." A phrase often used by soccer coaches and journalists, it is now, more often than not, used as a lament. For in watching modern players with polished but plastic skills, they wonder at the passing of soccer *genius*—Pele, deStefano, Puskas—players whose minds and bodies in not so rare moments created something unfound in coaching manuals, a new and continuously changing game for others to aspire to.

It is a loss they explain many ways. In the name of team play, there is no time or place for individual virtuosity, they say; it is a game now taken over by coaches, by technocrats and autocrats who empty players' minds to control their bodies, reprogramming them with X's and O's, driving them to greater *efficiency* and *work rate,* to move *systems* faster, to move games faster, until achieving mindless pace. Others fix blame more on the other side: on smothering defenses played with the same technical sophistication, efficiency, and work rate, but in the nature of defense, easier to play. Still others argue it is the professional sports culture itself which says that games are not won on good plays, but by others' mistakes, where the safe and sure survive, and the creative and not-so-sure may not.

But a few link it to a different kind of cultural change, the loss of what they call "street soccer": the mindless hours spent with a ball next to your feet, walking with it as if with a family pet, to school, to a store, or anywhere, playing with it, learning new things about it and about yourself, in time, as with any good companion, developing an *understanding.* In a much less busy time undivided by TV, rock music, or the clutter of modern lessons, it was a child's diversion from having nothing else to do. And, appearances to the contrary, it was creative diversion. But now, with more to do, and with a sophisticated, competitive society pressing on the younger and younger the need for training and skills, its time has run out. Soccer has moved away from the streets and playgrounds to soccer fields, from impromptu games to uniforms and referees, from any time to specific, scheduled time; it has become an *activity* like anything else, organized and maximized, done right or not at all. It has become something to be taught and learned, then tested in games; the answer at the back of the book, the one and only answer. So other time, time not spent with teams in practices or games, deemed wasteful and inefficient, has become time not spent at soccer.

Recently, in Hungary, a survey was conducted asking soccer players from 1910 to the present how much each practiced a day. The answer, on a gradually shrinking scale, was three hours early in the century to eight minutes a day today. Though long memories can forget, and inflate what they don't forget, if the absolute figures are doubtful, the point is none the less valid. Today, except in the barrios of Latin America, in parts of Africa and Asia, "street soccer" is dead, and many would argue that with it has gone much of soccer's creative opportunity.

When Guy Lafleur was five years old, his father built a small rink in the backyard of their home in Thurso, Quebec. After school and on weekends, the rink was crowded with Lafleur and his friends, but on weekdays, rushing through lunch before returning to school, it was his alone for half an hour or more. A few years later, anxious for more ice time, on Saturday and Sunday mornings he would sneak in the back door of the local arena, finding his way unseen through the engine room, under the seats, and onto the ice. There, from 7:30 until just before the manager awakened about 11, he played alone; then quickly left. Though he was soon discovered, as the manager was also coach of his team Lafleur was allowed to continue, by himself, and then a few years later with some of his friends.

The Canadian game of hockey was weaned on long northern winters uncluttered by things to do. It grew up on ponds and rivers, in big open spaces, unorganized, often solitary, only occasionally moved into arenas for practices or games. In recent generations, that has changed. Canadians have moved from farms and towns to cities and suburbs; they've discovered skis, snowmobiles, and southern vacations; they've civilized winter and moved it indoors. A game we once played on rivers and ponds, later on streets and driveways and in backyards, we now play in arenas, in full team uniform, with coaches and referees, or to an ever-increasing extent we don't play at all. For, once a game is organized, unorganized games seem a wasteful use of time; and once a game moves indoors, it won't move outdoors again. Hockey has become suburbanized, and as part of our suburban middle-class culture, it has changed.

Put in uniform at six or seven, by the time a boy reaches the NHL, he is a veteran of close to 1,000 games—30-minute games, later 32-, then 45-, finally 60-minute games, played more than twice a week, more than seventy times a year between late September and late March. It is more games from a younger age, over a longer season than ever before. But it is less hockey than ever before. For, every time a twelve-year-old boy plays a 30-minute game, sharing the ice with teammates, he plays only about ten minutes. And ten minutes a game, anticipated and prepared for all day, travelled to and from, dressed and undressed for, means ten minutes of hockey a day, more than two days a week, more than seventy days a hockey season. And every day that a twelve-year-old plays only ten minutes, he doesn't play two hours on a backyard rink, or longer on school or playground rinks during weekends and holidays.

It all has to do with the way we look at free time. Constantly pre-occupied with time and keeping ourselves busy (we have come to answer the ritual question "How are you?" with what we apparently equate with good health, "Busy"), we treat non-school, non-sleeping or non-eating time, unbudgeted free time, with suspicion and no little fear. For, while it may offer opportunity to learn and do new things, we worry that the time we once spent reading, kicking a ball, or mindlessly coddling a puck might be used destructively, in front of TV, or "getting into trouble" in endless ways. So we organize free time, scheduling it into les-sons—ballet, piano, French—into organizations, teams, and clubs, fragmenting it into impossible-to-be-boring segments, creating in ourselves a mental metabolism geared to moving on, making free time distinctly unfree.

It is in free time that the special player develops, not in the competitive expedience of games, in hour-long practices once a week, in mechanical devotion to packaged, processed, coaching-manual, hockey-school skills. For while skills are necessary, setting out as they do the limits of anything, more is needed to transform those skills into something special. Mostly it is time—unencumbered, unhurried, time of a different quality, more time, time to find wrong answers to find a few that are right; time to find your own right answers; time for skills to be practiced to set higher limits, to settle and assimilate and become fully and com-pletely yours, to organize and combine with other skills comfortably and easily in some uniquely personal way, then to be set loose, trusted, to find new instinctive directions to take, to create.

But without such time a player is like a student cramming for exams. His skills are like answers memorized by his body, specific, limited to what is expected, random and separate, with no overviews to organize and bring them out together. And for those times when more is demand-ed, when new unexpected circumstances come up, when answers are asked for things you've never learned, when you must intuit and piece together what you already know to find new answers, memorizing isn't enough. It's the difference between knowledge and understanding, be-tween a super-achiever and a wise old man. And it's the difference be-tween a modern suburban player and a player like Lafleur.

For a special player has spent time with his game. On backyard rinks, in local arenas, in time alone and with others, time without short-cuts, he has seen many things, he has done many things, he has *experienced* the game. He understands it. There is *scope* and *culture* in his game. He is not a born player. What he has is not a gift, random and otherworldly, and unearned. There is surely something in his genetic make-up that allows him to be great, but just as surely there are others like him who fall short. He is, instead, *a natural*.

"Muscle memory" is a phrase physiologists sometimes use. It means that for many movements we make, our muscles move with no message from the brain telling them to move, that stored in the muscles is a learned capacity to move a certain way, and, given stimulus from the spinal cord, they move that way. We see a note on a sheet of music, our fingers move; no thought, no direction, and because one step of the transaction is eliminated—the information-message loop through the brain—we move faster as well.

When first learning a game, a player thinks through every step of what he's doing, needing to direct his body the way he wants it to go. With practice, the repetition, movements get memorized, speeding up, growing surer, gradually becoming part of the muscle's memory. The great player, having seen and done more things, more different and personal things, has in his muscles the memory of more notes, more combinations and patterns of notes, played in more different ways. Faced with a situation, his body responds. Faced with something more, something new, it finds an answer he didn't know was there. He *invents the game.*

Listen to a great player describe what he does. Ask Lafleur or Orr, ask Reggie Jackson, O. J. Simpson, or Julius Erving what makes them special, and you will get back something frustratingly unrewarding. They are inarticulate jocks, we decide, but in fact they can know no better than we do. For ask yourself how you walk, how your fingers move on a piano keyboard, how you do any number of things you have made routine, and you will know why. Stepping outside yourself you can think about it and decide what *must* happen, but you possess no inside story, no great insight unavailable to those who watch. Such movement comes literally from your body, bypassing your brain, leaving few subjective hints behind. Your legs, your fingers move, that's all you know. So if you want to know what makes Orr and Lafleur special, watch their bodies, fluent and articulate, let them explain. They know.

When I watch a modern suburban player, I feel the same as I do when I hear Donnie Osmond or René Simard sing a love song. I hear a skillful voice, I see closed eyes and pleading outstretched fingers, but I hear and see only fourteen-year-old boys who can't tell me anything.

Hockey has left the river and will never return. But like the "street," like an "ivory tower," the river is less a physical place than an *attitude,* a metaphor for unstructured, unorganized time alone. And if the game no longer needs the place, it needs the attitude. It is the rare player like Lafleur who reminds us.

The Deep Discontent of the Working Woman

The popular image of working women is that of swinging white-collar careerists who juggle challenging jobs, cultural interests, and romance. But to the 80 percent of all working women who are not professionals but who hold factory, service, or clerical jobs, reality is strikingly different, as a Senate committee will learn on January 31.

According to a study by the National Commission on Working Women (NCWW), the average woman worker is a lonely person in a dead-end job, seething with frustration over her lot. Home and children only deepen her dissatisfaction, because they raise problems of housework and child care. With the number of women at work rising to 48.4 percent in 1977 from less than 40 percent in 1960—and projected to rise to 60 percent in the next decade—Congress is beginning to take heed.

Child Care

The Senate Human Resources Committee, headed by Senator Harrison Williams (D-N.J.), will hear a parade of witnesses testify on a broad range of women-related concerns in the hearings, which start on January 31 and lead off with depressing evidence unearthed by the NCWW. Separately, Senator Alan Cranston (D-Calif.) will open hearings on February 5 on a child care bill he introduced. Cranston thinks that chances for passage of the bill, which would lay the groundwork for federal aid for child care, have vastly improved since the last go-around in 1974, when such a bill never made it to a vote. "People used to say women would be drawn away from the family if offered child care help," says a Cranston aide. "It is clear by now that they are going to work anyway."

The Williams hearings will feature such headline stars as Bella Abzug, who was recently fired by Carter as chairperson of his Advisory Committee on Women. But the presentation that could most affect the future of women and men will be that of W. Willard Wirtz, former Labor Secretary, chairman of the National Manpower Institute, and, in this case, witness for the NCWW.

Wirtz will tell senators the preliminary results of a survey of 150,000 women who responded to questionnaires that the NCWW placed in women's magazines and union publications last September. Not only was the response so overwhelming that computers have still not completed tabulations, but several thousand women wrote unsolicited letters detailing their grievances. "Imagine people so isolated and upset that they will write to a post office box for solace, and you have an idea of the women we touched," says an NCWW staffer.

Some of the NCWW's findings about ordinary women workers:

- Forty percent felt that their jobs were boring and did not utilize their skills, and nearly half said they had no chance to train for better jobs. One-third reported receiving no counseling about other jobs or training. Because of failure to advance and what they had been told about women's capabilities, one in four said they lacked the self-confidence to get ahead. Among those who had problems with their jobs, 60 percent named as their primary problem their lack of opportunity to advance.
- Fifty-five percent had no leisure time and 39 percent had no time to pursue education. Presumably their after-work hours were devoted to housework. A study by the University of Michigan's Institute for Social Research found that on days when the wife works, only 5 percent of husbands spent as much as three and one half hours on home chores. Only 14 percent of women in the commission survey could say that job and family life did not interfere with each other.
- Among women with young children who already had jobs and presumably had made some arrangement for child care, almost one-third said they needed additional child care help. Wirtz will say that when the data on child care are finally tabulated, he expects to see a "much higher" figure for women who are not working, but who wish to.

More vivid than the survey results were the letters. "I'm on sick leave from my job, and my problems are directly related to having to work, run a household, and care for children," complained a Michigan woman, who said that she and many of her coworkers are "tired, don't have time to express ourselves."

Single parents, said a New York woman, experience "great frustration" in advancing because of educational deficiencies, then find that they cannot remedy this lack. "I have tried to attend school at night while working full time and raising my children," the New Yorker wrote, "but have been forced to postpone my education until the time when my children are older." A Massachusetts woman wrote that "retirement income is a function of earnings, and this is where the working woman is hurt. . . . The day I stop working is the day that my home of 30 years goes on the market. It frightens me."

Neither Wirtz nor Williams predicts that women workers will take to the streets in rage. But as their frustration is translated increasingly into political and legal action, they are likely to seek changes in such areas as counseling, training, and child care help that could be costly to employers or society and prompt some painful readjustment.

Raiders Slightly, ah, Different

Gary Myers

The cassette tape arrives from Phil Villapiano in Buffalo. It's time for the Los Angeles Raiders training camp Air Hockey Tournament where cheating is encouraged.

"We have 30 rules," Howie Long says. "The first one is you have to be drunk to play. The second one is Mormons can't win."

The other 28 are just as ridiculous. The Mormon rule doesn't please Todd Christensen, the Raiders' best air hockey player, who is a Mormon, does not drink and enjoys quoting Thoreau. But he wins every year, anyway.

The tournament begins when Villapiano's tape is played in the Bamboo Room bar, the Raiders' camp hangout. Villapiano was the originator of the tournament and remains active spiritually although he was traded to the Bills.

"He gives a speech, which is sort of like throwing out the first ball in baseball," Long said. "Everybody in the bar stands up. It's really pretty moving. Then it's time to play."

This, of course, has been preceded by the Air Hockey Parade through the streets of downtown Santa Rosa, Calif. The cars are decorated in ribbons and there is an Air Hockey Queen.

The Raiders, who play the Washington Redskins in Super Bowl XVIII Sunday in Tampa, are different in a humorous way.

And it stems from the top. Al Davis doesn't set but one rule. Win.

"We're like the guys in senior class that take wood shop," Matt Millen said. "We get the project done, but nobody cares how we do it. Individually, we have a bunch of guys with the demeanor of axe murderers."

"When I got traded here from Cleveland, there were rumors that I had mental problems. Well, I have a few," Lyle Alzado said. "My mind is never clear. I like it that way. Sane people are obnoxious people."

The Raiders have 19 players who have played with other NFL teams. They are the second-chance organization, willing to gamble on players considered too old, too slow, too fat or, in many cases, too crazy. Their image is fortified by the black uniforms, the renegade image Davis portrays and the fact that many of their players have no problem admitting they are slightly off-centre.

How else to explain Ted Hendricks answering John Madden's complaint a few years ago that the team wasn't intense by riding to practice

---

one day on a white horse in a white knight's outfit. Or Hendricks showing up for practice on Halloween with a pumpkin fitted to his head. Or
the time a stripper was hired to prance around the practice field.

"She was running around the field nude," Long said. "Can you imagine that happening in Dallas?"

Probably not.

"Every team has characters," Millen said. "The difference is here they
don't care what you do. I mean, they don't want you to be a degenerate,
but as long as any off-the-field problems don't carry onto the field, they
leave you alone. We have as many, if not more, conscientious guys here.
We're not big on being on time for meetings. But everybody gets there."

No security directors, either.

"We don't have any bad attitudes," Millen said. "We want to work
and we want to win. When you put that black shirt on, you are viewed
differently and it brings something out in you. I know Drew Pearson real
well and he would be a perfect Raider. I am very spoiled being here."

At Penn State, Millen was regarded as an outlaw by coach Joe
Paterno. "Paterno tried to recruit the same type players. He just missed
on me," Millen said. "I was more independent and outspoken than he
would have liked. I was regarded as a radical there. Here, I'm one of the
guys.

"When the Raiders drafted me as a linebacker (he played the line in
college), Paterno said to me, 'Millen, you can't play linebacker.' And I
said, 'Joe, you can't coach, but that hasn't stopped you.' "

It didn't take much time for Long, an all-pro defensive end in his third
year, to realize the Raiders were going to be a whole new experience.
"Day in and day out, you can see something here that is different. Football is supposed to be fun. There is an overemphasis on the non-smiling.
As long as we work hard, there is room for humor," he said. "On rookie
day, I guzzled three straight pitchers of beer. I ran around the parking lot
and got sick. But I was the hit of the party, and we place a lot of value on
those things."

That's why the Raiders often walk the 200 yards to the Bamboo Room
straight from the practice field. "Sometimes we take a shower first,"
Long said. Thursday night during the season is Comraderie Night, where
everybody is encouraged to congregate for a couple of cocktails in a
Manhattan Beach bar. "The coaches are invited," Mike Haynes said,
"but they're usually watching films."

Haynes went through NFL culture shock after the conservative
Patriots traded him to the Animal House Raiders, where he had no trouble recognizing Bluto, Flounder and Otter.

"When I first got here and saw guys before the game listening to music
or playing cards, it was pretty different to what I was used to," Haynes
said. "In New England, there were offensive buses and defenses buses.
You couldn't go out of the hotel on road trips. Here, it's real loose."

When the Raiders played in Denver in September, Hendricks called a timeout for no apparent reason. When he was questioned why by teammates, Hendricks stuck out his lower lip and said, "I miss Howie." Long was on the sideline after taking a shot to the head.

"I was just sitting on the bench looking off into the mountains," Long said. "A couple of the guys came over and said Ted wouldn't play unless I came back in."

He did.

"We're pretty close here," Alzado said. "Guys dance with each other in the locker room. Slow and fast, it just depends. Todd and I dance slow. You got to see it to believe what goes on in there before a game. Guys sing, play cards, yell and curse at each other. There's no mention of the game."

The Raiders, executive assistant Al LoCasale says, don't consider themselves a reclamation home. They are only concerned if a player can help them win. But Davis seems more willing to gamble with diverse personalities than most owners.

"The reputation in the NFL is if you want to be happy, this is the place to be," LoCasale said. "Players are well treated and well paid.

"I remember Howie Long got a call from a friend of his in Philadelphia who was worried that he wasn't making the adjustment to living in Los Angeles. Howie told him: 'As I stand here on the balcony of my Mediterranean villa overlooking the Pacific Ocean with the sun setting over my Mercedes with my arm around a USC law student, I would say, yes, things are working out well for me.' "

And for the Raiders, too, making their fourth appearance in the Super Bowl. "We are a menagerie of misfits," said Christensen, a former Cowboy who led the NFL and set a record for tight ends with 92 catches. "Al Davis is a great football owner because he's a football man. We are not one of his corporations. Al is a player's friend, a maverick willing to violate the status quo."

The comparison between the Raiders and Cowboys?

"Both teams have been very successful," Christensen said. "Dallas' clinical approach is excellent. Nobody knows more about film study than Tom Landry. But they make the team adapt to the system. I remember in a pre-season game, Pat Donovan recovered a fumble and he got yelled at because if he was in position, he wouldn't have recovered it. I thought that was very entertaining. Here, they adapt the system to the players.

"This is more fun."

Chicago Sun-Times, January 23, 1984.

Mistakes Murder Redskins

By RON RAPOPORT

TAMPA—Put me in a foxhole during an enemy barrage, and I will not put out a call for artillery cover. All I want is a Los Angeles Raider out there with me.

Send me out in a rainstorm 50 miles from the nearest lightning rod, and I will not be afraid for a moment. Not if a Raider is by my side.

I'd like to shrink one of those guys who beat up on the Washington Redskins in the Super Bowl Sunday down to a size where I could mount him on my dashboard. Or maybe I could dangle him from my keychain or put him near my front door, where I could pat him on the head on my way out.

One thing is sure: If you could bottle the good fortune the Raiders were exuding all over the Redskins during their 38-9 victory, you'd soon have enough money to retire to a yacht in the Grecian Isles. Either that or put on a Super Bowl halftime show. I'm not sure which costs more.

Life at the Bottom, Alias the Minimum Wage

Paul Lieberman and Chester Goolrick

Hardworking people like Clifford Giles, Buddy Lane, and Daisy Stripling are among the estimated 9 million American workers who get paid below or just at the federal minimum wage level. Some of these workers are covered by the federal Fair Labor Standards Act, some are not.

But in either case, they are not earning very much money. In 1977, the average full-time male worker in the U.S earned almost $17,000, and the average woman earned $9,353. In 1979, a worker being paid the federal minimum wage could earn $6,032 by working 40 hours a week for 52 weeks; the poverty level for a family of four in 1979 was $6,700.

Abridged from the AFL-CIO *American Federationist* (February, 1981), pp. 13–18, whose article was excerpted from a series of articles in the *Atlanta Constitution* written by Paul Lieberman and Chester Goolrick and entitled, "The Underpaid and Under-Protected."

But even the annual figure of $6,032 as the income for a minimum wage earner can be misleadingly high. Many workers who receive only the minimum wage, or even less, do not work a full 40-hour week, 52 weeks a year, because of the limited or unpredictable availability of work. A man who loads tobacco bales onto trucks gets paid when there are bales to load. There may not be any bales on a given day, and the worker is not paid for the time he must spend waiting to find this out.

Many other workers earning the minimum wage or less have a somewhat opposite situation: there is no upper limit to the time they might have to put in on the job. Although their pay is fixed to reflect a 40-hour, five-day week, in actuality they are expected to be available almost day or night, seven days a week, 52 weeks a year. This may come about in cases where employers find it convenient to provide housing for their employees adjacent to the work place, as when poultry workers are settled in houses perhaps only yards from the chicken sheds they are hired to look after.

Underemployment and, conversely, lack of time off are not the only potential drawbacks accompanying certain low-paying jobs. Some workers find their pay falling below the minimum guaranteed wage because of deductions their employers feel justified in taking from their paychecks. Other workers may be entitled to the minimum wage but accept less, having no idea a federal minimum wage law applies to their work. And where workers are aware they are not being paid what the law provides, they are often reluctant to complain; they fear gaining a reputation as a troublemaker, or they wish to be loyal to an employer they may have known all their lives.

And finally some workers are simply outside the umbrella of the federal law and must accept whatever pay is offered them. While they may still be covered by a state minimum wage law, such pay is not likely to be a living wage.

What is life like for these underpaid, often overworked wage earners? What is their daily routine like? What do they expect from their work and from their employers, and what do they expect to give?

When their places of work are visited and observed, and details are recorded, vivid pictures emerge in which the generalities of low pay, long hours, or unpredictably fluctuating income take on particular meaning in the lives of individuals who are at or near the bottom of the economic system. These workers appear to have few choices; they not only take what they can get in the way of work and pay, but often must accept extra tasks and conditions arbitrarily imposed by their employers. Indeed, for certain workers employer-provided living arrangements lead to an association between employee and employer reminiscent in some ways of supposedly long-dead economic systems: feudalism and slavery.

But there is another side to this story. Some of these same people in America's lowest-paid groups express, directly or indirectly, considerable satisfaction with their lives. They appear to go about their work and their lives without reflecting at all upon their situation or seeing it as something to be changed or even deplored. They may even extol the independence of their working lives, as some did in interviews with the *Atlanta Constitution*.

TURPENTINE MAN

After a grueling day of gathering pine gum, turpentine worker Clifford Giles uncomplainingly tosses hay until nightfall to supplement his pay. If there is one job many men resist at almost all costs, it is turpentining. Experts on the turpentining industry say the people who are willing to do the work are mostly those who "like the woods," or simply don't know anything else. Still, there is admiration for the men who are proficient at collecting the gum.

Clifford Giles is a turpentine man. He works in pine woods in the deep South, collecting gum from trees. Using a dipping iron, he scoops the sticky gum from tin cups attached to each tree, filling a large bucket he carries from tree to tree. When the bucket is full, he empties it into one of several large metal barrels that wait on a mule-drawn wooden cart. Each barrel weighs about 435 pounds when full, and on an average day Giles may fill two of them.

For every barrel Giles fills he is paid $8. At the turpentine distillery, the boss will receive about $80 per barrel, an amount Giles may make in an average week. In a very good week, working from 7 A.M. until 3 or 4 P.M., Monday through Friday, Giles may fill 13 barrels and thus make as much as $104.

The work is hard. On a hot midsummer day, Clifford Giles has to slosh through swamp water and fight off thorny bush, mosquitoes and horseflies, and an occasional rattlesnake. Sweat will pour from his body; his gummy, wet clothes will become like a second skin.

Giles is the son and the grandson of turpentine men, black laborers working in an industry that has changed little in a hundred years, with its hand labor, mule-drawn carts, and company-provided living arrangements. Although their operation is covered by the Fair Labor Standards Act, the minimum wage means little to Giles and his co-workers, who live in the turpentine "quarters" of a tiny southern town and are trucked daily to and from the pine forests by the company foreman.

The quarters, hidden from the main street of the town, are a cluster of faded, ramshackle clapboard shacks where Giles and 15 other workers and their families live. The shacks, like the turpentining rights, are leased to the turpentine company by the landowners; the laborers pay the company no rent.

Showing only traces of their original red paint, the shacks have tin roofs and one or two chimneys. Fireplaces supply the heat in winter. Covered porches in varying states of decay are in front of the shacks. On some porches, junk—automobile tires and rims, boxes, old chairs —leaves little room for sitting.

A wooden, tin-roofed outhouse is behind each shack. The outhouse behind Clifford Giles' four-room shack is overrun with maggots. Several small pigs root around one shack, and scrawny dogs have free run of the entire quarters.

On weekday mornings the company foreman drives his truck through the quarters at dawn, swinging through once to wake the workers with his horn, then a second time to pick them up. Carrying lunch, water jugs, and other supplies, the men climb into the back of the truck and bounce over the route to the edge of the woods, where they transfer to mule carts and slowly penetrate deeper among the trees.

On a summer day, Clifford Giles will probably be working in 90-degree heat by late morning. Swamp water will flow from his boots through holes cut into them for just that purpose. He will take one break, at noon, from his steady progress from tree to tree. Finally, at 3 or 4 P.M., he will drive the barrel-laden mule cart out of the woods, and feed and settle the animals in their corral. It may be 5 or 6 o'clock when the truck brings him and his coworkers back to the quarters. He may have filled two 435-pound barrels and earned $16 for the grueling labor.

Part of the $16 will go for deductions the boss figures in, deductions for water and electricity, perhaps for money advanced, perhaps for other services. Giles does not compute his deductions himself: "The boss adds it up." Nor does Giles add up and record his hours worked. It's barrels, not hours, that count; most turpentine men have only a vague notion of how much time they put in on the job.

Thirteen barrels, or $104 a week—before deductions—is a good week for a hard-working turpentine veteran. There are many weeks when the pay is considerably less. One group of turpentine men has estimated that during a busy summer season they were earning an average of $70 a week.

The work is relatively solitary and silent. "Chippers" and "pullers" go off to an assigned section of the woods to prepare the trees by scraping off bark. Giles, as a "dipper," works alone or in a two-man team. With vast numbers of trees to work, turpentine men often see none of their colleagues, except possibly during a lunch break. When the men do meet in the woods, exchanges are apt to be complaints about the scarcity of gum in the tin cups—which means a scarcity of earnings—or gossip about the previous weekend. There is rarely any complaining about pay or working conditions, or any talk about finding better jobs.

While the men work, the foreman monitors their progress on horseback. It's slow and exhausting in stifling summer weather. But if it rains, there is no work, and thus no pay, at all.

Most of the men are anxious to work. Only one worker in Clifford Giles' group expresses open dissatisfaction with the system, and urges a new worker to "get your money and save it up and get the hell out. 'Cause you ain't going to make nuthin' here." The rest of the experienced turpentine men consider the complainer a misfit; many believe he doesn't really want to work, and he is criticized for getting food stamps. When Clifford Giles is asked about food stamps, he says, "Yeah, I could get them free stamps, but I ain't got time to go sign up. I'm too busy workin'."

Indeed, Giles seems to be. When he returns from a full day in the woods, he and several other men take a short break, then head out for several hours of loading hay for a farmer in town.

But if it's Friday, there won't be any evening work. On Friday afternoon, it's payday, and a sense of quickening anticipation is evident as the men quit the trees earlier than usual. They must have time to load the barrels for transport to the distillery and return the mules from their five-day stay in the woods, where they spend the night in their corral, to an old wooden stable next to the quarters. A $10 fine can be incurred for hurrying the hard-working mules, so the drive back is slow and long.

When the stable is finally reached, the men spend an hour caring for the animals and the wagons. Some men begin washing up, someone goes for liquor, the first drinking begins, and men line up on the porch of the pay house. On one Friday, the forman starts, then stops, the pay process, announcing that men are needed to get the boss's truck out of the mud. When nobody volunteers, the boss emerges from the pay house to make it clear that no more wages will be paid out until the truck is freed. Five men leave to work on the truck, and when they return the boss starts paying again. One by one, the workers go into the pay house, advancing according to the foreman's repeated invitation, "Anybody who's out here, go on in."

The top dipper for this week filled 13 barrels and earned $104. Clifford Giles had a bad week: $56. Two other dippers earned $72 and $40.

POULTRY WORK

Poultry worker Buddy Lane speaks matter-of-factly about no days off for several years. A whole family working for the normal salary of one person is not uncommon on some chicken farms. The family is provided with a house close to the chicken sheds. In return for the family's labor, the head of the household receives a single weekly salary, typically between $100 and $125.

David Babb, his wife Sandy, and their three children lived and worked on a poultry farm for 14 months. As a result of their experience, the five members of the Babb family filed suit against the farm, alleging that its employment practices had violated the federal minimum wage law.

It was David Babb who was hired as "flock tender." He accepted the job with enthusiasm because a small, wood-frame house near the chicken shed, where they tended the layers and collected the eggs, was provided for him and his family. Babb says the man who hired him had made it clear that both husband and wife would have to work in the six chicken sheds to pick up the eggs laid by 15,000 chickens every day. The pay would be $100 a week, with a week's vacation sometime during the year. For the Babbs, the house and the opportunity to work together made the seven-day work week appear acceptable.

For the first three months, Sandy and David Babb spent three hours together every morning, and perhaps another three or four hours in the afternoon, making their way through the row of long, low chicken sheds a short downhill distance from their house. On a typical day, they might pick up some 12,000 freshly laid eggs and place them into cartons to be taken to the packer. There were other responsibilities, like checking on the layers' feed, and David Babb would make repairs on the house during the evenings.

David Babb says he was asked after these first three months by one of his two bosses if Sandy could pick up the eggs alone. The boss wanted David to do some odd jobs around the farm, for which David would receive the minimum wage on an hourly basis. The arrangement seemed fine to the Babbs: Sandy was glad to be working, and the extra money David would be making—sometimes as much as $90 a week—was welcome in a time of rising prices.

Although Babb recalls that the boss's original instructions had called for the three Babb children to stay away from the chicken house, the children started helping Sandy collect eggs. David would also help Sandy when there were no odd jobs. It did not occur to the Babbs to question their work arrangements or the pay.

It took the near loss of Sandy's left hand to make it plain that while her labor was useful to the poultry farm operators, as a worker entitled to compensation she was nonexistent in their eyes.

Sandy Babb's left hand got caught in an automatic feeder one day while she was making her rounds. The children heard her screams and got someone to turn off the machine. She was rushed to a hospital where doctors were able to save her hand. But they said that nerve damage would prevent her from using her hand for a long time. Since she was left-handed, Sandy faced considerable disability.

Sandy's hospital bill came to $1,680, her doctor's bill was $825, and ongoing therapy was $171 for every three days of treatment. But the poultry farm's insurance company refused to pay for anything. Since Sandy had never been placed on the payroll, as far as the insurance company was concerned she had never worked at all. It didn't matter that some days she was the sole "flock tender."

It was David Babb, the poultry farm operator said, "who signed the workers' compensation card. He was the one who was hired." The operator said he knew that poultry workers often had family members or even friends help them in the sheds, but he implied that the practice was beyond the control of the employer. He said Sandy Babb was not supposed to work in the sheds at all.

After the accident and the insurance company's refusal to pay, an angry David Babb packed up his family and left the chicken farm. Wondering how they would pay the medical bills, the Babbs began wondering too about the entire arrangement under which at times the whole family was working for David Babb's regular salary plus earnings for odd jobs. The family finally filed suit in federal court alleging that their bosses "were in a position to know and did, in fact, know" that each of the family members were working. The suit asked that Babb be paid $23,000 "as difference paid to his family and minimum wages." The Babbs had hoped that the suit would at least win them a settlement covering the medical bills.

Several months after the accident, with a new job and living with his family in a trailer—it was the house on the poultry farm that had made the poultry work especially attractive—David Babb had allowed his initial anger to subside somewhat. He said, "I've learned my lesson. There should be a written contract and everything should have been clearly understood from the first."

And he suggested another lesson from the job he had held for 14 months: "As long as there are people who will work, there will be some cotton pickin' turkey who will work for next to nothing."

MOTEL MAID

Motel maids comprise one of the nation's largest, and most visible, groups of underpaid workers. Thousands of women are paid less than the federal minimum wage—sometimes legally, sometimes illegally—to clean rooms in motels and hotels across America. One of them, Daisy Stripling, is proud of her long years of nearly unbroken service at a tourist inn, years for which she got little more than $1 an hour.

Daisy Stripling had been working at the Almar Tourist Inn for more than 15 years. The inn is more a boarding house, really, located about five miles from a southern coastal city. Miss Stripling walks there every morning, perhaps wearing a polyester dress over a pair of trousers and sporting a brown paper bag as headgear, to clean some of the inn's 10 rooms and do whatever else Mrs. Willie Shurling, the proprietor, has in mind.

After 15 years, Miss Stripling does the job almost automatically, without instruction. She resents it when Mrs. Shurling tells her what to do. She works hard, if slowly, and she gets paid very little for her work.

On one particular day, she can be seen keeping careful watch over a pile of leaves she is burning in the yard. The day before, she says, she worked from 10 until 5, and was given $3.50 for the day. She adds that "it seems like I should make more than that."

But since the Almar Tourist Inn grosses far less than $250,000 a year, Daisy Stripling is not covered by the Fair Labor Standards Act. Neither does she have any of the job protections, benefits, retirement plans, paid sick days, and vacations that millions of Americans routinely expect from their employers.

One summer day recently, Mrs. Shurling dismissed Miss Stripling after the maid apparently failed to heed warnings not to come to work accompanied by some dogs that were becoming nuisances around the inn. When a reporter gathering material for a newspaper story learned of the opening at Mrs. Shurling's establishment, she took the maid's job and worked there for three days.

Riding to work on an early-morning bus filled with maids headed for their own jobs in motels and private homes, the reporter found that most of the workers would not discuss their wages. But one woman said she made $10 a day for about six hours' work, and another said $7 a day. Mrs. Shurling at the Almar Tourist Inn was offering the new maid $1.25 an hour.

Mrs. Shurling greeted her new employee pleasantly at 7:30 A.M. on the first day and started her cleaning a bathroom, checking her progress periodically. After an hour, the maid was next assigned to a bedroom to wash and polish walls, woodwork, and baseboards, and vacuum the rug. Continuing under Mrs. Shurling's instructions, she cleaned out the closet and polished the floor and furniture. Before lunch, she moved on to vacuum the main living room and put a load of Mrs. Shurling's clothes into the washer in the laundry.

Mrs. Shurling then provided a light lunch, for which the maid took 20 minutes. In the afternoon she was asked to pick pole beans in the garden, then to wash dishes and fold laundry.

The maid began her second and third days in the back yard, picking up pears that dropped overnight from the pear tree. She would later carry the fruit to the house of Mrs. Shurling's sister for preserving. When the yard work was finished on the second day, the maid cleaned three of the rented rooms, finishing her tasks at 5 P.M.

On the third day, after picking up pears, the maid spent an hour clearing debris from an empty trailer lot in back of the inn. Next she scoured the garbage cans and washed windows. Then beds had to be stripped and remade, and the sheets machine-washed and dried. Emptying trash baskets and changing towels completed the morning. After a few minutes for another light lunch provided by Mrs. Shurling, the maid swept and scrubbed floors, cleaned the kitchen, and watered plants.

Mrs. Shurling was friendly as she prepared to pay the new employee at the end of the third day. "That's about 25 hours, isn't it?" she asked, stating the time on the job correctly. Mrs. Shurling paid the maid $30 for the three days, $20 in cash and $10 by check because, she said, she didn't have change "for another $20."

One day shortly thereafter Daisy Stripling reappeared at the Almar Tourist Inn, and Mrs. Shurling took her back. Later Mrs. Shurling willingly discussed her longtime maid's good qualities but refused to say what she paid her. Mrs. Shurling said she and Miss Stripling get along pretty well; she gives Miss Stripling lunch, and they "talk about things." Together, the 70-year-old employer and her employee are able to maintain the tourist inn in a condition suitable for boarders. As Mrs. Shurling talks about their arrangement, Miss Stripling rakes leaves and watches them burn in the bright autumn air. It is not known how much this day's work will pay her. Yesterday's work paid, according to Miss Stripling, about 50 cents an hour.

Institutional Bigotry

Roger Wilkins

A Federal court in the District of Columbia recently ordered the Air Force to reinstate Leonard P. Matlovich, a former sergeant who was dismissed five years ago because he admitted that he was a homosexual. Though it is on a narrower and more technical ground than I would have liked, I am delighted by the judge's decision.

Leonard Matlovich was a superb airman. He was a decorated Vietnam veteran whose service ratings were always excellent. There was nothing in Sergeant Matlovich's behavior in the service to single him out from anybody else except that he did his job far better than most people in the Air Force did theirs. But his spirit bothered him. He wasn't being honest with the world about himself. Part of his identity as a human being was his homosexuality. But he was hiding it, pretending it didn't exist, pretending he was something other than what he was. He was behaving as if he was ashamed of what he was and that made him ashamed of himself.

So he did a courageous thing: He announced his homosexuality. And the Air Force promptly threw this distinguished airman out of the service. The Air Force had a regulation prohibiting the retention of homosexuals in the service unless "the most unusual circumstances exist." The judge said the Air Force had engaged in "perverse behavior" in being unable to explain its policy, and ordered Matlovich reinstated.

I met Matlovich and another homosexual airman back when they were both fighting their original expulsions from the Air Force. The other airman, Skip Keith, was a mechanic trained to work on C-5A engines. He loved his work and had been judged to be good at it, but when he felt he had enough of hiding part of himself from the world, he too was tossed out of the Air Force.

I am not surprised that the Air Force could not explain its position clearly. Shortly after I met Matlovich and Keith, I had lunch with a group of journalists and an Air Force lieutenant general. During the course of the lunch, I asked the general why the Air Force tossed homosexuals out on their ears. He practically choked on his food. The best I could get from him was that when he was flying he wanted a wing man he could rely on. He couldn't answer why gay airmen would be more unreliable than anybody else. He just got more incoherent.

The general was black. If I had closed my eyes and changed his words a little bit, I could have imagined that tirade coming from a white general in 1940 trying to explain why the Army couldn't be integrated. Institutional bigotry in any form stinks, and men like Len Matlovich and Skip Keith are heroes to have stood up to it.

Chicago Tribune March 9, 1979.

Male Nurses Battle Prejudice

By JACK MABLEY

One of the most blatant examples of sexual discrimination is in nursing, male nurses say.

A male nurse is a man in a woman's world. The trials he faces are as real as those of the woman in business who gets pinched at the water cooler instead of seated in the board room.

Male nurses often are not allowed to care for female patients, although the doctors are men. Male nurses endure snide remarks at work and in their social life. Their opportunities are reduced significantly.

There are somewhere between 26,000 and 52,000 males among the nation's 1.3 million nurses.

Some of these men—some succesful, others not—were interviewed. Luther Christman is dean of the nursing school at Rush-Presbyterian-St. Luke's Medical Center in Chicago.

"My career has been very mixed," he said. "There's been either a lot of positive support or automatic rejection.

"I compare it to the way the National Organization for Women says men discriminate against women.

"Whoever's in power doesn't want to share.

"It's economic fear, the same thing that makes men chauvinists . . . A man has to be two or three times as good to get recognition. It's the same thing blacks complain about. Even if you are very competent, there's a reluctance to accept you.

"I've had to take a great many remarks, almost entirely from women nurses, comments like "You're only successful because you're a man, not because you're any good.""

Reprinted, Courtesy of the *Chicago Tribune*.

March 7, 1984.

Disabled Aussie Swimmer Sunk for Lack of an Arm

SYDNEY (UPI)—Australian swim officials have disqualified a one-armed swimmer because he failed to touch the end of the pool with two hands.

Greg Hammond, 16, a member of Australia's Disabled Olympic team scheduled to compete in New York in June, was disqualified from second place in the open men's 100-metre breaststroke championship Sunday at Narooma, 285 kilometres south of Sydney.

The championship's referee, Pauline Gill, reluctantly disqualified Hammond following the protest of coach Paul Pike under a rule that states "the touch should be made with both hands at the same time."

The disqualification has caused an uproar. The Sydney Daily Mirror condemned the disqualification in its editorial Wednesday:

'The history of competitive swimming in this country is littered with more than enough controversial blunders caused by rules that are bad or interpretations that are even worse."

Pike, whose protest led to the disqualification, said Tuesday he had no regrets about his action. "Greg has to meet the letter of the law, which he didn't do.''

The Wall Street Journal, May 22, 1984.

Dancing on the Job

Dancing on the job and tight dress led to discrimination, a judge rules.

Elizabeth Bellissimo, a 26-year-old attorney for Westinghouse Electric Corp., accepted an invitation to dance with a fellow worker while on a business trip. When she returned, her superior warned her about "unprofessional behavior." He told her she should have faked a headache and retired to her room, she later testified. He also thought her clothes were too tight and the colors too "flashy."

The attorney was fired when she threatened to tell a company vice president. She sued her supervisor, claiming sex discrimination, and won. A federal court judge awarded her $121,670 for lost pay and future wages. Westinghouse, which declines comment on the verdict, has until June to appeal.

Two Women, Three Men on a Raft

What really happened to raft no. 4 on an
Outward Bound trip down the Rogue River?

Robert Schrank

One afternoon in June, I left the cloistered halls of the Ford Foundation and within 36 hours found myself standing on the pebbled banks of the Rogue River in Oregon with three other uncertain souls who had embarked on a week of "survival training" sponsored by Outward Bound. It was a cloudy, cold day, and as we pumped up our rubber raft and contemplated the Rogue, we also wondered about each other.

Before embarking on a Greyhound for the raft launching site, we had gathered the night before at the Medford Holiday Inn. That night, the Outward Bound staff had distributed individual camping gear and waterproof sleeping/storage bags to the 20 of us, almost all novices, and had given us a short briefing on the perils of going down the Rogue River on a raft.

As they explained the nature of the trip, the Outward Bound staffers reminded me of seasoned military men or safari leaders about to take a group of know-nothings into a world of lurking danger. Their talk was a kind of machismo jargon about "swells," rattlers, safety lines, portages, and pitons. Because they had known and conquered the dangers, it seemed they could talk of such things with assurance. This kind of "man talk" called to a primitive ear in us novices, and we began to perceive the grave dangers out there as evils to be overcome. In our minds, we planned to meet "Big Foot" the very next day, and we were secretly thrilled at the prospect.

If the Outward Bound staff briefing was designed to put us at ease, its effect, if anything, was the opposite. Hearing the detailed outline of what would be expected of us increased our anxiety. "You will work in teams as assigned to your raft," said Bill Boyd, the Northwest Outward Bound director, "and you will be responsible for running your raft, setting up camp each night, cooking every fourth meal for the whole gang, and taking care of all your personal needs."

The staff divided the 20 of us into four groups, each of which would remain together for the week on the raft. How we were grouped was never explained, but of the five rafts on the river, No. 4 was the only one

---

that ended up with two women and three men. One of the men was a member of the Outward Bound staff, a counselor and guide who was considerably younger than his four charges.

The four of us on Raft No. 4 were all in our middle fifties. Each of us had experienced some modicum of success in his or her life, and Outward Bound had invited each of us in the hope that after a week of living on the Rogue River we would go back from that trip as Outward Bound supporters and promoters.

Outward Bound exists because of the surprising fact that during World War II fewer younger men survived being torpedoed on the Murmansk, Russia convoy run than older men. Dr. Kurt Hahn, C.B.E., an emigrant German educator living in England, had observed that the older men did things to help themselves survive, such as collecting rain water for drinking, building shelters in the lifeboats, catching and eating raw fish, and learning to care for each other.

Dr. Hahn found that many of the younger seamen, by contrast, tended to sit and wait for somebody to come and rescue them. If no one came, which was often the case, they died just sitting there. Dr. Hahn felt that these seamen must have lacked a certain self-confidence or an awareness that they could take action that would result in survival, and founded Outward Bound to help young people learn that they can take charge of their own survival and lives.

The worldwide organization has been operating in the United States for 14 years; its 35,000 graduates attest to its popularity. During this time, however, Outward Bound has evolved into more of a learning institution than a survival training organization. It now operates under a variety of different notions, one of them being that industrial man has lost and should regain the art of living with nature. The organization believes that the wilderness can teach people about themselves by providing a different backdrop against which they can gain insight into their day-to-day behavior.

This article is about what happened to two women and three men on a raft for a week on the Rogue River in Oregon.

ON THE RIVER

Like most of the other 19 people on the trip, at the outset I had little or no idea of what to expect. I had participated in a few human growth encounter workshops, so I was prepared for, although again surprised at, how willingly people seem to accept the authority of a completely unknown group leader. Most people seem able to participate in all kinds of strange and, in many instances, new behaviors with no knowledge regarding the possible outcomes. This group was no exception. All of us had some notion of Outward Bound, but we knew nothing about each other, or our raft leader John, or the Rogue River.

Even though their preembarkation talk was filled with the machismo jargon I mentioned, the staff did not describe what we might actually expect to happen, nor did they talk about the many other river trips they had been on. I suppose the staff leaders assumed that the best way for a group of people to learn about themselves and each other is to let the experience talk to them directly.

The two women assigned to Raft No. 4 were named Marlene and Helen. Marlene was a recently divorced mother of five kids from Washington, whom a number of us had observed in her pink bikini in the Holiday Inn pool when we had arrived. Most of us acknowledged that because of that build we would love to have her along. Marlene used to wear her red ski suit at night and talked a lot about times she'd spent on the slopes. A top-notch skier, she said she divorced her husband because she was tired of making believe he was a better skier than she was.

Helen, a big blonde woman with a fierce sense of humor and a divorced mother of two grown boys, was at the time of our trip the president of the Fund Center in Denver, a coordinating body for local foundations, as well as a political activist. She and I became each other's clowns, and one night at a campfire she leaned over and asked me, "Bobbie, is this just another plaything of the bored rich, or can we really learn something out here in this godforsaken wilderness?" I told her I wasn't sure but we ought to give it a chance, which we did.

One of the two other men was Bill, a very successful lawyer from Darien, Connecticut. He was the only one of the four passengers who was still happily married, since I too was divorced. Bill was a busy executive, but he managed to find time for hiking, skiing, and fishing. While Outward Bound took care of all our food requirements and most of our medical needs, Raft No. 4 had its own supply officer in Bill. His backpack was organized like a Civil War surgeon's field kit. He had all his changes of clothing scheduled, and when it rained, his extra plastic rainjacket kept me dry since mine leaked like a sieve. Though he and Marlene were obviously attracted to each other from the start, it was clear from his "happy family" talk that nothing was going to change, and it didn't.

The other man was John Rhoades, our heavily mustached, vigorous leader, in his early thirties, who saw himself as a teacher, educator, and trainer. As a progressive educator, John was overdedicated to the notion that no one can learn from anyone else since learning is a singular, unique experience. At night John slept away from the rest of us under a very fancy Abercrombie and Fitch drop cloth which was made to be strung up in many different ways. Trying a new fancy pitch, John would say to Bill and me, "Be imaginative in how you pitch your tarpaulin." As we had nothing but pieces of plastic as tarpaulins, we would greet John's injunction with amused silence.

The men and women of Raft No. 4 were a warm, friendly, outgoing bunch, each of whom helped create a nice supportive atmosphere.

When we arrived at the river, each was anxious to pitch in and do his or her part. The staff distributed the rafts, each of which had a small foot pump, and Bill and I, with instruction from John, proceeded to inflate ours. It was one of our first chores, and we did it with a machismo fervor that suggested either previous knowledge, or that it was man's work, or both. Marlene and Helen carried food bags, buckets, and ropes. It was a cold day, a gray mist hung over the towering Oregon pines, and I had a feeling that at least some of us, given a choice, would have opted for going back to the Holiday Inn. There was a lot of forced joking and kidding, with which we attempted to overcome some of our anxieties—we were whistling in the dark.

John gave each of us a Mae West-type life preserver and instructed us on how to use it. He told us, "You are not to go on the raft without it." Now with all of us bulging out of our Mae Wests, a Richter scale applied to anxiety would have registered eight or a full-scale breakdown. Postponing the inevitable, we shivered, fussed, and helped each other get adjusted to our life jackets. The trip down the Rogue was beginning to have a serious quality.

The rafts we used were small, about 10 feet long and 4 feet wide. The passengers sit on the inflated outer tube with their feet on the inside. Everyone is very close together with little or no room to move around. Also, unlike a boat, a raft has no keel or rudder mechanism, which means that it tends to roll and bobble around on top of the water. Unless the occupants work as a team and use their paddles in close coordination, it is very difficult to control.

While we were still on shore, John perched himself in the helmsman position at the back of the raft and said, "OK, I am going to teach you how to navigate the Rogue. When I say 'right turn,' the two people on the left side of the raft are to paddle forward and the two on the right are to backpaddle. When I say 'left turn,' the two people on the right are to paddle forward and the two on the left are to backpaddle. When I say 'forward,' I want everyone digging that paddle in like his life depended on it, and when I say 'backpaddle,' everyone paddle backward. When I say 'hold,' all paddles out of the water. Now you got it, or should we go over it again?" We pushed the raft out over the beach pebbles and paddled out into the Rogue, which at this point seemed like a nice pond. John barked his commands, and the team did just fine in the quiet water.

John told us that we were Raft No. 4 of five rafts, and it was important to everyone's safety that each raft maintain its position so that we could make periodic personnel checks to make sure no one was missing. John gave the command "forward," and because No. 3 raft was already far ahead of us and out of sight, Marlene, Helen, Bill, and I paddled vigorously.

As we proceeded down the river, John announced, "Each of you will take turns at being the helmsman." After some comment by Helen, this term was quickly corrected to conform to the new non-discriminatory linguistics, as well as for the EEOC, to "helmsperson." John said that this person would be in charge of the raft—steering from the stern and issuing the commands.

As John talked, my mind drifted. I was suddenly overwhelmed by the grandeur and beauty of this great wilderness river road we were traveling. In awe of the hugeness of the trees, I did not hear nor respond to a command. John, a very earnest fellow, was somewhat annoyed at my daydreaming and upbraided me saying, "Look, we all have to concentrate on our job or we will be in trouble." And then he explained the nature of the rapids up ahead.

He told us how to recognize a rapid's tongue (entrance), how to avoid "sleepers" (hidden rocks), and then how to ride the "haystacks" (the choppy waves that form at the outlet of the rapids) as you come through the rapids. He said that the most important art we would learn would be how to chop our paddles into the waves as we rode the haystacks. Since a raft has no seatbelts, or even seats for that matter, unless you chop down hard the rough water can bounce you right out of it.

As we paddled through the still calm waters, trying to catch up with Raft No. 3, Helen began to complain that she was already getting tired. "I'm just not used to pushing a paddle, but I'm damn good at pushing a pencil," she said. I too was beginning to feel the strain of the paddle, but rather than admit it, I just laughed saying, "Why this is nothing, Helen. You should canoe the St. John in Maine. That would teach you." Bill chimed in with "Yeah, this is nothing compared to climbing Pike's Peak."

As we moved down the river a faint distant roar broke the silence of the forest. And as we drew nearer to it, our excitement grew bigger. One might have thought that rather than a 4-foot rapids, Niagara Falls lay dead ahead. I was relieved when, some distance before the rapids, John told us to head for the bank where we would go ashore and study the rapids. As a team we would then decide what kind of course to take through them.

We had been on the river for a few hours, and, as it would be many times during the trip, getting on dry land was a great relief. Life on a small rubber raft consists of sitting in ankle-deep cold water, anticipating a periodic refill over both the side of the raft and one's genitals. If there was not time to bail out, we would just sit in the cold water. And even if there were time we would still be soaking wet and cold from the hips down. Though this was our first chance to escape the cold water treatment, we quickly learned to look forward to such opportunities. The physical discomfort we felt together on the raft was overcoming our sense of being strangers; by the time we disembarked that first time, we were a band of fellow sufferers.

At that point on the river, the bank was very steep, so we had a tough climb up a high rock cliff to get a good look at the rapids. Just before the rapids, the river makes a sharp 90-degree bend creating an additional danger. The swiftly running river could pile the raft up on the bank or into a hidden rock. After considerable discussion, during which Bill and I tried to demonstrate to Helen and Marlene our previous if not superior knowledge of boating, we agreed on taking a left course into the tongue while at the same time trying to bear right to avoid being swept onto the bank.

Coming up and down the steep river bank Bill helped Marlene over the rocks, holding her elbow. A ways behind them Helen commented to me, "Honestly, Bob, Marlene isn't that helpless." As we climbed into the raft, Bill helped Marlene again, and I, smiling sheepishly, offered my arm to Helen. I said, holding the raft, "Well, if we go, we all go together, and may we all end up in the same hospital room." Sitting herself down, Helen said, "Who will notify next of kin since no one will be left." After they were seated, Bill and I huddled and agreed that if anything went wrong, he would look after Marlene and I would look after Helen.

Once back on the river, with John at the helm, we paddled into the rapid's tongue, where the raft picked up speed. Staying to the left but maintaining our right orientation, before we knew what had happened, we were roaring through the tongue, roller coasting through the haystacks, screaming with excitement. Flushed with our first real achievement, the raft awash with ice-cold water, we patted each other on the back on our first great success. While bailing out the raft we paid each other compliments and convinced ourselves that we could master the Rogue River.

But this was our first set of rapids, and while John assured us that we had done well, he also reminded us of the meaner rapids yet to come with such potent names as Mule Creek Canyon, Blossom Bar, Big Bend, Copper Canyon, and Grave Creek. My God, I thought, did we really have to go through all of those terrible places?

Life on the Rogue included many other things besides shooting rapids. We pitched tarpaulins every night, lugged supplies in and out of the raft, and became accustomed to the discomforts of having no running water and of being absolutely frozen after sitting in cold water for a whole day. Nothing cements a group together like collective misery, and the people of Raft No. 4 had a *real* concern for each other as mutually suffering humans.

Each raft carried a watertight supply bag of sleeping bags and personal clothing. The bag was strapped to the front of the raft and had to be carried to and fro every morning and night. When we tied up at our first campsite, Marlene and Helen each took an end and started to carry the bag from the raft up the bank. Bill ran after them yelling, "Hey, hold it. That's too heavy for you," and grabbed the bag. Throwing it over his shoulder, he said, "You shouldn't try to do that heavy stuff." Marlene smiled and said, "Bill, anytime, be my guest." Helen, who was a little annoyed, commented sarcastically, "Well, it's great to have these big, strong men around now, ain't it though?"

When we came off the raft at night, most everybody instantly undressed to put on dry clothes, caring not one fig for a leaf or modesty. But even though on the surface it looked as though the physical sex differences had disappeared, the emergency nature of things exerted a different pressure, forcing each of us to "do what you know best."

Bill and I, for example, would pitch the tarpaulins each night and haul water, while Marlene and Helen would make the beds, clean the ground, and arrange the sleeping bags. Our mutual concern was evident; it was a beautiful experience of caring for one's fellow sisters and brothers, and I loved it.

After pitching our plastic tarpaulins (which were not much bigger than queen-size beds) as protection against the rain, the four of us would wiggle into our sleeping bags for the night. The first night Helen said she thought we were "four wonderful people gone batty sleeping on the hard cold ground when they could all be in soft feather beds." We laughed and helped each other zip up, arranged sweaters as pillows, and made sure we were all protected. Raft No. 4 was a real team.

During the days, I was beginning to learn some basics about rafts and rapids. Once the raft starts down the river and enters a swiftly moving rapid, the helmsperson must give and the crew respond to commands in quick succession in order to avoid hidden rocks, suck holes, boulders, and other obstacles, which can either flip the raft over or pull it under, bouncing it back like a ball.

As we approached the second rapids, we again went ashore to "look over our approach." It was a bad situation as the rapids planed out over a very rocky riverbed. Helen suggested that we let John take the raft through while we watch. "Now, Bob," she said, "do we really care about this damn river? I don't care if we can squeak through these rocks or not. Hit your head on them or something and you could really get hurt." Bill, John, and I cheered us on.

When I became helmsperson, I discovered quickly how difficult it is to steer a raft. The helmsperson can have some effect on the direction in which the raft goes, and because Bill and I had some boating experience, we were at least familiar with the idea of using the paddle as a rudder. Neither Helen nor Marlene seemed to understand how to use a paddle that way, nor did they have the experience.

When one of the two women on our raft, more so Marlene than Helen, was the helmsperson, she would chant, "I can't do it; I can't do it." Each time they cried out neither Bill nor I would answer right away, but we would eventually try to convince them that they could. Typically, Marlene would say, "I don't know right from left. One of you guys do it; you're so much better."

At Copper Canyon we needed a "hard right" command. With Marlene at the helm, we got a "hard left" instead. Bill and I looked at each other in utter disgust.

He asked Marlene, "What's the matter, honey?"

She said, "I don't know right from left. You be the helmsperson."

He said, "Why don't we write on the back of your hands 'right' and 'left'?"

Bill was kidding, but the next thing I knew, they were doing it.

Helen was mad and said to me, "Is it really necessary to make a baby out of her?"

"No," I said, "of course not. But she really doesn't know right from left."

As Marlene would say, "I can't do it," Bill and I would say, "Of course you can do it. It's easy; you're doing fine." All the time we were speaking, we were thinking, "Ye gods! When is she going to give up?" Each time either Marlene or Helen would be helmsperson, we'd have the same conversation; each time Bill's and my reassurances would be more and more halfhearted. Before long we weren't responding at all.

As the days wore on, Bill and I proceeded subtly but surely to take charge. The teamwork was unraveling. When we approached a tongue, if either Marlene or Helen were helmsperson, Bill and I would look at each other, and with very slight headshakes and grimaces we would indicate agreement that things were not going well at all. Once we had established that things were not going well, we then felt free to take our own corrective measures, such as trying to steer the raft from our forward paddle positions, an almost impossible thing to do. Not only is running the raft from the front not at all helpful to the person at the helm, but also if the helmsperson is not aware of the counterforces, the raft can easily turn around like a carousel. The unaware helmsperson is then totally out of control. When that would happen, Marlene would say, "I just don't know what's wrong with me," and Helen would echo, "I don't know what's wrong with me either." Bill's and my disgust would mount.

Eventually, John became fed up with the inability of the bunch on Raft No. 4 to work together, which was mainly a result, he said, of the two "captains" in the front. As a last resort he ordered each one of us to give a single command that he or she would shout as needed. My command was "hold," Bill's command was "left," Marlene's was "right," and Helen's was "backpaddle." John's teaching objective was to get the four of us working together, or else. Needless to say, "or else" prevailed.

On the fifth day, Marlene was helmsperson. Bill and I were in the bow, silently anxious. Even voluble Helen was silent as the raft approached a fast-moving chute. At that time only a clear, concise, direct command and a rapid response would be of any use at all.

Instead of a "hard right" command, we had no command. Marlene froze, the raft slid up on a big boulder, and in an instant we flipped over like a flapjack on a griddle. The current was swift and swept the five of us away in different directions. As I splashed around in the cold water, cursing that "goddamned dumb Marlene," I spotted Bill nearby. The two of us began together to look for Marlene and Helen, whom we found each grappling with paddles and gear they'd grabbed as the raft had gone over. We assured each other we were OK and expressed relief at finding each other.

Cold, wet, and shivering uncontrollably, we made our way out of the river. To warm us and to keep us moving, John chased us around the bank to get wood for a fire. He stuffed us with candies and other sweets to give us energy. As we stood around the fire, chilled and wet, unable to stop shaking, we talked about what had happened, and why.

There was mutiny in the air now and a consensus emerged. The four of us were furious at John and blamed him for our predicament. John retreated, but finally we were agreed that we would not have any more of this kind of thing. Regardless of John's wishes, anyone who did not want to be helmsperson could simply pass. Marlene was certain that she wanted no part of being at the helm, and Helen, though less sure, was happy to say, "Yeah, I just want to stay dry. Let you guys take the helm."

After becoming somewhat dry, sober, and a bit remorseful, the crew of Raft No. 4 returned to the river to resume our run down the Rogue. We had lost our No. 4 position, the other rafts having run past us. John was helmsperson. Helen and Marlene were settled into the backpaddle seats. Bill and I, miffed over our mishap, felt self-conscious and fell silent thinking of the inevitable joshing we'd receive from the other rafts.

We slowly overcame the tensions of our crisis, and as the trip came to an end, we were friends again; the fifth day was forgotten. As we climbed out of the raft for the last time, Marlene said, "Well, the next raft trip I take, it will be as a passenger and not as a crew member."

That last night on the Rogue, we celebrated with a big party. The women dressed up in improvised bangles and baubles. I was the maitre d', and none of us thought much about what really had happened on Raft No. 4.

5

ALIGNMENTS
AND REALIGNMENTS

In a complex corporate situation, the individual requires and deserves the support of the group. If people cannot find such support from their organization, they don't know how to act.

—Bowen H. McCoy

T he title of this section was inspired by the central argument in Culbert and McDonough's award winning book, *The Invisible War.* A selection from their book explaining and illustrating the concept of alignment or matching the needs of the individual with those of the job, is the first piece in the section. Our other selections illustrate how individuals in other settings seek, with varying degrees of success, to construct their personal alignments in the situations with which they are confronted, or how they strive for a successful realignment when their personal needs dictate such action.

Sometimes the pressures managers experience from senior management to maintain production on the one hand, and from a volatile, militant, and unionized labor force on the other, make it impossible for these individuals to achieve and maintain a satisfactory alignment between their needs and the demands of their job. Matt Zaleski, the principal character in the selection from Arthur Hailey's *Wheels* provides a vivid illustration of just such a situation. Those who have read Hailey's book will recall that ultimately the pressures Zaleski experienced led to his untimely death.

In "Memo to White-Collar Workers," Adam Fisher underscores Culbert and McDonough's message concerning the importance of congruence between one's personal values and the occupational choices we make. Speaking in favor of self-employment, he argues that work itself is not the important issue. What is important is knowing "Who am I?" and doing whatever is compatible with one's personal values and experience.

The next two selections illustrate the very real problems some individuals may experience when the work they do runs counter to their moral convictions. The first piece relates the plight of some engineers who are employed in companies whose work is largely defense related. Yet in the case of the engineers discussed in this piece, circumstances are such that the individuals feel boxed in, unable to find a satisfactory alternative. Indeed, the price of exercising one's moral convictions may be very high. John Madeley presents this type of case in "Whistle-blower Paid High Price."

Stanley Adams is the whistle-blower who revealed the illicit trading practices of a giant international firm and as a consequence suffered almost incredible harassment, the tragic loss of his wife, and financial ruin.

Yet as the next two pieces illustrate, many individuals do break out successfully from situations in which their alignment has crumbled. In "Life Without Work," Bernard Lefkowitz relates several incidents of this sort as does Walter Kiechel III in "Starting Over."

Mid-life career changes, we are told, are becoming increasingly common. Those of us who teach in MBA programs can think of many individuals who in their mid-thirties or early forties decided on a drastic occupational change. Within the past few years we have encountered MBA students who have abandoned successful careers as teachers, school administrators, lawyers and even a psychiatrist and a general surgeon, both of whom had been earning excellent incomes in their previous professions. Such a change, however, is not without risk as Kiechel points out in his "Starting Over" piece.

The necessity of adjusting our alignment as we age is the subject of "Fighting Off Old Age" by John Leo. While modern geriatric medicine has greatly increased our life expectancy, Leo argues that our mental attitude and changing the organization of our lives to conform with our changed physical capabilities is critical.

The final piece in this section, the "Parable of the Sadhu" by Bowen H. McCoy is perhaps the most provocative. Here the frequent conflict between individual and corporate ethics is brought into sharp focus. The author leaves us with some penetrating questions that merit serious thought by all those who would seek to manage either business or government organizations.

The Invisible War: Pursuing Self-Interest at Work

Samuel A. Culbert and John J. McDonough

Each time people enter a new work situation they engage in the implicit process of *aligning* personal values, interests, and skills with what they perceive to be the task requirements of their job. They seek an orientation that maximizes self-pursuits and organizational contribution. *Alignment* is our term for the orientation that results from such an effort, however implicitly this takes place. Once such an orientation has been evolved, it becomes a self-convenient lens through which all organizational happenings are viewed. That is, once people hit on an alignments—an orientation that lines self-interests up with the task requirements of their jobs—this alignment serves to alert them to meanings they can use in promoting and supporting their personal and organizational endeavors, and to meanings put forth by others which threaten the credibility and relevance of what they are pursuing.

Not all alignments are effective. That is, the orientation some people use is too far removed either from the needs and obligations of their jobs or from expressing the inner themes that can make their jobs personally meaningful. We say an individual possesses an "effective" alignment when the orientation directing that person's actions and view of reality allows him or her to represent important self-interests while making a contribution to the organization. We say an individual lacks an effective alignment when important discrepancies exist between what that person inwardly values, endeavors to express, does well, and needs to do in order to satisfy what he or she perceives to be the task requirements of the job.

Now we can return to the questions raised at the beginning of this chapter.

Why do people with the same job perform their assignments so differently?

Easy, they have unique interests, values, and competencies to bootleg into their jobs at every opportunity.

Why do people with comparable organizational goals see the same situation differently and fight unyieldingly over which interpretation is correct?

Easy, while they may be striving to attain comparable organizational objectives, what they are striving to attain in their lives and careers is very different. This causes them to attend differently to each of the elements in a given situation. Finally,

What determines the specific way individuals decide to perform their jobs and how they interpret each situation?

Easy again, it's what we've termed alignment. People proceed with a job orientation that spontaneously spins out interpretations and meanings that serve the unique way they need reality constructed in order to be a "success." How individuals do a job and what they see are influenced by what they find personally interesting, by the concepts they can master and the skills they can perform with excellence, by the self-ideals and values they seek to attain, by their unique ideas of what constitutes career advancement, by what they believe will score on the checklist that others will use in evaluating their performance, and by what they genuinely believe the organization needs from someone in their role.

Few people are all that aware of their alignment. Even fewer are conscious of the fact that systematic biases permeate their view of the organizational world. And, almost no one understands that such biases play a major role in making organizations effective. All this is because most people work their alignment out implicitly and take its presence for granted until a change in the external scene, in other people's views of their effectiveness, or in their own sense of satisfaction show it to be obsolete. Then they can appreciate what they lost and strive for a new alignment that will again allow them to satisfy self-interests and personal pride while getting acclaim for doing a good job. For example, consider what happened to a middle manager named Pete who had a marvelous alignment until he got promoted and suddenly found himself faced with a serious gap between his own and the organization's definition of success.

Pete was one of twenty in his corporation who, some five years ago, agreed to take on a newly created mission, that of improving communications and managerial competence within his company. This function seemed right up Pete's alley. He'd attended sensitivity training sessions, had a reputation of being genuinely concerned with people, and was respected up and down the ranks for his leadership ability even though he had not burned up the track with his progress.

Pete saw the new assignment as a chance to bolster a lagging career. He had never been overly concerned with rising in the hierarchy, but his failure to take a fast track to the top was presenting him with daily redundancies that left him feeling somewhat stale. At forty-five he needed another challenge and this assignment held the potential to revitalize his career. Eagerly he accepted.

Pete threw himself into the new position. He enrolled in outside courses and hired skilled consultants to design training programs for the corporation's managers. Whenever possible he assisted the consultants and within a short time he understood their technology and was able to play a role in tailoring their inputs to the specific needs of his corporation. His learning continued and soon he was running programs on his own, involving personnel from each divisional level. Almost immediately his reputation as a man who genuinely cared was enhanced by widespread recognition of his competence in the management development technologies. And he was no soft touch either. He aggressively challenged managers on their "self-sealing" logics and constructed boat-rocking experiments to confront higher-ups with the demotivating and profit-eroding consequences of their autocratic styles.

Pete's involvements took an exciting turn with the advent of minority and women's consciousness. If the corporation's managers weren't racist, their de facto hiring and promotion policies were. This meant a greater volume of work and warranted an increase in the size of his staff. From a resource base that started with himself and a secretary, his department increased to two professionals, an administrative assistant, and two secretaries. Their operation hummed. They did career development counseling with secretaries. They got involved with the corporation's recruiters, both to encourage the hiring of blacks and females and to create programs that would support the new employees' progress in an essentially all white male management structure. They hired racial-awareness consultants to get managers in touch with their prejudices and help them work these out. And with this heightened workload, Pete even found time to continue his efforts in getting managers to identify areas in which their style intruded on the effectiveness of others.

Pete also had marvelous latitude in job definition which he exploited to match his interests and values. He enrolled in personal growth courses, attended conventions, joined professional associations, and on occasion even used the company plane. Because Pete identified both with the welfare of people and the productivity of the corporation and was concerned that his work produce tangible outcomes, his indulgences were hardly noticed—rather they were seen as part of his power. The people on his staff looked up to him and nondefensively brought him their toughest problems for coaching and support. His credibility with people lower in the hierarchy provided him a position of influence with those at the highest corporate levels. And, delightfully for Pete, his reputation among blacks and women was impeccable.

Within a couple of years Pete had worked out an ideal *alignment*. He had a way of engaging each constituency that allowed them to see how his actions related to results they valued. There seemed to be a 99 percent overlap between his personal definition of success and the missions and responsibilities assigned to him, and no one in the company could perform them better.

The other nineteen managers receiving the same charter as Pete, but working elsewhere in the corporation, didn't fare nearly as well. Perhaps lack of know-how, perhaps enculturation in the corporation's way of doing things, or perhaps a different tolerance for conflict had made them reluctant to aggressively challenge higher-ups. With time, to a greater or lesser degree, their roles degenerated to those of commiserator and management "go-for." They always seemed to be on the defensive, trying to prove themselves rather than challenging others to be more excellent. Their weakness and low-keyed tactics made Pete's strength and accomplishments look all the more potent.

Eventually those sitting in upper corporate echelons took notice of the overall situation and decided that Pete was the role model of what they were trying to achieve. They approached Pete with an offer of a promotion if he would agree to supervise and train the other nineteen managers. Pete's first reaction was to accept, but something held him back. At the time, he didn't understand his hesitancy, so he merely used it to negotiate a sweeter deal. He would not take responsibility for the others, there were too many bad habits to overcome. But he would step up a level in his current territory and accept overall responsibility for recruitment, career planning, minority advancement, and improved managerial functioning.

Pete's promotion put him on the same level with other line managers. He became a regular member of the management team and now directly supervised three managers who were responsible for about forty professional employees and oversaw the hiring of outside consultants.

Unfortunately, at this point, his alignment fell apart and his work life became filled with aggravation. *First*, his former associates began treating him like their boss, which he was, and this severely undermined his ability to coach and openly suggest. Now his suggestions were heard as orders and his inadvertent questions were received as well-thought-out criticisms.

Next, his relationships with blacks and women went to pot. His elevation in the hierarchy caused him to be seen as manager rather than human rights worker and he was treated to rounds of Mau-Mauing and confrontations, as what formerly had been received as his in-group remarks were interpreted as racial and sexist slurs.

Next, Pete found that the added amount of time his new job required for supervision, staff meetings, and report writing reduced the time available for the internal consulting role he prized.

On top of everything else, a "screw-up" in another division involving a racial-awareness consultant set off a reactionary wave up to an executive vice-president who responded by ordering sharp cutbacks in the use of outside consultants. For Pete, this had the personal effect of cutting off sources of his support and learning and the task effect of withdrawing the quality resources needed to keep his operation competently stationed and challenging to the status quo.

To top these disappointments, after about three months in the new job, Pete's boss called him in for a coaching session where he received word that his new peers were concerned that he was hurting his career by appearing to be such a deviant and advocate for minorities. Pete returned to his office screaming, "What the hell is going on here, these are the same jokers who wanted me promoted because I *was* such a deviant?!"

This was the last straw. Not only were his former constituents treating him like one of the "other guys" but the "other guys" were claiming that he was too much of a deviant for them.

From our perspective Pete was caught without either a personally effective or an organizationally successful alignment. His personal viewpoint wasn't registering anywhere. Nowhere was he actively shaping reality. His alignment had become obsolete. He was in the same position his nineteen former counterparts had found themselves in when they were charged with a mission to which they could not personally relate and thus could not confidently assert an articulate point of view.

Incidentally, and no pun intended, this is not a case of the "Peter Principle." We know Pete and he's anything but a person who had been promoted above his level of competence. We believe it is just a matter of time before Pete constructs a new alignment, one that allows him to use his new job for personal expression and to further the mission he values. But until he gets realigned, the self-deliberations entailed in trying to match self-interests with what seems to be required by his job will provide him with many lonely hours of unhappiness and frustration.

Pete's story was chosen because it illustrates the active dimension of the orienting process we call alignment. It shows the importance of an individual's commitment to inner values. That Pete could succeed, both inwardly and outwardly, where nineteen others could not is a tribute to his success in finding a good match between his personal needs and interests and what he saw as needed by the job. He had an effective alignment. The nineteen others lacked an effective alignment and most of them became either *cynics* or *careerists.* The cynics converged on alignments that subordinated the organization's needs to their own interests and values. They saw management's view as constraints to be navigated around, not perspectives to be joined and possibly learned from. Conversely, the careerists adopted alignments that subordinated their personal interests and values to what they thought would score on the organization checklist. They ground out workshop after workshop, training event after training event, but without the conversations and conflicts that could budge the status quo.

The concept of alignment, and Pete's story, provides support for most people's contention that repackaging themselves to fit a particular job or role does not constitute a sell-out to the job, although to an outsider their compromises frequently appear fatal. As Pete's situation illustrates, people need to shift alignments when they change jobs or experience a new set of external demands, even though their interests, skills and values remain the same. While self-interests remain relatively constant, the form in which they are pursued and expressed must shift. How often we've seen people criticize the way their boss operates only to themselves embody much of the same behavior as they shift alignments upon moving up to the boss's level in the organization.

In summary, we see the concept of alignment as a key addition to how people should be thinking about organizations. There's a level of organization residing within each individual that explains how that person does his or her job and views external organization events. If there's an external organization that determines how groups of people relate in doing work together then there's an *internal organization*, far more encompassing than an individual's personality, that determines how individuals within groups transact their business and work for the greater institutional good. Moreover, despite their lack of prominence in how people present themselves, self-interests are a dominant factor in determining what gets produced in the name of organizationally required product and how what is produced is received. And you don't need the skills of a psychoanalyst to understand these self-interests. You merely need to comprehend what an individual is trying to express personally and achieve in his or her career, and what he or she perceives as making a valuable contribution to the job. At every point personal needs and organization goals impact on one another, and it's always up in the air whether the needs of the job or the interests of the individual will swamp the other or whether a synergy of interests will evolve.

Thus *alignment* is our term for the highly personal orientation one takes to the job that must be known before we can comprehend the meaning and intent of someone's actions. Sometimes people do different things for the same reason. Sometimes people do the same things for different reasons. Without knowing people's alignment, taking their actions on face value—even those with a direct connection to bottom-line product—leads to erroneous conclusions. The only way to comprehend what people are about is to know what they are trying to express and achieve personally and what assumptions they are making about the organizational avenues for doing so.

At this point we provide a guide to comprehending the personal side of an individual's orientation to the job. It's a set of questions which, when thoughtfully answered, provide a new perspective on why an individual does his or her job the way he or she does it, and why that person views organization events in a particular way. Add in the task requisites of the job, as the individual sees them, and you've got that person's alignment. Incidentally, we've had marvelous results using an abbreviated list of these questions as preparation for team-building meetings at which a boss and his or her subordinates get together for a long session to discuss opportunities for improving their work-group's effectiveness. Twenty to forty minutes each, around the group, and the edge comes off many premeeting criticisms. Instead of being programmed to fault one another for inadequacy, the discussion takes a constructive turn as participants contrast the fit between an individual's needs and talents with what participants see as the task requisites of that person's job.

The questions we use in seeking to understand the self-interest side of an individual's alignment fall into three categories: personal, career, and organizational. Specifically we ask questions drawn from, but not limited to, the following list.

SELF-INTEREST QUESTIONS

Personal

- What are you trying to prove to yourself and, very importantly, why?
- What are you trying to prove to others? Give an instance that illustrates why and how.
- What style of life are you trying to maintain or achieve? (Does this entail a change in income? geography? family size? etc.)
- Name the people who have played significant roles in your life and say what those roles were.
- What dimensions would you like to add to your personal life and why?
- What motto would you like to have carved on your tombstone and how do you want to be remembered by the people who are close to you?

Career

- What profession do you want to wind up in? (If you are an engineer and you say "management," tell why. If you are not in that profession, say how you plan to get into it.)
- How did you, or will you, develop competency in that profession?
- What do you want to accomplish in that profession?
- What honor or monument would you like to have symbolize your success in that profession? Say why it would constitute a personal hallmark.

Organizational

- What has been your image in your organization and what would you like it to be?
- Describe a bum-rap or overly simplistic category others have used in describing you and tell either why you are different now or why their statement was simplistic or too categorical.
- What is the next lesson you need to learn and what are your plans for doing so?
- What would you like to be doing two to five years out?*
- What would you like to be doing ten years out?*

While we encourage people to share perspectives generated by these questions with work associates whom they trust, we do not recommend that they reveal specific instances in which self-interests played a role in determining one of their organizational actions. We don't because we fear that others, however well-intentioned, will inadvertently misuse such candor later on. What we advocate is that each individual simply provide associates a more valid context for viewing his or her goals and accomplishments. . . .

CONCLUSION

It's appropriate that we've saved our favorite story for the end. It's a story about a manager who embodies the best of both the subjective and the rational approaches to leadership and for us is a symbol that it can be done. This manager is able to go toe to toe with hard-boiled characters like Charlie and at the same time remain sensitive to the contributions made by leaders like Fred.** He's a manager who searches for ways of relating to the uniqueness of those reporting to him while he shuns calling "objective" that which he sees as arbitrary and a matter of personal convenience.

The manager we have in mind demonstrated the effectiveness of much that we are advocating in three distinct settings: industry, education, and public service. First, he fought his way through the highly competitive world of consumer products where he became chairman of the board of one of the nation's largest and most successful conglomerates. Next, in the educational field, he became the dean of a large and prestigious professional school, instituting changes that brought national recognition to that institution. And most recently he was the President's choice to head a world-renowned agency and this appointment brought instant acclamation from the Senate Hearings Committee. All this took place before his forty-seventh birthday!

In our view the key to this manager's success lies in his ability to see the connection between personal effectiveness and organizational efficiency. To him, these are highly related issues. He believes that organizations exist to serve people, not the other way around, and he constantly searches to understand what people are trying to achieve in the way of personal meaning and career success. Nevertheless, his style is one which frequently gets misinterpreted as soft and permissive leadership and does not produce an easy route to universal love and appreciation. His understanding of personal projects allows him to penetrate many of the facades people construct, and this makes him the target of behind-the-scenes ambivalence and face-to-face suspicion. Let's examine his impact more closely.

In the first place, he resists spending the bulk of his energies responding to problems defined by others as "crises." This orientation allows him to take tough stands with respect to the succession of "crises" any top administrator faces, and which, if passed down through the organization, can make it impossible for anyone to align self-interests with the task requirements of their job in a way that's constructive for the institution. In the short run his "nonresponsiveness" makes him vulnerable to the charge that he is not on top of a situation. In the long run, however, he frees himself and the people in his organization from the oppressive burden of always responding to someone else's fire drill.

We certainly don't want to mislead you into thinking that our hero, or any other leader, could emerge from each of these settings totally unscarred. To the contrary, on his way to the board chairmanship he spent more than three years going eyeball to eyeball with a manager whose style was the antithesis of his own and whose subordinates consider him to be "the biggest prick you're ever going to find in a chief executive's office." When our leader realized that he was going to be locked in mortal combat for as long as he stayed with the conglomerate, he began to look around. That's when he got into education. Some say things got too hot for him to handle. In our minds his decision revealed that he saw more to life than surviving corporate death struggles.

It's interesting to contrast the subordinates who value his leadership style with those who don't. Those who see flexibility in the construction of their own alignments generally appreciate his style. But he causes fits among those with careerist and martyr mentalities. These people are confused by his respect for the personal side of their alignments. They mistake his sensitivity to what is personally meaningful to them as agreement with their self-beneficial formulations of what the organization needs to do. Consequently they experience small betrayals when learning of a decision he takes after surveying their perspective. What they don't understand is that our hero seriously considers competing perspectives prior to making a decision and that his integration is almost always original, with even the people who influenced him the most finding themselves unable to identify their input in what he prints out. But for those with open-ended questions, his print-outs are almost always educational. By factoring out what he added, they deduce what his leader sees as the limitations in their formulations.

For almost everyone, his style is disarming. His searching respect for the subjective side of an individual's participation is responded to as a warm and irresistible invitation to tell all. This makes it quite difficult to fragment. Knowing that he knows their subjective interests causes most people to tell their whole story—either out of a fear of looking stupid or one of getting caught telling a half-truth. In subtle ways this leader conveys the message that he's not there simply to serve the self-indulgent needs of individuals but to provide another perspective on what the organization needs and to challenge people to find a more synergistic means of relating their needs to organization product. And he's been able to do this and still score on the traditional checklist.

In many ways this leader is bigger than life; certainly his accomplishments surpass what most of us are externally striving to achieve. Today's society seems to worship external success, yet each of us knows that we're up to so much more. Our hero often strikes us as a very lonely man and we can't help but think that a major part of what appears to be a self-imposed solitude derives from an understanding that, in today's world, his accomplishments are valued for reasons which bear little resemblance to what he sets out to do. But help should be on the way. We believe the evaluation categories which convey illusions of objectivity and overemphasize externals will gradually change. And as more people demonstrate an enhanced appreciation for the subjective involvements that everyone brings to organization life, this leader, together with the rest of us, will have an easier time being himself and gaining recognition for just that.

NOTES

*Think of "doing" in terms of a specific assignment (job, position, status) and specify it in terms of a specific role (player, coach, expert) and how you would like to be performing it.

**Charlie and Fred are characters introduced earlier in the book from which this excerpt is taken.—Eds.

Wheels

Arthur Hailey

At a car assembly plant north of the Fisher Freeway, Matt Zaleski, assistant plant manager and a graying veteran of the auto industry, was glad that today was Wednesday.

Not that the day would be free from urgent problems and exercises in survival—no day ever was. Tonight, like any night, he would go homeward wearily, feeling older than his fifty-three years and convinced he had spent another day of his life inside a pressure cooker. Matt Zaleski sometimes wished he could summon back the energy he had had as a young man, either when he was new to auto production or as an Air Force bombardier in World War II. He also thought sometimes, looking back, that the years of war—even though he was in Europe in the thick of things, with an impressive combat record— were less crisis-filled than his civil occupation now.

Already, in the few minutes he had been in his glass-paneled office on a mezzanine above the assembly plant floor, even while removing his coat, he had skimmed through a red-tabbed memo on the desk—a union grievance which he realized immediately could cause a plant-wide walkout if it wasn't dealt with properly and promptly. There was undoubtedly still more to worry about in an adjoining pile of papers—other headaches, including critical material shortages (there were always some, each day), or quality control demands, or machinery failures, or some new conundrum which no one had thought of before, any or all of which could halt the assembly line and stop production.

Zaleski threw his stocky figure into the chair at his gray metal desk, moving in short, jerky movements, as he always had. He heard the chair protest—a reminder of his growing overweight and the big belly he carried around nowadays. He thought ashamedly; he could never squeeze it now into the cramped nose dome of a B-17. He wished that worry would take off pounds; instead, it seemed to put them on, especially since Freda died and loneliness at night drove him to the refrigerator, nibbling, for lack of something else to do.

But at least today was Wednesday.

First things first. He hit the intercom switch for the general office; his secretary wasn't in yet. A timekeeper answered.

"I want Parkland and the union committeeman," the assistant plant manager commanded. "Get them in here fast."

Parkland was a foreman. And outside they would be well aware which union committeeman he meant because they would know about the red-tabbed memo on his desk. In a plant, bad news traveled like burning gasoline.

The pile of papers—still untouched, though he would have to get to them soon—reminded Zaleski he had been thinking gloomily of the many causes which could halt an assembly line.

Halting the line, stopping production for whatever reason, was like a sword in the side to Matt Zaleski. The function of his job, his personal *raison d'être*, was to keep the line moving, with finished cars being driven off the end at the rate of one car a minute, no matter how the trick was done or if, at times, he felt like a juggler with fifteen balls in the air at once. Senior management wasn't interested in the juggling act, or excuses either. Results were what counted: quotas, daily production, manufacturing costs. But if the line stopped he heard about it soon enough. Each single minute of lost time meant that an entire car didn't get produced, and the loss would never be made up. Thus, even a two- or three-minute stoppage cost thousands of dollars because, while an assembly line stood still, wages and other costs went rollicking on.

But at least today was Wednesday.

The intercom clicked. "They're on their way, Mr. Zaleski."

He acknowledged curtly.

The reason Matt Zaleski liked Wednesday was simple. Wednesday was two days removed from Monday, and Friday was two more days away.

Mondays and Fridays in auto plants were management's most harrowing days because of absenteeism. Each Monday, more hourly paid employees failed to report for work than on any other normal weekday; Friday ran a close second. It happened because after paychecks were handed out, usually on Thursday, many workers began a long boozy or drugged weekend, and afterward, Monday was a day for catching up on sleep or nursing hangovers.

Thus, on Mondays and Fridays, other problems were eclipsed by one enormous problem of keeping production going despite a critical shortage of people. Men were moved around like marbles in a game of Chinese checkers. Some were removed from tasks they were accustomed to and given jobs they had never done before. A worker who normally tightened wheel nuts might find himself fitting front fenders, often with the briefest of instruction or sometimes none at all. Others, pulled in hastily from labor pools or less skilled duties—such as loading trucks or sweeping—would be put to work wherever gaps remained. Sometimes they caught on quickly in their temporary roles; at other times they might spend an entire shift installing heater hose clamps, or something similar—upside down.

The result was inevitable. Many of Monday's and Friday's cars were shoddily put together, with built-in legacies of trouble for their owners, and those in the know avoided them like contaminated meat. A few big city dealers, aware of the problem and with influence at factories because of volume sales, insisted that cars for more valued customers be built on Tuesday, Wednesday, or Thursday, and customers who knew the ropes sometimes went to big dealers with this objective. Cars for company executives and their friends were invariably scheduled for one of the midweek days.

The door of the assistant plant manager's office flung open abruptly. The foreman he had sent for, Parkland, strode in, not bothering to knock.

Parkland was a broad-shouldered, big-boned man in his late thirties, about fifteen years younger than Matt Zaleski. He might have been a football fullback if he had gone to college, and, unlike many foreman nowadays, looked as if he could handle authority. He also looked, at the moment, as if he expected trouble and was prepared to meet it. The foreman's face was glowering. There was a darkening bruise, Zaleski noted, beneath his right cheekbone.

Ignoring the mode of entry, Zaleski motioned him to a chair. "Take the weight off your feet, then simmer down."

They faced each other across the desk.

"I'm willing to hear your version of what happened," the assistant plant chief said, "but don't waste time because the way this reads"—he fingered the red-tabbed grievance report—"you've cooked us all a hot potato."

"The hell I cooked it!" Parkland glared at his superior; above the bruise his face flushed red. "I fired a guy because he slugged me. What's more, I'm gonna make it stick, and if you've got any guts or justice you'd better back me up."

Matt Zaleski raised his voice to the bull roar he had learned on a factory floor. "Knock off that goddam nonsense, right now!" He had no intention of letting this get out of hand. More reasonably, he growled, "I said simmer down, and meant it. When the time comes I'll decide who to back and why. And there'll be no more crap from you about guts and justice. Understand?"

Their eyes locked together. Parkland's dropped first.

"All right, Frank," Matt said. "Let's start over, and this time give it to me straight, from the beginning."

He had known Frank Parkland a long time. The foreman's record was good and he was usually fair with men who worked under him. It had taken something exceptional to get him as riled as this.

"There was a job out of position," Parkland said. "It was steering column bolts, and there was this kid doing it; he's new, I guess. He was crowding the next guy. I wanted the job put back."

Zaleski nodded. It happened often enough. A worker with a specific assignment took a few seconds longer than he should on each operation.

As successive cars moved by on the assembly line, his position gradually changed, so that soon he was intruding on the area of the next operation. When a foreman saw it happen he made it his business to help the worker back to his correct, original place.

Zaleski said impatiently, "Get on with it."

Before they could continue, the office door opened again and the union committeeman came in. He was a small, pink-faced man, with thick-lensed glasses and a fussy manner. His name was Illas and, until a union election a few months ago, had been an assembly line worker himself.

"Good morning," the union man said to Zaleski. He nodded curtly to Parkland, without speaking.

Matt Zaleski waved the newcomer to a chair. "We're just getting to the meat."

"You could save a lot of time," Illas said, "if you read the grievance report."

"I've read it. But sometimes I like to hear the other side." Zaleski motioned Parkland to go on.

"All I did," the foreman said, "was call another guy over and say, 'Help me get this man's job back in position.'"

"And I say you're a liar!" The union man hunched forward accusingly; now he swung toward Zaleski. "What he really said was 'get this *boy's* job back.' And it so happened that the person he was speaking of, and calling, 'boy,' was one of our black brothers to whom that word is a very offensive term."

"Oh, for God's sake!" Parkland's voice combined anger with disgust. "D'you think I don't know that? D'you think I haven't been around here long enough to know better than to use that word that way?"

"But you *did* use it, didn't you?"

"Maybe, just maybe, I did. I'm not saying yes, because I don't remember, and that's the truth. But if it happened, there was nothing meant. It was a slip, that's all."

The union man shrugged. "That's your story now."

"It's no story, you son-of-a-bitch!"

Illas stood up. "Mr. Zaleski, I'm here officially, representing the United Auto Workers. If that's the kind of language . . ."

"There'll be no more of it," the assistant plant manager said. "Sit down, please, and while we're on the subject, I suggest you be less free yourself with the word 'liar.'"

Parkland slammed a beefy fist in frustration on the desk top. "I said it was no story, and it isn't. What's more, the guy I was talking about didn't even give a thought to what I said, at least before all the fuss was made."

"That's not the way *he* tells it," Illas said.

"Maybe not now," Parkland appealed to Zaleski. "Listen, Matt, the guy who was out of position is just a kid. A black kid, maybe seventeen.

I've got nothing against him; he's slow, but he was doing his job. I've got a kid brother his age. I go home, I say, 'Where's the boy?' Nobody thinks twice about it. That's the way it was with this thing until this other guy, Newkirk, cut in."

Illas persisted, "But you're admitting you used the word 'boy.' "

Matt Zaleski said wearily, "Okay, okay, he used it. Let's all concede that."

Zaleski was holding himself in, as he always had to when racial issues erupted in the plant. His own prejudices were deep-rooted and largely anti-black, and he had learned them in the heavily Polish suburb of Wyandotte where he was born. There, the families of Polish origin looked on Negroes with contempt, as shiftless and trouble makers. In return, the black people hated Poles, and even nowadays, throughout Detroit, the ancient enmities persisted. Zaleski, through necessity, had learned to curb his instinct; you couldn't run a plant with as much black labor as this one and let your prejudices show, at least not often. Just now, after the last remark of Illas, Matt Zaleski had been tempted to inject: *So what if he did call him "boy"? What the hell difference does it make? When a foreman tells him to, let the bastard get back to work.* But Zaleski knew it would be repeated and maybe cause more trouble than before. Instead, he growled, "What matters is what came after."

"Well," Parkland said, "I thought we'd never get to that. We almost had the job back in place, then this heavyweight, Newkirk, showed up."

"He's another black brother," Illas said.

"Newkirk'd been working down the line. He didn't even hear what happened; somebody else told him. He came up, called me a racist pig, and slugged me." The foreman fingered his bruised face which had swollen even more since he came in.

Zaleski asked sharply, "Did you hit him back?"

"No."

"I'm glad you showed a little sense."

"I had sense, all right," Parkland said. "I fired Newkirk. On the spot. Nobody slugs a foreman around here and gets away with it."

"We'll see about that," Illas said. "A lot depends on circumstances and provocation."

Matt Zaleski thrust a hand through his hair; there were days when he marveled that there was any left. This whole stinking situation was something which McKernon, the plant manager, should handle, but McKernon wasn't here. He was ten miles away at staff headquarters, attending a conference about the new Orion, a super-secret car the plant would be producing soon. Sometimes it seemed to Matt Zaleski as if McKernon had already begun his retirement, officially six months away.

Matt Zaleski was holding the baby now, as he had before, and it was a lousy deal. Zaleski wasn't even going to succeed McKernon, and he knew it. He'd already been called in and shown the official assessment of himself, the assessment which appeared in a loose-leaf, leather-bound book which sat permanently on the desk of the Vice-President, Manufacturing. The book was there so that the vice-president could turn its pages whenever new appointments or promotions were considered. The entry for Matt Zaleski, along with his photo and other details, read: "This individual is well placed at his present level of management."

Everybody in the company who mattered knew that the formal, unctuous statement was a "kiss off." What it really meant was: *This man has gone as high as he's going. He will probably serve his time out in his present spot, but will receive no more promotions.*

The rules said that whoever received that deadly summation on his docket had to be told; he was entitled to that much, and it was the reason Matt Zaleski had known for the past several months that he would never rise beyond his present role of assistant manager. Initially the news had been a bitter disappointment, but now that he had grown used to the idea, he also knew why: He was old shoe, the hind end of a disappearing breed which management and boards of directors didn't want any more in the top critical posts. Zaleski had risen by a route which few senior plant people followed nowadays—factory worker, inspector, foreman, superintendent, assistant plant manager. He hadn't had an engineering degree to start, having been a high school dropout before World War II. But after the war he had armed himself with a degree, using night school and GI credits, and after that had started climbing, being ambitious, as most of his generation were who had survived *Festung Europa* and other perils. But, as Zaleski recognized later, he had lost too much time; his real start came too late. The strong comers, the top echelon material of the auto companies—then as now—were the bright youngsters who arrived fresh and eager through the direct college-to-front office route.

But that was no reason why McKernon, who was still plant boss, should sidestep this entire situation, even if unintentionally. The assistant manager hesitated. He would be within his rights to send for McKernon and could do it here and now by picking up a phone.

Two things stopped him. One, he admitted to himself, was pride; Zaleski knew he could handle this as well as McKernon, if not better. The other: His instinct told him there simply wasn't time.

Abruptly, Zaleski asked Illas, "What's the union asking?"

"Well, I've talked with the president of our local . . ."

"Let's save all that," Zaleski said. "We both know we have to start somewhere, so what is it you want?"

"Very well," the committeeman said. "We insist on three things. First, immediate reinstatement of Brother Newkirk, with compensation for time lost. Second, an apology for both men involved. Third, Parkland has to be removed from his post as foreman."

Parkland, who had slumped back in his chair, shot upright. "By Christ! You don't want much." He inquired sarcastically, "As a matter of interest, am I supposed to apologize before I'm fired, or after?"

"The apology would be an official one from the company," Illas answered. "Whether you had the decency to add your own would be up to you."

"I'll say it'd be up to me. Just don't anyone hold their breath waiting."

Matt Zaleski snapped, "If you'd held your own breath a little longer, we wouldn't be in this mess."

"Are you trying to tell me you'll go along with all that?" The foreman motioned angrily to Illas.

"I'm not telling anybody anything yet. I'm trying to think, and I need more information than has come from you two." Zaleski reached behind him for a telephone. Interposing his body between the phone and the other two, he dialed a number and waited.

When the man he wanted answered, Zaleksi asked simply, "How are things down there?"

The voice at the other end spoke softly. "Matt?"

"Yeah."

In the background behind the other's guarded response, Zaleski could hear a cacophony of noise from the factory floor. He always marveled how men could live with that noise every day of their working lives. Even in the years he had worked on an assembly line himself, before removal to an office shielded him from most of the din, he had never grown used to it.

His informant said, "The situation's real bad, Matt."

"How bad?"

"The hopheads are in the saddle. Don't quote me."

"I never do," the assistant plant manager said. "You know that."

He had swung partially around and was aware of the other two in the office watching his face. They might guess, but couldn't know, that he was speaking to a black foreman, Stan Lathruppe, one of the half dozen men in the plant whom Matt Zaleski respected most. It was a strange, even paradoxical, relationship because, away from the plant, Lathruppe was an active militant who had once been a follower of Malcolm X. But here he took his responsibility seriously, believing that in the auto world he could achieve more for his race through reason than by anarchy. It was this second attitude which Zaleski—originally hostile to Lathruppe—had eventually come to respect.

Unfortunately for the company, in the present state of race relations, it had comparatively few black foremen or managers. There ought to be more, many more, and everybody knew it, but right now many of the black workers didn't want responsibility, or were afraid of it because of young militants in their ranks, or simply weren't ready. Sometimes Matt Zaleski, in his less prejudiced moments, thought that if the industry's top brass had looked ahead a few years, the way senior executives were supposed to do, and had launched a meaningful training program for black workers in the 1940s and '50s, there would be more Stan Lathruppes now. It was everybody's loss that there were not.

Zaleski asked, "What's being planned?"

"I think a walkout."

"When?"

"Probably at break time. It could be before, but I don't believe so."

The black foreman's voice was so low Zaleski had to strain to hear. He knew the other man's problem, added to by the fact that the telephone he was using was alongside the assembly line where others were working. Lathruppe was already labeled a "white nigger" by some fellow blacks who resented even their own race when in authority, and it made no difference that the charge was untrue. Except for a couple more questions, Zaleski had no intention of making Stan Lathruppe's life more difficult.

He asked, "Is there any reason for the delay?"

"Yes. The hopheads want to take the whole plant out."

"Is word going around?"

"So fast you'd think we still used jungle drums."

"Has anyone pointed out the whole thing's illegal?"

"You got any more jokes like that?" Lathruppe said.

"No." Zaleski sighed. "But thanks." He hung up.

So his first instinct had been right. There wasn't any time to spare, and hadn't been from the beginning, because a racial labor dispute always burned with a short fuse. Now, if a walkout happened, it could take days to settle and get everybody back at work; and even if only black workers became involved, and maybe not all of them, the effect would still be enough to halt production. Matt Zaleski's job was to keep production going.

As if Parkland had read his thoughts, the foreman urged, "Matt, don't let them push you! So a few may walk off the job, and we'll have trouble. But a principle's worth standing up for, sometimes, isn't it?"

"Sometimes," Zaleski said. "The trick is to know which principle, and when."

"Being fair is a good way to start," Parkland said, "and fairness works two ways—up and down." He leaned forward over the desk, speaking earnestly to Matt Zaleski, glancing now and then to the union committeeman, Illas. "Okay, I've been tough with guys on the line because I've had to be. A foreman's in the middle, catching crap from all directions. From up here, Matt, you and your people are on our necks every day for production, production, more production; and if it isn't you it's Quality Control who say, build 'em better, even though you're building faster. Then there are those who are working, doing the jobs—including some like Newkirk, and others—and a foreman has to cope with them, along with the union as well if he puts a foot wrong, and sometimes when he doesn't. So it's a tough business, and I've been tough; it's the way to survive. But I've been fair, too. I've never treated a guy who worked for me differently because he was black, and I'm no plantation overseer with a whip. As for what we're talking about now, all I did—so I'm told—is call a black man 'boy.' I didn't ask him to pick cotton, or ride Jim Crow, or shine shoes, or any other thing that's supposed to go with that word. What I did was help him with his job. And I'll say another thing: if I did call him 'boy'—so help me, by a slip!—I'll say I'm sorry for that, because I am. But not to Newkirk. Brother Newkirk stays fired. Because if he doesn't, if he gets away with slugging a foreman without reason, you can stuff a surrender flag up your ass and wave goodbye to any discipline around this place from this day on. That's what I mean when I say be fair."

"You've got a point or two there." Zaleski said. Ironically, he thought, Frank Parkland *had* been fair with black workers, maybe fairer than a good many others around the plant. He asked Illas, "How do you feel about all that?"

The union man looked blandly through his thick-lensed glasses. "I've already stated the union's position, Mr. Zaleski."

"So if I turn you down, if I decide to back up Frank the way he just said I should, what then?"

Illas said stiffly, "We'd be obliged to go through further grievance procedure."

"Okay." The assistant plant manager nodded. "That's your privilege. Except, if we go through a full grievance drill it can mean thirty days or more. In the meantime, does everybody keep working?"

"Naturally. The collective bargaining agreement specifies . . ."

Zaleski flared, "I don't need you to tell me what the agreement says! It says everybody stays on the job while we negotiate. But right now a good many of your men are getting ready to walk off their jobs in violation of the contract."

For the first time, Illas looked uneasy. "The UAW does not condone illegal strikes."

"Goddamit, then! Stop this one!"

"If what you say is true, I'll talk to some of our people."

"Talking won't do any good. You know it, and I know it." Zaleski eyed the union committeeman whose pink face had paled slightly; obviously Illas didn't relish the thought of arguing with some of the black militants in their present mood.

The union—as Matt Zaleski was shrewdly aware—was in a tight dilemma in situations of this kind. If the union failed to support its black militants at all, the militants would charge union leaders with racial prejudice and being "management lackeys." Yet if the union went too far with its support, it could find itself in an untenable position legally, as party to a wildcat strike. Illegal strikes were anathema to UAW leaders like Woodcock, Fraser, Greathouse, Bannon, and others, who had built reputations for tough negotiating, but also for honoring agreements once made, and settling grievances through due process. Wildcatting debased the union's word and undermined its bargaining strength.

"They're not going to thank you at Solidarity House if we let this thing get away from us," Matt Zaleski persisted. "There's only one thing can stop a walkout, and that's for us to make a decision here, then go down on the floor and announce it."

Illas said, "That depends on the decision." But it was plain that the union man was weighing Zaleski's words.

Matt Zaleski had already decided what the ruling had to be, and he knew that nobody would like it entirely, including himself. He thought sourly: these were lousy times, when a man had to shove his convictions in his pocket along with pride—at least, if he figured to keep an automobile plant running.

He announced brusquely, "Nobody gets fired. Newkirk goes back to his job, but from now on he uses his fists for working, nothing else." The assistant plant manager fixed his eyes on Illas. "I want it clearly understood by you and by Newkirk—one more time, he's out. And before he goes back, I'll talk to him myself."

"He'll be paid for lost time?" The union man had a slight smile of triumph.

"Is he still at the plant?"

"Yes."

Zaleski hesitated, then nodded reluctantly. "Okay, providing he finishes the shift. But there'll be no more talk about anybody replacing Frank." He swung to face Parkland. "And you'll do what you said you would—talk to the young guy. Tell him what was said was a mistake."

"An apology is what it's known as," Illas said.

Frank Parkland glared at them both. "Of all the crummy, sleazy backdowns!"

"Take it easy!" Zaleski warned.

"Like hell I'll take it easy!" The burly foreman was on his feet, towering over the assistant plant manager. He spat words across the desk between them. "You're the one taking it easy—the easy out because you're too much a godddam coward to stand up for what you know is right."

His face flushing deep red, Zaleski roared, "I don't have to take that from you! That'll be enough! You hear?"

"I hear." Contempt filled Parkland's voice and eyes. "But I don't like what I hear, or what I smell."

"In that case, maybe you'd like to be fired!"

"Maybe," the foreman said. "Maybe the air'd be cleaner some place else."

There was a silence between them, then Zaleski growled, "It's no cleaner. Some days it stinks everywhere."

Memo to White-Collar Workers

Adam Fisher

The other day, a publishing executive whose apartment I was painting said to me: "Boy, it must be nice to be your own boss, have a skill and actually see things get done." I said something pleasant and noncommittal in reply—after all, the man was paying me to paint his apartment, not wax contemplative.

But later, when I chewed a bit on what he'd said, on the implications of it, there seemed to me to be a good many people who would agree with him, from the business-suited onlookers at construction sites here in New York to the admirers of sporting events throughout the country. For the desk jockey, the allure of physical labor can be intense. Frankly, I think you could use some cheering up.

My own work record includes packing Popsicles, construction, installing aluminum siding, translating (when I was in the Army), publicity and editing for a large publishing house, and five years as a reporter in Massachusetts. Now I paint apartments and feel I can lay some claim to having seen both sides of the fence. Based on experience, I offer this conclusion: the grass is greener on both sides.

DIRECTION

What is attractive about physical labor—from swinging a bat to wielding a paintbrush—is that it is straightforward. Skill, training and judgment are aimed in one direction only: completion of the task. In physical activity, byzantine artifice must be cleared from the mind. It is the time of the fabled "100 percent." It is impossible, for example, to actually play a good game of tennis if one is constantly thinking, "I am playing a good game of tennis." In the midst of physical effort, labeling, mental or otherwise, is seen for what it is: irrelevant.

Office life appears different. Here, the task itself does not necessarily take precedence over everything else, and labeling can be important. Here, skill, training and judgment are often aimed in several directions at once, split between the goal itself and the necessary maneuvers among other workers required to achieve it. In addition, there is a far greater distance between the individual and the result of his labor. A "good" job in the office may offer the worker a chance to glow, but it seldom gives the opportunity to shine. Everyone would like to shine—hit a homer—once in a while.

At the risk of offending those who resist or resent examining attitudes, I would like to offer several of my observations on the ways we look at the various jobs we do.

- The Protestant work ethic runs strong, deep and subtle in American society, but the plain fact is that work itself has no intrinsic value at all. Others may praise or criticize its results, there may be rewards or reprimands, but the work itself does not necessarily make a person better or worse, more or less admirable, more or less responsible. The horse is the worker; the cart is the work.

- Power and money may be part of a "better" life, but they do not ensure that life. As the saying goes, "There are two ways to be rich; one is to have more, the other is to want less." If there is any doubt about this, look at those who retire to Florida with full pockets only to die of what doctors are almost willing to call a "broken heart."

- Being your own boss has its advantages, but it severely disrupts one of the great American pastimes: griping about the boss. Being responsible is not easy, whatever the position.

- Success is possible. Failure is possible. But which is more sensible: to make a million dollars or to enjoy the attempt? An attitude that only allows for success is probably a failure from the outset.

- A lot has been said about the Japanese economic juggernaut. What makes it possible? My own feeling is that the core of that power lies in a lack of confusion among human beings—the confusion between who I am and what I do. Again, the horse is the worker; the cart is the work.

I can hardly suggest that any of this is new or even very encouraging. Suggesting a change in attitudes, I've found, is only slightly less threatening than the mugger's old standby, "Your money or your life!"

And that, to my mind, is the point: your life.

My own feeling is that people's lives are far more interesting than a description of their work would indicate. The social pleasantry, "What do you do for a living?" cannot possibly elicit the rich complexity that might erupt if one were to try honestly to answer the question, "Who am I?"—a query that is often reserved in our society for college sophomores.

And yet, perhaps these introspective sophomores have a point. After all, to the man or woman who can answer this question thoroughly to his or her own satisfaction, work is a matter not only of identity but also of personal choice, a matter of attitude influenced not only by a society full of Joneses to keep up with, but also by a private stock of values and experience. You are not what you do, you are not what you eat. You are the person who makes those choices.

Work on Weapons Pains the Conscience of Some Engineers

A few leave defense field; they run into problems finding new employment

Bob Davis

John Seavey is troubled.

Mr. Seavey used to design radar-jamming gear for B-52 and B-1 bombers and parts for submarine-launched Trident missiles. All carry nuclear weapons. Reflecting on their destructive power during a recent peace vigil at Washington Cathedral, the 46-year-old engineer closed his eyes and prayed for nuclear disarmament along with a thousand other worshipers.

For 10 years Mr. Seavey has anguished about working on military projects. Now, he says, he is ready to leave the field.

Not many engineers have actually sworn off defense work, and probably not many will. But talks with engineers at half a dozen companies indicate that, for the first time since the Vietnam War, the number of defense engineers agonizing over their work is growing. Even those who don't share the doubts, Leon Michelove for instance, agree that the doubts are spreading.

'LIVELY DISCUSSIONS'

"We have lively discussions," says Mr. Michellove, a materials engineer at Raytheon Co.'s missile-systems division in Bedford, Mass. "They cycle along with the news. The more strident the debate in the news, the more it's discussed at work."

During the Vietnam War, Mr. Michelove worked at Itek Corp., building surveillance equipment. In those days, he says, "when there were people getting killed on TV at night, more people were opting out. Some felt it was a repugnant situation that they were responsible for." They were particularly upset over napalm and cluster bombs.

"Now it's slightly more academic," Mr. Michelove says. "The only people doing the killing with these weapons are the Russians in Afghanistan."

Today the concern centers on nuclear weapons and the extent of the United States' military buildup. Some engineers worry that the nuclear weapons they help build may be used in warfare rather than sit in silos as a deterrent. Others feel that the money appropriated for weapons, which among other things pays their salaries, could be better used to help the needy or balance the budget.

"I wiggle-waggle back and forth," says Thomas Forman, 63, a principal design engineer at Avco Corp.'s systems division in Wilmington, Mass. "Do I really add to peace and genuine deterrence? Or is that just a sop to my conscience?" Mr. Forman has helped to design parts of the reentry vehicles that protect missile-launched nuclear warheads from burning up as they enter Earth's atmosphere from space.

THE GEAR AND THE MACHINE

Engineers would seem to be the least likely group to be disturbed by defense work. They don't view themselves as protesters but as puzzle-solvers, the sort who as kids built radios and took apart small appliances to see how they worked. In college and on the job, they learn how to tackle a small part of large, complex projects. Few actually work on nuclear explosives. Their relationship to the weapons industry can be seen as that of the gear to the machine.

But "it's morally inescapable that if you conceive, design and build weapons, you play a role in the arms race," says Warren Davis, a physicist who used to work on missiles but quit for reasons of conscience. Mr. Davis formed High Technology Professionals for Peace, a Cambridge, Mass., group that tries to find nondefense jobs for engineers who want to leave defense work. The group has about 200 resumes on file but has placed only a handful of employees in other fields.

Some 330,000 engineers are working on defense research and development projects. Their bosses say employee dissatisfaction is minimal. John Lynch, the president and chief executive officer of Adams-Russell Co. in Waltham, Mass., calls it "a nonproblem." Richard J. Boyle, vice president and group executive for Honeywell Inc.'s defense and marine systems group in Hopkins, Minn., agrees. People with troubled consciences transfer about as frequently "as people who fuss about the length of their commute," he says.

There are signs, however, that defense contractors are in for a tougher time attracting and keeping talent. They are already at a recruiting disadvantage at the Massachusetts Institute of Technology partly because of students' growing concern about defense work, says Robert Weatherall, the school's director of career planning and placement. And Norman Skelton, Motorola Inc.'s director of staffing, says that although defense contractors still have a buyers' market, "the real question is, 'What happens in 1984 or 1985?'"

In addition, many churches are encouraging debates over disarmament issues. Mr. Forman has led discussions at a youth group of the United Church of Christ in Needham, Mass. Mr. Seavey first decided to give up defense work, a step he still hasn't fully taken, during a 24-hour retreat at an Episcopal convent in Boston.

The Catholic Church is especially active in this area. In May, the diocese of Norwich, Conn., began offering counseling to troubled defense workers and financial aid to those who quit. Some parishioners there help build Trident submarines at General Dynamics Corp.'s electric-boat division in Groton.

The diocese of Amarillo, Texas, has a $28,000 fund for those who want to leave defense. The area is the home of the U.S. government's Pantex factory, the final assembly point for all U.S.-made nuclear weapons. So far only one worker at the plant, a mechanic, has used the fund to find another job, but the publicity has made questioning the ethics of weapons work "a popular topic of discussion, almost like the Dallas Cowboys," says Leroy Behnke, the editor of the West Texas Catholic, a diocese newspaper.

PRESSURE AND ISOLATION

Speaking out on the subject can mean real sacrifices. At a minimum, there is a psychological pressure or isolation of breaking ranks with co-workers. "You are looked at like a Judas," says Mr. Forman, who spoke at a meeting of engineers and religious leaders in Andover, Mass., last Veterans Day. "You aren't part of the family when you come out in public." Moreover, speaking out may threaten the security clearance that these engineers need to continue their work—and most, Mr. Forman among them, do want to stay in the industry.

After he was quoted in the Boston Globe questioning the ethics of military work, Mr. Forman says, he was reinvestigated for a security clearance. It was the first time in more than 20 years that he had been quizzed by security agents, he says, adding that investigators also interviewed his neighbors.

"I was told, 'You've made certain statements in public and we want to know if you are someone who will safeguard secrets,' " Mr. Forman says. "It was frightening. You aren't at all sure you could find another job."

Avco calls the security check a "precautionary matter" and refers questions to the Department of Defense's investigative agency. That agency won't confirm or deny that Mr. Forman was the subject of an investigation, saying it notifies a person only after a review and only if a clearance may be withdrawn. "No news is good news," says Daniel Dinan, the deputy director of industrial security for the Defense Investigative Service.

OBSTACLES TO LEAVING

Those who want to leave the industry also face substantial obstacles. Because their work often is classified, they have nothing to show potential employers other than a resume and references. On top of that, the recession made jobs scarce in non-defense fields.

Of the engineers who leave defense work, says Joseph Vito, an employment recruiter in Lexington, Mass., 75% have problems finding other jobs. Asked what jobs they eventually find, Mr. Vito says: "We have some of the classiest real-estate brokers and insurance agents in New England that you'd ever want to meet."

Over breakfast in St. Louis Park, Minn., John McFarland, 43, opens a loose-leaf scrapbook full of hundreds of job applications, resumes and form rejection letters. The scrapbook represents his futile search for challenging work outside the defense area.

"Those damn recruiters," he mutters. "All my letters say don't call about defense." Nevertheless, he says that of his four or five hot prospects, all have been in the defense industry. He tries to deflect these inquiries by telling recruiters he would use a defense job as a springboard to other work but says he still hasn't received a single nondefense engineering offer.

Mr. McFarland had worked in the defense field almost continuously since 1967. In 1981, he was paid $33,000 a year as an engineer at Honeywell to help design warhead casings for cluster bombs that could be dropped from aircraft to destroy approaching tanks.

'SOMETHING KIND OF CLICKED'

By then, he was growing disillusioned by what he sees as military extravagance and waste. He also was disturbed by talk in the Reagan administration of fighting and winning a nuclear war. "Something kind of clicked in my head," he says.

So he asked for a transfer to Honeywell's technology strategy center, which develops energy-conservation systems, robotics and other futuristic technology. There were no openings. He left Honeywell in mid-1981 to work on computer software for Control Data Corp. But he found that job boring and quit later that year, confident he could land another nondefense engineering job.

He still hasn't. He says commercial firms find him overspecialized. "It's like I have knowledge of all the angels you could stick on the head of a pin," he says of his detailed understanding of weapons materials. And much of his best work is classified, so he has little to show a prospective employer to demonstrate his competence.

During his job search, Mr. McFarland has spent his $10,000 in savings. To get by, he depends on a small inheritance from his mother and on Social Security payments to his father, with whom he lives. He even worked for no pay for a month at a small woodworking company to learn how to strip, stain and mend furniture so that he could try for a $15,000 a year job in that field. He didn't get it. "I'm looking at engineering as a past part of my life," he says.

Whistle-blower Paid High Price

John Madeley

Stanley Adams suffers from the worst kind of nightmare—one that is real.

It began in 1973 when he told the European Economic Community about illicit trading practices of the giant international drug company Hoffman-La Roche. Adams had worked for the Swiss-based company for nine years and had recently been promoted to world product manager.

Although he enjoyed the luxurious lifestyle that goes with one of the top commercial jobs, some of his company's practices alarmed him, especially a policy of price-fixing and market-sharing with competitors, and an oppressive control of the worldwide vitamin market.

Adams had his opportunity to curb such practices when Switzerland signed a free-trade agreement with the EEC. The community was grateful for the information he gave them, and used it for an investigation into Roche. Three years later the company was fined about $430,000—less than a per cent of its annual sales—for breaking EEC laws on free competition.

But blowing the whistle on Hoffman-LaRoche wrecked Stanley Adams's life.

He left Roche and planned to start a pig farm in Italy. In December, 1974, he and his family were crossing the border into Switzerland from Italy when he was arrested. Given no reason for the arrest, Adams was put into solitary confinement in a Swiss jail. Roche had lodged a complaint that had led to the arrest.

In the days that followed, his wife Marilene tried unsuccessfully to contact her husband. She was interrogated by Swiss authorities and told that, if convicted, Stanley Adams faced up to 20 years in jail.

On what charge? Adams believed he was doing his duty to consumers of Roche products the world over by exposing the firm's practices. But in

---

© Gemini News Service. Reprinted by permission.

Switzerland big business is, it seems, a matter of national security—so Marilene Adams was told that her husband faced charges of industrial espionage and treason.

No one knows what pressure she was put under by the Swiss authorities. All that is known is that Marilene committed suicide.

In prison, bewildered and dazed, Adams was not told of the suicide until two days later. He was then denied the right to attend her funeral.

When finally released on bail almost three months later, Adams's nightmare continued. The bank facilities previously arranged for his new business in Italy were not forthcoming. He was unpopular for interviews he gave that told of the connection between Italian politicians and Roche over the dioxin chemical scandal in Seveso.

Given a three-year suspended sentence in Switzerland, Adams won the unanimous backing of the European Parliament for his actions, but nonetheless faced bankruptcy. The EEC paid him about $36,000 for his pains—it was the community who had betrayed Adams by disclosing that he had told them about Roche's practices.

Now Adams has written a book, entitled *Roche versus Adams*, which is a horrific story of how a large company has the power to effectively ruin a man's life, of the way an important western country like Switzerland defends the illicit trading practices of its companies; and—not least— of the sheer bungling incompetence of the European Economic Commission.

Adams worked for Roche for five years in Latin America, and has also travelled widely in other developing countries.

He writes of the business practices of Roche that led him to complain to the EEC—of how Roche eliminated fair competition and of the prices it was able to charge.

A vitamin H product, for example, that cost about 56 cents a gram to produce, was sold at almost 20 times as much, $10 a gram.

His book gives insights into the way Hoffman-LaRoche operates in the developing world.

Adams says: "When news came of an influenza epidemic, for instance in India, instead of putting vitamin C out in greater quantities, we (Roche) would control the quantities going out and usually increase the price."

Government economists in Colombia were puzzled because pharmaceutical companies were keen to expand when they appeared to be making only six-per-cent profit on their activities. An investigation revealed that foreign-owned internationals were overcharging their Colombia subsidiaries for ingredients by 155 per cent.

Librium, made by Roche, was "over-priced by a staggering 6,478 per cent" Adams says.

Had the internationals been charging their subsidiaries the right price, then those subsidiaries would have been making 79 per cent. So Colombia was cheated out of taxes on profits. "In moral terms," Adams writes, "this amounts to exploitation."

Adams now lives in Britain where he continues his struggle for justice against huge organizations that have damaged him.

"Not only for me," he says, "but for other potential whistle-blowers who think it's not worth it and keep silent. We need them. The fiercer the pressure to keep silent, the more urgent the need is."

Life Without Work

Bernard Lefkowitz

One night, ten years ago, my father was complaining about his job. After 40 years of selling women's hats on the same street in Manhattan, the pay was still lousy, his boss didn't give a damn about him and nobody bought hats anymore. I had heard it all many times and had never known what to do except listen silently. That night, I wanted to say something because I knew time was running out, that every morning he had to put a nitroglycerin tablet under his tongue to make it up the subway steps with his sample case. So I offered him some money and suggested he take time off to relax and perhaps think about another job. Secretly, I hoped to coax him into early retirement.

"I can't quit," he said.

"Why not?" I asked, impatiently.

"Because I'd miss it," he said.

About a year later, he died. For a long time after his death, I wondered what kept him working when he knew he was dying. I understand now that it was the sense of community, and his position as a tribal elder in it, that drew him to The Street even when his heart was failing.

As a kid I'd sometimes go with my father when he went out selling, and he had always seemed happiest when he was shmoozing—shmoozing about politics or sex or the price of felt with the counterman at the luncheonette, the black woman who sewed the hat bodies at the back of the shop, the kid who ran the boutique in the East Village and hit him up for a contribution to the Abbie Hoffman bail fund. He cared for the people who populated his work world.

PATTERNS

In his life, work was a seamless cloth that stretched from his childhood to his death at the age of 64. Today, the pattern of work in America is much more uneven and irregular, a patchwork of frequent shifts in jobs and even occupations. In a two-year national study supported by the Ford Foundation, I interviewed more than 100 men and women who had stopped working for a minimum of two years. Almost all of them were in their 30s, 40s and early 50s. The point of the study was to find out how their lives had been affected by their disengagement from work and how they reassessed their position in society from their vantage point outside the factory gates.

In one sense they were all conventional. They had begun their working lives with high hopes and swelling ambition. Like my father, they had proceeded along a traditional path; first you found a job, then you married, raised a family, achieved a measure of economic security and earned the respect of your colleagues and neighbors.

Now they had veered off onto unchartered ground. At first I thought that their most difficult adjustment would involve finding the money to survive and filling up the time that had been occupied by their work. But most of the people made the transition without great trauma. They put together a basic economic package which consisted of government assistance, contributions from family members who had not worked before and some bartering of goods and services. When they couldn't meet a mortgage payment, they sometimes took a temporary off-the-books job or rented out a room. Generally they seemed to be living almost as well as when they were drawing a salary.

Unlike the Depression-era image of the man who crumbles when he doesn't have a job, these people found plenty to do. When they were working they had daydreamed about other interests and enthusiasms. Quitting gave them the chance to live out their daydreams. The aeronautics engineer who was laid off by Boeing in 1971 after twenty years on the job never went back to work. Instead, he builds magnificent, high-power electronic telescopes in his basement. The government economist who was never quite certain of the purpose of the programs he was analyzing does not doubt his purpose today; it is to take moving, richly evocative photographs of the people who live in his neighborhood in Boston.

Starting Over

Racked by fantasies of opening a restaurant or running a vineyard? Here's what to expect of a second career.

Walter Kiechel III

We tend to admire the people who do it. "He just chucked it all," we think, "told the boss where to get off, quit, and headed out West. By now he's probably got that little lemming ranch he dreamed of, somewhere in the Rockies. I bet he's just floating." What audacity. What independence.

What a lot of trouble. As just about anyone who has tried to launch a second career will tell you, the process isn't carefree. The move usually springs not from insouciance but from unhappiness. Often it results in more unhappiness. With a little calculation, though, you can significantly improve your chances of making it work.

First, let's be clear about what a second career is. The term implies a first career, work the individual devoted himself to seriously for an appreciable period. For this reason, the job selling auto parts that your hitherto shiftless brother-in-law finally finds fulfillment in, after casting about in 12 other fields in as many years, doesn't qualify as a second career. Nor does a new job that entails mostly a change of employers. You were an accountant in a Big Eight firm; you became controller of a medium-size company or retired and set up your own practice. Enterprising of you, but no second career.

The number of managerial types seeking more radical departures from what they've been doing appears on the increase. The closest thing to experts on the subject—individuals and firms that counsel people on career change—report that their business is brisk. They attribute the heightened interest in second careers to several causes: erosion of the individual's loyalty to the company; erosion of the company's loyalty to the individual—they may fire you at any time, why not beat them to it; even the spread of the I've-got-to-be-me ethic from the you-know-what generation to just about everybody.

People who have attempted second careers confirm much of this sociology but go on to etch it more sharply with the acid of unhappiness. From a computer salesman who, at age 40, left IBM and soon got into the restaurant business: "I was a small cog in a large organization. I looked at the people who were working for retirement and realized they had no vitality. I didn't want to be like them." From a 35-year-old engineer who's getting ready to make the change: "I'm bored and I'm under continuous stress. When you've been doing something for eight to ten years it becomes repetitive. I'm not using my real abilities." Nearly all say they want to make more decisions on their own.

Psychologists who treat people wrestling with the possibility of a second career see such remarks as fitting into a pattern. The therapists confirm the common perception that most of the folks who want to make the leap are men around 40. Yes, Virginia, there is a mid-life crisis, at least for males. Psychological eminences such as Erik Erikson of Harvard or Daniel Levinson of Yale construe it as a predictable transition from one "life stage" to another. Beginning in the individual's late 30s, a self-transformation occurs that Levinson labels BOOM, for "becoming one's own man." The boomer throws off his old, pardon the expression, mentors—the boss, the colleague who taught him all he knows about marketing—and seeks to speak more in his own voice. This potentially explosive assertion of self can blow you right into a second career.

"A large issue is the imminence of death," explains James A. Wilson, a psychotherapist and professor at the University of Pittsburgh who at 35 left a thriving insurance business to take up psychology. "People see that they don't have that many years left and they'd better do what they want to do. They realize that they've chosen a career to please someone else."

Father always wanted you to be a lawyer; you knew your business school classmates would drop dead from envy if you landed that management consulting job. A look at where second-careerists come from does suggest that the careers most likely to be left behind are those in high-pressure, high-status industries—investment banking, consulting, almost anything on Wall Street. Observes Roderick Gilkey, a psychologist on the faculty of Dartmouth's Amos Tuck School of Business Administration, "Those are the jobs that it's easiest to get into for the wrong reasons."

The businesses that people choose for their second careers, or at least that they fantasize about most, are just about as predictable. If America were transformed in accordance with the dreams of its second-career wishers, the continent would shake and rend into a vast archipelago—this to accommodate all the marinas. On every island, several charming restaurants would beckon, and maybe a cozy inn or two. The rest of the land would be given over to vineyards.

Career changers, it turns out, are driven not only by the desire to be more independent, but also by what counselors call lifestyle considerations. Immured in the concrete canyons of the financial district, they begin to dream of the rolling hills of Vermont. Many second careers also grow out of avocations—sailing; cooking; collecting antiques; if not making wine, then at least drinking it. "I always had a desire to do something with my longstanding hobby, designing and making furniture," recalls Dietrich Baeu, formerly the president of a company that sold electro-optical devices. In 1980, at age 41, he left the corporate life and set up a custom-furniture business in New Jersey.

Most folks who embark on second careers quickly find that the dissatisfaction with the old career gives way to anxiety over new uncertainties. Indeed, psychologists say that it usually takes at least a year for most people to adjust and feel comfortable with the change. Brian Froelich, who in his mid-30s left a vice president's job at a big insurance company to start a travel agency catering to corporations, recounts what the first week on his own was like: "I'd lock the door and lie down on the floor—I thought I was going to have a heart attack. I was literally trembling as I reflected on what I had done."

False starts contribute to the misery. Many career changers report that before they found a second career that stuck, they tried one or two other kinds of work—real estate development being the most commonly cited misadventure. Others brought their old psychological devils to their new life. Psychologist Gilkey tells of a New York City investment banker who in his early 40s decamped for Vermont to launch a little maple syrup business. "He developed a maple syrup empire," Gilkey reports, "and soon found himself burdened by the same pressures he had tried to escape. By the time he came in to see me, he was suffering from agrarian burnout."

The second-careerist's biggest problem might seem to be maintaining his or her accustomed standard of living. Incomes from second careers tend to be low—often no more than one-third the annual compensation of the first career. "We did cut out a lot of things," says a man who deserted consulting for his original love, architecture. But few career changers seem to mind much; they treat the change as a return to their student days, as pioneering in the wilds, or even as a plunge into the life Bohemian. It is also universally conceded that having a spouse who brings in a paycheck helps enormously.

For all the difficulty that attends them, second careers can be made to work. Experts estimate that something like 70% to 80% of the people who attempt the change succeed—in the sense that they stick with the new career they settle on after all the transitional messiness. The trick is to make the move with the least possible heartache.

When the second-career bug gnaws at you, begin, the experts say, by figuring out what you *really* want—as if you could. One way to get at this elusive subject is to try to write your ideal obituary: Killed last night, at age 119, when his (or her) sports car plummeted off a cliff, Mr. (or Ms.) So-and-So was well known as . . . what? A retired former chief financial officer of Limbruck Sheet & Tubing? The crusty but beloved proprietor of the Inn-We-Go Tavern, a favorite local watering hole? The operator of the best damn marina in Newport Beach? If you consistently draw a blank, consider a visit to your friendly local psychological testing firm. It might be able, by virtue of a few inoffensive exercises, to help you uncover your true interests.

Once you have some sense of what you want to be when you finally grow up, work backward. What position will you need to reach to be within striking distance of your ultimate goal? What position to reach that position? And so on, back to a step you can take from your present miserable position.

Think, and act, incrementally—that is, with the smallest possible change that will get you where you want to go. Maybe you don't need to buy a marina. Some less drastic choices, while they might disqualify you from what purists consider a second career, may be better. You may find it simpler to take your investment banking skills and parlay them into ten hours a week of consulting, which would bring in enough to keep both you and your yawl barnacle-free.

If you contemplate a move into a completely new field, accumulate work experience in that area, preferably before you sever all your ties to your old career. Gary Smyth was trading corporate bonds on Wall Street when, at age 38, he was smitten by the urge to operate a restaurant. When the deal he was cooking up to start one in New York fell through, he took a job as a bartender at an East Side steakhouse instead. Within a few weeks, he became maitre d', responsible for closing the place up at night. After a sufficient number of 15-hour days, he began to understand why so many restaurants are run by first-generation immigrants. "After I got over the initial fantasy fulfillment," Smyth recalls, "I wasn't really happy doing the work." Now 43, he is back trading bonds. The difference? He's contented.

Fighting Off Old Age
A theory that exercise and positive thinking really works

John Leo

Ronald Reagan, say gerontologists, may do for old age what Henry VIII did for divorce. Not that the new President, who turned 70 last week, is about to lavish money on septuagenarian lobbyists, the Gray Panthers or age researchers. Those researchers, in fact, consider themselves prime targets for Reagan's budget cutting. The gerontologists, rather, think Reagan may actually help retard the rate of aging among senior citizens simply by remaining active and competent. Reason: after decades of work in the field, researchers have concluded that warding off old age is in large part a matter of self-image, positive thinking and staying active. Says Jack Botwinick, a psychologist and the author of *Aging and Behavior:* "There's a general feeling that people could have a self-fulfilling prophecy of decline. By keeping active they'll hang on longer."

Part of the problem, say the researchers, is the chilling power that certain numbers have come to possess: to many Americans, 65 means used up; 70 or 75 means ready for death. Yet today's 65-year-olds can expect to live 16 more years. In sports too, numbers have some of the same paralyzing power. A baseball player is considered old at 35, a basketball guard at 30. Athletic skills clearly erode with time just as everyday physical capabilities inevitably decline after, say, 65, but some researchers think that even in sports aging is nearly as much mental as physical. A baseball star, knowing that most players are washed up at 35 or 36, begins to expect a decline and helps produce it by a lack of concentration. Yet highly motivated athletes can keep their skills longer. Philadelphia Phillies First Baseman Pete Rose, who will be 40 in April, is still going strong. Quarterback George Blanda played pro football at age 48, and at age 52, Gordie Howe played pro hockey on the same team as his two sons.

Dr. James Fries of the Stanford University Medical Center talks of shifting the "markers" of age in much the same way the Rose talks about rejuvenating himself each spring: exercise plus an upbeat attitude equal success. At Stanford's arthritis clinic, says Fries, "I tell patients to exercise—use it or lose it. 'Run, not rest' is the new advice of the cardiologist."

Most progress in medicine, Fries maintains, has come from exchanging acute medical problems for chronic ones. For instance, people who might once have died from diseases such as smallpox and tuberculosis now live long enough to develop chronic ailments like atherosclerosis and emphysema. Since we are running out of acute problems to "exchange," Fries says, the job of medical researchers is to keep the steady decay of organs at a low level, and the task of everybody is to work at postponing or reducing the severity of their chronic problems—giving up smoking to delay emphysema, for example, or treating hypertension to delay problems with the arteries. Regular checkups are necessary to detect early signs of disease, and exercise is crucial. "The body is now felt to rust out rather than wear out," says Fries. Every organ has a reserve capacity that declines gradually. "If loss of reserve function represents aging in some sense, then exercising an organ presents a strategy for modifying the aging process."

That includes the brain. Fries thinks that memory loss can be successfully resisted by memory-training techniques and that mental agility in old age comes from giving the brain regular workouts. "You can't fight the trend entirely," he says, "but within the envelope of human potential, you can greatly slow that progress toward the end." Estimates are that 10% of Americans over age 65 show some signs of senility. According to a task force sponsored by the National Institute on Aging, some of this deterioration—perhaps 10% or 20%—can be cured if caught early enough. Says K. Warner Schaie, director of the Gerontology Research Institute at the University of Southern California: "We find that people who have been very active and involved in life tend to maintain their intellectual functions."

Senile dementia, a degenerative organic brain disorder, of which a major type is Alzheimer's disease, is not much affected by positive thinking, but some doctors think that quicker treatment may cut the rate of the disorder. Psychologist Botwinick, coinvestigator in a study of the early stages of senility, says families waste too much time fretting and trying to cope before calling in a doctor. "By the time a doctor sees an Alzheimer's patient, that patient is pretty far along. Getting to him early may make a big difference."

Genetics, socioeconomic status and luck all help determine who will live to a ripe old age. So does education, according to one theory. Sociologist George Maddox, director of the Center for the Study of Aging and Human Development at Duke University, argues that education "is associated with the notion of taking hold of the future in a special way, and it leads people to organize their lives differently." If that theory is correct, then rising national levels of education may mean that tomorrow's elderly will have an easier time of it than today's.

The Parable of the Sadhu

Bowen H. McCoy

Last year, as the first participant in the new six-month sabbatical program that Morgan Stanley has adopted, I enjoyed a rare opportunity to collect my thoughts as well as do some traveling. I spent the first three months in Nepal, walking 600 miles through 200 villages in the Himalayas and climbing some 120,000 vertical feet. On the trip my sole Western companion was an anthropologist who shed light on the cultural patterns of the villages we passed through.

Reprinted by permission of the *Harvard Business Review*. "The Parable of the Sadhu" by Bowen H. McCoy, Sept./Oct. 1983. Copyright © 1983 by the President and Fellows of Harvard College; all rights reserved.

During the Nepal hike, something occurred that has had a powerful impact on my thinking about corporate ethics. Although some might argue that the experience has no relevance to business, it was a situation in which a basic ethical dilemma suddenly intruded into the lives of a group of individuals. How the group responded I think holds a lesson for all organizations no matter how defined.

THE SADHU

The Nepal experience was more rugged and adventuresome than I had anticipated. Most commercial treks last two or three weeks and cover a quarter of the distance we traveled.

My friend Stephen, the anthropologist, and I were halfway through the 60-day Himalayan part of the trip when we reached the high point, an 18,000-foot pass over a crest that we'd have to traverse to reach to the village of Muklinath, an ancient holy place for pilgrims.

Six years earlier I had suffered pulmonary edema, an acute form of altitude sickness, at 16,500 feet in the vicinity of Everest base camp, so we were understandably concerned about what would happen at 18,000 feet. Moreover, the Himalayas were having their wettest spring in 20 years; hip-deep powder and ice had already driven us off one ridge. If we failed to cross the pass, I feared that the last half of our "once in a lifetime" trip would be ruined.

The night before we would try the pass, we camped at a hut at 14,500 feet. In the photos taken at that camp, my face appears wan. The last village we'd passed through was a sturdy two-day walk below us, and I was tired.

During the late afternoon, four back-packers from New Zealand joined us, and we spent most of the night awake, anticipating the climb. Below we could see the fires of two other parties, which turned out to be two Swiss couples and a Japanese hiking club.

To get over the steep part of the climb before the sun melted the steps cut in the ice, we departed at 3:30 A.M. The New Zealanders left first, followed by Stephen and myself, our porters and Sherpas, and then the Swiss. The Japanese lingered in their camp. The sky was clear, and we were confident that no spring storm would erupt that day to close the pass.

At 15,500 feet, it looked to me as if Stephen were shuffling and staggering a bit, which are symptoms of altitude sickness. (The initial stage of altitude sickness brings a headache and nausea. As the condition worsens, a climber may encounter difficult breathing, disorientation, aphasia, and paralysis.) I felt strong, my adrenaline was flowing, but I was very concerned about my ultimate ability to get across. A couple of our porters were also suffering from the height, and Pasang, our Sherpa sirdar (leader,) was worried.

Just after daybreak, while we rested at 15,500 feet, one of the New Zealanders, who had gone ahead, came staggering down toward us with a body slung across his shoulders. He dumped the almost naked, barefoot body of an Indian holy man—a sadhu—at my feet. He had found the pilgrim lying on the ice, shivering and suffering from hypothermia. I cradled the sadhu's head and laid him out on the rocks. The New Zealander was angry. He wanted to get across the pass before the bright sun melted the snow. He said, "Look, I've done what I can. You have porters and Sherpa guides. You care for him. We're going on!" He turned and went back up the mountain to join his friends.

I took a carotid pulse and found that the sadhu was still alive. We figured he had probably visited the holy shrines at Muklinath and was on his way home. It was fruitless to question why he had chosen this desperately high route instead of the safe, heavily traveled caravan route through the Kali Gandaki gorge. Or why he was almost naked and with no shoes, or how long he had been lying in the pass. The answers weren't going to solve our problem.

Stephen and the four Swiss began stripping off outer clothing and opening their packs. The sadhu was soon clothed from head to foot. He was not able to walk, but he was very much alive. I looked down the mountain and spotted below the Japanese climbers marching up with a horse.

Without a great deal of thought, I told Stephen and Pasang that I was concerned about withstanding the heights to come and wanted to get over the pass. I took off after several of our porters who had gone ahead.

On the steep part of the ascent where, if the ice steps had given way, I would have slid down about 3,000 feet, I felt vertigo. I stopped for a breather, allowing the Swiss to catch up with me. I inquired about the sadhu and Stephen. They said that the sadhu was fine and that Stephen was just behind. I set off again for the summit.

Stephen arrived at the summit an hour after I did. Still exhilarated by victory, I ran down the snow slope to congratulate him. He was suffering from altitude sickness, walking 15 steps, then stopping, walking 15 steps, then stopping. Pasang accompanied him all the way up. When I reached them, Stephen glared at me and said: "How do you feel about contributing to the death of a fellow man?"

I did not fully comprehend what he meant.

"Is the sadhu dead?" I inquired.

"No," replied Stephen, "but he surely will be!"

After I had gone, and the Swiss had departed not long after, Stephen had remained with the sadhu. When the Japanese had arrived, Stephen had asked to use their horse to transport the sadhu down to the hut. They had refused. He had then asked Pasang to have a group of our porters carry the sadhu. Pasang had resisted the idea, saying that the porters would have to exert all their energy to get themselves over the pass. He had thought they could not carry a man down 1,000 feet to the hut, reclimb the slope, and get across safely before the snow melted. Pasang had pressed Stephen not to delay any longer.

The Sherpas had carried the sadhu down to a rock in the sun at about 15,000 feet and had pointed out the hut another 500 feet below. The Japanese had given him food and drink. When they had last seen him he was listlessly throwing rocks at the Japanese party's dog, which had frightened him.

We do not know if the sadhu lived or died.

For many of the following days and evenings Stephen and I discussed and debated our behavior toward the sadhu. Stephen is a committed Quaker with deep moral vision. He said, "I feel that what happened with the sadhu is a good example of the breakdown between the individual ethic and the corporate ethic. No one person was willing to assume ultimate responsibility for the sadhu. Each was willing to do his bit just so long as it was not too inconvenient. When it got to be a bother, everyone just passed the buck to someone else and took off. Jesus was relevant to a more individualistic stage of society, but how do we interpret his teaching today in a world filled with large, impersonal organizations and groups?"

I defended the larger group, saying, "Look, we all cared. We all stopped and gave aid and comfort. Everyone did his bit. The New Zealander carried him down below the snow line. I took his pulse and suggested we treat him for hypothermia. You and the Swiss gave him clothing and got him warmed up. The Japanese gave him food and water. The Sherpas carried him down to the sun and pointed out the easy trail toward the hut. He was well enough to throw rocks at a dog. What more could we do?"

"You have just described the typical affluent Westerner's response to a problem. Throwing money—in this case food and sweaters—at it, but not solving the fundamentals!" Stephen retorted.

"What would satisfy you?" I said. "Here we are, a group of New Zealanders, Swiss, Americans, and Japanese who have never met before and who are at the apex of one of the most powerful experiences of our lives. Some years the pass is so bad no one gets over it. What right does an almost naked pilgrim who chooses the wrong trail have to disrupt our lives? Even the Sherpas had no interest in risking the trip to help him beyond a certain point."

Stephen calmly rebutted, "I wonder what the Sherpas would have done if the sadhu had been a well-dressed Nepali, or what the Japanese would have done if the sadhu had been a well-dressed Asian, or what you would have done, Buzz, if the sadhu had been a well-dressed Western woman?"

"Where, in your opinion," I asked instead, "is the limit of our responsibility in a situation like this? We had our own well-being to worry about. Our Sherpa guides were unwilling to jeopardize us or the porters for the sadhu. No one else on the mountain was willing to commit himself beyond certain self-imposed limits."

Stephen said, "As individual Christians or people with a Western ethical tradition, we can fulfill our obligations in such a situation only if (1) the sadhu dies in our care, (2) the sadhu demonstrates to us that he could undertake the two-day walk down to the village or (3) we carry the sadhu for two days down to the village and convince someone there to care for him."

"Leaving the sadhu in the sun with food and clothing, while he demonstrated hand-eye coordination by throwing a rock at a dog, comes close to fulfilling items one and two," I answered. "And it wouldn't have made sense to take him to the village where the people appeared to be far less caring than the Sherpas, so the third condition is impractical. Are you really saying that, no matter what the implications, we should, at the drop of a hat, have changed our entire plan?"

THE INDIVIDUAL VS. THE GROUP ETHIC

Despite my arguments, I felt and continue to feel guilt about the sadhu. I had literally walked through a classic moral dilemma without fully thinking through the consequences. My excuses for my actions include a high adrenaline flow, a superordinate goal, and a once-in-a-lifetime opportunity—factors in the usual corporate situation, especially when one is under stress.

Real moral dilemmas are ambiguous, and many of us hike right through them, unaware that they exist. When, usually after the fact, someone makes an issue of them, we tend to resent his or her bringing it up. Often, when the full import of what we have done (or not done) falls on us, we dig into a defensive position from which it is very difficult to emerge. In rare circumstances we may contemplate what we have done from inside a prison.

Had we mountaineers been free of physical and mental stress caused by the effort and the high altitude, we might have treated the sadhu differently. Yet, isn't stress the real test of personal and corporate values? The instant decisions executives make under pressure reveal the most about personal and corporate character.

Among the many questions that occur to me when pondering my experience are: What are the practical limits of moral imagination and vision? Is there a collective or institutional ethic beyond the ethics of the individual? At what level of effort or commitment can one discharge one's ethical responsibilities?

Not every ethical dilemma has a right solution. Reasonable people often disagree; otherwise there would be no dilemma. In a business context, however, it is essential that managers agree on a process for dealing with dilemmas.

The sadhu experience offers an interesting parallel to business situations. An immediate response was mandatory. Failure to act was a decision in itself. Up on the mountain we could not resign and submit our résumés to a headhunter. In contrast to philosophy, business involves action and implementation—getting things done. Managers must come up with answers to problems based on what they see and what they allow to influence their decision-making processes. On the mountain, none of us but Stephen realized the true dimensions of the situation we were facing.

One of our problems was that as a group we had no process for developing a consensus. We had no sense of purpose or plan. The difficulties of dealing with the sadhu were so complex that no one person could handle it. Because it did not have a set of preconditions that could guide its action to an acceptable resolution, the group reacted instinctively as individuals. The cross-cultural nature of the group added a further layer of complexity. We had no leader with whom we could all identify and in whose purpose we believed. Only Stephen was willing to take charge, but he could not gain adequate support to care for the sadhu.

Some organizations do have a value system that transcends the personal values of the managers. Such values, which go beyond profitability, are usually revealed when the organization is under stress. People throughout the organization generally accept its values, which, because they are not presented as a rigid list of commandments, may be somewhat ambiguous. The stories people tell, rather than printed materials, transmit these conceptions of what is proper behavior.

For 20 years I have been exposed at senior levels to a variety of corporations and organizations. It is amazing how quickly an outsider can sense the tone and style of an organization and the degree of tolerated openness and freedom to challenge management.

Organizations that do not have a heritage of mutually accepted, shared values tend to become unhinged during stress, with each individual bailing out for himself. In the great takeover battles we have witnessed during past years, companies that had strong cultures drew the wagons around them and fought it out, while other companies saw executives supported by their golden parachutes, bail out of the struggles.

Because corporations and their members are interdependent, for the corporation to be strong the members need to share a preconceived notion of what is correct behavior, a "business ethic," and think of it as a positive force, not a constraint.

As an investment banker I am continually warned by well-meaning lawyers, clients, and associates to be wary of conflicts of interest. Yet if I were to run away from every difficult situation, I wouldn't be an effective investment banker. I have to feel my way through conflicts. An effective manager can't run from risk either; he or she has to confront and deal with risk. To feel "safe" in doing this, managers need the guidelines of an agreed-on process and set of values within the organization.

After my three months in Nepal, I spent three months as an executive-in-residence at both Stanford Business School and the Center for Ethics and Social Policy at the Graduate Theological Union at Berkeley. These six months away from my job gave me time to assimilate 20 years of business experience. My thoughts turned often to the meaning of the leadership role in any large organization. Students at the seminary thought of themselves as antibusiness. But when I questioned them they agreed that they distrusted all large organizations, including the church. They perceived all large organizations as impersonal and opposed to individual values and needs. Yet we all know of organizations where peoples' values and beliefs are respected and their expressions encouraged. What makes the difference? Can we identify the difference and, as a result, manage more effectively?

The word "ethics" turns off many and confuses more. Yet the notions of shared values and an agreed-on process for dealing with adversity and change—what many people mean when they talk about corporate culture—seem to be at the heart of the ethical issue. People who are in touch with their own core beliefs and the beliefs of others and are sustained by them can be more comfortable living on the cutting edge. At times, taking a tough line or a decisive stand in a muddle of ambiguity is the only ethical thing to do. If a manager is indecisive and spends time trying to figure out the "good" thing to do, the enterprise may be lost.

Business ethics, then, has to do with the authenticity and integrity of the enterprise. To be ethical is to follow the business as well as the cultural goals of the corporation, its owners, its employees, and its customers. Those who cannot serve the corporate visions are not authentic business people and, therefore, are not ethical in the business sense.

At this stage of my own business experience I have a strong interest in organizational behavior. Sociologists are keenly studying what they call corporate stories, legends, and heroes as a way organizations have of transmitting the value system. Corporations such as Arco have even hired consultants to perform an audit of their corporate culture. In a company, the leader is the person who understands, interprets, and manages the corporate value system. Effective managers are then action-oriented people who resolve conflict, are tolerant of ambiguity, stress, and change, and have a strong sense of purpose for themselves and their organizations.

If all this is true, I wonder about the role of the professional manager who moves from company to company. How can he or she quickly absorb the values and culture of different organizations? Or is there, indeed, an art of management that is totally transportable? Assuming such fungible managers do exist, is it proper for them to manipulate the values of others?

I see the current interest in corporate culture and corporate value systems as a positive response to Stephen's pessimism about the decline of the role of the individual in large organizations. Individuals who operate from a thoughtful set of personal values provide the foundation for a corporate culture. A corporate tradition that encourages freedom of inquiry, supports personal values, and reinforces a focused sense of direction can fulfill the need for individuality along with the prosperity and success of the group. Without such corporate support, the individual is lost.

That is the lesson of the sadhu. In a complex corporate situation, the individual requires and deserves the support of the group. If people cannot find such support from their organization, they don't know how to act. If such support is forthcoming, a person has a stake in the success of the group, and can add much to the process of establishing and maintaining a corporate culture. It is management's challenge to be sensitive to individual needs, to shape them, and to direct and focus them for the benefit of the group as a whole.

For each of us the sadhu lives. Should we stop what we are doing and comfort him; or should we keep trudging up toward the high pass? Should I pause to help the derelict I pass on the street each night as I walk by the Yale Club en route to Grand Central Station? Am I his brother? What is the nature of our responsibility if we consider ourselves to be ethical persons? Perhaps it is to change the values of the group so that it can, with all its resources, take the other road.

6

THE COMPULSION TO PERFORM

Today's symbol of success is a schedule simmering with pressure. Carrying diaries jammed months ahead with commitments, we regiment our time— lunching for contracts, dining for contracts, reading only for business. Dripping with crocodile tears, successful men and their growing number of female colleagues brag about their surfeit of duties, their lack of time.

—*Ann Marie Cunningham*

Much of the work of organizational behaviorists has one common objective: to increase the performance of employees. Treatments of such topics as motivation, compensation, training, attitudes, leadership, and supervision, to name a few, commonly focus on how more input and hence more output can be induced (some might say squeezed) out of individual workers. More generally it appears that the institutions that socialize our young people (e.g., schools, churches, universities) are, in important ways, directed to the same outcomes—preparing people who are oriented to performing in modern organizations or who are at least willing to tolerate the discipline of the workplace. Given the number of people who are currently chanting about the decline of the work ethic, it is tempting to conclude that these efforts are not succeeding.

On the other hand, we are more concerned that these efforts might be too successful. We fear that many individuals are so fully indoctrinated with work values and routines that psychologically they are not free to make reasonable choices about how much work to do, how hard to work, and how central a role to let work play in their lives. The title of this section—the compulsion to perform—stems from this concern. The virtues of performing work roles are so deeply ingrained in people and the costs of commitments to work and careers are so little considered, that individuals appear to play work roles compulsively without considering how they might allocate their time and energies in a more fully satisfying manner. The readings in this section focus on this compulsion and on some of the costs people pay as a result of the irresistible impulse to perform.

Most of the selections in this section deal directly with the cost to the individual worker. "Cat's in the Cradle" by Harry Chapin demonstrates that these consequences extend to other people outside the work place and can lead to irreversible regrets later in life.

The next five selections reveal how the pressures to perform are experienced by people who play various roles in organizations. In "Owners' Isolation Can Result in Loneliness and High Stress" by Sanford L. Jacobs we see how many small business owners tend to be highly stressed and also very lonely. Ann Marie Cunningham provides a vivid account of the influence of maintaining hectic schedules in one's total life in "The Time Pressured Life."

"As the Recovery Gains, Compulsory Overtime Becomes a Rising Issue" provides several anecdotes illustrating how basic economic pressures and the desire for material possessions lead a number of American workers to work overtime on a regular basis. The selection also points out how many companies encourage overtime since it is cheaper because of the added benefit costs associated with hiring additional full time employees. Many of these workers who habitually work overtime have acquired all of the characteristics of workaholics. The article "Best Gift for Secretary" by Ellen Goodman shows how the pressures to perform are transmitted to individuals at lower levels in the hierarchy who are frustrated and deadended in their jobs.

Many of the issues raised by the compulsion to perform are treated in the mainstream business literature under the heading of stress. The fact that stress has become the word that serves as the most popular label for these problems is revealing because of what it connotes. For the most part stress is an individually oriented concept; as such it leads us to try to get people to adjust to systems rather than to adjust systems to people. Moreover, many of the topics included under treatments of stress (and more recently "burnout") have often been included in discussions of anxiety, neurosis, and other conditions, which have more pathological connotations. In a society dominated by a compulsion to perform, experiencing stress and being perceived by oneself and by others as able to cope with it can be indices of importance and sources of ego gratification. The same cannot be said when the underlying processes are described as anxiety or neurosis. We urge the reader to consider the last article in this section, "What Stress Can Do to You" by Walter McQuade using both sets of connotations—those suggested by stress and those suggested by the more pathologically oriented terms.

Cat's in the Cradle

Harry Chapin

My child arrived just the other day;
he came to the world in the usual way.
But there were planes to catch and bills to pay;
he learned to walk while I was away.
And he was talkin' 'fore I knew it,
and as he grew he'd say,
"I'm gonna be like you, Dad,
you know I'm gonna be like you."

And the cat's in the cradle and the silver spoon,
little boy blue and the man in the moon.
"When you comin' home Dad?"
"I don't know when, but we'll get together then,
you know we'll have a good time then."

My son turned ten just the other day;
he said, "Thanks for the ball, Dad,
come on let's play.
Can you teach me to throw?"
I said, "Not today, I got a lot to do."
He said, "That's okay."
But his smile never dimmed, it said,
"I'm gonna be like him, yeah,
you know I'm gonna be like him."

Chorus

Well he came from college just the other day;
so much like a man I just had to say,
"Son, I'm proud of you, can you sit for a while?"
He shook his head and he said with a smile,
"What I'd really like, Dad,
is to borrow the car keys;
see you later, can I have them please?"

Chorus

I've long since retired,
my son's moved away;
I called him up just the other day.

I said, "I'd like to see you if you don't mind."
He said, "I'd love to Dad, if I could find the time.
You see, my new job's a hassle and the kids have the flu,
but it's sure nice talkin' to you, Dad,
it's been sure nice talkin' to you."
As I hung up the phone,
it occurred to me,
he'd grown up just like me;
my boy was just like me.

Chorus

Owners' Isolation Can Result in Loneliness and High Stress

Sanford L. Jacobs

Here's a blueprint for loneliness: Don't join a large organization that provides a colleague-oriented atmosphere; instead, go off on your own. Let your business dominate your life to the detriment of relationships with family and friends. Confide in no one.

That describes a lot of small-business owners, according to the findings of researchers Daivd P. Boyd and David Gumpert, who have been studying stress and loneliness in entrepreneurs.

They found that such people tend to be highly stressed, exhibiting one or more symptoms: back or chest pain, headache, impaired digestion, insomnia. And a majority (54%) of the 156 company founders surveyed said they had a recurrent sense of loneliness.

Isolation is part of running your own company. There isn't a gaggle of equals to share problems with and to help shape decisions as there often is in a big corporation (where loneliness may exist only at the top).

People can feel lonely even when they deal with other people frequently and aren't alone. "Loneliness," says Mr. Boyd, an associate professor at Northeastern University, "is the *feeling* of being isolated." Psychologists have described it as feeling apart from other people; as a feeling of being unable to bridge the gap between oneself and others.

The study found that when business owners feel most lonely they also experience the most stress, says Mr. Boyd, an organizational behavior

---

specialist. (Mr. Gumpert is an associate editor of the Harvard Business Review.)

"There is no one with whom I can share my deepest concerns." Sixty percent of the owners in the survey agreed with that statement. And going into business with someone else is no guarantee there will be someone with whom to share worries. Of those in the survey who started with partners, two thirds had dumped them because of personal conflicts.

Some owners avoid feeling isolated by joining small-business groups that enable them to meet regularly with other owners. Discussing mutual problems helps dispel their feelings of loneliness. But some in the survey said they don't divulge their deepest feelings because they don't, as one respondent put it, want to seem to be crying in their beer.

"It seems," Mr. Boyd says, "that entrepreneurs seek out lonely situations."

Indeed, the survey found that owners gravitate to solitary sports and hobbies: flying, sailing, swimming, mountain climbing, woodworking. Even though they are solitary, Mr. Boyd says, such outside activities are a beneficial escape from business worries. "When I am on my boat," an owner told the researchers, "nothing else matters."

But small-business owners "can become entrapped in a self-destructive cycle," the researchers say. "Because there is no one to confide in, there is no ready way of venting cumulative stress. The end result may be physiological impairment."

There are ways to combat the excessive isolation that causes loneliness, the researchers suggest. First, recognize that loneliness is part of being an owner and can't be totally removed from this type of career. Ownership carries with it a degree of isolation. But owners can alter their behavior to prevent themselves from being so immersed in their businesses that they have little time for socializing.

Seek confidants. Owners of noncompeting businesses or a board of directors can serve this function.

Be attentive to the needs of family and friends. "Business loneliness may be palliated by fulfillment outside the workplace," Messrs. Boyd and Gumpert say in a report on their research, which they presented recently at the Entrepreneurship Research Conference at the Georgia Institute of Technology.

Lonesome pursuits should be balanced with social ones. One owner said he had solitary hobbies, woodworking, music and collecting information on colonial wars, but he balanced them with public activities such as being a scoutmaster, school committee member and museum trustee.

There's a payoff in reducing loneliness. If owners "come to terms with loneliness," the researchers say, "they can improve the quality of their lives and the performance of their firms."

The Wall Street Journal, May 22, 1984.

Top Executives Prefer the Office to the Beach, a New Study Shows.

William Theobald, professor of recreation studies at Purdue University, interviewed chief executives in 60 of the Fortune 500 companies. He found that most prefer work to leisure. Nearly 60% hadn't taken a vacation in the past three years. Those who had took work along, called the office every day, or returned home early. "They couldn't leave their psychological baggage behind at the office," the professor says.

Most of the executives worked more than 65 hours a week and averaged five hours sleep a night. Some put in 100-plus hours weekly: they called themselves "busy executives" rather than workaholics. Less than 30% had read a non-business book in the last year. But, says Mr. Theobald, "They're tremendously happy."

There was one woman in the study. "If anything, she worked harder than the men," the professor says.

The Time Pressured Life

Ann Marie Cunningham

Today's symbol of success is a schedule simmering with pressure. Carrying diaries jammed months ahead with commitments, we regiment our time—lunching for contracts, dining for contracts, reading only for business. Dripping with crocodile tears, successful men and their growing number of female colleagues brag about their surfeit of duties, their lack of time.

Thus, committed time translates easily into status, and "no time" is a sure sign that someone is doing something important. Once luxury was status, leisure was status, but nowadays overextension, not even overachievement, is the ironic equivalent of the Good Life.

As women rise to executive and professional status, they become as time-pressured as men. But man-time and woman-time are still far from equal. Woman-time generally means trying to integrate professional and

Abridged and reprinted from *Savvy*, December 1980. Reproduced by permission.

personal life, while man-time traditionally involves using the personal as a support system for the professional. Pressure to "improve each shining hour" by devoting it to work is hard enough on men; it is monstrous for women.

For roughly 25 years, the thinking in sociology ran that the more social roles we had, the more strain we suffered because each role carried obligations. Then in 1974, as more women entered the working world, Sam D. Sieber, a sociologist at Columbia University, noticed that the more roles we had, the more benefits, not just duties, we accrued. Sieber pointed out that privileges—meaning liberties or freedoms—are "part and parcel of every social role." The more roles you have, the more privileges you enjoy; quite simply, "more is more." One role's privileges become a kind of capital that can be reinvested—one job, one introduction, leads to others, "handsomely compensating," according to Sieber, "for the possible burden of multiple role obligations."

Among the advantages that go along with "more is more," Sieber points out, is the opportunity of placing social eggs in many baskets. With many roles, you may be spread thin but you have social security. Should you fail in one role, the others will buffer you. As you acquire more roles, you become more valuable to the people who know you in each role. Because you're valuable, and also less available, they will probably slacken their demands on you. Appreciated and even competed for, you will find your self-confidence ballooning. "Getting around" may leave you drained, but neither bored nor boring. Sieber would be surprised if we "did not often find that the tension engendered by conflict overload was totally overshadowed by the rewards" of many roles. He pointed out that demands for equality from women and minority groups seem to include "a desire for access to the profits and pleasures of role accumulation."

But, ultimately, more may not be more; there's the question of quality. How we choose to spend our time, which roles we adopt, means deciding on a set of values. If the prestigious life is spent as a pressured and divided human assembly line, then the heart of the American dream is dark indeed. From Sieber's description, all is not rosy in the multiroled world. There are distinct *sub rosa* tints of greed and predation. Your privileges may include connections, invitations, friends, lovers—"and by no means least, graft, bribes and payola." You will have to practice a fair amount of fancy footwork and quick exits to balance the demands of one set of "role partners" against another. Such privileges may mean liberties but they hardly seem freeing.

How does time pressure really affect women's lives? As they live lives more like those of men, are they adopting the very values of male society they formerly criticized? Are women being trained to ignore their traditional concerns? Because executives and professional women are recent arrivals on the sociological scene, no one knows how they go about balancing solid achievement and personal satisfaction. Behind the façade of the competent Superwoman, what is the life like, hour by hour, day by day?

Savvy asked fifteen successful women, aged 32 to 57—married and single, with and without children—to write dispatches from the front. These players of many roles were to keep track of their daily schedules from the alarm clock's ring to bedtime. *Savvy's* study meant to examine the quality of the lives of this vanguard group, women on the edge of time, who have achieved the female version of the American Dream. Accordingly, the participants were asked to log what they thought about and how they felt while carrying out the day's tasks. What did these women—who included a White House special assistant, a company president, and a management consultant earning "low six figures"—think they had? And what do they really have?

Allowing for individual differences, the logs give a general impression of constant activity, of virtual enslavement to schedule. True to Sieber's notion of the effects of role accumulation, every woman reported happiness and satisfaction with her personal and professional lot. But those days of austere, machine-like productivity create the suspicion that there are pitfalls in time-pressured terrain.

The participants were subject to a scale of time pressures, culminating in a high of virtually around the clock for two mothers with three small children each. But nonstop schedules were not unique to mothers. "When I arrive at work, I get on a merry-go-round," said Helen Klein, a single copywriter who works for a large agency. "Sometime before bedtime, I'm thrown off. Next morning, I pick myself up and get on the merry-go-round again." The logs offer evidence that women have surpassed even male whirling: The average high-level male executive works a 60-hour week. But Barbara Taylor, who is married, childless, and a partner in Cullen and Taylor, Ltd., a public relations firm that specializes in travel and, ironically, leisure accounts, reported "100 hours of work out of 122 logged—definitely workaholic." Having accepted the notion that time pressure gives importance and direction to life, have these women been sold a bill of goods? An inability to stop trying to beat the clock is not so much the price, as the stark reality of the way we live now—the nightmare side of the American Dream.

The idea that a slippery devil like time can be managed is peculiarly Western. "Remember that Time is money," Benjamin Franklin, our most pragmatic Founding Father, admonished in 1748, in *Advice to a Young Tradesman;* but it wasn't until more than 100 years later that the "science" of time management was born in the factories of the industrial revolution.

Until 150 years ago, human schedules coincided with daylight hours and the annual cycle of the seasons. Then, in the mid-nineteenth century, electric light and heat allowed work to continue 24 hours a day, 365 days a year. In 1875, a lawyer's son named Frederick W. Taylor arrived at one of the new factories in Philadelphia as an apprentice. Poor eyesight had forced him to abandon plans to go to Harvard. But Taylor, an ascetic, energetic man who eschewed stimulants of all kinds, set great store by self-discipline as a means of developing "character." His "character" stood him in good stead as he rose from machine-shop laborer to chief engineer in a Philadelphia steel plant.

There he noticed that workers, under the mistaken impression that working rapidly today would lead to layoffs tomorrow because there would be no work left, were "soldiering," or working as slowly as possible. As an antidote, Taylor introduced, in 1881, what he called "scientific management." He argued that it was the way both management and labor could get what they wanted: high wages and production, combined with low labor costs.

Taylor's method was to select "a first class man," the most energetic worker, and then break his job down into as many simple, elementary movements as possible, discarding useless motions and selecting the most effective. He would then reconstruct the job and train the worker in the most efficient way of doing it.

Neither organized labor nor management believed him. At Bethlehem Steel, where Taylor was consulting, workers threatened his children, his wife and his life. Unions—and a young socialist named Upton Sinclair—were convinced that Taylor "gave about a 61 percent increase in wages, and got a 362 percent increase in work." Management did not appreciate Taylor either, because he blamed low production and soldiering on their lack of planning. When Taylor tried to reorganize the sprawling Army and Navy bureaucracies, their concerted opposition and the unions' resentment led to a blistering Congressional investigation of his method.

A bruised Taylor survived to lecture at Harvard and to publish *Principles of Scientific Management*, which has been in print since its publication in 1911. Ultimately Taylorism flourished and led to the development of mass production techniques, which contributed to the great gains made by industrial production in the 1920s.

In 1973, Alan Lakein, who became a time management specialist when his computer business failed, took time management techniques one step further and applied them to personal life. In *How to Get Control of Your Time and Your Life*, Lakein urged readers to develop a "master plan for life," to rank each day's tasks *A*, *B*, or *C* in order of importance, and to concentrate only on accomplishing *A*'s. To fight the boredom inevitable in a life resembling Drucker's well-run factory, Lakein advised scheduling one exciting activity per day. He also suggested a wall sign bearing "Lakein's question": "What is the best use of my time right now?"

Lakein followed his own advice. The result sounded like a life spent in blinkers: He never watched television, talked over the phone rather than face to face, and seldom read beyond the first two paragraphs of a newspaper story. To gain more time, he slept less. Before finally dropping off, he programmed his unconscious mind to mull over an unsolved problem.

Lakein's book sold 150,000 copies in hardcover and there are 1,810,000 paperbacks currently in print. Like Taylor, Lakein used to lecture widely, but he has had no known address for more than a year. No one knows why he has disappeared. "We can only assume," said a sales manager at his paperback publisher, "that he found a better way to spend his time."

Despite his defection, Lakein remains the grand master of time management. Lesser gurus, often former workaholic women, sell time management to its new female audience with the zeal of the converted.

Does the training they offer work? When I told freelance time consultant Denise Racine that I planned to poll women who had heard her presentation at a conference, she said, "I can tell you what you will find. Changing the way you organize your time means changing habits, which is hard. Most women try everything I suggest and give up quickly. The trick is to do only one or two little things." A month after the conference, some women had done just one thing—had bought answering machines and had begun closing their office doors to work alone for an hour each day. But an equal number responded, "I haven't had time to get organized," and another third never called back, presumably having related my message to the C rank.

No time manager has great secrets for sale: Everyone advises that you plan ahead and do first things first. A chill lingers ominously around time management literature, however, because of its Taylorist emphasis on self-discipline. You're encouraged to think of yourself as a well-oiled machine, programmed with the proper software, and to speak always in the future tense. The purpose of the present—even if spent in sleep—is to think of the future. To time managers and their converts, life looks like an hourglass, whose two bulbs represent the fading past and the looming future. The tiny connecting neck is all that remains of the present.

The women who kept time logs for *Savvy's* study performed triumphs of time management, even though only two had attended formal seminars. Their logs held few surprises: They were well aware of how they spent their time. Careful planning, often years in advance, had enabled them to accumulate roles. Barbara Taylor, partner in her own public relations firm, summed up the mindset of the logs: "We're used to thinking ahead, not registering how we're reacting to what's going on now." Perhaps inevitably, two of these model planners had trouble envisioning a log that recorded how they felt. They were "not sure what you mean by emotions."

These women think ahead, rise early (7:00 A.M. at the latest), and know at what time of day they work best. Alice Haemmerli, vice president of Chase Manhattan Bank, N.A., currently dealing with projects involving China's economy, spent four years in France and found her planning "entirely at odds with the culture. It was a constant source of irritation." She liked to work on her doctoral thesis in the mornings, when she was freshest, and devote the afternoon to shopping. However, since all shops closed from 1 to 4 P.M. Haemmerli continued working through the hours when she would have preferred to do something "less intellectually demanding." While the French ate big lunches and napped, Haemmerli chose to work with an eye on the future. Ellen Futter, a lawyer who became acting president of Barnard College last August, had a job so new that she could not plan. Forced to live in the present, she was finding the experience painful: "I like to know what the day is going to look like."

Three women, schedules drawn tight as harp strings, were almost consumed by work. Financial consultant Virginia Gobats usually unwinds in front of Mary Tyler Moore reruns at 2:30 A.M., and wakes at 6:30 A.M. Her work involves "doing the same thing for hours and hours on end." She was so worried by her boring log that she lined up a substitute. Gladys Dobelle, who runs her own public affairs public relations agency, said her log did not communicate "the frenetic quality of my life. I never see the light at the end of the tunnel; I always feel I've left something unfinished." When we met at 10:00 A.M., Dobelle had already laid out her clothes for the next day and explained that she had "seven of everything" to keep her wardrobe simple. A management consultant, who insisted on remaining anonymous because of her company's emphasis on low visibility, didn't get to bed again until 39½ hours after her alarm first rang.

These women represent the extreme end of the time-pressure scale, where no seam separates work from life. Gobats said she felt worried if her business day did not start on time. She is not alone: Johanna Hawkins, a copywriter at Foote, Cone & Belding, commented, "Most people in advertising prefer a busy schedule. They get depressed otherwise."

In politically powerful Washington, D.C., nonstop schedules may seem especially attractive. But subtract names like Brzezinski and issues like the fate of the ERA from the log belonging to Sarah Weddington, Carter's special assistant in charge of women's concerns, and her workhorse schedule is as flat as Dobelle's or Gobat's. Because the center-of-empire feeling that pervades Washington encourages workaholic habits, many private offices there actively encourage their employees to end the day promptly at 5:00 P.M. One such company lured Suzanne Woolsey, mother of three boys, aged 7, 5 and 3. She left a job as associate director of the Federal Office of Management and Budget and is now a management consultant at Coopers & Lybrand, an accounting firm. Much of Woolsey's log records pleasure and relief over her new, easier schedule: "If you have an important job in government, leaving the office before 6:30 or 7:00 P.M. is considered lack of commitment." Woolsey sleeps as little as Gobats, but for different reasons. She wasn't sure whether to begin her log with the midnight feed or when she dressed for work.

Not surprisingly, several husbands had schedules as demanding as their wives. Consequently, some husbands seemed quite peripheral to their spouses' lives: One woman didn't mention her husband until her log's third page. Others scheduled their husbands in: Ellen Futter reserves Friday night. Barbara Taylor, married one year to a professional fund raiser, frequently reflected, "How lucky I am!" to have a stable personal life. She described a dinner with her husband, their first night alone in two weeks. He outlined his timetable for the previous two days: breakfast in New York, lunch Los Angeles, dinner in San Diego, breakfast in Chicago, lunch in Baltimore, and finally dinner in New York with his wife.

Two women, a journalist and a company president, lived with men who had less demanding schedules than they did and were willing to play supporting roles. The husband of *New York Times* science reporter Jane E. Brody was checking the galleys of her 500-page book against the original manuscript. He was also willing to comb through several years of her weekly columns to select those suitable for collection in another book. He generally volunteered when she needed this sort of help—"I'm not good at asking," she explained. Carole Herrscher, the president and controlling partner of a Houston-based firm that makes a quarter of a million dollars annually manufacturing chemicals for the oil pipeline industry, regularly checked with her fiancé, Chuck, on business problems. In her log she consistently misspelled his name as "Check."

Only two women, both married, reported sex (with their husbands, once each). One described it as "hug therapy," the other as a "matinée." While reticence may have been a factor in the low incidence of reported lovemaking, a management consultant pointed out that "fatigue is also a strong urge"—strong enough to cancel out the sexual one in those who work late and rise early. If the logs are accurate, many women who are hardly isolated from men are ignoring a source of replenishment and comfort.

A monthly period is every woman's reminder of the biological deadline—a factor that prompts women to think about the future more than men. Some married women had decided that the demands of their careers precluded children, but two single women agreed that they were prey to panic on the subject.

One goblin can never be vanquished: There were a surprising number of intimations of mortality in the logs. Alice Haemmerli cried one evening at the thought of her mother's death a year earlier. Ann Gaillard, a divorced account executive with two children, ended her log-keeping abruptly when her mother died. Jane Brody returned a phone call, heard about the death of an old friend and felt "vulnerable and scared. Can't stand to hear about any more deaths and fatal illnesses. Too many in one year." Mary Didie, a pediatrician, saw four patients and felt "lucky" when she compared them to her own three children.

Gloria Morris, a Houston freelance writer who also teaches, had been seriously ill in 1977 and had to take a day off to rest during her log-keeping. Morris's close brush with death had gotten her cracking; she is as busy as any corporate executive. "When you don't have much time, you don't waste it." Now she uses a flow chart of five parallel bars to keep abreast of roles she's acquired since her illness—freelance writing, teaching at two local universities, advising student publications, involvement in a local organization for women in communications, and personal life. Keeping the *Savvy* log made her realize how much she relies on her flow chart. "There's a pleasure in plotting. You feel less buffeted." But she thought about other things besides leaping new hurdles. Some women recorded the weather; Morris was the only one who commented on the scenery, and who booked a regular dinner "to press the flesh" with close female friends.

Asked what they would do if faced with the prospect of imminent death, these women generally preferred to keep on keeping on. Only two restless souls said that, given just six months to live, they would definitely quit their jobs. Helen Klein said, "I probably wouldn't believe I had only six months. Only if I had a death sentence would I stop." Fueled by coffee, exercised as regularly as race horses, these women feel "proud I can swing it."

Yet they lead rather austere lives. The logs suggest that while opportunities for women have burgeoned, quality of lives had declined. To do what we love best, we have sacrificed many simple pleasures, including sleep, privacy, friends, nest-building, pets, home-cooked food and in some cases, children. No log-keeper had time simply to sit and think—which sometimes was the very thing she was paid to do. Some had no time to spend their money in enjoyable ways. Others were obliged to pay heavily for housekeepers, surrogate wives and a plethora of other time-saving services. "Home" is stripped down to a place "that works"; "wardrobe," to clothes that function.

Having done well in school, we can't break the habit of living in dormitories and wearing school uniforms. Indeed, Gladys Dobelle's log described her stripped-down-to-work life as boarding school: "Stuck with old-fashioned, 'use-Sunday-night-to-get-ready-for-Monday.' " Perennially good girls, we are always doing for others—the children or the corporation. This is traditional feminine behavior, but nowadays it earns salaries and status.

The time logs excerpted here illustrate four good girls who have fallen into the traps of time pressure. Often, a multirole life becomes a soap opera, which Carole Herrscher's log strongly resembles. Before she met her fiancé, she relied heavily on her staff for companionship—and she ruefully confessed that she is paying now. She devotes two days to smoothing others' feathers, sorting out internecine squabbles among her staff. Herrscher's life is a cliff-hanger: In the aftermath of her 4:00 A.M. conference with Chuck, what will the next installment bring?

While Herrscher wonders who she has to pay off to get out of her serial, *New York Times* science reporter and personal health columnist Jane E. Brody, 39, glows with a good girl's rewards. Slim and rosy-cheeked from frequent exercise, she is the apple of editors' eyes because she writes prolifically and finishes on time. Once she was a pro-crastinator, but writing about the way stress eats at the heart and stomach made her work hard to avoid last-minute panic. "If you get your work done, your free time—sex, food, anything—feels like a wonderful reward. I go on vacation very, very easily," she said. "My goal now is to get pieces written early in order to have free weekends. If I succeed, only my husband knows about my extra time."

Brody does admit to anxiety in the face of big, unfamiliar freelance writing projects, which she tries to do only for "good reasons—either the subject appeals to me or it opens new markets." As the principal wage earner in her household—her husband, a lyricist, does most of the chores their ten-room house and eleven-year-old twin sons entail—Brody can-not afford to slow down in her career. "I don't want to be dependent on anything in my life, and that includes *The New York Times.*"

She had just completed a 500-page book on nutrition, a year-and-a-half project for which she set a strict schedule, writing from 5:00 A.M. to 6:30 A.M. weekday mornings and weekends. She does elaborate cooking for dinner parties, and because she abhors sitting still and finds chores a relief after writing, she goes without a dishwasher and is considering not repairing the clothes dryer.

While Brody's efficiency and productivity are undeniable, she sounds suspiciously like one of her own columns on the healthful life. She acknowledged that she censored herself during her log-keeping: "It puts you on good behavior because you don't want to put down that you went crazy." Indeed, although her emotions column is fairly sparse, she said that the evening after her log ended, she exploded at her family. "After 10 P.M. I had no cope left."

Unlike Brody, Mary Didie feels out of shape, and her cheeks are pale. Her list of professional responsibilities is exhausting. It includes an acting directorship of the pediatric outpatient clinic at New York Hospital, where she is also an assistant attending physician; an assistant professor-ship at Cornell University Medical College and a private practice. She puts in a 9:00 A.M. to 7:00 P.M. working day, for which her base salary is $35,000—"a man would earn at least $7,000 more."

At home, Didie and her husband, who works full time as a project engineer at *The New York Daily News,* have three children under the age of 5. Her babies were scheduled to arrive during periods of her training when she was either not on call for hospital night duty, or "when I would inconvenience the least number of people."

Unlike his older brother and sister, Didie's youngest child, now 13 months old, played havoc with his mother's careful clockwork. He is dysrhythmic: His walking and feeding times change from day to day. Because he is still nursing, Didie's lunch, which she normally doesn't have until 3:00 P.M., consists of a yogurt she eats at her desk while she expresses her milk. This she freezes for her son. While this sounds like an extreme scheduling sacrifice—an assembly-line mother—it is Didie's way of making a direct and irreplaceably personal gift to her son. Though her schedule could be essayed only by a woman who needs very little sleep, her emotions are consistent and of a piece with her experiences.

In the process of wringing everything she wants from life, Didie has somewhat wrung herself out. She knows her life has narrowed—"my conversation isn't what it used to be"—but "I have to say that I'm happy." She laughs frequently over her hair-raising schedule—"What would my mother say?"—and appreciated her *Savvy* interview as "another set of ears" to hear about it. As a teacher, a doctor and a mother, Mary Didie does for other people all her many waking hours, but she knows what she does makes a vital difference.

The most time-pressured log belongs to the most financially successful woman, a married, childless management consultant. Her log graphically depicts how the added burden of travel taxes mind, body and relationships in a multiroled life.

On the eve of a recent European trip, our management consultant is stoic: "Having revisited this situation for possibly the fifth time, I resign myself to an exhausting week." Her perennial anxiety is "where the energy is going to come from. The unknown is always just how tired I'm going to get."

Small wonder: She spends much of the trip battling jet lag and plane delays. Yet she succeeds in making her time-serving life even harder. On her return, she is determined to stay up so she won't spend her first day home asleep. She finally goes to bed when she's been up "some 21 hours." Before her trip she had a single exhausting workout on Nautilus machines and then no exercise the rest of the week, relying on caffeine to keep awake for the clients and unwinding in front of television.

Both this woman and her husband travel so much that they must preclude all but spontaneous, last-minute recreation. Over dinner, after the wife's week-long absence, they planned ahead, as usual, and discussed the goods and services they needed to keep themselves going: "our upcoming vacation, the weekend house we are trying to buy, the meeting with our accountant tomorrow, the type of telephone-answering machine we ought to get, and some documents my husband would like me to have my secretary mail for him." The consultant and her husband are not eager to have children because "we are used to the freedom that we have."

If this sort of enslavement to schedule spells freedom and the Good Life, then time management deals only with a topical rash, not the underlying malady. The management consultant's log is the portrait of a girl so dutiful that she no longer has a life of her own—even though she maintains that she is "doing what I love best." Surely we—for in all these women I see a mirror image—should stop once in a while—if only to enjoy the fruits of our labor.

As women take on many roles, we gain the considerable satisfaction of calling ourselves professionals or executives. We feel included in more parts of society. But we lose time—and perhaps the inclination—to think about what exactly we are doing. We work hard, but our work, may add up to killing time. Forced to emphasize productivity, we avoid the nasty worry about whether doing a lot equals achievement, whether "having it all" may mean losing it all.

As there are good reasons why time management doesn't work, there are also good reasons why it shouldn't. Philosopher Amelie Oksenberg Rorty writes, "Women who must juggle the demands of many different sorts of lives tend to become efficient, and so become competent, rather than original."

In *The Partners,* novelist and practicing attorney Louis Auchincloss, has given us a model in Felicia Currier, a beautiful and intelligent lawyer whose speedy mind darts to "the dead center of any tangle of circumstances." She never works evenings or weekends, yet does as well at her firm as her workaholic husband, whose long hours are spent birthing stale memos. "A law firm is only a tool to make a happy life," Felicia tells Marc, sensing that his "dark cloud of industriousness" has nothing to do with his "professional ambition or love of the law."

Time is all we have. We each choose different tools to build our lives, but surely the Good Life is nourished and replenished by time spent contemplating beauty, the landscape, ideas, dreams; enjoying children, friendship, sex; working for what we believe in.

Time-pressured lives are competent and productive. But they don't foster satisfaction; only more work, requiring more dutifulness. If we can stop being drudges, if we can run our own lives, we will accomplish a great deal. And should we fail to accomplish a great deal, perhaps we won't even care. For ultimately, time isn't money or status; time is life itself.

Savvy, December 1980.

A Case for Inefficiency

By Ann Marie Cunningham

Bertrand Russell thought that four hours of work a day was plenty for anyone. William Faulkner regretted it was possible to do more: "One of the saddest things is that the only thing a man can do for eight hours a day is work. You can't eat eight hours a day, nor drink eight hours a day, nor make love eight hours a day—all you can do is work."

Most great hunches and major breakthroughs seem to have popped into people's heads when they weren't working—when they were staring into space, goofing off or even sleeping. Stanislaw Ulam, the Polish expatriate physicist who, with Edward Teller, hit on the design for the hydrogen bomb in 1951, was considered spectacularly lazy by his colleagues at Los Alamos. While everyone else worked around the clock to win the Cold War, he never appeared at the lab before ten and was gone by four. When other scientists went hiking in the New Mexican mountains, he remained at the foot of the trail and watched through binoculars.

James D. Watson, one of the three unravelers of the structure of DNA, was too lazy a doctoral candidate to take chemistry or physics. He was drawn to science by the partying at conventions, and went to Cambridge, England, where he hooked up with Francis Crick and Maurice Wilkins, to learn biochemistry. The three were well matched: Crick girl-watched incessantly and subscribed only to *Vogue*. At the height of the race with Linus Pauling to decode DNA, Wilkins disappeared regularly for fencing lessons. Watson spent afternoons on the tennis court, showing up at the lab "for only a few minutes of minor fiddling before dashing away to have sherry with the girls at Pop's." He pondered DNA at the movies, where he spent almost every evening.

As the Recovery Gains, Compulsory Overtime Becomes a Rising Issue

Gregory Stricharchuk and Ralph E. Winter

Virgil Archer doesn't try to talk with his fellow workers. He is afraid it will start a fight.

"It's best to mind your own business in the plant," he says. "It's a rough place. People tend to stay to themselves."

The 42-year-old Mr. Archer doesn't work in a prison workshop, although he says his seven-day week "is like going to prison." He works in Chrysler Corp.'s auto plant in the Cleveland suburb of Twinsburg. Workers there have been working so much overtime that they explode over trifles at foremen, fellow workers, wives and even their dogs.

"You get on edge" after working seven-days a week for so long, Mr. Archer says. "Sometimes I ask my wife what day it is."

Walt Whitman heard America singing as people went about their work a hundred years ago. But there isn't any singing at the Chrysler plant. "It's solemn," Mr. Archer says. "You tread lightly because you don't know what kinds of problems the people have. The safest course is to say nothing except good morning," he suggests.

FEAST OR FAMINE

Workers got so angry about the long hours and other working conditions that they shut the plant down last fall, costing Chrysler as much as $90 million of profit. Some of the problems were ironed out in a new local contract, but the overtime continues. For these Chrysler workers, like many other Americans, the five-day, 40 hour week is a myth. One year they are laid off, and the next they are working 60 hours a week.

Americans with steady, white-collar jobs, many of whom also work 50 or 60 hours a week, often without extra pay, may find it hard to identify with factory workers bitter about working overtime following a recession when many were laid off. But office work tends to be more interesting than running a stamping press. And office workers are free to sit down, take a few minutes for coffee and if necessary, slip out to the dentist.

Manufacturing workers averaged 3.3 hours of overtime a week in November, up 43% from a year earlier, the Labor Department says. But that 3.3 hours is a statistic, not a typical situation. Fewer than a quarter of the workers put in most of those hours, which means that many worked 12 hours or more of overtime a week.

For some, like Russ, a slight, self-styled "long-haired country boy," working six days a week stamping out license-plate brackets permits a life that otherwise would be out of reach. "I'm making payments on a new stereo, a 1982 motorcycle and a 1978 Camaro," he says over a beer in a country-music bar. He smiles at his companion, a honey-blonde amateur poet who has a nine-month-old son. "I tell her I have no money, but with this overtime I could provide." She smiles back, but pretends not to notice the offer.

EFFECTS OF OVERTIME

Few people like overtime work though. Economists say it leads people to take on payments for cars, motorcycles and houses that they can't afford when they go back to 40 hours. Many union leaders hate overtime, especially if it is mandatory. Many companies fire workers who refuse overtime without a medical excuse.

Overtime work traditionally increases at the beginning of a recovery, but in this industry union leaders and others say it has been overdone.

"Compulsory overtime is an outrage, fumes Sherwood "Bob" Weissman, the president of United Auto Workers' Local 122, which represents workers at the Twinsburg plant. "It's an imposition on a worker's life that goes beyond the bounds of decency."

Owen Bieber, the president of the UAW, said recently that the union will attempt to curb overtime in contract negotiations this year, even though "some of our members want the overtime, no matter what the cost to their fellow workers." During much of 1983, he said, "irresponsible" auto-company managements scheduled enough overtime to provide 55,000 jobs.

Some company officials, though, do have qualms about employees' working overtime while millions of Americans are unemployed. Prolonged overtime often cuts productivity, moreover, because workers pace themselves to be able to stand the extra hours. Product quality can deteriorate, company officials say. "You don't care if the job's done right; you just go through the motions," one Ford worker concedes.

SAVING FOR EMPLOYERS

Nonetheless, overtime is a common way to meet rising demand as the recovery spreads. Union leaders say companies find it cheaper to pay time-and-a-half for extra hours to existing workers than to pay health insurance, pensions, vacation pay, payroll taxes and other benefits for new employees. John Hunter, the president of UAW local 2000, which represents workers at Ford Motor Co.'s van-body plant in Avon Lake, Ohio, says each recalled worker is "a $19,000 liability" in benefit costs. (Ford calls that figure too high.)

Employers say it isn't that simple. "Any company that's been through substantial layoffs, and saw the problems created in the communities as well as the costs to the company, is going to be reluctant to balloon the work force with new hires until they're certain they will need that labor force longterm," says John J. Nevin, the chairman of Firestone Tire & Rubber Co.

But Americans who have been working long overtime hours on the assembly line talk of the hardships and guilt feelings that diminish their sense of accomplishment.

"It isn't the American dream," says Allen Brett, a tool and die maker at Chrysler's Twinsburg plant. "We're going into the 21st century, and we're working the same hours our grandfathers worked."

At the van-body plant in Avon Lake, Dorothy Geason says she is grateful to be working when unemployment is still high. But she feels guilty about how much she is working—nine or 10 hours a day sometimes six days a week.

"It makes you feel bad that you're working overtime and others are desperate" because they aren't working at all, says the assembly-line worker. "I wish people could come in and work those hours" of overtime, she says. "Maybe if they could work a few hours a day, they could save their homes."

But Ford basically decides who works and how long. "I try to put it out of my mind," she says. She is reminded, however, "every time I pick up the paper or see my neighbors who are laid off. So many people are out of work," she says, including her son-in-law, who was laid off from a General Motors plant.

Unemployment in Lorain Country, which is 20 miles west of Cleveland and includes Mrs. Geason's home city of Lorain as well as Avon Lake, Elyria and other towns, was 14.3% in November. That was down from a staggering 23.2% a year earlier but still was far worse than the 8.1% national average.

"When people find out you're working overtime, they're bitter and they make comments," Mrs. Geason adds. "They feel that people who work overtime shouldn't be working that much."

Mrs. Geason eases her conscience by helping some of her relatives. I've given more to people and the Salvation Army than I can afford," she says. The divorced mother of three grown children, Mrs. Geason says she made about $28,000 last year.

NOT MUCH FUN

But she says the overtime pay doesn't bring her much fun. "There is no life other than working," she complains. "All you do is work and sleep. I still have friends, but I'm lucky to see them."

Mrs. Geason, who looks far younger than her 53 years, says she has been trying to get a haircut and permanent for three weeks and has had to cancel the appointment three times.

"I used to go to the ballet, but I haven't done that in years," Mrs. Geason says. "I'm a treasure hunter—I have a metal detector. But I haven't done that for years. I used to bowl, but I haven't done that. I used to go horseback riding, I used to take trips . . . ." All of that has been abandoned for a life of working, eating and sleeping.

People who work overtime talk a lot about sleeping. Mrs. Geason says that on breaks at Ford she grabs a clean piece of cardboard, lies down on a steel platform and meditates. "You can meditate for 20 minutes and feel like you've slept for three hours," she says. Nonetheless, she says of overtime workers, "Once we get to bed, we don't want to get up." On some of the rare occasions when she gets a two-day weekend, she spends one day sleeping. "I pass out for a whole day."

DEFENDERS OF THE SYSTEM

Others staunchily support the long overtime hours because of the life style they help to provide.

Bertis "Chuck" Hardway, for example, lives with his wife, Ruth, in a four-bedroom house on nearly an acre of land on the edge of Elyria, about 11 miles south of Ford's Lorain plant, where he works.

On the kitchen wall is a framed picture of the ramshackle house where he grew up in West Virginia.

"I never thought I'd get this far," he says in a soft West Virginia accent. "We were raised poor," the trim, silvery-haired son of a coal miner says of himself and his wife, who was one of 12 children reared in a log house in West Virginia. "That's no sin. But staying poor is a sin."

Mr. Hardway doesn't intend to commit that sin. He earned about $40,000 last year working seven days a week at the auto-assembly plant. A former assembly-line worker, Mr. Hardway at age 45 is an apprentice millwright, learning to install conveyors, repair machinery and work with engineers on plant modernization. In addition to the long hours at the plant, he attends three hours of classes twice a week to learn the new trade. And on the side, he and a cousin run a used-auto-parts business. "The harder you work, the more you'll have," he says. "Nobody can stop you."

Other than holidays and plant shutdowns, such as between Christmas and New Year's, "I try to keep [days off] to under five days a year," he says. He is proud of the life style. "The 40-hour guys can't afford things," he says.

THE HARDWAY LIFE STYLE

Mr. Hardway can. The kitchen of his remodeled home is spotless, indicating that Mrs. Hardway, a slim woman in tight jeans and a bright pink sweater, works almost as hard as her husband. The appliances, including a microwave oven, are nearly new. The Hardways, who have five children, including one who was adopted, have only their 17-year-old daughter living at home now.

The Hardways own a mobile home in West Virginia that they visit "occasionally." Mr. Hardway has a 1982 Ford pickup, and his wife drives a 1984 Mercury. They have a camper to use on their infrequent vacations. Mr. Hardway bought an 18-foot truck and a $5,000 used tractor with a hydraulic loader that he uses in the auto-parts business.

Overtime work "takes away from your family," he admits. "I like to think that Ford doesn't own me, but they do." He says there have been times when he was so tired he could hardly walk, and there have been "months at a time that are a blur." He and his wife stick together because of their similar backgrounds, he says, "but divorce is rampant" among overtime workers. "A lot of women don't understand why their husbands are gone so much," he says. Often, a man doesn't know when he leaves home what time he will be back. At best, that makes it hard for his wife to plan meals. At worst, it leads to suspicion, jealousy and divorce.

Mr. Hardway's auto-parts sideline earns him about $10,000 a year, and it is "an insurance policy against bad times at Ford," he says. It will also give him something to do after retirement.

He and a cousin, who teaches school in West Virginia, ship used tires and parts for older cars to Boogerhole, W.Va. Recently, the partners began shipping firewood back to Ohio on the return trip, mainly to make a little extra money to pay the driver of Mr. Hardway's truck.

Henry S. "Hank" Lewandowski is somewhere between the beleaguered Mrs. Geason and the driven Mr. Hardway. He may be the model overtime worker.

The bearded, pipe-smoking electrician works seven days a week at Ford's Avon Lake plant. "I don't mind the overtime," he says. "Mentally, I've accepted it." He should by now, as he has worked extensive overtime for 21 of the 24 years he has been at Ford. Skilled workers, who have more varied and interesting work than those on the assembly line, generally resent overtime less.

"Forty hours is the cake. Overtime is the frosting," says Mr. Lewandowski. "You have to have the overtime to lick the frosting. That's my outlook."

Mr. Lewandowski, 45, and his wife, Marcia, are careful only to lick a little of the frosting. They won't allow themselves to become accustomed to eating. They budget as though they were "a 40-hour couple," he says. That way they won't be in trouble if overtime ends.

FINANCIAL DISCUSSIONS

They discuss every purchase over $25. The latest big outlay, $11,600 for a 1984 Ford pickup to pull their camper, came after nine months of talking over the possibilities.

When Mr. Lewandowski got out of military service in 1959, Marcia was pregnant and they had $135. It took more than a year to repay money they had to borrow to pay maternity bills. Mr. Lewandowski decided that he didn't ever want to be in that situation again. He grabbed as much overtime as he could get to provide "a cushion." Now, though, he takes a weekend off now and then, he says, for an overnight trip in his camper. At Mr. Lewandowski's plant, workers are entitled to every 14th day off, and his good attendance record gives him additional leeway.

The Lewandowskis won't disclose their income. But union officials say an electrician working seven eight-hour days would make about $50,000 a year. Until last March, Mrs. Lewandowski worked 30 hours a week as a bookkeeper in a men's-clothing store a few blocks from home. She quit to enroll in nursing school, which she will finish in March.

PAYING OFF THE MORTGAGE

Mr. and Mrs. Lewandowski and their youngest daughter, Donna, who is 14, live in a well-maintained, 50-year-old house in Lorain, about 15 miles west of the van plant. Three older children have left home. The mortgage payment is $139 a month. In five more years, it will be paid off. They have two cars and the truck, but only a one-car garage.

Many overtime workers drink to unwind, and some develop an alcohol problem. But not Hank Lewandowski. "Why should my overtime money make some bartender rich?" he asks.

He says working weekends has prevented him from making many friends. But the family is very close. For the last 10 years, he has worked the midnight shift, so he gets to see his family every evening. "Along the way, we missed things," he admits. "So when we're together, we have a good time."

Besides, it won't always be like this. Mr. Lewandowski plans to retire six years from now at age 51. He will be eligible for full pension under the

UAW contract. Early retirement is to be his reward for all the extra hours and thrifty living.

What then? First, he says, he and Marcia will spend a year or so camping around the country. Then he will "go back to school" to learn more about robots and computers. The subject interests him partly because he maintains computerized welding equipment at Ford. Eventually, he may become a consultant, he says.

Best Gift for Secretary: An Electrocardiogram

Ellen Goodman

They used to say it with flowers or celebrate it with a somewhat liquid lunch. National Secretaries Week was always good for at least a token of appreciation. But the way the figures add up now, the best thing a boss can do for a secretary this week is cough up for her cardiogram.

"Stress and the Secretary" has become the hottest new syndrome on the heart circuit.

It seems that it isn't those Daring Young Women in their Dress for Success Suits who are following men down the cardiovascular trail to ruin. Nor is it the female professionals who are winning their equal place in intensive care units.

It is powerlessness and not power that corrupts women's hearts. And clerical workers are the number one victims.

In the prestigious Framingham study, Dr. Suzanne Haynes, an epidemiologist with the U.S. National Heart, Lung and Blood Institute, found that working women as a whole have no higher rate of heart disease than housewives. But women employed in clerical and sales occupations do. Their coronary disease rates are twice that of other women.

"This is not something to ignore," says Dr. Haynes, "since such a high percentage of women work at clerical jobs." In fact, 35 percent of all working women hold these jobs.

When Dr. Haynes looked into their private lives, she found the women at greatest risk—with a one in five chance of heart disease—were clerical workers with blue-collar husbands, and three or more children. When she then looked at their work lives, she discovered that the ones who actually developed heart disease were those with nonsupportive bosses who hadn't changed jobs very often and who had trouble letting their anger out.

In short, being frustrated, dead-ended, without a feeling of control over your life is bad for your health.

The irony in all the various and sundry heart statistics is that we now have a weird portrait of the Cardiovascular Fun Couple of the Office. The Type A Boss and his secretary. The male heart disease stereotype is, after all, the Type A aggressive man who always needs to be in control, who lives with a great sense of time urgency . . . and is likely to be a white-collar boss.

"The Type A man is trying to be in control. But given the way most businesses are organized there are, in fact, few ways for them to be in control of their jobs," says Dr. Haynes. The only thing the Type A boss can be in control of is his secretary who in turn feels . . . well, you get the picture. He's not only getting heart disease, he's giving it.

Now then, as if all this weren't enough to send you out for the annual three-martini lunch, clerical workers are increasingly working for a new Type A boss: the computer.

These days fewer women are sitting in front of bosses with notepads and more are sitting in front of video display terminals. Word processors, data processors, microprocessors . . . these are the demanding, time-conscious, new automatons of automation. According to the IBM Word Processing Plan, "In the office of 1985 . . . there are no secretaries." Just pools of processors.

There is nothing intrinsically evil about computers. I am writing this on a VDT and if you try to take it away from me, I will break your arm. But as Working Women, the national association of office workers, puts it in their release this week, automation is increasingly producing clerical jobs that are deskilled, downgraded, dead-ended and dissatisfying.

As Karen Nussbaum of the Cleveland office described it, the office of the future may well be the factory of the past. Work on computers is often reduced to simple, repetitive, monotonous tasks. Workers are often expected to produce more for no more pay, and there are also reports of a disturbing trend to processing speed-ups and piece-rate pay, and a feeling among clerical workers that their jobs are computer-controlled.

"It's not the machine, but the way it's used by employers," says Working Women's research director, Judith Gregory. Too often, automation's most important product is stress.

Groups like Working Women are trying to get clerical workers to organize in what they call "a race against time" so that computers will become their tools instead of their supervisors.

But in the meantime, if you are 1) a female clerical worker, 2) with a blue-collar husband, 3) with three or more children, 4) in a dead-end job, 5) without any way to express anger, 6) with a Type A boss, 7) or a Type A computer controlling your work day . . . YOU BETTER START JOGGING.

What Stress Can Do to You

Walter McQuade

It has long been a matter of common intuition that bottled-up anger can crack the bottle, prolonged strain can make people sick. This old folklore now has considerable scientific support. Working independently, several groups of medical researchers—both physicians and psychologists— have collected impressive evidence that emotional factors are primarily responsible for many of the chronic diseases that have been hitting American males hard in middle age, notably the big one, heart disease. Challenging medical dogma, these doctors deny that fatty diet, cigarette smoking, and lack of proper exercise pose the main perils to men in their working prime. Much more important, they say, is stress. Stress might be defined as the body's involuntary reactions to the demanding life that we Americans choose—or that chooses us.

These reactions are rooted deep in the prehistory of the human species. Early man survived in a brutal world because, along with an elaborate brain, he had the mechanism of instantaneous, unthinking physical response when in danger. Picture a primitive man, many thousands of years ago, lying in the sun in front of his cave after the hunt, digesting. Suddenly, he felt the cool shadow of a predatory carnivore, stalking. Without thinking, he reacted with a mighty surge of bodily resources. Into his blood flashed adrenal secretions that mustered strength in the form of both sugar and stored fats to his muscles and brain, instantly mobilizing full energy, and stimulating pulse, respiration, and blood pressure. His digestive process turned off at once so that no energy was diverted from meeting the threat. His coagulation chemistry immediately prepared to resist wounds with quick clotting. Red cells poured from the spleen into the stepped-up blood circulation to help the respiratory system take in oxygen and cast off carbon dioxide as the ancestral man clubbed at the prowling beast, or scuttled safely back into his cave.

A COOL MEMO FROM A V.P.

Today, say stress researchers, a man in a business suit still reacts within his skin, in much the same chemical way. He does so although today's threat is more likely to be in the abstract, for example, a cool memo from a vice president of the corporation: "The chairman wants a study of the savings possible in merging your division with warehousing and relocating to South Carolina."

Flash go the hormones into the blood; up goes the pulse beat—but the manager who receives the memo can neither fight physically nor flee. Instead his first tendency is to stall, which only induces guilt, before he plunges into a battle fought with no tangible weapons heavier than paper clips. Under his forced calm builds repressed rage without any adequate target—except himself.

If he is the kind of hard-driving, competitive perfectionist whom many corporations prize, and if this kind of stress pattern is chronic, the stress experts will tell you that he is a prime candidate for an early coronary (an even likelier candidate than American men in general, whose chances of having a heart attack before age sixty are one in five). If not a coronary, it may be mirgrane, ulcers, asthma, ulcerative colitis, or even the kind of scalp itch James V. Forrestal developed as he began to give way to interior pressure. Or perhaps a collision on the road—stressed people are more accident-prone.

Chronic strain is so common that there are conventional ways of fighting back. Millions of pills repose in desk drawers, ready to foster calmness or energy. The trouble with them, say the doctors, is that after the calm or the uplift there usually comes a period of depression. Martinis may be better, although they too involve dangers. Some people under stress try to vent their repressed anger in polite violence at a driving range or bowling alley, or by chopping wood or throwing themselves at ocean waves breaking on the beach. But the violent exercisers had better be careful of contracting another common stress symptom, low back pain.

Marriages have to accept a lot of stress, both in hurtful words and yet another symptom, temporary impotence. If a man coming under job stress has been on an anticholesterol diet he had better stay on it, but the competitive strain on him will be upping his serum cholesterol, whatever he eats. In broad terms, man the victorious predator now preys internally on himself.

LOST CONSOLATIONS

. . . Particularly destructive of the individual's sense of security have been the side effects of one of the industrial world's most precious products—social mobility. This bright trophy of our times has its deeply etched dark side. Social mobility has weakened the sense of belonging to a class, the sense of having a place in the social order. More important, social mobility implies that success depends on merit alone, and to the extent that a society believes in such correlation, individual bread-winners are thrust into an endless competition in which losing or lagging can be interpreted as a sign of personal inadequacy. . . .

DISCOVERING THE UBIQUITOUS

A pioneer investigator into the implications of stress was Dr. Hans Selye, a Canadian who has become the world's acknowledged authority on his subject. Selye, now sixty-four, defines stress as the non-specific response of the body to any demand made on it. He maintains that stress went unstudied in detail for centuries simply because it had always been so common. "Stress is ubiquitous, and it is hard to *discover* something ubiquitous."

Selye recalls that an intimation of his future specialty came to him in his youth. "I was a second-year medical student in Prague in 1926 when my professor brought in five patients for the student to diagnose—one with cancer, one with gastric ulcer, etc. It struck me that the professor never spoke about what was common to them all, only about what were the specifics of the diagnosis. All these patients had lost weight, lost energy, and lost their appetites."

Ten years later, as an assistant professor at McGill in Montreal, Selye observed that various kinds of insults to the bodies and nervous systems of laboratory animals had lasting effects in making them vulnerable to subsequent stress. "I was trying to isolate a hormone in the laboratory. I was working with extracts of cow ovaries and injecting them into rats. All of them, when later subjected to stress, had the same reaction—adrenal overaction, duodenal and gastric ulcers, and shrinking thymus, spleen, and lymph nodes. The worse the stress, the stronger the reaction. Then I tried injecting other materials, even simple dirt. I even tried electric shock, and got the same results." When he tried inducing fear and rage, results were again similar.

WHEN ALL THE RATS DIED

One of Selye's most significant breakthroughs came when he realized he could take two similar groups of rats and predispose one group to heart disease, uncommon in animals, by injecting an excess of sodium and certain types of hormones. Then he would expose both groups of rats to stress. None of the control group suffered. *All* the rats in the predisposed group died of heart disease.

In time, Selye came to the conviction that the endocrine glands, particularly the adrenals, were the body's prime reactors to stress. "They are the only organs which do not shrink under stress; they thrive and enlarge. If you remove them, and subject an animal to stress, it can't live. But if you then inject extract of cattle adrenals, stress resistance will vary in direct proportion to the amount of the injection, and can even be put back to normal."

Selye explains that when the brain signals the attack of a stressor— which could be either a predatory beast or a threatening memorandum —the adrenal and pituitary glands produce the hormones ACTH, cortisone, and cortisol, which stimulate protective bodily reactions. If the stress is a fresh wound, the blood rushes irritants to seal it off; if the stress is a broken bone, swelling occurs around the break. The pro-inflammatory hormones are balanced by anti-inflammatory hormones, which prevent the body from reacting so strongly that the reaction causes more harm than the invasion.

ENERGY THAT CAN'T BE REPLENISHED

So the initial reaction to any kind of stress is alarm. It is followed by an instantaneous rallying of the body's defenses. The fight is on—even if the body, in effect, is just fighting the mind. If the threat recedes or is overcome, stability returns. But if the attack is prolonged, deterioration sets in, as the defense system gradually wears down. Selye calls this process the General Adaptation Syndrome, and it is recognized in the field as a brilliant concept.

Stress is not only a killer, Selye teaches, but also a drastic aging force. Different men have different hereditary capacities to withstand stress, but once each man's "adaptation energy" has been expended, there is no way yet known to replenish it. Selye believes that some time in the future it may be possible to produce from the tissues of young animals a substance that could replenish human stress energy. "But that is for the Jules Verne future—soft research, like soft news, that *may* happen."

Selye likens each man's supply of life energy to deep deposits of oil; once the man has summoned it up and burned it in the form of adaptation energy, it is gone—and so, soon, is he. If he picks a high-stress career, he spends his portion fast and ages fast. "There are two ages," says Selye, "one which is chronological, an absolute, and the other which is biologic and is your effective age. It is astonishing how the two can differ. . . .

A QUEERLY CONTEMPORARY QUALITY

Stress research in the U.S. centers on heart disease, and for good reason. Cardiovascular ailments such as coronary heart disease now take an appalling annual toll in lives of American men in vigorous middle age. Of the 700,000 people who died from coronary heart disease in the U.S. last year, almost 200,000 were under sixty-five.

Yet until this century heart disease was virtually unknown anywhere in the world, and as late as the 1920s it was still fairly rare in the U.S. Dr. Paul Dudley White, the eminent cardiologist, recalls that in the first two years after he set up his practice in 1912 he saw only three or four coronary patients. The queerly contemporary quality of heart disease cannot be attributed to the ignorance of earlier doctors. As far back as the time of Hippocrates, most afflictions were described well enough to be recognized today from surviving records. A convincing description of heart disease, however, was not entered in medical records until late in the eighteenth century.

Some of the most important research on the effects of occupational stress in the U.S. has been carried out by the University of Michigan's Institute for Social Research, and the experts there are not impressed with the conventional medical wisdom regarding coronaries. Professor John R. P. French, Jr., an austere and plainspoken psychologist at the institute, says that the known risk factors do not come close to accounting for the incidence of the disease. He maintains that "if you could perfectly control cholesterol, blood pressure, smoking, glucose level, serum uric acid, and so on, you would have controlled only about one-fourth of the coronary heart disease." There is little solid evidence, he adds, "to show that programs of exercise substantially reduce the incidence of coronary heart disease or substantially reduce some of the risk factors."

To a great extent, argues French, the problem is the job. "The stresses of today's organizations can pose serious threats to the physical and psychological well-being of organization members. When a man dies or becomes disabled by a heart attack, the organization may be as much to blame as is the man and his family." A nationwide survey directed by French's colleague Robert L. Kahn found evidence of widespread occupational stress in the U.S. The results indicated that 35 percent of the employees had complaints about job ambiguity, meaning a lack of clarity about the scope and responsibilities of the work they were supposed to be doing. Nearly half—48 percent—often found themselves trapped in situations of conflict on the job, caught in the middle between people who wanted different things from them. Some 45 percent of the sample complained of overload, either more work than they would possibly finish during an ordinary working day, or more than they could do well enough to preserve their "self-esteem."

Other occupational stresses found by the survey included insecurity associated with having to venture outside normal job boundaries; difficult bosses or subordinates; worry over carrying responsibility for other people; the lack of a feeling of participation in decisions governing their jobs—a malaise, adds Dr. French, that distinctly lowers productivity.

Management jobs carry higher risks than most. In a detailed study done for NASA at the Goddard Space Flight Center, the investigators from Ann Arbor found that administrators were much more subject to stress than engineers or scientists. Responsibility for people, French explains, always causes more stress than responsibility for things—equipment, budgets, etc. The rise in serum cholesterol, blood sugar, and blood pressure among ground managers is much greater during manned space flights than during flights of unmanned satellites. Whatever their assignment, the administrators at Goddard, as a group, had higher pulse rates and blood pressure, and smoked more, than the engineers or scientists. Medical records revealed that administrators also had suffered almost three times as many heart attacks as either the scientists or the engineers.

THE CORONARY TYPE

In any occupation, though, people vary a great deal in the amounts of stress they can handle. Some researchers at the institute hope psychologists will be able to work out methods of screening employees for their tolerance of stress. There may even prove to be physiological methods of selection. Dr. French and his associates have discovered a direct correlation between "achievement orientation" and high readings or uric acid in the blood—regarded in the past principally as a sign of susceptibility to gout. "High serum uric acid persons," Frech reported, "tend not to see the external environment as a source of pressure. [They] tend to master their external environment, while high cholesterol persons are typified by the perception that the external environment is mastering them."

It is not a new observation that some people are more subject to stress than others. Sir William Osler lived too early to see many coronary cases, but he left a shrewd description of the angina type. "It is not the delicate, neurotic person who is prone to angina," he commented, "but the robust, the vigorous in mind and body, the keen and ambitious man, the indicator of whose engine is always at 'full speed ahead' . . . the well set man of from forty-five to fifty-five years of age, with military bearing, iron gray hair, and florid complexion."

This Osler quotation is a favorite of two California cardiologists, Meyer Friedman and Ray H. Rosenman, who are among the country's leading students of stress. In the past seventeen years they and their staff at the Harold Brunn Institute of Mount Zion Hospital in San Francisco have spent thousands of hours and hundreds of thousands of research dollars building up an impressive case that behavior patterns and stress are principal culprits in the high incidence of coronary heart attacks among middle-aged Americans—and that personality differences are of vital importance.

Until 1955, Friedman and Rosenman were conventional cardiologists, doing research in the standard heart risk factors: serum cholesterol, cigarette smoking, blood pressure, diet, and obesity. They also gave half their time to practice, however, and, says Friedman, "We finally began to look at the individuals. They were signaling us. More than 90 percent showed signs of struggle. An upholsterer came in to redo our waiting room, and pointed out that the only place the chairs were worn was at the front edge."

In studying reactions to stress, Friedman and Rosenman gradually came to the conviction that people can be divided into two major types, which they designate A and B. Type A, the coronary-prone type, is characterized by intense drive, aggressiveness, ambition, com-petitiveness, pressure for getting things done, and the habit of pitting himself against the clock. He also exhibits visible restlessness. Type B may be equally serious, but is more easygoing in manner, seldom becomes impatient, and takes more time to enjoy leisure. He does not feel driven by the clock. He is not preoccupied with social achievement, is less competitive, and even speaks in a more modulated style. Most people are mixtures of Type A and Type B characteristics, but a trained interviewer can spot one pattern or the other as predominant.

A RATHER GRIM CHUCKLE

The extreme Type A is a tremendously hard worker, a perfectionist, filled with brisk self-confidence, decisiveness, resolution. He never evades. He is the man who, while waiting in the office of his cardiologist or dentist, is on the telephone making business calls. His wife is certain he drives himself too hard, and she may be a little in awe of him. The world is a deadly serious game, and he is out to amass points enough to win.

He speaks in staccato, and has a tendency to end his sentences in a rush. He frequently sighs faintly between words, but never in anxiety, because that stage is strange to him. He is seldom out sick. He rarely goes to doctors, almost never to psychiatrists. He is unlikely to get an ulcer. He is rarely interested in money except as a token of a game, but the higher he climbs, the more he considers himself underpaid.

On the debit side, he is often a little hard to get along with. His chuckle is rather grim. He does not drive people who work under him as hard as he drives himself, but he has little time to waste with them. He wants their respect, not their affection. Yet in some ways he is more sen-sitive than the milder Type B. He hates to fire anyone and will go to great lengths to avoid it. Sometimes the only way he can resolve such a situa-tion is by mounting a crisis. If he himself has even been fired, it was probably after a personality clash.

Type A, surprisingly, probably goes to bed earlier most nights than Type B, who will get interested in something irrelevant to his career and sit up late, or simply socialize. Type A is precisely on time for appointments and expects the same from other people. He smokes cigarettes, never a pipe. Headwaiters learn not to keep him waiting for a table reservation; if they do, they lose him. They like him because he doesn't linger over his meals, and doesn't complain about quality. He will usually salt the meal before he tastes it. He's never sent a bottle of wine back in his life. Driving a car, Type A is not reckless, but does reveal anger when a slower driver ahead delays him.

Type A's are not much for exercise; they claim they have too little time for it. When they do play golf, it is fast through. They never return late from vacation. Their desk tops are clean when they leave the office at the end of each day.

AN UNRECOGNIZED SICKNESS

But in the competition for the jobs in their companies, says Dr. Friedman, A's often lose out to B's. They lose because they are too competitive. They are so obsessed with the office that they have attention for nothing else, including their families. They make decisions too fast—in minutes, rather than days—and so may make serious business mistakes. They are intoxicated by numerical competition: how many units were sold in Phoenix, how many miles were traveled last month. Also, says Friedman, Type A's frequently have about them an "existential" miasma of hostility, which makes others nervous.

Type B's differ little in background or ability from A's, and may be quietly urgent, but they are more reasonable men. Unlike Type A, Type B is hard to needle into anger. Friedman says, "A's have no respect for B's, but the smart B uses an A. The great salesmen are A's. The corporation presidents are usually B's."

What is most tragic of all in this picture of hopeful, driving, distorting energy is that the Type A's are from two to three times more likely than the Type B's to get coronary heart disease in middle age. In all of Sinclair Lewis' pitiless characterizations of the go-getting American businessman of another era, there is nothing so devastating as these doctors' cool, clinical statistics. Says Rosenman about the Type A condition: "It is a sickness, although it is not yet recognized as such."

The test program that Friedman and Rosenman offer as their strongest body of evidence was undertaken in 1960 with substantial backing from the National Institutes of Health. A total of 3,500 male subjects aged thirty-nine to fifty-nine, with no known history of heart disease, were interviewed and classified as Type A or Type B. Then came complete physical examinations, which are still being performed on a regular basis as the program continues to accumulate data. So far, 257 of the test group—who are roughly half A's and half B's—have developed coronary heart disease. Seventy percent of the victims have been Type A's.

Even more emphatic is the picture that emerged when A's and B's were evaluated with respect to the generally accepted risk factors for heart trouble. As a group the A's had higher cholesterol levels than the B's. But it was found that even A's whom the conventional wisdom would have rated safer in blood pressure, parental history, or any combination of the usual risk factors were more likely to develop coronary heart disease. Conversely, B's could show adverse ratings in blood pressure and other factors and still be relatively safe. Dr. Rosenman reported that any B whose level of cholesterol and other fatty acids was within normal limits "had complete immunity to coronary heart disease, irrespective of his high-fat, cholesterol diet, family history, or his habits of smoking or his lack of exercising."

What creates a Type B or Type A? These cardiologists do not profess to know the complete answer yet. But to them it is obvious that both heredity and environment are involved. A's are naturally attracted toward careers of aggressiveness and deadline pressure. American life today, Friedman and Rosenman observe, offers plenty of these. What Type A's need but cannot easily achieve is restraint, says Dr. Friedman, who himself suffered a heart attack in 1967.

The medical debate that the Brunn Institute and the other stress researchers have joined is a bitter one, with deeply entrenched positions. The most emphatic opponents of the stress theory are those nutrition experts who, over the past twenty years, have virtually convinced the nation that a diet high in saturated fat and cholesterol is responsible for the epidemic of heart trouble. One pointed criticism that opponents make against the Friedman-Rosenman studies is that their method of classifying individuals into Type A or Type B is subjective, relying heavily on signs of tension as observed by the interviewer. The two cardiologists do not deny this, but point out that a good deal of all medical analysis is subjective. Their independent appraisals of Type A's or Type B's agree, they say, at least as much as doctors' readings of identical X-ray films. Says Rosenman: "Most epidemiologists are incapable of thinking of anything that cannot be qualified. There are no positive links between diet or exercise and heart disease, either. A migraine is subjective, too."

LAST WORDS OF A GREAT MAN

Studies of stress and its effects are now under way around the world. In 1950 Hans Selye's pioneering work was the sole technical treatise published on stress; last year there were close to 6,000 separate reports on stress research. At the Brunn Institute, Dr. Rosenman says, "we can't keep up with the requests from all over the world to train people here." During recent years, courts of law in the U.S., in a highly significant switch, have begun to favor plaintiffs seeking compensation for damage related to heart attacks caused by alleged stress on the job.

Now that even cardiologists are beginning to believe heart disease can be traced to unrelenting competitiveness and baffled fury, will a wave of concern over stress sweep over this hypochondriacal country, to match the widespread interest in jogging and polyunsaturated oils? Quite likely. There is nothing more fascinating to the layman than folklore finally validated by reputable scientists. A murmur of assent rises faintly from the past. When the great Pasteur lay in terminal illness, in 1895, he relfected once again on his long scientific disagreement with Claude Bernard. Pasteur's dying words were: "Bernard was right. The microbe is nothing, the terrain is everything."

Vancouver Sun, January 29, 1981.

Whistle Stops Anger Office Staff

BOISE, Idaho (AP)—Seven times a day, someone blows a whistle at the Idaho health and welfare office. The secretaries have to stop and fill out a form saying what they're doing at that moment.

Administrators in the state department of health and welfare say it's a good way to check office efficiency, part of a drive to eliminate three secretarial positions in an economy move.

Secretaries call it insulting, degrading and disruptive.

The procedure began on Monday. That was when Theo Murdock, chief of the state's welfare division instructed aides to blow the whistle—literally—on the secretarial staff. He said the "random moment time study" would enable him to judge how the secretaries spend time on the job.

Murdock said he has been ordered by Gov. John Evans to cut the budget by $110,000. This means three secretaries have to go.

Efficient or not, the secretaries say they don't like the whistle stops.

"It's insulting to my intelligence the way they go about these things," said one of them, Lois Moreland.

Complained Angie Stelling: "Yesterday morning, there wasn't a single whistle. They all blew in the afternoon and everybody was sitting on pins and needles afraid to take a break or go to the bathroom."

Murdock, however, said he doesn't expect even the most dedicated secretary not to take a coffee break once in a while. "That's part of the working day. If none of those showed up, I would be concerned."

But the biggest objections appeared to be aimed at the chief whistle blower, Robert Jensen.

"They're paying him a good salary to lay off three of our people," said Lois Moreland.

The study is due to end in mid-February.

Reprinted by permission of the Associated Press.

7

CONTROL
AND RESISTANCE

I was beginning to learn the second lesson that would be taught me many times over in a variety of jobs. Don't do more work than is absolutely necessary.

—*Robert Schrank*

The struggle for control of people's behavior and their efforts to evade it have been noted throughout recorded history in almost every organizational setting. Managerial theorists and behavioral scientists of virtually every persuasion have written volumes on how to control, but resistance and evasion continue under even the most harsh and coercive circumstances. In most contemporary organizations, attempts to control behavior must be more subtle than in the past, but then so are many of the techniques subordinates use to frustrate the wishes of their superiors. Much of the waste and bad blood that result seem to us to be directly attributable to the shortsightedness of management, subterfuge, organizational politics, and attempts at exploitation that we have noted elsewhere in this book.

The articles in this section describe several of the less publicized systems organizations have evolved to control the behavior of their members and, as a counterpoint, techniques employees use to counter attempts at control.

In "The Art of Saying No," Izraeli and Jick identify four types of refusal ceremonies that managers use to say no to subordinates or other organizational members. Each ceremony is invoked with the intention of controlling employees while preserving their commitment to the organization and socializing their expectations and their behavior. To accomplish these objectives, no sayers strive to manage meanings and to define and to shape the realities of those who are making requests of managers and of the organization.

Izraeli and Jick point out that dysfunctions typically accompany such techniques of control. Subordinates may accept but not like the verdict. The manipulations may have deleterious effects on morale, commitment, and productive efforts of subordinates. The authors capture the messiness, the ethical aspects of saying no in this way in a graphic illustration of a scientist who, as a manager, is asked to lie to his employees, to tell them they cannot have salary increments that are in fact possible.

The short *Business Week* piece by Clark and Hall, "The Administration vs. the Scientists: A Dangerous Rift Over Locking Up 'Sensitive' Data," illustrates alienation and resistance that stem from introduction of measures that do not have credibility or validity in the eyes of those being controlled. The clash is between administrators and professionals, and between conflicting goals, values, and assumptions. Clark and Hall describe tactics being used by the scientists to try to avoid, remove, or minimize the controls being invoked by the United States Defense Department. That decisions on tactics are not always clear-cut or easy to determine, is clear from the conflict within the professional community involved. There are differences of opinion on the relative merits of hard line versus moderate responses to control.

James Thurber's story "The Catbird Seat," captures some of the finer nuances of resistance to organizational control attempts. It is a chronicle of survival. Mr. Martin, the department head whose organizational future is threatened by a new manager, Mrs. Barrows, resorts to stealth, subterfuge, and flexible responses in the face of control attempts that are rigid, unimaginative, and predictable. The outcome is both amusing and instructive.

Another humorous story, "Señor Payroll" by William E. Barrett illustrates resistance to control by lower level employees in an organization. The central characters are a group of Mexican stokers who foiled the best efforts at bureaucratic control of their work habits by the company's head office.

Organizational reality, as these two pieces show, can be shaped by resisters. Employees who feel threatened by management control attempts can find ways to "hold the line," often using the same raw materials of control, such as desire for and belief in a system of predictability and order, to "turn the tables" on their bosses. A further example of resistance techniques and the attitudes and beliefs that support them can be found in Robert Schrank's "Furniture Factory." Set in the early 1930s, Schrank's description of his life in a furniture factory is very evocative. He brings to the reader a sense of the sights, sounds, and smells of factory life as well as the tedium of the work and the social world of the workers. He is carefully instructed and socialized into a way of working that is intended to protect him from control and exploitation by factory management. He learns how to work smart rather than hard and to do no more work than is absolutely necessary.

Schrank provides a glimpse of the antagonism and suspiciousness between workers and management of that era. A more chilling and disturbing perspective on this condition and the extent to which managerial control of the worker took place in some organizational settings in and prior to the 1930s is provided in the LaFollette report which, in edited form, "Excerpts from Violations of Free Speech and Rights of Labor," follows Schrank's piece. The report and its excerpts in this book deal with the coercive and subversive strategies and tactics used by some managers to control their workers in the early part of this century. Under the guise of control objectives such as preventing sabotage, detecting theft, and improving efficiency in methods and workers, management employed labor spies provided by detective agencies, including Pinkerton's, to undermine and destroy unions and attempts at union organizing. (Note that Schrank in his article says that he was fired from the factory as soon as he signed a union card.)

The report includes a description of the tactics spy agencies used to hire employees into careers as spies. Shrewd manipulation by "hookers" gradually drew individuals, who typically were in financial difficulty or who felt aggrieved by their unions, into a life of informing management on their friends and colleagues. The excerpts make for sobering reading. An important question for us centers on the generalizability of the material in this report to the current era of work organizations. In what ways have legislation, education, and management practice in relation to unions and union organizing changed since the times reflected in the LaFollette report? In what ways have they remained the same? At the very least, the material should serve as a warning of how far out of control attitudes and approaches to control can stray when those in power feel seriously threatened by those in their employ. As is noted in the report, an organization that resorts to spying for information so that it may control its workers is buying a risky package. "Spies beget spies—lies beget more lies—distrust begets distrust—until all faith is gone."

We started the readings in this section on control and resistance with an article that focused on control through managing meanings in which managers say no to their employees in symbolic ceremonial organizational language. We end the section with another article in which the management of reality is once again important, although the levels of complexity of control and resistance in this case are much higher. In Greider's "The Education of David Stockman," we gain a glimpse of President Reagan's attempts, in 1981, to introduce through David Stockman, his young Director of the Office of Management and Budget, a federal budget which would permit a balanced budget by 1984.

Stockman provides to Greider a very candid picture of his experiences with the development of the budget. (His candor earned him a strong reprimand from President Reagan. The article from which this excerpt is taken caused considerable commentary among politicians and the press when it was published.)

Stockman's story reveals the manipulation of reality, as well as the pace and pressure involved in attempting to gain control and to change direction in organizations that are large, complex, and highly interdependent with others. We see control attempts in this case in terms of conflicts between ideology and practice, and it becomes evident that many compromises occur along the way. Control is not likely to be clear cut nor necessarily enduring when there are countervailing forces at work, when those attempting control do not have all the winning cards in their hands. The piece provides a wealth of insights into the dynamics of control and resistance in a complex system.

The Art of Saying No:
On the Management of Refusals
in Organizations

Dafna Izraeli and Todd D. Jick

INTRODUCTION

The study of organizational culture has recently been furthered by examination of the content, function, and underlying meanings of symbols, language, stories, ideologies, rituals and myths (e.g., Moch, 1980; Smircich and Morgan, 1982; Wilkins, 1983). It has been argued that these mechanisms of culture-building convey multiple meanings (Pettigrew, 1979; Louis, 1983). On one level, technical or instrumental information may be conveyed while, at another, one can characterize the ceremonial nature of communication in terms of its expression of values, premises, and interests embodied in the definition of the situation. This ceremonial level primarily "says things", conveys a message, rather than "does things" (Leach, 1968). Thus the construction and maintenance of these common understandings or shared meanings (Louis, 1983; Smircich, 1983) have become increasingly subject to political analysis as to their role in sustaining and legitimating authority, in securing or preserving a semblance of order, harmony, and consensus in organizations (Abravanel, 1983; Smircich and Morgan, 1982). Wilkins (1983) noted that stories commonly told in organizations are important indicators of the social prescriptions concerning how things are to be done, the consequences of compliance or deviance, and an overall guide to what kinds of people can do what. In more subtle ways, symbols of culture convey beliefs about the use and distribution of power and privilege as reflected in rituals and myths which legitimate those distributions (Pettigrew, 1979).

What becomes interesting is how people come to believe, accept, and legitimate power and authority. Multiple elements of everyday life in the organization serve to transmit and reaffirm the existence and legitimacy of authority and of the ability of some people to define for others who they are and what it is they are doing.

Management does not have an absolute monopoly over the definitional process. The framing of organizational problems, the interpretive schemes, and the basic definition of reality are rarely uncontroversial. Anthropological studies of life on the shopfloor are rich in their documentation of the world of workers who operate with a different cultural tool kit (Swindler, 1982) and whose version of "what is going on here" is frequently very different from that of management (Roethlisberger and Dickson, 1939; Lupton, 1963; Crozier, 1964; Cunnison, 1966; Izraeli, 1980).

In the face of such tensions and conflicts, management typically seeks to build and sustain consensus while reinforcing their control. (Abravanel, 1983) How is this done? Tools of management include selective recruitment, training, promotion, role modeling, organizational and physical design, and direct communication of desired norms and values (Baker, 1980).

But, according to Smircich and Morgan (1982), effective leadership perhaps relies most on the management of meaning to the extent that the leader's definition of the situation serves as a basis for action by others, actions oriented to the achievement of desirable ends from the leader's viewpoint. Thus, the manager's role is portrayed as "framer of contexts, a maker and shaper of interpretive schemes (who) must deal with multiple realities." (Smircich, 1983). This management of context and meaning is a far less visible form of control than traditional supervision in that it achieves compliance on the basis of value premises. (Smircich, 1983) But it is a critical ingredient in the glue which holds an organization together. Ultimately, these invisible controls powerfully influence what people do and don't do, what people say and can't say, and what people have and can't have.

THE CASE OF REFUSAL CEREMONIES
AND SCARCE RESOURCES

One arena in which these mechanisms are manifest is in the distribution of incentives in organizations. For those who manage the organization, mobilizing and sustaining the willing cooperation of participants is a core dilemma. (Clark and Wilson, 1961) Pfeffer (1981, xi-xii) similarly observed that "one of the major tasks of managers is to make organizational participants want and feel comfortable doing what they have to do." Managers are assisted in accomplishing this by the widely accepted ideology that their authority is legitimate as well as by controlling the distribution of incentives of resources of both a material and symbolic nature.

However, the task can be especially difficult because there are always some people in the organization receiving less than they expect or less than they deem themselves entitled. Thus, the organization seeks ways to "cool out" (Goffman, 1952) their frustration and disappointment so as to retain the commitment and willingness of employees to give energy and loyalty to the organization's desired goals and purposes (Pettigrew, 1979; Kanter, 1972). Members must be helped to see how things are different from what they perceived and to shift their behavior accordingly. Organizations thus attempt to influence members to want less, to delay their gratification, to set policies as to who should have what, etc.

Two environmental conditions increase the prevalence with which organizations must engage in such influence rituals: a shift from economically good times to times of relative economic scarcity and an expansion of perceived entitlement. Both conditions lead to a negative shift in the ratio of those to whom the organization says "yes" to those to whom it says "no".

Consider two contemporary examples: organizational retrenchment, in which given or expected resources are typically taken away, and quality circles, in which generated requests for incremental resources may be discouraged. In both cases, a culture must be "re-worked" and power and influence exercised. In the first case, an ethos of expansiveness must give way to an ethos of frugality, restraint, and sacrifice (Jick and Murray, 1982). In the second case, beliefs in opportunity and change— stimulated by the development of quality circles—whet the appetite and encourage participants to make demands on organizational resources. Yet, the organization inevitably finds itself setting limits, defining domains, and establishing controls over resource distribution. In both cases, "reality" is brought in line with management's new definition of "what this organization needs". The result is that persons who expected to receive some benefit and may even have been initially encouraged in their expectations, must be helped to accept the new reality.

The art of saying "no" then is a process of redefining the situation and of managing meaning. The situated activity in which this is done we call a "refusal ceremony". It is through such ceremonies that we will illustrate the process by which the dominant culture is reaffirmed.

Refusal ceremonies may be classified as a specific case of breaking bad news. They are usually defined as unpleasant events by all participants involved. They are part of the dirty work of a manager's job. The task of saying no is usually assigned to the immediate superior who is expected to absorb the stings and arrows of the subordinate's disappointment. Since refusing requests is a normal part of everyday life in organizations, the immediate superior has sufficient credibility for the task.*

Our presentation focuses on the negative response of a superior to an initiative taken by a subordinate. We are describing one phase in a com-

---

*This is not so for occasions on which less routine bad news must be broken such as informing the family of the death of a kin—where persons of greater authority are required to lend credibility in the presence of an incredulous audience.

munication process, that in which the superior's response gives meaning to the action of the subordinate (e.g., Moch, 1980). The superior's response is the definition of reality in which the subordinate is invited to share.

SAMPLE AND DATA COLLECTION

The data for this study were collected from a convenience sample of 89 respondents, 67 or whom were enrolled in graduate business courses and 22 in an undergraduate business course. Most were part-time students who were also currently employed. All have had some previous work experience and the number of organizations virtually equalled the number of respondents. Overall, though, the sample reflects individuals at relatively early stages of their careers. The great majority may be classified as lower participants. The data were collected anonymously.

Respondents were asked to describe an incident in which their request for resources was denied by someone superior to them. The specific instructions were as follows:

> You've asked for, or let it be known, you'd like something such as a budget increase, an additional secretary, larger office space, assignment of a new project, salary hike, etc. However, you found that it would not be granted.

> Please describe: (a) the nature of the request; (b) what was said to you regarding the refusal; (c) how it was said, (e.g., verbally, in memo form, grapevine), and, (d) your reactions and feelings.

> Please be as specific as possible about the chronology of events, the communications and/or dialogue between you and your supervisor(s), and the resolution.

Analysis of our data suggests four types of ceremonies are conducted to convey refusals: normative invocation, status denial, rites of attrition, and rites of benevolence.

I. NORMATIVE INVOCATION

The most prevalent ceremonial strategy to explain and legitimate a refusal is the appeal to higher order values, such as rationalism, and to their structural manifestations. Technical efficiency and functional rationality are aspects of organizational ideology which legitimate the division of labour and the system of authority. Decisions made on those grounds become legitimate and by implication, correct. "We can't afford to increase your budget this year", "It's against company policy", "It's the rule here", "The interests of the organization require that", are statements tendered as reasons for not granting a request.

Normative invocations are occasions for the superior to explicate "the organization's point of view" and in so doing, to reaffirm management's right to define what the prevailing point of view is in the situation. The following examples are taken from our data:

Subordinate 1:   "It's not in the budget."

"Requested to hire an additional manager to cover afternoon shift operations. Was told could not afford to add to head count during decline in sales. Response: frustrated because I was convinced of the need and felt that the expense could be justified."

Subordinate 2:   "It's against corporate policy."

"Requested a foreign car instead of the standard North American car (company vehicle). Was refused on grounds that corporate policy did not allow for exceptions of this nature. Response: Was only marginally disappointed—did not feel the request would be granted in any event."

Subordinate 3:   "You haven't the seniority."

"On the part-time job requested more hours of work for the summer. The request was refused as management replied that the number of hours allotted was based on seniority and individuals who had been with the firm longer than myself were able to obtain more hours of work. Response: I felt that work performance is a more important criterion than seniority, however, since the company places more importance on seniority, I accepted the explanation with reluctance."

Subordinate 4:   "In the interest of the company."

"Requested a transfer of work classification to be retrained in a different functional area of the organization. Was told 'no'—as you are effectively performing your current job to the satisfaction and best wishes of the organization. Response: Although I understood the organization's point of view and was happy they considered me a top performer, I was bothered that they did not consider my feelings regarding the present job."

Subordinate 5:   "The needs of the organization."

"Requested a subordinate be transferred for his and the Company's benefit. Was told no, not now. Needs of my boss' organization too great at this time to release him, perhaps later. Response: Felt as if I had been out of line in making the request (which I wasn't) and felt hesitant about any future requests."

Subordinate 6:   "We can't afford it."

"Requested a pay raise. Was told not possible due to budget constraints. Response: Did not believe my bureau chief, I knew there was money available for raises and that it was his discretion solely that determined that distribution."

In the above cases the refusal is rationalized in terms of the rules of behaviour generally followed. In no case was the right of the superior to make the decision, and impose it upon the subordinate, questioned. The wisdom of the decision was questioned, even the wisdom of the criterion used for making the decision was criticized. Subordinate and superior, however, share an understanding of how the organization works. That understanding includes the belief that each holds about his/her relative authority and power in the situation. The ceremonies of refusal are micro-events in which these beliefs are tested against the reality and then either validated and reinforced, or weakened and perhaps transformed.

There are a number of reasons why normative invocations are the most frequently used rhetoric for conveying refusals. First, as already noted, they have high legitimacy in the organizational culture. Furthermore, reference to rational considerations impersonalize the refusal and veil the power dimension in the interaction between subordinate and superior (Gouldner, 1954). They are, in addition, difficult to refuse, since lower participants are usually less knowledgeable about rules and budget allocations than are their superiors. However, even when the subordinate is fully aware that the explanation is dishonest, as in the case of subordinate 6, few are ready to challenge and announce that the king has no clothes.

II. STATUS DENIAL

Organizational cultures define what kind of people are entitled to what sort of treatment. People are sorted for entitlements according to their technical skills as well as many other less formalized criteria, such as class, race, sex, age, and personal connections. The subordinate who initiates a request is frequently making a claim to being a certain kind of person or to having a certain status which entitles him/her to make the request and expect that it be granted.

A status denial ceremony is an occasion when the rejection of the claim forms the basis for the refusal. The message conveyed is that "you are not what you present yourself to be." This strategy shifts the responsibility for the refusal from the organization to the individual. If effective, the subordinate will perceive the organization as acting equitably and him/herself as inadequate. When the inadequacy is defined as remediable, and the subordinate is led to believe that s/he may become what s/he has professed to be (provided s/he completes the project, gets more experience, etc.) then fervor of effort is likely to ensue.

Subordinate 7:   "You will get what you deserve."

"A better rating on my annual evaluation was requested. I was told it would not be granted because I did not 'stand out in the crowd'. I had a verbal interview. I was very angry. I requested and obtained a second verbal interview. I requested a full explanation of the evaluation process and criteria. I presented my case based on the criteria. At a third interview I was informed my rating had been improved as I had requested. I was informed that the improved rating was not due to my efforts but because my manager's superior thought I deserved the rating."

Another form of status denial is to insist that the subordinate has not met the time requirements for that which s/he requests, as in the following examples:

Subordinate 8:   You're not here long enough."

"I had requested an increase in salary from $160 to $200 per week. I had been employed a year and a half in what I considered an above average job. I was refused on the basis that no one got a raise until working two years."

Subordinate 9:   "You're not old enough."

"I worked in a commercial bank. Asked to be promoted to commercial banking officer from division assistant. I was told that I was too young and not ready for the position (I was only 22 years old.)."

Merton (1982) referred to such time considerations as "socially expected durations"; namely, culturally prescribed and socially patterned expectations about the amount of time something will or should take. They are not the same as actual durations. The enactment of a socially expected duration as a justification for refusal may reflect the belief that during a specified time something will occur which is not likely to occur in less (or more) time. Time then becomes the measurable substitute for whatever process is supposed to occur.

Status denial may also take the form of discrediting the subordinate's presentation of self and accrediting him/her with a less attractive identity. The superior may select from a variety of labels (too aggressive, too impatient, uncooperative, poor team worker), any or all of which might serve to disqualify the subordinate for the very benefits being sought. Discrediting has high fear arousal potential and in that sense may belong to the cagegory of intimidation ceremonies.

Intimidation rituals (O'Day, 1974)* aim to dissuade the subordinate

---

* O'Day (1974) describes the intimidation rituals (nullification, isolation, defamation and expulsion) performed in progression by middle level bureaucrats to control the reform initiatives of a subordinate.

from pursuing his/her claim to entitlement. The dominant emotion aroused is that of fear—of the consequences of not changing the course of action. Intimidation may be conveyed in many styles from that of direct overt threat to the light hearted manner in the following case:

> Subordinate 10:   "Things could get worse."

> "I worked as a bricklayer this summer for a small, single owner company. The owner was my boss, he worked beside me and one other employee. I was earning $6/hr as was the other guy. After six months we both approached the owner and asked him if he could give us a 50¢/hr. raise. The owner refused stating in a half joking, half serious way that we were lucky to have a job in the first place."

In sum, status denial represents the harshest threat to the personal identity and future role of the individual. In demeaning, threatening, or exposing the status of the individual, this tactic reinforces the sanctity and impenetrability of organizational rules, values, and stature.

III.   ATTRITION

Rites of attrition are a form of "non-violent" resistance in which refusal is frequently implicit but not openly voiced. If successful they produce motivational fatigue as the subordinate gets used to his/her condition and comes to accept it. Attrition takes two forms: avoidance and stalling.

Avoidance takes place when the subordinate's initiatives are disattended (Goffman, 1959). Telephone messages are not responded to, letters are not answered. After one or two attempts, the subordinate may either get discouraged or get the message and withdraw from further initiatives.

Avoidance is more likely to take this form in large organizations where relations are relatively formalized and the person to whom the communication is directed is not the immediate superior or at least not personally known to the subordinate. These conditions made the use of informal modes of access to those in authority more difficult. Such inaccessibility may be specifically fostered for that purpose. Avoidance, however, may also occur in face to face encounters as in the following example related by a newly tenured associate professor:

> "I wrote my Dean asking for an extended leave. He didn't reply. I met him several times after that at faculty meetings but each time he avoided raising the issue. I was forced to be the one to raise it. I began to feel like a nag. Last time he walked right by me as if I weren't there. I knew I better not raise the issue there."

Avoidance is most likely to deter only the more timid and those whose position in the organization is precarious. If the subordinate persists, the superior may be persuaded to shift to another ceremonial strategy.

"My hands are tied" or "It's not up to me" is another type of avoidance ritual in which the superior avoids dealing with the issue by pointing to other individuals, groups or organizations who may be, credibly, presented as constraining action on the part of the superior. Organizations that generate a large number of committees provide fertile ground for the use of this ritual. The superior may relate a dramatized description of the intricacies and complexities of the organization's decision making process to convince the subordinate that "It's not up to me". The superior may offer to "look into it" and thus shift from an avoidance to a stalling ceremony.

Stalling refers to tactics used to gain time, such as "I'll look into it", or "You look into it". As different from avoidance, stalling tactics convey the message that something is being done to remedy the situation. Stalling may also have an attritional effect but successful stalling rites sustain the subordinate's belief in the organization's good will toward him/her and the hope that at some time in the future the matter will be resolved to the subordinate's satisfaction, as in the following example:

Subordinate 11:   "I'll get back to you."

"Requested an increase in salary. The initial response was positive with the supervisor (owner of Co.) agreeing with my request and saying he would get back to me. A few weeks passed with no response so I approached him. Again a few weeks passed and then I was told it would come in the form of a bonus and pay increase at the end of the year. It's been 6 months since my request and although they haven't said no, I haven't seen any increase or been informed of the amount."

In "I'll look into it" the manager presumably takes it upon him/herself to pursue the matter further after the subordinate leaves. This expression of intent and good will may be lent greater credibility by a jotting down of a note as an indication to the subordinate that the manager is resolved to do something, as if once recorded "I'll look into it" takes on an "as good as done" quality.

"You look into it" transfers responsibility for the next step to the subordinate. S/he is asked to do something which is presented as necessary before anything else can be done. This may require preparing a report explaining his/her position on the issue or collecting data which may be difficult to obtain:

Subordinate 12:   "Bring me proof."

"I requested additional office help (1 person) for duties the junior marketing assistant had in addition to her researching and analyzing functions; since when her work load backs up, so does mine. (I am the senior marketing research assistant.) The refusal was based on the overall all-corporate freeze, in addition to the lack of long term history regarding the amount of work that such an extra person would have—in other words, I couldn't prove that there would always be 40 hours of work per week for a secretary."

Successful stalling may be extended for a relatively long time until either the superior is replaced or circumstances change so as to make the initial request no longer relevant. The following incident reveals how the first supervisor was spared the refusal while her replacement shifts responsibility for solving the problem to the subordinate, an implicit discrediting ritual:

Subordinate 13:   "Wait till things settle down."

"I requested an exchange of offices, to be nearer my boss and co-workers. My boss and co-workers were clustered at the other end of the building. I wanted to be more involved in their work. My boss said to wait until 'things settled down', then until the organizational development project was finished. I waited 12-18 months. My boss moved up to executive director, reporting to the Vice-President, and my new boss told me (2 weeks ago) that no change would be made; I was also told that it was up to me to overcome the obstacle of distance and to find ways to integrate myself into the activities of my co-workers."

Stalling ceremonies are successful when they convey a message of good will and get the manager off the hook, if only temporarily. The general cultural norm according to which it is not nice to refuse a request, makes it generally more difficult to say "no" than to say "yes". Thus, rites of attrition may reflect as much of the general culture as the local organizational values and norms.

IV. BENEVOLENCE

A refusal may take the form of a benevolence rite in which the organization affirms its concern for the subordinate as a human being. Examples of benevolence are "for your own good!!" (FYOG) and "See how fair we are." (SHFWA) In FYOG the meaning of the refusal is inverted and redefined as being in the real interest of the subordinate. In SHFWA the subordinate is offered a consolation prize.

In FYOG ceremonies the benevolence may be directed to the subordinate either as a member of the organization (the public career) or as a person and member of a family (the private career). In both, the presumption is that the superior's understanding of the subordinate's goals and the means for their achievement is greater than that of the subordinate. The primacy of the superior's concern for the subordinate's welfare is the dominant posture. In relation to the public career, typical statements are "the job is not right for you", "you think you'll like it but you won't", "a pay increase now will arouse a lot of hostility", etc. When the benevolence is strongly paternalistic scratching the surface reveals 'intimidation'. Statements like "If I raise this with the board, they'll think you're a trouble maker" or "I'm willing to do this for you but you will have to bear the responsibility."

"For your own good" as a private person is a tactic most likely to be used to mollify a married woman. It involves the debunking of the dominant ideology that links success with power and position and invokes an alternative value system that links success with happiness and family life: "For your own good, what do you need all that extra responsibility, it'll create tensions, at home" or "your husband might resent your having to work weekends". The manager's concern may extend beyond the woman to the welfare of her husband as in "how can we send you abroad, what will your husband do, make cocktail parties?"

"See how fair we are" is the implicit message when the subordinate is offered an alternative or consolation prize, one less costly to the organization. Consolation prizes include change in job title instead of a job, a trip to a conference, or half (quarter?) of whatever was asked for, whether time, money or some other resources. The prize may have greater symbolic than substantial value, as when the refusal is redefined as a compliment, another example of meaning inversal.

Subordinate 14: "You're too good for a better job."

"Perhaps one year ago I requested of my boss to be placed on a new project. I had been working on one project which was very large and important for a year and a half and I felt I was no longer learning what I should have been learning as a third year engineer. My boss himself explained to me that I was in a sort of catch-22 situation. In performing the responsibilities which had come to me I exhibited a consistency and reliability which caused upper management to feel confident in me handling my position. I had done so well at my job in terms of defining my role and my interrelationships with the other disciplines that I was irreplacable. I was told that I would have to follow the project through to completion. My boss did help to bring some change into my job by getting me involved with the college recruitment effort. Although this extra responsibility only took one day every three weeks it gave me the diversification I desired. The way my boss posed the explanation was very flattering."

Being irreplacable may also be a reflection of the lack of attractiveness of the tasks performed rather than of the special skills of the subordinate. In that case being irreplacable would not be perceived as a consolation.

"Cooling out" (Goffman, 1952) the subordinate is an important part of refusal ceremonies and may be done most painlessly by benevolent tactics. In Goffman's study the individual (mark) needs to be cooled out so that he does not "squawk", create a row, or be an embarrassment to the organization in some other way. Our concern has been with the refused member who needs to be "cooled out" and then "cooled in" to the culture so that his/her commitments are once again harnessed to the purpose of the organization (as defined by managers).

CULTURE-WORKING AND REFUSAL CEREMONIES: FINAL THOUGHTS

The lion and the calf shall lie down together but the calf won't get much sleep.

(Woody Allen, *Without Feathers*)

Refusal ceremonies have been shown to be an important part of the acculturation process. On one level, they convey explicit guidelines and information about "the way things are done around here" and they contribute to socialization (Louis, 1980). The employee, "learns", for example, the policies, priorities, and goals from the superior's viewpoint—and the rules of the game in that particular organization.

The art of saying no can also be characterized as a form of culture-working activity in so far as these ceremonies serve to define realities, who people are (e.g., their status), and what influence people can exercise. In this sense, we have indicated how culture is intertwined with structure (i.e., power and control), how defining the terms of reality can be a prominent tool in a manager's "cultural tool kit". This is what Pfeffer (1981) referred to as the institutionalization of organizational culture whereby ". . . the distribution of power, the making of certain decisions, or the following of certain rules of operation . . . become defined as part of the organization's culture." (p. 299) Similarly, Smircich and Morgan (1982) characterized this type of process as "power-based reality construction".

In a sense, it appears as if the subordinates have been "brought into" the dominant culture—i.e., accepted the legitimacy of the distribution of power and authority as shared social fact. Subordinates implicitly agree to operate according to certain rules and, to some extent, concede their autonomy. Thus, refusal ceremonies reaffirm the purposes, values, norms, beliefs (i.e., culture) of the organization as defined by managers, and sustain institutional order. Moreover, Pfeffer (1981) argues that the distribution of power ". . . is perpetuated because people come to believe that this is how things always were, always will be, and, always should be." (p. 299)

However, the reaffirmation and perpetuation of culture also arouses resentment and tensions—which may indeed test the strength of the dominant culture. Many of the refused subordinates in our study reported feeling frustrated, angry, alienated, and resentful. While part of the message of the refusal ceremony may indeed be to underscore the relative unimportance or powerlessness of the subordinates, it creates (perhaps) unintended consequences as well. In some few cases, the employee actually resigned. In others, employees tried to resist the refusal—albeit within the groundrules of "evidence" defined by management. For many, the disgruntlement resulted in demoralization, discouragement, and even some questioning of the derivation of policies, and authority positions. Thus, it was not always clear that these people were indeed appeased and discouraged from pursuing benefits denied them by the organization and willing to do what they were expected to do. (In fact, there is literature on the management of extreme cases of protest (e.g., O'Day, 1974; Ewing, 1983).)

Although the perception of the groundrules may be shared and the distribution of power generally accepted, this is not to suggest that there is complete harmony, collaboration and consensus. Accepting the cultural groundrules is different from liking them, or feeling part of them. Although the subordinates typically complied with the refusal and rarely confronted their superiors with their dissatisfaction, they clearly had not bought all the values. That is, being "in" the culture and enacting behaviour within its terms is distinct from being "of" the culture, internalizing the dominant values and definitions of reality. The subordinate is typically not an equal partner in the determination of the culture and thus the dialectic tension: the more the culture is reaffirmed, the more the potential for resentment and opposition.

In order to maximize the reaffirmation of culture and minimize the opposition, the effective management of refusal ceremonies is often a prerequisite for advancement in a managerial career. Breaking or reconfirming bad news to subordinates provides situations in which the tension between the organization's interest and human variability is most exposed. Managers are expected to attend to preserving organizational legitimacy and disattend any ethical doubt that may cause them uneasiness much as medical students acquire a look of professional cool when handling an exposed gut. Refusal ceremonies may require actions for managers that seem insincere, dishonest, or unfriendly but as Goffman (1952) observed, "certain kinds of role success require certain kinds of moral failure."

The following account reported in Margolis (1979:126-7) is by a scientist who failed the test and consequently was forced to "jump off the managerial mainline and settle for a technical sideline."

You see, one can be very competent technically, but there are other skills. After two promotions I found that you just come up to a harsher level of reality than just doing your research.

The first time you're told to go tell a lie to a bunch of people, you make speeches to your boss about fairness and everything. I did that and he looked at me and said, "Frank, this is not the Supreme Court, and don't you tell me about fair and not fair. This is it and this is the story."

What happened was this. We were making some new rules about raises which were screwing some people. I had to say that you couldn't get more than one raise a year. Since I had been involved in giving some people three raises in one year, some of the people would have known that I couldn't honestly tell them that one raise was all you could get in a single year. At least I couldn't say that that was consistent with our past—the way things had always been done. So I was told to say that nobody was being hurt and that that was the way things had always been done. I said I couldn't and that we couldn't lie to our people since they'd know it and that would be like asking them to join your lie. You know, you say it and then you see who reacts and mostly people don't say anything because they don't want to get into trouble. Well, I wouldn't say it so my boss announced it. I was there though; I was listening and I didn't say anything.

The scientist in this narrative is sensitive not only to his own complicity in what he considers an unethical act, but also to the complicity of the subordinates who by their silence "join the lie" and consequently reaffirm the implicit theories which generate it (Argyris, 1982). Garfinkel (1967) used the term "reflexivity" to describe the ways in which the very acceptance of the usage of a familiar term or rule, by being understood as intended, reinforces the term of rule's familiarity and further assures the actors of its reality and propriety.

Refusal ceremonies are rather routine occurrences in organizations which through their regularity and importance transmit and reaffirm the organizational culture. They are micropolitical events through which those who invoke facts and arguments, or rules of reason, not sanctioned by the culture—or contemplate the possibility of doing so—are typically brought in line and serve as examples for others. Nevertheless, it must also be suggested that further research on organizational culture should identify the conditions under which the very reaffirmation of culture hardens resistance and provokes redefinition of the underlyng structure of power and control.

The Administration vs. the Scientists: A Dangerous Rift Over Locking Up 'Sensitive' Data

Evert Clark and Alan Hall

In its drive to prevent the export of U.S. technology to the Soviet bloc, the Reagan Administration may be shooting itself in the foot: It is trying zealously to lock up "sensitive," but unclassified, scientific research. In the process, the White House has alienated both university and industry scientists, the very creators of the technological supremacy that the Administration seeks to safeguard.

"Things are getting so larded up that you wonder if the definition of national security is getting lost," says Ralph J. Thomson, senior vice-president of the American Electronics Assn. In the name of national security, 44 separate federal offices have taken a confused and often conflicting approach to building a fence around U.S. technology. Defense Dept. zealots have forced withdrawal of technical papers from several scientific meetings and imposed contract restrictions that caused one major university to decline a key military-research contract.

"An obsession with preventing leakage of our technology will cripple our ability to remain the leader," warns Roland W. Schmitt, senior vice-president for corporate research and development at General Electric Co. Schmitt, who also heads the National Science Board, and others protest that the key to the vitality of U. S. technology is its very openness.

TURMOIL FOR SCHOOLS

Their arguments have fallen on deaf ears at the Pentagon, where Richard N. Perle, Assistant Defense Secretary for international security policy, in the absence of a national policy, has become the de facto czar of technology transfer in the U. S. (BW—May 21). With the backing of the White House, he has outflanked his counterparts at Commerce, Treasury, and State.

Perle also has overwhelmed milder Pentagon research colleagues who have been trying to lure schools back into the Defense fold in critical research areas. Notes one veteran science administrator: "I think the problem will continue to get worse; there is no way you can attract universities back into defense research with this kind of boiling turmoil."

Ever since retired Admiral Bobby R. Inman warned in 1981 of an impending crackdown on technical communication to halt what he called "the hemorrhage of U. S. technology," the scientific community has tried to reach an accommodation with government hardliners. Because they depend heavily on government dollars, scientists have often taken great care not to ruffle feathers.

The National Academy of Sciences assembled a panel, headed by Dale R. Corson, president emeritus of Cornell University, to examine the clash, but it could find little evidence that open communication of basic scientific information had benefited the Soviet military. The panel offered an olive branch to the Pentagon, however. It conceded there might be some "gray areas" of research—such as cryptography and advanced microelectronics—that might warrant oversight by the military, short of classification. And a group called the Defense Dept./University Forum was set up to work out how such technology could be controlled.

The panel's concession has backfired badly, however. Perle's followers have virtually ignored the conclusions of the report and are moving aggressively to lock up a broad range of research that they consider "sensitive." Even Corson now speaks despairingly about "creeping grayness," and business is becoming increasingly alarmed that it may find itself in the same boat. "Once you let the barriers down, people are going to rush through and make the hole very wide," says Corson. "And I think that is what is happening."

As a result, negotiations between universities and the Pentagon have reached an impasse. "We are back to Square One," says Leo Young, Defense's director for research and laboratory management. The most recent snag is a Defense proposal that unclassified technical papers on applied research be cleared for publication by the Pentagon. That move caused the presidents of three major universities to fire off a letter threatening that "our institutions would be unable to accept any research contracts subject to such a restriction."

Pentagon hardliners are also trying to limit the role that foreigners can play in so-called sensitive research. Because many U. S. scientists and students are not citizens, a proposal to keep research results from all foreigners recently compelled Cornell to turn down a $450,000 research contract.

FORTRESS APPROACH

Industry, too, is becoming increasingly alarmed by the shift to secrecy, but it also is taking a conciliatory approach. The National Academy of

Sciences is forming a new 20-member panel to study the impact of national security controls on industrial competitiveness here and abroad. The prospect of an 18-month second study, when the first one seems to have had almost no effect, is drawing criticism from some frustrated participants in the debate. "I don't see much to be served by yet another study," says Marvin L. Goldberger, California Institute of Technology president.

Others, however, remain adamant that continued dialogue is the best course of action. "I think the business community, rather than standing on the sidelines sniping, needs to see if there can't be an off-camera dialogue and see what the government's problem is," says Lewis M. Branscomb, chief scientist at International Business Machines Corp.

Still, as long as Richard Perle dominates the government's export-control actions, the hardliners clearly have the edge. And even some of the most ardent advocates of conciliation see little chance of agreement. Corson adds glumly: "There are two things I'd like to see—a coherent policy for the nation and a coherent policy that I believe in. I don't think we are likely to get either." And Inman, now president of Microelectronics & Computer Technology Corp., tends to agree. Perle, he says, "is driving Defense, and he is taking a Fortress America approach that will not work."

The Catbird Seat

James Thurber

Mr. Martin bought the pack of Camels on Monday night in the most crowded cigar store on Broadway. It was theater time and seven or eight men were buying cigarettes. The clerk didn't even glance at Mr. Martin, who put the pack in his overcoat pocket and went out. If any of the staff at F & S has seen him buy the cigarettes, they would have been astonished, for it was generally known that Mr. Martin did not smoke, and never had. No one saw him.

It was just a week to the day since Mr. Martin had decided to rub out Mrs. Ulgine Barrows. The term "rub out" pleased him because it suggested nothing more than the correction of an error—in this case an error of Mr. Fitweiler. Mr. Martin had spent each night of the past week working out his plan and examining it. As he walked home now he went over it again. For the hundredth time he resented the element of imprecision, the margin of guesswork that entered into the business. The project as he had worked it out was casual and bold, the risks were considerable. Something might go wrong anywhere along the line. And therein lay the cunning of his scheme. No one would ever see in it the cautious, painstaking hand of Erwin Martin, head of the filing department of F & S, of whom Mr. Fitweiler had once said, "Man is fallible but Martin isn't." No one would see his hand, that is, unless it were caught in the act.

Sitting in his apartment, drinking a glass of milk, Mr. Martin reviewed his case against Mrs. Ulgine Barrows, as he had every night for seven nights. He began at the beginning. Her quacking voice and braying laugh had first profaned the halls of F & S on March 7, 1941 (Mr. Martin had a head for dates). Old Roberts, the personnel chief, had introduced her as the newly appointed special adviser to the president of the firm, Mr. Fitweiler. The woman had appalled Mr. Martin instantly, but he hadn't shown it. He had given her his dry hand, a look of studious concentration, and a faint smile. "Well," she had said, looking at the papers on his desk, "are you lifting the oxcart out of the ditch?" As Mr. Martin recalled that moment, over his milk, he squirmed slightly. He must keep his mind on her crimes as a special adviser, not on her peccadillos as a personality. This he found difficult to do, in spite of entering an objection and sustaining it. The faults of the woman as a woman kept chattering on in his mind like an unruly witness. She had, for almost two years now, baited him. In the halls, in the elevator, even in his own office, into which she romped now and then like a circus horse, she was constantly shouting these silly questions at him. "Are you lifting the oxcart out of that ditch? Are you tearing up the pea patch? Are you hollering down the rain barrel? Are you scraping around the bottom of the pickle barrel? Are you sitting in the catbird seat?"

It was Joey Hart, one of Mr. Martin's two assistants, who had explained what the gibberish meant. "She must be a Dodger fan," he had said. "Red Barber announces the Dodger games over the radio and he uses those expressions—picked 'em up down South." Joey had gone on to explain one or two. "Tearing up the pea patch" meant going on a rampage; "sitting in the catbird seat" meant sitting pretty, like a batter with three balls and no strikes on him. Mr. Martin dismissed all this with an effort. It had been annoying, it had driven him near to distraction, but he was too solid a man to be moved to murder by anything so childish. It was fortunate, he reflected as he passed on to the important charges against Mrs. Barrows, that he had stood up under it so well. He had maintained always an outward appearance of polite tolerance. "Why, I even believe you like the woman," Miss Paird, his other assistant, had once said to him. He had simply smiled.

A gavel rapped in Mr. Martin's mind and the case proper was resumed. Mrs. Ulgine Barrows stood charged with willful, blatant, and persistent attempts to destroy the efficiency and system of F & S. It was competent, material, and relevant to review her advent and rise to power. Mr. Martin had got the story from Miss Paird, who seemed always able to find things out. According to her, Mrs. Barrows had met Mr. Fitweiler at a party, where she had rescued him from the embraces of a powerfully built drunken man who had mistaken the president of F & S for a famous retired Middle Western football coach. She had led him to a sofa and somehow worked upon him a monstrous magic. The aging gentleman had jumped to the conclusion there and then that this was a woman of singular attainments, equipped to bring out the best in him and in the firm. A week later he had introduced her into F & S as his special adviser. On that day confusion got its foot in the door. After Miss Tyson, Mr. Brundage, and Mr. Bartlett had been fired and Mr. Munson had taken his hat and stalked out, mailing in his resignation later, old Roberts had been emboldened to speak to Mr. Fitweiler. He mentioned that Mr. Munson's department had been a "little disrupted" and hadn't they perhaps better resume the old system there? Mr. Fitweiler had said certainly not. He had the greatest faith in Mrs. Barrows' ideas. "They require a little seasoning, a little seasoning, is all," he had added. Mr. Roberts had given it up. Mr. Martin reviewed in detail all the changes wrought by Mrs. Barrows. She had begun chipping at the cornices of the firm's edifice and now she was swinging at the foundation stones with a pickaxe.

Mr. Martin came now, in his summing up, to the afternoon of Monday, November 2, 1942—just one week ago. On that day, at 3 P.M., Mrs. Barrows had bounced into his office. "Boo!" she had yelled. "Are you scraping around the bottom of the pickle barrel?" Mr. Martin had looked at her from under his green eyeshade, saying nothing. She had begun to wander about the office, taking it in with her great, popping eyes. "Do you really need *all* these filing cabinets?" she had demanded suddenly. Mr. Martin's heart had jumped. "Each of these files," he had said, keeping his voice even, "plays an indispensable part in the system of F & S." She had brayed at him, "Well, don't tear up the pea patch!" and gone to the door. From there she had bawled, "But you sure have got a lot of fine scrap here!" Mr. Martin could no longer doubt that the finger was on his beloved department. Her pickaxe was on the upswing, poised for the first blow. It had not come yet; he had received no blue memo from the enchanted Mr. Fitweiler bearing nonsensical instructions deriving from the obscene woman. But there was no doubt in Mr. Martin's mind that one would be forthcoming. He must act quickly. Already a precious week had gone by. Mr. Martin stood up in his living room, still holding his milk glass. "Gentlemen of the jury," he said to himself, "I demand the death penalty for this horrible person."

The next day Mr. Martin followed his routine, as usual. He polished his glasses more often and once sharpened an already sharp pencil, but not even Miss Paird noticed. Only once did he catch sight of his victim; she swept past him in the hall with a patronizing "Hi!" At five-thirty he walked home, as usual, and had a glass of milk, as usual. He had never drunk anything stronger in his life—unless you could count ginger ale. The late Sam Schlosser, the S of F & S, had praised Mr. Martin at a staff meeting several years before for his temperate habits. "Our most efficient worker neither drinks nor smokes," he had said. "The results speak for themselves." Mr. Fitweiler had sat by, nodding approval.

Mr. Martin was still thinking about that red-letter day as he walked over to the Schrafft's on Fifth Avenue near Forty-sixth Street. He got there, as he always did, at eight o'clock. He finished his dinner and the financial page of the *Sun* at a quarter to nine, as he always did. It was his custom after dinner to take a walk. This time he walked down Fifth Avenue at a casual pace. His gloved hands felt moist and warm, his forehead cold. He transferred the Camels from his overcoat to a jacket pocket. He wondered, as he did so, if they did not represent an unnecessary note of strain. Mrs. Barrows smoked only Luckies. It was his idea to puff a few puffs on a Camel (after the rubbing-out), stub it out in the ashtray holding her lipstick-stained Luckies, and thus drag a small red herring across the trail. Perhaps it was not a good idea. It would take time. He might even choke, too loudly.

Mr. Martin had never seen the house on West Twelfth Street where Mrs. Barrows lived, but he had a clear enough picture of it. Fortunately, she had bragged to everybody about her ducky first-floor apartment in the perfectly darling three-story red-brick. There would be no doorman or other attendants; just the tenants of the second and third floors. As he walked along, Mr. Martin realized that he would get there before nine-thirty. He had considered walking north on Fifth Avenue from Schrafft's to a point from which it would take him until ten o'clock to reach the house. At that hour people were less likely to be coming in or going out. But the procedure would have made an awkward loop in the straight thread of his casualness, and he had abandoned it. It was impossible to figure when people would be entering or leaving the house, anyway. There was a great risk at any hour. If he ran into anybody, he would simply have to place the rubbing-out of Ulgine Barrows in the inactive file forever. The same thing would hold true if there were someone in her apartment. In that case he would just say that he had been passing by, recognized her charming house and thought to drop in.

It was eighteen minutes after nine when Mr. Martin turned into Twelfth Street. A man passed him, and a man and a woman talking. There was no one within fifty paces when he came to the house, halfway down the block. He was up the steps and in the small vestibule in no time, pressing the bell under the card that said "Mrs. Ulgine Barrows." When the clicking in the lock started, he jumped forward against the door. He got inside fast, closing the door behind him. A bulb in a lantern hung from the hall ceiling on a chain seemed to give a monstrously bright light. There was nobody on the stair, which went up ahead of him along the left wall. A door opened down the hall in the wall on the right. He went toward it swiftly, on tiptoe.

"Well, for God's sake, look who's here!" bawled Mrs. Barrows, and her braying laugh rang out like the report of a shotgun. He rushed past her like a football tackle, bumping her. "Hey, quit shoving!" she said, closing the door behind them. They were in her living room, which seemed to Mr. Martin to be lighted by a hundred lamps. "What's after you?" she said. "You're as jumpy as a goat." He found he was unable to speak. His heart was wheezing in his throat. "I—yes," he finally brought out. She was jabbering and laughing as she started to help him off with his coat. "No, no," he said. "I'll put it here." He took it off and put it on a chair near the door. "Your hat and gloves, too," she said. "You're in a lady's house." He put his hat on top of the coat. Mrs. Barrows seemed larger than he had thought. He kept his gloves on. "I was passing by," he said. "I recognized—is there anyone here?" She laughed louder than ever. "No," she said, "we're all alone. You're as white as a sheet, you funny man. Whatever *has* come over you? I'll mix you a toddy." She started toward a door across the room. "Scotch-and-soda be all right? But say, you don't drink, do you?" She turned and gave him her amused look. Mr. Martin pulled himself together. "Scotch-and-soda will be all right," he heard himself say. He could hear her laughing in the kitchen.

Mr. Martin looked quickly around the living room for the weapon. He had counted on finding one there. There were andirons and a poker and something in a corner that looked like an Indian club. None of them would do. It couldn't be that way. He began to pace around. He came to a desk. On it lay a metal paper knife with an ornate handle. Would it be sharp enough? He reached for it and knocked over a small brass jar. Stamps spilled out of it and it fell to the floor with a clatter. "Hey," Mrs. Barrows yelled from the kitchen, "are you tearing up the pea patch?" Mr. Martin gave a strange laugh. Picking up the knife, he tried its point against his left wrist. It was blunt. It wouldn't do.

When Mrs. Barrows reappeared, carrying two highballs, Mr. Martin, standing there with his gloves on, became acutely conscious of the fantasy he had wrought. Cigarettes in his pocket, a drink prepared for him—it was all too grossly improbable. It was more than that; it was impossible. Somewhere in the back of his mind a vague idea stirred, sprouted. "For heaven's sake, take off those gloves," said Mrs. Barrows. "I always wear them in the house," said Mr. Martin. The idea began to bloom, strange and wonderful. She put the glasses on a coffee table in front of a sofa and sat on the sofa. "Come over here, you odd little man," she said. Mr. Martin went over and sat beside her. It was difficult getting a cigarette out of the pack of Camels, but he managed it. She held a match for him, laughing. "Well," she said, handing him his drink, "this is perfectly marvelous. You with a drink and a cigarette."

Mr. Martin puffed, not too awkwardly, and took a gulp of the highball. "I drink and smoke all the time," he said. He clinked his glass against hers. "Here's nuts to that old windbag, Fitweiler," he said, and gulped again. The stuff tasted awful, but he made no grimace. "Really, Mr. Martin," she said, her voice and posture changing, "you are insulting our employer." Mrs. Barrows was now all special adviser to the president. "I am preparing a bomb," said Mr. Martin, "which will blow the old goat higher than hell." He had only had a little of the drink, which was not strong. It couldn't be that. "Do you take dope or something?" Mrs. Barrows asked coldly. "Heroin," said Mr. Martin. "I'll be coked to the gills when I bump that old buzzard off." "Mr. Martin!" she shouted, getting to her feet. "That will be all of that. You must go at once." Mr. Martin took another swallow of his drink. He tapped his cigarette out in the ashtray and put the pack of Camels on the coffee table. Then he got up. She stood glaring at him. He walked over and put on his hat and coat. "Not a word about this," he said, and laid an index finger against his lips. All Mrs. Barrows could bring out was "Really!" Mr. Martin put his hand on the doorknob. "I'm sitting in the catbird seat," he said. He stuck his tongue out at her and left. Nobody saw him go.

Mr. Martin got to his apartment, walking, well before eleven. No one saw him go in. He had two glasses of milk after brushing his teeth, and he felt elated. It wasn't tipsiness, because he hadn't been tipsy. Anyway, the walk had worn off all effects of the whisky. He got in bed and read a magazine for a while. He was asleep before midnight.

Mr. Martin got to the office at eight-thirty the next morning, as usual. At a quarter to nine, Ulgine Barrows, who had never before arrived at work before ten, swept into his office. "I'm reporting to Mr. Fitweiler now!" she shouted. "If he turns you over to the police, it's no more than you deserve!" Mr. Martin gave her a look of shocked surprise. "I beg your pardon?" he said. Mrs. Barrows snorted and bounced out of the room, leaving Miss Paird and Joey Hart staring after her. "What's the matter with that old devil now?" asked Miss Paird. "I have no idea," said Mr. Martin, resuming his work. The other two looked at him and then at each other. Miss Paird got up and went out. She walked slowly past the closed door of Mr. Fitweiler's office. Mrs. Barrows was yelling inside, but she was not braying. Miss Paird could not hear what the woman was saying. She went back to her desk.

Forty-five minutes later, Mrs. Barrows left the president's office and went into her own, shutting the door. It wasn't until half an hour later that Mr. Fitweiler sent for Mr. Martin. The head of the filing department, neat, quiet, attentive, stood in front of the old man's desk. Mr. Fitweiler was pale and nervous. He took his glasses off and twiddled them. He made a small, bruffing sound in his throat. "Martin," he said, "you have been with us more than twenty years." "Twenty-two, sir," said Mr. Martin. "In that time," pursued the president, "your work and your—uh—manner have been exemplary." "I trust so, sir," said Mr. Martin. "I have understood, Martin," said Mr. Fitweiler, "that you have never taken a drink or smoked." "That is correct, sir," said Mr. Martin. "Ah, yes." Mr. Fitweiler polished his glasses. "You may describe what you did after leaving the office yesterday, Martin," he said. Mr. Martin allowed less than a second for his bewildered pause. "Certainly sir," he said. "I walked home. Then I went to Schrafft's for dinner. Afterward I walked home again. I went to bed early, sir, and read a magazine for a while. I was asleep before eleven." "Ah, yes," said Mr. Fitweiler again. He was silent for a moment, searching for the proper words to say to the head of the filing department. "Mrs. Barrows," he said finally, "Mrs. Barrows has worked hard, Martin, very hard. It grieves me to report that she has suffered a severe breakdown. It has taken the form of a persecution complex accompanied by distressing hallucinations." "I am very sorry, sir," said Mr. Martin. "Mrs. Barrows is under the delusion," continued Mr. Fitweiler, "that you visited her last evening and behaved yourself in an—uh—unseemly manner." He raised his hand to silence Mr. Martin's little pained outcry. "It is the nature of these psychological diseases," Mr. Fitweiler said, "to fix upon the least likely and most innocent party as the—uh—source of persecution. These matters are not for the lay mind to grasp, Martin. I've just had my psychiatrist, Dr, Fitch, on the phone. He would not, of course, commit himself, but he made enough generalizations to substantiate my suspicions. I suggested to Mrs. Barrows when she had completed her—uh—story to me this morning, that she visit Dr. Fitch, for I suspected a condition at once. She flew, I regret to say, into a rage, and demanded—uh—requested that I call you on the carpet. You may not know, Martin, but Mrs. Barrows had planned a reorganization of your department—subject to my approval, of course, subject to my approval. This brought you, rather than anyone else, to her mind—but again that is a phenomenon for Dr. Fitch and not for us. So, Martin, I am afraid Mrs. Barrows' usefulness here is at an end." "I am dreadfully sorry, sir," said Mr. Martin.

It was at this point that the door to the office blew open with the suddenness of a gas-main explosion and Mrs. Barrows catapulted through it. "Is the little rat denying it?" she screamed. "He can't get away with that!" Mr. Martin got up and moved discreetly to a point beside Mr. Fitweiler's chair. "You drank and smoked at my apartment," she bawled at Mr. Martin, "and you know it! You called Mr. Fitweiler an old windbag and said you were going to blow him up when you got coked to the gills on your heroin!" She stopped yelling to catch her breath and a new glint came into her popping eyes. "If you weren't such a drab, ordinary little man," she said, "I'd think you'd planned it all. Sticking your tongue out, saying you were sitting in the catbird seat, because you thought no one would believe me when I told it! My God, it's really too perfect!" She brayed loudly and hysterically, and the fury was on her again. She glared at Mr. Fitweiler. "Can't you see how he has tricked us, you old fool? Can't you see his little game?" But Mr. Fitweiler had been surreptitiously pressing all the buttons under the top of his desk and employees of F & S began pouring into the room. "Stockton," said Mr. Fitweiler, "you and Fishbein will take Mrs. Barrows to her home. Mrs. Powell, you will go with them." Stockton, who had played a little football in high school, blocked Mrs. Barrows as she made for Mr. Martin. It took him and Fishbein together to force her out of the door into the hall, crowded with stenographers and office boys. She was still screaming imprecations at Mr. Martin, tangled and contradictory imprecations. The hubbub finally died out down the corridor.

"I regret that this has happened," said Mr. Fitweiler. "I shall ask you to dismiss it from your mind, Martin." "Yes, sir," said Mr. Martin, anticipating his chief's "That will be all" by moving to the door. "I will dismiss it." He went out and shut the door, and his step was light and quick in the hall. When he entered his department he had slowed down to his customary gait, and he walked quietly across the room to the W20 file, wearing a look of studious concentration.

Señor Payroll

William E. Barrett

Larry and I were Junior Engineers in the gas plant, which means that we were clerks. Anything that could be classified as paperwork came to that flat double desk across which we faced each other. The Main Office downtown sent us a bewildering array of orders and rules that were to be put into effect.

Junior Engineers were beneath the notice of everyone except the Mexican laborers at the plant. To them we were the visible form of a distant, unknowable paymaster. We were Señor Payroll.

Those Mexicans were great workmen: the aristocrats among them were the stokers, big men who worked Herculean eight-hour shifts in the fierce heat of the retorts. They scooped coal with huge shovels and hurled it with uncanny aim at tiny doors. The coal streamed out from the shovels like black water from a high pressure nozzle, and never missed the narrow opening. The stokers worked stripped to the waist, and there was pride and dignity in them. Few men could do such work, and they were the few.

The Company paid its men only twice a month, on the fifth and on the twentieth. To a Mexican, this was absurd. What man with money will make it last 15 days? If he hoarded money beyond the spending of three days, he was a miser—and when, Señor, did the blood of Spain flow in the veins of misers? Hence it was the custom for our stokers to appear every third or fourth day to draw the money due to them.

There was a certain elasticity in the Company rules, and Larry and I sent the necessary forms to the Main Office and received an "advance" against a man's paycheck. Then, one day, Downtown favored us with a memorandum:

"There have been too many abuses of the advance-against-wages privilege. Hereafter, no advance against wages will be made to any employee except in a case of genuine emergency."

We had no sooner posted the notice when in came stoker Juan Garcia. He asked for an advance. I pointed to the notice. He spelled it through slowly, then said, "What does this mean, this 'genuine emergency'?"

I explained to him patiently that the Company was kind and sympathetic, but that it was a great nuisance to have to pay wages every few days. If someone was ill or if money was urgently needed for some other good reason, then the Company would make an exception to the rule.

Juan Garcia turned his hat over and over slowly in his big hands. "I do not get my money?"

"Next payday, Juan. On the 20th."

He went out silently and I felt ashamed of myself. I looked across the desk at Larry. He avoided my eyes.

In the next hour two other stokers came in, looked at the notice, had it explained and walked solemnly out; then no more came. What we did not know was that Juan Garcia, Pete Mendoza and Francisco Gonzalez had spread the word and that every Mexican in the plant was explaining the order to every other Mexican. "To get the money now, the wife must be sick. There must be medicine for the baby."

The next morning Juan Garcia's wife was practically dying, Pete Mendoza's mother would hardly last the day, there was a veritable epidemic among children and, just for variety, there was one sick father. We always suspected that the old man was really sick; no Mexican would otherwise have thought of him. At any rate, nobody paid Larry and me to examine private lives; we made out our forms with an added line describing the "genuine emergency." Our people got paid.

That went on for a week. Then came a new order, curt and to the point: "Hereafter employees will be paid ONLY on the fifth and the 20th of the month. No exceptions will be made except in the cases of employees leaving the service of the Company."

The notice went up on the board and we explained its significance gravely. "No, Juan Garcia, we cannot advance your wages. It is too bad about your wife and your cousins and your aunts, but there is a new rule."

Juan Garcia went out and thought it over. He thought out loud with Mendoza and Gonzales and Ayala, then, in the morning, he was back. "I am quitting this company for different job. You pay me now?"

We argued that it was a good company and that it loved its employees like children, but in the end we paid off, because Juan Garcia quit. And so did Gonzales, Mendoza, Obregon, Ayala and Ortez, the best stokers, men who could not be replaced.

Larry and I looked at each other; we knew what was coming in about three days. One of our duties was to sit on the hiring line early each morning, engaging transient workers for the handy gangs. Any man was accepted who could walk up and ask for a job without falling down. Never before had we been called upon to hire such skilled virtuosos as stokers for handy gang work, but we were called upon to hire them now.

The day foreman was wringing his hands and asking the Almighty if he was personally supposed to shovel this condemned coal, while there in a stolid, patient line were skilled men—Garcia, Mendoza and others—waiting to be hired. We hired them, of course. There was nothing else to do.

Every day we had a line of resigning stokers, and another line of stokers seeking work. Our paperwork became very complicated. At the Main Office they were jumping up and down. The procession of forms showing Juan Garcia's resigning and being hired over and over again was too much for them. Sometimes Downtown had Garcia on the payroll twice at the same time when someone down there was slow in entering a resignation. Our phone rang early and often.

Tolerantly and patiently we explained: "There's nothing we can do if a man wants to quit, and if there are stokers available when the plant needs stokers, we hire them."

Out of chaos, Downtown issued another order. I read it and whistled. Larry looked at it and said, "It is going to be very quiet around here."

The order read: "Hereafter, no employee who resigns may be rehired within a period of 30 days."

Juan Garcia was due for another resignation, and when he came in we showed him the order and explained that standing in line the next day would do him no good if he resigned today. "Thirty days is a long time, Juan."

It was a grave matter and he took time to reflect on it. So did Gonzales, Mendoza, Ayala and Ortez. Ultimately, however, they were all back—and all resigned.

We did our best to dissuade them and we were sad about the parting. This time it was for keeps and they shook hands with us solemnly. It was very nice knowing us. Larry and I looked at each other when they were gone and we both knew that neither of us had been pulling for Downtown to win this duel. It was a blue day.

In the morning, however, they were all back in line. With the utmost gravity, Juan Garcia informed me that he was a stoker looking for a job.

"No dice, Juan" I said. "Come back in 30 days. I warned you."

His eyes looked straight into mine without a flicker. "There is some mistake, Señor," he said. "I am Manuel Hernandez. I work as the stoker in Pueblo, in Santa Fe, in many places."

I stared back at him, remembering the sick wife and the babies without medicine, the mother-in-law in the hospital, the many resignations and the rehirings. I knew that there was a gas plant in Pueblo, and that there wasn't any in Santa Fe; but who was I to argue with a man about his own name? A stoker is a stoker.

So I hired him. I hired Gonzalez, too, who swore that his name was Carrera, and Ayala, who had shamelessy become Smith.

Three days, later, the resigning started.

Within a week our payroll read like a history of Latin America. Everyone was on it: Lopez and Obregon, Villa, Diaz, Batista, Gomez, and even San Martin and Bolivar. Finally Larry and I, growing weary of staring at familiar faces and writing unfamiliar names, went to the Superintendent and told him the whole story. He tried not to grin, and said, "Damned nonsense!"

The next day the orders were taken down. We called our most prominent stokers into the office and pointed to the board. No rules any more.

"The next time we hire you *hombres*," Larry said grimly, "come in under the names you like best, because that's the way you are going to stay on the books."

They looked at us and they looked at the board; then for the first time in the long duel, their teeth flashed white. *"Si, Señores,"* they said.

And so it was.

Furniture Factory

Robert Schrank

It was 1932 and we were in the depths of the depression. If you were lucky enough to find a job, it was usually through a friend, and that was how I got my first full-time job in a Brooklyn factory that made frames

Reprinted from *Ten Thousand Working Days* by Robert Schrank by permission of The MIT Press, Cambridge, Massachusetts. Copyright © 1978 The MIT Press.

for upholstered furniture. I was fifteen years old and lived in the Bronx, traveling on the subway for an hour and fifteen minutes each way, every day, six days a week for twelve dollars. I considered myself to be the luckiest boy in the world to get that job. When Mr. Miller the owner of the Miller Parlor Frame Company, interviewed me and agreed to hire me, he made it quite clear that he was doing a favor for a mutual friend and did not really care much about giving me a job.

Like most small factory offices, Mr. Miller's was cluttered with catalogs, samples of materials, some small tools, a rolltop desk with a large blotter pad worn through the corners. The whole place was in a sawdust fog with a persistent cover of dust over everything. Mr. Miller was a short fat man who chewed cigars and sort of drooled as he talked to me. He sat on the edge of his big oak swivel chair. I had a feeling he might slip off anytime. He never looked at me as we spoke. He made it clear that he was annoyed at people asking favors, saying that he did not like people who were "always trying to get something out of me."

The sour smell of the oak sawdust comes back to fill my nose as I recall the furniture factory. It is a smell I always welcomed until I had to live in it eight hours a day. There were days, especially when it was damp or raining, when the wood smell was so strong you could not eat your lunch. Next to the smell I remember getting to the factory and back as being an awful drag. But the New York subway that I rode to and from work for many years had two marked positive effects on me. First, I felt part of a general condition that nobody seemed to like. I was part of a group and we were all in the same fix, busting our asses to get to work in the morning and home at night. While I felt unhappy, it was made easier through the traditional "misery loves company," and there was plenty of that. And second, if I had a lucky day, there was the chance of seeing or being pressed up against some sweet-smelling, young, pretty thing who would get me all excited. Sometimes I tried a pickup, but it usually did not work because the situation was too public. With each person rigidly contained, it was surprising if anyone tried to move out of his shell. Everyone in the train would be staring to see what would develop. Almost nothing did.

To be at the furniture factory in Brooklyn by 8 A.M., I would leave my house in the Bronx by 6:30 A.M. While it was always a bad trip it became less so in the long spring days of the year as contrasted with December, when I most hated getting up in the dark. It was very important to be very quiet as I would feel my way around our old frame house, so as not to wake people up who had another thirty or forty minutes to sleep. I would sleepily make a sandwich for lunch, preferably from a leftover or just bologna, grab a cup of coffee—always with one eye on the clock—and run for the station. Luckily, we lived at the end of a subway line, and in the morning I was usually able to get a corner seat in the train. The corner seat was good for sleeping because I could rest against the train wall and not have the embarrassment of falling asleep on the person sitting next to me. It meant being able to sleep the hour-long trip to Brooklyn, and it was critical to set my "inner clock" so it would wake me up at Morgan Avenue station in Brooklyn. If it failed or was a little late, which sometimes happened, panic would ensue, as I usually would wake up just as the train was pulling out of Morgan Avenue. I would make a quick, unsuccessful dash for the door, and people would try to help by grabbing at the door. Then I would burn with anger for being late and maybe losing the job. When I would end up past my stop, I would have to make a fast decision to either spend another nickel and go back or go on to a double station where I could race down the steps to the other side of the tracks and catch a train going the other way without paying an additional fare.

The trip home from work on the New York subway in the evening rush hour is an experience most difficult to describe. The train, packed full of people, hurtles into a station. The doors slide open. There is always an illusion that someone may be getting out. That never seems to happen while a mass of people begin to push their way in. All strangers, we are not packed like sardines in a can, as is often suggested; the packing of sardines is an orderly process. The rush hour subway is more like a garbage compacter that just squeezes trash and rubbish into a dense mass and then hurtles it at very high speeds through a small underground tube. Unlike the morning, at night when I was exhausted from the day's work I never was able to get a seat, and that meant standing on my dog-tired feet for more than an hour and trying not to lean on the person next to me, an almost impossible thing to do. . . .

As I walked from the subway in the morning I could smell the furniture factory a block away. It was a powerful smell; as I said, I loved that oak at first. It was a perfume from the woods: a combination of skunk, mushrooms, and honeysuckle blended to a musk, a sweet contrast to the steel-and-oil stink of the subway. Yet, by the end of a day's work, the factory, its smells, its noise, its tedium all became so terribly tiresome and exhausting that leaving every day was an act of liberation.

The factory was a five-story loft building about half a city block long. The making of furniture frames began on the bottom floor where the rough cuts were made from huge pieces of lumber. As the cut wood moved along from floor to floor, it was formed, shaped, carved, dowled, sanded, and finally assembled on the top floor into completed frames. The machines in the plant included table saws, band saws, planers, carving machines, routers, drills, hydraulic presses, all run by 125 machine operators who were almost all European immigrants. My job was to keep the operators supplied with material, moving the finished stuff to the assembly floor, a sort of human conveyor. When I wasn't moving pieces around, I was supposed to clean up, which meant bagging sawdust into burlap bags. Sometimes the foreman would come and say, "Hey, kid, how would you like to run the dowling machine?" At first I thought that was a real break, a chance to get on a machine and become an operator. I told him enthusiastically, "Yeah, that would be great." I would sit in front of this little machine, pick up a predrilled piece, hold it to the machine, which would push two glued dowels into the holes. I soon found that I preferred moving parts around the plant and cleaning up to sitting at that machine all day, picking up a piece of wood from one pile, locating the holes at the dowel feeder that pushed in two preglued dowels, then dropping it on the other side. The machine had a sort of gallump, gallump rhythm that made me sleepy and started me watching the clock, the worst thing you can do in a factory. It would begin to get to me, and I would just sit and stare at the machine, the clock, the machine, the clock.

Those first few weeks in that factory were an agony of never-ending time. The damn clock just never moved, and over and over again I became convinced that it had stopped. Gradually, life in the furniture factory boiled down to waiting for the four work breaks: coffee, lunch hour, coffee, and quitting time. When the machines stopped, it was only in their sudden silence that I became aware of their deafening whine. It was almost impossible to hear each other talk while they were running, and all we were able to do was to scream essential information at one another.

The breaks were the best times of the day, for I could become intoxicated listening to the older men talk of rough, tough things in the big world out there. Being accepted was a slow process, and I was just happy to be allowed to listen. When I had been there for a couple of weeks, Mike the Polack said, "Hey, kid, meet in the shit house for talk." I was making it all right.

The coffee- and lunch-break talks centered around the family, sports, politics, and sex, in about that order. The immigrants from Middle Europe, and especially the Jews, were the most political. Most of them seemed to believe that politicians were crooks and that's how it is. The Jews talked the least about sex and the Italians the most. Luigi would endlessly bait Max (who would soon be my friend), saying that what he needed most was "a good woman who make you forget all dat political shit." There were a whole variety of newspapers published in New York at that time and one way workers had of figuring out each other's politics, interests, and habits was by the papers they read.

Max Teitelbaum would say to me, "See Louie over there. You can tell he's just a dummy, he reads that *Daily Mirror*. It fills his head with garbage so he can't tink about vot is *really* happening in the vorld." Arguing strongly in the defense of Franklin Roosevelt, probably too strongly, Mike the Polack told me with his finger waving close to my nose, "Listen, kid, vot I tink and vot I do is my business, and nobody, no politician or union or smart-ass kid like you is gonna butt into dat. You got it? Don't forget it!"

As people began to trust me, I was slowly making friends. Their trust was expressed in small ways, like when Luigi called me over to his workbench, held up a picture of Jean Harlow for me to look at as he shook his big head of black hair, all the time contemplating the picture together with me, and said, "Now, whaddya tink, boy?" . . . Then he said, "OK, kid, you gotta work hard and learn something. See all those poor bastards out there outa work. Watch out or you could be one of dem." Luigi was a wood-carver who made the models for the multiple-spindle carving machine and was probaby the only real craftsman in the place.

One day as I distributed work in process to the operators and picked up their finished stuff, I received one of my first lessons in the fundamentals of working that I would relearn again and again in almost every job I have had: How to work less hard in order to make the task easier.

Max Teitelbaum, a band saw operator just a few years out of Krakow, Poland, a slightly built man with sort of Mickey Mouse ears, twinkling eyes, and a wry smile, would upbraid me repeatedly with such passing comments as, "You are a dummy," or "You're not stupid, so what's da matter vit you?" Finally one day he stopped his machine, turned to me, and said, "Look, come over here. I vant to talk vit you. Vy you are using your back instead your head? Max Teitelbaum's first rule is: Don't carry nuttin' you could put a veel under. It's a good ting you wasn't helpin' mit der pyramids—you vould get crushed under the stones."

I said, "But Max, if the hand truck is on the third floor and I'm on the fifth, I can't go all the way down there just for that."

"You see," he said, "you are a dummy. Vy you can't go down dere? Huh, vy not? You tell me!"

"Well," I said, "it would take a lot of time—"

He cut me off. "You see, you are vorrying about da wrong tings, like da boss. Is he vorrying about you? Like da Tzar vorried about Max Teitelbaum. Listen, kid, you vorry about you because no von else vill. Understand? You vill get nuttin' for vorking harder den more vork. Now ven you even don't understand someting, you come and ask Max. OK?" Max became my friend, adviser, and critic.

By the end of my first weeks in the factory I began to feel as if I was crushed under stones. My body helped me to understand what Max was saying. I would come home from work on Saturday afternoon and go to bed expecting to go out later that night with a girl friend. For some weeks when I lay down on Saturday I did not try, nor was I able, to move my body from bed until some time on Sunday. The whole thing just throbbed with fatigue: arms, shoulders, legs, and back were in fierce competition for which hurt the most. I began to learn what Max meant by "Always put a veel under it and don't do more than you have to."

My third or fourth week at the factory found me earnestly launched in my quest for holding the job but doing less work—or working less hard. This was immediately recognized and hailed by the men with "Now you're gettin' smart, kid. Stop bustin' your ass and only do what you have to do. You don't get any more money for bustin' your hump and you might put some other poor bastard outa job." Remember this was the depression. Most workers, while aware of the preciousness of their jobs, felt that doing more work than necessary could be putting someone else, even yourself, out of a job. "Only do what you have to" became a rule not only to save your own neck but to make sure you were not depriving some other soul like yourself from getting a job.

In the next few weeks, I was to be taught a second important lesson about working. One day while picking up sawdust, I began to "find" pieces in the sawdust or behind a woodpile or under a machine. The first few times, with great delight, I would announce to the operator, "Hey, look what I found!" I should have figured something was wrong by the lack of similar enthusiasm from the operator. Sam was a generally quiet Midwesterner who never seemed to raise his voice much, but now when I showed him my finished-work discovery behind his milling machine he shouted, "Who the fuck asked you to be a detective? Keep your silly ass out from behind my machine; I'll tell you what to pick up. So don't go being a big brown-nosing hero around here."

Wow, I sure never expected that. Confused, troubled, almost in tears, not knowing what to do or where to go, I went to the toilet to hide my hurt and just sat down on an open bowl and thought what the hell am I doing in this goddamned place anyway? I lit a cigarette and began pacing up and down in front of the three stalls, puffing away at my Camel. I thought, What the hell should I do? This job is terrible, the men are pissed off at me. I hate the place, why don't I just quit? Well, it's a job and you get paid, I said to myself, so take it easy.

While I'm pacing and puffing, Sam comes in, saying, "Lissen, kid, don't get sore. I was just trying to set you straight. Let me tell you what it's all about. The guys around, that is the machine operators, agree on how much we are gonna turn out, and that's what the boss gets, no more, no less. Now sometimes any one of us might just fall behind a little, so we always keep some finished stuff hidden away just in case." The more he talked, the more I really began to feel like the enemy. I tried to apologize, but he just went on. "Look, kid, the boss always wants more and he doesn't give a shit if we die giving it to him, so we [it was that "we" that seemed to retrieve my soul back into the community; my tears just went away] agree on how much we're going to give him—no more, no less. You see, kid, if you keep running around, moving the stuff too fast, the boss will get wise about what's going on." Sam put his arm on my shoulder. (My God! I was one of them! I love Sam and the place. I am in!) "So look," he says, "your job is to figure out how to move and work no faster than we turn the stuff out. Get it? OK? You'll get it." I said, "Yes, of course, I understand everything." I was being initiated into the secrets of a work tribe, and I loved it.

I was beginning to learn the second work lesson that would be taught me many times over in a variety of different jobs: Don't do more work than is absolutely necessary. Years later I would read about how people in the Hawthorne works of Western Electric would "bank work" and use it when they fell behind or just wanted to take it easy. I have seen a lot of work banking, especially in machine shops. In some way I have felt that banking work was the workers' response to the stopwatches of industrial engineers. It is an interesting sort of game of hide the work now, take it out later. In another plant, would you believe we banked propellor shafts for Liberty ships!

I learned most of the rules, written and unwritten, about the furniture factory, but I never got to like the job. After I had been there six or seven months, the Furniture Workers Union began an organizing drive. I hated the furniture factory, the noise, the dust, and the travel, so I, too, quickly signed a union card. I was just as quickly out on my ass. It was a good way to go, since my radical friends considered me a hero of sorts, having been victimized for the cause. The first time I ever considered suicide in my life was in that furniture factory as I would stare at the clock and think to myself, "If I have to spend my life in this hellhole, I would rather end it." Well, of course, I didn't; and as I look back, it was not the worst place I worked, but I was young and unwilling to relinquish childhood.

Violations of Free Speech and Rights of Labor
Report of the Committee on Education and Labor

INTRODUCTION

The committee has previously issued two reports. Report No. 46, Seventy-fifth Congress, first session, submitted on February 8, 1937, was a preliminary account of the committee's inquiries and studies from its inception on June 6, 1936, through its first set of public hearings, which were held in August and September 1936. Report No. 46, part 2, Seventy-fifth Congress, first session, dated July 22, 1937, dealt solely with the subcommittee's investigation of the Chicago Memorial Day incident.

From the United States Government Printing Office, 1938.

The present report on industrial espionage is first of a series which describes the major work of the committee to date, sets forth the findings and recommendations arising out of its inquiries, and points out avenues for further investigation.

SCOPE AND METHOD OF THE INVESTIGATION

The bulk of the committee's investigations and hearings has been confined, for reasons stated below, to the related fields of industrial espionage, strikebreaking, and the furnishing of munitions to private industry.

Industrial espionage was found to be a common, almost universal, practice in American industry. The forms of espionage differed from firm to firm but the objectives remain identical, however euphemistically described. Strikebreaking methods varied with localities. Industrial munitioning was likewise found to be widespread, secretive in its methods, and available in many forms to all types of industry. But the promotional and sales activities of all munitioning firms were markedly similar; their purpose identical.

Three investigative procedures were available to the committee, limited as it was to studying typical instances: (1) To examine labor and labor organizations as the victims of the three antilabor practices; (2) to examine management as the customer and client of the detective agency, the strikebreaker, and the munitions firm; and (3) to examine the detective agency, the strikebreaking firm, and munitions company as functional organizations themselves.

The first two methods entailed investigations of such magnitude and generality that they were beyond the resources of the committee's staff. The committee, therefore, deemed it desirable to examine in detail large representative organizations supplying labor spies, strikebreakers, and munitions to industry, supplemented, where possible, by additional information from labor organizations and from firms known to have employed detective agencies, strikebreakers, and munitions.

In all of the hearings of the committee, which were public, witnesses were summoned from every party having an interest in the proceedings. Thus, the committee conducted, in many of its hearings what may be called a "round-table" interrogation. For example, in the General Motors-Pinkerton hearings there were as many as 14 witnesses on the stand before the committee at one time. These represented the employer, the employees, the labor organization, the detective agency and its representatives and operatives. Full opportunity was given to each witness, without exception, to present his case and to refute or rebut any damaging testimony or evidence. The witnesses were all further advised that the record of the committee was open to them for insertion of any pertinent data they desired to submit. Many of the witnesses took advantage of this opportunity. These data appear in the printed volumes of the committee's record.

The testimony of the witnesses varied considerably in reliability and credibility. Certain of the spies and strikebreakers, apparently either friendly or penitent, gave testimony concerning their own activities, their betrayals of confidence and their deeds of violence, which assumes significance because of the fact that it was so clearly against their own interests. The subcommittee has, however, been careful not to accept such testimony at its face value, unless it could be verified from other sources. On the whole, the most important facts have been established through the grudging testimony of reluctant and sometimes hostile witnesses, both among the officials of the detective agencies and among the employers. Their very evasiveness and frequent hostility make their admissions evidence of unquestioned accuracy.

REASONS FOR MAKING THE INVESTIGATION

So much has been written about the committee and its investigations have received so much public notice that a statement of its policies and course seems appropriate. Under Resolution 266 the Senate authorized the committee to investigate "violations of the right of free speech and assembly and undue interference with the right of labor to organize and bargain collectively." The preliminary hearings on this resolution brought forth an array of evidence which demonstrated that the right, guaranteed labor by the National Labor Relations Act, to organize free from employer restraint and interference, was being denied by force and stealth.

The hearings further indicated that the denial of this right was the most important problem of civil liberties before the Nation, because denying workers the right to organize almost invariably meant denying them the fundamental civil rights which are the basis of our democratic system. As the report on the preliminary hearings established, "wage earners attempting to take advantage of their legal right to organize (under the National Labor Relations Act) find that to do so imperils their right to peaceable assembly, to freedom of speech, and to vote, no less than to keep their job."

But a second and even more disturbing conclusion derived from the preliminary hearings was that denial of these rights to workers simultaneously endangered the rights of other citizens in no way concerned with particular labor controversies. Nowhere were the civil rights guaranteed all Americans under the Constitution more seriously in jeopardy than in those communities where employers invoked instruments of violence and coercion against workers who sought to express the right to organize.

The first of these consequences is more obvious, the second no less implicit, in every attempt to prevent workers from freely exercising the right to organize. The exercise of this right and the achievement of certain of the aims of organization and collective bargaining—job securities, fair wages, and decent living conditions—necessarily involves workers in a practical, day-to-day assertion of the rights of free speech, free association, and free assembly. In fact, the committee's studies strongly suggest that the right to organize is indeed fundamental, if only because the practices invoked by employers to nullify this right—spying, strikebreaking, and munitioning—are so subversive of our most vital law and democratic processes. But the tides of organization could not be stayed. Employers have therefore resorted to espionage to prevent their employees from joining bona fide unions, to ascertain, fire, and blacklist those who did join, and to subvert their organizing plans. If a union withstood these preliminary barrages and engaged in a strike, it found itself pitted against a small army of notorious strikebreakers, recruited from the gutter with criminal records as their certificates of proficiency. The employer has armed these strikebreakers, often illegally, with tear gas and vomiting gas, pistols, and machine guns.

He has turned them loose on defenseless and peaceable citizens, men and women alike, often after influencing local officials to swear them in as regularly constituted "peace" officers. And finally, when even his private armed mercenaries have failed him, the employer has sometimes been able to resort to the presumably impartial armed force of the State to "settle the strike" through the complaisance of public officials.

Neither the textbooks on labor and on management practices, nor the writings and speeches of industrial leaders and employers' groups, mentioned the practices. It is therefore important to stress that these are the methods, not of criminals and sadists, but of employers high in the esteem of the Nation, possessing wealth and power over millions of men and women; and that these practices are not the sporadic excesses of mismanagement, but rather the chosen instruments of a deliberate design to thwart the concrete expression of the right of collective action by individual workers who, without that right, have no rights.

SCOPE OF INQUIRY INTO LABOR ESPIONAGE

This report on industrial espionage is based on the committee's study of the services supplied to industry by five of the largest private detective agencies in this country. These agencies included among their clients the largest and most representative American industrial corporations. The committee developed testimony and facts from sources: (1) From the records of the agency and the testimony of its officials; (2) from the records, and officials of the firms or corporations employing the agency;

(3) from a number of the employees or operatives of the agency who performed the espionage service; and (4) from the workers, union members or officials upon whom the detective agency, at the direction of the employing firms, conducted its spying activities. Two of the agencies—Railway Audit & Inspection Co. and the National Corporation Service—also supply strikebreakers through subsidiaries. Some data regarding the labor espionage work of hundreds of other detective agencies was obtained from questionnaires and the investigation of other topics.

The reluctance of the detective agencies to yield their documents and their hostility to the investigation made it necessary to examine certain of their clients in great detail. The General Motors Corporation and the Chrysler Motors Corporation were investigated as soon as it was determined that they were the largest clients of Pinkerton's and Corporations Auxiliary Co., respectively.

A sample of a different form of spy service, that performed by an employers' association, was also studied in the investigation of the National Metal Trades Association, which has had a long history serving employers in the metal fabricating industry east of the Mississippi. Incidental to the Goodyear Tire & Rubber Co. study, some data was obtained on the somewhat similar espionage activities carried on by the Akron (Ohio) Employers' Association.

The committee did not investigate the private espionage systems maintained by certain large corporations, evidence of whose existence was encountered in the course of other investigations. This study remains to be done and is included in the committee's agenda.

PURPOSE AND EXTENT OF INDUSTRIAL ESPIONAGE

Purpose of Industrial Espionage

Since its inception in the 1870's labor espionage has spread throughout practically the whole of American industry. One national labor leader expressed it in these terms: "There is no gathering of union members large enough to be called a meeting that is small enough to exclude a spy." That statement from a labor leader is confirmed by spokesmen from industry itself. Herman L. Weckler, vice president and general manager of the De Soto Corporation (division of Chrysler Corporation) and himself a worker "up from the ranks" stated to the committee:

> It (labor espionage) has been a practice that has been in existence for years. It is a practice we have grown up with.

J. H. Smith, president for almost 40 years of the Corporations Auxiliary Co., largest espionage agency devoted solely to industrial work, testified that the nature of his business "has changed slightly, but not very much" in the last four decades.

Why has American industry resorted, during this period of its most active growth and consolidation of power, to a practice that every congressional and State inquiry has condemned since it came to public notice? Your committee can only conclude from its investigations that this practice is an infallible index of the stubborn and irreconcilable opposition of a considerable section of American industry to the recognition of labor's right to organize. The indefensible practices assumed by industry in its opposition to labor's right to organize form a striking contrast to the growth of horizontal combinations in industry itself.

In addition to the increase in the size and strength of individual business units there has been a continual growth in the number of employer combinations. Today the Department of Commerce lists more than 7,000 associations of employers. Many of these associations, united primarily by common economic interests, are organized ostensibly to propagate lofty ideals of responsible business ethics, fellowship, and Americanism. Their business ethics do not countenance, as many of them testified, the introduction of spies, informers, and saboteurs in the ranks of their own organizations; yet countless members of these associations, citizens of repute, beset their own employees with paid spies. Their view of the responsibilities of management permits them, while proclaiming the virtues of American industry, to betray their workingmen. Neither their speeches nor their advertising label their products "made by spied-on labor."

Employer resistance to organization has taken many forms. These vary from company unions and other types of "welfare" organizations through blacklisting and espionage down to open displays of force. Espionage is the most efficient method known to management to prevent unions from forming, to weaken them if they secure a foothold, and to wreck them when they try their strength. Its use by management is an entirely "natural growth" in the long struggle to keep unions out of the shop.

The chief reasons advanced by employers and detective agency officials for the use of labor spies were: (1) Protecting industry against radicalism and Communism; (2) preventing sabotage (closely linked to the first); (3) detecting theft; (4) improving efficiency in methods and workers; merging into (5) improving relations between employers and workers, or "human engineering." These "legitimate" reasons for the employment of labor spies were strenuously advanced by officials of the detective agencies and, with diminished enthusiasm, by representatives of industry. These "reasons" were of so little merit that after examination by the committee they were repudiated by the same officials who advanced them. They are, however interesting to examine for the light they shed on the actual motive.

No employer seriously defended his use of labor spies by the well-worn excuse of a crusade against radicalism and sabotage. The Pinkerton and Burns officials, on the other hand, regarded ferreting out radicals as their private and real endeavor.

Raising the red scare is a common practice with detective agencies, not because of any profoundly felt fear of radicalism among employers, but more because the identification of labor with radicalism and sabotage neatly serves their antilabor policy. Radicalism is more opprobrious than labor-unionism; therefore, the employer opposed to unions is more than anxious to plead his cause in public by stigmatizing all unions as radical. This type of reasoning places an initial handicap on the organizing campaigns of unions from which only the hardiest can survive.

A revealing example of this technique is to be found in the following inter-office correspondence of the William J. Burns International Detective Agency, Inc. The first is a letter from W. Sherman Burns, secretary-treasurer of the agency, to G. H. Fleming, manager of the Portland, Oreg., office:

> There is no doubt but what in view of the strikes on the Pacific Coast, business men have come to appreciate that these strikes are fostered and agitated by the extreme radical element. Heretofore, the average business man has taken only a more or less academic interest in communism and radicalism. It has merely been something to read about. However, I think there is a different view being taken by these business men today. They appreciate that if the agitators and communists could be weeded out of employment, wherever they have found employment, the movement would soon die out or it would at least lose its influence over the other employees.
>
> With this growing understanding upon the part of business as to what this movement is all about, I think there is a splendid opportunity for a number of the offices to place industrial undercover operatives, as the use of these industrial undercover operatives is the only effective method by which the identity of the communists and agitators can become known.

The more realistic reply of the Portland manager to the above letter stamps this subterfuge for what it really is:

> I acknowledge receipt of your letter of August 9th. * * *
>
> The main proposition out here in which the employers are interested is not the Communist but the labor agitators, who may be Communists, and what influence their agitation has on the men. There has been a continuous battle since the NRA was organized here in Oregon between the so-called company unions and the A. F. of L.
>
> I have inserted in the second line of the second paragraph of your letter the word "labor" in the letters which we are sending out, making that paragraph read "The problem of determining the identity of any Communists or radical labor agitators who might be in your employ, * * *.

Another reason advanced to justify the employment of labor spies was detecting and preventing theft and sabotage. Reference has already been made to the Pinkerton bookkeeping entries for industrial work which frequently carried the designation "sabotage" or "detection of theft and other irregularities."

What at first sight appears to be a perfectly legitimate reason for industry's employment of detective agencies was revealed, upon examination, to be of minor consequence, if not completely misleading. Aside from the regularly constituted police officers available for such work most of the larger clients of the detective agencies maintain their own special police and patrol services. General Motors, for example, has an extensive and, as Harry W. Anderson, in charge of General Motors labor relations testified, well-trained plant police force in each factory.

By comparing specific bookkeeping entries reading "detection of theft" with reports of actual operations for the same accounts, it was conclusively shown that the operations were in all cases concerned with securing union information. "Theft detection" was, it seems, another of the conceits so freely employed by the agencies to conceal reprehensible industrial espionage.

The Corporations Auxiliary Co. claimed that its operations were largely concerned with welfare, efficiency, and consulting engineering work in plants. Their articles of incorporation also give as their purpose, "To assist employers and employees in promoting harmonious relations * * *." When it was shown that their work was in no sense technical engineering, both J. H. Smith, president, and Dan G. Ross, general manager, defended the use of their agents as tending to develop such harmonious relations—"human engineering."

"Human engineering" or another contribution to the lexicography of espionage? Only the actual operations and the operatives—or their victims—could provide an adequate answer.

Clearly the work of Corporations Auxiliary Co. operatives was not engineering in any professional sense. None even of the major officials were engineers.

As numerous operatives of the Corporations Auxiliary Co. were uncovered and their major work found to be obtaining information about unions and worming their way into high positions in them, it became clear that "human engineering" was another blind to conceal their real activities. The reluctant admission of Dan G. Ross finally confirmed the duties of these "human engineers."

Senator LA FOLLETTE. You stated that these operatives would report the names of men who were active in union activities, and that you would send that on to their employers.

Mr. Ross. Yes.

. . . the Pinkerton detective agency and Louis G. Seaton of the General Motors Corporation to Senators La Follette and Thomas as follows:

Mr. CLARK. I think that is the Corporation Auxiliary Co.

Senator LA FOLLETTE. What were you doing on that job?

Mr. CLARK. Well, we were trying to find out whether or not information they were securing was being passed to a competitor.

Senator LA FOLLETTE. Who authorized that? Mr. Anderson?

Mr. ANDERSON. No sir.

Senator LA FOLLETTE. Mr. Hale?

Mr. HALE. No, sir.

Senator LA FOLLETTE. Mr. Seaton?

Mr. SEATON. I didn't authorize anything in a specific manner. We were interested at that particular time, if I remember it, in what you might call a product leak and information.

Senator LA FOLLETTE. Tell us about it.

Mr. SEATON. There was a feeling—we have had feelings, and I imagine most people get them once in a while—that some of our engineering or design information was getting out, before our new models came out.

The Pinkerton officials did not seem surprised by the assignment.

Senator LA FOLLETTE. Was that on the theory that any agency that would use undercover methods to get secrets of unions would be willing to do the same job getting trade secrets?

Mr. CLARK. No; I wouldn't say that.

Senator LA FOLLETTE. There is no difference in moral values there, is there, Mr. Clark?

Mr. CLARK. I would not want to say about that, Senator.

Here is the essence of spy stuff. These are the risks American industry assumes when it buys labor espionage. Yet, in spite of these risks, so ineradicable is the spy habit that when faced with the evils it produces management seems to have only one answer—more spies. Spies beget spies—lies beget more lies—distrust begets distrust—until faith in all is gone. Even faith in self is lost. Industry cannot survive this endless dependence upon unreliable knowledge which begets fear of all things and of all men.

THE INDUSTRIAL SPY

The whole espionage system is based upon the possibility of securing men to engage in the betrayal of their fellows for hire. It is with the character, motives, and careers of such men that we are now concerned.

The public at large, both employer and employee, are unsparing in their condemnation of such men. Officials of the detective agencies, although reluctantly, were compelled to acknowledge that such condemnation is universal and severe. Indeed, once a spy has been exposed he is no longer useful to the agency, which promptly severs its connections with him and leaves him to drift. He is a social pariah, seeking to practice his despised profession in communities where he is not known.

Mr. Richard Frankensteen, vice president of the United Automobile Workers of America, cited a particular instance from the workers' point of view:

> I want to specifically mention the next situation. The next concerns a man named Roy Williams. He was, I believe, the best-liked and most popular man in Graham-Paige Motor Co. He worked there for 17 years. He was very well thought of. He was elected to the position of recording secretary and this year is chairman of the board of trustees. He had worked there for 17 years, and only during the last 3 years has he been hired by the Corporations Auxiliary. He was hooked into it. By that I mean they got him in; they roped him. He did not know what it was about until they got him in. Then when he tried to get out I understand that a Mr. H. L. Madison urged him to stay in—told him his work was perfectly all right, that he should stay, there was nothing wrong, that the Corporations Auxiliary was not the same type as the other agencies and he should certainly stay there. So the fellow, after 17 years in the plant, with two children, is out on the street, without a job. I don't know whether the Corporations Auxiliary will take care of him or not.
>
> That man was not a typical spy. It was not his ambition to become a stool pigeon, or spy, or, as we call them, a rat. He did not mean to be that at all, he was just hooked into it.

The story of Roy Williams is typical of many cases brought to the attention of the committee. Dan G. Ross, general manager of the Corporations Auxiliary Co., confirmed Mr. Frankensteen's statement.

> It causes them (the spies) to be really social outcasts as Mr. Frankensteen testified himself.

The rest of the testimony of Mr. Ross served to emphasize this point:

Senator Thomas: You wish to change then your statement to the effect that a man who is a spy and has been caught spying has his whole social status hurt?

Mr. Ross. Very much impaired; yes.

Senator Thomas. No; I mean hurt.

Mr. Ross. Hurt; yes, he has his social status hurt.

Senator Thomas. There is no doubt about that?

Mr. Ross. I will testify to that; yes.

Senator Thomas. Therefore, in any part of your record where you have implied that the espionage may be an honorable business, in the sense that it does not damage people, we are to change that whole thing, and you are going to admit that it is not only a damaging proposition but it hurts the individual himself?

Mr. Ross. Damaging to the individual himself when he is found out?

Senator THOMAS. And he can never make his place again in society?

Mr. Ross. I would not go that far as to say that he can never make his place again in society, but it subjects him, at the time it subjects him to not only embarrassment, but to the possibility of violence, injury of limb, and everything else.

Senator THOMAS. All right. You see, you are getting very close to what we want to find out.

Despite universal condemnation, spies of the different espionage agencies are secured from and operate in every section of society. The bulk of the spies are undoubtedly drawn from the ranks of workers in the large industrial plants. The lists of spies disclosed to the committe also includes a liberal sprinkling who were not employed by industry.

The spies of the National Metal Trades Association included two women, Mrs. D. D. Anastasis, Operative 568, and Bertha Rutter, Operative 619. The National Corporation Service employed 11 women among its active operatives apart from those doing office work. One of them, named Mary Javorsky, alias Mary Jay, who was assigned the number 585, was among the most proficient of the agency's operatives. The list of her assignments is impressive:

> Street and undercover operative on behalf of the following firms: American Fork & Hoe Co., Ashtabula Hide & Leather Co., American Bow Socket Co. Aetna Rubber Co., all in Ashtabula, Ohio, 1934; Lake Erie Power & Light Co. Bellevue, Ohio, 1934; Val Decker Packing Co., Piqua, Ohio, 1934; Cloverleaf Dairy Co., Toledo, Ohio, 1935; Youngstown Auto Dealers Association, Youngstown, Ohio, 1935; Dayton Auto Dealers Association, Dayton, Ohio, 1936. Is now statutory agent for Hulbert & Wood, Inc., detective agency, Room 513, Bulkley Building, Cleveland, Ohio.

In addition, the National Corporation Service carried on its payroll a minister, the Reverend Bunch, of Leavittsburg, Ohio, whose function was to "spread propaganda for the company union" at the Taylor-Winfield Co. in Warren, Ohio. Another employee was Wallace Metcalf, whose ostensible employment was with the Civil Service Commission of Mahoning County, at Youngstown, Ohio.

Spies, because of the nature of their work, are difficult to classify. As was stated above, a minister of the gospel or a government employee may in truth be a labor spy. A spy may pose as a workingman in a factory and later masquerade as a salesman with offices adjacent to the union office. Then again the spy may appear as a bitter opponent of genuine labor organization and as the guiding genius of a plant company union. Spies may be anything or many things at once, but the unifying principle behind the myriad guises assumed by the spy is the fact that he is always acting in the interest of the espionage agency and its client and against the interest of the client's employees. It is with relation to this principle that one method of classification suggests itself.

The professional spy can be distinguished from what is known in the espionage vocabulary as "the hooked man." The professional spy knows he is acting in the employer's interest. He has definitely thrown his lot in with the spy agency and he pursues his union-smashing devices with conscious treachery.

"Hooked man," however, is a term used to designate the man who is led innocently to betray the confidence placed in him by his friends. The typical hooked man does not know that his reports are sent to the employer and usually is serene in the belief that he is actually helping his fellow employees. But once caught in the toils of the spy business through a constant and subtle training the hooked man is developed by espionage agencies into a matured professional spy.

In between the professional spy and the hooked man stands the spy who is hired with the understanding that he is to act as an industrial detective but who is led to believe at first that he is to prevent thefts and not to destroy labor unions. His moral aversion to labor espionage is broken down by the spy agencies with the same technique used in developing the hooked man.

Hooking is an elaborate and difficult operation. The average person has deep-rooted scruples against betraying his friends and conspiring against their efforts to better their wages and working conditions. The experienced hooker is skilled in lulling these scruples to rest and in breaking down the moral sensibilities of his victim. The bait he uses is money. But a crude offer of a bribe would in most cases be met with an indignant refusal. For this reason, the hooker uses a "pretext," a plausible story intended to reassure the to-be-hooked man that he is really acting in the best interests of his fellow employees. Once the man has been hooked and has signed a receipt the hooker drops his pleasant mask. He applies pressure and insists that the hooked man report more and more in detail on the plans of the union. The hooked man becomes caught in the trap. Attacted by the money, still hoping that the pretext was true, fearing exposure by the hooker if he tries to break away, the hooked man slides further and further down the path of treachery that leads him into deliberate espionage.

The hooker is skilled in the business of espionage.

R. L. Burnside, one of the Pinkerton hookers, testified that when he was persuaded to give up his practice as an insurance salesman and work for Pinkerton's, he was told:

> The only way you can ever get anywhere with the agency is to start as an operative.

The hooker is also thoroughly conversant with the labor situation. Lawrence Barker, a Pinkerton operative, testified to the familiarity which Robert Mason, Pinkerton hooker in the Detroit area, showed with the affairs of the United Automobile Workers.

The hooker also builds up a familiarity with the labor movement as he progresses with his work. He has available a string of hooked men on whom he can depend when the agency succeeds in selling its business.

In addition to maintaining a wide circle of contacts, the hooker is on the alert for new men. R. L. Burnside told the committee:

> We always have to be on the lookout for good material.

It was for this reason that Burnside approached Charles Forwerck, a member of the executive board of the flat plate glass workers' union in Toledo, Ohio. Burnside said:

> As a matter of fact, for Mr. Forwerck—we had no client at that time for him either. It was merely a case of trying to employ him because he seemed to be a suitable man for the work.

The hookers of the espionage agencies are thus constantly lurking in the neighborhood of union workers watching for a proper moment to move in and take advantage of the difficulties in which a worker finds himself.

The most common factor on which the hooker depends in seeking to corrupt a worker is financial hardship. A worker in need of money ordinarily does not scrutinize too carefully a windfall which comes his way. The hooker mercilessly plays upon the temptation of the worker to find relief from the poverty which torments him. Another factor is personal pique. Then, too, the factions and differences of opinion which naturally arise in any organization are grist to the hooker's mill. A union member smarting from personal defeat in the union is ripe for the unscrupulous blandishments of the spy agency.

C. M. "Red" Kuhl, former hooker for the National Corporation Service, gave a much blunter statement of the technique.

> Well, first you look your prospect over, and if he is married that is preferable. If he is financially hard up, that is number two. If his wife wants more money or he hasn't got a car, that all counts. And you go offer him this extra money, naturally you don't tell him what you want him for.

This technique was employed by R. L. Burnside of the Pinkerton Agency in his attempt to hook Charles Forwerck as related above.

A union member who is disgruntled because of fractionalism in the union is easy prey to the accomplished hooker. W. H. Gray, hooker of the Railway Audit & Inspection Co., on May 23, 1935, wrote a revealing letter to the superintendent of the agency's office in Atlanta. Referring to a conversation he had had with Operative 723, E. E. Miller, Gray said:

> He states that Bulick, the U. T. W. Org. has returned from Dan-

ville, Va. and stated that he was disgustd with the heads of the Union, as they are not playing fair with the workers and etc. Wish that business was good maybe this chap could be hooked.

It was by such tactics that A. L. Pugmire, Pinkerton officials in the Detroit office, hooked Arthur G. Dubuc, president of the Chevrolet local of the United Automobile Workers in Flint, Mich.

Pugmire told Dubuc "that he was representing some financiers in New York, big financiers * * *" Dubuc was astonished that Pugmire was so thoroughly acquainted with his background. "How do you know me so well?" Dubuc asked. "Well," he replied, "do you think I approach you blindly? In fact, I know more about you than you know yourself." The details that Pugmire knew of Dubuc's life were suprisingly minute. At the first interview he sympathized with Dubuc because of his ill health. He knew that Dubuc had been discriminated against by the Chevrolet Co. in 1934 for union activity. But in particular he knew that Dubuc was having difficulties as an officer within the union.

Experienced hookers, like R. L. Burnside and A. L. Pugmire, find their own victims. The letter of W. H. Gray quoted above, shows how, through information received from other operatives, the hooker is able to get the names of union men who are ripe for his advances.

The usual method of securing a list of prospective hooked men, however, is through the employer. This was the testimony of Asher Rossetter of the Pinkerton agency given before Senators La Follette and Thomas.

Various pretexts are used by hookers. W. H. Gray of the Railway Audit & Inspection Co. disclosed several to the committee.

The hooker takes great pains to make the hooked man feel that his reports are going to a group that are not identified with the operating staff of the plant. The common pretext of the "minority stockholders," "the financial house" or the "insurance set-up" are useful because they are identified with interests which, to a certain extent, are adverse to the operating group. The hooker explains that the group he represents is interested in getting a check on the conduct of the supervisory officers in order to put an end to mismanagement. C. M. Kuhl, who formerly acted as a hooker for the National Corporation Service, testified in this respect as follows:

> You have got some story that you are representing some bankers or some bondholders or an insurance company and they want to know what goes on in there. You probably tell him, "I want to know more of what these foremen and superintendents do than your fellow workmen."

At times, the hooker even persuades the hooked man that he represents a philanthropic agency that in some vague way is acting in the direct interest of the workers.

The use of pretexts is a necessary part of the hooking process. Mr. Pugmire, of the Pinkerton agency, protested to the committee that in his dealings with undercover men "I was truthful except when I was under pretext." Without a pretext, workers could scarcely be enlisted as spies. As Dan G. Ross, general manager of the Corporation Auxiliary Co. stated:

> You would run a chance of losing them, Senator, if at that time you told them they were working for the Corporations Auxiliary. You run a chance. I do not see why it makes any difference whether they work for somebody else, or whether their understanding is that they were working for some investment house.

The reports of the hooked man are frequently handled by a different official of the agency from the man who did the hooking. The official in the office borrows the alias of the hooker and continues the correspondence with the hooked man, who remains under the impression that he is still dealing with the man who called upon him.

The use of aliases and blind addresses serves as an almost impenetrable fog behind which it is practially impossible to trace the operations of the espionage agency. Least of all does the hooked man have a clear picture. Arthur G. Dubuc who had been hooked by A. L. Pugmire, alias Palmer, of the Pinkerton agency, testified that he had reported to a bewildering series of Pinkerton officials.

> Mr. DUBUC. Well, to start with it was Pugmire and then a man by the name of Matthews, but since then I know is Mason. Of course, that might be a different alias, but I know him as Mason now. Then Parker, but now I know he is Peterson. Then Sullivan came in the picture and then after Sullivan there was a man by the name of—no, Roberts came in the picture and then Sullivan came and finally a man by the name of Riley, but Pugmire told me that it was Riley and to call him Ed, that his real name was John, and, at a later date, that he did not know who Riley was, but it was Riley, so I think it was a fictitious name.

Once hooked the spy is put through an elaborate educational process which leads him into labor espionage work. At first he is told that he is to report on various innocuous matters dealing with plant efficiency and conduct of the supervisory officers.

The hooked man soon discovers that his employment is leading him into betraying his friends. C. M. Kuhl, of the National Corporation Service, estimated that within 2 or 3 months the hooked man is fully aware of what he is doing.

> Mr. KUHL. . . . I think maybe 70 percent, or next to it, from the start know, but in no time at all, say, 90 percent, say, in 2 or 3 months, know what they are really doing, because you have got to go back to this

fellow and school him and train him to bring in facts that this particular client wants to know. And today it is all as regards unions and the activities of unions.

Senator LA FOLLETTE. That is most of the work now?

Mr. KUHL. That is most of the work.

Occasionally the hooked man withdraws when he discovers the true nature of the work. There eventually comes a point where every hooked man must make up his mind as to whether or not he will be a spy. The spy agency does everything in its power to overcome his reluctance.

It is not simple, however, for the operative to quit.

The hooked man, once he has continued to render his reports after he is fully aware of the significance of his work, has matured into the professional spy. Once his moral integrity is gone and he has definitely alienated himself from the interests of his fellow worker, he becomes dependent upon the spy agency. He becomes a callous and unscrupulous informant. His whole moral fiber weakens. This is perhaps best illustrated in the case of John Davison, spy No. 880 of the Railway Audit and Inspection Co. Davison worked in the Carnegie-Illinois Steel Co., in Farrell, Pa., and was hooked by Pete Godino, alias Peter Goodman, of this agency in May 1936. On August 10, 1936, he had become so enmeshed in the spy business that he wrote in his daily report that

> I may as well state right here that George Ferguson who is a movie operator and an office holder in his local union and Darrell Kepler, a movie operator, who is secretary of the local union, are personal friends of mine. I have known Ferguson for twenty years and Kepler for ten years and now I am selling them out as they tell me most anything.

The moral tragedy implicit in this confession is magnified when it is realized that such corruption of needy or ignorant union men is the principal source of industrial spies. Evidence amassed by the committee reveals that every detective agency under examination engaged in the practice of hooking. Estimates by officials of the agencies themselves indicated that from 50 to 70 percent of all industrial spies are hooked men.

The advantage of the hooked man is that he is already settled in the community and enjoys the confidence of the men he is to betray. There are occasions, however, when conditions permit the sending of a stranger into the community. The delicacy and difficulty of the hooking operations make it preferable in such cases either to send a professional spy to the job, or to engage or detail a new operative outright.

Detective agencies at times detail their investigative employees to undercover industrial work. Conscious of their position from the start such operatives enter a plant as new employees and report in the customary fashion to the agency. If they display proficiency in the undercover role they may advance to the status of a professional spy and ultimately to a supervisory position.

Agencies engaged in legitimate criminal or investigating work may occasionally engage new men for industrial work under the representation that they are to act as detectives in ferreting out criminals. The process bears many resemblances to hooking. Only after the employee has been rendering reports for some time on such matters as theft, efficiency, or sanitary facilities is he required to report on union activities.

Agencies which engage in nothing but industrial espionage, such as Corporations Auxiliary Co., cannot lure workers into their trade through the pretext of legitimate criminal or investigative work. They must, therefore, resort to blind advertisements. Applications in response to such advertisements are answered by the detective agency on the letterhead of a fictitious corporation.

Practically all of the hooking subterfuges are employed to turn such applicants for work into industrial spies. One document in the committee's record charged that a representative of the National Metal Trades Association impersonated an officer of the United States Government in the Intelligence Service as a pretext.

Occasionally a detective agency will insert an advertisement designed to draw the attention of the professional spy or the worker versed in industrial espionage. One such advertisement used by the National Metal Trades Association simply called for machinists "with experience along industrial lines." Even so slight a departure from the norm of "help wanted" phrasings drew responses from several ex-spies who were then in need of employment.

Professional spies normally maintain their contacts with the detective agencies who have employed them, but since fear of exposure drives them from place to place they may often be separated from sources of employment. The carefully worded ad offers the means to draw such wanderers back into the service.

The professional spy deserves extended comment. None of the excuses that may be pleaded for the hooked man can be applied to him. His business is the conscious and deliberate exercise of deceit and treachery. He is a constant menace not only to the existence of unions but to the security and livelihood of every fellow employee at whose side he works. Yet his is often a lucrative and prosperous career. Many of the supervisory and executive officers of the great detective agencies have been recruited from his ranks. Every spy agency maintains a staff of skilled operatives, shifting them from assignment to assignment, perfecting their skill in antiunion activities as their experience broadens.

THE PROCESS OF UNION BUSTING

The furtive and despicable character of the spy springs logically, as we have seen, from the nature of espionage and its objectives. What the spy, so formed and directed, does to organizations of labor in the interests of employers must now be examined. A few examples of the techniques practiced by spies in destroying unions, wrecking organizing efforts, and preventing workers from exercising their civil rights will suffice.

The spy's work centers in the union. In his quest for information he naturally seeks membership in the local union, if he is not already a member. Once a member, his activities take on a new direction and impetus. He is then in a position to become an active agent of destruction.

That the spy should be a regular attendant at union meetings and active in the union's work is not surprising. Indeed the union is of more importance to him than his work in the factory. Since success as a spy depends upon advancement in union confidences, the spy has every incentive to press forward as a unionist. In time, he comes to make the union his chief business. In this he has the assistance and training of the agency officials who guide his career and have themselves been similarly educated in union affairs. He becomes an expert in labor matters, a professional parliamentarian, a tactician, and often obtains a position of leadership in the local union.

The first job is to ascertain, not only the names of union members but particularly those who are most active or who play a leading part. The uses the employer makes of such information has been described above. A callous account of one such series of discriminatory discharges, told in the reports of the spy who brought them about, is found in the records of the Burns agency concerning its operations for the Tubize Chatillon Co., in Hopwell, Va., in 1934. In that case wholesale discharges, instigated by the spy, were part of a successful design to force the union into a premature strike in order to weaken its strength. The entire testimony of this willful union destruction by a Burns operative should be contrasted with the declarations of Raymond J. Burns that the agency would reject business that sought to disrupt a union.

Ascertaining the names of union members is sometimes difficult. But in this, his initial task, the spy must not fail. If need be, therefore, he will bribe janitors or custodians, rifle files or desks, burglarize offices to secure access to union records. Such was the practice of Robert Coates, operative C-24, Burns spy for the Master Bakers Association, Pittsburgh in 1933.

A position as a custodian or sergeant at arms in the union offers opportunity to purloin the necessary records, carry them to the agency office for copying, and return them undisturbed to the files, as was done in Atlanta and Cincinnati by Pinkerton agents. Election to the office of financial or recording secretary is naturally of even greater importance. In that capacity the spy learns of every applicant for membership. At least 38 Pinkerton spies held such union offices.

The betrayal of union membership to the employer is implemented by the spy's day to day observation of union members in the plant for the infraction of plant rules. The employer today seldom dares to discharge outright for union activity. He must wait until the active unionist has given some plausible excuse for dismissal. Here the spy is of invaluable assistance. If the intended victim's work is beyond criticism the spy watches for such offenses as stepping over the conveyor belt, or smoking in the toilet—offenses which are customarily condoned, except where they offer the excuse for discrimination against union men.

Within the ranks of the union, however, in addition to reporting men for discriminatory discharge, the spy can be even more effective in disrupting the organization. One of the favorite devices is to seek to discredit the union leaders or frame them on false charges. The experienced spy knows that weakening the members' confidence in their leaders often leads to loss of confidence in the union and impairing the morale of the rank and file.

In another instance, the infamous Brady faked a photograph of his union president leaning on the bar of a saloon and then preferred charges of drunkenness. The spy may attack fellow members for being aliens or for their alleged radical political beliefs, the latter a standard technique constantly employed by the detective agencies.

In the councils of the union the spy often assumes the role of the agent provocateur. He incites to violence, preaches strikes, inflames the hotheaded and leads the union to disaster. Spies attempt to call abortive and premature strikes which will result in crushing the union before it has become stronger. They seek to discredit the union by attempting to associate it with violence and sabotage.

More subtle than the role of the open provocateur but no less damaging is that of the contentious dissenter who, under the cloak of plausibility, creates a breach in the ranks of the membership. He attempts to discredit leaders, particularly aggressive ones who are seeking to increase the strength of the union. An able spy may be able to create a following for ideas opposed to the best interests of the union. He readily shifts from one side to another in a local struggle, prolonging contention and dissuading from positive actions which will build the union.

Particularly a spy who has attained office is certain to have supporters. These he will use to create strife and conflict, often over minor matters. His chief interest is obtaining greater personal power and delaying aggressive organizing efforts which his employer fears. A spy of the Corporations Auxiliary Co., accomplished in his trade, rose rapidly to the presidency of the local of the United Automobile Workers in Toledo, Ohio, embracing the Electric Autolite plant, in which he worked, and a number of other plants. In this position he sought a separate charter for his plant and provisions in the constitution of the national union that would have severed his local from connection with the rest of the union and surrendered it to his control.

Another spy, employed by the National Metal Trades Association, entering a local of the International Association of Machinists in Erie, reported to his employers:

> This local is an easy one to handle as there are only about two men in it that are really interested in the Organization work and they are *easily discouraged.*

Subsequently he succeeded in preventing this local from undertaking an organizing campaign that would have increased its membership.

It is not always necessary for the spy to enter the arena of public debate and foment movements that will hinder the union. In an executive position he sabotages the union through the deliberately improper performance of the duties of his office. As chairman of the grievance committee he can delay and refuse to handle grievances, spreading discontent, distrust and dissatisfaction through the membership. His presence on a bargaining commmittee is equally dangerous. In a crucial situation he betrays the interests of those who have chosen him to represent them.

As one union witness stated—

> These people built themselves up as labor leaders, took an active part until some crucial time, and then they would take an opposite stand, thereby breaking the morale of the men and lots of times disrupting meetings and diverting the real purpose of the meeting off to some tangent whereby nothing could be done.

Perhaps the most anomalous position held by the spy is that of labor organizer. Some spies, reluctant to increase the strength of the organization it is their purpose to destroy, fail to recruit members. Others show activity but report the names of new members to the employer before they reach the union. Such an organizer, a spy for the Railway Audit & Inspection Co., appeared in the mill town of West Point, Ga., shortly before the textile strike in September 1934. The union did not gain a foothold in the town, both because of the spy's activities, and because those sympathetic to the union were beaten up by a gang of imported sluggers also furnished by the Railway Audit & Inspection Company.

Such conduct is nothing less than entrapment. The employer who deliberately unleashes a spy upon his workers in the guise of an organizer provoking expressions of sympathy for unionization which may serve as a basis of discharge or violence, is guilty of the utmost in double dealing. Human treachery can sink no lower. Yet a spy-organizer is a highly valuable asset to the business of industrial espionage. He is able to thwart the union drive at its very inception.

The spy, from his position in the union, is able to direct the full force not only of dismissal but even of intimidation and violence at his fellow workers. A Pinkerton spy, named Weinandy, assigned to a strike at the Closure plant of the Owens Illinois Glass Co. in Toledo in 1936 recommended in one of his reports that if certain named union leaders were "eliminated" the strike would collapse. Shortly thereafter an officer of the union was assaulted and severely beaten. Similarly, the spy within the union will point out and identify union officers or organizers to "shadow men" assigned by the agency to dog their footsteps. Such shadowing is often intended to intimidate. In such cases the detectives harass the subject openly and threateningly, following his every move.

The above instances have been selected from among a host of similar ones. It is abundantly clear that the spy's object is to disrupt the union and that his method is suited to the circumstances in which he finds himself. He may counsel either for and against strikes, advocate violence or urge workers to abandon a strike for fear of violence by the employer.

The cumulative effects of the myriad spy activities we have discussed create a nightmare of fears in the industrial community. Men who know they are being spied upon lose their morale. For this reason the management frequently lets it be known that spies are in the plant. For example, in the Pratt & Whitney Aircraft Mfg. Co. of Hartford, Conn., a spy of the National Metal Trades Association reported to the management the names of the members who attended union meetings. According to James Matles, grand lodge representative of the International Association of Machinists, as soon as employees would come to work following a union meeting

> a foreman by the name of Rice in that department would go over to our members and tell them everything that happened at the meeting, and they should keep their mouths shut and stay away from meetings or they would be fired. This resulted in intimidation, and that was the reason the employees stayed away from meetings.

Occasionally employees learn they are being spied upon from friendly foremen. Robert Thurlow, an employee of the Chevrolet Motor Division of General Motors describes how his foreman told him that he was being put under surveillance by two—"I do not know whether Pinkerton men or Brunswick men, or who it was"—and cautioned him against soliciting members for the union during the recess for meals. Thurlow added that the foreman told him he

> was cautioned to watch me by the management for any move I might make that would give them an opportunity to fire me. I think, as he expressed himself, he did not want anything to occur which would cause him to fire me because he and I had always gotten along well, he wanted our relationship to continue as it had been. He told me my job was good there as long as his job was good, if nothing happened that would force him to fire me.

Sometimes employees learn that they are being spied upon through incidents occurring in the plant. Richard Frankensteen, vice president of the United Automobile Workers of America, described one instance which was typical of many.

> A bonus * * * was paid by the Chrysler Corp. This fellow Mike Dragon, came into work one morning, went into the coat room and hung his coat up, and one of the fellows said, a non-union man, by the way—he said 'I suppose Dragon, you are going to tell us that the union was responsible for getting the bonus.' Dragon said, 'Of course it was responsible for getting the bonus. You know damned well it was.' For that he was called in the office and discharged and told the reason why they discharged him, which was a slip on somebody's part.

The effects of spy activity show themselves in a plant by the fear, suspicion, and terror in the minds of the workers. No better proof of the truth of these statements can be found than in the reports of the spies themselves. For example, John Seglar Operative 3787 of the Railway Audit & Inspection Co., reported to its client, the Jewish Hospital in Brooklyn, N. Y., on August 11, 1936, as follows:

> It seems to me that of late, leaders are becoming more secretive. They do not go around talking about the union matters openly as they were doing when I first came. Now when there is something they want to discuss they go off into a corner. In the dining room, they all sit at the same table, usually—that is, Steve, John Spleen, Jim Graham, and his brother, Leo, Tommy, the houseman, and Jimmy from the engine room,—but all they talk about is Olympics, etc.

Spy Number 765 of the Railway Audit & Inspection Co., named "Andy" Anderson, employed by the Woodward Iron & Coal Co. at Bessemer, Ala., also protested in his report that the men were oversuspicious and he was unable to get them to talk. He wrote:

> I * * * went to the blacksmith shop. This is the hardest place I have ever struck to make friends. Those fellows in the blacksmith shop don't have anything to say they act like they are afraid of something.

The terror inspired by spies spreads from the plant to the union meetings. L. L. Letteer, Jr,. a Pinkerton spy, described the temper of the workers in the Chevrolet plant of the General Motors plant at Atlanta, Ga., in the following terms:

> Of course, those labor unions were so hot, crying about spies, that everything was at fever pitch and they looked at each other with blood in their eye.

So demoralizing is the effect of spies upon members in unions that it is sometimes impossible to persuade members to attend meetings at all. Such was the testimony of Chester L. Robertson, general business director of the Detroit chapter of the Society of Designing Engineers; with reference to operative H-72 of the Corporation Auxiliary Co., W. G. Eckert, who was recording secretary of his chapter, director on the Detroit Board of Directors of the Society, and alternate to the National Board of Directors:

Mr. ROBERTSON. The effects of his (the spy's) activities in the records rendered by both operatives have been to place the members of the organization who were employed by Chrysler in a position of fear, so that they are too terror-stricken to appear at our headquarters, for fear of detection, and a great many of them send in their dues by mail rather than—

Senator LA FOLLETTE. (interrupting) As a result of your experience, what would you say caused this fear on the part of members of your organization when they became suspicious that a spy was in their midst?

Mr. ROBERTSON. Because they felt to have their membership in our organization known to the company would place their jobs in jeopardy.

The union members, indeed, often become persuaded that, far from being an organization for mutual protection, as a result of the activity of the spy their union has become a trap, causing them to lose their livelihood. Such a situation was reported with satisfaction by a spy, Number D-11, of the Washington D. C. branch office of the Burns agency. As a result of dismissals following his reports, D-11, who was located at the Tubize Chatillon Co. plant in Hopewell, Va., in April 27, 1934, noted:

> I saw Mr. Finlayson after leaving the plant. He says that Mr. Johnson of the nitrating department was laid off today and also a bunch of the spinning and twisting departments. He says that it seems like the Company will get rid of all Union members and if the Union doesn't do something pretty soon they will break the union.

> The meeting on Wednesday night did not draw so many members as I was expecting to see as they had at least three-fourths of the employees that were not working and could have attended if they cared but only a small number was there compared to the number they claim to have signed up as members. Either they have a lot of members afraid to come out and attend the meeting or the leaders are misleading what to intend to believe that they have more members than they have.

The demoralization of the union was soon complete. D-11 wrote on June 8, 1934:

> They are not in favor of any strike here and the most of them wish they had never joined any Union. Some of them don't know just what

to do or they would get out of the union if they knew just how to go about it.

Pending actual exposure, mere suspicion does not harm the spy. Indeed, part of the technique of the spy rests upon his ability to brazen out suspicion, and to break up meetings by his attendance in spite of the fact that he is distrusted. James Matles, grand lodge representative of the International Association of Machinists, described further the effect on a union at the Pratt & Whitney Aircraft Co., of Hartford, Conn., of a spy named John Cole, of the National Metal Trades Association, who persisted in attending meetings. Eventually the union was forced to hold a special meeting for Cole's benefit, and then hold a regular meeting to transact union business. Mr. Matles testified:

> We became very suspicious because of the fact that he pushed himself too much to the front trying to get himself elected as an officer of the organization. The employees began suspecting him and began staying away from the meetings. It was common talk that there was something wrong with John Cole, and that resulted in a drop of attendance in meetings from 300 to 400 down to a dozen, which meetings I have attended personally, and when it dwindled down to a dozen, John Cole was still one of the loyal members attending all the meetings.

> It reached the point that when I came to attend the meeting of the lodge I saw no important business taken up at the meeting of the lodge, and then the meeting was officially closed. I saw groups of members remaining in the hall and they asked me to remain and stay for a while, and after John Cole would leave they would convene another meeting. That was the official meeting, without John Cole, in order to take up the business of that meeting. Everything would go blank while John Cole was around there. That was in the later months of his membership in the organization.

Mr. Matles continued with reference to the difficulty of eliminating the spy:

> It happens that the men are influential people that the Metal Trades Association sends into our association. They have good personalities, they happen to get in good with the boys, they secure the confidence of a portion of the membership, and you are running the risk, when you haven't got conclusive evidence that they are spies and rats, that if you throw them out a portion of your membership will support them and create dissension in the organization, and it is for this reason that we have to be extremely cautious before we are in the position to eliminate or expel anyone on the suspicion of being a stoolpigeon.

James H. Mangold, employed at the Chevrolet division of the General Motors Corporation in Flint, Mich., who had experienced the effects of this espionage during this time, testified that, under surveillance by industrial spies, employees, even during their leisure periods—

> are very quiet, they are skeptic about anything you have to say, they do not take any part in activities at all. If you ask them to read anything that pertains to organization, or to give them any pamphlets, stuff like that, they just glance over it and throw it aside because they figure someone is looking at them.

Senator THOMAS. Are they afraid to talk to their neighbors?

Mr. MANGOLD. Yes. You don't know whom you are talking to.

Senator THOMAS. You never take a chance?

Mr. MANGOLD. You never take a chance.

Senator THOMAS. You get suspicious of everybody?

Mr. MANGOLD. You get suspicious of everybody.

As a result in 1936 the membership of this Flint local had fallen to 120. In August of that year the United Automobile Workers of America undertook to resuscitate the organization. A Pinkerton operative attached himself like a leech to the new organizers, Robert C. Travis and Wyndham Mortimer and attempted to worm out of them every new organizing move.

Travis and Mortimer found the community in a state of terror. A union meeting with Polish workers had to be advertised as a lecture on Poland in order to induce any employees to attend. The organizers had to operate underground like a band of conspirators. They could not risk entrusting their organizing plans to the spy-ridden executive board of the local. They were forced to call street meetings as Robert Travis testified:

> When I first went into Flint I could not get more than 25 or 30 people together, and I was very much interested in the reason. So I made personal calls all through the city to find out why they would not come. They were afraid. They knew there was spies in the local union because they had seen the movement go from 26,000 to 122. They knew they were being watched. Therefore it was necessary for me to organize little home meetings in members' basements after work, sometimes with the lights out; they were so skeptical; we would sit in the dark and talk to these people. One week end we had 19 home meetings, all day Saturday and Sunday. After we were strong enough we tied the meetings together and came out in the open, but in the first meetings it was necessary to work along those lines because of the spy system built up so effectively it had broken the labor movement in Flint.

To such lengths were free American workmen forced in the exercise of their guaranteed rights under the National Labor Relations Act.

The Education of David Stockman

William Greider

I. HOW THE WORLD WORKS

Generally, he had no time for idle sentimentality, but David A. Stockman indulged himself for a moment as he and I approached the farmhouse in western Michigan where Stockman was reared. With feeling, he described a youthful world of hard work, variety, and manageable challenges. "It's something that's disappearing now, the working family farm," Stockman observed. "We had a little of everything—an acre of strawberries, an acre of peaches, a field of corn, fifteen cows. We did everything."

This winter weekend was a final brief holiday with his parents; in a few weeks he would become director of the Office Management and Budget in the new administration in Washington. Technically, Stockman was still the U.S. congressman from Michigan's Fourth District, but his mind and exceptional energy were already concentrated on runing OMB, a small but awesomely complicated power center in the federal government, through which a President attempts to monitor all of the other federal bureaucracies.

Stockman carried with him a black binder enclosing a "Current Services Budget," which listed every federal program and its current cost projections. He hoped to memorize the names of 500 to 1,000 program titles and major accounts by the time he was sworn in—an objective that seemed reasonable to him, since he already knew many of the budget details. During four years in Congress, Stockman had made himself a leading conservative gadfly, attacking Democratic budgets and proposing leaner alternatives. Now the President-elect was inviting him to do the same thing from within. Stockman had lobbied for the OMB job and was probably better prepared for it, despite his youthfulness, than most of his predecessors.

He was thirty-four years old and looked younger. His shaggy hair was streaked with gray, and yet he seemed like a gawky collegian, with unstylish glasses and a prominent Adam's apple. In the corridors of the Capitol, where all ambitious staff aides scurried about in serious blue suits, Representative Stockman wore the same uniform, and was frequently mistaken for one of them.

Atlantic Monthly (December 1981). Reprinted by permission of the author.

II. A RADICAL IN POWER

Three weeks before the inauguration, Stockman and his transition team of a dozen or so people were already established at the OMB office in the Old Executive Office Building. When his appointment as budget director first seemed likely, he had agreed to meet with me from time to time and relate, off the record, his private account of the great political struggle ahead. The particulars of these conversations were not to be reported until later, after the season's battles were over, but a cynic familiar with how Washington works would understand that the arrangement had obvious symbiotic value. As an assistant managing editor at *The Washington Post*, I benefited from an informed view of policy discussions of the new administration; Stockman, a student of history, was contributing to history's record and perhaps influencing its conclusions. For him, our meetings were another channel—among many he used—to the press. The older generation of orthodox Republicans distrusted the press; Stockman was one of the younger "new" conservatives who cultivated contacts with columnists and reporters, who saw the news media as another useful tool in political combat. "We believe our ideas have intellecutal respectability, and we think the press will recognize that," he said. "The traditional Republicans probably sensed, even if they didn't know it, that their ideas lacked intellectual respectability."

In any case, for the eight months that followed, Stockman kept the agreement, and our regular conversations, over breakfast at the Hay-Adams, provided the basis of the account that follows.

In early January, Stockman and his staff were assembling dozens of position papers on program reductions and studying the internal forecasts for the federal budget and the national economy. The initial figures were frightening—"absolutely shocking," he confided—yet he seemed oddly exhilarated by the bad news, and was bubbling with new plans for coping with these horrendous numbers. An OMB computer, programmed as a model of the nation's economic behavior, was instructed to estimate the impact of Reagan's program on the federal budget. It predicted that if the new President went ahead with his promised three-year tax reduction and his increase in defense spending, the Reagan Administration would be faced with a series of federal deficits without precedent in peacetime—ranging from $82 billion in 1982 to $116 billion in 1984. Even Stockman blinked. It those were the numbers included in President Reagan's first budget message, the following month, the financial markets that Stockman sought to reassure would instead be panicked. Interest rates, already high, would go higher; the expectation of long-term inflation would be confirmed.

Stockman saw opportunity in these shocking projections. "All the conventional estimates just wind up as mud," he said. "As absurdities. What they basically say, to boil it down, is that the world doesn't work."

Stockman set about doing two things. First, he changed the OMB computer. Assisted by like-minded supply-side economists, the new team discarded orthodox premises of how the economy would behave. Instead of a continuing double-digit inflation, the new computer model assumed a swift decline in prices and interest rates. Instead of the continuing pattern of slow economic growth, the new model was based on a dramatic surge in the nation's productivity. New investment, new jobs, and growing profits—and Stockman's historic bull market. "It's based on valid economic analysis," he said, "but it's the inverse of the last four years. When we go public, this is going to set off a wide-open debate on how the economy works, a great battle over the conventional theories of economic performance."

The original apostles of supply-side, particularly Representative Jack Kemp, of New York, and the economist Arthur B. Laffer, dismissed budget-cutting as inconsequential to the economic problems, but Stockman was trying to fuse new theory and old. "Laffer sold us a bill of goods," he said, then corrected his words: "Laffer wasn't wrong—he didn't go far enough."

The great debate never quite took hold in the dimensions that Stockman had anticipated, but the Reagan Administration's economic projections did become the source of continuing controversy. In defense of their counter-theories, Stockman and his associates would argue, correctly, that conventional forecasts, particularly by the Council of Economic Advisers in the preceding administration, had been consistently wrong in the past. His critics would contend that the supply-side premises were based upon wishful thinking, not sound economic analysis.

But, second, Stockman used the appalling deficit projections as a valuable talking point in the policy discussions that were under way with the President and his principal advisers. Nobody in that group was the least bit hesitant about cutting federal programs, but Reagan had campaigned on the vague and painless theme that eliminating "waste, fraud, and mismanagement" would be sufficient to balance the accounts. Now, as Stockman put it, "the idea is to try to get beyond the waste, fraud, and mismanagement modality and begin to confront the real dimensions of budget reduction." On the first Wednesday in January, Stockman had two hours on the President-elect's schedule to describe the "dire shape" of the federal budget; for starters, the new administration would have to go for a budget reduction in the neighborhood of $40 billion. "Do you have any idea what $40 billion means?" he said. "It means I've got to cut the highway program. It means I've got to cut milk-price supports. And Social Security student benefits. And education and student loans. And manpower training and housing. It means I've got to shut down the synfuels program and a lot of other programs. The idea is to show the magnitude of the budget deficit and some suggestion of the political problems."

How much pain was the new President willing to impose? How many sacred cows would he challenge at once? Stockman was still feeling out the commitment at the White House, aware that Reagan's philosophical commitment to shrinking the federal government would be weighed against political risks.

Stockman was impressed by the ease with which the President-elect accepted the broad objective: find $40 billion in cuts in a federal budget running well beyond $700 billion. But, despite the multitude of expenditures, the proliferation of programs and grants, Stockman knew the exercise was not as easy as it might sound.

Consider the budget in simple terms, as a federal dollar representing the entire $700 billion. The most important function of the federal government is mailing checks to citizens—Social Security checks to the elderly, pension checks to retired soldiers and civil servants, reimbursement checks for hospitals and doctors who provide medical care for the aged and the poor, welfare checks for the dependent, veterans checks to pensioners. Such disbursements consume forty-eight cents of the dollar.

Another twenty-five cents goes to the Pentagon, for national defense. Stockman knew that this share would be rising in the next four years, not shrinking, perhaps becoming as high as thirty cents. Another ten cents was consumed by interest payments on the national debt, which was fast approaching a trillion dollars.

That left seventeen cents for everything else that Washington does. The FBI and the national parks, the county agents and the Foreign Service and the Weather Bureau—all the traditional operations of government—consumed only nine cents of the dollar. The remaining eight cents provided all of the grants to state and local governments, for aiding handicapped children or building highways or installing tennis courts next to Al Stockman's farm. One might denounce particular programs as wasteful, as unnecessary and inneffective, even crazy, but David Stockman knew that he could not escape these basic dimensions of federal spending.

As he and his staff went looking for the $40 billion, they found that most of it would have to be taken from the seventeen cents that covered government operations and grants-in-aid. Defense was already off-limits. Next Ronald Reagan laid down another condition for the budget-cutting: the main benefit programs of Social Security, Medicare, veterans' checks, railroad retirement pensions, welfare for the disabled—the so-called "social safety net" that Reagan had promised not to touch—were to be exempt from the budget cuts. In effect, he was declaring that Stockman could not tamper with three fourths of the forty-eight cents devoted to transfer payments.

No President had balanced the budget in the past twelve years. Still, Stockman thought it could be done, by 1984, if the Reagan Administration adhered to the principle of equity, cutting weak claims, not merely weak clients, and if it shocked the system sufficiently to create a new political climate. He still believed that it was not a question of numbers. "It boils down to a political question, not of budget policy or economic policy, but whether we can change the habits of the political system."

The struggle began in private, with Ronald Reagan's Cabinet. By inaugural week, Stockman's staff had assembled fifty or sixty policy papers outlining major cuts and alterations, and, aiming at the target of $40 billion, Stockman was anxious to win fast approval for them, before the new Cabinet officers were fully familiar with their departments and prepared to defend their bureaucracies. During that first week, the new Cabinet members had to sit through David Stockman's recital—one proposal after another outlining drastic reductions in their programs. Brief discussion was followed by presidential approval. "I have a little nervousness about the heavy-handedness with which I am being forced to act," Stockman conceded. "It's not that I wouldn't want to give the decision papers to the Cabinet members ahead of time so they could look at them, it's just that we're getting them done at eight o'clock in the morning and rushing them to the Cabinet room. . . It doesn't work when you have to brace these Cabinet officers in front of the President with severe reductions in their agencies, because then they're in the position of having to argue against the group line. And the group line is cut, cut, cut. So that's a very awkward position for them, and you make them resentful very fast."

Stockman proposed to White House counselor Edwin Meese an alternative approach—a budget working group, in which each Cabinet secretary could review the proposed cuts and argue against them. As the group evolved, however, with Meese, chief of the staff James Baker, Treasury Secretary Donald Regan, and policy director Martin Anderson, among others, it was stacked in Stockman's favor. "Each meeting will involve only the relevant Cabinet member and his aides with four or five strong keepers of the central agenda," Stockman explained at one point. "So on Monday, when we go into the decision on synfuels programs, it will be [Energy Secretary James B.] Edwards defending them against six guys saying that, by God, we've got to cut these back or we're not going to have a savings program that will add up."

In general, the system worked. Stockman's agency did in a few weeks what normally consumes months; the process was made easier because the normal opposition forces had no time to marshal either their arguments or their constituents and because the President was fully in tune with Stockman. After the budget working group reached a decision, it would be taken to Reagan in the form of a memorandum, on which he could register his approval by checking a little box. "Once he checks it," Stockman said, "I put that in my safe and I go ahead and I don't let it come back up again."

The check marks were given to changes in twelve major budget entitlements and scores of smaller ones. Eliminate Social Security minimum benefits. Cap the runaway costs of Medicaid. Tighten eligibility for food stamps. Merge the trade adjustment assistance for unemployed industrial workers with standard unemployment compensation and shrink it. Cut education aid by a quarter. Cut grants for the arts and humanities in half. "Zero out" CETA and the Community Services Administration and National Consumer Cooperative Bank. And so forth. "Zero out" became a favorite phase of Stockman's; it meant closing down a program "cold turkey," in one budget year. Stockman believed that any compromise on a program that ought to be eliminated—funding that would phase it out over several years—was merely a political ruse to keep it alive, so it might still be in existence a few years hence, when a new political climate could allow its restoration to full funding.

"I just wish that there were more hours in the day or that we didn't have to do this so fast. I have these stacks of briefing books and I've got to make decisions about specific options. . . I don't have time, trying to put this whole package together in three weeks, so you just start making snap judgments."

III. THE MAGIC ASTERISK

On Capitol Hill, ideological consistency is not a highly ranked virtue but its absence is useful grounds for scolding the opposition. David Stockman endured considerable needling when his budget appeared, revealing that many programs that he had opposed as a congressman had survived. The most glaring was the fast-breeder nuclear reactor at Clinch River, Tennessee. Why hadn't Stockman cut the nuclear subsidy that he had so long criticized? The answer was Senator Howard Baker, of Tennessee, majority leader. "I didn't have to get rolled," Stockman said, "I just got out of the way. It just wasn't worth fighting. This package will go nowhere without Baker, and Clinch River is just life or death to Baker. A very poor reason, I know."

Consistency, he knew, was an important asset in the new environment. The package of budget cuts would be swiftly picked apart if members of Congress perceived that they could save their pet programs, one by one, from the general reductions. "All those guys are looking for ways out," he said. "If they can detect an alleged pattern of preferential treatment for somebody else or discriminatory treatment between rural and urban interests or between farm interests and industrial interests, they can concoct a case for theirs."

Even by Washington standards, where overachieving young people with excessive adrenalin are commonplace, Stockman was busy. Back and forth, back and forth he went, from his vast office at the Old Executive Office Building, with its classic high ceilings and its fireplace, to the cloakrooms and hideaway offices and hearing chambers of the

Capitol, to the West Wing of the White House. Usually, he carried an impossible stack of books and papers under his arm, like a harried high school student who has not been given a locker. He promised friends he would relax—take a day off, or at least sleep later than 5 A.M., when he usually arose to read policy papers before breakfast. But he did not relax easily. What was social life compared with the thrill of reshaping the federal establishment?

In the early skirmishing on Capitol Hill, Stockman actually proposed a tight control system: Senator Baker and the House Republican leader, Robert Michel, of Illinois, would be empowered to clear all budget trades on particular programs—and no one else, not even the highest White House advisers, could negotiate any deals. "If you have multiple channels for deals to be cut and retreats to be made," Stockman explained, "then it will be possible for everybody to start side-dooring me, going in to see Meese, who doesn't understand the policy background, and making the case, or [James] Baker making a deal with a subcommittee chairman." Neither the White House nor the congressional leadership liked his idea, and it was soon buried.

By March, however, Stockman could see the status quo yielding to the shock of the Reagan agenda. In dozens of meetings and hearings, public and private, Stockman perceived that it was now inappropriate for a senator or a congressman to plead for his special interests, at least in front of other members with other interests. At one caucus, a Tennessee Republican began to lecture him on the reduced financing for TVA; other Republicans scolded him. Stockman cut public-works funding for the Red River project in Louisiana, which he knew would arouse Russell Long, former chairman of the Senate Finance Committee. Long appealed personally at the White House, and Reagan stood firm.

One by one, small signals such as these began to change Stockman's estimate of the political struggle. He began to believe that the Reagan budget package, despite its scale, perhaps because of its scale, could survive in Congress. With skillful tactics by political managers, with appropriate public drama provided by the President, the relentless growth rate of the federal budget, a permanent reality of Washington for twenty years, could actually be contained.

Stockman's analysis was borne out a few weeks later, in early April, when the Senate adopted its first budget-cutting measures, 88-10, a package close enough to the administration's proposals to convince Stockman of the vulnerability of "constituency-based" politics. "That could well be a turning point in this whole process," Stockman said afterward.

Still, Stockman was even more impressed by the performance of the new Republican majority in the Senate. After a week of voting down amendments to restore funds for various programs—"voting against every motherhood title," as Stockman put it—moderate Republicans from the Northeast and Midwest needed some sort of political solace. Led by Senator John Chaffee, of Rhode Island, the moderates proposed an amendment spreading about $1 billion over an array of social programs, from education to home-heating assistance for the poor. Stockman had no objection. The amendment wouldn't cost much overall, and it would "take care of those people who have been good soldiers." Senator Pete Domenici, of New Mexico, the Senate budget chairman, decided, however, that the accommodation wasn't necessary, and he was right. The Chaffee amendment lost.

"It was the kind of amendment that should have passed," Stockman reflected afterward. "The fact that it didn't win tells me that the political logic has changed."

The vulnerability of Stockman's ideology was always that the politics of winning would overwhelm the philosophical premises. But after the Senate victory, Stockman devoted his energy to the tactical questions—winning again in the House of Representatives, which was controlled by the Democrats. "This is pure politics," he said. "It's a question of whether the President can prevail on the floor of the House, because if he can't, then the committee chairmen know they have license to do anything they want."

Stockman watched with admiration as his principal intellectual rival, Jim Jones, the Democratic chairman of the House Budget Committee, attempted to fashion a budget resolution that would hold the Democratic majority together. The budget director calculated that Jones had an impossible task, but he could see that the Oklahoma congressman was going to come closer than he had expected. The Democrats, by Stockman's analysis, were really three groups: the old-line liberal faithful, who would follow the party leadership and defend against any or all budget cuts; a middle group, including Jones and other younger members, who recognized that federal deficits were out of control and were willing to confront the problem (Stockman referred to them as "the progressives"); and, finally, the "boll weevils," the thirty-eight southerners who were pulled toward Reagan both in conservative philosophy and by the politics of their home districts, which had voted overwhelmingly for the President. Jones was drawing up a resolution that would restore some funds to social programs, to keep the liberals happy; that projected a smaller deficit than Stockman's, to appear more responsible in fiscal terms; and that did not touch the defense budget, which would offend the southerners.

Artful as it was, the Jones resolution was, according to Stockman, a series of gimmicks: economic estimates and accounting tricks. "Political numbers," he called them. But Stockman was not critical of Jones for these budget ploys, because he cheerfully conceded that the administration's own budget numbers were constructed on similar shaky premises, mixing cuts from the original 1981 budget left by Jimmy Carter with new baseline projections from the Congressional Budget Office in a way that, fundamentally, did not add up. The budget politics of 1981, which produced such clear and dramatic rhetoric from both sides, was, in fact, based upon a bewildering set of numbers that confused even those, like Stockman, who produced them.

"None of us really understands what's going on with all these numbers," Stockman confessed at one point. "You've got so many different budgets out and so many different baselines and such complexity now in the interactive parts of the budget between policy action and the economic environment and all the internal mysteries of the budget, and there are a lot of them. People are getting from A to B and it's not clear how they are getting there. It's not clear how we got there, and it's not clear how Jones is going to get there."

These "internal mysteries" of the budget process were not dwelt upon by either side, for there was no point in confusing the clear lines of political debate with a much deeper and unanswerable question: Does anyone truly understand, much less control, the dynamics of the federal budget intertwined with the mysteries of the national economy? Stockman pondered this question occasionally, but since there was no obvious remedy, no intellectual construct available that would make sense of this anarchical universe, he was compelled to shrug at the mystery and move ahead. "I'm beginning to believe that history is a lot shakier than I ever thought it was," he said, in a reflective moment. "In other words, I think there are more random elements, less determinism and more discretion, in the course of history than I ever believed before. Because I can see it."

The "random elements" were working in Stockman's behalf in the House of Representatives. He had a good fix on what Jones would produce as the Democratic alternative, in part because he had a spy in the Democratic meetings—Phil Gramm, of Texas, a like-minded conservative and friend who agreed to co-sponsor the administration's substitute resolution. Did Jones know that one of his Democratic committee members was really on the other side? "No," said Stockman. "That's how I know what's in Jones's budget."

Stockman was also dealing with the recognized leaders of the "boll weevils." He thought that the southerners could be won to the President's side with a minimum of trading, but he was prepared to trade. He agreed with G. V. "Sonny" Montgomery, chairman of the House Veterans' Affairs Committee and a genuine leader among the southern Democrats, to acquiesce in the restoration of $350 to $400 million for staffing at veterans' hospitals. Once Montgomery announced he was with the President, it would be a respectable position, which other southerners could embrace, Stockman felt. Still, he was confident that he could defend the agenda against general trading for votes.

The underlying problem of the deficits first surfaced, to Stockman's embarrassment, in the Senate Budget Committee in mid-April, when committee Republicans choked on the three-year projections supplied by the nonpartisan Congressional Budget Office. Three Republican senators refused to vote for a long-term budget measure that predicted continuing deficits of $60 billion, instead of a balanced budget by 1984.

Stockman thought he had taken care of embarrassing questions about future deficits with a device he referred to as the "magic asterisk." (Senator Howard Baker had dubbed it that in strategy sessions, Stockman said.) The "magic asterisk" would blithely denote all of the future deficit problems that were to be taken care of with additional budget reductions, to be announced by the President at a later date. Thus, everyone could finesse the hard questions, for now.

But, somehow or other, the Senate Budget Committee staff insisted upon putting the honest numbers in its resolution—the projected deficits of $60 billion-plus running through 1984. That left the Republican senators staring directly at the same scary numbers that Stockman and the Wall Street analysts had already seen. The budget director blamed this brief flare-up on the frantic nature of his schedule. When he should have been holding hands with the Senate Budget Committee, he was at the other end of the Capitol, soothing Representative Delbert Latta, of Ohio, the ranking Republican in budget matters, who was pouting. Latta thought that since he was a Republican, his name should go ahead of that of Phil Gramm, a Democrat, on the budget resolution: that it should be Latta-Gramm instead of Gramm-Latta.

After a few days or reassurances, Stockman persuaded the Republican senators to relax about the future and two weeks later they passed the resolution—without being given any concrete answers as to where he would find future cuts of such magnitude. In effect, the "magic asterisk" sufficed.

But the real problem, as Stockman conceded, was still unsolved. Indeed, pondering the reactions of financial markets, the budget director made an extraordinary confession in private: the original agenda of budget reductions, which had seemed so radical in February; was exposed by May as inadequate. The "magic asterisk" might suffice for the political debate in Congress, but it would not answer the fundamental question asked by Wall Street: How, in fact, did Ronald Reagan expect to balance the federal budget? "It's a tentative judgment on the part of the markets and of spokesmen like Kaufman that is reversible because they haven't seen all our cards. From the cards they've seen, I suppose that you can see how they draw that conclusion."

"It means," Stockman said, "that you have to have some recalibration in the policy. The thing was put together so fast that it probably should have been put together differently." With mild regret, Stockman looked back at what had gone wrong:

"The defense numbers got out of control and we were doing that whole budget-cutting exercise so frenetically. In other words, you were juggling details, pushing people, and going from one session to another, trying to cut housing programs here and rural electric there, and we were doing it so fast, we didn't know where we were ending up for sure . . . In other words, we should have designed those pieces to be more compatible. But the pieces were moving on independent tracks—the tax program, where we were going on spending, and the defense program, which was just a bunch of numbers written on a piece of paper. And it didn't quite mesh. That's what happened. But, you see, for about a month and a half we got away with that because of the novelty of all these budget reductions."

Reagan's policy-makers knew that their plan was wrong, or at least inadequate to its promised effects, but the President went ahead and conveyed the opposite impression to the American public. With the cool sincerity of an experienced television actor, Reagan appeared on network TV to rally the nation in support of the Gramm-Latta resolution, promising a new era of fiscal control and balanced budgets, when Stockman knew they still had not found the solution. This practice of offering the public eloquent reassurances despite privately held doubts was not new, of course. Every contemporary President—starting with Lyndon Johnson, in his attempt to cover up the true cost of the war in Vietnam—had been caught, sooner or later, in contradictions between promises and economic realities. The legacy was a deep popular skepticism about anything a President promised about the economy. Barely four months in office, Ronald Reagan was already adding to the legacy.

Indeed, Stockman began in May to plot what he called the "recalibration" of Reagan policy, which he hoped could be executed discreetly over the coming months to eliminate the out-year deficits for 1983 and 1984 that alarmed Wall Street—without alarming political Washington and losing control in the congressional arena. "It's very tough, because you don't want to end up like Carter, where you put a plan out there and then, a month into it, you visibly and unmistakably change postures. So what you have to do is solve this problem incrementally, without the appearance of reversal, and there are some ways to do that."

IV. OLD POLITICS

The President's televised address, in April, was masterly and effective: the nation responded with a deluge of mail and telephone calls, and the House of Representatives accepted Reagan's version of budget reconciliation over the Democratic alternative. The final roll call on the Gramm-Latta resolution was not even close, with sixty-three Democrats joining all House Republicans in support of the President. The stunning victory and the disorganized opposition from the Democrats confirmed for Stockman a political hunch he had first developed when he saw the outlines of Representative Jim Jones's resolution, mimicking the administration's budget-cutting. The 1980 election results may not have been "ideological," but the members of Congress seemed to be interpreting them that way.

This new context, Stockman felt, would be invaluable for the weeks ahead, as the budget-and-tax issues moved into the more complicated and vulnerable areas of action. The generalized budget-cutting instructions voted by the House were now sent to each of the authorizing committees, most of them chaired by old-line liberal Democrats who would try to save the programs in their jurisdictions, but their ability to counterattack was clearly limited by the knowledge that President Reagan, not Speaker Tip O'Neill, controlled the floor of the House. Stockman expected the Democratic chairmen to employ all of their best legislative tricks to feign cooperation while actually undermining the Reagan budget cuts, but he was already preparing another Republican resolution dubbed "Son of Gramm-Latta," to make sure the substantive differences were maintained—the block grants that melded social programs and turned them over to the states, the "caps" on Medicaid and other open-ended entitlement programs, the "zeroing out" of others.

In the first round, Stockman felt that he had retreated on very little. He made the trade with Representative Montgomery on VA hospitals, and his old friend Representative Gramm had restored some "phase-out" fund for EDA, the agency Stockman so much wished to abolish. "He put it in there over my objections," Stockman explained, "because he needed to keep three or four people happy. I said okay, but we're not bound by it." The Republican resolution also projected a lower deficit than Stockman thought was realistic, as a tactical necessity. "Gramm felt he couldn't win on the floor unless they had a lower deficit, closer to Jones's deficit, so they got it down to $31 billion by hook or by crook, mostly the latter."

Stockman was supremely confident at that point. The Reagan Administration had taken the measure of its political opposition and had created a new climate in Washington, a new agenda. Now what remained was to follow through in a systematic way that would convince the financial markets. In the middle of May, he made another prediction: the bull market on Wall Street, the one he had expected in April, would arrive by late summer or early fall.

"I think we're on the verge of the response in the financial markets. It takes one more piece of the puzzle, resolution of the tax bill. And that may happen relatively quickly, and when it does, I think you'll start a long bull market, by the end of the summer and early fall. The reinforcement that the President got politically in the legislative process will be doubled, barring some new war in the Middle East, by a perceived economic situation in which things are visibly improving. I'm much more confident now."

Stockman was wrong, of course, about the bull market. But his misinterpretation of events was more profound than that. Without recognizing it at the time, the budget director was headed into a summer in which not only financial markets but life itself seemed to be absolutely perverse. The Reagan program kept winning in public, a series of well-celebrated political victories in Congress—yet privately Stockman was losing his struggle.

Stockman was changing, in a manner that perhaps he himself did not recognize. His conversations began to reflect a new sense of fatalism, a brittle edge of uncertainty.

"There was a certain dimension of our theory that was unrealistic. . ."

"The system has an enormous amount of inertia. . ."

"I don't believe too much in the momentum theory any more. . ."

"I have a new theory—there are no *real* conservatives in Congress. . ."

The turning point, which Stockman did not grasp at the time, came in May, shortly after the first House victory. Buoyed by the momentum, the White House put forward, with inadequate political soundings, the Stockman plan for Social Security reform. Among other things, it proposed a drastic reduction in the benefits for early retirement at age sixty-two. Stockman thought this was a privilege that older citizens could comfortably yield, but 64 percent of those eligible for Social Security were now taking early retirement, and the "reform" plan set off a sudden tempest on Capitol Hill. Democrats accused Reagan of reneging on his promise to exempt Social Security from the budget cuts and accused Stockman of trying to balance his budget at the expense of Social Security recipients, which, of course, he was. "The Social Security problem is not simply one of satisfying actuaries," Stockman conceded. "It's one of satisfying the here-and-now of budget requirements." In the initial flurry of reaction, the Senate passed a unanimous resolution opposing the OMB version of how to reform Social Security, and across the nation, the elderly were alarmed enough to begin writing and calling their representatives in Congress. But Stockman seemed not to grasp the depth of his political problem; he still believed that congressional reaction would quiet down eventually and Democrats would cooperate with him.

"Three things," he explained. "First, the politicians in the White House are over-reacting. They're overly alarmed. Second, there is a serious political problem with it, but not of insurmountable dimensions. And third, basically I screwed up quite a bit on the way the damn thing was handled."

Stockman said that Republicans on Ways and Means were urging him to propose an administration reform plan as an alternative to the Democrats'; Stockman misjudged the political climate. The White House plan, put together in haste, had "a lot of technical bloopers," which made it even more vulnerable to attack, Stockman said. "I was just racing against the clock. All the office things I knew ought to be done by way of groundwork, advance preparation, and so forth just fell by the wayside. . . Now we're taking the flak from all the rest of the Republicans because we didn't inform them."

Despite the political uproar, Stockman thought a compromise would eventually emerge, because of the pressure to "save" Social Security. This would give him at least a portion of the budget savings he needed. "I still think we'll recover a good deal of ground from this. It will permit the politicians to make it look like they're doing something *for* the beneficiary population when they are doing something *to* it which they normally wouldn't have the courage to undertake."

But there was less "courage" among politicians than Stockman assumed. Indeed, one politician who scurried away from the President's proposed cuts in Social Security was the President. Stockman wanted him to go on television again, address the nation on Social Security's impending bankruptcy, and build a popular constituency for the changes. But White House advisers did not.

"The President was very interested [in the reform package] and he believed it was the right thing to do. The problem is that the politicians are so wary of the Social Security issue per se that they want to keep him away from it, thinking they could somehow have an administration initiative that came out of the boondocks somewhere and the President wouldn't be tagged with it. Well, that was just pure naive nonsense. . . My view was, if you had to play this thing over, you should have the President go on TV and give a twenty-minute Fireside Chat, with some nice charts. . . You could have created a climate in which major things could be changed."

The White House rejected that idea. Ronald Reagan kept his distance from the controversy, but it would not go away. In September, Reagan did finally address the issue in a televised chat with the nation: he disowned Stockman's reform plan. Reagan said that there was a lot of "misinformation" about in the land, to the effect that the President wanted to cut Social Security. Not true, he declared, though Reagan had proposed such a cut in May. Indeed, the President not only buried the Social Security cuts he had proposed earlier but retreated on one reform measure—elimination of the minimum benefits—that Congress had already, reluctantly, approved. As though he had missed the long debate on that issue, Reagan announced that it was never his intention to deprive anyone who was in genuine need. Any legislative action toward altering Social Security would be postponed until 1983, after the 1982 congressional elections, and too late to help Stockman with his stubborn deficits. In the meantime, Reagan accepted a temporary solution advocated by the Democrats and denounced by Stockman as "irresponsible"—borrowing from another federal trust fund that was in surplus, the health-care fund, to cover Social Security's problems. Everyone put the best face on it, including Stockman. The tactical retreat, they explained, was the only thing Reagan could do under the circumstances—a smart move, given the explosive nature of the Social Security protest. Still, it was a retreat, and, for David Stockman, a fundamental defeat. He lost one major source of potential budget savings. The political outcome did not suggest that he would do much better when he proposed reforms for Medicare, Social Security's twin.

The final reconciliation measure authorized budget reductions of $35.1 billion, about $6 billion less than the President's original proposal, though Stockman and others said the difference would be made up through shrinking "off-budget" programs, which are not included in the appropriations process. The block grants and reductions and caps that Reagan proposed were partially successful—some sixty major programs were consolidated in different block-grant categories—though Stockman lost several important reforms in the final scrambling, among them the cap on the runaway costs of Medicaid, and user fees for federal waterways. The Reagan Administration eliminated dozens of smaller activities and drastically scaled down dozens of others.

In political terms, it was a great victory. Ronald Reagan became the first President since Lyndon Johnson to demonstrate both the tactical skill and the popular strength to stare down the natural institutional opposition of Congress. Moreover, he forced Congress to slog through a series of unique and painful legislative steps—a genuine reconciliation measure—that undermined the parochial baronies of the committee chairmen. Around Washington, even among the critics who despised what he was attempting, there was general agreement that the Reagan Administration would not have succeeded, perhaps would not even have gotten started, without the extraordinary young man who had a plan. He knew what he wanted to attack and he knew Congress well enough to know how to attack.

Yet, in the glow of victory, why was David Stockman so downcast? Another young man, ambitious for his future, might have seized the moment to claim his full share of praise. Stockman did appear on the Sunday talk shows, and was interviewed by the usual columnists. But in private, he was surprisingly modest about his achievement. Two weeks after selling Congress on the biggest package of budget reductions in the history of the republic, Stockman was willing to dismiss the accomplishments as less significant than the participants realized. Why? Because he knew that much more traumatic budget decisions still confronted them. Because he knew that the budget-resolution numbers were an exaggeration. The total of $35 billion was less than it seemed, because the "cuts" were from an imaginary number—hypothetical projections from the Congressional Budget Office on where spending would go if nothing changed in policy or economic activity. Stockman knew that the CBO base was a bit unreal. Therefore, the total of "cuts" was, too.

Stockman explained: "There was less there than met the eye. Nobody has figured it out yet. Let's say that you and I walked outside and I waved a wand and said, I've just lowered the temperature from 110 to 78. Would you believe me? What this was was a cut from an artificial CBO base. That's why it looked so big. But it wasn't. It was a significant and helpful cut from what you might call the moving track of the budget of the government, but the numbers are just out of this world. The government never would have been up at those levels in the CBO base."

Stockman was proud of what had been changed—shutting down the $4 billion CETA jobs program and others, putting real caps on runaway programs such as the trade adjustment assistance for unemployed industrial workers. "Those were powerful spending programs that have been curtailed," he said, "but there was a kind of consensus emerging for that anyway, even before this administration."

All in all, Stockman gave a modest summary of what had been wrought by the budget victory: "It has really slowed down the momentum, but it hasn't stopped what you would call the excessive growth of the budget. Because the budget isn't something you reconstruct each year. The budget is a sort of rolling history of decisions. All kinds of decisions, made five, ten, fifteen years ago, are coming back to bite us unexpectedly. Therefore, in my judgment, it will take three or four or five years to subdue it. Whether anyone can maintain the political momentum to fight the beast for that long, I don't know."

Stockman, the natural optimist, was not especially optimistic. The future of fiscal conservatism, in a political community where there are "no real conservatives," no longer seemed so promising to him. He spoke in an analytical tone, a sober intellect trying to figure things out, and only marginally bitter, as he assessed what had happened to his hopes since January. In July, he was forced to conclude that, despite the appearance of a great triumph, his original agenda was fading, not flourishing.

"I don't believe too much in the momentum theory any more," he said. "I believe in institutional inertia. Two months of response can't beat fifteen years of political infrastructure. I'm talking about K Street and all of the interest groups in this town, the community of interest groups. We sort of stunned it, but it just went underground for the winter. It will be back . . . Can we win? A lot of it depends on events and luck. If we got some bad luck, a flareup in the Middle East, a scandal, it could all fall apart."

Stockman's dour outlook was reinforced two weeks later, when the Reagan coalition prevailed again in the House and Congress passed the tax-cut legislation with a final frenzy of trading and bargaining. Again, Stockman was not exhilarated by the victory. On the contrary, it seemed to leave a bad taste in his mouth, as though the democratic process had finally succeeded in shocking him by its intensity and its greed. Once again, Stockman participated in the trading—special tax concessions for oil-lease holders and real-estate tax shelters, and generous loopholes that virtually eliminated the corporate income tax. Stockman sat in the room and saw it happen.

"Do you realize the greed that came to the forefront?" Stockman asked with wonder. "The hogs were really feeding. The greed level, the level of opportunism, just got out of control."

Indeed, when the Republicans and Democrats began their competition for authorship of tax concessions, Stockman saw the "new political climate" dissolve rather rapidly and be replaced by the reflexes of old politics. Every tax lobby in town, from tax credits for wood-burning stoves to new accounting concessions for small business, moved in on the legislation, and pet amendments for obsure tax advantage and profit became the pivotal issues of legislative action, not the grand theories of supply-side tax reduction. "The politics of the bill turned out to be very traditional. The politics put us back in the game, after we started making concessions. The basic strategy was to match or exceed the Democrats, and we did."

But Stockman was buoyant about the political implications of the tax legislation: first, because it put a tightening noose around the size of the government; second, because it gave millions of middle-class voters tangible relief from inflation, even if the stimulative effects on the economy were mild or delayed. Stockman imagined the tax cutting as perhaps the beginning of a large-scale realignment of political loyalties, away from old-line liberalism and toward Reaganism.

And where did principle hide? Stockman, with his characteristic mixture of tactical cynicism and intellectual honesty, was unwilling to defend the moral premises of what had occurred. The "idea-based" policies that he had espoused at the outset were, in the final event, greatly compromised by the "constituency-based" politics that he abhorred. What had changed, fundamentally, was the list of winning clients, not the nature of the game. Stockman had said the new conservatism would pursue equity, even as it attempted to shrink the government. It would honor just claims and reject spurious ones, instead of simply serving powerful clients over weak clients. He was compelled to agree, at the legislative climax, that the original moral premises had not been served, that the new principles of Reaganism were compromised by the necessity of winning.

"I now understand," he said, "that you probably can't put together a majority coalition unless you are willing to deal with those marginal interests that will give you the votes needed to win. That's where it is fought—on the margins—and unless you deal with those marginal votes, you can't win."

In order to enact Reagan's version of tax reduction, "certain wages" had to be paid, and, as Stockman reasoned, the process of brokering was utterly free of principle or policy objectives. The power flowed to the handful of representatives who could reverse the majority, regardless of the interests they represented. Once the Reagan tacticians began making concessions beyond their "policy-based" agenda, it developed that their trades and compromises and giveaways were utterly indistinguishable from the decades of interest-group accommodations that had preceded them, which they so righteously denounced. What was new about the Reagan revolution, in which oil-royalty owners win and welfare mothers lose? Was the new philosophy so different from old Republicanism when the federal subsidies for Boeing and Westinghouse and General Electric were protected, while federal subsidies for unemployed black teenagers were "zeroed out"? One could go on, at great length, searching for balance and equity in the outcome of the Reagan program without satisfying the question; the argument will continue as a central theme of electoral politics for the next few years. For now, Stockman would concede this much: that "weak clients" suffered for their weakness.

"Power is contingent," he said. "The power of these client groups turned out to be stronger than I realized. The client groups know how to make themselves heard. The problem is, unorganized groups can't play in this game."

When Congress recessed for its August vacation and President Reagan took off for his ranch in the West, David Stockman had a surprising answer to one of his original questions: could he prevail in the political arena, against the status quo? His original skepticism about Congress was mistaken; the administration had prevailed brilliantly as politicians. And yet, it also seemed that the status quo, in an intangible sense that most politicians would not even recognize, much less worry over, had prevailed over David Stockman.

V. "WHO KNOWS?"

Autumn was cruel to David Stockman's idea of how the world should work. The summer, when furious legislative trading was under way, had tattered his moral vision of government. Politics, in the dirty sense, had prevailed. Now he was confronted with more serious possibilities—the failure of the economic strategy and the political unraveling that he had feared from the beginning. On Capitol Hill, where Stockman was admired and envied for his nimble mind, where even critics conceded that his presence in the Cabinet was essential to Ronald Reagan's opening victories, politicians of both parties were beginning to reach a different conclusion about him. Despite the wizardry, Stockman did not have all the answers, after all. The wizard was prepared to agree.

His failed expectations were derived from many events. In August, when enactment of the Reagan program was supposed to create a boom, instead, the financial markets sagged. Interest rates went still higher, squeezing the various sectors of the American economy. Real-estate sales were dead, and the housing industry was at a historic low point. The same was true for auto sales. Farmers complained about the exorbitant interest demanded for annual crop loans. Hundreds of savings-and-loan associations were at the edge of insolvency. The treasury secretary, perhaps also losing his original faith in the supply-side formulation, suggested that it was time for the Federal Reserve Board to loosen up on its tight monetary policy. Donald Regan saw a recession approaching.

Stockman's prospects for balancing the budget were getting worse, not better. The optimistic economic forecast made in January to improve his original budget projections came back to haunt him in September. The inflation rate was down considerably (a prediction fortuitously correct because of oil and grain prices) but interest rates were not: the cost of federal borrowing and debt payments went still higher.

Stockman was boxed in, and he knew it. Unable to cut defense or Social Security or to modify the overly generous tax legislation, he was forced to turn back to the simple arithmetic of the federal budget—and cut even more from that smaller slice of the federal dollar that pays for government operations and grants and other entitlements. For six months, Stockman had been explaining to "the West Wing guys" that this math wouldn't add. When Reagan proposed his new round of $16 billion in savings, the political outrage confirmed the diagnosis. Stockman was accused of breaking the agreements he had made in June: Senate Republicans who had accepted the "magic asterisk" so docilely were now talking of rebellion—postponing the enormous tax reductions they had just enacted. While the White House promised a war of vetoes ahead, intended to demonstrate "fiscal control," Stockman knew that even if those short-range battles were won, the budget would not be balanced.

Disappointed by events and confronted with potential failure, the Reagan White House was developing a new political strategy: wage war with Congress over the budget issues and, in 1982, blame the Democrats for whatever goes wrong.

The budget director developed a new wryness as he plunged gamely on with these congressional struggles; it was a quality more appealing than certitude. Appearing before the House Budget Committee, Stockman listed a new budget item on his deficit sheet, drolly labeled "Inaction on Social Security." With remarkable directness and no "magic asterisks," he described the outlook: federal deficits of $60 billion in each of the next three years. Some analysts thought his predictions were modest. In the autumn of 1981, despite his great victories in Congress, Ronald Reagan had not as yet produced a plausible answer to John Anderson's question.

Still, things might work out, Stockman said. They might find an answer. The President's popularity might carry them through. The tax cuts would make people happy. The economy might start to respond, eventually, to the situation of the tax cuts. "Who knows?" Stockman said. From David Stockman, it was a startling remark. He would continue to invent new scenarios for success, but they would be more complicated and cloudy than his original optimism. "Who knows?" The world was less manageable than he had imagined; this machine had too many crazy moving parts to incorporate in a single lucid theory. The "random elements" of history—politics, the economy, the anarchical budget numbers—were out of control.

Where did things go wrong? Stockman kept asking and answering the right questions. The more he considered it, the more he moved away from the radical vision of reformer, away from the wishful thinking of supply-side economics, and toward the "old-time religion" of conservative economic thinking. Orthodoxy seemed less exciting than radicalism, but perhaps Stockman was only starting into another intellectual transition. He had changed from farm boy to campus activist at Michigan State, from Christian moralist to neo-conservative at Harvard; once again, Stockman was reformulating his ideas on how the world worked. What had he learned?

"The reason we did it wrong—not wrong, but less than the optimum—was that we said, Hey, we have to get a program out fast. And when you decide to put a program of this breadth and depth out fast, you can only do so much. We were working in a twenty or twenty-five-day time frame, and we didn't think it all the way through. We didn't add up all the numbers. We didn't make all the thorough, comprehensive calculations about where we really needed to come out and how much to put on the plate the first time, and so forth. In other words, we ended up with a list that I'd always been carrying of things to be done, rather than starting the other way and asking, What is the overall fiscal policy required to reach the target?"

That regret was beyond remedy now; all Stockman could do was keep trying on different fronts, trying to catch up with the shortcomings of the original Reagan prospectus. But Stockman's new budget-cutting tactics were denouced as panic by his former allies in the supply-side camp. They now realized that Stockman regarded them as "overly optimistic" in predicting a painless boom through across-the-board tax reduction. "Some of the naive supply-siders just missed this whole dimension," he said. "You don't stop inflation without some kind of dislocation. You don't stop the growth of money supply in a three-trillion-dollar economy without some kind of dislocation . . . Supply-side was the wrong atmospherics—not wrong theory or wrong economics, but wrong atmospherics . . . The supply-siders have gone too far. They created this nonpolitical view of the economy, where you are going to have big changes and abrupt turns, and their happy vision of this world of growth and no inflation with no pain."

The "dislocations" were multiplying across the nation, creating panic among the congressmen and senators who had just enacted this "fiscal revolution." But Stockman now understood that no amount of rhetoric from Washington, not the President's warmth on television nor his own nimble testimony before congressional hearings, would alter the economic forces at work. Tight monetary control should continue, he believed, until the inflationary fevers were sweated out of the economy. People would be hurt. Afterward, after the recession, perhaps the supply-side effects could begin—robust expansion, new investment, new jobs. The question was whether the country or its elected representatives would wait long enough.

His exasperation was evident: "I can't move the system any faster. I can't have an emergency session of Congress to say, Here's a resolution to cut the permanent size of government by 18 percent, vote it up or down. If we did that, it would be all over. But the system works much more slowly. But what can I do about it? Okay? Nothing. So I'm not going to navel-gaze about it too long."

Still trying, still energetic, but no longer abundantly optimistic, Stockman knew that congressional anxieties over the next election were already stronger, making each new proposal more difficult. "The 1982 election cycle will tell us all we need to know about whether the democratic society wants fiscal control in the federal government," Stockman said grimly.

The alternative still energized him. If they failed, if inflation and economic disorder continued, the conservative reformers would be swept aside by popular unrest. The nation would turn back toward "statist" solutions, controls devised and administered from Washington. Stockman shrugged at that possibility.

"Whenever there are great strains or changes in the economic system," he explained, "it tends to generate crackpot theories, which then find their way into the legislative channels."

8

HUMOR

When a computer engineer gets old, he gets turned out to pasture or else made into dog food.

—*Young Computer Engineer,
Data General Co.*

This section of the book is short. We'd like it to be longer. However, there does not appear to be much literature on humor in the work place. Donald Roy's description in 1960 of humor at work, "Banana Time: Job Satisfaction and Informal Interaction," is an often cited work, but little else has caught the attention of students of organization in subsequent years. We hope that the reemergence, recently, of interest in organizations as cultures and in organizational symbolism as an area of study, will draw scholars to the study of humor.

Humor conveys messages and meanings to people in ways that allow listeners to be surprised, intrigued, or persuaded by information they might otherwise resist, reject, or ignore. Humor presents information about individuals and groups in a form that they often find difficult to contest or to refute. The damage done in this way cannot easily be repaired by denial or logical argument. It is also a vehicle for tension release and for communicating aggression in a socially acceptable manner.

Do executives have a sense of humor? Do executives use humor as a part of their managerial/administrative style? Walter Kiechel III's "Executives Ought to Be Funnier," suggests that executives are not funny and that they are not perceived to be so by many of those with whom they interact. Paradoxically, executive head hunters look for a sense of humor as a necessary characteristic in candidates they screen for important administrative appointments in organizations. There is an assumed association here between the ability to joke, which entails joining two previously unconnected ideas, events, and so forth with executive vision, which entails in part making unexpected connections between phenomena that occur in and around the work place. Kiechel provides an outline and some illustrations for several ways that executives can and do use humor as an organizational tool.

One role Kiechel describes for humor is that of facilitating team building in an organization. In "Midnight Programmer," an excerpt from Tracy Kidder's *Soul of a New Machine*, we see a rich description of the use of humor in this way. Kidder tells us of the games played by Carl Alsing and his team of young computer engineers at Data General. These engineers worked on a project to create a new computer, the Eagle, under difficult and very competitive conditions. Alsing used humor to defuse some of his tensions and he created games intended to develop and to direct his team. They in turn played games designed to outwit him and to shape his behavior and attitudes. Along the way, humorous events also emerged spontaneously. The excerpt is amusing and informative.

Humor can also be used to define situations, to signal pecking orders in a group or in an organization, and to convey to workers in an acceptable form the extent and the limits of their control over difficult and dangerous tasks. These and other themes are delightfully displayed in Boland and Hoffman's description of "Humor in a Machine Shop." The new worker who fails to interpret such humor correctly risks isolation from the work group and perhaps even failure on the job.

Kiechel examines humor and executives, Kidder describes the humor of white collar professionals and of the middle manager, and Boland and Hoffman focus on blue collar humor. Taken together, the three pieces convey some of the richness and diversity of this concept which is in our view an integral and important part of organizational life.

Executives Ought to Be Funnier

*Every manager's bag of tricks should include
a sense of humor. But you'd better know
how and when to use it.*

Walter Kiechel III

Heard the one about the three executives? Probably not. Executives
aren't funny. At least, they're not supposed to be. Ask the person on the
street, ask the corporate underlings, ask the wives of senior managers—
they'll tell you that the people at the top, while perhaps admirable in
other respects, are hardly a barrel of laughs. Work is work, after all; let's
get serious.

In his sneaky heart of hearts, the intelligent executive knows better.
Not that it's all giggles in the corner office, but the potential for mirth is
usually there, frequently lurking just below the surface, sometimes erupt-
ing into the light of day. Indeed, people who hire executives look for a
sense of humor. But canny execs also realize that humor can easily
backfire, that its application has to be carefully calculated.

Just how widespread is this kept-under-pinstriped-wraps humor?
David Baum, a teaching fellow at Temple University in Philadelphia who
also consults on the managerial uses of humor, offers an instructive
story. In a workshop for 60 executives from a bank, he asked how many
of them felt they had a sense of humor. Each of the 60 bankers raised his
or her hand. "When the hands were up," Baum reports, "everyone was
looking around at his neighbors with shock on his face. You know, like
'What the hell, what do you have your hand up for?' or 'I know you,
forget it, get your hand down.' "

The way the bankers were expected to act at work—what social scientists, with their customary light touch, call the behavioral norm—effectively prevented underground springs of laughter from bubbling to the
surface. Norms vary from industry to industry, of course. Banking tends
to be on the somber side—"When you're dealing with people's money,"
comments one observer, "the clients don't want to see the spitballs flying." In advertising, by contrast, if all the folks in an agency come on like
church elders, you just might wonder how creative their product is likely
to be.

Being funny seems most acceptable in industries and companies that
are relatively new, growing fast, and innovating a lot. In Silicon Valley,

it may be noted, employees at all levels commonly come to work on Halloween in humorous costumes—the receptionist as a ghoulie, say, the computer engineer as a ghostie, the executive V.P. as a long-legged beastie.

While one can't quite envision that happening in the steel business, most experts on managerial horseflesh—executive recruiters, business-school professors, and the high muckety-mucks themselves—regard a sense of humor as essential in an executive, whatever the industry. William Gould, a headhunter with his own New York City firm and the executive vice president of the Association of Executive Search Consultants, explains why he would never offer a client a humorless job candidate: "What companies are seeking is someone who can see issues clearly. If a person can laugh, particularly at himself, he can probably step back and get the right perspective on things."

Academics, noting research that shows managers get things done mostly by working a network of contacts, point out the usefulness of mirth in building such networks. Other experts call attention to the similarity between making a joke—yoking two utterly disparate things—and that much prized managerial attribute, vision, which at least partly consists of seeing unexpected connections.

More visceral benefits to the humorist include the chance to relieve himself of aggressive feelings in a more or less acceptable way, reduce stress, even display philosophical composure, Renn Zaphiropoulos, co-founder and president of Versatec Inc., a manufacturer of computer printers and now a Xerox subsidiary, is thought by many to be the funniest executive in Silicon Valley. That may be an overstatement, but the man does have refreshing views on certain subjects. For example, he defines business as providing a service for a profit. "If you provide the service and make no profit," he goes on, "it's philanthropy. If you make a profit and provide no service, it's thievery." When asked recently what his sense of humor had done for his career, Zaphiropoulos replied simply, "It has given me the courage to go through the rough times."

The trick, as Zaphiropoulos admits, is knowing when and how to use it. Being a clown—compulsively responding with a joke to everything that comes up—won't get you to the corner office; it'll keep you from it.

The first proper managerial use of humor is to defuse tense situations. When he was president of Chrysler, Eugene Cafiero traveled to England to meet with workers at a troubled plant there. Ushered in to meet the burly unionist, he was confronted with a man who loudly proclaimed, "I'm Eddie McClusky and I'm a Communist." The Chrysler executive extended his hand and said. "How do you do. I'm Eugene Cafiero and I'm a Presbyterian." A burst of laughter clears the air, all can focus anew on the tasks at hand. The tension-dispelling effects of humor lead some experts to conclude that it's particularly important for female and minority-group managers to cultivate their funny streaks. By their very presence, these executives may, in certain benighted quarters, generate a bit of awkwardness.

A second use, so near akin to the first as to be almost identical, is to create rapport. Here's where perhaps the most admirable form of executive humor, the self-deprecating jest, comes in. Research indicates that in encounters between people of different status, the high-status individual almost always initiates the joshing. If Mr. Big uses his prerogative to mock himself in a genuinely funny way, then for a moment differences in status are eclipsed, and high and low have a better chance of really talking. Sandra Kurtzig, the founder and president of ASK Computer Systems Inc., a California software company, has a gift for just this technique. A typical Kurtzigism: "When I started this company, my long-range planning consisted of figuring out where I'd go to lunch." Asked if she'd serve on another company's board, she has replied, "I don't do boards or windows."

Somewhat paradoxically, certain types of humor can, by contrast, serve to reduce rapport and heighten status differences, or at least endow the joke maker with a slight nimbus of power. Jacqueline Goodchilds, an associate professor of psychology at UCLA, has found that in small groups, people who make sarcastic witticisms at the expense of others are seen as powerful. Before you sign up to take Don Rickles lessons, however, be aware of two caveats. First, the sarcasm has to be funny. As Goodchilds puts it, "If the humor falls flat, the power dissipates too." Second, no one in the group *likes* the sarcastic so-and-so; they're merely afraid of him or her. Given a chance, the jest-whipped worms may turn.

You're much better off using humor to make difficult messages more agreeable to the recipients. You don't want to couch reports of tragedy in a joke—"I've got bad news and good news; the bad news is that we're closing your plant and laying off all the workers . . ." But putting a humorous face on less serious ill tidings can help in two ways. First, it softens the blow. Second, it protects the messenger by creating a we're-all-in-this-together bond.

Even if the news is good, the lubricant of humor can assist in avoiding potentially sticky situations. Suppose that 28-year-old woman MBA you hired has been working like a demon. If you, her male boss, stand up at staff meeting and announce, "I wish to single out Ms. Crinziki for special attention—congratulations on your herculean efforts," approximately the following will happen: three middle-aged males will have strokes; everyone will conceive undying enmity toward the object of your attentions; Crinziki herself will be pleased for a moment, but mostly embarrassed; and they'll all wonder just what *is* your relationship to this tyro. So much more politic to simply let drop, "Well, I guess we'd better get the energy conservation boys in again—with the long hours Crinziki has been putting in, our light bill is going to be obscene."

Humor is also a perfect accompaniment when you want to let the troops know that you're aware something's up, and that you're concerned, but you don't want to hammer away at the point. "Gosh, guys," you might say, "I just figured out the message in your latest inventory figures—you want a new warehouse for Christmas." Enough said. Research on presentations shows that people most clearly remember points driven home with laughter.

Almost all these managerial uses of humor are elements in perhaps the most important use: building team cohesion, spirit, and performance. Jim Kouzes, the director of the Executive Development Center at the University of Santa Clara, sees many Silicon Valley managers who use laughter to, in his lovely phrase, encourage the heart of their workers—to help them get through a routine 16-hour workday. Zaphiropoulos of Versatec sums the matter up nicely: "I use a sense of humor to produce an informal situation, and I do that primarily because informality encourages communication," he says. "A person who doesn't laugh may be a ruler, but he would get only what he asked for—nothing more. In high-tech companies you can't survive by having people do merely what you ask them to. You hope for pleasant surprises."

Perhaps the most secret thing about executive jocularity is how easy it is to achieve: if you indicate the slightest willingness to laugh, jokes will walk right up to you, delivered by subordinates, peers, maybe the boss. Look for humor, expect it. Soon you'll probably see its laughing face everywhere, even smirking from behind the solemn, workaday visages of your fellow managers.

Who knows—you may even learn the answer to that timeless question, "How many executives *does* it take to change a light bulb?"

Midnight Programmer

Tracy Kidder

Looking around the basement, some of the team's brand-new engineers would sometimes wonder what would happen to them when they turned thirty. Being young, they could make light of the question, and say, as one did, "When a computer engineer gets old, he gets turned out to pasture or else made into dog food." Data General was a young company, and so its engineers tended to be young. There really was such a thing in the world as a practicing middle-aged computer engineer. It did

From *The Soul of a New Machine*, by Tracy Kidder. © 1981 by John Tracy Kidder. By permission of Little, Brown and Company in association with the *Atlantic Monthly Press*.

appear, however—mangement handbooks say so—that many engineers experience a change of life when they reach the age of thirty or so.

Among engineers generally, the most common form of ambition—the one made most socially acceptable—has been the desire to become a manager. If you don't become one by a certain age, then in the eyes of many of your peers you become a failure. Among computer engineers, I think, the wish to manage must be a virtual instinct. The industry's short product cycles lend to many projects an atmosphere of crisis, so that computer engineering, which is arduous enough in itself, often becomes intense. The hours are long. Emotions get taxed. Moreover, the technology of computers changes constantly; every year it's a struggle to keep up with the youngsters fresh out of school. What another of West's old hands called "a long-term tiredness" can easily creep over computer engineers in their thirties.

From the start of Eagle, Alsing disengaged himself from much of the technical work on the machine. He was running the Microteam, but from a little distance. Eagle would contain more code than any Data General machine before it—as much code as Alsing had written in his entire career. Alsing could not write all of it, even if there were time. He simply could not generate the excitement he used to feel about gates and bits. Moreover, he believed that since he could not write all of the code, then he couldn't write any of it. These new kids, he saw, approached the job in a way he never had. They worked steadily, day after day, night after night. That was fortunate, for the sake of the team. Alsing admired their discipline. He believed that it exceeded his by far. So he left the writing of the code to half a dozen new recruits, and most of the supervision of their work to submanagers.

Sometimes Alsing worried about his detachment. "Although I sometimes say I don't care too much this time around, if I were to lose this—if I were to be fired or transferred to another project more mundane—I would be, uh, very unhappy. Maybe I'm starting to take this place for granted," he said once.

For a time, when he was still in college, Alsing had wanted to become a psychologist. He adopted that sort of role now. Although he did keep track of his team's technical progress, he acted most visibly as the social director of the Microteam, and often of the entire Eclipse Group. Fairly early in the project, Chuck Holland had complained, "Alsing's hard to be a manager for, because he goes around you a lot and tells your people to do something else." But Holland also conceded: "The good thing about him is that you can go and talk to him. He's more of a regular guy than most managers."

Alsing created the Microteam. He chose its members and he gave them their first training, with some help from Rosemarie Seale. Nowadays it takes a computer to build a new computer, especially when it comes to writing microcode for one. Alsing figured that before the Microkids did anything else, they must learn how to manipulate Trixie. He didn't want simply to give them a stack of manuals and say, "Figure it out." So he made up a game. As the Microkids arrived, in ones and twos, during the summer of 1978, he told each of them to figure how to write a certain kind of program in Trixie's assembly language. This program must fetch and print out the contents of a certain file, stored inside the computer. "So they learned the way around the system and they were very pleased," said Alsing. "But when they came to the file finally, they found that access to it was denied them."

The file in question lay open only to people endowed with what were called "superuser privileges." Alsing had expected the recruits to learn how to find this file and, in the process, to master the system. He was equally interested in seeing what they would do when they found they couldn't get the file.

One after the other, they came to him and said, "I almost have it."

"Okay," said Alsing, "but you don't have it."

In the end, most Microkids went to Rosemarie. Alsing had conferred with her beforehand. She was to help the Microkids find the file, if they asked. They learned something, Alsing felt. "If a person knows how to get the right secretary, he can get everything. It was a resourceful solution—one of the solutions I hoped they'd find."

This first game led to others. Not long after the recruits arrived, the "Tube Wars" began. As a rule, it was the kids against Alsing. In one commonly used gambit, a Microkid would sit down at a terminal and order Trixie to open up Alsing's files. The Microkid would then move the files to a new location. Returning from coffee or lunch, Alsing would find his files gone. He'd hear tittering from the cubicles nearby. And he would know he'd been "tubewarred."

"What did you do to me?" he'd cry.

"Find out, stupid," a voice would answer.

The Microkids weren't the only ones playing games with the computers in the basement. A young woman worked for Rosemarie. She was unmarried and, by general consensus, good-looking. Every day for a couple of weeks during the Eagle project, she was "assaulted" at her desk. She would be doing her electronic paperwork when suddenly everything would go haywire, all her labor would be spoiled, and on the screen of her cathode-ray tube would appear cold, lascivious suggestions. "Whoever was doing it," said West, had "the mentality of an assassin."

West put Alsing on the case. Alsing had some members of the team lay traps inside the computer system—traps designed to leave a trail back to the masher's terminal. But the masher spotted all of these; one time he made his escape by bringing to an abrupt halt the entire system on which most of the engineering departments relied. He had to be stopped, and eventually Alsing found a strong suspect, a young man outside the group. Alsing had a casual chat with him about all the marvelous tricks that could be played with the in-house computing system; afterward, the obscene messages ceased. Wholesomeness, in this regard, returned to the basement. Indeed, said one young engineer, the place seemed antiseptic.

The masher's game had been especially nasty and unfair, Alsing pointed out, because the victim could not fight back. But Tube Wars pitted worthy adversaries against each other. The jousting did no harm, and, on the contrary, released tension. One day Alsing came back from lunch and went to work at his terminal. Everything looked right, all his files seemed to be in place—until he tried to do something with them. Then, to his surprise, he found that all of them were vacant. "It was like opening a filing cabinet and finding all the folders empty. They were dummy files. It took me an hour to find the real ones. So now I can never be sure, when I log on the system, that what I see is real."

Alsing struck back. He created an encrypted file and tantalized the team, "There's erotic writing in there and if you can find it, you can read it." They tried, and ultimately all gave up, including Bob Beauchamp. Alsing taunted Beauchamp, though. So Beauchamp tried again. This time he wrote a program that broke Asling's encryption system. "He beat me," Alsing said. "But I think he was too much of a gentleman to read what was inside."

Alsing doubled-encrypted the secrets in his files after that, and for many months he assumed they were safe. Beauchamp abandoned his first approach, feeling that it was a little crude. Now he made a slight revision in Trixie's operating system. In essence, he instructed the machine that whenever Alsing encrypted a message, the operating system should send to Beauchamp's files an unencrypted copy. This was the ultimate victory in Tube Wars, not least of all because Alsing never learned what Beauchamp had done to him until Beauchamp himself spilled the beans.

Tube Wars died out slowly. At their height, whenever I visited Alsing, I'd take a look at the screen of his cathode-ray tube and almost always see something peculiar written on it, some message or picture sent to him by a young engineer at play. I'd come into Alsing's cubicle and there on the screen would be a picture of a fist with the middle finger extended; or there'd be a little story on his screen:

SEX LIFE OF AN ELECTRICIAN (PART 3) FULLY EXCITED
MILLIE AMP MUMBLED OHM! OHM! OHM! . . .

Alsing arranged several sorts of social gatherings, among them a weekly meeting of the Microteam held around a table in a barren little conference room that contained one tiny window. I went to a couple of these convocations. Alsing would call the assembly to order, read a few announcements, and then submit to teasing.

"I read about someone who did a study of his company and discovered that he was the least important employee. So he quit," Alsing said.

"So long, Carl!" cried one of the Microkids.

There was a lot of talk about Alsing's idea that they should hand out Honorable Member of the Microcode Group Awards.

"I think we oughta give one to West," said one of the team. "So that when we get pissed off at him, we can take it back."

"No," said another, "because now he'll be a member of the Microteam. He can solve his own problems."

They did do some business, using the beautiful and, to me, inscrutable language of the microelectronic era: *hexaddresses, default redix, floating-point mantissas, swapbites, sys log, sim dot, scratch pad.*

"The scratch pad doesn't come alive on CPD until one-sixteen," said one.

"That means all the stack tests go away!" cried another.

"That's right."

There was laughter all around the table.

When it died away, a Microkid said, "Look, we can speed up Eagle's stack stuff by putting in a scratch pad."

"Can we," asked another, "also plant a little bomb in the thing?"

Alsing sat with his hands folded, smiling subtly. He looked like a big contented cat. No one actually called an end to the meeting. It simply petered out in laughter.

And yet there was bad feeling among some of them, much of it directed toward Alsing; and even then, petty intrigue was in progress. Some of the team would eventually describe the weekly micromeetings as "Alsing's weekly—No-Op" being the name of an assembly-language instruction that accomplishes nothing. For a long time, however, almost all of the recruits enjoyed these meetings, the Tube Wars and other entertainments that Alsing arranged. He made a point of sharing lunchtime with some of them several days a week. And they appreciated Alsing's friendliness; they could always talk to him.

Alsing believed that the team's managers, in handling the new recruits, really were practicing what was called "the mushroom theory of management." It was an old expression, used in many other corners of corporate America. The Eclipse Group's managers defined it as follows: "Put 'em in the dark, feed 'em shit, and watch 'em grow." It was a joke with substance, Alsing felt; and he believed that their mushroom management needed an occasional antidote. Alsing in effect had signed up to provide the kids with some relief from their toil. West warned him several times, "If you get too close to the people who work for you, Alsing, you're gonna get burned." But West didn't interfere, and he soon stopped issuing warnings.

One evening, while alone with West in West's office, Alsing said: "Tom, the kids think you're an ogre. You don't even say hello to them."

West smiled and replied, "You're doing fine, Alsing."

Humor in a Machine Shop: An Interpretation of Symbolic Action

Richard J. Boland, Jr. and Raymond Hoffman

THE MACHINE SHOP

The basis for this study is a small, privately owned machine shop. Such shops are found in almost every town that has an industrial or agricultural base, but are especially prevalent in the midwest where they provide custom tooled steel parts to nearby manufacturing firms. A typical shop size ranges from 10 to 50 machinists, working with large lathes, surface grinders, drill presses and other automatic machines to transform tubes and bars of steel into a wide variety of finished products.

The shop we observed works primarily with steel tubing (from ½″ to 12″ outer diameter) producing component parts (mostly steel bushings) for agricultural and earth moving equipment manufacturers. As a job shop, almost no request is too small and their customers and order sizes range from the single individual to the largest industrial firms. This shop (M shop) has 20 machinists in 15,000 square feet of floorspace. It has concrete floors and walls, 18 to 24 foot ceilings, and overhead conduits connecting the machines. Approximately 20 percent of the shop is used for stockpiling raw steel in racks 12 feet high. Overhead cranes move the required steel stock in bundles up to 6,000 pounds to the appropriate machining areas. A given order may require a dozen or more separate machining operations.

Like most machine shops, M is characterized by noise, dirt and constant threat of injury. Machine operations and steel handling create a loud whining and clanging, and the nature of the steel and the machines gives a pervasive sense of grease, oil and dust. There is a strong element of danger in the work. Lathes rotate the steel tubing at a high speed and a stationary cutting tool is applied to the softer steel stock. The result is heat, with the machined steel turning blue hot and peeling off at the tool's edge in coiled ribbons that can cause immediate third-degree burns. Other machines create equal amounts of hot steel discharge in the form of chips and shavings.

Abridged from "Humor in a Machine Shop: An Interpretation of Symbolic Action" by Richard J. Boland, Jr. and Raymond Hoffman forthcoming in *Organizational Symbolism* by Louis Pondy, Peter Frost, Gareth Morgan, and Thomas Dandridge (eds.). Reprinted by special permission of the authors.

No matter how "boring" or "monotonous" a job in the shop may seem, no matter how simple and routine an operation may appear to an observer, there is an element of danger that always exists. There's an old saying that puts it well: "Take the machine for granted and it'll take your hand; pay attention and you'll be a whole man." The machines may take off an arm or hand, or severely cut an individual, while the steel itself may fall from its stacked piles and crush a foot, ankle, leg or arm. If a loose piece of clothing or long hair gets caught in a machine, the individual himself is quickly pulled in. Most injuries take place when the individual stops respecting or paying full attention to the machine. The older the machinist, the lower the accident rate. Minor accidents may be humorous to the other workers, evoking an "I told you so" look on the face. But nobody likes to get burned by blue-hot steel shavings that stick to the skin. Most machinists realize that at best the machine is a double-edged sword, capable of being controlled to an extent, but also capable of inflicting unexpected injury to its operator.

The steel itself is important in creating the atmosphere of the machine shop. Virtually everything the men work with is steel in one firm or another. Steel tubing is the raw material. High carbon steel tools cut and shape the tubing on steel lathes and drill presses. Steel drums store the finished pieces and work in process. Steel is the scrap, and even work boots are lined with steel. Machinists live in a steel world for eight to ten hours every day. They make the steel take a certain form, and yet the steel shapes them. A machinist's hands become strong and thick with calluses from all the cuts, slivers, and burns he receives. Nonetheless, to a machinist, his hands are a prized possession. He is proud of them, no matter what they look like to other people. The machinist is physically altered by the process of shaping the steel, and comes to respect its inert strength. It is the "immovable object" that he struggles with.

There is also an important cognitive component to being a machinist. Steel as a raw material has a wide range of hardness, tensile strength, and malleability. The machines and tools have varied rates of material feed, cutting speed and steel removal, and a specific job order may demand tolerances of plus or minus five ten-thousandths of an inch. Being a machinist includes developing the special ability to take these standard specifications plus other, more subtle aspects of a particular piece of steel, machine, and tool into account in producing the desired result.

The machinists at M shop range in age from late fifties to late teens, and shop experience ranges from thirty-five years to no experience at all. A hierarchy exists within the shop based on experience with machines. One exception to this is the foreman, who, at forty years of age, finds himself at the top of the formal hierarchical structure even though he has less experience than several of the machinists. The foreman does not take his position as implying that he is the most experienced, however, and often calls on the advice of older machinists in problem situations.

Several other hierarchies exist in the social world of M shop, including ones based on strength and intelligence.

M shop was founded in the summer of 1972. At first, much of the work was subcontracted, but in the fall of 1973 the shop began full service operation with three machinists and one owner/manager. From that point through August of 1974 the second author worked in the shop as an apprentice. He continued to work as an apprentice machinist during summers and holidays for the next five years, including the most recent summer of observation. During this time, the shop had grown to twenty full-time machinists and he has continued to be an accepted, though intermittent, member of the work force. The examples of humor discussed here are based on recorded observations, but they are elaborated with recollections of the five preceding years of work experience.

OBSERVATIONS

We do not pretend to have developed a taxonomy of all the instances of humor that were observed, but some natural headings would include language jokes, physical jokes, and machine jokes. In this paper we will deal only with physical and machine jokes as they are the easiest to relate specifically to the work place. Language jokes, especially at lunchtime and breaks, run the full spectrum of an individual's social life, including hobbies, family, personal history, etc. Taking them into account is beyond our ability here. We would argue, however, that our narrowing to these specific behaviors is to study a particular language—a bodily and object-mediated one—not to ignore language.

Purely physical jokes include one or more individuals in direct or indirect contact with another. For example, each machinist has a rag tucked into his back pocket for use in wiping himself, the steel, or the machine. Taking his rag, without his notice, is a common and effective joke—especially when he reaches to clean a hand full of grease. Or, because lidded steel drums are put on a dolly for movement to the next machine operation, replacing a full drum with an empty one can cause the individual to fall flat on his face when he gives the heave ho. Another frequent physical joke is the goose. A broom handle or steel tube, not so delicately placed, will bring any machinist up short. Many of the physical jokes play on the desire to keep clean in the dirty shop environment. A rag wet with machine coolant or grease set on a chair or lobbed across the shop onto a clean shirt back is one example, and dropping large pieces of steel into a vat of coolant or cleaning fluid and splashing those around it is another.

Physical humor is also evident in mimicry. While the shop is in full production with all men at their machines, an extended sequence of mimicked jokes are taking place. Imitating unique physical gestures or characteristics of those stationed at other machines or walking in the aisles is a frequent form of humor. Besides the parody of unique physical gestures or abnormalities of others, mimicry often has sexual or intellectual overtones. Other machinists are often portrayed as either sexually incompetent or as sexually perverted, using bars of steel or pieces of the machine as mock sex objects to pantomime another's missing or insatiable appetites. The pantomimes may also refer to another's mental powers, as in "you are looking (acting) so stupidly."

The other major category of humor relates to the machines themselves. These are primarily jokes played on an individual through his machine. Each machinist will spend approximately 60 percent of his time on one particular machine. He will come to see the machine as his and will often give it a name, paint a unique decoration on it, and in general come to have an intimate understanding of its unique operating characteristics. Because of this relationship, the machine is an ideal medium for pulling jokes. It is an important element in establishing the individual's identity as a machinist, and therefore a powerful medium for pulling jokes about the definition of self. "Blueing" is a popular trick in which an indelible steel marking ink is rubbed on the handles or knobs of a machine. This is especially funny when the individual touches his face or clothes after grabbing the "blued" knob or handle. The natural blackened color of the knobs and handles makes this "blueing" difficult to detect. In a similar vein, the hose which sprays a fine stream of coolant over the raw steel as it is being machined can be adjusted to spray at high pressure directly onto the machine operator. Other machine jokes include removing fuses or gears from a machine, thus making them inoperable, or reversing the direction in which a machine rotates. Slightly more adventurous jokes include the outright removal of key operating parts from another's machine, or recalibrating the measurement instruments he uses for checking the narrow tolerances.

These machine tricks are best when pulled while a machinist is in the middle of a production run but has turned off and left his machine for a few minutes. When he returns, the trick pullers are watching for his reaction when the machine doesn't start, runs backwards, soaks him with coolant, or when he discovers he has "blueing" on his hands, and has just touched his face. One joke that requires a running machine is the cannon trick. Here, the running machine becomes an amusing toy for the machinist. By plugging one end of the steel tubing with a rubber ball, the air pressure is built up until a cannonlike explosion blows it out. . . .

We take the position that the instances of humor observed in M shop are seen as being funny by the individuals involved to the extent that each individual finds in "getting the joke," that two incongruous frames of reference for interpreting the self are meaningfully resolved. The problems of self-definition that this humor is dealing with are inferred from the frames of reference the jokes juxtapose. While this is ultimately each individual's unique experience in "getting the joke," we will summarize what appears to us to be the most conspicuous frames involved.

Each worker, over time, establishes a strong self-identity in the shop. In these self-identities, the definition of the individual as a worker is our primary concern, but this is deeply intertwined with other, more personal aspects of their life and we cannot separate them. The self-definition includes such things as his manner and type of dress, morning ritual of arrival, dressing, having coffee, checking his machine, etc. It also includes his identity as a machinist—the level of skills and capabilities he asserts. We see these self-identities as structured in sets of hierarchies. Humor plays both an initiating and reversing role in these nested sets of hierarchically structured self-definitions. It initiates structure by affirming an individual's place, and it also reverses structure when played on an individual's previously established identity. For instance, a new worker will have jokes played on him so he learns his place, but once established, the jokes are played to reverse his place. The ambiguity of self confirmed by humor allows for movement through the established hierarchies. While humor serves to celebrate an individual's existing identity, it also asserts its fragility and ultimate equivocality. The machinist who prides himself on being the cleanest in M shop, with a pressed uniform and scrubbed hands, is great for a wet rag, blueing, or coolant hose trick. Of course, this particular machinist defines himself by many of the structured hierarchies of the shop. He is also seen as one of the best joke pullers and one of the most difficult to pull one on. While this may or may not add to the reversal effect of a joke played on him, it does provide for multiple frames of reference that can be used as a basis for "getting the joke."

Other examples of humor used to reverse the established order are found at the lunch table. Some men will bring exactly the same lunch every day (salami on white bread, two carrots, two celery sticks, one packet of twinkies). They eat these items in the same order every day, and a good joke is to divert their attention, so that they eat their food in a different order. One man went so far as to arrange with another worker's wife to pack a different lunch for her husband as part of the trick. (He refused to eat it.)

This use of jokes to deny an asserted self-identity is a major theme of the mimicry mentioned earlier. The individual's position in the hierarchies of sexual prowess, physical strength, intelligence, or skilled machinist is a basis for much of the mimicry. The joker is saying "you're not so smart (strong, skilled)." The machine jokes (removing parts, changing adjustments, etc.) are also reversing the individual's position, but, like the lunch jokes, have a ritual interruption component also. That is, each machinist develops a highly rigid, sequenced set of actions for setting up his machine or for running a particular job. Any joke pulled on him while he is in the middle of this sequence will force him to go back to the beginning and start over again. This starting over again is an integral part of "getting the joke" and emphasizes the disparity of the several frames that must be involved.

There is an important sense in which the joke must "fit" the existing hierarchy. In order to pull a joke, an individual must himself be well established in the relevant hierarchy. For instance, a new apprentice cannot really pull a joke on anyone. Once he *is* seen as fit for pulling jokes, he only plays certain kinds, rag jokes or dirty and clean jokes, but not machine jokes. Only the machinists pull machine jokes. On the other hand, then, jokes are primarily directed against an individual's self-identity, but on the other, the joke is asserting or confirming the indentity of the joke puller. . . .

9

HAZARDS

Most of us are unaware that we have the following unspoken contract with life: the world is inherently orderly and predictable. . . Imagine the shock that occurs to an individual or to a corporation when something so terrible and unpredictable happens that it shatters our belief in the orderliness of the world.

—*Ian I. Mitroff and*
Ralph H. Kilmann

We are all accustomed to newspaper and television stories about the heavy toll extracted by accidents at work and illnesses caused by exposure to hazardous materials in the work environment. Periodically we see statistical summaries of occupational accidents, disabilities, and deaths. Since these events are removed from the lives of most of us, they tend to make little lasting impression. After all, Workman's Compensation and OSHA were created to insure that justice is done on the one hand and that dangerous working conditions are corrected on the other. To be sure, our perceptions of the latter agency are diluted by news stories of the misdirected bureaucratic zeal with which its efforts are sometimes addressed to trivial conditions in the work environment, correction of which is annoying and expensive to employers.

We think it is important, however, that our look at organizational reality include first a brief summary of the cost to society of health and safety problems and some graphic illustrations of these costs to the individuals concerned. The selection by Sayles and Strauss presents the former and notes that the workplace is in fact becoming more, not less, hazardous. "How to Keep Safe" brings the statistics to life through accounts of the damage to individuals and property through criminal negligence on the part of employees—damage that usually could have been avoided had management taken seriously its obligation for occupational safety. The cavalier manner in which such infractions are treated by the courts is a shocking indictment of society's attitude toward the preservation of life and property in the course of day to day business. While the illustrations in this selection are from Great Britain, perusal of the North American record reveals a similar situation.

On the other hand, programs negotiated by employers and unions with the best interests of employees at heart can become a two edged sword. "Auto Firm's Blue-Collar Transfers Result in Troubles at Work, Home" documents how a program designed to maintain continuity of employment for workers displaced by plant closures has boomeranged with serious effects for the employees concerned as well as for their families, and has created disruptive conditions in the plants to which these individuals were transferred. As the restructuring of industry that is taking place continues, what greater hazards must employees and managers face whose jobs are simply terminated and whose skills are redundant or obsolete?

The next two selections are concerned with problems women can encounter in the workplace. Sexual harassment by supervisors and fellow workers has received a great deal of attention in recent years. However, "Voices in the Night" reports a particularly frightening form of sexual harassment. We wonder how many women who work alone at night are confronted with similar unwelcome attentions.

"Managers and Lovers" by Eliza G. C. Collins addresses the situations that arise when reasonably senior managers in an organization come to love one another. The author, an associate editor of the *Harvard Business Review*, presents four case studies in support of her view that one of the parties should either be transferred or leave the organization. This article created quite a stir when it was first published. We include the readers' responses to Ms. Collins' views that were printed in a subsequent issue of the *Harvard Business Review*.

Finally, "Corporate Tragedies: Teaching Companies to Cope with Evil" moves to the level of the corporation and addresses three questions: Is there a list of unthinkables that can beset any business; why is the unthinkable more prevalent in today's world; and what can businesses do to cope more effectively with the unthinkable? Mitroff and Kilmann identify four basic types of unthinkables and provide illustrations of each. They then argue that the unthinkable is happening more often both because business is operating in a vastly different environment today and because most organizations simply are not prepared to deal with the unthinkables. They are sharply critical of business education for the inability of organizations to respond to these situations appropriately. Finally, the authors offer some provocative suggestions for improving organizations' abilities to cope.

Safety and Occupational Health

Leonard R. Sayles and George Strauss

SCOPE OF THE PROBLEM

A decade ago there was considerable optimism about "curing" industry's safety problems. Between 1926 and 1956, the accident frequency rate in manufacturing had declined by about 50 percent. But by the beginning of this decade, accidents were occurring 26.77 percent more frequently than a decade earlier. Further, we have recently learned that a number of terrible diseases are associated with industrial and mining processes—for example, black lung, cancer, and asbestosis.[1] The scope of this growing challenge to management can be inferred from these annual statistics for the United States:

- 3 million (out of 8) workers become ill or are injured
- 2 million workers are disabled
- 14,000 deaths occur in work accidents
- 100,000 deaths occur from occupationally caused illnesses
- 400,000 new cases of disabling illness occur
- These illnesses and injuries cost $9 billion, including 45 million man-days of work lost

Shocking as these figures are, they understate industry's true costs from health and safety problems. Worker productivity suffers as a result of fear of accidents and resentment over uncorrected hazards. Companies pay high insurance premiums to cover their liabilities for accidents. Injuries mean reduced productivity and possible break-in and training costs for substitute employees. Some authorities have estimated that for serious accidents there may be $4 of indirect costs associated with every dollar of direct costs.

Obviously, some accidents just happen. In a world filled with moving vehicles, rotating equipment, exotic chemicals, and tall buildings, injuries are bound to occur. We have all read about how dangerous the average home is, and most of us have seen friends take needless chances in the routines of everyday living.[2] However, we should certainly not be content to permit a "that's life" attitude to excuse a problem of the magnitude of the current one. Furthermore, the law requires that management pay close attention to its safety and health records, and violations are costly.

NOTES

1. One of the more gruesome accounts of unsolved safety problems in industry is provided by Rachel Scott, *Muscle and Blood* (New York: Dutton, 1974).

2. One of the authors sustained his most serious work-related injury while leaning against a wall in a steel chair while only two of the legs were on the floor. A slight shift in weight and the chair slipped, throwing the surprised occupant to the concrete floor.

How to Keep Safe

'The health and safety of the people is the highest law.' So said Cicero. Most people, however, tend to see safety law as being 'different' to other law. Mugging is quite clearly a 'crime' in everyone's mind. Running a machine without guards is also a 'crime,' but people see it in a different way. The result is that safety legislation is not something to which many managers give a lot of thought in their daily lives. This question of the perception of the offence, one of the biggest problems in safety, has never really been satisfactorily resolved, despite the efforts of legislators.

Cicero may well have defined the basic principle, but it was not until the Industrial Revolution that legislation was thought necessary in Britain. An Act for the Preservation of the Health and Morals of Apprentices and Others Employed in Cotton and Other Factories appears to have been the first legislation in the field. It required apprentices to have (among other things) sufficient and suitable clothing, fresh air and quick-limed factories in which to work. Nightwork was prohibited, and the apprentices were to be instructed in the principles of the Christian religion. Concern for moral welfare appears to be the basis of much safety legislation; it may be this philosophy which has led to the clouding of the perception of the crime committed.

Between 1802 and 1974, a considerable body of statues developed to support the now famous Factories Acts, the first of which was the Factory and Workshop Act 1878 and the most recent the Factories Act 1961. This legislation gave detailed instructions about what was or was not permitted. A century later, in 1974, a new approach was adopted. Instead of giving details, the new Health and Safety at Work, etc. Act attempted to put responsibility in the right place by establishing general rules to be supported by Regulations and Codes of Practice.

In all this legislation penalties have been stipulated for infringement. Up to the 1970s, most offences were dealt with summarily, with a £60

From *Management Today*, February 1984. Reprinted with permission.

fine as the limit. Since then, penalties have been more serious: the Health and Safety at Work Act provides for fines of £1,000 on summary conviction; after indictment, the penalty is imprisonment for up to two years, or a fine, or both, or separately an unlimited fine.

The 1974 Act also clarified the question of individual responsibility, making it clear that 'an offence . . . to have been attributable to any neglect on the part of any director, manager . . . shall be liable to be proceeded against and punished accordingly'. It may be that the legislators intended to get away from the code of civil liability which the judges had established. In any event, the penalties are actually quite severe. The legislators obviously intended people to be aware that offences against safety legislation were serious. The Courts have the power to act. The question is do they use it; and if not, why not?

It is accepted that people are fallible. If people were infallible, there would be no need for safety legislation and therefore no need for Courts to hear offences against safety legislation. Since magistrates and judges are people, too, they are also fallible. You would not expect exactly the same penalty to be applied for offences under the same sections of the legislation in every Court. You would, however, expect an element of consistency to emerge—and this does not appear to have happened.

Here are some examples. A roofing contractor was using a bitumen boiler on a roof. The gang went off to lunch, leaving a 16-year-old with instructions to keep an eye on the boiler and to go down the five storeys to ground level to bring up new roofing felt. How he was to keep an eye on the boiler while going up and down was not explained. While he was away, the wind caused the flame from the boiler to blow back and ignite bitumen on an unprotected rubber hose. The hose burnt and in turn set fire to rubbish on the roof. A 47kg liquid petroleum gas cylinder overheated and exploded. A nearby block of flats was evacuated. Action was taken under Section 3 (i) of the Act. The company was fined £500.

Another roofing contractor transported a lit asphalt boiler along with 47kg propane cylinders, roofing felt and asphalt on the back of a truck. The crew went through heavy traffic across London before stopping at a café for a break. The men all went into the café, leaving the truck on the roadside with the burner still burning. The truck caught fire, and the gas cylinders exploded, causing damage to nearby property. Action was taken, again under Section 3 (i) of the Act. The company was fined £1,000.

Another company was involved in the recovery of solvents from contaminated highly flammable liquids. Cooling during the recovery process was vital. The normal plant cooling water supply had failed, and a temporary supply (which had proved erratic in the past) was established. A director set up the plant, and then left the site with a partially-trained operator in charge. No member of the management was present. Faults occurred which led to an explosion. One man was killed, another seriously injured, and a building demolished. Damage was caused to residential property, 37 fire appliances were called in, and local residents were evacuated. Action was taken under Section 2. The company was fined £900.

A further incident involving gas occurred at a leisure centre. The staff were changing chlorine cylinders for a swimming pool purification system. Chlorine escaped after a valve had been left open on the cylinder. When the gas got into the changing room area, 34 people had to be taken to hospital. Grass over a 100-yard radius around the area was burnt brown. Vegetables were affected in gardens 180 yards away. No action was taken.

In another case, two men were being lifted by crane onto an almost complete oil-rig. A cage in which the men were being lifted was attached to the crane hook by a D shackle and wire rope. The cage became detached and fell about 240 feet into the sea. Both men died. The company operating the yard, prosecuted under Section 3, was fined £700.

Then, a crane driver experienced in the use of track-mounted cranes was transferred by his employers to a wheel-mounted crane which had to use outriggers when lifting loads. The driver was given no extra training and was then called upon to use the crane to carry out a lift. He did not use the outriggers. The crane overturned, killing one man and seriously injuring two others. The company was prosecuted under Section 2 (i) of the Act. Fine £500.

On the railways a signalman was found drunk in his signal box. Five trains in his section were delayed for an hour until a frustrated driver went to the signal box and found the signalman 'unconscious'. The signalman was prosecuted and sentenced to two months' imprisonment. Nobody had been hurt because the railway safety system was effective.

Another signalman had a young railway buff who came to see him in the signal box. The signalman went off for a few moments, instructing the youngster to shout for him if anything happened. A buzzer sounded, and the young railway enthusiast, on his own initiative, operated the system, sounding a warning bell, closing barriers and signalling a train through. As he shouted to the signalman through the window, two passing plainclothes policemen overheard. The signalman was prosecuted and sentenced to two months' imprisonment, suspended for two years. Nobody had been hurt. Both the signalment were prosecuted under railway legislation, by the British Transport Police rather than Health and Safety inspectors.

The eight safety offences in the sample attracted a range of punishments from two months in jail to no action at all. All the prosecutions under the Health and Safety at Work Act were against companies. Only in the prosecutions by police were individuals pursued. Yet in each case an individual was responsible for setting in motion the actions which led to the offences. In the industrial offences, a manager had decided what was to be done, who was to do it, and when it was to happen. Otherwise, there would have been no activities to cause the offences in the first place. So, although the 1974 Act has provision for putting the responsibility where it should lie, this does not seem to be happening. The perception of the crimes appears different; certainly the perception of the amount of punishment seems to belong to different scales.

People perceive things in different ways. Psychological tests make use of the fact that different subjects see two different things in the same cunningly plotted drawing. The same principle applies to industrial safety versus other law. People's stored information tells them that mugging is a serious crime and should be dealt with severely. The reaction to news of a mugging will be 'Poor Jack, he was mugged. They should bring back the birch'. Jack, who may have severe bruising, will recover in a week and perhaps suffer residual damage consisting of a fear of walking home alone at night. The same observers will have stored information which tells them that a person who is drawn into a machine and loses the use of both hands as a result has had an industrial accident. There will be no thought initially that this damage is the result of a crime. The likely reaction will be 'Poor Jack, he got hurt at work'.

In each case, there is an injured party. In each case, there is a crime. The perception of the 'wrong-doing' is, however, crucially different. The mugging is quite clearly an illegal act. The removal or nonfitting of the guard which led to the industrial accident is not so clearly an illegal act, although the requirement to guard machines is an absolute duty under Section 14 of the 1961 Factories Act. However, although the Factories Acts were, and are, criminal statutes in form, they have been adapted by generations of judges into a code of civil liability governing the relations between employers and employees in factories. This appears to reduce the absoluteness of perceptions.

Whether these perceptions are in fact valid or not is open to discussion. But clearly, if the perception of the crime involved in an industrial accident is blurred, it is likely that the trail to the person responsible will be, too. And yet in every case someone is directly responsible: that someone is normally a manager.

The philosophy behind the Health and Safety at Work Act was that those who created the risks and worked with them would be responsible for reducing them. Most professional managers accept this responsibility in principle, but in day-to-day activity often allocate a low priority to the task. Managers countenance the running of machines without guards, the storage of flammable liquids on the shopfloor, the employment of young people without adequate training, the running of pilot plants without adequate precautions—to mention but a few of the industrial 'crimes' committed each day.

Every working day, a manager somewhere says, 'OK, run it for now'; 'Complete that batch, and we'll get it right later'; 'Be careful while that guard is off'; 'Get the fitter to fix it as soon as possible'; 'I know the brakes are not too good, that's why it's going to the garage. Just be careful on the way'; or, 'I know the scaffold has no toe-boards, they'll be here tomorrow'. Just choose the industry and select the appropriate remark. No manager has not, at some stage in his life, made some such statement and hoped that it would be all right on the night.

THE AMPHORG IS BLAMED

Most of the time, it is. Occasionally it goes wrong, and someone is injured. Although a crime is committed each time that it happens, few managers would accept the criminal responsibility. When someone is injured, the manager truly feels that it is the fault of 'the company', because he, the manager, was only doing his job, and his job requires him to act that way. If an accident occurs, personal responsibility seems to float away; it becomes the amorphous organization (amphorg) which is at fault. Since it is unusual for an individual to be prosecuted, it must be assumed that the Health and Safety Executive supports this view.

Yet no company makes executive decisions. The decisions are made by the executives. It is axiomatic that the executive who decides is responsible for his action or for any action which follows his decision. The law says that this is so, and managers accept the principle. But the practice is far removed from the philosophy. For example, the punishment should presumably fit the crime as defined in the legislation, which also lays down the punishment, yet the punishments awarded for safety offences, when compared with other offences, do *not* fit the crime. The average 1981 fine was £187.

To illustrate, four men working for a water authority were sent to check a sewer. For some reason, as yet unknown (or at least unreleased), they all died. They were the victims of an industrial accident. It seems unlikely that there will be a public enquiry. Yet when the Penlee lifeboat sank, with the loss of all the crew, there was a national appeal for the families and a public enquiry lasting some weeks. The enquiry found that nobody was to blame, that the lifeboat sank as a result of events over which man had no control: i.e., it was a real 'accident'.

The four water board men, however, were involved in an unexpected event in an otherwise planned sequence of events. Furthermore, 'unexpected' does not mean unprecedented: there have been deaths before in similar circumstances. Organized bodies take precautions to preclude this particular unexpected event in the planned sequence by measuring the atmosphere before allowing entry.

The question now is 'What will happen next?' Past experience shows, in case after case, that if any action is taken, it is against the company (the amphorg). The manager who set the project in motion will not be penalized. Past experience shows that the proceedings, if any, are generally summary, with the probability of that average £187 fine. The amphorg time and again is found wanting, while the people who flesh it out can rest secure in the feeling of a job well done. The sequence will be the direct effect of the way people perceive the events.

The fact that the world's a dangerous place is freely and anxiously recognized. At Greenham Common, women demonstrate because they fear the ultimate catastrophe of a nuclear holocaust. The Central Electricity Generating Board is forced to hold open house at Sizewell to convince the public that the next generation of nuclear machines is both necessary and safe. There are multiple accidents on the motorways. Air liners crash, causing hundreds of deaths. Lead in the atmosphere is thought to cause delayed intellectual development in children. There are riots in the major cities. The crime rate goes on rising. In any year, 5,000 people will be killed in accidents in the home; no less than 39,000 will die of lung cancer; and about 700 will die in industrial accidents.

True, as the present recession has shown, people are willing to trade safety for jobs—up to a point. The research paper, *Public Attitudes to Risk*, showed that, while two-thirds of people thought that the risks created by industry were worth taking, both for the public and the worker, two-thirds also opted for the safest job at the lowest pay. In other words, work risks are all right so long as the other chap is taking them. Nevertheless, people do accept work risks and hope that the worst won't happen to themselves.

The same is not true of other risks. People believe that they should be safe to walk the streets. It follows that crimes against the person fit into a different frame of reference. The risk of an injury at work is two-thirds acceptable, while the risk of a mugging is totally unacceptable. The citizen requires the State to protect him after he has taken the risk of working. While some of the money he earns goes in taxes to fund the running of the State, which must protect him from crime, from riots, from lead in the air or from nuclear blast, he does not see it as the State's job to protect him at work (except that there should be factory inspectors to make sure that employers are not too careless).

On the other hand, safety at work is the responsibility of the man who gives the citizen the job: the manager (the 'boss') rather than the amphorg. When the injured man says, 'It was the company's fault,' he is normally thinking of a specific person. In every amphorg, employees associate 'the company' with a particular person. It may not be that specific person who is legally responsible for the infringement when an incident occurs. But dangers are associated with certain responsibilities, and most people have clear ideas about who is actually responsible. In safety, the responsibility becomes dispersed after the event.

MANAGERS ARE RESPONSIBLE

The unfortunate result of mild punishments and prosecution of the organization rather than the individual is that the people who are in fact responsible, and could influence matters rationalize their responsibility away. The transfer of responsibilty to the amphorg is reinforced and thus reduces the rate of improvement of safety in industry. Managers keep on making the same sort of decisions because after the event the responsibility for the decision is transferred. They suffer no penalty and feel no remorse. The amphorg, being inanimate, absorbs as much punishment as society cares to inflict, without any need for change. Until safety legislation is interpreted as it was intended to be in the 1974 Act, there will be no major improvements in the safety field. Each manager is responsible for his decisions; each employee is responsible for his acts. If progress is to be made, the individual responsibility must be accepted.

Auto Firms' Blue-Collar Transfers Result in Troubles at Work, Home

Dale D. Buss

In 1956, 19-year-old Sandor Rozsa fled Hungary to escape the Soviet occupation, leaving his parents behind for good. Now a 47-year-old auto worker who was transferred here nearly a year ago by General Motors Corp., Mr. Rozsa is undergoing an even more trying separation—from his wife and children. "I feel like I've deserted everyone who needs me," he says.

But Janice Rozsa, his wife, feels she has no choice but to stay in West Convina, Calif., 1,300 miles from her husband's new job. A move would disrupt her seniority as a hospital nurse, the education of their learning disabled child and her own treatments for Addison's disease. Twice since her husband's transfer, she has been hospitalized for stress-induced flare-ups of the disease. "I never had to be hospitalized when he was still here," she whispers, breaking into sobs.

Not long ago, none of this would have happened to the Rozsas. When factories were closed, no one gave serious thought to transferring the affected workers. Companies and unions both assumed that most blue-collar workers had deep roots in their communities, and wouldn't move.

Since 1982, GM, Ford Motor Co. and the United Auto Workers have been testing those assumptions. That year, in exchange for wage and benefit concessions, certain high-seniority UAW workers won protection against plant closings and production cutbacks. The only condition: They must accept a transfer, if it's offered, to another plant.

So far, the experiences of many of the 3,600 GM and Ford workers who have accepted transfers under the program have been far from encouraging. Many have had problems adjusting to their new jobs. The combination of their high seniority in their companies with their low seniority in their new plants has kindled angry disputes with new workmates. Here in Oklahoma City, locals have even complained that the influx of transferees has driven up food and housing prices.

The transfers have been even harder on the workers' families. They suffer many of the problems experienced by white-collar families during transfers, but with the added burden that moving allowances have been less than generous. GM gives a married blue-collar transferee $2,075 and will loan him an additional $1,000. Lacking attractive options, some spouses have been forced to give up lucrative jobs. Other families, like the Rozsas, have been separated.

"We're just like a yo-yo on a string," says Mr. Rozsa. "That's what we get for giving most of our lives to the company." Says John Malicki, a 49-year-old GM worker who turned down a transfer: "I think the whole plan was to offer you a job in some distant place where you couldn't take it so they could cut you off and save money."

Officials at the UAW and GM, which has done most of the transferring, generally defend the programs, while conceding they could stand improvement. The union says it will bargain for those improvements during this summer's negotiations. A GM manager agrees that "some things haven't gone so well" with the implementation, though "the intent is very good."

But some of the program's underlying problems won't be easy to solve. Unlike white-collar workers, the auto companies' blue-collar transferees usually move en masse: Mr. Rozsa, for example, was only one of 600 GM workers transferred here from two plants closed in California. Because there are only so many openings at other plants—and because moves are so expensive—companies limit both the number of people eligible for transfers and the moving allowances paid to each.

Those limitations, in turn, cause problems. For instance, the programs protect only workers with at least 10 years' seniority, people who have grown accustomed to doing the more-desirable jobs at their former plants. In their new jobs, their corporate seniority remains intact for retirement and other purposes, but they have the same plant seniority as new hires. So the transferees, most in their late 30s to early 50s, get some of the hardest, most-tedious assembly-line jobs, and most work nights.

The transferees have been pressing for recognition of their seniority at the plant here; the change, which would have given all the transferees seniority over the Oklahomans, was overwhelmingly rejected at a union meeting last fall. Later, there were fisticuffs between the new workers and the natives, and the bad feelings persist.

"I know they need jobs, too, but the ones they take here could be filled by our relatives and friends," says A. C. Lackey, sitting in his pickup truck one afternoon before starting his night-shift painting job at the plant. "You go down the line and there's nobody from here any more. One's from St. Louis and one's from Ohio and the next one's from California."

For many transferees, tense working relationships come on top of strained family ties. Faced with pressures such as the limited moving allowance, the need for a spouse to keep a good job, the reluctance of children to change schools and problems in selling homes, many workers feel they have little choice but to leave their families behind.

Two such workers—46-year-old Gary Peoples and 50-year-old Donald Johnson—have spent the past year as roommates, living together like a pair of over-aged boot-campers in a Spartan apartment a few minutes from the plant. Outside of work, they spend most of their time eating, sleeping, playing racquetball or scrubbing the thick, red prairie mud from their cars—a frequent pastime of the Californians here.

They also spend a lot of time worrying. (Heavy drinking and first encounters with high blood pressure aren't uncommon among the transferees.) Mr. Peoples is making about $400 a week because of all the overtime he's putting in, but he says his family has rarely been in such financial straits. He makes house payments in California as well as rent payments here, piles up phone bills of $200 or more a month, and spends $350 every few months for short, harried visits home.

More troubling than the money, he says, is the separation from his family. "I went to high school about a block from the South Gate plant and then went right to work there," he recalls. "I had a real base in California, coaching football and everything. The worst thing is: I'm used to sleeping with my wife." In Los Angeles, Shirley Peoples sometimes wonders how much their "wonderful" relationship can stand.

This day, at least, Mr. Peoples is cheered by the receipt of a package of lemons his wife plucked from their backyard tree. But for his roommate, the afternoon turns sour: Mr. Johnson gets a call about a household money matter from his wife, who is a computer-company supervisor in Los Angeles. Her frantic tone upsets him. "I think sometimes that she's about ready to crack" because of the separation, Mr. Johnson says, worrying about the strains that it puts on their 24-year marriage. "I can see it. I can feel it. She can't even pick me up at the airport any more because it's too hard on her."

Still, for Messrs. Peoples and Johnson, there is hope for relief soon:

Each has less than two years to work until he qualifies for a GM pension of about $900 a month and can move back to California to enjoy retirement.

But for Robert Edelen, the long-term outlook isn't much rosier than his short-term prospects, the way he sees it. With only 16 years at GM, he needs to work nearly that long again to be eligible for a full pension. At 37, with a shock of crewcut, silver-gray hair and a "Born to Lose" tattoo on his right forearm, Mr. Edelen looks weary and much older than his years.

Mr. Edelen tried to bring his wife and children to Oklahoma City once, but a deal on a house fell through. He says he plans to try again within a year, though he hasn't convinced the family of that yet. Back in Rosemead, Calif., Sharon Edelen seems likely to resist the idea. "We can't just shuffle our kids in and out of schools," she sighs. "With GM these days, it seems like you're just a nomad."

Voices in the Night

Bob Greene

On the night she finally knew she was in trouble, Alix Lacy was near the end of her shift. It was almost two A.M.; she had been on the air for four hours. As usual, she was alone in the studios of KBCO-FM, in Boulder, Colorado. She worked without an engineer; there was no one else in the building.

The light on her telephone was blinking again; like the phones in most sound studios, hers was wired to flash a light rather than to ring. She knew it was him. By this time, she thought she could feel it when he called.

She spoke into the microphone. In her soft, unthreatening voice—perfect for Boulder—she announced the next record. For all the listeners who were waiting, she put an album on one of the two studio turntables. The music played, and the telephone light kept blinking, and with the microphone turned off she started to sob.

It is a phenomenon of American late-night radio: the female voice wafting over the airwaves, comforting and stirring at the same time, offering a promise of companionship for listeners who are lonelier than they might want to admit. For women disc jockeys with the right kind of voice, the night shift offers professional opportunity; men want to hear women play them music when it is dark outside, and the station managers all across the United States are aware of this.

Alix Lacy is one of the women who sought a career doing this kind of work. Lacy, twenty-seven, worked the ten P.M.–two A.M. shift at KBCO. Her voice was not overtly sexual; in the words of one of her bosses, she came across on the air "like the typical Boulder lady—beautiful, yet simple and wholesome."

Ray Skibitsky, who is the KBCO station manager, said, "I think some listeners have a fantasy in the back of their minds that the female late-night disc jockey is sitting there talking to them, and them alone."

There are no surveys that measure that type of attitude. But one thing Skibitsky and Dennis Constantine, KBCO's program director, were sure of: when they walked the steets of their town and stopped in at bars and restaurants, people would find out what they did for a living, and one of the first questions was always, "What does Alix Lacy look like?"

When the calls started, Alix Lacy barely noticed them. As a matter of routine, she gave out the station's telephone number during her show. The purpose was to allow listeners to call with requests.

At some point—she does not remember precisely when—she realized that someone was calling and hanging up on her, and that a pattern was beginning to emerge. Right when she would start her shift, the phone would blink, she would answer it—and the caller would hang up. This would occur several times. Nothing would happen until the middle of her shift. Then the caller would do it again; a flurry of calls. Things would get quiet. Then near the end of the shift, another flurry. She would answer; the caller would hang up.

The KBCO studio is in an office complex that is deserted at night. Alix Lacy worked alone in a room on the second floor, up a flight of stairs. The only entrance or exit for her was the glass door at the top of the stairs. As the hang-up calls continued, night after night, she found herself, for the first time, thinking about that.

One night, after her shift, she left a note on the bulletin board: HEY, EVERYBODY, IS ANYONE ELSE GETTING HANG-UP CALLS A LOT? She asked the other on-air performers to initial the note if they were receiving similar harassment. No one else was.

The caller never said anything. Lacy told herself that "he'll burn out pretty soon. At least he'll say something." She realized she had already decided the caller was a man.

Station employees went on vacation, and Lacy was shifted to fill in for some of them. One week she was on the air from six A.M. until ten A.M. Just after six, the phone flashed. She answered it. The caller hung up. Then again in the middle of the shift. Then just before ten. Another week she was assigned to the two P.M.–six P.M. shift. The caller did it again.

She felt something funny happening inside of her. The caller was beginning to become a person to her—a man—and she was frightened of him. She asked her superiors to authorize a phone trace on the calls, which they did; but the telephone company said that, because of technical limitations, they were unable to isolate the calls.

Against her will, she began to feel her stomach knot every time she arrived at the studio for her show. The caller had never threatened her, had never said a word. Yet he was reaching her. She began to refuse to answer the phone during the first hour of her shift. She would see the phone blink, and she would know it was the caller, and she would not pick it up. She would talk on the air and play the records, and all the time she would be looking at the light on the phone. Finally, she would make herself pick it up. Then the caller would hang up. Sometimes the caller would let the phone ring for an hour and a half before she picked it up; when he heard her voice, he would replace the receiver.

There were other callers, too, of course; KBCO listeners who wanted her to play records for them. When she looked at the lights blinking, she thought she could tell which callers were normal, and which was the one. "I kind of know what his calls feel like," she said. She realized that such a thing sounded absurd. "I know that something like this can run away with you, but once it's happening, knowing that doesn't help." She had become obsessed with the blinking light: "Every time it blinks, it's like a knife going into me again and again."

He bosses knew that something was wrong. "I listened to her tapes, and it was clear that she was distracted," said Dennis Constantine. "It's fairly easy to tell when a disc jockey isn't paying attention to what she is doing."

To Alix Lacy's great consternation, the presence of the caller was taking over the hours she spent at the studio. "I feel as if he is trying to touch me," she said. "He's not touching me by saying anything; he's touching me by getting me to react to his consistency." Ray Skibitsky told her that by refusing to answer the phone when she thought it was the caller, she was only encouraging him; she was verifying to him that he was getting to her. She knew this was true; still, when she felt it was the caller on the other end, she could not pick up the receiver. She could only stare at the light and try to get through her show.

Her conviction grew stronger. She was fearful that the caller was going to come to the studio with a gun, shoot his way through the door, and come up the stairs to where she sat before the microphone. One afternoon she called Peter Rodman, a KBCO host and Boulder journalist. She told him about her fear about the gun; Rodman said, "Alix the door is glass. If anyone wants to do anything, all he has to do is kick the door in. Why are you thinking about a gun?" Rodman's talk persuaded her to ask the station management to have a man answer her phone for one night; maybe if the caller heard a man's voice, he would stop.

Ray Skibitsky agreed to do it. He came to work with Lacy one evening; when the phone began to blink, he picked it up. Whoever was on the other end hung up. He sat with Lacy throughout her shift. Near the end, the caller hesitated before hanging up. The caller let out an exasperated sigh. It was definitely the sigh of a male. Then the line went dead.

The next two nights, he did not call. Alix Lacy was ecstatic. She thought she had been silly in the extreme for worrying about it. At the end of the week she worked an earlier shift than usual and her voice on KBCO was replaced that night by fellow disc jockey Rick Lofgren. Lofgren worked his shift. When he finished and walked out to his car in the parking lot, one tire had been slashed and all the air let out of another.

Both Lacy and her bosses knew they had a problem. It was not so much a horror story as something even more disturbing: the idea that someone with access to a medium of mass communication could become mentally trapped by one person in the audience with a will to disrupt her life. When Lacy had gone into radio work, she had liked the idea that, sitting behind a microphone in an isolated room, she could reach thousands upon thousands of strangers. Now one of the strangers was reaching her.

"I sensed there was a guy out there doing this," Ray Skibitsky said. "But what was there to do? He obviously gets his gratification and his kicks by doing this to her. But there have been no overt threats. When you look at it objectively, it's just an annoyance. If she could just ignore it, she would see that. But she can't."

When Lacy arrived at work one day, there was a letter addressed to her from Bob Greenlee, the owner of the station.

"I am not unaware of your concern over the belief you are being harassed by a telephone caller," the letter began.

Ray mentioned that he came in this week to answer the phones while you were here and he too senses that there may be someone on the phone who, for whatever reason, gets off on having you answer the phone and then hang up.

As you know, we have little control over sick minds who would do this to someone. Try as we might, it is impossible for us to do anything to trace or catch up with the person calling you. And even though you are upset by having to put up with this situation, I believe it is a continuing disruption of your work at this station and must now step into the matter. I have authorized Dennis Constantine to find a person to answer the phone for you during your shift for the next week. If, at the end of that time, you cannot pull yourself together and live in peace with yourself, the situation is not correctable by any further actions from us. I will need to address the matter of finding another person to do your work. . . . You are an excellent employee, we all like you very much, and hope you can find the inner strength it will require to get over the fear you have.

Alix Lacy decided to take a vacation. As of this writing, that is where she was.

She was sick at heart. She knew that when she returned to work, the caller would be waiting for her; and she knew she could not continue to live her life thinking about him. To her, the only logical solution seemed to be to leave Boulder, or to get out of radio work. It almost made her shake to think about it; the best thing about the vacation was that she did not have to see the phone blink at her every night. She had talked to Constantine and Skibitsky about a possible leave of absence, but she knew that was only delaying her final decision.

She had gotten some jobs around Boulder playing records at parties; it was a big step down from talking to the listeners of KBCO, but at least she could see her audience. She was also studying jazz piano; something was telling her that she had to come up with an alternative way to make a living.

"My voice . . ." she said. "I've always had a voice that people commented on. I just think it's a pleasant and conversational voice. I've never felt it necessary to project my sexuality through my voice. The last thing I ever wanted to do was provoke someone with it.

"I know that if I don't quit, I'm going to get fired. It's funny, isn't it. . . . I know how foolish all of this sounds, and I know that everyone thinks I should just ignore it. I feel like a fool for letting it get to me."

But it has. All over America, there are voices being sent out into the night; all the voices entering all the bedrooms and automobiles and bars. Implicit in the voices is a sense of power; the power to reach people, to touch their minds and change them, if only in small ways. Seldom do you hear about someone touching the voices back.

"There is this movie, *Forbidden Planet*," Lacy said. "It's about this invisible monster that attacks a spaceship. They try to find the monster, but it turns out that there's really nothing there. See, the monster was the subconscious mind of the scientist himself. I've been thinking about that a lot. Why am I creating this invisible monster in my life? And then I realize how far it's gone. I'm even questioning myself."

One thing bothers Lacy most of all, she said. It is a belief she holds—a belief that goes beyond all the rationalizing and all the intellectual understanding of what has happened.

"I'm not afraid, but I know I will meet him someday," she said. "I know how that sounds, but I've thought about it and I know it's true and there's nothing I can do about it. He's created this thing between us, and he's out there, and someday we'll meet."

Managers and Lovers

When mature love blooms in the organization,
top managers must face—and deal
with—its consequences

Eliza G. C. Collins

Two executives, a man and a woman, arrived back at the office after a three-week business trip. Feeling quite pleased with their work, they looked forward to the next day's operations committee meeting, at which the senior executive was to present a report summing up their progress on this first phase of a year-long project. But the pair was not prepared for the reception they met.

The senior executive's briefing got much less attention than did the particulars of his time away from the office. The junior executive's input, which she was sure would be good for her career, was practically ignored. While the two executives had been away, the project had become an office joke.

It was clear that everyone believed "something" had happened on the trip. In this case, "something" had not happened, but because of others' reactions, the two executives decided not to travel together again, even though the project would take longer to complete and might not turn out as well. Other, bigger, things were at stake: the project and their careers.

Many executives might have handled the situation differently. With the influx of women to high managerial positions, it becomes increasingly likely that something will happen on a business trip or during a long night's work. Most often it will be a brief sexual encounter that the two will gladly forget. Although a sexual liaison may be considered immoral, unless it leads to harassment it presents a minor problem to the organization. But on occasion an encounter will develop into a love relationship, which constitutes a threat to the business.

Organizational life has not been known for its abundance of close personal relationships. To maintain objectivity and avoid conflicts of interest, managers have learned to keep a protective distance from the people they work with. Even when executives run into people with whom they share common interests and points of view, they tend to keep their personal likes and dislikes separate from their professional judgments. If they cannot maintain that distance, their business lives are in trouble long before the most difficult of personal relationships intrudes: that of romantic and sexual love.

It is not immediately apparent to some that love between two people in the same company can be either a problem for top management or a threat to the organization. After all, love is a positive emotion that is supposed to make the world go 'round, not under. It is negative emotions, like jealousy or feelings of inferiority, that usually cause the messy personal relationships between people working at the same place.

However messy these kinds of relationships, usually everyone understands who has the most power when the relationships are between bosses and subordinates or peers in an organization. Love between managers is dangerous because it challenges—and can break down—the organizational structure. (The accompanying insert describes what I mean by "love.") For instance, even in this day and age, when a man and a woman fall in love, the relationship often takes on a traditional cast; the male is superior to the female. In a company where the two are high-level managers who are supposed to work together as equals, love's old sexist hierarchy is disruptive. Also, because the lovers are managers, their romance affects the organization's power alliances.

In the past, organizations defended themselves against love's buzz saw. In most companies, executives indulging their power in a sexual way lost not only the esteem of others and credibility but also their jobs. Where sexual liaisons did arise at work, most male executives tacitly agreed that these relationships were only for sexual gratification and that if they threatened the organizational order, the woman could go. Today, because of several factors, neither the abrupt dismissal of the man nor the class-sanctioned attitude toward the woman will work.

One factor is the changing status of, attitudes toward, and numbers of women at work. Another is men's growing awareness and acceptance of how adult males develop and how their needs change. For these reasons, relationships between men and women will more and more concern love between powerful managers, not merely sex or love only between lower-level peers. Executives will need new ways to think about this phenomenon; neither the old sex-laden concepts nor simplistic policies will apply to what is already occurring and will continue to occur in organizations.

Of course, wherever a diversity of people congregates, a diversity of relationships will spring up. In corporations the possibilities are numerous; what develops depends on the characteristics of the partners. There can be intimate relationships between heterosexuals or homosexuals. They can be based on friendship, sex, or love and be between peers, persons at different levels, or persons of different marital status. Here I am concerned with relationships between men and women who both have some authority over others. When one or both of the partners is married, the impact on the organization is likely to be more intense.

How should management react when a man and a woman, both competent and successful executives, fall in love? Should a top executive intervene and discuss the relationship with the participants, and, if so, what should he or she propose?

Before answering these questions, let's look first at a few of the cases that have led me to decide that love between two executives can create a problem in the organization because of what happens to the people involved. I base my observations on actual situations that severely threatened careers and organizational effectiveness. I do not mean to imply that every outcome I describe in the following paragraphs will occur when a high-level man and woman in the same company fall in love, but that some of the same patterns will emerge and their repercussions will be great.

OPPORTUNITY & NEED

People generally fall in love and marry others who are like them in some important ways. In the old days, most male executives who had sexual relationships with women at work did not consider them potential mates. In all likelihood, the differences in the men's and women's actual or aspired-to social status ruled out marriage; any alliance was seen as play.

The ambitious young man in search of a place in the sun was more likely to fantasize about the boss's daughter than about the girl next door who became a secretary. When the college-educated careerist married the girl of his dreams, she didn't go to work. She had the option to stay home and raise a family, and almost invariably chose to. Of course, numbers of male executives did marry their secretaries and have lived very happy lives. But the lingering perception that it is OK for men—but not for women—to sow a few wild oats reinforced the notion that men at work were on the lookout for ripe fields to cultivate.

Because the mythical female at work was unlikely to be a mate and was not taken seriously, the office relationships that occurred were, for the most part, short-term sexual sprees. Only under a few conditions would an affair lead to an important long-term commitment: when the woman's social class outside the company was higher than her class role inside or when she was extraordinarily attractive or talented.

What Has Changed?

Today things are different. Regardless of their backgrounds, women are less willing to accept the playmate role in which the man invests less in the relationship than they do. Even if she starts out as a willing partner, a woman may not just go quietly away when an affair becomes disruptive; she may sue, file sexual harassment charges, or simply make the executive's workday a series of unpleasant confrontations and embarrassing moments.

Through education, acceptance by industry, and affirmative action, more working women have jobs that are equal, or nearly equal, to men's, and they are more often seen as appropriate partners for long-term relationships. Four cases highlight these changes. In each, the woman involved has a higher status than she might have had in the past, when her position would have been filled by a man:

- At a large diversified company, a group manager, Daniel Brown, fell in love with a woman, Sheila Murray, who reported to one of his vice presidents. Although not on the same organizational level as Daniel, Sheila was close to his and was well educated, so her social eligibility was not in question.
- Sam Dunn, a high-level executive in the headquarters of a bank, fell in love with a woman, Judith Green, who was a vice-president.
- A woman who was being considered for a top executive post in a large company fell in love with an executive in another division.
- A female associate in a large law firm fell in love with a partner in the firm.

The dynamics of any relationship in which the woman is an equal of the man outside the company and has enough status inside to be a colleague are very different from those of a relationship between unequals. It is more probable that sexual attraction between two people will lead to genuine love; for instance, many of the characteristics of a good working relationships between superiors and subordinates—frequent interaction, mutual respect and trust—can contribute to the development of a romantic attachment.[1] When two managers experience this interaction and have close contact, they have to consider the possibility of a long-term relationship, and recognition of the possibility increases the probability.

While, for example, group manager Daniel found Sheila, the assistant to the vice president, very attractive, he probably wouldn't have approached her if he had been merely looking for a sexual fling. The office affair has many mundane as well as moral constraints. Anyone looking for a good reason not to act out sexual fantasies or satisfy lust inside the organization can find one. One reason is practical: it usually doesn't work very well. Another is that it is frequently actionable.

But Daniel did approach Sheila for the most compelling reason of all; like the men in the other cases, he was emotionally receptive. He had

---

1. According to James G. Clawson and Kathy E. Kram, "Managing Cross-Sex Developmental Relationships," *Business Horizons,* forthcoming.

reached a time in his life when a desire for intimacy outweighed his need to achieve.

Transitions

During a man's 30s, work is often far more important than any other thing in his life.[2] Such a man relegates other aspects of his life, such as concern with relationships, feelings, nurturing, equality, and love, to his wife. All the men in the four cases had at one time or another been married. The group manager was married when he met the assistant to the vice president; the bank executive was also married; the division executive had been married but divorced three or four years before meeting the female executive; and the lawyer was divorced.

In all these examples, the men were or had been married to women who might be characterized as conventional—they played a traditional, passive role so that their husbands could move up in their organizations. The marriages came apart because *both* parties in each decided it was over.

As men approach their 40's, work may suddenly lose its emotional hold, and they start caring more about a personal life. If a man turns to his wife at this time he may find nobody at home. In these cases, the men were in mid-life transition when they became involved with women at work; the youngest was 39 and the oldest, 46. Early in their careers they had made choices about the dreams they wished to pursue, had achieved them, and were reevaluating the fundamental values by which they were going to live. With organizational status came the realization that they could choose what they did all day long. A top executive has freedom, power, and money and, with them, the potential for emotional affluence. Richer in resources, he can ask more of life.

Available and willing, the men in these cases became involved with senior females who were not passive put powerful equals. The women were not only sources of acceptance and love but also people who understood—and did not try to pull them away from—the executives' worlds.

Even if both the man and woman knew that love in the office was a dangerous thing, they could not avoid each other. In all the cases their jobs required frequent contact; opportunity and need eventually wore down prudence.

THE LOVE AFFAIR

Love is blind, so they say, and older lovers are only slightly more perceptive than younger ones. Both are blind about the persons they love and

---

2. Daniel H. Levinson, *The Seasons of a Man's Life* (New York: Knopf, 1978).

about the reactions of other people. This blindness makes the lovers unaware of their impact on others and of possible repercussions on them and their careers.

After a few months of unplanned and then planned encounters, the two executives in the first case arrived at that point where sexual activity is not merely gratifying but also loving. Despite occasional feelings of intense guilt (he was married) and anxiety, they saw their affair as loving. Like most lovers, they thought they were essentially innocent and under love's protective umbrella. The two were first blissfully unaware that anyone noticed and, as no news to the contrary came, that anyone cared. Ultimately, however, people came to know about the affair, and trouble began.

Warning bells finally rang out when the lovers attended a presentation ceremony dinner along with the company's top people. Using Sheila's job as a justification, group manager Daniel arranged to have her go along. During dinner somebody suggested to him that it was inappropriate to bring Sheila, whose formal status was not the same as that of the other guests. So the first objection to the affair was couched in organizational terms. Daniel remembers hearing the objection and thinking, "Can't they see that this is different? Organizational politics have nothing to do with it."

In his innocence about his feelings, Daniel misinterpreted the depth of others' anxiety. From the organization's point of view, however, the actions and feelings of others had now become as important as those of the lovers themselves.

Anxious Outsiders

In the first place, others in the organization hadn't been as blind as the lovers. Almost from the beginning they'd been aware that something was going on. In all the cases the female executives expected surprise when they finally discussed the affair with their immediate superiors but instead found that the superiors had not only known but had also been deeply disturbed. People in love look different. They glow. But those on the outside don't always see the glow as love; sometimes it appears to be a stigma left by the seamiest kind of sex. Particularly in one case some onlookers projected their own nonloving sexual fantasies onto the lovers. Through a filter of lust, they saw the romance as a danger to the social order.

The degree of organizational anxiety is determined by a number of variables. Whether the male executive's leadership style is such that he has close, warm relationships with subordinates and peers or is coolly distant, his coworkers are likely to be made quite anxious by such an affair. If they fancy themselves as protégés, they will see any redirection of the executive's affection—to a woman or to anyone else—as a loss. If they feel removed from the executive, they will see anyone getting close as an extra threat. They will be jealous and angry and feel abandoned. To alleviate these feelings they'll politicize them and assert that the affair disrupts the social order. In all these cases, subordiantes and peers started making moral judgments, such as, "He shouldn't do this at work" and "It isn't right."

The second source of anxiety is the way the affair threatens the home lives of others, especially if one or both lovers are married. When executives of a company and their spouses get together on social occasions and the lovers appear, couples whose marriages are shaky can become anxious and angry. To avoid dealing with the problems in their own marriages, coworkers and their spouses may project their anxiety onto the executives who are in love.

Open about the fact that they were becoming very close, bank executive Sam Dunn and vice president Judith Green made a fellow vice president, Jim Silver, exceedingly uncomfortable. Judith would sit in Sam's office and chat during part of the day, and the couple frequently spent evenings with people from the bank. Unfortunately, Jim Silver's wife, Alice, was one of Sam's wife's closest friends. The two married couples had socialized often and lived near one another.

The lover's relationship progressed at work, but Sam's wife, Marie, did not know about it. Alice knew about the affair, however, and felt disloyal to Marie. She felt she was being asked to live a lie—at least by omission. When Marie finally expressed concern that something was very wrong with her marriage, Alice didn't know what to say. In her distress she blamed Jim for being friends with "such a man" and asserted that she would be the next wife to go. Pots on the back burner began to bubble over.

Outsiders also fear that the formal and informal communication networks of the organization will be crossed by pillow talk. If the male executive has a higher position than the female, his immediate subordinates as well as her peers can fear that their own confidences have been broken. The subordinates begin to fantasize: "Does she know something about me?" "Is she smirking?" "How does the boss see me?" "I've got to be careful with her; whatever I say might get back to him."

In one case, the female executive was one of a group that met regularly to air complaints by grousing to one another at lunch. Whereas before the group could openly complain, "We can't figure this out because the old man doesn't know what the hell he wants," now they fell silent. In the silence, they withheld other information as well; the organization's informal communications network started going awry.

The fourth source of pain relates to the third. In the case of the affair in the bank, Judith's male colleagues engaged in some outrageous behavior. Having difficulty imagining that the relationship might proceed toward love, they saw it as smut. The male peers saw the banker, "papa" (who was enormously respected, competent, and much liked), take up with a colleague who was not only attractive but also unabashedly sexy. Her peers did not know how to handle their own relationships with her; she was unusual, both assertive and sexual, and very threatening. A few coworkers fancied that she was attracted to them and became angry and hostile when the affair became public. Judith received a number of hate notes in the inter office mail and on at least one occasion was insulted by an angry peer. Over time such incidents caused unbearable tension, even for many who were not directly involved.

Another source of subordinates' anxiety is the possibility that the male executive will lose power and the ability to influence on their behalf. To many, love flies in the face of power, and power may lose. We want our leaders to be pleasant but also tough when they have to be. We fear that a manager who loves a person we consider taboo has lost his or her judgment and may stop exercising authority. In the bank, people saw their boss losing power to a woman who was also very threatening. Some assumed that equity would go and she would receive special consideration. The organization began to tremble.

As the affair ripens into something important, more and more people learn of it and anxiety becomes widespread. People may really care about the man, be glad that he's having what appears to be a wonderful experience, and hope it will be important to his life. They may also care about the woman and feel the same things. In the bank case, however, subordinates were so threatened that they became increasingly ambivalent and suffered the pain this emotion brings. Because it wouldn't go away, they tried to resolve the conflict by driving out what they saw as its source.

The Woman as Scapegoat

In the bank case, Judith suffered attacks from within the organization. Men began to look at her and think, "How could Sam possibly fall for that one? She's a pushy, aggressive broad." They began to make comments about the old man being "off his rocker" for falling for someone "who's a real bitch." (Other women in the organization may also try to sabotage the female executive.[3]) In picking up on these attacks, Judith realized her worst fears, and her self-doubts began to surface.

At the beginning of an affair, a woman, like a man, is in a state of heightened sensual awareness, loses critical faculties, and almost willingly gives up judgment and reason. As reason, like knowledge in the garden of Eden, returns she will question whether others know, and curiosity about other people's knowledge represents a real wish to tell them, to go public.

---

3. Robert E. Quinn, "Coping with Cupid: The Formation, Impact and Management of Romantic Relationships in Organizations," *Administrative Science Quarterly.* March 1977, p. 34.

In these cases, for example, male peers and superiors expressed subtle hostility, first marked by withdrawal. They didn't ask the women to lunch as often, stopped conversations when the women approached, and tinged their smiles with sarcasm. The women were being iced, and they knew it. Because they were cut out, they felt illicit, immoral, or dirty. At the worst times, these women believed what others implied: that they were no better than the secretarial meat of the corporate-caveman era.

As a rule, members of minorities look over their shoulders with caution; many executive women think "there but for the grace of God go I" about the secretarial pool. A terrible double bind underlies many problems women have in organizations. To get in the arena with men, many women believe they must pretend to be comfortable playing a lot of roles, roles they—or any other woman—have never played before. The affair threatens to reveal the pretense: that she is just a woman after all. Making the affair public legitimizes the woman's position again; at least she doesn't have to worry about being taken for a ride.

When the affairs I'm discussing went public (as most eventually do), the female executives thought they should be included in the settings that were important to their lovers. Intellectually, the women understood that they did not hold the same organizational status as their men. In one case the woman agreed to skip the annual meeting functions and attend only social events, where she would behave very much like a wife. But playing a part that they had ruled out irritated the women, especially because they thought they had brought knowledge of the business and some power to the relationship.

At the same time these female executives agreed to play the wifely role, they were aware that the men in the company didn't want them at social or business functions. These assertive, powerful women who had risen to high levels were not going to be snubbed without fighting back. Survivors, they first became angry at their peers and their peers' wives and, finally, the company.

The women were mainly angry, however, because others viewed them as playthings. That made them afraid; it raised suspicions that they were risking their careers for nothing. Each woman had sacrificed a personal life for her career; now they seemed near to sacrificing their careers for threatened relationships. They felt victimized. In anger, the women in these cases turned to their men and confronted them with the insensitivity of the louts they worked with. Like the organizational outsiders who projected their fears on the women, the women turned theirs onto the onlookers. The male lover was then in the middle.

The Male Executive's Quandary

Caught between loyalty to his subordinates and peers and to the woman he loves, the male executive begins to feel something he hasn't felt for a long time: out of control. The organization is threatened in another way.

If the female executive escalates her demands that she be with him and he capitulates, he may begin to think his fellow executives are unworthy and unfair. That can produce organizational chaos. If he says, on the other hand, "Wait a minute, I have to put the organization first," she will automatically feel slighted. Their relationship may suffer, since they began it in part because they were equals.

In one case the male executive decided that it would be better that the female executive not join him on a business trip even though she had a good business excuse. The female could see the point—in part. But once he had gone, she decided he cared more about his work than about her, that his love was contingent and had limitations. She remembers that she began to see every option as a catastrophe; her emotional needle swung between extremes of abandonment and submission.

In such predicaments, the male executives become angry that they cannot protect the women they love. In the four cases, all the male managers felt indignant and guilty that the women had to take the risks and pay the prices while they could do nothing. They lost not only a sense of control but also their view of themselves as protectors.

Ultimately the lovers may turn their anger at the corporation onto each other; as they begin to doubt the relationship's value, they lose confidence in it and begin to treat each other differently. One man remembers beginning to believe what his subordinates had hinted—that his lover really was a bitch. The female executive's response was to subscribe to a lot of feminist rhetoric about powerful males. Innocent attraction became organizational and emotional turmoil.

FROM DEATH TO LIFE

Because the lovers are blind and others around them are anxious, resolution of the conflict falls into the hands of the top manager to whom both executives ultimately report. In the long run, the most fragile thing is probably not the corporation or the people but the love relationship. The top manager must decide whether and how to act and needs to keep one inescapable reality in mind. Regardless of what the manager does, it will be judged at a deep emotional level by others, and most harshly if the relationship suffers. Despite fears, ambivalence, and anxiety, everyone still loves a love affair.

At the outset the decision to intervene seems to pose the thorniest problem. An unwritten rule states that managers do not become involved in the private lives of their subordinates, especially highlevel subordinates. Most managers are inclined to look away from a subordinate's personal problem and hope it will clear itself up.

In the case of purely sexual, transitory affairs, that attitude has worked and may still. A manager can reasonably assume that a high-level executive, whether male or female, will soon tire of a romp. Even if a transitory sexual liaison has organizational repercussions, no one doubts what comes first or what the solution will ultimately be if it doesn't stop.

But when genuine love is involved, the solution isn't so obvious. Can a manager afford to ignore the situation? I don't think so. Ignoring the problem means the top manager has no control over the outcome. Moreover, others will feel the loss of control and resent the fact that he or she has not acted in a situation that causes them pain and disrupts work.

In the case of Sam and Judith, the pair first decided that he would leave the bank despite his superior position. They thought he had a better chance to obtain a good job elsewhere. But most important, they wanted to take a stand that would explicitly favor the woman, whom they both saw as more the victim. They presented their decision to the bank's CEO, who remembers thinking: "I can't afford to lose him. This couple understands my position but won't accept it."

The CEO was so upset about losing Sam that he called him into his office and said, "You work it out; I'm not going to take any action." In effect, he pushed the problem down into the organization. Sam eventually decided to stay, but the repercussions of the CEO's inaction were vast. Jim and Alice Silver felt such stress that they had to get outside help and were understandably very angry at the CEO for not dealing with the problem. Jim was unable to talk to either Sam or Judith about his difficulties. A friend of both, he thought they had enough problems of their own.

The question of when to intervene is easier to answer: as soon as the manager knows about the relationship. If the rule is that the person at the top is the last to know, by the time he or she does, you can assume that everyone else has known for weeks or months. Repercussions have already been felt. Of course, the superior must rule out the possibility that the relationship is simply a long-playing dalliance. A short discussion with the senior member of the pair will make the affair's status apparent. If it is merely a sexual liaison, a word of warning will most likely be sufficient to stop it.

What to do in the case of real love is more difficult to say. The manager's task is to protect the interests of the corporation and preserve the careers of the two people if possible. It is a difficult juggling act.

Much depends on how managers deal with their subordinates. If the chief is open and can talk candidly, he or she ought to arrange to discuss the affair with the couple as soon as organizational consequences are apparent. In any case, the boss's attitude and conduct of the meeting are crucial to the outcome. Here are some guidelines that may help:

1. Treat the relationship as a conflict of interest. In deciding what to do, a top manager needs to understand how the pain is distributed.

When two vice presidents love each other, the other vice presidents who compete for remaining resources and power may feel outweighed. They are now up against a coalition. Also, if the two departments supervised by the two executives often conflict, resolution becomes more and more difficult. The couple's respective subordinates may have trouble being candid with their bosses, and the couple may be unable to confront one another even when it's necessary to protect their people.

The top manager needs to be clear in his own mind before he can help the two people see that their love affair represents a conflict of interest in the organization. In talking to couples, managers must stress that they are going to deal with the romance as they would any business problem—as equitably as possible.

This stance has two virtues. First, it is realistic. The love affair between two executives with status and at least some power is a conflict of interest. They cannot be, and should not be expected to be, objective in their decisions when someone they love might be hurt or put at a disadvantage by the outcome. Second, this point of view takes the focus off the romance, puts it on the business issue, and does not force the two managers to go on the defensive about the affair.

The top manager should not attack the love relationship. Ultimately both the corporation and the people involved will survive, but the relationship may not. Because of its fragility and because both executives will fight to protect it, the boss must not denigrate it.

It may be difficult for top managers to be supportive. They may feel that the affair is immoral, especially if one or both of the partners is married. Bosses may judge people against their own interpretations of God's law. Top managers' spouses may also feel threatened and try to convince the managers to take a judgmental position. Or the spouse may become so vexed that the executive takes the discomfort at home out on the couple.

Even for the boss whose principles are offended, it is more humane to deal compassionately with the tendency to "sin" than to judge harshly. All of us have principles we hold dear. But to act on them in a business situation may be unwise. In approaching what has become a business decision, executives often have to subordinate personal moral stances to resolve organizational conflicts fairly. If bosses can see the relationship in a light not cast with purple overtones, they will give the couple a chance to decide what they want to do, free of organizational pressures.

Another difficulty is that the manager may simply be unable to imagine the experience. The top manager in the diversified company where Daniel and Sheila worked admitted that he couldn't "catch" the feelings, couldn't remember the innocence, the luminosity, the clear restructuring of what was important in life. After talking with the couple and suspending his own belief system, however, he was able to see that perhaps the liaison was not silly and that the couple was enjoying one of life's great experiences.

2. Advise the couple to get outside help.   Because the boss is a member of the organization, the executives may not trust his or her assessment of the situation no matter how good their personal relationship. Their hackles raised, the two executives will be unable to accept their boss's judgment on the messiness of the situation. They see it as yet another attack. A specialized counselor can help the couple see the situation more clearly and understand that what happened makes emotional sense. The boss needs to realize that the primary relationship is between two people; of itself, the feeling they share is not an organizational phenomenon. First the pair needs a chance to determine whether their relationship can or should survive.

3. Persuade the couple that either the person least essential to the company or both have to go.   Coming to the recognition that someone must go is painful but, I regret to say, inevitable. To some this resolution may seem obvious and straightforward. But real cases like the ones I've been discussing raise so many personal and difficult issues that no solution is obvious or easy.

In the first place, many younger women and men simply will not understand that letting the less important person—in almost all cases a woman—go is the fairest action. Younger people are committed to equality; they would see a love-related termination as pure recidivism. Though I arrived at it with great reluctance, the conclusion is inescapable. At present, most people in organizations are not trained to handle such relationships or their own responses to them. That makes it improbable that a high-level love relationship will survive in today's organization.

In collegial, nonhierarchical, or professional organizations, where power and communications networks are less important, the relationship may survive, especially if the couple marries. I know of places where it has happened—not always smoothly, but with everyone still in one place. Love may also survive organizational tensions if it arises between two people in divisions that don't interact often, but it is unlikely that executives in those divisions will meet often enough to begin a love affair. In a large organization where resources are scarce and power is important, the chances of both partners staying with the company are minimal, no matter how equal their status.

In cases of two equals, one must leave, and I recommend that it should be the less effective person from a business point of view. If both really are equal, the woman should stay and the man go because although it might not be sexist to let the woman go, it can appear that way. When the status is unequal, however, the lower-ranking person must leave. Taking this stand is difficult and often heartbreaking. But bosses must not be swayed by emotion or think they are merely clearing up misunderstandings between subordinates or between subordinates and themselves. No matter how much everyone understands the beauty of a love relationship, it can't survive if the less valuable person stays.

If the couple chooses to stay and live through the consequences and doesn't have the power to change the organizational structure, I can predict how the relationship will end. It will come under more stress; she (assuming the lower-ranked lover is a woman) will start seeing the organization as the enemy; he will resent how others in the organization are treating her; he will start to resent her for attacking people he cares about. If the affair ends, others in the organization will move in for the kill. She will be cut out of power and may end up a skeleton in the organizational closet. At that point she has no option but to leave if she wants to save her relationship and nurture her career.

One woman became aware that she simply couldn't handle the hostility of her peers. Friends to whom she had looked for help and support withdrew. Increasingly she realized she couldn't even go into her lover's office for support. Finally, she knew she had to get out. Once she had left, the company gradually returned to normal. It took a while for people to forgive him and for him to forgive those who had been mean to her. But he gradually understood that her perception of the events may not have been exact.

If the male executive insists on going, the female may become an outcast. Most likely she'll lose much of her influence. Her superiors will blame her for the loss of an executive they see as more valuable. Very often, if the higher-status person leaves, the lower will soon go as well.

The simple fact is that for the business's purpose, the most valuable person ought to stay, and in today's organization, considering seniority and time as investments, that person is probably the man. Managers need to believe in the inevitability of this outcome because they will have to counter endless entreaties and pleas for fairness.

The woman who has fought her way to an executive position may think she is being asked to leave simply because she's a woman. She doesn't like that, doesn't want to get out, doesn't want to transfer. She has relationships and friends she wants to keep, especially if the love affair is not at a point where she's certain she wants to stay with him forever. She faces an enormous career risk without knowing whether it will be worthwhile. Of course the man takes a risk that even after the woman goes, others may think that he is in the wrong. He may lose respect and never regain it.

4. Help the ousted executive find a new and perhaps better job.   The top manager must help the person asked to leave because of romance. Any boss should want to resolve a conflict of interest to everyone's advantage. Moreover, the top manager will want to boost the ego of the person departing, especially if the organization has treated the couple as if they had committed a crime instead of as valuable contributors.

Finally, the manager should not ignore the feelings of the executive who stays behind or of those who have witnessed and taken part in the decision. Regardless of how right they think they are, everyone but the most callous will, after the threat is removed, feel guilty. To assuage those feelings, the top manager must assure everyone that the organization has done everything it can to make certain the departing executive is not tossed out on the street.

A Happy Ending

Let's look at the outcome of the cases to find out if fariness is really the most important consideration.

It became clear to group manager Daniel Brown that he must seek a divorce. He did and moved out of his home, while the assistant to his vice president, Sheila Murray, got a good job in another company. Their subsequent marriage seems quite stable and satisfying.

In the bank case, Judith Green, the female vice president, also quit. Uncertain about the maturity of their relationship, Judith and Sam Dunn decided not to live together for a while. She wanted to keep her independence in case things didn't work out. Judith got a job that was as good as, if not better than, the one she left. For six months before deciding to marry, they spent a lot of time in one place or the other. Eventually they married, bought a new house together, and began a new life.

Once Jim Silver stopped agonizing about Judith and Sam and his wife stopped fantasizing about being deserted, things calmed down. Jim and Alice were able to spend more time with each other and found out how much more they needed one another.

The two executives in the large company are also married now. She has a job with another company and received a major promotion in the past year.

At the law firm the outcome was equally bright. The woman was on the track to a high-level job when she and a partner in the firm decided to marry. She informed her boss and he helped her find a good job with another firm, where she is now on her way to becoming a partner. Colleagues in the original firm are still friends.

'TIS BETTER TO HAVE LOVED

The issues cases like these raise are numerous, but I'd like to summarize those I see as most important:

- Until more women are at high executive levels, the woman will usually be the prime victim when two executives fall in love, even if she is a senior member in the organization.[4] Although it is realistic that the least valuable person leave, because that person is so often a woman, it is a sexist solution. Organizations should, therefore, try to defuse the gender issue. In part, they should deal with the problem as a conflict of interest. Increasing the numbers of women at high levels will make it more likely, though in no way guarantee, that resolutions are not sexist.

- Male executives attracted to lower-level female executives will be in a painful and serious dilemma. To begin a flirtation, to see her outside of work and expose her to gossip, could be to end her career in that company. The female executive also has some responsibility, but it is less onerous because she will mainly hurt herself. Both have to be aware of the impact their affair will have on the employment policies of the company.

- The "gentlemanly" hands-off way of approaching personal matters disrupts the goals of the corporation. Such love relationships will not go away if ignored; they will most likely lead to organizational stress. Executives must learn to deal with these messy human problems. In fact, the way they approach sensitive issues like love and sex will influence in part the way people view management.

Sadly, most people lack the skills to deal with these issues. More people will need to be aware of the effect of the love affair on the organization, its implications if it lasts, and their own likely responses to it. Until people reach this level of sophistication, even close, platonic friendships between men and women will be affected. As more women enter higher levels in organizations these issues will surface and have to be dealt with. Ultimately we will all be less squeamish, and male-female friendships will form without arousing suspicion.

Until then, clear-cut company policies should outline the conflicts and probable consequences of these romances. Explicit policies will make executives understand that to break a taboo, a relationship should be worth the price they will pay. Moreover, a policy allays the fears of others in the organization that things will get completely out of control and will mitigate some of the potential organizational chaos.

Top managers have to take the lead in dealing with these complicated situations. Regardless of how clumsy their attempts, it is better to have tried and failed than never to have tried at all.

---

4. "Coping with Cupid,"
ibid., p. 44.

Letters to the Editor

edited by Julie A. Fernandez

MANAGERS AND LOVERS

In "Managers and Lovers" (September-October 1983) Eliza G. C. Collins makes no mention of the non-executive woman in the male manager's life—his wife. The executive would not in most cases have reached his high-paying, attractive position unless someone kept his kids off his back, ran an efficient home for him, and catered to his demanding life. But when that someone is about to reap the rewards for this harrowing period, in steps a beautifully dressed, intelligent, and usually younger woman, an executive, who walks off with the spoils and leaves the devastated spouse to her meager life.

Ms. Collins eliminates from her discussion the most important elements of all—the high cost and the pain of infidelity, immorality, and broken hearts.

Anonymous

I am troubled that Ms. Collins believes that even love cannot surmount corporate interests. As a manager who has experienced "love at work," I can only assure her the Freud was right when he said that *Lieb und Arbeit* (love and work) are essential for a well-adjusted, mature existence. Admittedly, they usually appear in our lives in separate little boxes, if we are lucky enough to find love at all.

Eric Fromm extols love as an ennobling experience that "breaks through the walls which separate man from his fellow men." I know of no better way for managers to understand what goes on in the company than to get themselves "unseparated" with the help of love.

I am appalled by the author's suggestion that given a love situation in the company, the woman will probably get sacked because she is lower on the totem pole. This seems like a reversion to the medieval notion that the woman in an affair is a harlot, an adultress, a seducer, while the man is just having a little fun. I hope we are not reinventing that.

But since we agree that love, at least in the abstract, is a good thing, my question is, whose business is it anyway? I think it is the business of those in love—period. If love in the corporation is to be defined as dysfunctional, are we now to have "love hunts" as the successor to "witch hunts"? Will we hear "I believe those two are in love so let's get rid of her"?

In a lifetime of working I have managed enough people to develop my own golden rule for performance evaluation: judge people by how well they do their jobs. The further we stray from that basic consideration, the closer we come to invading individual rights concerning such things as religion, sexual preference, politics, and race, none of which is the corporation's business.

Robert Schrank
Visiting Professor
Cornell University
School of Industrial and Labor
Relations
Ithaca, New York

While I, too, have seen negative results of love relationships within organizations such as those the author reports, I find her position and her advice to top management highly questionable, if not irresponsible. In her advice (curiously subtitled "From death to life") Ms. Collins assumes that a love relationship is a conflict of interest.

For a policy such as the author advocates to be accepted as nondiscriminatory, it would have to be established that a personal relationship between a man and a woman poses a greater potential conflict of interest than the relationship between intimate friends of the same sex or of different sexes or between family members, all of which exist in many organizations. I cannot imagine how Ms. Collins can defend, let alone enforce, a policy that discriminates against those who are in love rather than those who are involved in a sexual liaison.

The fact that people often lack the skills to deal effectively with issues of intimacy should not force management to make arbitrary policies. Rather, the standard for all employees, whether colleagues, friends, family members, or lovers, should be one that calls for business-like conduct, responsible and equitable decision making, effective performance, and professional integrity. The challenge is to set standards of adult, ethical behavior and to help men and women learn to work together productively.

We are all still learning. Thinking about and discussing these issues together helps. It is possible for love and professional integrity to coexist.

Jeanne Bosson Driscoll
Partner
Driscoll Consulting Group
Williamstown, Massachusetts

In her article, Eliza G. C. Collins writes movingly of the complications of love among executives. But the article took a gratuitous sideswipe at secretaries, with whom executives, by *droit du seigneur,* may dally but—good heavens—couldn't possibly respect as equals.

After almost two bitter and impoverished years of being locked out of professional employment, I know that to many, perhaps most, employers, support staff is "secretarial meat." On the other hand, for the author to take this outrageous attitude for granted suggests that she is either so cynical or so supine that she will willingly placate the white male gatekeepers of privilege at the expense of female proles.

Recently we have seen all sorts of vicious efforts made to impose a self-fulfilling economic caste system on women and other relatively powerless groups. When my modest professional position disappeared, I faced a climate in which I could not get reemployed. In a desperate effort to survive, I was forced to labor on piecework for poverty wages with no security, no schedule, no benefits, no rights, and no recognition.

I soon noticed that my applications for even low-level positions in my field or for jobs with prospects for advancement were routinely rejected, often in favor of the applications of younger women with fewer qualifications but whose combination of wide-eyed deference and perky executive pretentions seemed to gratify the middle-aged male ego.

These women are often favored and patronized by male mentors who find female peers threatening. Such women are merely ornamental in meetings and luncheons and, as they usually do not have children to support, they can afford "success costumes." Many are able and talented, and all are completely convinced that their superior intelligence and education alone account for the preferential treatment they receive.

In short, I found that my qualifications often were irrelevant because of a hankering for romance in the executive suite and because, at 50, I was not "tender" meat. On the other hand, every office was willing to use and abuse my secretarial skills, provided I subscribed to the myth that my low pay was for skills and labor, not for the knowledge, experience, and judgment I shared with other professionals.

Thus, employers carefully ignore the corrections a good secretary routinely makes in their spelling, grammar, and syntax. Yet an "editor" making the same changes is praised and well paid for doing so because the status of the person who does the work determines how it will be valued.

I am sure that there are many middle-aged women like myself who have been forced to play the martyr while others further their careers. Some women resign themselves and embrace the role thrust on them: doing the worst tasks and being paid in the devalued coin of backhanded praise. (Why are "indispensable" people always underpaid?)

Those professional young women who recoil from any identification with secretaries, in or out of a pool, may be fortunate enough to continue to enjoy and consolidate their advantages. But, on the other hand, they may not always be immune to job segregation and other types of

discrimination against women. If they lose their jobs at middle age, they may find that only tender meat sells in the job market.
Winifred Scheffler
(Address and affiliation withheld)

Corporate Tragedies: Teaching Companies to Cope with Evil

Ian I. Mitroff and Ralph H. Kilmann

Most of us are unaware that we have the following unspoken compact with life: "The world is inherently orderly and predictable. It will behave as it always has; the worst will not happen to me." Imagine the shock that occurs to an individual or to a corporation when something so terrible and unpredictable happens that it shatters our belief in the orderliness of the world.

Of events in recent memory, the one that best captures the nature of this shock is the Tylenol incident. This event shows just how fragile the assumptions are on which we base our daily actions. No other phenomenon presents more of a challenge to the education of future managers and to the attitudes of current managers toward the surrounding world.

Ever since the Tylenol tragedy first broke, we have been engaged in a study of the wider range of tragedies that can befall business organizations. The Tylenol case is an example of a larger class which we call "the unthinkable." We have been asking three questions:

- Is there a list of the unthinkables that can beset any business?
- Why is the unthinkable more prevalent in today's world?
- What can business do to cope more effectively with the unthinkable?

Our study of corporate tragedies shows that, although it is virtually impossible to prevent all tragedies from occurring, one can think about nearly every aspect of them prior to their occurrence. We believe that thinking about the unthinkable is absolutely vital if a business is to be in a position to cope more effectively with such tragedies. Coping is thus the key; prevention is not.

From *New Management*, Vol. I, No. 4, 1984, pp. 48–53. Reprinted by permission.

CATEGORIZING EVIL

We have been able to identify four basic types of unthinkables that have recently befallen businesses. We make no claim that these exhaust all the kinds of unthinkable acts that could occur, but these four are sufficient to get an organization thinking about the worst that could happen to it. The four kinds of evils are:

- Tampering (the evil from without);
- Unplanned, unwanted defects (the evil from within);
- Unwanted compatibility (the evil of the parasite);
- Projection (the evil in the mind's eye).

Let us look at examples of each.

Tampering, the Evil From Without: Tylenol   On September 29, 1982, **Mary Kellerman** and the brothers **Adam** and **Steve Janus**, all of suburban Chicago, died from taking Extra-Strength Tylenol capsules. Cyanide had been injected in the capsules. In time, five more deaths were to be linked directly to cyanide-laced Tylenol capsules.

Johnson and Johnson (J&J), the parent company of McNeil (the maker of Tylenol), then recalled some 31 million bottles of the product with a retail value of over $100 million. As a consequence, J&J thirdquarter earnings dropped from 78 cents a share in 1981 to 51 cents in 1982. The company had originally projected that Tylenol would garner a billion dollars in sales in 1983. After the tragedy, analysts estimated that the product would earn half of that.

The major dimensions of this kind of tragedy stand out in sharp relief: the loss of eight lives and tremendous amounts of money. If these are not enough to get business to think seriously about the unthinkable then perhaps nothing will.

The Evil From Within: P&G's Rely   All manufacturers know the fear that one of their products might somehow become responsible for widespread harm or even death. What's worse, this could occur despite the best of intentions, and with no actions on the part of evil external actors, but because lurking somewhere within the product, there is an unknown evil. It happened to Procter and Gamble (P&G).

In September 1980, after a wave of unfavorable publicity, P&G was forced to withdraw its Rely tampons product from the market. According to a *Fortune* article, "government researchers reported that over 70% of toxic-shock patients in one study had worn [the] single brand [Rely]." While P&G's top scientists strongly disputed the government's findings, P&G nevertheless took a $75-million loss on its Rely business. Although Rely accounted for less than 1% of P&G's total annual sales of over $10 billion, taking it off the market still cut nearly a dollar off P&G's net earnings per share of $7.78.

What's most frustrating is that other than an "association" with tampons in general (and with P&G's Rely in particular), no one knows for sure why tampons "cause" TSS, and there is no definitive proof that they do. The best thinking of the research community is that a toxin produced by a bacteria, staphylococcus aureus, is the underlying cause.

Similar to the Tylenol incident, this is a case of an unknown killer. The difference is that the Tylenol killer was an evil *human agent*, whereas the Rely killer was an impersonal *biological mechanism* that was triggered by the interaction between the physical properties of the product and the biological properties of its users.

The Evil of the Parasite: Atari   Suppose your business was based upon providing clean entertainment for the entire family. Suppose also that someone made an unauthorized X-rated component that was compatible with your product. This happened to Atari, the well-known maker of video games and equipment, when American Multiple Industries released an "adult" game cartridge called *Custer's Revenge.* In the "game" a naked General Custer dodges flying arrows and various obstacles to have sexual intercourse (some outraged groups have contended "rape") with an Indian maiden tied to a stake.

While X-rated cartridges are the most flagrant example of unwarranted intrusion in what seemed like a closed business loop, they are by no means an isolated exception. The very success of both Atari and Mattel, who at one time made all of the game cartridges used in their home computers, have prompted others to exploit their exceedingly attractive market.

The Evil in the Mind's Eye: P&G Logo   According to two of the most recent best selling books on management, Procter and Gamble is one of America's "excellent" companies. It is also one of the clearest examples of an organization with a strong culture. One of the distinguishing marks of its culture is its unwavering commitment to customers. P&G learned early the value of a distinctive logo in communicating its strong commitment to "listening to its customers." **Terrence Deal** and **Allan Kennedy** described the lesson in *Corporate Cultures:*

"One morning in 1851, **William Procter** noticed that a wharfhand was painting black crosses on P&G's candle boxes. Asking why this was done, Procter learned that the crosses allowed illiterate wharfhands to distinguish the candle boxes from the soap boxes. Another artistic wharfhand soon changed the black cross to a circled star. Another replaced the single star with a cluster of stars. And then a quarter moon was added with a human profile. Finally, P&G painted the moon and star emblem on all of their candles.

"At some later date, P&G decided that the 'man in the moon' was unnecessary so they dropped it from their boxes. Immediately P&G

received a message from New Orleans that a jobber had refused delivery of an entire shipment of P&G candles. Since these boxes lacked the full "moon and stars' design, the jobber thought they were imitations. P&G quickly realized the value of the 'moon and stars' emblem and brought it back into use by registering it as a trademark. It was the beginning of brand name identification for P&G, and the first of many times that P&G listened to its customers."

Imagine the shock when P&G found that a religious sect had declared that P&G was in cahoots with the devil—because the "man in the moon" symbol was "obviously a sign of Satan!"

Such incidents are far from isolated. Sears Roebuck, the nation's largest retailer, was also accused of being in league with the devil. According to a report on the ABC-TV program "20-20," the first three digits on all of Sears' innumerable plastic credit cards were "666." As anyone who has had even a fleeting acquaintance with the "Omen" films knows, the number "666" is how the devil shall be recognized!

In many ways, this category of evil is the most unthinkable of all. It involves one of the most incredible features of the human mind, its ability to project onto other persons and inanimate objects symbolic urges which emanate from the innermost recesses of the human psyche. It's bad enough for manufacturers to contemplate how they protect their products from the invasion of unintended substances, or even from unintended uses, but how in the world do they protect their companies from the invasion of unintended *thoughts?*

WHY THE UNTHINKABLE IS HAPPENING MORE

It is infinitely easier to describe the unthinkable than it is to specify why today's corporations are more susceptible to it. Still, three factors probably deserve mention:

- Today's business environment is vastly different from earlier ones;
- traditional business education has neither kept pace with the radically-changing nature of the world, nor has it prepared students and practitioners for thinking about the unthinkable; and
- most organizations do not have cultures that facilitate coping with the unthinkable.

Factor One: It's A Wholly Different World   The environment in which today's businesses operate is radically different from that of previous eras. Today's businesses are subject to the impact of more volatile and unpredictable forces than ever before. It could once be said that the major forces operating on an organization were those of the stockholders and management itself. As a result, it was easier both to formulate business strategies and to stick to them. In contrast, the forces today are almost too numerous to list: government regulatory agencies, labor unions, suppliers, competitive forces of all kinds, international cartels, educational institutions, the news media, financial institutions, environmentalist groups, consumer interest groups, and so forth. Any one of these groups can exert a tremendous influence on business. In contrast to the single group "stockholders," all of these broader forces can be termed "stakeholders."

With the growth in the number of stakeholders who can potentially affect a business has come an accompanying lack of predictability and certainty. It has become harder to know exactly from where a force in the environment will strike and to know for sure what the consequences will be.

All of the this reflects a society that has become more complex. In the words of social critic **Philip Slater,** American society has been transforming itself from a *community* into a *network.* The differences between the two are profound.

A community tends to be a small, tightly-knit group of persons who know one another on sight. One of its essential properties is that it contains persons of all kinds who are forced to interact with one another. They are akin to the members of an extended family. There are rich ones and poor ones, smart and dull ones. But all the members of a community depend on one another.

Networks, in distinction, tend to be homogeneous. Within each network one tends to find the same kinds of people communicating with one another, increasingly by computer. Since the members of a network tend to think alike, they tend to share the same blind spots as well as strengths. As a consequence, they are vastly more susceptible to disruptions emanating from forces outside the network.

A society that is organized along the lines of networks also tends to be more permissive than one that is organized along the nature of communities. A series of networks allows for a greater range of behavior and, therefore, more deviant kinds of behavior. While every society or community has psychopaths and sociopathic behavior, a networked society is less directly in contact with such forces than is a community where the deviant members are more likely to be known, cared for, and even tolerated. The paradox is that the more we have attempted to exclude and isolate sociopaths from our networks the more we have, in turn, become susceptible to them.

There is no single class of people that business today is more dependent on, and yet knows less about, than psychopaths. The challenge facing business today is not just that the world is more complex because of conflicting pressures from more stakeholders, but also that some stakeholders are more bizarre and evil. Clearly, it is impossible to understand why anyone would inject poisonous substances into food or medicinal products without studying psychopathic behavior.

Factor Two: The Depressing State of Management Education   With few exceptions, management education today is largely geared to training students to solve exercises that are predicated on a simple, stable view of the world. Unlike real problems, such exercises are designed to have a single correct answer. Furthermore, the answers to such artificial exercises tend to be measured by their impact on a single criterion, the "bottom line." As a result, the bulk of students and practitioners of management today are unprepared to face the kinds of intellectual and emotional challenges that the unthinkable presents.

Most managers find the unthinkable too depressing to consider seriously. It is clear that they would prefer to dismiss the whole phenomenon rather than to grapple with it. Whether managers like to think about the unthinkable or not is irrelevant. The fact is that it is increasingly a part of our world and, as such, it must be dealt with. That current managers do not wish to face up to it must be taken as a serious defect in the way we educate them.

The intellectual challenges of facing the unthinkable are formidable. Unlike artificial exercises, real problems can always be looked at from more than one angle. Indeed, the more critical the problem, the more it demands to be viewed from as many different perspectives as possible in order to avoid missing essential aspects. The worst thing that can be done in solving complex problems is to pick one view and to ignore all the others.

Thus, the first kind of intellectual challenge that the unthinkable poses is the ability to view phenomena from several radically distinct and divergent vantage points. For the most part, we just don't train people to do this.

The second intellectual challenge arises because students and managers are generally not trained to handle even moderate amounts of uncertainty. As a result, they fall prey to the worst kind of rigid either/or thinking. For instance, while it is perfectly true that one cannot locate with certainty the exact whereabouts of the psychopath who is contemplating evil against a business, we can nevertheless study the general behavior patterns of the kinds of persons who are most likely to engage in evil acts. Because we lack *perfect* knowledge, it does not therefore follow that we can have *no* knowledge whatsoever. That's the devil's proposition. Wisdom, in contrast to mere technical competency, consists of making the best of what one has at hand.

Factor Three: The Tragedy of Current Corporate Cultures   For all the foregoing reasons and more, the unthinkable raises great anxiety in individuals. If individuals generally are not prepared either intellectually or emotionally to confront the unthinkable, there is no help to be found at the organizational level, either.

All corporate cultures are composed of a combination of silent as well as overt signals. Overt signals are written rules of behavior and structured patterns of reward. The silent signals constitute the "unwritten rules of the game." While not found in formal rules or manuals, they guide the behavior of people in organizations as powerfully as anything that is recorded. They carry the real messages of the culture—what people will *really* get rewarded for doing, whether it's *really* OK to disagree with the boss, whether creativity is *really* valued, whether the organization *really* believes in equal pay regardless of sex, race, religion, and so on.

Thinking about the unthinkable demands a different set of silent and overt signals from those that govern most organizations. It demands that people be encouraged and rewarded for creative, divergent thinking. It demands that people not be punished for raising anxiety-provoking issues. It demands that people be rewarded for anticipating issues of strategic importance to the organization. It demands that people be encouraged to monitor the environment for strange trends, bizarre events, and so forth. It demands that organizations bring in outsiders who can shake up and challenge conventional ways of thinking.

THE $64 BILLION QUESTION: WHAT CAN BE DONE?

There are actions organizations can take to cope more effectively with the unthinkable. Businesses are not as powerless as one might think.

First, they must recognize the existence of psychopathic behavior. In fact, managers, must ask, how does our organization look when viewed from the vantage point of a psychopath? What are its strengths, its weaknesses, when viewed from this perspective? How can it be protected?

Second, they need to develop early-warning, environmental scanning mechanisms for monitoring the environment for bizarre acts committed against any kind of organization. Very few psychopaths walk up and directly announce their intentions. However, *all human behavior is contagious*. All human beings are influenced by the actions of others, and disturbed persons are even more susceptible to social influence. Thus, the fact that even one organization has been attacked is likely to call forth destructive tendencies, especially from those, like copycat killers, who are on the borderline of controlling their destructive impulses.

At a minimum, organizations need to develop an inventory of the kinds of evil acts (and the frequency of their occurrence) committed against organizations inside and outside of their industry. We are not saying that all acts committed against organizations are the result of psychopaths. However, a significant proportion of such acts can only be understood in terms of psychopathic behavior. This is certainly true in the cases of Tylenol and P&G's logo.

Indeed, it may come as a real surprise that of all the types of unthinkable evil, the case of P&G's logo (undesired projection) is the most treatable of all. If organizations were willing to hire such unconventional consultants as specialists in mythology and religious symbolism, then they could probably predict those aspects of their logos that are most susceptible to misinterpretation by religious fanatics. There are even detailed guides for thinking about undesired projection. In fact, we have used these guides with MBA students to ferret out "Satanic signs" in corporate logos and product labels. We are amazed to find just how many labels contain such devilish symbols as pentagrams or hexagrams.

By the same token, new schemes have recently been developed which allow one to think more comprehensively than before about the full range of technological hazards, such as toxic shock syndrome, that can develop in products.

Third, organizations need to develop *intellectual skunk works!* Companies need to encourage individuals and groups to think about the unthinkable. Participation in such groups should be regarded as an essential step up the corporate ladder. Since evil is contagious, it is important to realize that persons participating in such groups need special training to inoculate themselves against being overwhelmed by the very disease against which they are trying to protect the organizations. For this same reason, the involvement of outsiders is, again, necessary to help the organization deal with the anxiety the unthinkable inevitably raises.

Finally, and most important of all, coping with the unthinkable must be seen as part of a total, integrated program of strategic thinking about the entire range of issues with which the modern organization must deal. Thinking about evil is, in fact, no different from thinking about any longrange or low-probability event that might have high impact on the corporation. The subject matter is merely more bizarre.

We believe that corporations have the means to think about nearly every aspect of the unthinkable. New and powerful techniques have recently been developed for getting at, and challenging, the core assumptions that organizations hold about themselves and their environment. Therefore, the issue is whether corporations have the will to use these tools to face their deepest fears and anxieties. The fact that all tragedies cannot be prevented does not relieve us from the basic responsibility of learning to cope with the unthinkable.

St. Louis Post-Dispatch, December 4, 1983.

'Snooping' Reporters Snap
at Baited White House Trap

Washington (AP)—Tired of reporters stealing glances at White House memos, presidential spokesman Larry Speakes got his revenge when two reporters "bit like snakes" at fake memos planted on a press aide's desk.

One of the fake documents contained a proposal to move the press corps from the White House next door to the Old Executive Office Building, said Speakes, who disclosed his caper at Friday's press briefing.

The other proposed that President Ronald Reagan announce his reelection bid during halftime of a New Year's Day football game, because "halftime audiences are one of the biggest . . . (and) most representative," Speakes said.

The two reporters who perused the memos "bit like snakes," even though the documents were "facetious on their face," he said.

"They both made calls all over this White House about relocating the press," Speakes said. "We held the line on it for two days here, and we wouldn't tell them anything."

The hoax "was prompted by one reporter here who very often goes to a desk and goes through a person's desk while you're sitting there," Speakes said. He did not identify the reporter and would not say whether that individual was one of the victims of his hoax.

The false information was not published or broadcast.

One reporter took a fake memo off a press aide's desk and into the briefing room, Speakes said. "The second reporter sat on the desk until she could read the two memos while pretending to read the news summary."

After realizing he or she has been hoodwinked, one reporter called and asked Speakes why he had perpetrated the hoax, the spokesman said.

"We have always had sort of an understanding, unwritten rule, honor system where you don't read things on our desk," he said. "You don't read things on our computer. You don't look over our shoulder. And if you happen to see something, it's considered off the record."

St. Louis Globe-Democrat, December 20, 1983.

EPA Inspectors Want to Carry Guns
Job is 'one of most violent in nation,' officials from 2 states say

Washington (AP)—Criminal investigators for the Environmental Protection Agency, seeking full police authority and the right to carry guns, were backed Monday by state authorities who called the hazardous waste business "one of the most violent . . . in the nation today."

Authorities from Pennsylvania and New Jersey, testifying before a House subcommittee in favor of the EPA request, said their state investigators are armed because the job is too dangerous without police authority.

"I would not under any circumstances direct investigators of mine to do investigations like these without being armed," said Steven Madonna, New Jersey's deputy attorney general in charge of toxic waste enforcement.

"I believe that the waste industry is probably one of the most violent industries in the nation today," Madonna added. "There have been murders, threats, arson. Organized crime plays a major role. . . . Weapons are commonplace, if not the rule; intimidation and violence are fairly commonplace."

Keith Welkes, Pennsylvania's deputy attorney general for toxic wastes, said his state tried the federal method of having investigators seek help from regular law enforcement officials when needed. But the process was abandoned in favor of giving the state investigators police authority, and Welkes urged that the same authority be given EPA's criminal investigators.

"Without it, all the urgings of Congress and the good intentions of EPA will still result in exceedingly limited results," Welkes said.

But the Justice Department, which has refused since April to grant EPA's request to deputize its federal investigators, said it wanted more time to study the problem. A department official said EPA was not the only agency seeking such authority, and the number should be limited.

In one case cited in testimony, that procedure forced an agency investigator to watch as a truck leaked toxic PCBs for 50 miles along a highway between Seattle and Portland, Ore., the EPA car following behind, until a sheriff's deputy arrived who had the authority to pull the truck over.

In addition, witnesses said, some states refuse EPA investigators access to police files, making it impossible for them to check license plates of suspicious trucks or mug shots of suspected polluters. Many states deny agency investigators access to police radio bands.

Smiles of Flight Attendants Mask Hostility, Fatigue and Bodily Pain

Susan Harrigan

The next time a flight attendant smiles at you, smile back sympathetically. The friendly skies, it seems, are a seething cauldron of stress.

Attendants suffer from so much fatigue, bodily pain and other stress symptoms that at the end of many a day, they don't feel able to deal with emergencies, according to a study by the Aviation Safety Institute, a non-profit research group. The study drew on detailed records kept by 30 flight attendants—27 women and three men—over a two month period.

Constant travelers mightn't be surprised to learn that attendants don't always feel terrific. Some other findings of the study, however, are less predictable.

STRESSFUL ROUTES

For one thing, your smiling attendant actually may feel hostile toward you if you are on a southwesterly or northeasterly flight. Attendants' pulse rates and other stress indicators rise on such flights, according to the study, which couldn't find "plausible explanations" for the phenomena.

Flight attendants say such flights are more stressful because passengers on them are "higher-strung." Southwesterners tend to be "hustling" types who drink a lot and call stewardesses "baby," says Jean Bombach, an Eastern Airlines attendant. "You're always trying to shake that anyhow, and when somebody's blatant about it, you really get turned off," she says.

Northeasterners, by contrast, aren't "laid back" enough when they fly, attendants say. "They want everything (served to them) in the Northeast," Mrs. Bombach says. "You have to make sure they don't take the seats with them when they leave."

A little in-flight turbulence actually calms jumpy flight attendants, according to the study, which can't explain that finding, either. But Mrs. Bombach says, "It feels like being rocked—back-to-the-womb security."

WISDOM OF THE ELDERS

Mature years help, too. In general, older flight attendants report less fatigue than younger ones do, the study found. It hypothesizes that younger attendants tend to rush off to see the sights during layovers, while older and wiser ones rest up. Enid Grigg, an Eastern attendant for 14 years, says older attendants tend to fly the same routes continually and "know how to deal with passengers' hostility when it crops up."

And, in a finding sure to strike a sympathetic chord among fellow travelers, the study revealed that flight attendants suffer from "mild malnutrition." They don't eat enough on flights, partly because they don't have time, but mostly because they don't want to swallow "plastic food," as many of them call airline meals.

"It seems to me that the food is mostly fillers," one flight attendant says. "All the stuff congeals after a while, and the meat turns blue or various shades of purple and green. After you've seen that, you can't eat it."

10

COURAGE

Courage: the state or quality of mind or spirit that enables one to face danger with self-possession, confidence and resolution.

—*The Heritage Illustrated Dictionary of the English Language. New College Edition, 1975.*

In an organizational world which involves crises and conflict, which is an arena in which struggles are waged between and amongst different self-interested individuals and groups, which provides through its resources the rewards for success and the punishments for failure, and which reflects the meanings that organizational members give to events they create, witness, and evaluate, there is ample opportunity for people to display both courage and cowardice. In small ways, in large scale dramas, in handling the daily ongoing business of organizations, in grappling with single stark events, managers and workers, each in their own way, must deal with danger, with difficulty, and with ethical dilemmas.

It is surprising to us that we and our fellow students of organization have paid so little attention to the nature of courage, and to its possible role in organizational behavior and outcomes. The excerpts in this section are our first step toward recognizing and, hopefully, legitimating its place in any serious discussion of organizational reality. We are confident that managers, administrators, and workers would be quick to acknowledge and discuss their experience with courage.

The concept, of course, is far from simple. In part, what is and is not courageous will be defined subjectively by those who act and those who observe. For example, what a manager considers to be a difficult and courageous stand taken in the best interests of the organization may be interpreted by his or her employees as manipulative and self-interested. An action or gesture against organizational policies and practices, made on ethical principle by a worker, may be seen by management as disruptive and disloyal. Furthermore, courageous action may be difficult to detect by all but those closest to that action. In such circumstances, the courageous act involves doing, without fanfare or applause, things which are not rewarded by the organization and which may even draw censure and criticism from other members of the organization. The latter often respond to the external actions of individuals without being able to see or understand the inner workings of those actions. These and other aspects of courage are discussed in the articles that follow.

Blowing the whistle on dishonest or harmful organizational practices is an obvious and fertile territory for the examination of courage. Connie Lauerman's "One Woman's War on Corruption: A Testament to an Honest Official," describes the experiences of Marie Ragghianti, who was fired from her job as Chairman of the Tennessee Board of Pardons and Paroles, the first woman in history to hold that post. Ragghianti had much to lose by exposing the web of corruption in her organization, the selling and bartering or pardons, paroles, and clemencies to murderers, rapists, and other criminals, and much to gain by playing the game and remaining silent. Lauerman describes the pressures that were exerted on the whistle-blower (including a contract on Ragghianti's life). It is interesting to note the perceptions Ragghianti reports of her own actions. It was easier for her to blow the whistle than to walk away or remain silent. Her courage, and perhaps that of many like her, may come more from sticking with the decision than in making it in the first place. Perseverance in the face of adversity marks the quality of her action.

Tom Wolfe's "Becoming a Fighter Pilot," provides us with a chilling and insightful view of the courage of the fighter pilot. He captures the tension of the concept, the extent to which being courageous involves combining mind, body, and spirit to stare down and cope with an uncertainty that includes a realization that to back off means loss of face, and loss of career advancement up a seemingly endless pyramid. To proceed may mean physical injury and even death. His description of the trainee confronting for the first time the pitching heaving carrier on which he must land his aircraft graphically illustrates the condition.

Not all situations of organizational courage involve the individual in a choice between life and death, although the previous article on whistle-blowing makes it clear that it is not only fighter pilots who face that outcome. Nevertheless, the choice inevitably involves some degree of expected personal loss if the (courageous) action is undertaken. The loss of job, esteem, and friendships make perseverance painful. Wolfe's excerpt also captures the cultural influences that may determine what is courageous action.

Courage, as mentioned earlier, is sometimes associated with quiet actions that go unrewarded in some sense and that reflect resolute action repeatedly even though such behavior draws little recognition and attention by those who have a major say in determining who is successful, who is a hero. This "unsung hero" aspect of courage is nicely captured in two pieces. In "Bob Gainey," an excerpt from Ken Dryden's *The Game,* we meet a hockey player who scores few goals in a game in which most of the attention and accolades go to high scoring players. Despite the temptations to try to be like others and to score often, Gainey sticks to actions that make others do well, that allow them to score goals, and permit his team to win. Dryden describes him as the consummate team player. The article makes explicit many of the issues involved in achieving such a stature in an environment that encourages individualism.

The unglamorous, hard lot of the salesman, particularly in economically difficult times is the subject of the other piece on unsung heroes, "Life of a Salesman" by Bob Greene. This piece makes explicit the courageous act of sticking to personal goals and of striving against great odds. "They face what we dread most: flat, cold, rejection," says Greene. Their heroism goes unnoticed except to themselves and perhaps to their families. Read in conjunction with *Death of a Salesman* by Arthur Miller (section 12), it provides a compelling picture of a job that, like the fighter pilot in Wolfe's *The Right Stuff*, requires the individual to draw continually on inner resources of pluck and spirit in order to survive and to prosper. In both jobs the game is always on, it is never over until the player quits.

Finally, in an interesting and insightful article, Vice Admiral James Stockdale's, "The World of Epictetus" draws on his own experiences as a prisoner of war, and on his observations of others in that plight, to discuss some of the dimensions of courage and cowardice. Stockdale also speculates on ways to resist the efforts others make to break one's resolve to pursue a given path. His piece includes a strong statement stressing the role of a liberal education in the preservation of democratic values and of courageous leadership.

One Woman's War on Corruption: A Testament to an Honest Official

Connie Lauerman

At first glance, Marie Ragghianti might seem an unlikely whistle-blower—not so much because she is a demure, soft-spoken Southern lady with a dazzling smile, but rather because she had so much to lose. Everything, in fact.

After a disastrous marriage ended, she was supporting three children. Having put herself through college, she finally had a prestigious, well-paying job as chairman of the Tennessee Board of Pardons and Paroles, the first woman in history to hold that post. So a lot of people told her not to rock the boat, to play the game like everyone else. But Ragghianti couldn't.

It soon became clear that she was surrounded by a tangled conspiracy to sell or barter pardons, paroles and clemencies to murderers, rapists and other criminals that was being masterminded by officials in the governor's office. Ragghianti went to the FBI.

The corruption she exposed eventually cost her a job, jeopardized her life and left her a political outcast. She was tailed and constantly threatened with dismissal. Her secretary betrayed her. Rumors about her supposed drinking and sleeping around ran rampant. She was set up for two drunken-driving arrests. A friend and colleague on the board, who was to be her chief witness in the wrongful dismissal suit she later won, was found murdered in a motel room. An informant told the FBI there was a contract out on Ragghianti's life.

When she was fired, she was denounced as a liar, a cheat and a thief. In the end, though, the reputations of others would be shattered, indictments returned and prison sentences handed down.

"By failing to do anything, I myself would have felt that I shared in the responsibility for what was going on," said Ragghianti in an interview. "I don't think that I can be aware that something's going on that's within my control to alter—somthing that's very wrong—and ignore it.

"By the same token, the one thing I did briefly consider, resigning, was also impossible, because I don't think I could have lived with myself knowing that, if I resigned, what was going on would just get worse."

"People say, 'Wouldn't it have been easier to ignore what was going on or easier to quit?' but I did what was easiest for me. I don't think I could have lived with myself if I had resigned."

Reprinted, courtesy of the *Chicago Tribune*.

Marie Ragghianti is being hailed as a heroine these days. Her story is the subject of a book, "Marie: A True Story" [Random House, $16.95], written by Peter Maas, the best-selling author of "Serpico" and "The Valachi Papers." This tale of political corruption is in the tradition of Frank Serpico, the courageous New York City detective whose refusal to look the other way triggered a probe of police practices. Both are testaments that one person *can* make a difference.

"I don't consider myself a heroine," she says simply. "For people to call me that is a reflection of our times. I just did what was right, what anyone should do in those circumstances.

"I'm a pretty devout Catholic, which is not to say I'm particularly good or holy or anything, but I do take my faith seriously. And one of the things that has always disturbed me as a person who knows a lot of people who are very good and devoted Catholics—or Christians or Jews, for that matter—is their attitude, which is frequently: 'Stay away from politics. It's a dirty business.' That attitude offends me because I think we need [good] people to be involved in the political process. When they turn their back on it, they leave it open to corruption and dishonesty.

"There was a historian, Edmund Burke, who once said, 'All that is necessary for the triumph of evil is that enough good men do nothing.' I think that's very true. And Winston Churchill said, 'The malice of the wicked is reinforced by the weakness of the virtuous.' Those are very profound statements, and they're things that meant enough to me that they have been with me ever since I read them years ago. So my interest in politics has always included those kinds of concepts."

Ragghianti's belief in what the American democractic system can and should be was formed during her childhood.

The first of five children, she was born 41 years ago in Chattanooga, Tenn. Her mother, Virginia, was third generation Tennessee Scots-Irish whose people had been stone masons and blacksmiths. Ragghianti's grandfather, Roque Fajardo, was the Cuban-born son of a professor of Spanish at the University of Chattanooga. Her father was a newspaperman, a political reporter—first in Knoxville, then Nashville. She recalls growing up in a house filled with people and political talk and remembers watching Estes Kefauver, the Tennessee senator and vice-presidential candidate who investigated organized crime.

"Eventually my father was a speechwriter for [former Tennessee governor] Frank Clement," Ragghianti said. "He was there when Clement delivered the keynote address [at the Democratic Convention] back in '56. I stayed up all night to watch it. From that day to this I've always been fascinated by politics."

When Marie was 15, financial problems forced her father to quit journalism and move to Daytona Beach, Fla., to become an executive of a motel chain. She quickly adapted to languerous beach life. Pretty, vivacious and popular, she won beauty contests, posed for tourism photos. Boys swarmed around her.

She met David Ragghianti at a dance in Memphis, where she enrolled at Siena College, her mother's alma mater. He was an amateur boxer, had been kicked out of high school, allegedly was a lady killer. She thought he seemed to need help. She decided to drop out of school to marry him, help put *him* through college. Her mother was appalled; his parents were against it. She faked pregnancy. They were married at Christ the King Catholic Church in Nashville. She was 19; he was 18.

Almost immediately he began complaining about her cooking and housekeeping. His rowdy friends practically moved in with them, spilling beer on the floor and listening to rock music and passing around copies of Playboy magazine. She hated it but tried her best to please him. Soon there were arguments, and he began hitting her. Babies came: Dante, Therese, Ricky—three of them in as many years. Things would improve, then quickly sour. Violence, then remorse. Over and over again.

When she was 25, she took her three children and fled. She got a divorce and, later, an annulment. Broke and living on handouts, she started over in a shabby, bug-infested apartment in the poor section of Nashville. When all three children were in school, she enrolled at Vanderbilt University, majoring in English and psychology. To pay for it, she typed papers for graduate students, worked as a cocktail waitress on Friday and Saturday nights, and as the church librarian Sunday mornings at Christ the King. She joined the Young Democrats and wrote for the campus newspaper.

After her graduation in 1974, she got a job as Tennessee's extradition officer through Eddie Sisk, legal counsel to newly elected Gov. Ray Blanton. She had met Sisk through the Young Democrats, called to congratulate him on his appointment and asked to talk to him in person. Bedlam reigned in his office that day. There was a backlog of extradition cases, and the attorney general was upset. Sisk called someone to ask if the extradition officer had to be a lawyer [answer: no], then he turned to Marie and offered her the job. From the beginning, writes Maas, Sisk "figured he'd swatted a lot of flies at once. Marie was a good-looking woman . . . her Vanderbilt degree was class. And she was a little naive."

Ragghianti was thrilled. She knew little about Blanton, but had voted for him mainly because he was a Democrat. He was a three-term former congressman from rural West Tennessee who talked about his dirt-farm origins and vowed to advance blacks and women in his administration. Though he had an imposing presence, Nashville's wealthy crowd liked to ridicule him. They snickered over his oratorical gaffes [the "anals of history"], said the only thing he learned in Washingon was that it was all right to wear colored shirts with ties. His inner circle was dubbed "the redneck Mafia."

Blanton was an outsider and believed you couldn't really trust someone until you'd done something for him and he was in your debt. Blanton had said he didn't want a lawyer he didn't know. [Eddie Sisk had been coordinator of Blanton's unsuccessful 1972 Senate campaign. He lost to Howard Baker, now Senate majority leader.]

Marie dug into the job, reducing the backlog, tracking down papers and making sure the attorney general's office got them for review. But she began noticing altered records and incomplete files. It was, she told Sisk one day, "the sort of dumb, covered-wagon mentality that had led to Watergate." Very funny, he said.

Still, Blanton soon was thinking about appointing her to the Board of Pardons and Paroles. It involved more money and more independence, and she pursued it. She wrote to Blanton, telling him she wanted to be board chairman as well. She said her interest was seeing that his administration was viewed in the best possible light. She also rounded up support from key law enforcement people, legislators and important Blanton backers. She met with John Seigenthaler, publisher of the Tennessean, the state's most influential paper, to seek his support.

Blanton announced Ragghianti's appointment on May 11, 1976. He was effusive in his praise of her "mature judgment" in a "tough and often thankless job." She had been on the state payroll in an obscure job for little more than a year. In the corridors of the state capitol up on the hill in Nashville, there were snide remarks about just how "little Marie" had gotten so far so fast.

A year later, on Aug. 3, 1977, Blanton would fire her, falsely accusing her of bilking the state of $7,500. Privately he said: "She was the only woman who ever screwed me before I had a chance to screw her."

The scandal blew Blanton out of the governor's mansion. Three of his lieutenants, including Eddie Sisk, who was arrested with a payoff in his pocket, received prison sentences. As an outgrowth of that investigation, Blanton was convicted of conspiring to take kickbacks for liquor store licenses. And in the Tennessee legislature a reform bill was passed, creating a new pardons and parole board with its own attorney, budget and staff.

While in the thick of her ordeal with pressures mounting, Ragghianti told the corrections commissioner: "I want you to know this isn't the worst thing that ever happened to me."

There had been, of course, her violent marriage and the mysterious lung ailment that nearly killed her youngest child, Ricky. She had fought the misdiagnosis of his illness by doctors who wouldn't listen to her. And she watched over him all night, suctioning fluid from his lungs while roaches and bugs skittered on the floor and walls. At one point she herself was severely ill and doctors feared it was cancer.

"I had been through much worse," Ragghianti said, "and that was one reason I was able to endure all of that. I had a real perspective on just what things do matter most in this life; my baby's life or my health, or my internal faith and principles, not things like prestige or money or a job."

After her ouster from the pardons and paroles board, Ragghianti sold real estate in Nashville for a time, then decided to relocate in Florida, mostly to give her children a life outside the public spotlight where she "could just be mama." She has taught courses at Daytona Beach Community College and lives quietly in Sarasota. She plans to go to law school, but for now she is writing and preparing to lecture on college campuses. She says it makes her angry that Watergate figures, such as G. Gordon Liddy and others, lecture on campuses and advise young people to stay away from politics. 'They should advise them to stay away from corruption," she says sternly.

Becoming a Fighter Pilot

Tom Wolfe

A young man might go into military flight training believing that he was entering some sort of technical school in which he was simply going to acquire a certain set of skills. Instead, he found himself all at once enclosed in a fraternity. And in this fraternity, even though it was military, men were not rated by their outward rank as ensigns, lieutenants, commanders, or whatever. No, herein the world was divided into those who had it and those who did not. This quality, this *it,* was never named, however, nor was it talked about in any way.

As to just what this ineffable quality was . . . well, it obviously involved bravery. But it was not bravery in the simple sense of being willing to risk your life. The idea seemed to be that any fool could do that, if that was all that was required, just as any fool could throw away his life in the process. No, the idea here (in the all-enclosing fraternity) seemed to be that a man should have the ability to go up in a hurtling piece of machinery and put his hide on the line and then have the moxie, the reflexes, the experience the coolness, to pull it back in the last yawning moment—and then to go up again *the next day,* and the next day, and every next day, even if the series should prove infinite—and, ultimately, in its best expression, do so in a cause that means something to thousands, to a people, a nation, to humanity, to God. Nor was there *a test* to show whether or not a pilot had this righteous quality. There was, instead, a seemingly infinite series of tests. A career in flying was like climbing one of those ancient Babylonian pyramids made up of a dizzy progression of steps and ledges, a ziggurat, a pyramid extraordinarily high and steep; and the idea was to prove at every foot of the way up

Excerpt adapted from *THE RIGHT STUFF* by Tom Wolfe. Copyright © 1979 by Tom Wolfe. Reprinted by permission of Farrar, Straus and Giroux, Inc.

that pyramid that you were one of the elected and anointed ones who had *the right stuff* and could move higher and higher and even—ultimately, God willing, one day—that you might be able to join that special few at the very top, that elite who had the capacity to bring tears to men's eyes, the very Brotherhood of the Right Stuff itself.

None of this was to be mentioned, and yet it was acted out in a way that a young man could not fail to understand. When a new flight (i.e., a class) of trainees arrived at Pensacola, they were brought into an auditorium for a little lecture. An officer would tell them: "Take a look at the man on either side of you." Quite a few actually swiveled their heads this way and that, in the interest of appearing diligent. Then the officer would say: "One of the three of you is not going to make it!"—meaning, not get his wings. That was the opening theme, the *motif* of primary training. We already know that one-third of you do not have the right stuff—it only remains to find out who.

Furthermore, that was the way it turned out. At every level in one's progress up that staggeringly high pyramid, the world was once more divided into those men who had the right stuff to continue the climb and those who had to be *left behind* in the most obvious way. Some were eliminated in the course of the opening classroom work, as either not smart enough or not hardworking enough, and were left behind. Then came the basic flight instruction, in single-engine, propeller-driven trainers, and a few more—even though the military tried to make this stage easy—were washed out and left behind. Then came more demanding levels, one after the other, formation flying, instrument flying, jet training, all-weather flying, gunnery, and at each level more were washed out and left behind. By this point easily a third of the original candidates had been, indeed, eliminated . . . from the ranks of those who might prove to have the right stuff.

In the Navy, in addition to the stages that Air Force trainees went through, the neophyte always had waiting for him, out in the ocean, a certain grim gray slab; namely, the deck of an aircraft carrier; and with it perhaps the most difficult routine in military flying, carrier landings. He was shown films about it, he heard lectures about it, and he knew that carrier landings were hazardous. He first practiced touching down on the shape of a flight deck painted on an airfield. He was instructed to touch down and gun right off. This was safe enough—the shape didn't move, at least—but it could do terrible things to, let us say, the gyroscope of the soul. *That shape!—it's so damned small!* And more candidates were washed out and left behind. Then came the day, without warning, when those who remained were sent out over the ocean for the first of many days of reckoning with the slab. The first day was always a clear day with little wind and a calm sea. The carrier was so steady that it seemed, from up there in the air, to be resting on pilings, and the candidate usually made his first carrier landing successfully, with relief and even *élan*. Many young candidates looked like terrific aviators up to that very point—and it was not until they were actually standing on the carrier deck that they first began to wonder if they had the proper stuff, after all. In the training film the flight deck was a grand piece of gray geometry, perilous, to be sure, but an amazing abstract shape as one looks down upon it on the screen. And yet once the newcomer's two feet were on it . . . *Geometry*—my God, man, this is a . . . skillet! It *heaved*, it moved up and down underneath his feet, it pitched up, it pitched down, it rolled to port (this great beast *rolled!*) and it rolled to starboard, as the ship moved into the wind and, therefore, into the waves, and the wind kept sweeping across, sixty feet up in the air out in the open sea, and there were no railings whatsoever. This was a *skillet!*—a frying pan!—a short-order grill!—not gray but black, smeared with skid marks from one end to the other and glistening with pools of hydraulic fluid and the occasional jet-fuel slick, all of it still hot, sticky, greasy, runny, virulent from God knows what traumas—still ablaze!—consumed in detonations, explosions, flames, combustion, roars, shrieks, whines, blasts, horrible shudders, fracturing impacts, as little men in screaming red and yellow and purple and green shirts with black Mickey Mouse helmets over their ears skittered about on the surface as if for their very lives (you've said it now!), hooking fighter planes onto the catapult shuttles so that they can explode their afterburners and be slung off the deck in a red-mad fury with a *kaboom!* that pounds through the entire deck—a procedure that seems absolutely controlled, orderly, sublime, however, compared to what he is about to watch as aircraft return to the ship for what is known in the engineering stoicisms of the military as "recovery and arrest." To say that an F–4 was coming back onto this heaving barbecue from out of the sky at a speed of 135 knots . . . that might have been the truth in the training lecture, but it did not begin to get across the idea of what the newcomer saw from the deck itself, because it created the notion that perhaps the plane was gliding in. On the deck one knew differently! As the aircraft came closer and the carrier heaved on into the waves and the plane's speed did not diminish and the deck did not grow steady—indeed, it pitched up and down five or ten feet per greasy heave—one experienced a neural alarm that no lecture could have prepared him for: This is not an *airplane* coming toward me, it is a brick with some poor sonofabitch riding it (*someone much like myself!*), and it is not *gliding*, it is *falling*, a thirty-thousand-pound brick, headed not for a stripe on the deck but for *me*—and with a horrible *smash!* it hits the skillet, and with a blur of momentum as big as a freight train's it hurtles toward the far end of the deck—another blinding storm!—another roar as the pilot pushes the throttle up to full military power and another smear of rubber screams out over the skillet—and this is nominal!—quite okay!—for a wire stretched across the deck has grabbed the hook on the end of the plane as it hit the deck tail down, and the smash was the rest of the fifteen-ton brute slamming onto the deck, as it tripped up, so that it is now straining against the wire at full throttle, in case it hadn't held and the plane had "boltered" off the end of the deck and had to struggle up into the air again. And already the Mickey Mouse helmets are running toward the fiery monster . . .

And the candidate, looking on, begins to *feel* that great heaving sunblazing deathboard of a deck wallowing in his own vestibular system—and suddenly he finds himself backed up against his own limits. He ends up going to the flight surgeon with so-called conversion symptoms. Overnight he develops blurred vision or numbness in his hands and feet or sinusitis so severe that he cannot tolerate changes in altitude. On one level the symptom is real. He really cannot see too well or use his fingers or stand the pain. But somewhere in his subconscious he knows it is a plea and a beg-off; he shows not the slightest concern (the flight surgeon notes) that the condition might be permanent and affect him in whatever life awaits him outside the arena of the right stuff.

Those who remained, those who qualified for carrier duty—and even more so those who later on qualified for *night* carrier duty—began to feel a bit like Gideon's warriors. *So many have been left behind!* The young warriors were now treated to a deathly sweet and quite unmentionable sight. They could gaze at length upon the crushed and wilted pariahs who had washed out. They could inspect those who did not have that righteous stuff.

The military did not have very merciful instincts. Rather than packing up these poor souls and sending them home, the Navy, like the Air Force and the Marines, would try to make use of them in some other role, such as flight controller. So the washout has to keep taking classes with the rest of his group, even though he can no longer touch an airplane. He sits there in the classes staring at sheets of paper with cataracts of sheer human mortification over his eyes while the rest steal looks at him . . . this man reduced to an ant, this untouchable, this poor sonofabitch. And in what test had he been found wanting? Why, it seemed to be nothing less than *manhood* itself. Naturally, this was never mentioned, either. Yet there it was. *Manliness, manhood, manly courage . . .* there was something ancient, primordial, irresistible about the challenge of this stuff, no matter what a sophisticated and rational age one might think he lived in.

Perhaps because it could not be talked about, the subject began to take on superstitious and even mystical outlines. A man either had it or he didn't! There was no such thing as having *most* of it. Moreover, it could blow at any seam. One day a man would be ascending the pyramid at a terrific clip, and the next—bingo!—he would reach his own limits in the most unexpected way. Conrad and Schirra met an Air Force pilot who had had a great pal at Tyndall Air Force Base in Florida. This man had been the budding ace of the training class; he had flown the hottest fighter-style trainer, the T-38, like a dream; and then he began the routine step of being checked out in the T–33. The T–33 was not nearly as hot in aircraft as the T–38; it was essentially the old P–80 jet fighter. It had an exceedingly small cockpit. The pilot could barely move his shoulders. It was the sort of airplane of which everybody said, "You don't get into it, you *wear* it." Once inside a T–33 cockpit this man, this budding ace, developed claustrophobia of the most paralyzing sort. He tried everything to overcome it. He even went to a psychiatrist, which was a serious mistake for a military officer if his superiors learned of it. But nothing worked. He was shifted over to flying jet transports, such as the C–135. Very demanding and necessary aircraft they were, too, and he was still spoken of as an excellent pilot. But as everyone knew—and, again, it was never explained in so many words—only those who were assigned to fighter squadrons, the "fighter jocks," as they called each other with a self-satisfied irony, remained in the true fraternity. Those assigned to transports were not humiliated like washouts—*somebody* had to fly those planes—nevertheless, they, too, had been *left behind* for lack of the right stuff.

Or a man could go for a routine physical one fine day, feeling like a million dollars, and be grounded for *fallen arches.* It happened!—just like that! (And try raising them.) Or for breaking his wrist and losing on-ly *part* of its mobility. Or for a minor deterioration of eyesight, or for any of hundreds of reasons that would make no difference to a man in an ordinary occupation. As a result all fighter jocks began looking upon doctors as their natural enemies. Going to see a flight surgeon was a no-gain proposition; a pilot could only hold his own or lose in the doctor's office. To be grounded for a medical reason was no humiliation, looked at objectively. But it was a humiliation, nonetheless!—for it meant you no longer had that indefinable, unutterable, integral stuff. (It could blow at *any* seam.)

All the hot young fighter jocks began trying to test the limits them-selves in a superstitious way. They were like believing Presbyterians of a century before who used to probe their own experience to see if they were truly among *the elect.* When a fighter pilot was in training, whether in the Navy or the Air Force, his superiors were continually spelling out strict rules for him, about the use of the aircraft and conduct in the sky. They repeatedly forbade so-called hot-dog stunts, such as outside loops, buzzing, flat-hatting, hedgehopping and flying under bridges. But somehow one got the message that the man who truly *had* it could ignore those rules—not that he should make a point of it, but that he *could*—and that after all there was only one way to find out—and that in some strange unofficial way, peeking through his fingers, his instructor halfway expected him to challenge all the limits. They would give a lec-ture about how a pilot should never fly without a good solid break-fast—eggs, bacon, toast, and so forth—because if he tried to fly with his blood-sugar level too low, it could impair his alertness. Naturally, the next day every hot dog in the unit would get up and have a breakfast consisting of one cup of black coffee and take off and go up into a vertical climb until the weight of the ship exactly canceled out the upward thrust of the engine and his air speed was zero, and he would hang there for one thick adrenal instant—and then fall like a rock, until one of three things happened: he keeled over nose first and regained his aerodynamics and all was well, he went into a spin and fought his way out of it, or he went into a spin and had to eject or crunch it, which was always supremely possible.

Likewise, "hassling"—mock dogfighting—was strictly forbidden, and so naturally young fighter jocks could hardly wait to go up in, say, a pair of F–100s and start the duel by making a pass at each other at 800 miles an hour, the winner being the pilot who could slip in behind the other one and get locked in on his tail ("wax his tail"), and it was not uncommon for some eager jock to try too tight an outside turn and have his engine flame out, whereupon, unable to restart it, he has to eject . . . and he shakes his fist at the victor as he floats down by parachute and his million-dollar aircraft goes *kaboom!* on the palmetto grass or the desert floor, and he starts thinking about how he can get together with the other guy back at the base in time for the two of them to get their stories straight before the investigation: "I don't know what happened, sir. I was pulling up after a target run, and it just flamed out on me." Hassling was forbidden, and hassling that led to the destruction of an aircraft was a serious court-martial offense, and the man's superiors knew that the engine hadn't *just flamed out*, but every unofficial impulse on the base seemed to be saying: "Hell, we wouldn't give you a nickel for a pilot who hasn't done some crazy rat-racing like that. It's all part of the right stuff."

The other side of this impulse showed up in the reluctance of the young jocks to admit it when they had maneuvered themselves into a bad corner they couldn't get out of. There were two reasons why a fighter pilot hated to declare an emergency. First, it triggered a complex and very public chain of events at the field: all other incoming flights were held up, including many of one's comrades who were probably low on fuel; the fire trucks came trundling out to the runway like yellow toys (as seen from way up there), the better to illustrate one's hapless state; and the bureaucracy began to crank up the paper monster for the investigation that always followed. And second, to declare an emergency, one first had to reach that conclusion in his own mind, which to the young pilot was the same as saying: "A minute ago I still *had* it—now I need your help!" To have a bunch of young fighter pilots up in the air thinking this way used to drive flight controllers crazy. They would see a ship beginning to drift off the radar, and they couldn't rouse the pilot on the microphone for anything other than a few meaningless mumbles, and they would know he was probably out there with engine failure at a low altitude, trying to reignite by lowering his auxiliary generator rig, which had a little propeller that was supposed to spin in the slipstream like a child's pinwheel.

"Whiskey Kilo Two Eight, do you want to declare an emergency?"

This would rouse him!—to say: "Negative, negative, Whiskey Kilo Two Eight is not declaring an emergency."

Kaboom. Believers in the right stuff would rather crash and burn.

One fine day, after he had joined a fighter squadron, it would dawn on the young pilot exactly how the losers in the great fraternal competition were now being left behind. Which is to say, not by instructors or other superiors or by failures at prescribed levels of competence, but by death. At this point the essence of the enterprise would begin to dawn on him. Slowly, step by step, the ante had been raised until he was now involved in what was surely the grimmest and grandest gamble of manhood. Being a fighter pilot—for that matter, simply taking off in a single-engine jet fighter of the Century series, such as an F–102, or any of the military's other marvelous bricks with fins on them—presented a man, on a perfectly sunny day, with more ways to get himself killed than his wife and children could imagine in their wildest fears. If he was barreling down the runway at two hundred miles an hour, completing the takeoff run, and the board started lighting up red, should he (a) abort the takeoff (and try to wrestle with the monster, which was gorged with jet fuel, out in the sand beyond the end of the runway) or (b) eject (and hope that the goddamned human cannonball trick works at zero altitude and he doesn't shatter an elbow or a kneecap on the way out) or (c) continue the takeoff and deal with the problem aloft (knowing full well that the ship may be on fire and therefore seconds away from exploding)? He would have one second to sort out the options and act, and this kind of little workaday decision came up all the time. Occasionally a man would look coldly at the binary problem he was now confronting every day—Right Stuff/Death—and decide it wasn't worth it and voluntarily shift over to transports or reconnaissance or whatever. And his comrades would wonder, for a day or so, what evil virus had invaded his soul . . . as they left him behind. More often, however, the reverse would happen. Some college graduate would enter Navy aviation through the Reserves, simply as an alternative to the Army draft, fully intending to return to civilian life, to some waiting profession or family business; would become involved in the obsessive business of ascending the ziggurat pyramid of flying; and, at the end of his enlistment, would astound everyone back home and very likely himself as well by signing up for another one. What on earth got into him? He couldn't explain it. After all, the very words for it had been amputated. A Navy study showed that two-thirds of the fighter pilots who were rated in the top rungs of their groups—i.e., the hottest young pilots—reenlisted when the time came, and practically all were college graduates. By this point, a young fighter jock was like the preacher in *Moby Dick* who climbs up into the pulpit on a rope ladder and then pulls the ladder up behind him; except the pilot could not use the words necessary to express the vital lessons. Civilian life, and even home and hearth, now seemed not only far away but far *below*, back down many levels of the pyramid of the right stuff.

A fighter pilot soon found he wanted to associate only with other fighter pilots. Who else could understand the nature of the little proposition (right stuff/death) they were all dealing with? And what other subject could compare with it? It was riveting! To talk about it in so many words was forbidden, of course. The very words *death, danger, bravery, fear* were not to be uttered except in the occasional specific instance or for ironic effect. Nevertheless, the subject could be adumbrated in *code* or *by example*.

Every evening at bases all over America, there were military pilots huddled in officers clubs eagerly cutting the right stuff up in coded slices so they could talk about it. What more compelling topic of conversation was there in the world? In the Air Force there were even pilots who would ask the tower for priority landing clearance so that they could make the beer call on time, at 4 p.m. sharp, at the Officers Club. They would come right out and state the reason. The drunken rambles began at four and sometimes went on for ten or twelve hours. Such conversations! They diced that righteous stuff up into little bits, bowed ironically to it, stumbled blind folded around it, groped, lurched, belched, staggered, bawled, sang, roared, and feinted at it with self-deprecating humor. Nevertheless!—they never mentioned it by name. No, they used the approved codes, such as: "Like a jerk I got myself into a hell of a corner today." They told of how they "lucked out of it." To get across the extreme peril of his exploit, one would use certain oblique cues. He would say, "I looked over at Robinson"—who would be known to the listeners as a non-com who sometimes rode backseat to read radar—"and he wasn't talking any more, he was just staring at the radar, like this, giving it that *zombie* look. Then I *knew* I was in trouble!" Beautiful! Just right! For it would also be known to the listeners that the non-coms advised one another: "*Never* fly with a lieutenant. *Avoid* captains and majors. Hell, man, do yourself a favor: don't fly with anybody below colonel." Which in turn said: "Those young bucks shoot dice with death!" And yet once in the air the non-com had his own standards. He was determined to remain as outwardly cool as the pilot, so that when the pilot did something that truly petrified him, he would say nothing; instead, he would turn silent, catatonic, like a zombie. Perfect! *Zombie*. There you had it, compressed into a single word, all of the foregoing. I'm a hell of a pilot! I shoot dice with death! And now all you fellows know it! And I haven't spoken of that unspoken stuff even once!

Bob Gainey

Ken Dryden

The Leafs tie the game quickly, Boutette scoring after a penalty to Houle, but when the game resumes, the sloppy play continues. Already the fans, even some of the players, can sense that the real game is being played the one minute in every three that Jarvis, Gainey, and Chartraw play against Sittler, McDonald, and Williams. Because the Leafs depend on Sittler's line for a high percentage of their scoring, our approach is simple—stop Sittler, McDonald, and Williams and we will win. To do that, Bowman wants the Jarvis line, our best defensive line, to play them head-to-head. At home, with the advantage of the last change of players, Leafs coach Roger Neilson works to keep Sittler away from Jarvis, but finding he can do it only by moving him on and off the ice too quickly to be effective, he soon abandons the effort. Thereafter, whenever Sittler's line goes onto the ice, Jarvis's line follows. Within that match-up there is another, which for me has always been the best part of a Leafs-Canadiens game. It is when Lanny McDonald and Bob Gainey play against each other. They are two strong, proud, willful players, Gainey on left wing, McDonald on right, face to face, as if theirs is a personal test—skating, hammering at each other with shoulders and hips, hard and often in painful exhilaration, like two well-matched fighters taking their best shots, grim, respectful, and inside, grinning with enormous pleasure. As I watch them on the ice, uncomplaining, never acknowledging the other, friends competing as good friends often do, it is as if they understand what we can only sense—that whoever wins their private contest will win the game.

It is a great temptation to say too much about Bob Gainey. It comes in part from a fear, guilt-edged in all of us, that Gainey, a fifteen-goal scorer in a league full of do-nothing thirty-goal scorers, goes too often unrewarded. But mostly it is admiration. If there is such a thing as a "player's player," it would be Gainey. A phrase often heard and rarely explained, it is seldom applied to the best player of a sport, as Gainey is not, for performance is only a part of it. Instead, the phrase is for someone who has the personal and playing qualities that others wish they had, basic, unalterable qualities—dependability, discipline, hard work, courage—the roots of every team. To them, Gainey adds a timely, insistent passion, an enormous will to win, and a powerful, punishing playing style, secure and manly, without the strut of machismo. If I could be a forward, I would want to be Bob Gainey.

It took more than two years for Montreal's press, fans, coaches, and management to agree that Gainey had an indefinite future with the team doing simply what he had been doing. I remember a brief talk I had with Bowman on the way to an airport after a game in Gainey's second year. Gainey had just played what I thought was an outstanding game, characteristically without a goal or an assist, and I was talking extravagantly to Bowman about him. Bowman was agreeing, but once or twice, wincing, fighting his own feelings, he said that Gainey really needed to score more often, that a regular forward on the Canadiens team had to score at least 20 goals. The next year, after he had scored several times early in the season, when others were predicting 40 goals or more for him, Gainey talked of 25, not with any longing, but simply as a total that would remove the pressure from him, that would release him to play the game he knew he played best. Soon after, when the team was in the midst of a slump, he began to think differently. He said he had come to realize that if he was to do his job well, he couldn't score even 25 goals a season. He felt that if he did, the negative trade-off in goals against would make it a poor bargain for the team. He scored 15 goals that year.

The same year, Doug Jarvis joined the team, and with Gainey and a 35-year-old defenseman-right winger named Jim Roberts, they formed the "Jarvis line." Playing one minute in every three, on a team that scored more than 380 goals, they scored 33. But playing the first shift of every game, often the last shift of a period and the last minute of every game when the score was close, playing the Clarke, Sittler, Perreault, Dionne, Esposito, and Trottier lines, the league's best lines, head-to-head, they allowed even fewer. It seemed inconceivable to us. After losing just twelve games (eleven regular-season games, and one playoff game) and winning the Stanley Cup, there was a clear and unequivocal consensus by the end of the 1976 season—there was room for a low-scoring but peerless defensive forward, for a low-scoring but superb defensive line.

That is an important moment for a defensive player, particularly a forward—to know that his play will be judged against a standard suited to his natural game; to know that a general manager will ignore statistics, or emphasize different ones, and reward him for what he does for the team, not for what he doesn't do. If he scores only rarely, as he always has, it is important to know that the press and the fans won't wonder out loud why he is playing. To feel the pressure taken off, to feel accepted and appreciated for what he does, no longer feeling himself at a halfway house, safe for now, but getting older, and knowing he must soon be something else—that is decisive. For without that consensus, the incentives—more applause, more kind words, more money—are too much, tempting him away from what he can do to what he cannot, at great cost to the team, and to him.

He is the consummate team player. An often misunderstood phrase, it does not mean that Gainey is without the selfish interests the rest of us have. It means instead that without the team's tangible rewards, without the wins and the Stanley Cups, there are few tangible rewards for him. For Gainey's skills are a team's skills, ones that work best and show best when a team does well; ones that seem less important when it doesn't. While other players, in their roles, constantly battle the tension between team and self (it is surely good for Larry Robinson to score a goal; if the team is ahead and the score is close, it may not be good for the team that he try), simply put, what's good for Bob Gainey is good for the team; and vice versa. In many ways he is like former basketball star Bill Bradley. Without virtuoso individual skills, team play becomes both virtue and necessity, and what others understand as unselfishness is really cold-eyed realism—he simply knows what works best, for the team and for him.

Like a coach, like a goalie, Gainey plays with a constant perspective on a game. But unlike a coach or a goalie, he plays a game in its passionate midst, where perspective is rare, perhaps unique to him. He is sensitive to a game's tempos, to its moods, if it moves too fast or too slow, if we are in control, or they are, or no one is. And each time he goes on the ice, his role becomes the same. More than to score and to stop his man from scoring, it is one almost of stewardship. When he leaves the ice sixty seconds later, he wants the puck in his opponent's zone, the tempo of the game to be right for the score and for the time of the game; he wants the game under control. Then, as the next line comes on to do what it does best, Gainey stays with the game, watching for the link between what he has done and what comes next, and if a goal is scored a minute or two minutes later, he will find satisfaction or despair that is more than just vicarious.

Because of his style, because of the role he plays on a team, the moment a game is under control is the moment of Gainey's triumph. For us, that moment usually comes when we score so often that the gap of goals is so wide and the time so short that a comeback is no longer possible. On this night, we scored only four goals, the Bruins were never far behind, and there was always time for something to happen. But nothing could happen. The tempo of the game was set; the mood was set; our control was absolute. For more than half the game, Gainey could savor that moment in triumph.

One time, reading something which mentioned repeatedly that Gainey scored very few goals, Lynda turned to me a little surprised and said that while she had watched him play for almost five years, she had never realized that. Then she shrugged, and went on to something else, as if in Gainey's case it somehow wasn't relevant. While a team needs all kinds of players with all kinds of skills to win, it needs prototypes, strong, dependable prototypes, as examples of what you want your team to be. If you want it to be quick and opportunistic, you need a Lafleur and a Shutt, so that those who can be quick are encouraged to try, and those who cannot will move faster than they otherwise might. If you want a team to be cool and unflappable, you need at least one Savard, to reassure you, to let you know that the time and the team needed to do what you want are still there. If you want a team to be able to lift a game, to find an emotional level higher than any opponent can find, you need players like Lapointe and Tremblay, mercurial players who can take it there. And if you want a team game, where the goal is the team and the goal is to win, you need a player with an emotional and practical stake in a team game, a player to remind you of that game, to bring you back to it whenever you forget it, to be the playing conscience of the team. Like Bob Gainey.

Life of a Salesman

Bob Greene

For a while there, before we knew any better, we spoke of them with the deepest disdain. "I suppose I might be a *salesman* when I get out of school," we would say, kidding. Sometimes, in bars, we would continue the joke. A stranger would initiate a conversation and ask what we did; "I'm an insurance salesman," we would say, breaking our friends up.

To a whole generation the very word—"salesman"—conjured up the worst possibilities that life could offer. To be on the street day after day, making business calls trying to peddle a product one did not necessarily believe in—that was the depth of hypocrisy, or so we told ourselves. That was the ultimate in selling out—and boring besides. We were a generation that was going to be creative and alive and free of spirit. We may have been a lot of things, we thought, but we were not going to be a generation of salesmen.

Well . . . I am on the road a lot. One of the staples of my life is the moment when I get off a plane, or arrive at an airport to catch a flight, and spend my spare minutes at a pay telephone. The phones are generally in a line, close together; you are able to hear what your neighbors are saying, to your left and to your right.

And what I overhear, time after time, is one of the melancholy stories of our modern age: the salesman checking in with his home office to confess he has not been able to make the sale he was sent out to consummate.

There is a pattern; I have seen the drama acted out enough times that I can almost tell when it is coming. The man moves the receiver away from the wall, then hesitates before making his call. He is figuratively, if not literally, taking a breath. When his superior back home answers, he begins the conversation in a hearty tone of voice. But soon enough he is required to give the news—it usually comes in some variation of "They think they're going to have to pass on it for now"—and it is not long before the party on the other end terminates the call.

I see these same men at tables for one in hotel dining rooms, on stools in hotel bars. I see them heading out into a city not their own at eight A.M., dressed as if they are expected at a fancy dinner; I see them coming back late in the afternoon, their ties loosened, their eyes distracted.

I see them everywhere, and I have come to understand that they are among the bravest of us. They face on a daily basis what we all dread the most: flat, cold rejection. Even the best of them hears "No" more than he hears "Yes"; the unlucky ones hardly hear "Yes" at all. Yet all of them get up each morning and go out to do it again—move through a world where they usually are not welcome, usually are considered a nuisance. And they dare not ever let their fear show on their faces; once they do, they are dead.

Especially in the current economic climate, their task seems brutal. No one has extra money to spend; individuals don't have it, and corporations don't have it, and everyone has been advised to ride the bad times out and wait for a turnaround. But the salesmen can't do that. If they don't sell, their families don't eat; if they don't sell, they don't live. Before they walk out the door in the morning they know they are probably going to fail. But they have no choice other than to try.

The rest of us can ease through our bad days without being stuck in the ribs. If things are not going well, the signs are usually subliminal. The salesman, though—there is no subtlety in the way he is told the bad news. There are a million ways to paraphrase it, but the basic message never changes: We don't want what you're selling. Go away.

Even on the good days, it is hard to imagine that the salesman's sleep comes easily. Even on the days when someone has said the magic word—"Yes"—the salesman goes to bed knowing that he's got to do it all over again in the morning. Can he feel glory? Doubtful. The product is never his own. If he is able to sell it, the producer assumes that the product is so good it sells itself. When he is unable to sell it, the producer assumes that the salesman is lousy. Lousy, or getting old and tired.

So I see them everywhere—so will you, if you look. And it occurs to me that the salesmen are no longer only the older men so scorned by a generation. As I hear their tales on the pay telephones to either side of me, I glance over and see that more and more of them are a part of that generation. That generation is aging like every generation before it, and many of its dreamers are now salesmen, dreaming different dreams.

If there is something heroic about them—and I think that there is—it is a heroism that is destined to be felt only in their own hearts, or perhaps in the hearts of their families. They have learned to smile when they feel like cringing; they have learned to hit the streets when they feel like locking the door. Most of them may not have ever imagined they would end up doing precisely this. But as long as there is life and as long as there are businesses, there will be salesmen. When this generation is long forgotten, another generation's salesmen will be knocking on doors and taking a breath before phoning the home office. Trying to find a palatable explanation for that ugliest, most familiar word in their lexicon—"No."

The World of Epictetus
Reflections on survival and leadership
Vice Admiral James Bond Stockdale, USN

The author was the senior naval service prisoner of war and leader of American covert resistance in North Vietnamese prisons from 1965 to 1973. He was awarded the Congressional Medal of Honor and is currently a senior research fellow at the Hoover Institution at Stanford University. An award for "inspirational leadership" has been established in his name by the Navy for commanding officers below the grade of captain who are serving in command of fleet operational ships, submarines, or aviation squadrons.

In 1965 I was a forty-one-year-old commander, the senior pilot of Air Wing 16, flying combat missions in the area just south of Hanoi from the aircraft carrier *Oriskany*. By September of that year I had grown quite accustomed to briefing dozens of pilots and leading them on daily air strikes; I had flown nearly 200 missions myself and knew the countryside of North Vietnam like the back of my hand. On the ninth of that month I led about thirty-five airplanes to the Thanh Hoa Bridge, just west of that city. That bridge was tough; we had been bouncing 500-pounders off it for weeks.

The September 9 raid held special meaning for *Oriskany* pilots because of a special bomb load we had improvised; we were going in with our biggest, the 2000-pounders, hung not only on our attack planes but on our F-8 fighter-bombers as well. This increase in bridge-busting capability came from the innovative brain of a major flying with my Marine fighter squadron. He had figured out how we could jury-rig some switches, hang the big bombs, pump out some of the fuel to stay within takeoff weight limits, and then top off our tanks from our airborne refuelers while en route to the target. Although the pilot had to throw several switches in sequence to get rid of his bombs, a procedure requiring above-average cockpit agility, we routinely operated on the premise that all pilots of Air Wing 16 were above average. I test-flew the new load on a mission, thought it over, and approved it; that's the way we did business.

Our spirit was up. That morning, the *Oriskany* Air Wing was finally going to drop the bridge that was becoming a North Vietnamese symbol of resistance. You can imagine our dismay when we crossed the coast and the weather scout I had sent on ahead radioed back that ceiling and visibility were zero-zero in the bridge area. In the tiny cockpit of my A–4 at the front of the pack, I pushed the button on the throttle, spoke into the radio mike in my oxygen mask, and told the formation to split up and proceed in pairs to the secondary targets I had specified in my contingency briefing. What a letdown.

The adrenaline stopped flowing as my wingman and I broke left and down and started sauntering along toward our "milk run" target: boxcars on a railroad siding between Vinh and Thanh Hoa, where the flak was light. Descending through 10,000 feet, I unsnapped my oxygen mask and let it dangle, giving my pinched face a rest—no reason to stay uncomfortable on this run.

As I glided toward that easy target, I'm sure I felt totally self-satisfied. I had the top combat job that a Navy commander can hold and I was in tune with my environment. I was confident—I knew airplanes and flying inside out. I was comfortable with the people I worked with and I knew the trade so well that I often improvised variations in accepted procedures and encouraged others to do so under my watchful eye. I was on top. I thought I had found every key to success and had no doubt that my Academy and test-pilot schooling had provided me with everything I needed in life.

I passed down the middle of those boxcars and smiled as I saw the results of my instinctive timing. A neat pattern—perfection. I was just pulling out of my dive low to the ground when I heard a noise I hadn't expected—the *boom boom boom* of a 57-millimeter gun—and then I saw it just behind my wingtip. I was hit—all the red lights came on, my control system was going out—and I could barely keep that plane from flying into the ground while I got that damned oxygen mask up to my mouth so I could tell my wingman that I was about to eject. What rotten luck. And on a "milk run"!

The descent in the chute was quiet except for occasional rifle shots from the streets below. My mind was clear, and I said to myself, "five years." I knew we were making a mess of the war in Southeast Asia, but I didn't think it would last longer than that; I was also naive about the resources I would need in order to survive a lengthy period of captivity.

The Durants have said that culture is a thin and fragile veneer that superimposes itself on mankind. For the first time I was on my own, without the veneer. I was to spend years searching through and refinding my bag of memories, looking for useful tools, things of value. The values were there, but they were all mixed up with technology, bureaucracy, and expediency, and had to be brought up into the open.

Education should take care to illuminate values, not bury them amongst the trivia. Are our students getting the message that without personal integrity intellectual skills are worthless?

Integrity is one of those words which many people keep in that desk drawer labeled "too hard." It's not a topic for the dinner table or the cocktail party. You can't buy or sell it. When supported with education, a person's integrity can give him something to rely on when his perspective seems to blur, when rules and principles seem to waver, and when he's faced with hard choices of right or wrong. It's something to keep him on the right track, something to keep him afloat when he's drowning; if only for practical reasons, it is an attribute that should be kept at the very top of a young person's consciousness.

The importance of the latter point is highlighted in prison camps, where everyday human nature, stripped bare, can be studied under a magnifying glass in accelerated time. Lessons spotlighted and absorbed in that laboratory sharpen one's eye for their abstruse but highly relevant applications in the "real time" world of now.

In the five years since I've been out of prison, I've participated several times in the process of selecting senior naval officers for promotion or important command assignments. I doubt that the experience is significantly different from that of executives who sit on "selection boards" in any large hierarchy. The system must be formal, objective, and fair; if you've seen one, you've probably seen them all. Navy selection board proceedings go something like this.

The first time you know the identity of the other members of the board is when you walk into a boardroom at eight o'clock on an appointed morning. The first order of business is to stand, raise your right hand, put your left hand on the Bible, and swear to make the best judgment you can, on the basis of merit, without prejudice. You're sworn to confidentiality regarding all board members' remarks during the proceedings. Board members are chosen for their experience and understanding; they often have knowledge of the particular individuals under consideration. They must feel free to speak their minds. They read and grade dozens of dossiers, and each candidate is discussed extensively. At voting time, a member casts his vote by selecting and pushing a "percent confidence" button, visible only to himself, on a console attached to his chair. When the last member pushes his button, a totalizer displays the numerical average "confidence" of the board. No one knows who voted what.

I'm always impressed by the fact that every effort is made to be fair to the candidate. Some are clearly out, some are clearly in; the borderline cases are tough ones. You go over and over those in the "middle pile" and usually you vote and revote until late at night. In all the boards I've sat on, no inference or statement in a "jacket" is as sure to portend a low confidence score on the vote as evidence of a lack of directness or rectitude of a candidate in his dealings with others. Any hint of moral turpitude really turns people off. When the crunch comes, they prefer to work with forthright plodders rather than with devious geniuses. I don't believe that this preference is unique to the military. In any hierarchy where people's fates are decided by committees or boards, those who lose credibility with their peers and who cause their superiors to doubt their directness, honesty, or integrity are dead. Recovery isn't possible.

The linkage of men's ethics, reputations, and fates can be studied in even more vivid detail in prison camp. In that brutally controlled environment a perceptive enemy can get his hooks into the slightest chink in a man's ethical armor and accelerate his downfall. Given the right opening, the right moral weakness, a certain susceptibility on the part of the prisoner, a clever extortionist can drive his victim into a downhill slide that will ruin his image, self-respect, and life in a very short time.

There are some uncharted aspects to this, some traits of susceptibility which I don't think psychologists yet have words for. I am thinking of the tragedy that can befall a person who has such a need for love or attention that he will sell his soul for it. I use tragedy with the rigorous definition. Aristotle applied to it: the story of a good man with a flaw who comes to an unjustified bad end. This is a rather delicate point and one that I want to emphasize. We had very very few collaborators in prison, and comparatively few Aristotelian tragedies, but the story and fate of one of these good men with a flaw might be instructive.

He was handsome, smart, articulate, and smooth. He was almost sincere. He was obsessed with success. When the going got tough, he decided expediency was preferable to principle.

This man was a classical opportunist. He befriended and worked for the enemy to the detriment of his fellow Americans. He made a tacit deal; moreover, he accepted favors (a violation of the code of conduct). In time, out of fear and shame, he withdrew; we could not get him to communicate with the American prisoner organization.

I couldn't learn what made the man tick. One of my best friends in prison, one of the wisest persons I have ever known, had once been in a squadron with this fellow. In prisoners' code I tapped a question to my philosophical friend: "What in the world is going on with that fink?"

"You're going to be surprised at what I have to say," he meticulously tapped back. "In a squadron he pushes himself forward and dominates the scene. He's a continual fountain of information. He's the person everybody relies on for inside dope. He works like mad; often flies more hops than others. It drives him crazy if he's not liked. He tends to grovel and ingratiate himself before others. I didn't realize he was really pathetic until I was sitting around with him and his wife one night when he was spinning his yarns of delusions of grandeur, telling of his great successes and his pending ascension to the top. His wife knew him better than anybody else; she shook her head with genuine sympathy and said to him: 'Gee, you're just a phony.' "

In prison, this man had somehow reached the point where he was willing to sell his soul just to satisfy this need, this immaturity. The only way he could get the attention that he demanded from authority was to grovel and ingratiate himself before the enemy. As a soldier he was a miserable failure, but he had not crossed the boundary of willful treason; he was not written off as an irrevocable loss, as were the two patent collaborators with whom the Vietnamese soon arranged that he live.

As we American POWs built our civilization, and wrote our own laws (which we leaders obliged all to memorize), we also codified certain principles which formed the backbone of our policies and attitudes. I codified the principles of compassion, rehabilitation, and forgiveness with the slogan: "It is neither American nor Christian to nag a repentant sinner to his grave." (Some didn't like it, thought it seemed soft on finks.) And so, we really gave this man a chance. Over time, our efforts worked. After five years of self-indulgence he got himself together and started to communicate with the prisoner organization. I sent the message "Are you on the team or not?"; he replied, "Yes," and came back. He told the Vietnamese that he didn't want to play their dirty games anymore. He wanted to get away from those willful collaborators and he came back and he was accepted, after a fashion.

I wish that were the end of the story. Although he came back, joined us, and even became a leader of sorts, he never totally won himself back. No matter how forgiving we were, he was conscious that many resented him—not so much because he was weak but because he had broken what we might call a gentleman's code. In all of those years when he, a senior officer, had willingly participated in making tape recordings of anti-American material, he had deeply offended the sensibilities of the American prisoners who were forced to listen to him. To most of us it wasn't the rhetoric of the war or the goodness or the badness of this or that issue that counted. The object of our highest value was the well-being of our fellow prisoners. He had broken that code and hurt some of those people. Some thought that as an informer he had indirectly hurt them physically. I don't believe that. What indisputably hurt them was his not having the sensitivity to realize the damage his opportunistic conduct would do to the morale of a bunch of Middle American guys with

Middle American attitudes which they naturally cherished. He should have known that in those solitary cells where his tapes were piped were idealistic, direct, patriotic fellows who would be crushed and embarrassed to have him, a senior man in excellent physical shape, so obviously not under torture, telling the world that the war was wrong. Even if he believed what he said, which he did not, he should have had the common decency to keep his mouth shut. You can sit and think anything you want, but when you insensitively cut down those who want to love and help you, you cross a line. He seemed to sense that he could never truly be one of us.

And yet he was likable—particularly back in civilization after release—when tension was off, and making a deal did not seem so important. He exuded charm and "hail fellow" sophistication. He wanted so to be liked by all those men he had once discarded in his search for new friends, new deals, new fields to conquer in Hanoi. The tragedy of his life was obvious to us all. Tears were shed by some of his old prison mates when he was killed in an accident that strongly resembled suicide some months later. The Greek drama had run its course. He was right out of Aristotle's book, a good man with a flaw who had come to an unjustified bad end. The flaw was insecurity: the need to ingratiate himself, the need for love and adulation at any price.

He reminded me of Paul Newman in *The Hustler.* Newman couldn't stand success. He knew how to make a deal. He was handsome, he was smart, he was attractive to everybody; but he had to have adulation, and therein lay the seed of tragedy. Playing high-stakes pool against old Minnesota Fats (Jackie Gleason), Newman was well in the lead, and getting more full of himself by the hour. George C. Scott, the pool bettor, whispered to his partner: "I'm going to keep betting on Minnesota Fats; this other guy [Newman] is a born loser—he's all skill and no character." And he was right, a born loser—I think that's the message.

How can we educate to avoid these casualties? Can we by means of education prevent this kind of tragedy? What we prisoners were in was a one-way leverage game in which the other side had all the mechanical advantage. I suppose you could say that we all live in a leverage world to some degree; we all experience people trying to use us in one way or another. The difference in Hanoi was the degradation of the ends (to be used as propaganda agents of an enemy, or as informers on your fellow Americans), and the power of the means (total environmental control including solitary confinement, restraint by means of leg-irons and handcuffs, and torture). Extortionists always go down the same track: the imposition of guilt and fear for having disobeyed their rules, followed in turn by punishment, apology, confession, and atonement (their payoff). Our captors would go to great lengths to get a man to compromise his own code, even if only slightly, and then they would hold that in their bag, and the next time get him to go a little further.

Some people are psychologically, if not physically, at home in extortion environments. They are tough people who instinctively avoid getting sucked into the undertows. They never kid themselves or their friends; if they miss the mark they admit it. But there's another category of person who gets tripped up. He makes a small compromise, perhaps rationalizes it, and then makes another one; and then he gets depressed, full of shame, lonesome, loses his willpower and self-respect, and comes to a tragic end. Somewhere along the line he realizes that he has turned a corner that he didn't mean to turn. All too late he realizes that he has been worshiping the wrong gods and discovers the wisdom of the ages: life is not fair.

In sorting out the story after our release, we found that most of us had come to combat constant mental and physical pressure in much the same way. We discovered that when a person is alone in a cell and sees the door open only once or twice a day for a bowl of soup, he realizes after a period of weeks in isolation and darkness that he has to build some sort of ritual into his life if he wants to avoid becoming an animal. Ritual fills a need in a hard life and it's easy to see how formal church ritual grew. For almost all of us, this ritual was built around prayer, exercise, and clandestine communication. The prayers I said during those days were prayers of quality with ideas of substance. We found that over the course of time our minds had a tremendous capacity for invention and introspection, but had the weakness of being an integral part of our bodies. I remembered Descartes and how in his philosophy he separated mind and body. One time I cursed my body for the way it decayed my mind. I had decided that I would become a Gandhi. I would have to be carried around on a pallet and in that state I could not be used by my captors for propaganda purposes. After about ten days of fasting, I found that I had become so depressed that soon I would risk going into interrogation ready to spill my guts just looking for a friend. I tapped to the guy next door and I said, "Gosh, how I wish Descartes could have been right, but he's wrong." He was a little slow to reply; I reviewed Descartes's deduction with him and explained how I had discovered that body and mind are inseparable.

On the positive side, I discovered the tremendous file-cabinet volume of the human mind. You can memorize an incredible amount of material and you can draw the past out of your memory with remarkable recall by easing slowly toward the event you seek and not crowding the mind too closely. You'll try to remember who was at your birthday party when you were five years old, and you can get it, but only after months of effort. You can break the locks and find the answers, but you need time and solitude to learn how to use this marvelous device in your head which is the greatest computer on earth.

Of course many of the things we recalled from the past were utterly useless as sources of strength or practicality. For instance, events brought

back from cocktail parties or insincere social contacts were almost repugnant because of their emptiness, their utter lack of value. More often
than not, the locks worth picking had been on old schoolroom doors.
School days can be thought of as a time when one is filling the important
stacks of one's memory library. For me, the golden doors were labeled
history and the classics. The historical perspective which enabled a man
to take himself away from all the agitation, not necessarily to see a rosy
lining, but to see the real nature of the situation he faced, was truly a
thing of value.

Here's how this historical perspective helped me see the reality of my
own situation and thus cope better with it. I learned from a Vietnamese
prisoner that the same cells we occupied had in years before been lived in
by many of the leaders of the Hanoi government. From my history
lessons I recalled that when metropolitan France permitted communists
in the government in 1936, the communists who occupied cells in Vietnam were set free. I marveled at the cycle of history, all within my
memory, which prompted Hitler's rise in Germany, then led to the rise of
the Popular Front in France, and finally vacated this cell of mine halfway
around the world ("Perhaps Pham Van Dong lived here"). I came to
understand what tough people these were. I was willing to fight them to
the death, but I grew to realize that hatred was an indulgence, a very inefficient emotion. I remember thinking, "If you were committed to
beating the dealer in a gambling casino, would *hating* him help your
game?" In a pidgin English propaganda book the guard gave me,
speeches by these old communists about their prision experiences
stressed how they learned to beat down the enemy by being united. It
seemed comforting to know that we were united against the communist
administration of Hoa Lo prison just as the Vietnamese communists had
united against the French administration of Hoa Lo in the thirties. Prisoners are prisoners, and there's only one way to beat administrations.
We resolved to do it better in the sixties than they had in the thirties. You
don't base system-beating on any thought of political idealism; you do it
as a competitive thing, as an expression of self-respect.

Education in the classics teaches you that all organizations since the
beginning of time have used the power of guilt; that cycles are repetitive;
and that this is the way of the world. It's a naive person who comes in
and says, "Let's see, what's good and what's bad?" That's a quagmire.
You can get out of that quagmire only by recalling how wise men before
you accommodated the same dilemmas. And I believe a good classical
education and an understanding of history can best determine the rules
you should live by. They also give you the power to analyze reasons for
these rules and guide you as to how to apply them to your own situation.
In a broader sense, all my education helped me. Naval Academy
discipline and body contact sports helped me. But the education which I
found myself using most was what I got in graduate school. The
messages of history and philosophy I used were simple.

The first one is this business about life not being fair. That is a very important lesson and I learned it from a wonderful man named Philip Rhinelander. As a lieutenant commander in the Navy studying political science at Stanford University in 1961, I went over to philosophy corner one day and an older gentleman said, "Can I help you?" I said, "Yes I'd like to take some courses in philosophy." I told him I'd been in college for six years and had never had a course in philosophy. He couldn't believe it. I told him that I was a naval officer and he said, "Well, I used to be in the Navy. Sit down." Philip Rhinelander became a great influence in my life.

He had been a Harvard lawyer and had pleaded cases before the Supreme Court and then gone to war as a reserve officer. When he came back he took his doctorate at Harvard. He was also a music composer, had been director of general education at Harvard, dean of the School of Humanities and Sciences at Stanford, and by the time I met him had by choice returned to teaching in the classroom. He said, "The course I'm teaching is my personal two-term favorite—The Problems of Good and Evil—and we're starting our second term." He said the message of his course was from the Book of Job. The number one problem in this world is that people are not able to accommodate the lesson in the book.

He recounted the story of Job. It starts out by establishing that Job was the most honorable of men. Then he lost all his goods. He also lost his reputation, which is what really hurt. His wife was badgering him to admit his sins, but he knew he had made no errors. He was not a patient man and demanded to speak to the Lord. When the Lord appeared in the whirlwind, he said, "Now Job, you have to shape up! Life is not fair." That's my interpretation and that's the way the book ended for hundreds of years. I agree with those of the opinion that the happy ending was spliced on many years later. If you read it, you'll note that the meter changes. People couldn't live with the original message. Here was a good man who came to unexplained grief, and the Lord told him: "That's the way it is. Don't challenge me. This is my world and you either live in it as I designed it or get out."

This was a great comfort to me in prison. It answered the question "Why me?" It cast aside any thoughts of being punished for past actions. Sometimes I shared the message with fellow prisoners as I tapped through the walls to them, but I learned to be selective. It's a strong message which upsets some people.

Rhinelander also passed on to me another piece of classical information which I found of great value. On the day of our last session together he said, "You're a military man, let me give you a book to remember me by. It's a book of military ethics." He handed it to me, and I bade him goodbye with great emotion. I took the book home and that night started to read it. It was the *Enchiridion* of the philosopher Epictetus, his "manual" for the Roman field soldier.

As I began to read, I thought to myself in disbelief, "Does Rhinelander think I'm going to draw lessons for my life from this thing? I'm a fighter pilot. I'm a technical man. I'm a test pilot. I know how to get people to do technical work. I play golf; I drink martinis. I know how to get ahead in my profession. And what does he hand me? A book that says in part, 'It's better to die in hunger, exempt from guilt and fear, than to live in affluence and with perturbation.' " I remembered this later in prison because perturbation was what I was living with. When I ejected from the airplane on that September morn in 1965, I had left the land of technology. I had entered the world of Epictetus, and it's a world that few of us, whether we know it or not, are ever far away from.

In Palo Alto, I had read this book, not with contentment, but with annoyance. Statement after statement: "Men are distrubed not by things, but by the view that they take of them." "Do not be concerned with things which are beyond your power." "Demand not that events should happen as you wish, but wish them to happen as they do happen and you will go on well." This is stoicism. It's not the last word, but it's a viewpoint that comes in handy in many circumstances, and it surely did for me. Particularly this line: "Lameness is an impediment to the body but not to the will." That was significant for me because I wasn't able to stand up and support myself on my badly broken leg for the first couple of years I was in solitary confinement.

Other statements of Epictetus took on added meaning in the light of extortions which often began with our captors' callous pleas: "If you are just reasonable with us we will compensate you. You get your meals, you get to sleep, you won't be pestered, you might even get a cellmate." The catch was that by being "reasonable with us" our enemies meant being their informers, their propagandists. The old stoic had said, "If I can get the things I need with the preservation of my honor and fidelity and self-respect, show me the way and I will get them. But, if you require me to lose my own proper good, that you may gain what is no good, consider how unreasonable and foolish you are." To love our fellow prisoners was within our power. To betray, to propagandize, to disillusion conscientious and patriotic shipmates and destroy their morale so that they in turn would be destroyed was to lose one's power of good.

What attributes serve you well in the extortion environment? We learned there, above all else, that the best defense is to keep your conscience clean. When we did something we are ashamed of, and our captors realized we were ashamed of it, we were in trouble. A little white lie is where extortion and ultimately blackmail start. In 1965, I was crippled and I was alone. I realized that they had all the power. I couldn't see how I was ever going to get out with my honor and self-respect. The one thing I came to realize was that if you don't lose integrity you can't be had and you can't be hurt. Compromises multiply and build up when you're working against a skilled extortionist or a good manipulator. You can't be had if you don't take that first shortcut, or "meet them halfway," as they say, or look for that tacit "deal," or make that first compromise.

Bob North, a political science professor at Stanford, taught me a course called Comparative Marxist Thought. This was not an anticommunist course. It was the study of dogma and thought patterns. We read no criticisms of Marxism, only primary sources. All year we read the works of Marx and Lenin. In Hanoi, I understood more about Marxist theory than my interrogator did. I was able to say to that interrogator, "That's not what Lenin said; you're a deviationist."

One of the things North talked about was brainwashing. A psychologist who studied the Korean prisoner situation, which somewhat parallelled ours, concluded that three categories of prisoners were involved there. The first was the redneck Marine sergeant from Tennessee who had an eighth-grade education. He would get in that interrogation room and they would say that the Spanish-American War was started by the bomb within the *Maine*, which might be true, and he would answer, "B.S." They would show him something about racial unrest in Detroit. "B.S." There was no way they could get to him; his mind was made up. He was a straight guy, red, white, and blue, and everything else was B.S.! He didn't give it a second thought. Not much of a historian, perhaps, but a good security risk.

In the next category were the sophisticates. They were the fellows who could be told these same things about the horrors of American history and our social problems, but had heard it all before, knew both sides of every story, and thought we were on the right track. They weren't ashamed that we had robber barons at a certain time of our history; they were aware of the skeletons in most civilizations' closets. They could not be emotionally involved and so they were good security risk.

The ones who were in trouble were the high school graduates who had enough sense to pick up the innuendo, and yet not enough education to accommodate it properly. Not many of them fell, but most of the men that got entangled started from that background.

The psychologist's point is possibly oversimplistic, but I think his message has some validity. A little knowledge is a dangerous thing.

Generally speaking, I think education is a tremendous defense; the broader, the better. After I was shot down my wife, Sybil, found a clipping glued in the front of my collegiate dictionary: "Education is an ornament in prosperity and a refuge in adversity." She certainly agrees with me on that. Most of us prisoners found that the so-called practical academic excercises in how to do things, which I'm told are proliferating, were useless. I'm not saying that we should base education on training people to be in prison, but I am saying that in stress situations, the fundamentals, the hard-core classical subjects, are what serve best.

Theatrics also helped sustain me. My mother had been a drama coach when I was young and I was in many of her plays. In prison I learned how to manufacture a personality and live it, crawl into it, and hold that role without deviation. During interrogations, I'd check the responses I got to different kinds of behavior. They'd get worried when I did things irrationally. And so, every so often, I would play that "irrational" role and come completely unglued. When I could tell that pressure to make a public exhibition of me was building, I'd stand up, tip the table over, attempt to throw the chair through the window, and say, "No way. Goddammit! I'm not doing that! Now, come over here and fight!" This was a risky ploy, because if they thought you were acting, they would slam you into the ropes and make you scream in pain like a baby. You could watch their faces and read their minds. They had expected me to behave like a stoic. But a man would be a fool to make their job easy by being conventional and predictable. I could feel the tide turn in my favor at that magic moment when their anger turned to pleading: "Calm down, now calm down." The payoff would come when they decided that the risk of my going haywire in front of some touring American professor on a "fact-finding" mission was too great. More important, they had reason to believe that I would tell the truth—namely, that I had been in solitary confinement for four years and tortured fifteen times—without fear of future consequences. So theatrical training proved helpful to me.

Can you educate for leadership? I think you can, but the communists would probably say no. One day in an argument with an interrogator, I said, "You are so proud of being a party member, what are the criteria?" He said in a flurry of anger, "There are only four: you have to be seventeen years old, you have to be selfless, you have to be smart enough to understand the theory, and you've got to be a person who innately influences others." He stressed that fourth one. I think psychologists would say that leadership is innate, and there is truth in that. But, I also think you can learn some leadership traits that naturally accrue from a good education: compassion is a necessity for leaders, as are spontaneity, bravery, self-discipline, honesty, and above all, integrity.

I remember being disappointed about a month after I was back when one of my young friends, a prision mate, came running up after a reunion at the Naval Academy. He said with glee, "This is really great, you won't believe how this country has advanced. They've practically done away with plebe year at the Academy, and they've got computers in the basement of Bancroft Hall." I thought, "My God, if there was anything that helped us get through those eight years, it was plebe year, and if anything screwed up that war, it was computers!"

11

LEADERSHIP

*If some found him tiresome . . . they were nonetheless bedazzled by his
vitality, guile, endurance, his powers of divination and ability to appeal to
the core interests of other people.*

—Doris Kearns

What makes a person an effective leader? How does the leadership
process work? Do leaders really make a difference to organizational
outcomes and to the lives and fortunes of people in the organization?
Nobody seems to have definitive answers to these questions. Indeed, many
behavioral scientists, after observing or being part of the innumerable
studies, debates, and theoretical formulations focused on leadership, have
thrown up their hands and turned to other concepts in an effort to understand and to explain organizational life. Yet the fascination and indeed
preoccupation with leadership remains for researchers and practitioners
alike. The search for effective leaders goes on. Training courses abound
which promise the development of improved leadership ability and research money is still allocated to its study. Owners of unsuccessful
organizations, such as some sports teams, regularly blame the managers
and replace them with "better leaders." People continue to attach their
hopes and hatreds to those chosen as leaders.

We do not have the answers to the questions posed at the beginning of
this section. We do feel, however, that one approach to a better
understanding of what leadership comprises is to examine what some
students of leadership have said recently, based on their research on leaders
in the field, and to take a close look at descriptions of some leaders in action in their organizations. Leaders described here and in other sections of
this book appear to be purposive, dynamic, durable individuals. Frequently leaders are manipulative, creating and interpreting realities and moving
people into those realities to accomplish their goals. They often are admired and respected by their followers, but sometimes they are feared and
hated by these same followers. Successful leaders typically are good
listeners; sometimes they listen in order to work with those who tell them
things, sometimes to take advantage of them, but always because they ar
relentless in their pursuit of information upon which to base their future
ideas and actions.

We suspect that most people will have encountered, worked for, competed with or even acted as individuals having some or all of the leadership

characteristics evident in the pieces in this section. In the article, "Why Are Some Managers Top Performers? A Researcher Picks Out 16 Characteristics," Erik Larson discusses the research findings of leadership researcher Charles Garfield. While Garfield's research methods are apparently controversial, his findings make intuitive sense to managers and echo observations and actions reported in other articles in this section. Several characteristics are linked to effective leadership, including the ability of managers to plan ahead and to stay "lean and hungry" in their jobs. Two characteristics identified are: 1.) an ability to act, to reject perfectionism, to not be paralyzed by too much thinking or too much concern with a perfect blueprint or game plan and 2.) a capacity to enjoy the art in their work, to be playful and to retain a sense of fun in their jobs. These characteristics reappear frequently in this and other sections of the book, wherever the discussion turns to successful individual performance.

McCall and Lombardo augment the discussion of leadership characteristics in "What Makes a Top Executive?" They compare executives who have fufilled their potential and are seen as successful with those who have not reached the top, have plateaued or even have declined in their careers. Both categories of leaders studied had strengths and weaknesses. Perhaps the most important difference between the successful and unsuccessful managers studied was a reported insensitivity to others' needs and messages. Excessive ambition, betrayal of trust, and arrogance stalled the upward path of many managers in the McCall and Lombardo sample. The authors also point out that luck, in this case misfortune, can produce failure. Being in the wrong place at the wrong time, politically or economically can damage even those leaders who are personally effective. Luck may also produce successful outcomes for leaders.

Effective leaders appear able to acquire a base of power from which they can operate and succeed. They can read their environments perceptively. Doris Kearns' "The Politics of Seduction," describes former President Lyndon Johnson's abilities to build a power base (see also Campus Politico, section 2), his capacities to analyze people and situations, and to enter into the perspectives of others and to turn the knowledge gained to his own advantage.

The excerpt from "Boss" by Mike Royko provides interesting illustrations of tactics used by the late Mayor Richard Daley of Chicago to exert control over the decision making process in city government and to maintain and increase the bases of his power. Daley's sometimes insensitive behavior and his bullying tactics suggest that once at the top a successful leader may not display the qualities described earlier in this section. A close reading of Royko's book suggests that Daley behaved differently, that is with little of his later arrogance, on his way to the top.

Like Johnson, Vince Lombardi in "Winning Is the Only Thing" apparently had an ability to understand and to be sensitive to the needs and emotions of people. Lombardi was able to persuade and to coerce others to stretch their efforts and to accomplish the goals he set for them. He frequently took risks in handling his players, pushing them to their limits of patience and self-control in some of his encounters with them.

The Johnson, Daley, and Lombardi pieces bring into focus the issue of the costs of leadership. There appear to be costs to the leader, to the followers, to the organization and to the larger society when individuals as leaders exert the kind of forceful, yet often subtle behaviors described in these stories. Daley's style and system of leadership did not survive him; no effective subordinates developed to succeed him. Johnson and Lombardi suffered physically from the rigors of their endeavors. The Watergate cover-up during President Nixon's administration illustrated the disadvantages to individuals and to society of an unquestioning commitment to the creed of "Winning Is the Only Thing."

"The Calf Path" by Samuel Foss humorously depicts how sometimes strange and inefficient ways of doing things come into being and persist.

We end this section with a provocative, challenging, and essentially optimistic piece by Ray Bradbury, "Management from Within." He talks about the need to develop the magic, the creativity, and the child within us if we are to be effective leaders. His prescriptions for being creative, springing traps, and surviving in a healthy manner have distinct relevance to leadership. We like his admonition "don't think, don't try, just do!" It reinforces the point made by Larson, in the first piece in this section, about the importance of action for effective leadership. Of course, it is not only action that produces successful outcomes. Reflection is a vital part of the process. Bradbury addresses this too in his guides for creative being.

Why Are Some Managers Top Perfomers?

A Researcher Picks Out 16 Characteristics

Erik Larson

Berkeley, Calif.—Managers, take stock. Do you rule by terror? Do you whine that there's no time for planning? Have you been on the verge of perfecting your pet project for 15 years?

Then you aren't a peak-performing business manager, at least to Charles Garfield, president of the Peak Performance Center here and a researcher in human performance. About this time last year he described six characteristics of high-performance people in a variety of fields; now he's completed his work with a look at about 300 business managers—and has concluded that top performers in that field use more skills than anyone else.

Senior managers require 16 defined characteristics to work at the top of their form. "The corporate culture is much more complex and requires more skills than sports, arts or science cultures," says Mr. Garfield, who has also plotted five stages in the development of the most effective executives. He consented to name a few of these paragons, but more on that later.

THE SIX CHARACTERISTICS

Good business managers at any level have the same six characteristics that mark top performers in other fields, he notes. These people transcend previous performance, avoid getting too comfortable in their jobs, enjoy the art of their work, vividly rehearse coming events in their minds, don't hold trials to place blame for mistakes and examine the worst consequences of an action before taking the risk.

At the level of general manager of, say, sales, research or advertising, four more traits and skills come into play. Top performers at this level always have time for planning and didn't merely swing from crisis to crisis like monkeys caught in a forest fire. "Lower-performing managers would tend to get wrapped up in anything that looked like a crisis," says Mr. Garfield. "High performers were able to sift through and sort out the real crises."

They also were adept at selling their ideas, and sought responsibility instead of artfully dodging it, like bureaucrats. They bore rejection and loss well. Finally, they were inclined to champion new ideas and projects rather than letting them die untried.

In the upper reaches of management, the additional characteristic most apparent was an ability to reject perfectionism and act. "Many others were paralyzed by perfectionism," says Mr. Garfield. "They felt that if they tried it out and it didn't work, they'd be in trouble."

The best senior managers usually didn't have nicknames like Genghis Khan or Bloody Mary, either. They created a balance between autonomy and direction, setting goals for subordinates but not dictating how those goals were to be met. They were good team-builders too, limiting the number of staffers involved in projects to avoid "bureaucratic neutralization."

The most effective senior managers sought quality rather than just quantity in their work, and saw clearly that the training and development of other managers and employees was a vital function. "To them, it's more than just a nice thing to do to give people management training," adds Mr. Garfield.

On his climb to the corner office with five windows, Oriental rugs and live plants, the successful manager evolves through several stages, the researcher found. He illustrates them with the history of an electronics engineer named Joe who clambered up the beanstalk at a Silicon Valley computer company. His journey:

- Initiation Stage. A hotshot engineer, Joe catches the eye of senior officials who switch him into management. Joe must learn to think of himself as a manager and wean himself away from engineering, his first love. He tries.
- Fear of Success Stage. Joe begins to get good at his job—and is scared of being too good because that will pull him still further away from engineering. But he adapts.
- Team-Building Stage. Now fully engaged in management, Joe falls overboard. As boss, he treats subordinates with all the delicacy of Cromwell ruling Ireland. He calls his management style "reign of terror." But when dissension rises, he talks with subordinates, sees the light, and is able to forge them into a team.
- Affiliation Stage. Closely watched by management, Joe has to learn to relate to both upper and lower levels of the organization. The company gods like what they see; Joe is invited to senior management retreats and asked to write important reports. He builds a reputation as a guy you can count on.
- Elevation-Seniority Stage. Joe is tapped for a senior management post. He must learn to cope with his increased distance from both engineering and his former team, and to focus instead on more

abstract demands of the company—finance, strategic planning, the corporate good.

ARE LEADERS BORN OR MADE?

Mr. Garfield's work is only part of a maturing field of study whose roots lie in the old debate over whether great leaders are born or made. Others in that field have already criticized his earlier findings and methods, and his past seminars on peak performance haven't exactly blown executives out of their Brooks Brothers duds, according to some who've attended them.

His sole reliance on interviews has been questioned. Says Douglas Bray, director of human resources research at American Telephone & Telegraph Co. and a pioneer in long-range studies of managerial success factors: " I would be disinclined to place much emphasis on studies based on interviews. However, if Sigmund Freud were doing the interviewing I might change my mind."

But what Mr. Garfield *has* accomplished according to others, is a more scientific confirmation of what talent-spotters may have sensed only intuitively. "The things he is saying are things that have worked for us right along," says Joseph Murray, executive vice president of the San Francisco-based leasing unit of Security Pacific Corp. "What impressed me about Garfield is that he had really done his research. Of course, the other thing that impressed me was that he agreed with me."

And if Mr. Garfield is right, then who are the best of the best? He offers a partial list: Steven Jobs, chairman of Apple Computer Inc.; Gordan Sherman, former chief executive of Midas Muffler Inc.; Joseph and Benjamin Weider of Weider International Inc.; Leonard Krystal, director of Goldcrest-Multimedia Inc. in London, and Vittorio Floriani, chairman of Floriani International, Italy.

What Makes a Top Executive?

Morgan W. McCall Jr.
and Michael M. Lombardo

Senior Executive: At one time, Jim was the leading, perhaps the only , candidate for chief executive officer. And then he ran into something he'd never faced before—an unprofitable operation. He seemed to go on a downward spiral after that, becoming more remote each day, unable to work with key subordinates.

Interviewer: Why do you think he derailed?

Senior Executive: Some of it was bad luck, because the business was going down when he inherited it. Some of it was surrounding himself with specialists, who inevitably wear the blinders of their particular field. And some of it was that he had never learned to delegate. He had no idea of how to lead by listening.

The case of Jim is by no means unusual. Many executives of formidable talent rise to very high levels, yet are denied the ultimate positions. The quick explanations for what might be called their derailment are the ever-popular Peter Principle—they rose past their level of competence—or, more darkly, they possessed some fatal flaw.

The grain of truth in these explanations masks the actual complexity of the process. So we learned from a study that we recently did here at the Center for Creative Leadership, a nonprofit research and educational institution in Greensboro, North Carolina, formed to improve the practice of management.

When we compared 21 derailed executives—successful people who were expected to go even higher in the organization but who reached a plateau late in their careers, were fired, or were forced to retire early—with 20 "arrivers"—those who made it all the way to the top—we found the two groups astonishingly alike. Every one of the 41 executives possessed remarkable strengths, and every one was flawed by one or more significant weaknesses.

Insensitivity to others was cited as a reason for derailment more often than any other flaw. But it was never the only reason. Most often, it was a combination of personal qualities and external circumstances that put an end to an executive's rise. Some of the executives found themselves in a changed situation, in which strengths that had served them well earlier in their careers became liabilities that threw them off track. Others found that weaknesses they'd had all along, once outweighed by assets, became crucial defects in a new situation requiring particular skills to resolve some particular problem.

Our goal was to find out what makes an effective executive, and our original plan was to concentrate on arrivers. But we soon realized that, paradoxically, we could learn a lot about effectiveness by taking a close look at executives who had failed to live up to their apparent potential.

We and our associate, Ann Morrison, worked with several Fortune-500 corporations to identify "savvy insiders"—people who had seen many top executives come and go and who were intimately familiar with their careers. In each corporation one of us interviewed several insiders, usually a few of the top 10 executives and a few senior "human resources professionals," people who help to decide who moves up. We asked them to tell both a success story and a story of derailment.

FATAL FLAWS

Asked to say what had sealed the fate of the men (they were all men) who fell short of ultimate success, our sources named 65 factors, which we boiled down to 10 categories:

1. Insensitive to others: abrasive, intimidating, bullying style.
2. Cold, aloof, arrogant.
3. Betrayal of trust.
4. Overly ambitious: thinking of next job, playing politics.
5. Specific performance problems with the business.
6. Overmanaging: unable to delegate or build a team.
7. Unable to staff effectively.
8. Unable to think strategically.
9. Unable to adapt to boss with different style.
10. Overdependent on advocate or mentor.

No executive had all the flaws cited; indeed, only two were found in the average derailed executive.

As we have noted, the most frequent cause for derailment was insensitivity to other people. "He wouldn't negotiate; there was no room for countervailing views. He could follow a bull through a china shop and still break the china," one senior executive said of a derailed colleague.

Under stress, some of the derailed managers became abrasive and intimidating. One walked into a subordinate's office, interrupting a meeting and said, "I need to see you." When the subordinate tried to explain that he was occupied, his boss snarled, "I don't give a goddamn. I said I wanted to see you now."

Others were so brilliant that they became arrogant, intimidating others with their knowledge. Common remarks were: "He made others feel stupid" or "He wouldn't give you the time of day unless you were brilliant too."

In an incredibly complex and confusing job, being able to trust others absolutely is a necessity. Some executives committed what is perhaps management's only unforgivable sin: They betrayed a trust. This rarely had anything to do with honesty, which was a given in almost all cases. Rather, it was a one-upping of others, or a failure to follow through on promises that wreaked havoc in terms of organizational efficiency. One executive didn't implement a decision as he had promised to do, causing conflicts between the marketing and the production divisions that reverberated downward through four levels of frustrated subordinates.

Others, like Cassius, were overly ambitious. They seemed to be always thinking of their next job, they bruised people in their haste, and they spent too much time trying to please upper management. This sometimes led to staying with a single advocate or mentor too long.

When the mentor fell from favor, so did they. Even if the mentor remained in power, people questioned the executive's ability to make independent judgments. Could he stand alone? One executive had worked for the same boss for the better part of 15 years, following him from one assignment to another. Then top management changed, and the boss no longer fit in with the plans of the new regime. The executive, having no reputation of his own, was viewed as a clone of his boss and was passed-over as well.

A series of performance problems sometimes emerged. Managers failed to meet profit goals, got lazy, or demonstrated that they couldn't handle certain kinds of jobs (usually new ventures or jobs requiring great powers of persuasion). More important in such cases, managers showed that they couldn't change; they failed to admit their problems, covered them up, or tried to blame them on others. One executive flouted senior management by failing to work with a man specifically sent in to fix a profit problem.

After a certain point in their careers, managers must cease to do the work themselves, and must become executives who see that it is done. But some of the men we studied never made this transition, never learning to delegate or to build a team beneath them. Although over managing is irritating at any level, it can be fatal at the executive level. When executives meddle, they are meddling not with low-level subordinates but with other executives, most of whom know much more about their particular area of expertise than their boss ever will. One external-affairs executive who knew little about government regulation tried to direct an expert with 30 years' experience. The expert balked, and the executive lost a battle that should never have begun.

Others got along with their staff, but simply picked the wrong people. Sometimes they staffed in their own image, choosing, for instance, an engineer like themselves when a person with marketing experience would have been better suited for the task at hand. Or sometimes they simply picked people who later bombed.

Inability to think strategically—to take a broad, long-term view—was masked by attention to detail and a miring in technical problems, as some executives simply couldn't go from being doers to being planners. Another common failure appeared as a conflict of style with a new boss. One manager who couldn't change from a go-getter to a thinker/planner eventually ran afoul of a slower-paced, more reflective boss. Although the successful managers sometimes had similar problems, they didn't get into wars over them, and rarely let the issues get personal. Derailed managers exhibited a host of unproductive responses—got peevish, tried to shout the boss down, or just sulked.

In summary, we concluded that executives derail for four basic reasons, all connected to the fact that situations change as one ascends the organizational hierarchy:

1. *Strengths become weaknesses.* Loyalty becomes overdependence, narrowness, or cronyism. Ambition is eventually viewed as politicking and destroys an executive's support base.
2. *Deficiencies eventually matter.* If talented enough, a person can get by with insensitivity at lower levels, but not at higher ones, where subordinates and peers are powerful and probably brilliant also. Those who are charming but not brilliant find that the job gets too big and problems too complex to get by on interpersonal skills.
3. *Success goes to their heads.* After being told how good they are for so long, some executives simply lose their humility and become cold and arrogant. Once this happens, their information sources begin to dry up and people no longer wish to work with them.
4. *Events conspire.* A few of the derailed apparently did little wrong. They were done in politically, or by economic upheavals. Essentially, they just weren't lucky.

While conducting the interviews, we heard few stories about water-walkers. In fact, the executive who came closest to fitting that category, the one "natural leader," derailed precisely because everyone assumed that he could do absolutely anything. At higher levels of management, he became lost in detail, concentrated too much on his subordinates, and seemed to lack the intellectual ability to deal with complex issues. Still, no one helped him; it was assumed that he would succeed regardless.

In short, both the arrivers and those who derailed had plenty of warts, although these generally became apparent only late in the men's careers. The events that exposed the flaws were seldom cataclysmic. More often, the flaws themselves had a cumulative impact. As one executive put it, "Careers last such a long time. Leave a trail of mistakes and you eventually find yourself encircled by your past."

In general, the flaws of both the arrivers and the derailed executives showed up when one of five things happened to them: 1) They lost a boss who had covered, or compensated for, their weaknesses. 2) They entered a job for which they were not prepared, either because it entailed much greater responsibility or because it required the executives to perform functions that were new to them. Usually, the difficulties were compounded by the fact that the executives went to work for a new boss whose style was very different from that of his newly promoted subordinate. 3) They left behind a trail of little problems or bruised people, either because they handled them poorly or moved through so quickly that they failed to handle them at all. 4) They moved up during an organizational shake-up and weren't scrutinized until the shake-down period. 5) They entered the executive suite, where getting along with others is critical.

One or more of these events happened to most of the executives, so the event itself was telling only in that its impact began to separate the two groups. How one person dealt with his flaws under stress went a long way toward explaining why some men arrived and some jumped the tracks just short of town. A bit of dialogue from one interview underscores this point:

Senior Executive: Successful people don't like to admit that they make big mistakes, but they make whoppers nevertheless. I've never known a CEO [chief executive officer] who didn't make at least one big one and lots of little ones, but it never hurt them.

Interviewer: Why?

Senior Executive: Because they know how to handle adversity.

Part of handling adversity lies in knowing what *not* to do. As we learned, lots of different management behavioral patterns were acceptable to others. The key was in knowing which ones colleagues and superiors would find intolerable.

As we said at the beginning, both groups were amazingly similar: incredibly bright, identified as promising early in their careers, outstanding in their track records, ambitious, willing to sacrifice—and imperfect. A closer look does reveal some differences, however, and at the levels of excellence characteristic of executives, even a small difference is more than sufficient to create winners and losers.

THE ARRIVERS AND THE DERAILED COMPARED

In the first place, derailed executives had a series of successes, but usually in similar kinds of situations. They had turned two businesses around, or managed progressively larger jobs in the same function. By contrast, the arrivers had more diversity in their successes—they had turned a business around *and* successfully moved from line to staff and back, or started a new business from scratch *and* completed a special assignment with distinction. They built plants in the wilderness and the Amazonian jungle, salvaged disastrous operations, resolved all-out wars between corporate divisions without bloodshed. One even built a town.

Derailed managers were often described as moody or volatile under pressure. One could control his temper with top management he sought to impress, but was openly jealous of peers he saw as competitors. His too-frequent angry outbursts eroded the cooperation necessary for success, as peers began to wonder whether he was trying to do them in. In contrast, the arrivers were calm, confident, and predictable. People knew how they would react and could plan their own actions accordingly.

Two Executives: A Study in Contrast

The two case histories that follow are told in the words of corporate executives who knew them well.

	One who arrived	One who derailed
The man	"He was an intelligent guy with a delightful twinkle in his eye. He could laugh at himself during the toughest of situations."	"He got results, but was awfully insensitive about it. Although he could be charming when he wanted to be, he was mostly knees and elbows."
Notable strengths	"He was a superb negotiator. He could somehow come out of a labor dispute or a dispute among managers with an agreement everyone could live with. I think he did this by getting all around a problem so it didn't get blown. People knew far in advance if something might go wrong."	"He was a superb engineer who came straight up the operations ladder. He had the rare capability of analyzing problems to death, then reconfiguring the pieces into something new."
Flaws	"He was too easy on subordinates and peers at times. Line people wondered whether he was tough enough, and sometimes, why he spent so much time worrying about people."	"When developing something, he gave subordinates more help than they needed, but once a system was set up, he forgot to mind the store. When things went awry, he usually acted like a bully or stonewalled it, once hiring a difficult employee and turning him over to a subordinate. 'It's your problem now,' he told him."
Career	"He was thrown into special assignments—negotiations, dealing with the press, fix-it projects. He always found a way to move things off dead center."	"He rocketed upward through engineering/operations jobs. Once he got high enough, his deficiencies caught up with him. He couldn't handle either the scope of his job or the complexity of new ventures."

| *And ended up...* | Senior Vice President | "Passed over, and it's too bad. He was a talented guy and not a bad manager, either. I suppose that his overmanaging, abrasive style never allowed his colleagues to develop and never allowed him to learn from them." |

Although neither group made many mistakes, all of the arrivers handled theirs with poise and grace. Almost uniformly, they admitted the mistake, forewarned others so they wouldn't be blind-sided by it, then set about analyzing and fixing it. Also telling were two things the arrivers didn't do: They didn't blame others, and once they had handled the situation, they didn't dwell on it.

Moreover, derailed executives tended to react to failure by going on the defensive, trying to keep it under wraps while they fixed it, or, once the problem was visible, blaming it on someone else.

Although both groups were good at going after problems, arrivers were particularly single-minded. This "What's the problem?" mentality spared them three of the common flaws of the derailed: They were too busy worrying about their present job to appear overly eager for their next position; they demanded excellence from their people in problem-solving; and they developed many contacts, saving themselves from the sole-mentor syndrome. In fact, almost no successful manager reported having a single mentor.

Lastly, the arrivers, perhaps due to the diversity of their backgrounds, had the ability to get along with all types of people. They either possessed or developed the skills required to be outspoken without offending people. They were not seen as charming-but-political or direct-but-tactless, but as direct-and-diplomatic. One arriver disagreed strongly with a business strategy favored by his boss. He presented his objections candidly and gave the reasons for his concerns as well as the alternative he preferred. But when the decision went against him, he put his energy behind making the decision work. When his boss turned out to be wrong, the arriver didn't gloat about it; he let the situation speak for itself without further embarrassing his boss.

One of the senior executives we interviewed made a simple but not simplistic distinction between the two groups. Only two things, he said, differentiated the successful from the derailed: total integrity, and understanding other people.

Integrity seems to have a special meaning to executives. The word does not refer to simple honesty, but embodies a consistency and predictability built over time that says, "I will do exactly what I say I will do when I say I will do it. If I change my mind, I will tell you well in advance so you will not be harmed by my actions." Such a statement is partly a matter of ethics, but, even more, a question of vital practicality. This kind of integrity seems to be the core element in keeping a large, amorphous organization from collapsing in its own confusion.

Ability—or inability—to understand other people's perspectives was the most glaring difference between the arrivers and the derailed. Only 25 percent of the derailed were described as having a special ability with people; among arrivers, the figure was 75 percent.

Interestingly, two of the arrivers were cold and asinine when younger, but somehow completely changed their style. "I have no idea how he did it," one executive said. "It was as if he went to bed one night and woke up a different person." In general, a certain awareness of self and willingness to change characterized the arrivers. That same flexibility, of course, is also what is needed to get along with all types of people.

A final word—a lesson, perhaps, to be drawn from our findings. Over the years, "experts" have generated long lists of critical skills in an attempt to define the complete manager. In retrospect it seems obvious that no one, the talented executive included, can possess all of those skills. As we came to realize, executives, like the rest of us, are a patchwork of strengths *and* weaknesses. The reasons that some executives ultimately derailed and others made it all the way up the ladder confirm what we all know but have hesitated to admit: There is no one best way to succeed (or even to fail). The foolproof, step-by-step formula is not just elusive; it is, as Kierkegaard said of truth, like searching a pitch-dark room for a black cat that isn't there.

The Politics of Seduction

Doris Kearns

The authority that Johnson inherited as Senate Democratic majority leader had been rendered ineffective by the Senate's inner club. Johnson set about to change all that, and before long he had transformed the instruments at hand—the steering committee, which determined committee assignments, and a hitherto unimportant Democratic Policy Committee—into mechanisms of influence and patronage in his relations with his Democratic colleagues and of control in the scheduling of legislation.

Abridged and adapted from "Lyndon Johnson and the American Dream" by Doris Kearns, as it appeared in *The Atlantic Monthly*. Copyright © 1976 by Doris Kearns. Reprinted by permission of Harper & Row, Publishers, Inc.

From facts, gossip, observation—a multitude of disparate elements—he shaped a composite mental portrait of every senator: his strengths and his weaknesses; his place in the political spectrum; his aspirations in the Senate, and perhaps beyond the Senate; how far he could be pushed in what direction, and by what means; how he liked his liquor; how he felt about his wife and his family; and, most important, how he felt about himself. For Johnson understood that the most important decision each senator made, often obscurely, was what kind of senator he wanted to be; whether he wanted to be a national leader in education, a regional leader in civil rights, a social magnate in Washington, an agent of the oil industry, a wheel horse of the party, a President of the United States. Yet his entrepreneurial spirit encompassed not simply the satisfaction of present needs but the development of new and expanding ones. He would, for instance, explain to a senator that "although five other senators are clamoring for this one remaining seat on the congressional delegation to Tokyo, I just might be able to swing it for you since I know how much you really want it. . . . It'll be tough but let me see what I can do." The joys of visiting Tokyo may never have occurred to the senator, but he was unlikely to deny Johnson's description of his desire— after all, it might be interesting, a relaxing change, even fun; and perhaps some of the businesses in his state had expressed concern about Japanese competition. By creating consumer needs in this fashion, and by then defining the terms of their realization, Johnson was able to expand the base of benefits upon which power could be built.

Johnson's capacities for control and domination found their consummate manifestation during his private meetings with individual senators. Face to face, behind office doors, Johnson could strike a different pose, a different form of behavior and argument. He would try to make each senator feel that his support in some particular matter was the critical element that would affect the well-being of the nation, the Senate, and the party leader; and would also serve the practical and political interests of the senator. . . .

The arrangements that preceded a private meeting were elaborate indeed. A meeting with a colleague might seem like an accidental encounter in a Senate corridor, but Johnson was not a man who roamed through the halls in aimless fashion; when he began to wander he knew who it was he would find.

After the coincidental encounter and casual greetings, Johnson would remember that he had something he would like to talk about. The two men would walk down the corridor, ride the elevator, and enter an office where they would begin their conversation with small talk over Scotch. As the conversation progressed, Johnson would display an overwhelming combination of praise, scorn, rage, and friendship. His voice would rise and fall, moving from the thunder of an orator to the whisper reminiscent of a lover inviting physical touch. Transitions were abrupt.

He responded to hostility with a disconcerting glance of indignation; the next minute he would evoke a smile by the warmth of his expression and a playful brush of his hand. Variations in pitch, stress, and gesture reflected the importance which he attached to certain words. His appeal would abound with illustration, anecdote, and hyperbole. He knew how to make his listeners *see* things he was describing, make them tangible to the senses. And he knew how to sustain a sense of uninterrupted flow by parallel structure and a stream of conjunctions.

From his own insistent energy, Johnson would create an illusion that the outcome, and thus the responsibility, rested on the decision of this one senator; refusing to permit any implication of the reality they both knew (but which in this office began to seem increasingly more uncertain), that the decisions of many other senators would also affect the results.

Then too, Johnson was that rare American man who felt free to display intimacy with another man, through expressions of feeling and also in physical closeness. In an empty room he would stand or sit next to a man as if all that were available was a three-foot space. He could flatter men with sentiments of love and touch their bodies with gestures of affection. The intimacy was all the more excusable because it seemed genuine and without menace. Yet it was also the product of meticulous calculation. And it worked. To the ardor and the bearing of this extraordinary man, the ordinary senator would almost invariably succumb.

Johnson was often able to use the same behavior with the press as he did with his colleagues, dividing it into separate components, and carving out a special relationship with each of the reporters.

"You learn," he said, "that Stewart Alsop cares a lot about appearing to be an intellectual and a historian—he strives to match his brother's intellectual attainments—so whenever you talk to him, play down the gold cufflinks which you play up with *Time* magazine, and to him, emphasize your relationship with FDR and your roots in Texas, so much so that even when it doesn't fit the conversation you make sure to bring in maxims from your father and stories from the Old West. You learn that Evans and Novak love to traffic in backroom politics and political intrigue, so that when you're with them you make sure to bring in lots of details and colorful description of personality. You learn that Mary McGrory likes dominant personalities and Doris Fleeson cares only about issues, so that when you're with McGrory you come on strong and with Fleeson you make yourself sound like some impractical red-hot liberal."

Boss: Richard J. Daley of Chicago

Mike Royko

If there is a council meeting, everybody marches downstairs at a few minutes before ten. Bush and the department heads and personal aides form a proud parade. The meeting begins when the seat of the mayor's pants touches the council president's chair, placed beneath the great seal of the city of Chicago and above the heads of the aldermen, who sit in a semibowl auditorium.

It is his council, and in all the years it has never once defied him as a body. Keane manages it for him, and most of its members do what they are told. In other eras, the aldermen ran the city and plundered it. In his boyhood they were so constantly on the prowl that they were known as "the Gray Wolves." His council is known as "the Rubber Stamp."

He looks down at them, bestowing a nod or a benign smile on a few favorites, and they smile back gratefully. He seldom nods or smiles at the small minority of white and black independents. The independents anger him more than the Republicans do, because they accuse him of racism, fascism, and of being a dictator. The Republicans bluster about loafing payrollers, crumbling gutters, inflated budgets—traditional, comfortable accusations that don't stir the blood.

That is what Keane is for. When the minority goes on the attack, Keane himself, or one of the administration aldermen he has groomed for the purpose, will rise and answer the criticism by shouting that the critic is a fool, a hypocrite, ignorant, and misguided. Until his death, one alderman could be expected to leap to his feet at every meeting and cry, "God bless our mayor, the greatest mayor in the world."

But sometimes Keane and his trained orators can't shout down the minority, so Daley has to do it himself. If provoked, he'll break into a rambling, ranting speech, waving his arms, shaking his fists, defending his judgment, defending his administration, always with the familiar "It is easy to criticize . . . to find fault . . . but where are your programs . . . where are your ideas. . ."

If that doesn't shut off the critics, he will declare them out of order, threaten to have the sergeant at arms force them into their seats, and invoke *Robert's Rules of Order*, which, in the heat of debate, he once described as "the greatest book ever written."

All else failing, he will look toward a glass booth above the spectator's balcony and make a gesture known only to the man in the booth who operates the sound system that controls the microphones on each alderman's desk. The man in the booth will touch a switch and the offending critic's microphone will go dead and stay dead until he sinks into his chair and closes his mouth.

The meetings are seldom peaceful and orderly. The slightest criticism touches off shrill rebuttal, leading to louder criticism and finally an embarrassingly wild and vicious free-for-all. It can't be true, because Daley is a man who speaks highly of law and order, but sometimes it appears that he enjoys the chaos, and seldom moves to end it until it has raged out of control.

Every word of criticsm must be answered, every complaint must be disproved, every insult must be returned in kind. He doesn't take anything from anybody. While Daley was mediating negotiations between white trade unions and black groups who wanted the unions to accept blacks, a young militant angrily rejected one of his suggestions and concluded, "Up your ass!" Daley leaped to his feet and answered, "And up yours too." Would John Lindsay have become so involved?

Independent aldermen have been known to come up with a good idea, such as providing food for the city's hungry, or starting day-care centers for children of ghetto women who want to work; Daley will acknowledge it, but in his own way. He'll let Keane appropriate the idea and rewrite and resubmit it as an administration measure. That way, the independent has the satisfaction of seeing his idea reach fruition and the administration has more glory. But most of the independents' proposals are sent to a special subcommittee that exists solely to allow their unwelcome ideas to die.

The council meetings seldom last beyond the lunch hour. Aldermen have much to do. Many are lawyers and have thriving practices, because Chicagoans know that a dumb lawyer who is an alderman can often perform greater legal miracles than a smart lawyer who isn't. . . .

The afternoon work moves with never a minute wasted. The engineers and planners come with their reports on public works projects. Something is always being built, concrete being poured, steel being riveted, contractors being enriched.

"When will it be completed?" he asks.

"Early February."

"It would be a good thing for the people if it could be completed by the end of October."

The engineers say it can be done, but it will mean putting on extra shifts, night work, overtime pay, a much higher cost than was planned.

"It would be a good thing for the people if it could be completed by the end of October."

Of course it would be a good thing for the people. It would also be a good thing for the Democratic candidates who are seeking election in early November to go out and cut a ribbon for a new expressway or a water filtration plant or, if nothing else is handy, another wing at the O'Hare terminal. What ribbons do their opponents cut?

The engineers and planners understand, and they set about getting it finished by October.

On a good afternoon, there will be no neighborhood organizations to see him, because if they get to Daley, it means they have been up the ladder of government and nobody has been able to solve their problem. And that usually means a conflict between the people and somebody else, such as a politician or a business, whom his aides don't want to ruffle. There are many things his department heads can't do. They can't cross swords with ward bosses or politically heavy businessmen. They can't make important decisions. Some can't even make petty decisions. He runs City Hall like a small family business and keeps everybody on a short rein. They do only that which they know is safe and that which he tells them to do. So many things that should logically be solved several rungs below finally come to him.

Because of this, he has many requests from neighborhood people. And when a group is admitted to his office, most of them nervous and wide-eyed, he knows who they are, their leaders, their strength in the community. They have already been checked out by somebody. He must know everything. He doesn't like to be surprised. Just as he knows the name of every new worker, he must know what is going on in the various city offices. If the head of the office doesn't tell him, he has somebody there who will. In the office of other elected officials, he has trusted persons who will keep him informed. Out in the neighborhoods his precinct captains are reporting to the ward committeement, and they in turn are reporting to him.

His police department's intelligence-gathering division gets bigger and bigger, its network of infiltrators, informers, and spies creating massive files on dissenters, street gangs, political enemies, newsmen, radicals, liberals, and anybody else who might be working against him. If one of his aides or handpicked officeholders is shacking up with a woman, he will know it. And if that man is married and a Catholic, his political career will wither and die. That is the greatest sin of all. You can make money under the table and move ahead, but you are forbidden to make secretaries under the sheets. He has dumped several party members for violating his personal moral standards. If something is leaked to the press, the bigmouth will be tracked down and punished. Scandals aren't public scandals if you get there before your enemies do.

So when the people come in, he knows what they want and whether it is possible. Not that it means they will get it. That often depends on how they act.

He will come out from behind his desk all smiles and handshakes and charm. Then he returns to his chair and sits very straight, hands folded on his immaculate desk, serious and attentive. To one side will be somebody from the appropriate city department.

Now it's up to the group. If they are respectful, he will express sympathy, ask encouraging questions, and finally tell them that everything possible will be done. And after they leave, he may say, "Take care of it." With that command, the royal seal, anything is possible, anybody's toes can be stepped on.

But if they are pushy, antagonistic, demanding instead of imploring, or bold enough to be critical of him, to tell him how he should do his job, to blame him for their problem, he will rub his hands together, harder and harder. In a long, difficult meeting, his hands will get raw. His voice gets lower, softer, and the corners of his mouth will turn down. At this point, those who know him will back off. They know what's next. But the unfamiliar, the militant, will mistake his lowered voice and nervousness for weakness. Then he'll blow, and it comes in a frantic roar:

"I want *you* to tell *me* what to do. *You* come up with the answers. *You* come up with the program. Are we perfect? Are *you* perfect? We all make mistakes. We all have faults. It's easy to criticize. It's easy to find fault. But *you* tell me what to do. This problem is all over the city. We didn't create these problems. We don't want them. But we are doing what we can. *You* tell me how to solve them. *You* give me a program." All of which leaves the petitioners dumb, since most people don't walk around with urban programs in their pockets. It can also leave them right back where they started.

They leave and the favor seekers come in. Half the people he sees want a favor. They plead for promotions, something for their sons, a chance to do some business with the city, to get somebody in City Hall off their backs, a chance to return from political exile, a boon. They won't get an answer right there and then. It will be considered and he'll let them know. Later, sometimes much later when he has considered the alternatives and the benefits, word will get back to them. Yes or no. Success or failure. Life or death.

Some jobseekers come directly to him. Complete outsiders, meaning those with no family or political connections, will be sent to see their ward committeemen. That is protocol, and that is what he did to the tall young black man who came to see him a few years ago, bearing a letter from the govenor of North Carolina, who wrote that the young black man was a rising political prospect in his state. Daley told him to see his ward committeeman, and if he did some precinct work, rang doorbells, hustled up some votes, there might be a government job for him. Maybe something like taking coins in a tollway booth. The Rev. Jesse Jackson, now the city's leading black civil rights leader, still hasn't stopped smarting over that.

Others come asking him to resolve a problem. He is the city's leading labor mediator and has prevented the kind of strikes that have crippled New York. His father was a union man, and he comes from a union neighborhood, and many of the union leaders were his boyhood friends. He knows what they want. And if it is in the city's treasury, they will get it. If it isn't there, he'll promise to find it. He has ended a teachers' strike by promising that the state legislature would find funds for them, which surprised the Republicans in Springfield, as well as put them on the spot. He is an effective mediator with the management side of labor disputes, because they respect his judgment, and because there are few industries that do not need some favors from City Hall. . . .

Winning Is the Only Thing

Jerry Kramer

FRANK GIFFORD: "I WAS ALWAYS TRYING TO PLEASE HIM"

When Vince joined the New York Giants in 1954, he walked into a disaster area. Their defense was a shambles; their offense was worse. The year before, they had lost nine out of twelve games and had scored only 179 points, the fewest of any team in the league. Vince immediately molded a new offense and, in the process, created a superstar: Frank Gifford, a halfback who could run, block, pass and catch passes.

An All-American at the University of Southern California, Gifford had been used almost exclusively on defense in 1952, his rookie season. Under Vince, he became the most exciting offensive halfback in the National Football League. In each of the five years he played for Vince, Gifford was nominated for the Pro Bowl. In those five years, the Giants never had a losing record, never scored fewer than 246 points. . . .

In the spring of 1970, before we knew of Vince's illness, I sat down with Frank Gifford in his office at CBS. After thirteen seasons with the Giants, Frank is now a highly successful sportscaster, covering everything from the Masters to the Super Bowl. . . .

To be honest, very few of the guys liked him at first. For one thing, he had us running like we had never run before. But the main thing was that we resented a guy coming in from college and telling us what to do. And he was completely in charge. Jim Lee never interfered; he left the offense entirely to Vinny and the defense entirely to Tom Landry. As Jim Lee himself said many times, "I'm just here to take the roll and blow up the balls."

The first two or three weeks, we weren't too impressed by Vinny's Here's-how-we-did-it-at-St.-Cecilia-High-or-at-Army attitude. . . .

But it didn't take us long to realize that even though Vinny's approach to football was very basic—fundamentals: hit, block and tackle—he was somebody special. His enthusiasm, his spirit, was infectious. We really began to dig him when he started coming up to our rooms at night after he'd put in a new play during a chalk talk. I was rooming with Charlie, and Vinny'd come to our room, after putting in an off-tackle play, and say, "Well, what do you think? Will it work?" He was very honest. When he put in the power sweep, he'd ask, "Can the halfback get down and hold that defensive end and stop the penetration?" That was my job on one side and Alex Webster's on the other. We'd say, "Oh, sure, coach, we can do it." And then he'd just drill the hell out of us.

I can remember sneaking out some nights after curfew in Oregon, and sometimes I'd come back in pretty late, and the lights would still be on in his room. I realized then the kind of work he was putting in. He had to be exhausted, but he never showed it. He'd be out on the field the next day, going full speed, driving himself every minute.

We never feared Vinny in New York. It wasn't like in Green Bay later, when he came in with you guys as a winner, as an established person. To us, he was just an assistant coach from Army and St. Cecilia High. There are maybe twelve or fifteen of us who were the core of the offense, and we were kind of a clique, and Vinny liked to hang around with us. He'd eat dinner with us on the road and laugh with us when we won and die with us when we lost. We used to tease him and raise hell with him. We'd hide his baseball cap, things like that, just to see him get his emotions worked up. When he was showing us films, we used to bait him, lead him on to the point where he'd smash a table or throw an eraser at the blackboard. He'd break two or three projectors a year when he got angry. . . .

He was always a great psychologist, great at analyzing individuals, knowing which players needed to be driven and which ones needed a friendly pat on the fanny. When he was with us, we had a few players who needed driving. One was Mel Triplett. Mel used to exasperate Vinny. He could've been a great player—he had a fantastic year in 1956—but he never played up to his potential, except on certain occasions, like against the Cleveland Browns after they got Jimmy Brown.

Mel always felt that he was better than Jimmy. You and I both know that he wasn't, but he was a fine football player.

Vinny used to ride Mel pretty good, especially in the movies. You know how he is with that projector. You could miss a block, and he'd never say a word sometimes, but he'd run the film back and forth, back and forth, till every guy in the room felt like he'd done something wrong. It was sort of like going to a revival meeting. A preacher will fire some buckshot out there, and everybody is going to feel it. Everybody is the guilty party.

Well, Mel used to think that Vinny was persecuting him something awful. All he really was trying to do was help Mel along. But one time he went a little too far with Mel, who was kind of a frightening guy when he got hot. Vinny kept running this one play back and forth, back and forth, back and forth—with Mel missing a block—and about the eighth or tenth time, Mel said, loud and hard, "Move on with that projector."

You could have heard a pin drop. We all wondered what was going to happen. Mel had told the rest of us a few times what he intended to do to Mr. Lombardi someday. And Mel was the kind of guy who was emotional and might do just what he said he would. He was at the breaking point right then. Vince didn't say a word. He went on to the next play. He read Mel just right. They never did have a confrontation. I heard a lot of guys over the years say they were going to punch Vinny out at the end of the season, but no one ever did. You've got to end up loving a guy who can build a team, put it all together—and you share in the rewards. But Vinny walked a very dangerous line at times.

He ruled us all equally—with one exception. He loved Charlie Conerly. He never said a harsh word to Charlie. And, again, he was really getting the proper reading, because Charlie didn't need it. You couldn't fire Charlie up with a branding iron. But you couldn't cool him off, either. Charlie was his own person.

When Charlie used to throw a couple of interceptions or blow an automatic—which really fried Vinny—Vinny wouldn't say a word. He'd get on Don Heinrich—Don was our other quarterback, and he was a little younger and a little wilder than Charlie—but never to the point where he got totally angry. I think he has a special fondness for his quarterbacks. A quarterback is his own extension on the field. I think he looked at Bart Starr as Vinny Lombardi out there. I think he feels the same way about Sonny Jurgensen.

But the rest of us got equal treatment. I remember when he put in the nutcracker drill: A defensive lineman sets himself in between two big bags, and an offensive lineman tries to lead a ballcarrier through. Everybody always used to say, "Oh, that poor offensive lineman." Nobody ever thought about the poor offensive back, who was just getting the hell knocked out of him. After an hour of banging heads, those defensive linemen were so hot and mad they didn't care what they did to you. Maybe you were a star, or thought you were a star, but you ran the nutcracker as often as the rookie trying to make the team. Vinny kept track of it, close track, and if you tried to get out of one run at it, his teeth'd be grinning at you, and he'd be yelling. "Get in here, get in here," and there'd be no way you could escape. . . .

And Vinny could put his finger on these elements in a personality. He knew exactly how to motivate. He knew just what buttons to push. You see, I didn't hide anything from him. I was always just as open as I could be with him, because I liked him so much. I know that after a while it got to the point where I was playing football for just one reason: I was always trying to please him. When we played a game, I could care less about the headlines on Monday. All I wanted was to be able to walk into the meeting Tuesday morning and have Vinny give me that big grin and pat me on the fanny and let me know that I was doing what he wanted me to do. A lot of our guys felt that way. We had guys who would run through a stadium wall for him—and then maybe cuss him in the next breath. . . .

I can remember very clearly the happiest I've ever seen Vinny. It wasn't after a game. It was in the middle of a week during the 1956 season. We'd gotten up over .500 in 1954 and 1955, but we hadn't finished first or second in our division. Then, in 1956, we won four of our first five games, and on a Wednesday—we were getting ready to play Pittsburgh—he called us all around him, the whole offense. He just couldn't restrain himself. He was bubbling. He was bursting with pride. "By God," he said, "we've really got something going." His eyes were shining. He just felt that we were going to win everything, and he knew it was his baby, and he had to tell us, and, of course, he was right. We did go on to win everything that year. . . .

People are always asking me what makes Vince Lombardi different from other coaches, and I've got one answer: He can get that extra ten percent out of an individual. Multiply ten percent times forty men on a team times fourteen games a season—and you're going to win. He proved that last year at Washington. That's not a talented team, and my God, they hadn't had a winning team since 1955. But he made them winners. He made them believe they could win. Sonny Jurgensen loved him. He had no right to succeed in Washington. There are twenty-six teams now, not twelve like there were when he sent to Green Bay. It's a hell of a lot harder to find good ballplayers. You can't trade the way you used to; you can't draft the way you could. There just isn't the same material available for every team. And the quality of coaching has been upgraded throughout the league. And, still, he did it. Nobody else could've done it. There are four or five coaches that know as much strategically and tactically as Lombardi, but they don't get that extra ten percent.

Vinny believes in the Spartan life, the total self-sacrifice, and to succeed and reach the pinnacle that he has, you've got to be that way. You've got to have total dedication. The hours you put in on a job can't even be considered. The job is to be done, and if it takes a hundred hours, you give it a hundred hours. If it takes fifteen minutes, you give it fifteen minutes. I saw the movie *Patton*, and it was Vince Lombardi. The situation was different, but the thought was the same: We're here to do a job, and each and every one of us will put everything we've got into getting the job done. That was Vince. . . .

KYLE ROTE: "HE WAS SEARCHING FOR A RELATIONSHIP WITH US"

During Vince's years with the New York Giants, Kyle Rote was more than one of his stars: He was Vince's kind of ballplayer. Kyle had a bad left knee that forced him, after a few pro seasons, to forget about playing halfback, to give up the brilliant running and passing that had made him college football's most spectacular All-American in 1950. He became a flanker instead and, through hard work and despite his painful knee, made himself one of the finest receivers in the league.

You may find this hard to believe, but Vince Lombardi impressed me as a shy person when he first came to the Giants.

When I look back at those days now, I suppose that I mistook caution for shyness. Vinny was a perfectionist, and to his credit, I think he wanted to make sure his feet were on solid ground before he asserted himself. He was feeling his way until he was positive of what he was doing.

His previous experience had been limited to high school and college football, and in his first exhibition season with the pros, Vinny was rather careful in his dealings with the players, especially the older players. I don't mean he was timid, but I do think he was searching for a relationship with us that would make us both feel acceptable to each other. He was perceptive enough to sense that, because of the absence of any arena for physical give and take, it's often more difficult for a rookie coach to be accepted by the veterans than it is for a rookie player.

Some of us tested Vinny in his first few weeks. Charlie Conerly and I were not above trying to play as little as possible in the pre-season games, and I can recall Vinny, during one exhibition, coming to Conerly and me on the sidelines and asking if we thought we'd like to get in a little work. "Maybe in a couple of more series, Coach," we replied.

What Vinny didn't realize—or, at least, what we thought he didn't realize—was that Charlie and I were trying to pick our spot. We knew that before the game was over, we'd have to go in, and we were studying the opposing team's rookie defensive backs, trying to find one with a weakness we could take advantage of.

Fortunately for Charlie and me, we usually were able to find what we were looking for, and when we felt our club was in good field position, we'd tell Vinny we were ready. In we'd go, and more times than not, we were able to complete a pass on the rookie we'd been watching.

I honestly think Vinny, at the beginning, held most of the older players in slight awe, and when we'd pull off a stunt like that, it enhanced his image of us.

Of course, that was only the first few weeks. After a while, Vinny would turn to us and say, "You and Charlie ready to go in now?"

"Give us just a few more downs," I'd say.

"Go in there now," he'd say.

The shyness or the cautiousness wore off quickly, and as Vinny began to realize that pro ball is actually a less complicated game than college ball—that the tactics and skills of the opposition are much more predictable—the Lombardi confidence began to emerge. And in direct ratio to the emergence of his confidence, our little "confidence game" submerged. . . .

One year, when we were training at Bear Mountain, New York, we lost most of our exhibition games, and Vinny decided that we were too tight. So just before our opening game, when Jim Lee Howell, our head coach, was off scouting or something, Vinny threw a beer blast for the whole team in the basement of the Bear Mountain Inn. We all loosened up, and we went on to win the Eastern championship.

Kyle's mention of the beer blast and of how much Vince enjoyed being with the Giant players made me think of how difficult it must have been for him to divorce himself from the players in Green Bay. I think he really would have liked to have been close to us—I think he felt, as I did, that the special appeal of football was the comaraderie among men with a common goal—but he knew he couldn't allow himself that luxury. To fufill his commitment to victory, he had to go against his nature and stay aloof from us.

I remember how much he enjoyed Rookie Night, the one night when we all really relaxed together, when the rookies staged a show and made fun of training camp in general and of Vince in particular. They could be pretty rough in their caricatures, and they portrayed Vince as a dictator, and they ridiculed his manner and his physical appearance, and he sat and watched and laughed as heartily as anyone. It took a big man, and a strong man, to see himself through others' eyes, to see his foibles exposed and attacked, but Vince seemed to love it. He would have liked more opportunities to relax and laugh with his players, but he knew, in Green Bay, he couldn't be one of the boys anymore. He wasn't an assistant coach anymore. He had to be a leader.

WILLIE DAVIS: "HE MADE ME FEEL IMPORTANT"

When I first saw Willie Davis, with his big torso and his relatively slender legs—his "getaway sticks," we called them—I was skeptical about his reputation for speed. I challenged him to a race. We both got down in three-point stances, and someone yelled, "Go," and he jumped and just beat me. We did it again, and I jumped and just beat him. That was enough for me; I didn't race Willie anymore

Willie broke into our starting lineup right away, and by 1962, he was an All-Pro defensive end. Willie made All-Pro five out of six years and, in 1966, became captain of our defensive team, by then the toughest defensive unit in pro football.

Football is a game of emotion, and what the old man excels at is motivation. I maintain that there are two driving forces in football, and one is anger, and the other is fear, and he capitalized on both of them. Either he got us so mad we wanted to prove something to him or we were fearful of being singled out as the one guy who didn't do the job.

In the first place, he worked so hard that I always felt the old man was really putting more into the game on a day-to-day basis than I was. I felt obligated to put something extra into it on Sunday; I had to, just to be even with him.

Another thing was the way he made you a believer. He told you what the other team was going to do, and he told you what you had to do to beat them, and invariably he was right. He made us believe that all we had to do was follow his theories on how to get ready for each game and we'd win.

I knew we were going to win every game we played. Even if we were behind by two touchdowns in the fourth quarter, I just believed that somehow we were going to pull it out. I didn't know exactly how or when, but I knew that sooner or later, we'd get the break we needed—the interception or the fumble or something. And the more important it was for us to win, the more certain I was we would win. . . .

Probably the best job I can remember of him motivating us was when we played the Los Angeles Rams the next-to-last game of 1967. We had already clinched our divisional title, and the game didn't mean anything to us, and he was worried about us just going through the motions. He was on us all week, and in the locker room before the game, he was trembling like a leaf. I could see his leg shaking. "I wish I didn't have to ask you boys to go out there today and do the job," he said. "I wish I could go out and do it myself. Boy, this is one game I'd really like to be playing in. This is a game that you're playing for your pride." He went on like that and he got me so worked up that if he hadn't opened that locker-room door quick, I was going to make a hole in it, I was so eager.

And we played a helluva game. We had nothing to gain, and the Rams were fighting for their lives, and they just did manage to beat us. They won by three points when they blocked a punt right near the end. . . .

You never could predict how he was going to act. The days you really expected him to go through the ceiling, he'd come in and be very soft. He'd say something like, "You're a better football team than you showed today." Or he'd blame himself and the other coaches for not preparing us properly. He'd never let us slip into a defeatist attitude. But then sometimes, when you figured you'd played pretty decent—maybe you'd lived up to what you thought he expected of you—he'd come in and drop the bomb on you. Like one time we beat Minnesota, and didn't play all that bad even though they scored a lot of points, and he walked into the locker room and said, "I'd like our front four to apologize to the rest of the team. You cheated on us today. You should apologize. You didn't play the kind of football you're capable of playing." His words kind of froze me. I felt awful.

One time, when we thought we'd played a good game, he started in on us, "Who the hell do you think you are? The Green Bay Packers? The Green Bay Nothings, that's who you are. You're only a good football team when you play well together. Individually none of you could make up a team. You'd be nothing without me. I made you, mister."

How about the day we beat the Rams, 6-3, in Milwaukee in 1965? We'd broken a two-game losing streak, and we were all kind of happy and clowning around, and he came in and you saw his face and you knew nothing was funny anymore. He kicked a bench and hurt his foot, and he had to take something out on somebody, so he started challenging us. "Nobody wants to pay the price," he said. "I'm the only one here that's willing to pay the price. You guys don't care. You don't want to win."

We were stunned. Nobody knew what to do, and, finally, Forrest Gregg stood up and said, "My God, I want to win," and then somebody else said, "Yeah, I want to win," and pretty soon there were forty guys standing, all of us shouting, "I want to win." If we had played any football team in the world during the next two hours, we'd have beaten them by ten touchdowns. The old man had us feeling so ashamed and angry. That was his greatest asset: His ability to motivate people.

He never got me too upset personally. Of course, I had pretty thick skin by the time I got to Green Bay. Paul Brown had chewed on me so much in Cleveland that when I got to the Packers, Vince was a welcome sight. Vince and Paul Brown were similar in the way they could cut you with words and make you want to rise up to prove something to them.

I think Vince got on me sharp maybe twice in eight years. I remember once, after the Colts had been hooking me on the sweep, he ate me up, and Max McGee said "Well, I've seen everything: Vince got on Willie Davis."

Maybe he wasn't as tough on me as he was on some people, but I'll tell you, I hated to have him tell me I was fat. I hated to have him tell me I didn't have the desire anymore. He'd just say those things to the whole team—"You're fat; you don't want to win anymore"—and I'd get so angry I couldn't wait till I got out on the field.

I guess maybe my worst days in football were the days I tried to negotiate my contracts with the old man. I'd get myself all worked up before I went in to see him. I'd drive up from my home in Chicago, and all the way, I'd keep building up my anger, telling myself I was going to draw a hard line and get as much money as I deserved.

One year, I walked into his office feeling cocky, you know, "Roll out the cash, Jack, I got no time for small change." All he had to do was say one harsh word, and I was really going to let him have it. I never got a word in. Soon as he saw me, he jumped up and began hugging me and patting me and telling me, "Willie, Willie, Willie it's so great to see you. You're the best trade I ever made. You're a leader. We couldn't have won without you, Willie. You had a beautiful year. And, Willie, I need your help. You see, I've got this budget problem. . . ."

He got me so off-balance, I started feeling sorry for him. He had me thinking, "Yeah, he's right, he's gotta save some money for the Kramers and the Greggs and the Jordans," and the next thing I knew, I was saying, "Yes, sir, that's fine with me," and I ended up signing for about half what I was going to demand. When I got out of that office and started driving back to Chicago, I was so mad at myself, I was about to drive off the highway.

The next year, finally, I got him. I went into his office and I said, "Coach, you're quite a guy. I got to be very frank, Coach, I just can't argue with you. You know, you just overwhelm me. So I've jotted down a few things I want to tell you." And I handed him a letter I'd written.

He started reading the letter—and I'd put a lot of stuff in it, like how I felt about the fans and what he'd done for me and how many years I had left—and, at first, he gave me that "heh . . . heh . . . heh" of his. Then, when he got around to how much money I wanted, he put his frown on me. He looked at me and said, "I can't argue with what you say here, Willie, but I can't pay you that much money."

"Well, coach," I said, "I really feel that way."

He thought it over a little and said, "I'll tell you what I'll give you," and named a figure not too much below what I was willing to settle for. "You'd be one of the highest-paid linemen in the whole league," he whispered, like he was afraid somebody might hear him.

"Look, Coach," I said, "I really thought hard about this, and I got to have a thousand dollars more than that. It's only a thousand dollars, but it's the difference between me driving back to Chicago today feeling real good and driving back to Chicago wanting to go head-on into somebody. It's really what I feel like I'm worth."

"If it's that important to you," he said, "you got it."

I felt good. I had my letter in my hand and started to walk out, and he said, "Hey, wait a minute. Let me have that letter. Let me keep it. I don't want you giving it to anybody else."

The Calf Path
Samuel Foss

One day thru the primeval wood
A calf walked home, as good calves should;
But made a trail, all bent askew,
A crooked trail, as all calves do.
Since then 300 years have fled,
And I infer the calf is dead.
But still, he left behind his trail
And thereby hangs my mortal tale.

The trail was taken up next day
By a lone dog, that passed that way.
And then a wise bell weathered sheep
Pursued the trail, o'er vale and steep
And drew the flocks behind him too
As good bell weathers always do.
And from that day, o'er hill and glade
Thru those old woods, a path was made.

And many men wound in and out,
And dodged, and turned, and bent about,
And uttered words of righteous wrath
Because 'twas such a crooked path.
But still they followed, do not laugh
The first migrations of that calf.
And thru the winding woods they stalked
Because he wobbled when he walked.

This forest path became a lane
That bent, and turned, and turned again.
This crooked lane became a road
Where many a poor horse with his load
Toiled on beneath the burning sun
And traveled some three miles in one.
And thus a century and a half
They trod the footsteps of that calf.

The years passed on in swiftness fleet,
The road became a village street.
And this, before men were aware,
A city's crowded thoroughfare.
And soon the central street was this
Of a renowned metropolis.
And men, two centuries and a half
Trod the footsteps of that calf.

Each day a 100 thousand route
Followed the zig-zag calf about,
And o'er his crooked journey went
The traffic of a continent.
A 100 thousand men were led
By one calf, near three centuries dead.
They followed still his crooked way
And lost 100 years per day.
For this such reverence is lent
To well established precedent.

A moral lesson this might teach
Were I ordained, and called to preach.
For men are prone to go it blind
Along the calf paths of the mind,
And work away from sun to sun
To do what other men have done.
They follow in the beaten track,
And out, and in, and forth, and back,
And still their devious course pursue
To keep the paths that others do.

They keep the paths a sacred groove
Along which all their lives they move.
But how the wise old wood gods laugh
Who saw that first primeval calf.
Ah, many things this tale might teach,
But I am not ordained to preach.

Management from Within

Ray Bradbury

People ask me what I am, and I give various answers, as should we all. A writer, after all, is not merely a writer, nor an artist an artist, nor an actor an actor.

I have learned finally, more often than not, to reply:

I am a magician.

And not only a magician, but a boy-magician with a false moustache that falls at my feet as I finish an illusion. It is that boy, and not me, who works the miracles, traps life, shouts with amazement, and hands the whole incredible stuff on to the man I'm supposed to be.

So should it be with managers and management. If, when asked what they were, such chaps responded with, "I'm a manager," or "I'm a businessman," I would write them off as doomed. Or, at least, in my magic book.

For, really, isn't it true, we are all up to the *same* business? We go about it differently, but the result is the same. We are survivors who learn and live and teach survival, this man this way, that woman another. But all of us inhabit one earth and the sum of us is life itself, and all of us on our way through that life must find his or her way to survive. When we learn that lesson well, we can pass it on to our friends and children.

Books, printing, typing, writing, reading are ways of trapping time and information and funneling it on to the present and future generations, thus hoping to improve their chances at survival and enhance their lives while they do it.

It follows then that a manager is not a manager nor is management a coterie of managers, but single human beings and a great mob of humans engaged in their own effort of survival, singly and by the numbers.

Let me go back to that boy-magician, if you will allow.

Have you ever, as employee or employer, powerless or with power, sat at a meeting with your peers, as I have, and looked around suddenly in a panic to think:

What am I doing here!? These people are all forty-five, fifty, and fifty-five years old! They know what they're doing! And I? I am ten, twelve, thirteen at the most, and know *nothing!*

Sound familiar?

From *New Management*, Vol. I, No. 4, 1984, pp.12-15. Reprinted by permission.

It happens to me all the time. Not just once a month, or once a week, but almost daily when people turn to look at me and ask my opinion. At museum conferences, in film studios, following plays where I am asked onstage to be part of an analytical panel, or when my daughters come to look in my face to chart the future. Sometimes a large moment of panic ensues. If not that, at least a small one, and then I regain my calm and think: But we are all this age, aren't we, trapped in the older self, still feeling a lack of education, still sensing we have not yet learned to think? Yet here are all these curious folks, craning their heads like dinosaurs in a swamp, staring at me as if I were Tyrannosaurus rex, when at most I am simply the boy who holds the nervous rabbit on his lap, waiting for others to begin.

It is to this boy, the boy who inhabits your blood even as you read this, that I will seize you back again and again. For if he has not survived, your own ability to write, act, paint, husband, father, or manage will be impaired if not crippled. If you have starved him, if you have forgotten how to have fun, how to play, how to love, then no matter what you set out to do, you will not do it well.

How do you feed and sustain that kid? What is there in diet and intellectual nutrition that differs as between a writer like myself and you who read these pages and hope to learn how better to creatively manage whatever business it is you are part of (in order for all of it to enjoy your creativity)?

I contend that we are not different in any way and proceed with amiable arrogance to give you my recipes. . . .

FEEDING CREATIVITY

Well now, when was the last time you ran to a library and took home more books than you could read, like stacked loaves of bread, warm in the arms, waiting to be chewed? When, for that matter, was the last time you opened a book, placed it to your nose and gave a great sniff? Heaven! The smell of bread, baking.

When was the last time that you found a really great old book store and wandered through it hour after hour, alone, finding yourself on the shelves. With no list, no intellectual priorities, just wandering, snuffing the dust, plucking the pigeon books off the shelves to read their entrails and, not in love, putting them back, or in love, toting them home? To be lost in time is to find your roots. How long ago was that? How long ago did you try? How long ago did you simply do?

When was the last time you told your son (or daughter) that you loved him (or her)? When was the last time you said the same thing, bless his grey head, to your living father?

When was the last time you went into a stationery store and bought forty bucks worth of stationery you didn't really need, because it looked rainbow bright and all noonday sun?

When was the last time you ate lunch alone, so you could find your own thoughts and maybe know just who in hell you were, instead of giving your energy away at lunch with people you really didn't want to be with?

When was the last time you took a train across country only two-and-one-half days away from telephones, with that book you've been wanting to read, and a bottle of champagne at midnight to be drunk as you watch the little towns go by and wonder who in hell all those people are in the houses with the bright windows? Here they *come,* there they *go!*

When was the last time. . . ?

When was the last time you stuck your head in at an office meeting just after lunch and said, everyone the hell out, go swim, go make love, come back at four for that meeting!

Because if you do that, and people go swim, jog, run, jump, love, and come back refreshed, did you ever figure maybe you might get more done in one hour of chat than in three hours of pressure?

For that matter, did you ever think that maybe taking your whole staff to the desert to sit around a pool and swim and figure out problems might be better than those damned meetings you sit at and terrify one another with, and sweat with and try to solve problems with? For we all know, don't we, I mean *don't* we, that the harder you try the less you do, and the more you try to think the less thinking gets done?

I've had these signs by my typewriter for 40 years:

DON'T THINK. DON'T TRY. JUST DO.

For in doing, in the process, thought evolves. There's plenty of time to think after the doing, after the action, after the fun. To approach problem solving grimly, in business or anywhere else, is to be non-creative. Do you run your business like the Inquisition, condemning ideas by being too serious?

I hate serious people. When I see someone sitting down with me or anyone else to have a serious discussion, I know the Muse will be dead by noon, carried out with the trash by three, buried by dusk, forgotten by dawn.

I have seen more problems destroyed by overthinking than I have seen solutions created.

If I were to toss out another motto it would be:

LEAVE PEOPLE ALONE!

If we gave each other more breathing space, we would all create better, work better, live better. Don't nag. Suggest. That means to yourself, too.

Stay away from newspapers, television, radio, and telephone calls early in the morning. It's your best time, your creative time. Depending, of course, on the business you're in. If it's the stock market, forget it, you're sunk already.

Stay away, then, from anything you can't even begin to solve, which is why I mention TV, radio and newspapers, because it's too late for the rapes, murders, and robberies, right? If you carry that burden into your life, at breakfast, you might as well go back to bed. Okay to read *Barron's* and *The Wall Street Journal.* But try them at night, okay?

Stop watching the 6:00 News, or the 6:30 News, or come to think of it, sometimes even the 7:00 Intercontinental and National News. Stop watching the 11:00 News. If you must, watch **Ted Koppel** on *Nightline* at 11:30 at night on ABC. Or the *McNeil/Lehrer Report.*

Why this advice? We have become a nation of doomsayers and thought destroyers. We are no good, we say, we are beneath notice, we are dustworms, we are graveyard dirt, we are lousy, we are the world's worst.

Well, son, and daughter, it follows that if you believe that, you will stop living. You won't be able to manage your zipper, much less a small business or a medium corporation.

Instead of the French intellectual's dictum—oppose in order to learn and be enlightened—we oppose out of easy cynicism, rampant self-detestation, and the will *not* to listen.

Creativity cannot exist in an acid-rain of murder, rape, suicide, car-crash, and nuclear meltdown. For Christ's sake, the world isn't ALL that. Come off it. Jump from the Bubonic Plague Express and join us plain peasants on the road, getting our work done, and with some small hope, no matter how pitiful, for the future.

After all, think of it, every single leader in the history of the world has been an optimist. Can you name one that wasn't? Did any of them run on the ticket Doom and Gloom, tomorrow will be lousier than yesterday? There's no hope? Give up? Lie down? Fester? Don't bother to repent? Die?

They did not. Not even Hitler. He was out to bust the world, buster, or know the reason why. And, by God, he almost did it, while others stood around and said nothing could be done.

TURNING JOB INTO PLAY

Now if none of the above things seem to apply to you, don't be so certain-sure!

After all, what is life supposed to be about? Love and fun, isn't it? Good grief, if everything isn't fun, why do it? Or most things, anyway. There's always a certain amount of drudgery connected with any work, business, art, or even playing basketball. The latter isn't easy, but unless you frolic at it, like a healthy animal, you had better hit the showers.

If someone told me that, from now on, for the rest of my life, I must write only serious novels and be a serious thinker thinking deep long thoughts, I would either kick the son of a bitch, run like hell, or quit writing. Even my serious novels, and I have done a few, were absolute delights to write, were delicious enterprises that surprised and shocked me as I went. If life isn't cracker-jack, the more you eat the more you want, what the hell *is* it?

Yes, yes, I can hear you, this is some damn fool aging Martian maniac running around laughing all the time and making people want to drown him in the nearest pool. Not so. It's just that I absolutely love my work so much I want to pass the secret on. When you love work it's no longer work, we all know that. Love is the lubricant that turns Job into Play.

And we stop loving work when we ignore the long cliche-ridden list I have laid out for you in this essay. We forget sometimes. This article is to remind you where you lost yourself along the way.

If your meeting room, your board room, or your office (take your pick) isn't a nursery for ideas, a rumpus room where seals frolic, forget it. Burn the table, lock the room, fire the clerks. You will rarely come up with any solutions worth entertaining. The dull room with the heavy people trudging in with long faces to solve problems by beating them to death is very death itself. Serious confrontations rarely arrive at serious ends. Unless the people you meet with are funloving kids out for a romp, tossing ideas like confetti, and letting the damn bits fall where they may, no spirit will ever rouse, no notion will ever birth, no love will be mentioned, no climax reached. You must swim at your meetings, you must jump for baskets, you must take hefty swings for great or missed drives, you must run and dive, you must fall and roll, and when the fun stops get the hell out. The whole idea of brainstorming, unless it is a storm of hilarity and ideas clamoring to be born, is silly and non-productive. God deliver me from such.

That just about does it. Save to add one immense irony: Even insane people like the world so much they don't want to leave it. How's that? Rather than to commit suicide people hole up in madness, hide away in insanity, in order to survive. Anything, they say, is better than nothing. Being crazy is better than being dead. There's a lesson there, if we want to take it.

You are neither mad nor bad nor dead. You are alive, but sometimes you forget it. Life is running through your fingers and you forget to mould, touch, shape it as it passes. Touch it, mould it, shape it.

Or, conversely, on certain days, emulate Darwin.

What did he do? He strolled out to stand in the middle of fields waiting for a bird to land on his shoulder, watching for the foxes to come home at dawn, listening to the sounds of the world and knowing delight as well as discovery.

Tomorrow, go stand in a field somewhere. You might just meet yourself, coming home, at noon, or as the sun sets, and your heart will know delight.

12

RISES
AND FALLS

CHARLEY: *It was a very nice funeral. . .*

LINDA: *I can't understand it. At this time especially. First time in thirty-five years we were just about free and clear. He only needed a little salary. He was even finished with the dentist.*

CHARLEY: *No man only needs a little salary.*

—Arthur Miller

C onventional textbooks on management and organizational work concentrate for the most part on upward mobility and how to achieve it. Comparatively little recognition is given to the frequency with which hitherto successful managers "fall from grace." The economic disasters associated with the recent recession have led to increased recognition of this aspect of organizational life in the popular press and business oriented media. The selections in this section contain a small set of pieces that describe various types of "falls," some of the reasons for these falls, and their impact on the individuals concerned.

One topic that has attracted widespread attention is the organization's culture, its importance to organizational effectiveness, and the difficulties entailed in changing an established culture (see for example *Corporate Cultures* by Terence E. Deal and Allan A. Kennedy).

As the vast AT&T system found its historic virtual monopoly on telephone communication eroding through deregulation, competition from other firms in the industry, and the impending breakup ordered by the Supreme Court, it became apparent to a number of senior executives that the established AT&T culture was no longer viable. It was recognized that drastic changes were necessary in the marketing strategy that had been effective for so many years. But changing that culture has proven to be a formidable task. Old ways of thinking die slowly and many of the individuals who have been charged with bringing about that change have found their efforts frustrated, often times to their personal detriment. Our first piece, "AT&T Manager Finds His Efforts to Galvanize Sales Meets Resistance" by Monica Langley reports the experiences of one such senior executive that led to his transfer to "an obscure planning position."

Organizations have always found it necessary to fire certain individuals. The volume of terminations associated with the recent recession has led to the coining of such euphemisms as "dehiring" and the emergence of individuals and firms that specialize in easing the trauma of being fired and helping the terminated employee to readjust and to find alternative employment. In "When the Axe Falls . . . ," Dale Burg describes her termination and subsequent outplacement experiences. She also provides interesting information about the outplacement industry and some data concerning the fate of those who are fired.

Judith Bardwick points out the rule of 99%. That is, "less than 1% of managers make it to the top of an organization." Further, she notes that in the future, for a variety of reasons, increasing numbers of managers will find themselves plateaued somewhere in middle management. The picture she presents is an important one both for students aspiring to managerial careers and the present incumbents of middle management positions.

The selection from Arthur Miller's classic, *Death of a Salesman,* emphasizes the consequences of a reason for the withdrawal of work which has received far too little attention: obsolescence. This process is often more brutal than retirement because it has few of the humane, social institutions that make retirement a somewhat graceful process. In contrast to obsolescence, retirement is an expected event for which organizations can plan and which they can handle through routine procedures. As a result, any sense of personal failure can often be submerged by gifts, parties, and speeches. However, there are few such procedures for handling the individual such as Willy Loman, whom the organization defines as obsolete.

Our next selection, "The Human Cost of Plant Closings," discusses yet another aspect of "falls." It is widely known that profound restructuring of our economy is well underway. Employment in manufacturing has been declining for some years. New technologies and industries are on the rise. Obsolete plants in the former north and central industrial hub increasingly are being relocated in the southern and southwestern sunbelts. As a consequence, more and more employees are being subjected to the trauma of plant closing, job loss, and the necessity of mid-life occupational change or relocation. Finally, Betsy Morris gives us a graphic illustration of the impact of a plant closing on one individual in "Like Many, a Production Scheduler Agonizes over Choosing New Career." When the steel plant closed where this individual had been employed for twenty years, he decided to look for employment outside the steel industry but wished to capitalize on his present know how, rather than undertaking expensive retraining without a reasonable assurance of being able to use newly acquired skills. At age thirty-eight, he is typical of thousands of workers, many of whom are in their forties or fifties, who are displaced from aging smokestack industries and passed over by potential employers in favor of younger people. (This article should be considered with "Starting Over" in section 5.)

The reader is invited to contrast the readings in this section with other materials on work life quality, job enrichment, participative management, and employee development.

AT&T Manager Finds His Effort to Galvanize Sales Meets Resistance

A Visionary or a Maverick?

Monica Langley

William F. Buehler looks back on the past year and speaks in elegiac tones about his "noble experiment."

Here he was, 43 years old, just named a vice president at American Telephone & Telegraph Co., given a work force of 3,000 and put in charge of marketing phone systems to small businesses all over the U.S. What's more, his bosses at AT&T gave him considerable freedom to break with the Bell way of doing things.

And that's exactly what he did. In place of Bell's rigmarole of endless memos, interminable meetings and strict chain of command, the boyish-looking Mr. Buehler discarded planning manuals, threw out employee tests, put salespeople on the highest commission-based compensation plan in AT&T history and fired those who couldn't meet his tough quotas.

It worked. Salespeople say they caught "Buehler fever," and sales figures soared off the charts. His boss and the chairman of AT&T Information Systems, Charles Marshall, concedes that the Buehler unit that sold the smaller business systems is outperforming the rival unit selling larger ones.

But today, 12 months later, Mr. Buehler isn't bathing in accolades. Instead, he is being removed from his job and put in an obscure planning position, though he remains a vice president.

"I argued to the management that the system should stay in place and I should continue leading it," he says. "I win most of my arguments around here, but I lost this one."

As a result, the new corporate culture that he created has been weakened, if not snuffed out, and many of his subordinates are apprehensive even though they often found him difficult to work for. "We're all upset and worried that we'll lose our new culture," says James R. Lewis, an AT&T account executive in Southfield, Mich. Moreover, many observers wonder whether AT&T isn't discouraging the kind of competitive zeal it is going to need as it tries to change from a regulated monopoly into a company that can take on the likes of International Business Machines Corp.

VARIED EXPLANATIONS

Why Mr. Buehler lost his position depends on whom you talk with. If you talk with Robert J. Casale, who ran the rival sales group along traditional lines and recently became his boss, the change was designed "to integrate the two discrete sales staffs in order to eliminate duplication in central support services."

But Mr. Marshall disagrees with that explanation. He says he favored moving Mr. Buehler so that the small-system sales force would report up the same channels as the large-systems division.

To many within the company, however, Mr. Buehler was removed because he was too menacing to the old Ma Bell culture. Despite his bottom-line success, he was viewed more as a maverick than a visionary, they say.

"Bill Buehler ruffled some feathers at the top. I wouldn't rule out that his different style of leadership caused him to be pushed out of a line position," Mr. Lewis speculates. "In the field, we knew there was a power struggle going on at the top."

PREDICTABLE BATTLE?

That change may have set off a struggle doesn't surprise David A. Nadler, the president of Organizational Research & Consultation Inc., a New York management-consulting firm. "Frequently in entrenched organizations where something new and entrepreneurial is tried," he says, "the experiment may not survive because it's too threatening to the old line."

When first meeting Mr. Buehler, you instantly see that he loves the limelight. He deems himself a born leader and constantly postures to dominate conversations, meetings and corporate strategies.

"I am blessed. I am a charismatic leader, I'll just tell you. I've always been able to get up in front of a group of people and motivate them to follow me," Mr. Buehler says unabashedly.

But at a recent press briefing in Washington, D.C.—where his superiors and not his subordinates were present—Mr. Buehler was visibly uncomfortable about taking a back seat. Sitting at the dais with AT&T Information Systems officers, Mr. Buehler was the only one not asked to speak by the chairman, Mr. Marshall. Mr. Buehler fidgeted in his seat throughout the briefing until, finally unable to contain himself, he started waving his arms to get the chairman's attention.

During his 19 years with the Bell System, Mr. Buehler hasn't had any trouble gaining attention as a dynamic manager. Always considered on the fast track by people who have known him over the years, he received promotion after promotion. Some describe him as "Kennedyesque."

When AT&T Information Systems was created last Jan. 1 to become the unregulated equipment-marketing unit for AT&T, which was preparing to divest itself of its Bell operating companies this Jan. 1, Mr. Buehler was tapped as a vice president. He was to head General Business Systems, which would sell smaller systems at high volume, while Mr. Casale would oversee sales of large accounts at National Business Systems.

Not seeing his wife and two sons very much, and putting aside his love for skiing, playing touch football and reading spy novels, Mr. Buehler began working 16-hour days to install a new corporate culture in his unit.

In setting up GBS, Mr. Buehler used as a road map a book "In Search of Excellence: Lessons from America's Best-Run Companies." He read the best seller twice and confesses that he "stole from it liberally." Last January, in fact, he handed out to his new force a typewritten sheet of marching orders that was titled "What We Aspire to Be" and contained verbatim phrases from the book. They included such mottoes as "customer is king," "reward results, not process," "staff supports the line" and "keep it simple."

"That little list of points was the only guide I gave my new work force in January—no detailed plans or directives," Mr. Buehler says. "I wanted the team to know from the start that this was an entrepreneurial venture, and they were to abide by these points in a way that worked best for them."

Also from the start, Mr. Buehler was highly visible. He traveled across the country to his 27 branches to meet his people.

"The staffers in my branch have been with Bell for years, but this was the very first time any of them had ever even seen an AT&T vice president," says Robert L. Focazio, the GBS branch manager for New Jersey. "And then he actually sat down with the billing staff and ate hoagie sandwiches. This was radical by AT&T standards, but we came to know it was perfectly natural by Bill Buehler's standards."

Mr. Focazio, who says he is "personally dissapointed" that Mr. Buehler won't be his boss after Jan. 1, says Mr. Buehler didn't pay any attention to hierarchical lines. "That's the kind of guy you'd want to kill for," he says. "It almost doesn't matter what Bill Buehler says."

Mr. Buehler's troops initially had trouble not only picking up his way of thinking but also bringing in the results. GBS made few sales in the first quarter, while the more traditional NBS was meeting its quota. "It was gut-wrenching those first months, watching the results come in," Mr. Buehler says.

As bad as the initial results were, Mr. Buehler was bothered as much by the reception that his new unit was getting from other AT&T units. "Employees in different parts of the country enjoyed seeing us fail," he recalls.

About the same time, Archie McGill, then the president of AT&T Information Systems and the man who had persuaded Mr. Buehler to leave

Pacific Telephone Co., resigned. Insiders said then that Mr. McGill had left rather than to be pushed into a less important role because higher-ups found him difficult to control. (He denied this and said it was simply time to move on.) With the departure of the man who had given him autonomy to run his unit, Mr. Buehler was the only one left at AT&T trying to shake up the sleepy giant, some insiders say. (Other inside observers speculate that the recent shake-up concerning Mr. Buehler was a move to expunge the last remnant of Mr. McGill's leadership.)

But shortly after Mr. McGill's resignation, Mr. Buehler's team caught "Buehler fever" and started bringing in the numbers. His salespeople were exceeding quotas and began taking home $40,000 to $45,000 a year.

As the salesmen wrote more orders and the managers got the hang of this new free-wheeling atmosphere, they started making more demands on Mr. Buehler—and he responded. When they needed prompter deliveries, Mr. Buehler guaranteed that the phones would be delivered even if a decorative feature was missing. When they refused to spend time filling out contract forms, Mr. Buehler reduced the standard contract to one page from four. When they wanted quicker approvals of customer designs and bids, he organized a small committee to respond within days.

"Decisions that would have taken two years in the Bell System were made in days by Bill Buehler," marvels Diane Allen, an account executive in Monterey, Calif. "Bias for action," an "In Search of Excellence" buzzword, had taken hold. Unlike the tradition-bound AT&T, where planning is often an end in itself, a "try it, fix it, don't study it to death" kind of attitude prevailed.

But sometimes Mr. Beuhler's managers didn't like what the boss was saying. Mr. Focazio remembers a meeting where the branch managers were complaining about how some nonsales employees were paid. "Bill rejected our proposal," Mr. Focazio recalls, "and we were upset with his decision. So he told us to go outside right then, kick rocks and come back ready to support the decision as if it were our own."

Mr. Buehler minces no words to demonstrate his demand for obedience. "If I found one of my managers trying to sabotage any decision I made, I'd cut his neck off," he says.

His toughness extends to his choice of whom he allows to work for him. Each month, he makes keep-or-cut determinations based strictly on sales performance. More than one-third of his sales force has quit, been transferred or been fired. "Results are what count," Mr. Buehler says. "If a salesman can't meet quota, he doesn't belong here." Edward R. Hodges, an account executive in Dallas, says, "It's tough to meet Bill's standards, and I've seen a lot of salesmen in Dallas put back in the streets."

The GBS sales force receives compensation based 50% on straight salary and 50% on sales commissions, while the NBS force has a 70%-30%

salary-commission mix. In addition, all GBS salespeople have the same quota, while NBS conducts complex, time-consuming quota reviews for each salesman to allow for differences in sales territories.

In this performance-driven regime, Mr. Buehler's salespeople say they feel more competitive pressure from their fellow salesmen than from product competitors such as TIE/Communications Inc., Mitel Corp. and ITT Corp.

To ensure that peer pressure, not the boss's orders, motivated his salespeople, Mr. Buehler demanded that individual sales results be posted. "One of the few things I insisted on was a sales board to be prominently displayed in every office," Mr. Beuhler says. "As hokey as it sounds, when a person comes to work every day and sees his red tab isn't the highest one up there, he will work that much harder."

But some branches worked harder at how the sales board looked than what it said—the "Bell-shaped head" mentality lingered on. "My God, you wouldn't believe it! My managers wanted to know whether the boards should be magnetic or chalk, colored or black and white, large or small," Mr. Buehler complains. "They were so used to detailed corporate orders in the Bell System, they wanted to be led by the hand. Hell, I just wanted any kind of board up there, and then the results."

But many salespeople fear that all this will come to an end when Mr. Buehler moves to his planning job next month. "All of us would have liked to go into 1984 with Bill at the helm," Mr. Hodges says. And Mr. Buehler says, "There were tears around here. But I lost on this, and I can live with that."

Mr. Buehler may not be the only loser. Many inside and outside observers say AT&T is making a mistake by stifling Mr. Buehler and the new corporate culture that he tried to create despite the huge bureaucracy. "I would have kept Bill as a leader of the sales force," Mr. McGill says. Mr. Nadler, the consultant, agrees. "Bill Buehler is the kind of leader AT&T needs to develop," he says. And Dennis Lukas, who resigned as marketing director at AT&T Information Systems "in part" because of the recent changes at GBS and has just become an assistant vice president at GTE Corp., predicts "that AT&T will try this kind of experiment again because it was so right."

But for now, this battle between corporate traditionalism and innovation has produced a victory for the old line at AT&T. Yet Buehler makes it clear that his campaign to create a new corporate culture there hasn't ended.

"I'm already meeting with my new planning staff," he says, "and they've never had an operations type like me leading them. So we're having a difference of opinion on how we view the world, but I'm used to this kind of resistance. Hey, it's not stopped me before, and it won't now."

When the Ax Falls . . .

Dale Burg

When my boss asked if he could meet with me in my office at precisely 1:30 on a recent Thursday afternoon, I knew I shouldn't order lunch for the two of us. The request, in fact seemed ominous. My boss had inherited me (rather than hired me) when he joined the company not long before; a takeover by another company had changed the nature of the department's work; and lately he'd taken to making picayune complaints about my performance—that is, when he bothered to acknowledge my presence at all. I knew enough about corporate style to realize the signs were there: I was about to be fired.

Sure enough, by 1:40 Thursday I was without a job. "We're eliminating your position," he said, and, in case I didn't get it, "You won't be working here anymore." My boss briefly reviewed the financial arrangements, assured me I'd have time to pack up my personal belongings, relieved me of any further responsibilities and then said: "The company has hired an outplacement service to assist you with your job search. And right now, I'd like you to meet your counselor."

He opened the door of my office. A pleasant-looking man with a briefcase (filled with Kleenex, I imagined) entered and shook my hand. This was evidently the "outplacement counselor." He seemed to me like an unwelcome guest at a funeral.

He settled into a chair across from me, as my now ex-boss fled. "Did you have any sense this was coming?" The counselor began. Civility compelled me to respond, and soon I found myself talking about my career in general and my job history with this company in particular. He was drawing me out. While I was calm—I had anticipated and perhaps even welcomed this turn of events—I sensed that he would have been unruffled by any reaction from a fit of rage to a tearful outburst. I was conscious of telephone calls I wanted to make—to my husband, my mother, my business and personal contacts—but he had an agenda to follow and tacitly won my cooperation. In the next two and a half hours, he introduced me to the outplacement process.

THE SWELLING RANKS

Until I became an outplacement "candidate" (the diplomatic term for one who is fired; one is newly a "candidate" for another job), I hadn't even

---

been aware that my company offered the benefit. I eventually wondered why, since the cost of the service (usually 15 percent of an ex-employee's annual salary) is not small. William J. Morin, chairman of Drake Beam Morin, Inc., in New York (which with $20 million in annual billings is probably the country's largest outplacement firm), enumerates the reasons for outplacement.

One is public relations, both external and internal. The community won't regard the company as a monster and an ex-employee won't bad mouth the company or industry, and employees who remain will see that their former associates are being treated well. Another is avoiding lawsuits; a former employee who is focusing on getting that next job is less likely to think about suing her employer for firing her in the first place.

Finally, there is a financial advantage. Companies hoping to trim their payrolls find that managers are less reluctant to terminate employees if they feel those people will be helped in finding new jobs. And with the aid of outplacement, ex-employees are likely to find those jobs more quickly than they might on their own. For companies that pay severance until a former worker locates a new job, outplacement may mean substantial corporate savings. Such savings may be especially high for law firms, which traditionally have kept on staff the attorneys who didn't make the grade as partners. Finding this sort of noblesse oblige too costly, many firms now hold onto their less-favored lawyers only until they find other positions through outplacement.

An estimated three-fourths of Fortune 500 companies, "if not more," provide outplacement services, according to James E. Challenger, president of Challenger, Gray & Christmas, Inc., whose main Chicago office and 13 branches work with some 1,200 to 1,500 people per year. His firm is one of 54 that accept compensation only from employers, according to the 1982 *Directory of Outplacement Firms.* These companies are different from businesses known in the industry as "retail services"—outplacement firms that take payment from terminated employees; such firms occasionally make falsely extravagant claims for finding jobs. Sometimes executive-search firms also provide outplacement, but this activity violates the standards of the Association of Executive Recruiting Consultants, which sees a conflict of interest.

Job counselors believe that anyone who has a job today may well become an outplacement candidate tomorrow, for one consequence of living in our "future-shock" society is that no one can be assured of spending a lifetime with a single employer. Drake Beam Morin reports that its clients average 11 years at the jobs from which they were terminated, and other firms report similar statistics.

Drake Beam Morin's clientele also average 47 years of age and a $48,000 annual salary. At one time, outplacement was an exclusive perk of upper-level managers (upper-level seems to be defined generally as above $60,000, middle at $30,000), but this is no longer so. Robert M. Hecht, PhD, of Lee-Hecht & Associates in New York, says that even people at the $15,000 level may get some version of outplacement—"perhaps not the intensive, classical counseling, but rather they will be part of a one-, two-, or three-day group program." Drake Beam Morin has provided group-out placement services for companies that have let go hundreds of people at once; their clients have included Allied Corporation, Hooker Chemical, Hudson Stores, Montgomery Ward, Rockwell, Sears Roebuck and Xerox.

THE COUNSELING PROCESS

Classical, one-on-one outplacement counseling generally starts before the termination. For example, when a client tells J. J. Gallagher Associates in New York that an employee is about to be let go, he or an associate meets with a member of the personnel department and with the line manager who actually will do the firing. He or his representative offers pointers regarding the firing: where (not in the manager's office; the manager should retain the option of leaving), when (never on Friday, holidays or anniversaries) and how (among other things, make sure the situation is clear, even if you must say, as my boss did, "You won't be working here anymore").

Then attention shifts to the candidate. Following the termination interview and the candidate's first meeting with the counselor, the candidate receives a number of interest and aptitude tests that she must complete and mail to a testing service for evaluation.

Gallagher is among the companies that use testing to help identify the candidate's real interests, possibly with a view toward seeking another kind of job. Hecht says his staff (composed largely of industrial psychology PhDs with experience in industry) do testing, but he feels it is sometimes of limited value in terms of assessment for career change. "Most people finally decide to play the same game, or a variation of it, though in a different ballpark." He finds that only about 5 percent of his clients actually change professions and even fewer become free-lancers. Challenger, Gray & Christmas says 30 to 50 of its 1,200 to 1,500 annual clients go off on their own. Most executives are too specialized or have too expensive a life-style to take such risks.

In addition to filling out tests, Gallagher Associates' clients complete a questionnaire about past successes, both business and personal. In the first meeting at the outplacement firm's office, this questionnaire is used to help identify the client's strong points and subsequently to reiterate them in a résumé. The counselor and candidate discuss job possibilities which the candidate then rates from one to ten in terms of desirability and attainability.

Once they have established a job goal, the counselor helps the candidate review her contacts, both business and social (for the latter will lead to the former), and begin the process of attempting to secure interviews—even when no specific job may be available. The theory is that, in the course of the interview, the candidate may get a referral to someone else, and that this process eventually will lead to a job. It is a rule of thumb among outplacement specialists that 80 percent of jobs exist in the "hidden job market"—that is, they never are advertised publicly. Hecht, who doesn't use the term, still says that "most jobs come through personal contact—who you know, or who you can approach in a persuasive and selling way." A smaller number of jobs is filled through search and employment agencies, still fewer through ads in newspapers.

The various firms estimate they spend between 25 and 50 hours on the first steps of the outplacement process. While the particulars vary in some respects from Gallagher Associates' procedure, all the firms help with preparing a résumé, practicing interviewing and so forth; all help in ascertaining important data (life and work history, results of standardized tests, defining strongest skills), training and motivating. Also, says Challenger, a lot of time is spent simply making the client feel good. "It's therapy." If there are marital or drinking problems, the firm might suggest extra counseling; occasionally, says Hecht, "We pick up charges: for example, for an outside tax expert or a relocation expert" to help a highly paid executive (whose fee warrants the firm's expenditure).

The first steps completed, the outplacement firms stay on the case, meeting with the candidate in the counselor's office for one to three hours a week. The association continues through possible assistance in salary negotiation for the new job, and counseling during the first weeks of reemployment, while the client settles in.

According to J. J. Gallagher Associates, a senior-level executive making $60,000 to $80,000 a year can expect to find another job in five to nine months with outplacement help. For midlevel executives in the $40,000 to $60,000 annual-income range, the job search should be completed in four to six months. Other firms report slightly different figures. Reflecting the improving economy, the *Challenger Outplacement Index* reports that the average job-search time for rehired managers declined 9 percent in the second quarter of 1983, to 3.3 months, compared with 3.6 months in the previous quarter. Drake Beam Morin's most recent statistics still reflect economically hard times: job searches that used to average 4.3 months now take 5.2 months, at which point 80 to 85 percent of their clients are placed.

Echoing other counselors, Morin points out that, in the end, getting a job depends on the attitude of the individual. "If you work the plan—networking, getting organized—you find jobs. But if you hang up on any part of it—'I haven't told my friends, I don't want them to know I lost my job,' or 'I mailed my résumé to only three companies'— it doesn't work that way."

He adds that depression is a big part of the picture. Losing a job always is painful—Morin refers to it as "going through the vale"—and outplacement counselors provide some balm when they tell you, as they generally will, that no matter what the reason given (cutbacks, mergers, reorganization), you lost your job for reasons of chemistry. "I don't know how you write this down," says Hecht, "but the top reason people get fired is, 'I don't like your face. I used to, but I don't anymore.' Outplacement counseling helps ease the pain of losing a job and, more important, it helps you look toward the future."

Genevieve Bazelmans, a partner in J. J. Gallagher Associates, cautions managers who are enthusiastic about outplacement that they should avoid telling fired employees that they are giving them "a terrific opportunity"—somehow that's not what you want to hear as you're getting the ax—but, in fact, outplacement counseling may be just that. It's a chance to assess one's career, both present and future, with the guidance of people who have both corporate and counseling expertise. Often, you jump forward. Some 86 percent of Drake Beam Morin's clients "relocate" to another job at equivalent or better salaries; Challenger, Gray & Christmas reports similar figures. Gallagher Associates finds that 60 percent of recent clients topped their previous salary, and a fifth of that group achieved increases in excess of 40 percent. Challenger cautions, though, that one shouldn't expect too much—a 20 percent increase is "outstanding."

Hecht proposes two questions a candidate should ask in evaluating the outplacement process: Did you get a job in timely fashion? And did you learn from the process things that are beneficial in your life in general? According to him, the answer to both questions should be a resounding yes.

Rather than handing new employees a booklet that contains termination policies, suggests Morin, companies would be better advised to state clearly that, if things don't work out, they offer career guidance and counseling in the form of outplacement. A woman on the way up ought to inquire whether a firm she might join offers such a valuable benefit. Certainly this is a realistic concern in view of the volatility of business in a rapidly changing workplace.

When Ambition Is No Asset

Judith M. Bardwick

"I'm 44. I think that's young. The prime of life, as a matter of fact. But right now I seem to be getting some kind of message. Oh, nobody has said anything outright. But, hell, Bob just got promoted to the head of the section, and he's only 36. I hate to have a kid over me. I have to admit that he is good. Real good. But I could have done that job. The truth is, I was sure I was going to get that spot. I've been in this job for over six years. The guy before me was promoted after only three. . . .

"There's talk about giving me a slot in San Francisco, but Marjorie and the kids would be really upset if we left New York. You know, they said it would be a 'terrific opportunity' but I'm not really sure it's a promotion. There's more money in it, but the truth is, the work would be just the same—only in another city . . . .

"When I joined this company, it was terrific. I was promoted every few years, faster than anybody who started with me. I made more money than anybody my age. The sky was the limit. And I worked. Did I work! Nights, weekends. We moved four times in the first ten years. And it was worth it . . . .

"Was it? Was it worth it? Hell, I don't know. Is this it? Am I on the shelf? Forty-four and gone as far as I'm going. I don't feel too good. As a matter of fact, I feel lousy."

This man is plateaued.

What does that mean? If you are *structurally plateaued,* it means that promotions have ended. While your job may change, there will be no significant increases in responsibilities, status, money, or power as long as you remain in the same organization. Any future moves will be horizontal at best (and demotion is even a possibility). If you are *content plateaued,* it means that your work doesn't change much—it doesn't challenge you or require that anything new be learned.

In workshops on plateauing I have run for managers, there are moments when the tension is palpable. The room is silent, no one moves, and no one looks at anyone else. People sit rigidly as they think, "My God, they're talking about me." Closet fears—often expressed as hostile jokes—come out in the open.

Being plateaued is the cause of widespread (but generally unacknowledged) stress for people whose self-esteem depends upon success.

From *New Management,* Vol. I., No. 4, 1984, pp. 22–28. Reprinted by permission.

The fear (or the fact) of being plateaued can result in hard times, especially for those whose careers were once fast-track, those who were once assured that they were the best and the brightest. Those are the people who may feel plateaued not only at work, but plateaued in life in general. Without the exhilaration of triumph at work, *nothing* feels exciting. Instead, life seems to be made up of routines, none of which provides any sense of vivid pleasure.

MANAGERIAL INTERVENTION

As the manager of plateaued people, when do you need to do or say something? You need to intervene whenever someone's productivity, involvement, and creativity fall off significantly. That often happens when people are under great stress, because when people are truly upset they have trouble managing anything other than their own emotions.

When being plateaued is the source of stress, then symptoms of the condition are likely to emerge at work. These symptoms can include coming late, leaving early, absenteeism, and frequent illness. Other symptoms are irritability and hypersensitivity to criticism. Sometimes people drink or smoke excessively. . . they may eat or sleep a lot or very little . . . their dress can change. Perhaps the most serious symptom is withdrawing from the job or from people. Any marked change in personality or behavior can be a symptom of major stress—for example, a sudden interest in philosophic questions such as "the meaning of life," or in pop-psychology. Classically, men have love affairs, usually with younger women. Currently, athletics has become a way of coping with stress. When it is used as a way of coping with life, it can lead to excessive behavior. We all know 50-year-old men who suddenly become marathon runners, transforming their frustrated competitiveness from work to the road.

Some symptoms of stress are easy to identify. But not everyone who is plateaued will be stressed, and plateauing is not the only cause of stress. And, in many cases, neither the stressed individual nor the person's superior is likely to recognize the most common and psychologically-efficient response to the chronic pain of being plateaued: The person increases the amount of time spent at work. Depressed and angry, the person works long—but doesn't work well.

WHAT THE BOSS NEEDS TO KNOW

Ambition is no asset when it cannot be fulfilled. Instead, it can become a burr, resulting in chronic dissatisfaction and feelings of frustration. Hence, those managers who regard promotion as the only significant reward are likely to become frustrated, because promotions end long before retirement for almost everyone. This structural plateauing is virtually inevitable because of "the Rule of 99%": Less than 1% of the people in an organization make it to the highest level of decision-making.

While most people know these odds, some persist in pursuing promotion right to the end of their careers. Such people tend to think of themselves as exceptions. That is, because they were successful at the beginning of their careers, they developed expectations that they would continue to climb. Very few of these managers will accept the fact that it is much easier to be promoted on the lower rungs of the organizational pyramid, because there are many more opportunities for promotion nearer the base, and a much greater breadth of ability among those with whom one is competing. The higher a manager climbs, the harder it becomes to look outstanding.

Further, promotion became the most important organizational reward during the past three decades because of a unique set of circumstances. Those who are now 45-60 years old were born around the time of the Great Depression. At that time, America had the lowest birth rate in its history. And when the Depression Kids went to work after World War II, they participated in the longest sustained economic boom America has ever had. As organizations expanded during this boom, a large number of promotional opportunities were created for a small number of people. As a result, managers were promoted at an unusually rapid pace. In addition, since prosperity continued for about 25 years, these unusual conditions came to be perceived as typical. Thus, a career of abnormally swift promotions came to be seen as normal.

Plateauing is now increasing because conditions in the 1980's are exactly the opposite. There are too many managers. By 1985, there will be a 45% increase in the number of people aged 30-39 (as compared with the preceding generation). While some members of the current generation have non-traditional values that are less dominated by the need for a career success, that trait is *not* characteristic of those who have chosen to work in competitive organizations. In addition to the sheer number of people in their 30's, the number of managers in actual competition has increased greatly because of the reduction in discrimination against women and blacks. While members of these two groups did not constitute a significant part of the pool of managers before mid-1970's, 20% of the MBA degrees that will be granted in 1985 will be earned by women and 5% by blacks.

Given the increasing number of those in the managerial pool—and the fact that the ranks of management are not expanding in most organizations—competitive pressures are likely to increase. Hence, while the average age of those who became structurally plateaued was about 45 in the late 1970's, today there are managers in their early 30's who are plateaued.

The population increase, the rising number of educated people, the stagnant economy, and certain aspects of technological change dictate that the high rates of promotion that once existed will not exist in the near future. Although promotions have been the major organizational reward for outstanding performance in expanding organizations, in the future promotions will be the exception rather than the rule.

One of the first traumas for those who were once successful in the promotion game is the realization that they are no longer regarded as exceptional. For those who were once treated as exceptions, being regarded as ordinary can be shattering. For those once regarded as promising, being seen as merely dependable and competent is a tremendous come-down.

PLATEAUED MEN

If the plateaued individual is an executive, his negative emotions may be increased by the responses of those he manages. A plateaued manager who occupies the same slot for a long time is often viewed as a "road block" by his subordinates. Plateaued managers are also frequently seen as powerless because they aren't able to do anything to help themselves. Put yourself in the shoes of such an executive: If the people who work for you think that you block their promotions, see you as powerless, and don't want to work for a loser—then their resentment will add to your negative self-esteem.

The managers who are most likely to become seriously alienated when promotions end are those who have been so well rewarded by the organization in the past that they let their lives become dominated by work. These people have no other emotional resources or significant activities from which they can derive good feelings about themselves. This typically happens to men in upper-middle to upper-level management—almost all of whom are married and are fathers and have a comfortable and comforting relationship with their wives and children. Psychologically, they *need* their families. But, for many, *passion* is restricted to work.

Most men whose work has dominated their lives inevitably come to feel that they gave less time and less emotional involvement to their wives and children than would have been ideal. It is very common for men to feel guilty about this. Guilt is especially likely if their children's lives did not turn out as they had hoped, if their marriage is comfortable but somewhat boring, or if their wives are unhappy. As men contemplate how they have spent their lives, it is no doubt the case that very few children or marriages or wives fulfill early expectations. Thus, adding disappointment with personal accomplishments to disappointment associated with work, a man may feel that he has failed in all the important aspects of his life.

Men have a special vulnerability when they can no longer feel successful through work. Masculinity is normally gained through success in competition, and work is the most important competitive arena for middle-class men. Masculinity has to be earned; it is not a quality that we attribute to men simply because they are male. In this society, the gut level fear of plateaued men is that they are no longer men.

One of the most dramatic indications of the relationship between success at work and how men experience themselves can be found in their perceptions of how old they are. In interviews with men whose ages range from 36 to 59, I find that chronological age is *not* significant. Instead the men who say, "I am plateaued," are the ones who say, "I am middle-aged." No matter what their actual age, those who are not plateaued and who expect further promotions usually say they are not middle-aged.

In my workshops, I often ask corporate managers how they spend their days. They usually say that they get to the office between 7:30 and 8:00 in the morning and return home at 7:00 or 7:30 at night. They frequently bring work home and, whether they do anything with it or not, work is on their minds. So even when they are not at work, they continue to think about it. What, then, is home? Home is the haven to which they repair before they go back into competition; home, which includes family, is terribly important even when little attention is paid to it.

PLATEAUED WOMEN

In this regard, women managers are likely to have a vulnerability which most men do not. When I ask corporate men how many are married, about 95% will raise their hands. When I ask the same question of corporate women who are in middle management or above, the percentage who are married is very low. Census data tell us that the rates of "never-marrying," "divorcing," and "remaining childless" are highest for women who are economically successful and who have five or more years of college. In brief, the chances are good that the plateaued, successful woman will realize that the cost to her success was not, as it is for men, a *less-fulfilling* family life than might have been but, rather, *no* family at all. The gut-level fear of these women is that they might not be women.

Women who combine marriage, maternity, and a career are usually less vulnerable to the stress of plateauing. Women who continue to have their traditional home as well as job responsibilities do not focus on work as exclusively as men and unmarried women. Still, their lives are hardly free from stress. Since the social rules governing dual-career marriages are not really established, such marriages require continuous compromise and endless discussion about the division of responsibilities. That is a tense way to live. Thus, while these women are less likely to feel as angry as unmarried women when they plateau, the quality of their home lives will nonetheless have been affected by the demands of work.

Like married men, married women, too, are likely to question the value of how they have spent their lives when they realize they are plateaued.

PLATEAUING AND SUPPORTIVE RELATIONSHIPS

Since most of the people in middle management and above are men, I've had more exposure to the problems of plateaued men than women. I find that those men who have emotionally-sustaining personal relationships do not necessarily have less need for recognition and success on the job. On the other hand, the *absence* of emotionally-affirming relationships usually relates to a very intense need for confirmation from the organization. Those men who seem unable to be emotionally close to anyone— wives, children, or friends—ask the organization for the good feelings about themselves they don't get elsewhere. Hence, while a workaholic may look like an organizational asset in the short run, in the long haul the organization will not be able to meet his emotional needs. Managers have to realize that meeting the needs of a workaholic requires more than a promotion—he needs insight into his problem and new sources of esteem and fulfillment.

WHAT CAN BE DONE?

While plateauing is a painful subject, it must be taken out of the closet. That's the responsibility of the manager of the plateaued individual. Being open about plateauing means encouraging managers at all levels to accept the reality that promotions do not go on forever. When confronted with this reality, it is possible that some very good people may decide to leave the organization. That is not a problem. The problem in most organizations is that there are too many good people to promote them all. The organization can afford to lose some good people. The organization can't afford to lose its stars. But there are very few stars, and they can be retained if they are well rewarded.

One way to reward them (everyone, really—not just stars) is to value their professionalism and competence. Since they must find pride in mastering their work and in learning new tasks without seeing this as an instrumental step to a promotion, their knowledge, wisdom, perspectives, skills, and experience have to be esteemed for themselves. In essence, corporations must be careful not to couple structural *and* content plateauing. Opportunities for the expansion of experience have to be available in the absense of opportunities for moving up in the hierarchy.

When managers are asked what is important to them in their jobs, their most frequent answers are "challenge and change." People say that they need to learn, to grapple, and to cope with difficult new problems that are important to the organization. The opportunity to do that is a major reward. Therefore, plateaued people should not be confined to the same task for so long that the feelings of boredom replace their sense of mastery.

Plateaued managers should be encouraged to think about job changes. While an organization cannot promise that their wishes will always be granted, the objective should be to replace their passivity with activity. Passivity increases the sense of powerlessness, depression, and resentment. Activity generates a sense of mastery and optimism—as long as some positive change does, in fact, occur. For that reason, plateaued managers should be encouraged to think about what work alternatives might exist for them, what they might prefer to do, and how those changes could be created.

Organizations can use lateral transfers to alleviate the stress of constant plateauing. In addition to the stimulation that such transfers generate, these job changes also assure people that the organization is confident that they can handle different responsibilities. Although changing people's jobs always involves some loss of productivity while new tasks are being mastered, the possibility of significantly increasing their involvement because of new challenges far outweighs this loss.

Lateral transfers should be thought of on three dimensions: horizontal, vertical, and in terms of time. The simplest changes are horizontal; people are transferred from one job to another.

More complex horizontal changes involve altering jobs. This can be designed so that new positions involve a combination of old and new responsibilties.

More elaborate changes can involve vertical as well as horizontal positions (if status differences are not great).

Finally, horizontal or vertical changes can vary from short-term assignments to permanent new positions.

In some organizations, it is appropriate to create teams to handle projects. Since members of a team have both common and unique skills, the group can handle a broader range of projects than can the same number of individuals working singly. Working in teams is a way to increase the amount of change in the content of tasks all group members do.

Organizations often choose to increase the rate of promotions by increasing the number of levels in the hierarchy. The alternative, of course, is to reduce the importance of promotions by reducing the number of levels in the hierarchy. The latter is usually a better strategy—for when there are fewer levels, power is distributed more horizontally than vertically and this lessens the importance of promotion. For example, a team is a small unit in which power is essentially horizontal. Being a member of a team can reduce the individual's need for promotion and for solo success.

It is crucial to pay constant attention to plateaued people, especially those who are so dependable that they tend to be taken for granted. To this end, an annual or biannual performance evaluation is inadequate in terms of frequency of feedback. Worse, performance reviews are often inadequate because many supervisors are uncomfortable conveying criticism, and thus they avoid saying anything negative. We all understand that people resent too much criticism. Less easily understood is the fact that people also resent it when they feel that they do not get *enough* criticism. They wonder: "If I am praised so much, and I'm as good as people say I am, why haven't I been more successful?"

Mostly, people feel anxious when they don't get critical feedback. Because they know they are not perfect, the absence of criticism leaves them uncertain about how they are really regarded. Most people want to know how they are really being judged and what their future is likely to be. Plateaued people, too, need that information.

Given the vulnerability of those whose psychological investments are restricted to work, corporations should be prepared to counsel people about personal issues, particularly if that can be done within the context of work. While management should not probe into personal lives, personal problems can easily affect the quality of work. For example, corporate counselors might give advice on participation in community organizations, in athletic activities, or on making more time for family and friends.

Organizations can prepare people financially and psychologically for early retirement. Since an enforced early retirement often generates bitter resentment, it is most desirable for people to volunteer to retire. That will only happen when there is a supportive program that enables people to see early retirement as an opportunity to begin a second career or to start a new life.

In essence, the organization can reduce the negative feelings of managers by giving them information about plateauing that lessens their sense of failure. Their uncertainty can be reduced by giving them candid evaluations. They can be remotivated by giving them challenging new work assignments that tell them the organization has confidence in their abilities. They can be encouraged to increase other involvements. All of this gives them the message that they are valued.

Those who are depressed about being plateaued are trying to redefine ambition. The decline of ambition is usually seen in the negative—as giving something up. This has to be transformed into the positive—as the possibility to gain aspects of the self and of life which one didn't have before.

Since plateauing is inevitable for all but the one percent, the organizational climate has to change so that it becomes permissible to say, "I like my job and I do it well. I'm willing to work hard, but work won't run my life any more. I've got some other things I need to do."

Organizations benefit when they remove (or prevent) the stigma of failure and the despair of frustration among their plateaued managers. The necessary first step is for the organization to acknowledge the problem. Only then can the issues be confronted and resolved. I have never held a workshop on plateauing that didn't begin with palpable tension. But, then, I have never held a workshop that didn't end optimistically—with a great relief.

Death of a Salesman
Arthur Miller

From the right, Willy Loman, the Salesman, enters, carrying two large sample cases. The flute plays on. He hears but is not aware of it. He is past sixty years of age, dressed quietly. Even as he crosses the stage to the doorway of the house, his exhaustion is apparent. He unlocks the door, comes into the kitchen, and thankfully lets his burden down, feeling the soreness of his palms. A word-sigh escapes his lips—it might be "Oh, boy, oh, boy." He closes the door, then carries his case out into the living room, through the draped kitchen doorway.

Linda, his wife, has stirred in her bed at the right. She gets out and puts on a robe, listening. Most often jovial, she has developed an iron repression of her exceptions to Willy's behavior—she more than loves him, she admires him, as though his mercurial nature, his temper, his massive dreams and little cruelties, served her only as sharp reminders of the turbulent longings within him, longings which she shares but lacks the temperament to utter and follow to their end.

LINDA, *hearing Willy outside the bedroom, calls with some trepidation:* Willy!

WILLY: It's all right. I came back.

LINDA: Why? What happened? *Slight pause.* Did something happen, Willy?

WILLY: No, nothing happened.

LINDA: You didn't smash the car, did you?

WILLY: *with casual irritation:* I said nothing happened. Didn't you hear me?

LINDA: Don't you feel well?

WILLY: I'm tired to death. *The flute has faded away. He sits on the bed beside her, a little numb.* I couldn't make it. I just couldn't make it, Linda.

LINDA, *very carefully, delicately:* Where were you all day? You look terrible.

WILLY: I got as far as a little above Yonkers. I stopped for a cup of coffee. Maybe it was the coffee.

LINDA: What?

WILLY, *after a pause:* I suddenly couldn't drive any more. The car kept going off onto the shoulder, y'know?

LINDA, *helpfully:* Oh. Maybe it was the steering again. I don't think Angelo knows the Studebaker.

WILLY: No, it's me, it's me. Suddenly I realize I'm goin' sixty miles an hour and I don't remember the last five minutes. I'm—I can't seem to—keep my mind to it.

LINDA: Maybe it's your glasses. You never went for your new glasses.

WILLY: No, I see everything. I came back ten miles an hour. It took me nearly four hours from Yonkers.

LINDA, *resigned:* Well, you'll just have to take a rest, Willy, you can't continue this way.

WILLY: I just got back from Florida.

LINDA: But you didn't rest your mind. Your mind is overactive, and the mind is what counts, dear.

WILLY: I'll start out in the morning. Maybe I'll feel better in the morning. *She is taking off his shoes.* These goddam arch supports are killing me.

LINDA: Take an aspirin. Should I get you an aspirin? It'll soothe you.

WILLY, *with wonder:* I was driving along, you understand? And I was fine. I was even observing the scenery. You can imagine, me looking at scenery, on the road every week of my life. But it's so beautiful up there, Linda, the trees are so thick, and the sun is warm. I opened the windshield and just let the warm air bathe over me. And then all of a sudden I'm goin' off the road! I'm tellin' ya, I absolutely forgot I was driving. If I'd've gone the other way over the white line I might've killed somebody. So I went on again—and five minutes later I'm dreamin' again, and I nearly—*He presses two fingers against his eyes.* I have such thoughts, I have such strange thoughts.

LINDA: Willy, dear. Talk to them again. There's no reason why you can't work in New York.

WILLY: They don't need me in New York, I'm the New England man. I'm vital in New England.

LINDA: But you're sixty years old. They can't expect you to keep traveling every week.

WILLY: I'll have to send a wire to Portland. I'm supposed to see Brown and Morrison tomorrow morning at ten o'clock to show the line. Goddammit, I could sell them! *He starts putting on his jacket.*

LINDA, *taking the jacket from him:* Why don't you go down to the place tomorrow and tell Howard you've simply got to work in New York? You're too accommodating, dear.

WILLY: If old man Wagner was alive I'd a been in charge of New York now! That man was a prince; he was a masterful man. But that boy of his, that Howard, he don't appreciate. When I went north the first time, the Wagner Company didn't know where New England was!

LINDA: Why didn't you tell those things to Howard, dear?

WILLY, *encouraged:* I will, I definitely will. Is there any cheese?

LINDA: I'll make you a sandwich.

WILLY: No, go to sleep. I'll take some milk. I'll be right away. . . .

[*Editor's note:* The scene shifts to Howard Wagner's office the following day.]

WILLY: Pst! Pst!

HOWARD: Hello, Willy, come in.

WILLY: Like to have a little talk with you, Howard.

HOWARD: Sorry to keep you waiting. I'll be with you in a minute.

WILLY: What's that, Howard?

HOWARD: Didn't you ever see one of these? Wire recorder.

WILLY: Oh. Can we talk a minute?

HOWARD: Records things. Just got delivery yesterday. Been driving me crazy, the most terrific machine I ever saw in my life. I was up all night with it.

WILLY: What do you do with it?

HOWARD: I bought it for dictation, but you can do anything with it. Listen to this. I had it home last night. Listen to what I picked up. The first one is my daughter. Get this. *He flicks the switch and "Roll out the Barrel" is heard being whistled.* Listen to that kid whistle.

WILLY: That is lifelike, isn't it?

HOWARD: Seven years old. Get that tone.

WILLY: Ts,ts. Like to ask a little favor if you . . .

The whistling breaks off, and the voice of Howard's daughter is heard.

HIS DAUGHTER: "Now you, Daddy."

HOWARD: She's crazy for me! *Again the same song is whistled.* That's me! Ha! *He winks.*

WILLY: You're very good!

The whistling breaks off again. The machine runs silent for a moment.

HOWARD: Sh! Get this now, this is my son.

HIS SON: "The capital of Alabama is Montgomery; the capital of Arizona is Phoenix; the capital of Arkansas is Little Rock; the capital of California is Sacramento . . ."*and on, and on.*

HOWARD, *holding up five fingers:* Five years old, Willy!

WILLY: He'll make an announcer some day!

HIS SON, *continuing:* "The capital . . ."

HOWARD: Get that—alphabetical order! *The machine breaks off suddenly.* Wait a minute. The maid kicked the plug out.

WILLY: It certainly is a—

HOWARD: Sh, for God's sake!

HIS SON: "It's nine o'clock, Bulova watch time. So I have to go to sleep."

WILLY: That really is—

HOWARD: Wait a minute! The next is my wife.

They wait.

HOWARD'S VOICE: "Go on, say something." *Pause.* "Well, you gonna-talk?"

HIS WIFE: "I can't think of anything."

HOWARD'S VOICE: "Well, talk—it's turning."

HIS WIFE, *shyly beaten:* "Hello." *Silence.* "Oh, Howard, I can't talk into this . . ."

HOWARD, *snapping the machine off:* That was my wife.

WILLY: That is a wonderful machine. Can we—

HOWARD: I tell you, Willy, I'm gonna take my camera, and my band-saw, and all my hobbies, and out they go. This is the most fascinating relaxation I ever found.

WILLY: I think I'll get one myself.

HOWARD: Sure, they're only a hundred and a half. You can't do without it. Supposing you wanna hear Jack Benny, see? But you can't be home at that hour. So you tell the maid to turn the radio on when Jack Benny comes on, and this automatically goes on with the radio . . .

WILLY: And when you come home you . . .

HOWARD: You can come home twelve o'clock, one o'clock, any time you like, and you get yourself a Coke and sit yourself down, throw the switch, and there's Jack Benny's program in the middle of the night!

WILLY: I'm definitely going to get one. Because lots of time I'm on the road, and I think to myself, what I must be missing on the radio!

HOWARD: Don't you have a radio in the car?

WILLY: Well, yeah, but who ever thinks of turning it on?

HOWARD: Say, aren't you suposed to be in Boston?

WILLY: That's what I want to talk to you about, Howard. You got a minute? *He draws a chair in from the wing.*

HOWARD: What happened? What're you doing here?

WILLY: Well . . .

HOWARD: You didn't crack up again, did you?

WILLY: Oh, no. No . . .

HOWARD: Geez, you had me worried there for a minute. What's the trouble?

WILLY: Well, tell you the truth, Howard. I've come to the decision that I'd rather not travel any more.

HOWARD: Not travel! Well, what'll you do?

WILLY: Remember, Christmas time, when you had the party here? You said you'd try to think of some spot for me here in town.

HOWARD: With us?

WILLY: Well, sure,

HOWARD: Oh, yeah, yeah. I remember. Well, I couldn't think of anything for you, Willy.

WILLY: I tell ya, Howard. The kids are all grown up, y'know. I don't need much any more. If I could take home—well, sixty-five dollars a week, I could swing it.

HOWARD: Yeah, but Willy, see I—

WILLY: I tell ya why, Howard. Speaking frankly and betwen the two of us, y'know—I'm just a little tired.

HOWARD: Oh, I could understand that, Willy. But you're a road man, Willy, and we do a road business. We've only got a half-dozen salesmen on the floor here.

WILLY: God knows, Howard, I never asked a favor of any man. But I was with the firm when your father used to carry you in here in his arms.

HOWARD: I know that, Willy, but—

WILLY: Your father came to me the day you were born and asked me what I thought of the name of Howard, may he rest in peace.

HOWARD: I appreciate that, Willy, but there just is no spot here for you. If I had a spot I'd slam you right in, but I just don't have a single solitary spot.

He looks for his lighter. Willy has picked it up and gives it to him. Pause.

WILLY, *with increasing anger:* Howard, all I need to set my table is fifty dollars a week.

HOWARD: But where am I going to put you, kid?

WILLY: Look, it isn't a question of whether I can sell merchandise, is it?

HOWARD: No, but it's a business, kid, and everybody's gotta pull his own weight.

WILLY, *desperately:* Just let me tell you a story, Howard—

HOWARD: 'Cause you gotta admit, business is business.

WILLY, *angrily:* Business is definitely business, but just listen for a minute. You don't understand this. When I was a boy—eighteen, nineteen—I was already on the road. And there was a question in my mind as to whether selling had a future for me. Because in those days I had a yearning to go to Alaska. See, there were three gold strikes in one month in Alaska, and I felt like going out. Just for the ride, you might say.

HOWARD, *barely interested:* Don't say.

WILLY: Oh, yeah, my father lived many years in Alaska. He was an adventurous man. We've got quite a little streak of self-reliance in our family. I thought I'd go out with my older brother and try to locate him, and maybe settle in the North with the old man. And I was almost decided to go, when I met a salesman in the Parker House. His name was Dave Singleman. And he was eighty-four years old, and he'd drummed merchandise in thirty-one states. And old Dave, he'd go up to his room, y'understand, put on his green velvet slippers—I'll never forget—and pick up his phone and call the buyers, and without ever leaving his room, at the age of eighty-four, he made his living. And when I saw that, I realized that selling was the greatest career a man could want. 'Cause what could be more satisfying than to be able to go, at the age of eighty-four, into twenty or thirty different cities, and pick up a phone, and be remembered and loved and helped by so many different people? Do you know? when he died—and by the way he died the death of a salesman, in his green velvet slippers in the smoker of the New York, New Haven and Hartford, going into Boston—when he died, hundreds of salesmen and buyers were at his funeral. Things were sad on a lotta trains for months after that. *He stands up. Howard has not looked at him.* In those days there was personality in it, Howard. There was respect, and comradeship, and gratitude in it. Today, it's all cut and dried, and there's no chance for bringing friendship to bear—or personality. You see what I mean? They don't know me any more.

HOWARD, *moving away, to the right:* That's just the thing, Willy.

WILLY: If I had forty dollars a week—that's all I'd need. Forty dollars, Howard.

HOWARD: Kid, I can't take blood from a stone, I—

WILLY, *desperation is on him now:* Howard, the year Al Smith was nominated, your father came to me and—

HOWARD, *starting to go off:* I've got to see some people, kid.

WILLY, *stopping him:* I'm talking about your father! There were promises made across this desk! You mustn't tell me you've got people to see—I put thirty-four years into this firm, Howard, and now I can't pay my insurance! You can't eat the orange and throw the peel away—a man is not a piece of fruit! *After a pause:* Now pay attention. Your father—in 1928 I had a big year. I averaged a hundred and seventy dollars a week in commissions.

HOWARD, *impatiently:* Now, Willy, you never averaged—

WILLY, *banging his hand on the desk:* I averaged a hundred and seventy dollars a week in the year of 1928! And your father came to me—or rather, I was in the office here—it was right over this desk—and he put his hand on my shoulder—

HOWARD, *getting up:* You'll have to excuse me, Willy, I gotta see some people. Pull yourself together. *Going out:* I'll be back in a little while.

On Howard's exit, the light on his chair grows very bright and strange.

WILLY: Pull myself together! What the hell did I say to him! My God, I was yelling at him! How could I! *Willy breaks off, staring at the light, which occupies the chair, animating it. He approaches this chair, standing across the desk from it.* Frank, Frank, don't you remember what you told me that time? How you put your hand on my shoulder, and Frank . . . *He leans on the desk and as he speaks the dead man's name he accidentally switches on the recorder, and instantly*

HOWARD'S SON: ". . . of New York is Albany. The capital of Ohio is Cincinnati, the capital of Rhode Island is . . ." *The recitation continues.*

WILLY, *leaping away with fright, shouting:* Ha! Howard! Howard! Howard!

HOWARD, *rushing in:* What happened?

WILLY, *pointing at the machine, which continues nasally, childishly, with the capital cities:* Shut it off! Shut it off!

HOWARD, *pulling the plug out:* Look, Willy. . . .

WILLY, *pressing his hands to his eyes:* I gotta get myself some coffee. I'll get some coffee . . .

Willy starts to walk out. Howard stops him.

HOWARD, *rolling up the cord:* Willy, look. . .

WILLY: I'll go to Boston.

HOWARD: Willy, you can't go to Boston for us.

WILLY: Why can't I go?

HOWARD: I don't want you to represent us. I've been meaning to tell you for a long time now.

WILLY: Howard, are you firing me?

HOWARD: I think you need a good long rest, Willy.

WILLY: Howard—

HOWARD: And when you feel better, come back, and we'll see if we can work something out.

WILLY: But I gotta earn money, Howard. I'm in no position to—

HOWARD: Where are your sons? Why don't your sons give you a hand?

WILLY: They're working on a very big deal.

HOWARD: This is no time for false pride, Willy. You go to your sons and you tell them that you're tired. You've got two great boys, haven't you?

WILLY: Oh, no question, no question, but in the meantime . . .

HOWARD: Then that's that, heh?

WILLY: All right, I'll go to Boston tomorrow.

HOWARD: No, no.

WILLY: I can't throw myself on my sons. I'm not a cripple!

HOWARD: Look, kid, I'm busy this morning.

WILLY, *grasping Howard's arm:* Howard, you've got to let me go to Boston!

HOWARD, *hard, keeping himself under control:* I've got a line of people to see this morning. Sit down, take five minutes, and pull yourself together, and then go home, will ya? I need the office, Willy. *He starts to go, turns, remembering the recorder, starts to push off the table holding the recorder.* Oh, yeah. Whenever you can this week, stop by and drop off the samples. You'll feel better, Willy, and then come back and we'll talk. Pull yourself together, kid, there's people outside. . . .

REQUIEM

[*Editor's note:* Biff & Happy are Willy's sons. Charley is a neighbor.]

CHARLEY: It's getting dark, Linda.

Linda doesn't react. She stares at the grave.

BIFF: How about it, Mom? Better get some rest, heh? They'll be closing the gate soon.

Linda makes no move. Pause.

HAPPY, *deeply angered:* He had no right to do that. There was no necessity for it. We would've helped him.

CHARLEY, *grunting:* Hmmm.

BIFF: Come along, Mom.

LINDA: Why didn't anybody come?

CHARLEY: It was a very nice funeral.

LINDA: But where are all the people he knew? Maybe they blame him.

CHARLEY: Naa. It's a rough world, Linda. They wouldn't blame him.

LINDA: I can't understand it. At this time especially. First time in thirty-five years we were just about free and clear. He only needed a little salary. He was even finished with the dentist.

CHARLEY: No man only needs a little salary.

LINDA: I can't understand it.

BIFF: There were a lot of nice days. When he'd come home from a trip; or on Sundays, making the stoop; finishing the cellar; putting on the new porch; when he built the extra bathroom; and put up the garage. You know something, Charley, there's more of him in that front stoop than in all the sales he ever made.

CHARLEY: Yeah. He was a happy man with a batch of cement.

LINDA: He was so wonderful with his hands.

BIFF: He had the wrong dreams. All, all, wrong.

HAPPY, *almost ready to fight Biff:* Don't say that!

BIFF: He never knew who he was.

CHARLEY, *stopping Happy's movement and reply. To Biff:* Nobody dast blame this man. You don't understand: Willy was a salesman. And for a salesman, there is no rock bottom to the life. He don't put a bolt to a nut, he don't tell you the law or give you medicine. He's a man way out there in the blue, riding on a smile and a shoeshine. And when they start not smiling back—that's an earthquake. And then you got yourself a couple of spots on your hat, and you're finished. Nobody dast blame this man. A salesman is got to dream, boy. It comes with the territory.

BIFF: Charley, the man didn't know who he was.

HAPPY, *infuriated:* Don't say that!

BIFF: Why don't you come with me, Happy?

HAPPY: I'm not licked that easily. I'm staying right in this city, and I'm gonna beat this racket! *He looks at Biff, his chin set.* The Loman Brothers!

BIFF: I know who I am, kid.

HAPPY: All right, boy. I'm gonna show you and everybody else that— Willy Loman did not die in vain. He had a good dream. It's the only dream you can have—to come out number one man. He fought it out here, and this is where I'm gonna win it for him.

BIFF, *with a hopeless glance at Happy, bends toward his mother:* Let's go, Mom.

LINDA: I'll be with you in a minute. Go on, Charley. *He hesitates.* I want to, just for a minute. I never had a chance to say good-by.

Charley moves away, followed by Happy. Biff remains a slight distance up and left of Linda. She sits there, summoning herself. The flute begins, not far away, playing behind her speech.

LINDA: Forgive me, dear. I can't cry. I don't know what it is, but I can't cry. I don't understand it. Why did you ever do that? Help me, Willy, I can't cry. It seems to me that you're just on another trip. I keep expecting you. Willy, dear, I can't cry. Why did you do it? I search and search and I search, and I can't understand it, Willy. I made the last payment on the house today. Today, dear. And there'll be nobody home. *A sob rises in her throat.* We're free and clear. *Sobbing more fully, released:* We're free. *Biff comes slowly toward her.* We're free . . . We're free . . .

Biff lifts her to her feet and moves out up right with her in his arms. Linda sobs quietly. Bernard and Charley come together and follow them, followed by Happy. Only the music of the flute is left on the darkening stage as over the house the hard towers of the apartment buildings rise into sharp focus, and The Curtain Falls

The Human Cost of Plant Closings

Arthur Shostak

Union members are by now all too familiar with the tremendous social and economic consequences of a plant closing. Yet when they look to academia for help in sorting out the antidotes, for ways to ease the pain, for remedies to heal the hurt, they are likely to be seriously disappointed.

The necessary research work has still not been done. Our library of materials is paltry and inadequate. We do know some helpful things, however, and with the assistance of the trade union movement this subject could soon get the research attention it deserves.

Our case studies of plant closings were largely done in the 1960s, and are still quite sound. The difference in being unemployed in the 1960s and being unemployed in the 1980s appears a matter of degree, rather than one of kind.

Here are some of the highlights of what we found in the 1960s in the aftermath of plant closings:

- Social Hardships—People were reluctant to move, and geographic mobility was low. Relocating represented an incredible challenge for the individual. They were not only reluctant to move from the frost belt to the sun belt, for example, but were unwilling to move even a few hundred miles. We soon secured anecdotal data about what it cost people to be weekend husbands, to be without family, to leave familiar settings for a savage-appearing new city.

  In the 1960s we had considerable failure to regain steady and satisfactory employment after plant closings. Men and women who readily found jobs showed up disproportionately later as frequent job changers, discontented and restless. Large numbers of re-employed workers suffered real losses from previous levels of economic attainment. If they had been working for $7 an hour, they were soon working for $4.50 or $5.25. And many of the others laid off with them struggled to survive protracted unemployment.

- Health Problems—Health research is difficult. You've got to talk people in the home or the factory into giving urine samples, take blood from them, measure blood pressure, and do a lot of things that appear not so much for their benefit as for the benefit of "ivory tower" research needs. That's tough. Thus the little research we got from the 1960s indicated high uric acid levels, increased cholesterol, elevations in blood pressure, and elevations in pulse rate

Abridged and reprinted from *AFL-CIO American Federationist,* August 1980. Reproduced by permission.

among the suddenly unemployed. We also found the rich man's disease of gout, which, in fact, was no longer exclusively a rich man's disease. We connected data on plant closings to heart disease, hypertension, and pervasive tension. At the bottom of all of this we found an increase in drinking—hard drinking—and we found a tragic increase in self-destruction and inexplicably fatal accidents.

At a reductionist level of analysis, each of us is a social system. As such we promote an equilibrium, a pattern of habitual behavior and attitudes. There are certain times of day when all of us like our morning coffee. You may prefer to brush your teeth before or after breakfast; you probably take a particular route to work every day. All of us like to minimize stress through such repeatable behaviors. One of the major consequences of plant closing, then, is that it shatters habitual worklife patterns.

There's a terrible story about the Russian troops moving through the remains of Berlin at the end of World War II. They are supposed to have found at the Civil Service headquarters of the shattered Third Reich civil servants at their desks preparing requisitions for next year's paper clips, rubber bands, note pads and that sort of thing. I don't know if it's true, but I've been told that certain elderly Berlin postal workers continued to walk their mail rounds after the city was destroyed, even though they had no mail to deliver, because it helped fill out the day and it made sense to them—delivering nonexistent mail to bombed-out addresses, the better to cling to routine and help time pass in a meaningful, familiar way.

That is the kind of deep-reaching psychological attachment to worklife habits that can get shattered in the aftermath of a plant closing.

- Reduced Social Interaction—People begin to withdraw into themselves in the aftermath of a plant shutdown. They begin to withdraw from family contacts; many begin to withdraw from union meetings and even from a passive interest in union matters.
- Political Alienation—A worker caught in a plant closing can become bitter in every direction. They feel betrayed and sold out, and he or she may demand to know where organized labor has been all that time. Where was COPE? And how did it come down this way?
- Openness to Economic Radicalism—Sociologists have noted a new openness to economic radicalism among workers when capitalism gets them in the neck; one is receptive to hearing something radical and even revolutionary in the aftermath of a plant closing, the research suggests.

That's about the sum of what we know from the case studies of plant closings in the 1960s. There are some new research strategies now in the

1980s, one of which focuses on closings as a type of separation experience, a trauma with about six phases.

In the opening phase, a plant is "up and going." You may hear we used to have 8,700 on the payroll, and now we've got 1,800; we used to have 9,000 now we have 3,000, but the plant's still "up and going."

That's a preclosing state of affairs, and in preclosing time you may get what workers perceive as company blackmail: "we need more productivity." In this preclosing phase some workers will urge the union to take the issue to the mayor, government, or the press. Employees know when a closedown is coming. Certain kinds of strategic stock materials are not being reordered; certain kinds of maintenance are not being done; farming out of contracts is increasing. So, a proactivist set of possibilities exists in the preclosing phase.

Then comes the news of the closedown over the loudspeaker, in the mail, or in a general auditorium session. Some are stunned; others say, "I told you so." The cynics may rise to power in the local union; the optimists are likely to fall in stature.

Then is the phase of unemployment itself, the search for a new job, and a new definition of "success," as a wage-earner. This "success" becomes highly individual. We might look at the job-seeker's new job and think it second rate; but that's not legitimate—only the individual can tell us whether it's second rate or not, and why, and we must learn to listen and suspend our judgment.

The next and last phase is the rehired worker's adjustment to the new job, a stage that is often overlooked by researchers, union leaders, and counselors. Not only is the job new, but the worker has the equivalent of a new family and a new community. Once you get a new job, your family may be altered by that event and its aftermath.

A psychologist told me recently about his practice, which now includes an increasing number of plant closing cases. One of his clients, for example, came off traditional factory work and found a job driving a panel truck. This gave him independence and autonomy, removed him from supervision, put him out in the open air, allowed him to choose his own coffee breaks, and go to his favorite diner. It was all wonderful, except for one minor problem: he was now employed as an exterminator, complete with a can and a hose, and his wife now said that at the end of the day, he stunk. He hadn't smelled badly before; he had always been clean, even fastidious.

So, what did our reemployed worker have now? A different wife and a different family, because of an odor problem unadvertised and unavoidably part of his otherwise desirable new job.

In our 1980s research we should focus on certain problems regretfully unexplored in the 1960s material, such as the sense of self-punishing personal guilt that may come with plant closings. In the book *The Hidden Injuries of Class*, Richard Sennett and Jonathon Cobb explain that

America encourages us to hold ourselves responsible for what happens to us, the better to exonerate its social order: "It isn't capitalism. It isn't federal favoritism to regions. It isn't corporate board decisions. It's probably some flaw in you and me that explains our plight. We picked the wrong plant to work in; we picked the wrong industry to identify with; we didn't get out in time; people told us 10 years ago we should leave. The handwriting was on the wall."

When all that nonsense comes together, a laid-off worker can derive a profound sense of guilt from it, a notion that he or she has let the family down. This sense of guilt for those caught in plant closings is something humanists and capitalists alike should worry about.

Another problem for new research attention is that individuals involved in plant closings often suffer from diminished attention span. If a local union meeting has an agenda that puts something else on ahead of the subject of a shutdown's impact, you are likely to discover 35 minutes into the meeting that people are wandering out of the hall. People involved in a plant shutdown have little patience for any other topic. It had better come early in the meeting's agenda.

Then there is the widespread feeling of loneliness, especially in the sense of abandonment, that often accompanies a factory shutdown. If there is guilt, if there is self-blame, then loneliness and abandonment on top of it can be hard for many ex-workers to handle.

In the 1980s we've begun to find evidence of the notion that "they've done it to me again." "They," those incredibly vague "others," include the government, Congress, union staffers—somebody. The worker begins to pull from memory a host of past failures: "I should have gone to get that associate degree" or "I should have taken that training program" or "When I was offered the stewardship, I should have said 'yes'." And so on. Such an individual may begin to wallow in "I-should-haves," and in much self-blame, all at a great cost to mental well-being.

Since the critical success of Gail Sheehy's book, *Passages*, we've begun to give a lot of attention to middle age crisis. Beginning at about age 40, social events begin to shift away from weddings, bar mitzvahs, and baptisms to the funerals of friends and acquaintances. And that shift is easily exacerbated by plant closings. Middle-aged unemployed adults begin to think of themselves as over-the-hill; plant closings invite a morbidity in one's mind set, a new sense of personal frailty, a heightened recognition of the uncertainties of life and, the allure of a stress-resolving death.

Work gives many people the indispensable leverage they need to contain self-destructive habits and behaviors. Certain people who used to drink to excess get a job and sober up; the pressure that comes from knowing alcoholism isn't accepted on the job is enough to help keep them from further drinking, at least during working hours. Similarly, people who are chronic gamblers, or on occasion abuse a spouse or a child may control the situation through the discipline of their employment: after a closing, however, they may find the loss of a job severely weakens the control mechanisms they so desparately need.

For these reasons we may see more and more men whose anxiety on losing their jobs appears disproportionate, as it is, after all, "only a job." But, such men may understand that this loss could mean a return to alcoholism or to gambling, or to other comparable terrors, even if they've been sober and self-regulating for many years. And that specter, for them, is the end, the sentence of a living death, a fate being forced back into their lives by the reverberating disaster of a plant closing.

When we focus our research on family life one of the things that worries us is the possibility of "cabin fever." Blue-collar wives do not welcome having the male hanging around home, particularly during conventional working hours. And when a male displaced by a plant closing does stay home, cabin fever is highly predictable . . . as when an ex-aspereated unemployed worker says: "It isn't anything that she's said or done; it's the way she puts the coffee on the table in the morning." His wife, in turn, may say: "I don't know what the hell he's talking about. He hasn't been the same for three months, since the plant closed. There's nothing that I can do that can make a difference, even a little difference. And when I put a cheaper cut of meat on the table, he almost destroyed the kitchen. I thought I was doing good; he behaved like I was destroying him."

Finally, one of the major 1980s research frontiers may concern how men and women relate in their sexuality. Many working class women seem to have absorbed new attitudes in the sexual realm, and their sexual agendas are different today from the 1960s; they expect their husbands to be better lovers, and their lovers to be more sensitive than before, and both husbands and lovers to be more open to their female sexuality than was true in earlier decades. In good times, all of this could be a fine prescription. In a recession, however, especially one combined with plant layoffs, it can prove a prescription for interpersonal disaster: men who are cut off from work may have self-esteem hurt by the loss of the central role in the male life, that of the primary breadwinner, and it also hurts self-esteem in the bedroom.

Given all these historic, ongoing, and readily anticipated social problems, what are some possible reforms worth research attention?

- Social Impact Legislation: Harry Levinson, a leading industrial psychologist, identified the presence of the "psychological contract" some years ago while doing research on a Kansas utility company and its workers. The "psychological contract" is never put in writing, but it assures an injured worker a claim on the company for another post in the company compatible with the worker's remaining capabilities. This is one way we get factory gatekeepers, watchmen and messengers, many of whom are former employees who have been crippled in work-related accidents, and even sometimes in a nonwork-related accident. This pledge of readjusted work is a tradition, a "psychological contract" that we might add to social impact legislation. Employers might pledge to provide new jobs and compensation, under the "psychological contract," to cover counseling costs entailed in helping workers recover any emotional and social well-being undermined by a plant closing.

- Career and Community Continuation Teams: You cannot adequately help workers in a plant closing unless you also help the larger surrounding community. The federal government should therefore have, on a stand-by basis, several career and community aid teams of economists, counselors, psychologists, job-location and job-retraining experts, all trained in crisis theory and intervention techniques.
- Rehabiliataion for the Reemployed: People who are rehired should not fade out of our concern.

First, many rehired workers become sensitive to the idea that the new employer expects them to be obligated for the job. The rehired workers may soon resent a new foreman, a new regimen, a new set of expectations that makes it seem the new boss is lording it over the new worker. And the new worker may determine not to put up with this. A troubled person, a troubled union member, a person under a lot of stress, is a very real possibility here, though no one ever intended this, and few intervene in time to avert avoidable trouble.

Another thing we find is loss of morale: some reemployed workers may privately say: "For 27 years I worked for one employer, and I gave him everything. I was there on time, accepted overtime with a smile, never stole a thing. I put suggestions in the suggestion box. I'm not going to do any of that again; I'm not going to do one little part of that again. They fooled me the last time. They're not going to get anything from me this time but eight hours of regular output, and they damn well better accept that because it's all they've got coming this time around."

The last kind of reaction for which postrehiring counseling would seem necessary involves the gunshy new worker. This individual comes in expecting his new work place to close, even though the plant is in a great industry, is healthy, has a Dun & Bradstreet rating of AAA plus—but, if this worker has known disaster, he is sure that if something can go wrong for this company, it will. The presence of such a person can bring the local workforce stress, trouble, bad vibes. Such workers need remedial counseling, concerned "outsiders" who can help notice this troubled worker and help guide him or her to a source of counseling help.

In sum, then, plant closings are still far too under-researched. We in academic work are going to need labor's help if this subject is soon going to get the research attention that its quotient of human problems deserves. Only as organized labor reaches out to concerned researchers at colleges and universities will we really have any chance of it soon happening.

In every locale with a major plant, there are at least a few academics nearby who will respond to labor's request. At first, of course, they will be astonished that you've asked; they will be pleased; then they will ask how can they help. America needs the case studies they can do—and workers need them.

The subject grows daily too important to continue without this research. The impact of plant closings can be lessened, provided some fresh lessons are soon drawn from collaborative labor-academic research into this topic—possibly the most important domestic issue of the 1980s.

Like Many, a Production Scheduler Agonizes over Choosing New Career

Betsy Morris

Robert Pillar doodles on a pad of paper beside the telephone and speaks haltingly.

"Ah, ma'am . . . I'm calling in response to the newspaper ad regarding employment. I'm currently laid off from the steel industry. I had some experience in production control and data processing. Ma'am, I'm wondering if there might be some need for somebody such as myself."

The personnel woman in Florida tells him to send a resume. That will make close to 500 resumes he has sent out. Mr. Pillar, who got his job the day he applied at the local Crucible Inc. steel plant 20 years ago, never dreamed that at age 38 he'd be desperate for work. But last year, the Crucible plant closed, and job security dissipated just like the black smoke that used to blanket this steel town.

"Hey, there has to be something for this guy out there somewhere. There has to be," he says. But all the resumes and scores of humiliating telephone calls have led to only four job interviews. The skills that earned $29,000 last year don't seem to be worth much to other employers.

THRASHING WITHOUT RESULT

Many workers who find that their old jobs in aging industries have collapsed move swiftly to enter new careers. But untold thousands follow Mr. Pillar's course: Uncertain of direction, they go one way and then another. Sometimes indecisive, but sometimes caught in agonizing dilemmas, they can't settle on a clear plan to escape their predicament.

Day after day, Mr. Pillar mulls over and rejects the same choices. He wants to find something outside the steel industry, but he believes he can't afford to start over and retrain with no guarantee of finding a job. Although he has lowered his expectations significantly, he still isn't willing to work for minimum wage. His lifetime savings are dwindling, and his unemployment benefits expire next month.

At first, he says, he wanted a job just like his old one as a production scheduler, but in a healthy industry like pharmaceuticals. He wanted a salary of at least $16,000. But lately, he has applied for mail clerk and secretarial jobs paying a lot less—and been turned down.

"I'm reaching a panic situation," Mr. Pillar says. "Sometimes I wonder whether I'm doing the best job of marketing myself." He has revised his resume six times. The most recent version emphasizes his bookkeeping and data-processing skills. "Every time I get depressed, I think of revising my resume," he says.

It's all a far cry from the life he lived for two decades. Over the years, the steelworker advanced to a skilled job scheduling the movement of raw materials and equipment through the plant to turn huge pieces of steel into tractor blades and discs. He could afford private Catholic schooling for his two children, and new cars. In a steel town where living high on the hill reflects a worker's position, he owned a small but neatly kept brick house—high on the hill. He even owned an $8,000 fishing boat.

But a year ago, he sold the boat and bought a more modest one. Several weeks ago, he sold that one, too.

These days, after nearly a year out of work, he is more preoccupied with his daily job-hunting routine than with fishing anyway. Most mornings, David Wilson, a friend who also is a laid-off steelworker, stops at Mr. Pillar's house, and the two men begin the job search together. They often dress in suits and ties and carry vinyl briefcases purchased especially for the search. Usually, they drive first by the mailbox on Main Street to mail resumes, then to Migliore's, a local shop, to buy the newspaper and their lottery tickets. As Mr. Wilson drives, Mr. Pillar scans the newspaper want ads.

'SKINNY COLLEGE KIDS'

As they drive by the airport on a typical day, the men look longingly at the hustle and bustle. But the day they interviewed with an airline, "there were already 2,000 people there, all of them young, skinny college kids," Mr. Pillar says. "Here we were a couple of old, fat steelworkers. We didn't have a snowball's chance in hell."

They stop the car at a metal manufacturing company near New Castle, Pa. The personnel manager glances at their resumes and says, "What we could really use here is a mechanical engineer. Do you know any?"

Down the road, a secretary at a concrete plant won't even take their resumes. "We're going to be closing down for a while next week," she tells them.

In the hours they spend driving, the men cook up ideas. Mr. Wilson has considered a fast-food fried catfish franchise he has heard about. Mr. Pillar researched the cost of displaying the two men's resumes on a billboard. "I haven't scrapped that idea yet," he says.

DWINDLING RESOURCES

Lately, the two men have been running out of companies to visit, and Mr. Pillar is nervous. Although his wife, Jeanne, has gone to work as a savings and loan association secretary/receptionist, her $8,000 annual salary doesn't begin to meet the family's expenses. The Pillars have been drawing about $300 a month from their savings, which have dwindled to around $3,000. The $2,600 after taxes that Mr. Pillar received in severance pay is long gone. Expiration of the $198 weekly unemployment benefits next month will add to the squeeze. Mr. Pillar worries about how he will pay for the college education he has promised his teenage children.

The tension has spilled into the family life. Mrs. Pillar says she believes she must be the family cheerleader even though she is really feeling "frustration, bitterness, disgust and disappointment. I've never felt like this before."

One of her daily tasks at work, calling people who are delinquent on mortgage payments, makes it all the harder. "Believe me, I know what goes on," she says, dabbing away tears. "I have to wonder, are they going to come and take my house?"

The Pillars' 17-year-old daughter, Paula used to burst into tears at the thought of leaving Midland. Now she'd like to escape it. "I want to move down to Florida really badly—to the warm climate, and live in a condo near the beach," she says. "Everything would be so much simpler."

Her 14-year-old brother, Bobby, says the uncertainty of the family's situation can dispel his best moods. He says: "Even when I'm really having a good day and everything is going right at school, I come home and think, 'What if in several months my father still doesn't have a job?' It brings me back to earth. Every day the 'what if' gets closer."

Mr. Pillar feels the effects of frustration, too. In periods of depression, he just sits and stares. As much as anything, he is stung by the indifference of employers in other industries to the skills he feels sure could be put to good use.

SKILLS REQUIRED

"If anyone could find a job, you'd think it would be Bob Pillar," said Kenneth Weslager, his supervisor at Crucible, who has since retired. Mr. Pillar's old job demanded considerable planning ability, and even required some computing and data processing skills.

Mr. Pillar says he considered retraining and starting over, but has rejected the idea for now. "I'd hate like hell to take a two-year data-processing course and come out to find that two million other kids out there had the same idea," he says. Besides, he adds, "it's a matter of pride. I'd hate to think that for 19 years all I was doing was collecting a paycheck."

Yet the current approach has produced nothing. Even the employer response that Mr. Pillar considered the most promising turned out to be a total washout. Shortly after he began his search, Mr. Pillar received a polite letter from Motorola Inc. electronics division in Scottsdale, Ariz. It rejected him for an $18,000 production scheduling job, but promised that Motorola would contact him "when a suitable position develops." It added: "We sincerely hope to be in touch with you soon."

Mr. Pillar recalls, "I thought, 'Hey, this is going to be easy. It's all downhill from here.' "

But Chris Kumlin, the Motorola employee who wrote the letter, recently re-examined the application. She says the company hires first from its local labor supply and had "more than plenty of people right here who could do this job," including a number with electronics experience.

"I'm sure this gentleman could learn to do this job. But a company is not going to hire the person who is going to take three to six months to train when there are others who could learn in a week," Mrs. Kumlin says. Mr. Pillar, she adds, "didn't have a chance."

13

ORGANIZATIONAL EFFECTIVENESS

Corporate leaders often tell their charges that hard work will lead to success. Indeed this theory of reward being commensurate with effort has been an enduring belief in our society, one central to our self image as a people where the 'main chance is available to anyone of ability who has the gumption and persistance to seize it.'

—*Robert Jackall*

Recent years have seen a number of instances of the decline of organizations that long have been important to our society. The effectiveness of an organization is a "bottom-line measure." It is a term used to summarize the overall success of the organization in acquiring, transforming, and using resources to establish favorable reactions with its important constituents. Of course, bottom-line measures often interfere with understanding underlying dynamic processes. So it has been with effectiveness.

Almost all books on management, whether they are written by presidents, accountants, economists, engineers, or behavioral scientists, place the goal of organizational effectiveness (or some related goal such as efficiency) at the core of their analysis. Most writers stress some set of rational designs, decisions, controls, policies, or models which organizations use or ought to use in the pursuit of effectiveness. However correct these ideas may be as normative approaches, they provide only limited insight into what organizations actually do in their efforts to achieve "effectiveness" and provide little insight into the social processes that are major determinants of effectiveness.

Frequently, writers have failed to realize that "organizational effectiveness" is more than a pervasive goal of almost all organizations; it is also a constraint upon how organizational members use resources. Members most frequently define, justify, and defend their decisions and actions in terms of "effectiveness." Our first selection, "Organizational Psychology and the World Series," by Edwin A. Locke, a distinguished organizational psychologist, illustrates one formula for the pursuit of effectiveness. Although it is written very much with tongue in cheek, we have encountered many managers to whom the question is just that simple.

Of course, it is a mistake to conclude that the explicit concern with effectiveness leads directly to organizations which are well managed and achieve their goals. There are many aspects of organizations that can go astray. Generations of Americans have been taught that the way to move up in corporate management is to work hard and make sound decisions. Has the bureaucratic world changed all that? Has the connection between work and reward become more capricious? Robert Jackall, the author of "Moral Mazes: Bureaucracy and Managerial Work" interviewed more than a hundred managers seeking answers to these and other questions. Based on his interviews he believes that there are many unintended consequences associated with the way our large scale organizations are managed.

Corporate espionage as a means of gathering information to gain an advantage on one's competitors has been recognized as part of the organizational scene for many years. In "How to Snoop on Your Competitors," Steven Flax details a number of ways that companies may snoop on one another—some legal, even ethical, and a number of ways that are certainly much more questionable. On the other hand, "Mum's the Word" by Susan Chace and James A. White provides interesting details as to how the giant IBM Corporation seeks to safeguard proprietary information concerning its research, product lines, and maintenance systems.

Each of the articles in the section contain suggestions for organizational participants to consider. However, the most comprehensive approach is outlined and illustrated in Culbert's "A General Strategy for Getting Out of Traps." Fundamental to his approach is the need to recognize that when one is in an organizational trap, the reasons for one's unhappiness and ineffective responses do not necessarily lie with oneself, but are more likely to reside in the pattern of surrounding influences which must be detected and made explicit and then responded to in a coherent fashion.

All of us are familiar with the vast number of mergers, acquisitions, and takeovers that characterize the contemporary corporate scene. It is equally obvious to most of us that often these maneuvers create financial carnage for the acquired company if indeed it survives at all. "Of Boxes, Bubbles, and Effective Management" by David K. Hurst is a frank report of how the senior management of an acquired steel company found themselves in extremely difficult financial straits and how, through a major shift in their management style, they managed to survive. We believe that this is an excellent case study for students of organizational behavior and management.

Our final selection is another case study. This piece by David McClintick documents the true story of the high level conflict that can occur when big business meets show business, when corporate self-interest challenges personal ethics, and when a top decision maker is unable to decide.

Clearly, the selections in this section give only a glimpse of some of the processes that influence the effectiveness of organizations. Most of these processes have been given little attention by students of management, who sought to understand effectiveness through traditional economic, management, and behavioral science models. We hope that the direct look at the behavior of organizations themselves provides the reader with a greater understanding of the actual dynamics of processes that influence organizational effectiveness.

Organizational Psychology and the World Series

Edwin A. Locke

As scientists we should not be closed to any source of information which bears upon validity of our theories. For example, consider what we can learn from the victory of the Yankees in the World Series:

1. authoritarian management can be quite effective, providing it is both smart and rich;
2. lack of group cohesion (intragroup conflict) does not inhibit short-term success, providing the members have talent and do their jobs;
3. intragroup conflict is unpleasant and may lead to high turnover;
4. on the other hand, if enough money is offered to stay, it may not.

What more do you need to know to run a successful organization?

Moral Mazes: Bureaucracy and Managerial Work

With Moral Choices Tied to Personal Fates, how does Bureaucracy Shape Managerial Morality?

Robert Jackall

Corporate leaders often tell their charges that hard work will lead to success. Indeed, this theory of reward being commensurate with effort has been an enduring belief in our society, one central to our self-image as a people where the "main chance" is available to anyone of ability who has the gumption and the persistence to seize it. Hard work, it is also frequently asserted, builds character. This notion carries less conviction because businessmen, and our society as a whole, have little patience with those who make a habit of finishing out of the money. In the end, it is success that matters, that legitimates striving, and that makes work worthwhile.

What if, however, men and women in the big corporation no longer see success as necessarily connected to hard work? What becomes of the social morality of the corporation—I mean the everyday rules in use that people play by—when there is thought to be no "objective" standard of excellence to explain how and why winners are separated from also-rans, how and why some people succeed and others fail?

This is the puzzle that confronted me while doing a great many extensive interviews with managers and executives in several large corporations, particularly in a large chemical company and a large textile firm. (See the insert for more details.) I went into these corporations to study how bureaucracy—the prevailing organizational form of our society and economy—shapes moral consciousness. I came to see that managers'

Author's note: I presented an earlier version of this paper in the Faculty Lecture Series at Williams College on March 18, 1982. The intensive field work done during 1980 and 1981 was made possible by a Fellowship for Independent Research from the National Endowment for the Humanities and by a Junior Faculty Leave and small research grant from Williams College.

Editor's note: All references are listed at the end of the article.

rules for success are at the heart of what may be called the bureaucratic ethic.

This article suggests no changes and offers no programs for reform. It is, rather, simply an interpretive sociological analysis of the moral dimensions of managers' work. Some readers may find the essay sharp-edged, others familiar. For both groups, it is important to note at the outset that my materials are managers' own descriptions of their experiences.[1] As it happens, my own research in a variety of other settings suggests that managers' experiences are by no means unique; indeed they have a deep resonance with those of other occupational groups.

WHAT HAPPENED TO THE PROTESTANT ETHIC?

To grasp managers' experiences and the more general implications they contain, one must see them against the background of the great historical transformations, both social and cultural, that produced managers as an occupational group. Since the concern here is with the moral significance of work in business, it is important to begin with an understanding of the original Protestant Ethic, the world view of the rising bourgeois class that spearheaded the emergence of capitalism.

The Protestant Ethic was a set of beliefs that counseled "secular asceticism"—the methodical, rational subjection of human impulse and desire to God's will through "restless, continuous, systematic work in a worldly calling."[2] This ethic of ceaseless work and ceaseless renunciation of the fruits of one's toil provided both the economic and the moral foundations for modern capitalism.

On one hand, secular asceticism was a ready-made prescription for building economic capital; on the other, it became for the upward-moving bourgeois class—self-made industrialists, farmers, and enterprising artisans—the ideology that justified their attention to this world, their accumulation of wealth, and indeed the social inequities that inevitably followed such accumulation. This bourgeois ethic, with its imperatives for self-reliance, hard work, frugality, and rational planning, and its clear definition of success and failure, came to dominate a whole historical epoch in the West.

But the ethic came under assault from two directions. First, the very accumulation of wealth that the old Protestant Ethic made possible gradually stripped away the religious basis of the ethic, especially among the rising middle class that benefited from it. There were, of course, periodic reassertions of the religious context of the ethic, as in the case of John D. Rockefeller and his turn toward Baptism. But on the whole, by the late 1800s the religious roots of the ethic survived principally among independent farmers and proprietors of small businesses in rural areas and towns across America.

In the mainstream of an emerging urban America, the ethic had become secularized into the "work ethic," "rugged individualism," and especially the "success ethic." By the beginning of this century, among most of the economically successful, frugality had become an aberration, conspicuous consumption the norm. And with the shaping of the mass consumer society later in this century, the sanctification of consumption became widespread, indeed crucial to the maintenance of the economic order.

Affluence and the emergence of the consumer society were responsible, however, for the demise of only aspects of the old ethic—namely, the imperatives for saving and investment. The core of the ethic, even in its later, secularized form—self-reliance, unremitting devotion to work, and a morality that postulated just rewards for work well done—was undermined by the complete transformation of the organizational form of work itself. The hallmarks of the emerging modern production and distribution systems were administrative hierarchies, standardized work procedures, regularized timetables, uniform policies, and centralized control—in a word, the bureaucratization of the economy.

This bureaucratization was heralded at first by a very small class of salaried managers, who were later joined by legions of clerks and still later by technicians and professionals of every stripe. In this century, the process spilled over from the private to the public sector and government bureaucracies came to rival those of industry. This great transformation produced the decline of the old middle class of entrepreneurs, free professionals, independent farmers, and small independent businessmen—the traditional carriers of the old Protestant Ethic—and the ascendance of a new middle class of salaried employees whose chief common characteristic was and is their dependence on the big organization.

Any understanding of what happened to the original Protestant Ethic and to the old morality and social character it embodied—and therefore any understanding of the moral significance of work today—is inextricably tied to an analysis of bureaucracy. More specifically, it is, in my view, tied to an analysis of the work and occupational cultures of managerial groups within bureaucracies. Managers are the quintessential bureaucratic work group; they not only fashion bureaucratic rules, but they are also bound by them. Typically, they are not just *in* the organization; they are *of* the organization. As such, managers represent the prototype of the white-collar salaried employee. By analyzing the kind of ethic bureaucracy produces in managers, one can begin to understand how bureaucracy shapes morality in our society as a whole.

PYRAMIDAL POLITICS

American businesses typically both centralize and decentralize authority. Power is concentrated at the top in the person of the chief executive officer and is simultaneously decentralized; that is, responsibility for decisions and profits is pushed as far down the organizational line as possible. For example, the chemical company that I studied—and its structure is typical of other organizations I examined—is one of several operating companies of a large and growing conglomerate. Like the other operating companies, the chemical concern has its own president, executive vice presidents, vice presidents, other executive officers, business area managers, entire staff divisions, and operating plants. Each company is, in effect, a self-sufficient organization, though they are all coordinated by the corporation, and each president reports directly to the corporate CEO.

Now, the key interlocking mechanism of this structure is its reporting system. Each manager gathers up the profit targets or other objectives of his or her subordinates, and with these formulates his commitments to his boss; this boss takes these commitments, and those of his other subordinates, and in turn makes a commitment to *his* boss. (Note: henceforth only "he" or "his" will be used to allow for easier reading.) At the top of the line, the president of each company makes his commitment to the CEO of the corporation, based on the stated objectives given to him by his vice presidents. There is always pressure from the top to set higher goals.

This management-by-objectives system, as it is usually called, creates a chain of commitments from the CEO down to the lowliest product manager. In practice, it also shapes a patrimonial authority arrangement which is crucial to defining both the immediate experiences and the long-run career chances of individual managers. In this world, a subordinate owes fealty principally to his immediate boss. A subordinate must not overcommit his boss; he must keep the boss from making mistakes, particularly public ones; he must not circumvent the boss. On a social level, even though an easy, breezy informality is the prevalent style of American business, the subordinate must extend to the boss a certain ritual deference: for instance, he must follow the boss's lead in conversation, he must not speak out of turn at meetings, and must laugh at the boss's jokes while not making jokes of his own.

In short, the subordinate must not exhibit any behavior which symbolizes parity. In return, he can hope to be elevated when and if the boss is elevated, although other important criteria also intervene here. He can also expect protection for mistakes made up to a point. However, that point is never exactly defined and always depends on the complicated politics of each situation.

Who Gets Credit?

It is characteristic of this authority system that details are pushed down and credit is pushed up. Superiors do not like to give detailed instructions to subordinates. The official reason for this is to maximize subordinates' autonomy; the underlying reason seems to be to get rid of tedious details and to protect the privilege of authority to declare that a mistake has been made.

It is not at all uncommon for very bald and extremely general edicts to emerge from on high. For example, "Sell the plant in St. Louis. Let me know when you've struck a deal." This pushing down of details has important consequences:

1. Because they are unfamiliar with entangling details, corporate higher echelons tend to expect highly successful results without complications. This is central to top executives' well-known aversion to bad news and to the resulting tendency to "kill the messenger" who bears that news.
2. The pushing down of detail creates great pressure on middle managers not only to transmit good news but to protect their corporations, their bosses, and themselves in the process. They become the "point men" of a given strategy and the potential "fall guys" when things go wrong.

Credit flows up in this structure and usually is appropriated by the highest ranking officer involved in a decision. This person redistributes credit as he chooses, bound essentially by a sensitivity to public perceptions of his fairness. At the middle level, credit for a particular success is always a type of refracted social honor; one cannot claim credit even if it is earned. Credit has to be given, and acceptance of the gift implicitly involves a reaffirmation and strengthening of fealty. A superior may share some credit with subordinates in order to deepen fealty relationships and induce greater future efforts on his behalf. Of course, a different system is involved in the allocation of blame, a point I shall discuss later.

Fealty to the 'King'

Because of the interlocking character of the commitment system, a CEO carries enormous influence in his corporation. If, for a moment, one thinks of the presidents of individual operating companies as barons, then the CEO of the parent company is the king. His word is law; even the CEO's wishes and whims are taken as commands by close subordinates on the corporate staff, who zealously turn them into policies and directives.

A typical example occurred in the textile company last year when the CEO, new at the time, expressed mild concern about the rising operating costs of the company's fleet of rented cars. The following day, a stringent system for monitoring mileage replaced the previous casual practice.

Great efforts are made to please the CEO. For example, when the CEO of the large conglomerate that includes the chemical company visits a plant, the most important order of business for local management is a fresh paint job, even when, as in several cases last year, the cost of the paint alone exceeds $100,000. I am told that similar anecdotes from other organizations have been in circulation since 1910; this suggests a certain historical continuity of behavior toward top bosses.

The second order of business for the plant management is to produce a complete book describing the plant and its operations, replete with photographs and illustrations, for presentation to the CEO; such a book costs about $10,000 for the single copy. By any standards of budgetary stringency, such expenditures are irrational. But by the social standards of the corporation, they make perfect sense. It is far more important to please the king today than to worry about the future economic state of one's fief, since if one does not please the king, there may not be a fief to worry about or indeed any vassals to do the worrying.

By the same token, all of this leads to an intense interest in everything the CEO does and says. In both the chemical and the textile companies, the most common topic of conversation among managers up and down the line is speculation about their respective CEO's plans, intentions, strategies, actions, styles, and public images.

Such speculation is more than idle gossip. Because he stands at the apex of the corporation's bureaucratic and patrimonial structures and locks the intricate system of commitments between bosses and subordinates into place, it is the CEO who ultimately decides whether those commitments have been satisfactorily met. Moreover, the CEO and his trusted associates determine the fate of whole business areas of a corporation.

Shake-ups & Contingency

One must appreciate the simultaneously monocratic and patrimonial character of business bureaucracies in order to grasp what we might call their contingency. One has only to read the *Wall Street Journal* or the *New York Times* to realize that, despite their carefully constructed "eternal" public image, corporations are quite unstable organizations. Mergers, buy-outs, divestitures, and especially "organizational restructuring" are commonplace aspects of business life. I shall discuss only organizational shake-ups here.

Usually, shake-ups occur because of the appointment of a new CEO and/or division president, or because of some failure that is adjusted to demand retribution; sometimes these occurrences work together. The first action of most new CEOs is some form of organizational change. On the one hand, this prevents the inheritance of blame for past mistakes; on the other, it projects an image of bareknuckled aggressiveness much appreciated on Wall Street. Perhaps most important, a shake-up rearranges the fealty structure of the corporation, placing in power those barons whose style and public image mesh closely with that of the new CEO.

A shake-up has reverberations throughout an organization. Shortly after the new CEO of the conglomerate was named, he reorganized the whole business and selected new presidents to head each of the five newly formed companies of the corporation. He mandated that the presidents carry out a thorough reorganization of their separate companies complete with extensive "census reduction"—that is, firing as many people as possible.

The new president of the chemical company, one of these five, had risen from a small but important specialty chemicals division in the former company. Upon promotion to president, he reached back into his former division, indeed back to his own past work in a particular product line, and systematically elevated many of his former colleagues, friends, and allies. Powerful managers in other divisions, particularly in a rival process chemicals division, were: (1) forced to take big demotions in the new power structure; (2) put on "special assignment"—the corporate euphemism for Siberia (the saying is: "No one ever comes back from special assignment"); (3) fired; or (4) given "early retirement," a graceful way of doing the same thing.

Up and down the chemical company, former associates of the president now hold virtually every important position. Managers in the company view all of this as an inevitable fact of life. In their view, the whole reorganization could easily have gone in a completely different direction had another CEO been named or had the one selected picked a different president for the chemical company, or had the president come from a different work group in the old organization. Similarly, there is the abiding feeling that another significant change in top management could trigger yet another sweeping reorganization.

Fealty is the mortar of the corporate hierarchy, but the removal of one well-placed stone loosens the mortar throughout the pyramid and can cause things to fall apart. And no one is ever quite sure, until after the fact, just how the pyramid will be put back together.

SUCCESS & FAILURE

It is within this complicated and ambiguous authority structure, always subject to upheaval, that success and failure are meted out to those in the middle and upper middle managerial ranks. Managers rarely spoke to me of objective criteria for achieving success because once certain crucial points in one's career are passed, success and failure seem to have little to do with one's accomplishments. Rather, success is socially defined and distributed. Corporations do demand, of course, a basic competence and sometimes specified training and experience; hiring patterns usually ensure these. A weeding-out process takes place, however, among the lower ranks of managers during the first several years of their experience. By the time a manager reaches a certain numbered grade in the ordered hierarchy—in the chemical company this is Grade 13 out of 25, defining the top 8½% of management in the company—managerial competence as such is taken for granted and assumed not to differ greatly from one manager to the next. The focus then switches to social factors, which are determined by authority and political alignments—the fealty structure—and by the ethos and style of the corporation.

Moving to the Top

In the chemical and textile companies as well as the other concerns I studied, five criteria seem to control a person's ability to rise in middle and upper middle management. In ascending order they are:

1. Appearance and dress. This criterion is so familiar that I shall mention it only briefly. Managers have to look the part, and it is sufficient to say that corporations are filled with attractive, well-groomed, and conventionally well-dressed men and women.

2. Self-control. Managers stress the need to exercise iron self-control and to have the ability to mask all emotion and intention behind bland, smiling, and agreeable public faces. They believe it is a fatal weakness to lose control of oneself, in any way, in a public forum. Similarly, to betray valuable secret knowledge (for instance, a confidential reorganization plan) or intentions through some relaxation of self-control—for example, an indiscreet comment or lack of adroitness in turning aside a query—can not only jeopardize a manager's immediate position but can undermine others' trust in him.

3. Perception as a team player. While being a team player has many meanings, one of the most important is to appear to be interchangeable with other managers near one's level. Corporations discourage narrow specialization more strongly as one goes higher. They also discourage the expression of moral or political qualms. One might object, for example, to working with chemicals used in nuclear power, and most corporations today would honor that objection. The public statement of such objections, however, would end any realistic aspirations for higher posts because one's usefulness to the organization depends on versatility. As one manager in the chemical company commented: "Well, we'd go along with his request but we'd always wonder about the guy. And in the back of our minds, we'd be thinking that he'll soon object to working in the soda ash division because he doesn't like glass."

   Another important meaning of team play is putting in long hours at the office. This requires a certain amount of sheer physical energy, even though a great deal of this time is spent not in actual work but in social rituals—like reading and discussing newspaper articles, taking coffee breaks, or having informal conversations. These rituals, readily observable in every corporation that I studied, forge the social bonds that make real managerial work—that is, group work of various sorts—possible. One must participate in the rituals to be considered effective in the work.

4. Style. Managers emphasize the importance of "being fast on your feet"; always being well organized; giving slick presentations

complete with color slides; giving the appearance of knowledge even in its absence; and possessing a subtle, almost indefinable sophistication, marked especially by an urbane, witty, graceful, engaging, and friendly demeanor.

I want to pause for a moment to note that some observers have interpreted such conformity, team playing, affability, and urbanity as evidence of the decline of the individualism of the old Protestant Ethic.[3] To the extent that commentators take the public images that managers project at face value, I think they miss the main point. Managers up and down the corporate ladder adopt the public faces that they wear quite consciously; they are, in fact, the masks behind which the real struggles and moral issues of the corporation can be found.

Karl Mannheim's conception of self-rationalization or self-streamlining is useful in understanding what is one of the central social psychological processes of organizational life.[4] In a world where appearances—in the broadest sense—mean everything, the wise and ambitious person learns to cultivate assiduously the proper, prescribed modes of appearing. He dispassionately takes stock of himself, treating himself as an object. He analyzes his strengths and weaknesses, and decides what he needs to change in order to survive and flourish in his organization. And then he systematically undertakes a program to reconstruct his image. Self-rationalization curiously parallels the methodical subjection of self to God's will that the old Protestant Ethic counseled; the difference, of course, is that one acquires not moral virtues but a masterful ability to manipulate personae.

5. Patron power. To advance, a manager must have a patron, also called a mentor, a sponsor, a rabbi, or a godfather. Without a powerful patron in the higher echelons of management, one's prospects are poor in most corporations. The patron might be the manager's immediate boss or someone several levels higher in the chain of command. In either case the manager is still bound by the immediate, formal authority and fealty patterns of his position; the new—although more ambiguous—fealty relationships with the patron are added.

A patron provides his "client" with opportunities to get visibility, to showcase his abilities, to make connections with those of high status. A patron cues his client to crucial political developments in the corporation, helps arrange lateral moves if the client's upward progress is thwarted by a particular job or a particular boss, applauds his presentations or suggestions at meetings, and promotes the client during an organizational shakeup. One must, of course, be lucky in one's patron. If the patron gets caught in a political crossfire, the arrows are likely to find his clients as well.

Social Definitions of Performance

Surely, one might argue, there must be more to success in the corporation than style, personality, team play, chameleonic adaptability, and fortunate connections. What about the bottom line—profits, performance?

Unquestionably, "hitting your numbers"—that is, meeting the profit commitments already discussed—is important, but only within the social context I have described. There are several rules here. First, no one in a line position—that is, with responsibility for profit and loss—who regularly "misses his numbers" will survive, let alone rise. Second, a person who always hits his numbers but who lacks some or all of the required social skills will not rise. Third, a person who sometimes misses his numbers but who has all the desirable social traits will rise.

Performance is thus always subject to a myriad of interpretations. Profits matter, but it is much more important in the long run to be perceived as "promotable" by belonging to central political networks. Patrons protect those already selected as rising stars from the negative judgments of others; and only the foolhardy point out even egregious errors of those in power or those destined for it.

Failure is also socially defined. The most damaging failure is, as one middle manager in the chemical company puts it, "when your boss or someone who has the power to determine your fate says: 'You failed.'" Such a godlike pronouncement means, of course, out-and-out personal ruin; one must, at any cost, arrange matters to prevent such an occurrence.

As it happens, things rarely come to such a dramatic point even in the midst of an organizational crisis. The same judgment may be made but it is usually called "nonpromotability." The difference is that those who are publicly labeled as failures normally have no choice but to leave the organization; those adjudged nonpromotable can remain, provided they are willing to accept being shelved or, more colorfully, "mushroomed"—that is, kept in a dark place, fed manure, and left to do nothing but grow fat. Usually, seniors do not tell juniors they are nonpromotable (though the verdict may be common knowledge among senior peer groups). Rather, subordinates are expected to get the message after they have been repeatedly overlooked for promotions. In fact, middle managers interpret staying in the same job for more than two or three years as evidence of a negative judgment. This leads to a mobility panic at the middle levels which, in turn, has crucial consequences for pinpointing responsibility in the organization.

Capriciousness of Success

Finally, managers think that there is a tremendous amount of plain luck involved in advancement. It is striking how often managers who pride themselves on being hardheaded rationalists explain their own career patterns and those of others in terms of luck. Various uncertainties shape this perception. One is the sense of organizational contingency. One change at the top can create profound unheaval throughout the entire corporate structure, producing startling reversals of fortune, good or bad, depending on one's connections. Another is the uncertainty of the markets that often makes managerial planning simply elaborate guesswork, causing real economic outcome to depend on factors totally beyond organizational and personal control.

It is interesting to note in this context that a line manager's credibility suffers just as much from missing his numbers on the up side (that is, achieving profits higher than predicted) as from missing them on the down side. Both outcomes undercut the ideology of managerial planning and control, perhaps the only bulwark managers have against market irrationality.

Even managers in staff positions, often quite removed from the market, face uncertainty. Occupational safety specialists, for instance, know that bad publicity from one serious accident in the workplace can jeopardize years of work and scores of safety awards. As one high-ranking executive in the chemical company says, "In the corporate world, 1,000 'Attaboys!' are wiped away by one 'Oh, shit!' "

Because of such uncertainties, managers in all the companies I studied speak continually of the great importance of being in the right place at the right time and of the catastrophe of being in the wrong place at the wrong time. My interview materials are filled with stories of people who were transferred immediately before a big shake-up and, as a result, found themselves riding the crest of a wave to power; of people in a promising business area who were terminated because top management suddenly decided that the area no longer fit the corporate image desired; of others caught in an unpredictable and fatal political battle among their patrons; of a product manager whose plant accidentally produced an odd color batch of chemicals, who sold them as a premium version of the old product, and who is now thought to be a marketing genius.

The point is that managers have a sharply defined sense of the *capriciousness* of organizational life. Luck seems to be as good an explanation as any of why, after a certain point, some people succeed and others fail. The upshot is that many managers decide that they can do little to influence external events in their favor. One can, however, shamelessly streamline oneself, learn to wear all the right masks, and get to know all the right people. And then sit tight and wait for things to happen.

'GUT DECISIONS'

Authority and advancement patterns come together in the decision-making process. The core of the managerial mystique is decision-making prowess, and the real test of such prowess is what managers call "gut decisions," that is, important decisions involving big money, public exposure, or significant effects on the organization. At all but the highest levels of the chemical and textile companies, the rules for making gut decisions are, in the words of one upper middle manager: "(1) Avoid making any decisions if at all possible; and (2) if a decision has to be made, involve as many people as you can so that, if things go south, you're able to point in as many directions as possible."

Consider the case of a large coking plant of the chemical company. Coke making requires a gigantic battery to cook the coke slowly and evenly for long periods; the battery is the most important piece of capital equipment in a coking plant. In 1975, the plant's battery showed signs of weakening and certain managers at corporate headquarters had to decide whether to invest $6 million to restore the battery to top form. Clearly, because of the amount of money involved, this was a gut decision.

No decision was made. The CEO had sent the word out to defer all unnecessary capital expenditures to give the corporation cash reserves for other investments. So the managers allocated small amounts of money to patch the battery up until 1979, when it collapsed entirely. This brought the company into a breach of contract with a steel producer and into violation of various Environmental Protection Agency pollution regulations. The total bill, including lawsuits and now federally mandated repairs to the battery, exceeded $100 million. I have heard figures as high as $150 million, but because of "creative accounting," no one is sure of the exact amount.

This simple but very typical example gets to the heart of how decision making is intertwined with a company's authority structure and advancement patterns. As the chemical company managers see it, the decisions facing them in 1975 and 1979 were crucially different. Had they acted decisively in 1975—in hindsight, the only rational course—they would have salvaged the battery and saved their corporation millions of dollars in the long run.

In the short run, however, since even seemingly rational decisions are subject to widely varying interpretations, particularly decisions which run counter to a CEO's stated objectives, they would have been taking a serious risk in restoring the battery. What is more, their political networks might have unraveled, leaving them vulnerable to attack. They chose short-term safety over long-term gain because they felt they were judged, both by higher authority and by their peers, on their short-term performances. Managers feel that if they do not survive the short run, the long run hardly matters. Even correct decisions can shorten promising careers.

By contrast, in 1979 the decision was simple and posed little risk. The corporation had to meet its legal obligations; also it had to either repair the battery the way the EPA demanded or shut down the plant and lose several hundred million dollars. Since there were no real choices, everyone could agree on a course of action because everyone could appeal to inevitability. Diffusion of responsibility, in this case by procrastinating until total crisis, is intrinsic to organizational life because the real issue in most gut decisions is: Who is going to get blamed if things go wrong?

'Blame Time'

There is no more feared hour in the corporate world than "blame time." Blame is quite different from responsibility. There is a cartoon of Richard Nixon declaring: "I accept all of the responsibility, but none of the blame." To blame someone is to injure him verbally in public; in large organizations, where one's image is crucial, this poses the most serious sort of threat. For managers, blame—like failure—has nothing to do with the merits of a case; it is a matter of social definition. As a general rule, it is those who are or who become politically vulnerable or expendable who get "set up" and become blamable. The most feared situation of all is to end up inadvertently in the wrong place at the wrong time and get blamed.

Yet this is exactly what often happens in a structure that systematically diffuses responsibility. It is because managers fear blame time that they diffuse responsibility; however, such diffusion inevitably means that someone, somewhere is going to become a scapegoat when things go wrong. Big corporations encourage this process by their complete lack of any tracking system. Whoever is currently in charge of an area is responsible—that is, potentially blamable—for whatever goes wrong in the area, even if he has inherited others' mistakes. An example from the chemical company illustrates this process.

When the CEO of the large conglomerate took office, he wanted to rid his capital accounts of all serious financial drags. The corporation had been operating a storage depot for natural gas which it bought, stored, and then resold. Some years before the energy crisis, the company had entered into a long-term contract to supply gas to a buyer—call him Jones. At the time, this was a sound deal because it provided a steady market for a stably priced commodity.

When gas prices soared, the corporation was still bound to deliver gas to Jones at 20¢ per unit instead of the going market price of $2. The CEO ordered one of his subordinates to get rid of this albatross as expeditiously as possible. This was done by selling the operation to another party—call him Brown—with the agreement that Brown would continue to meet the contractual obligations to Jones. In return for Brown's assumption of these costly contracts, the corporation agreed to buy gas from Brown at grossly inflated prices to meet some of its own energy needs.

In effect, the CEO transferred the drag on his capital accounts to the company's operating expenses. This enabled him to project an aggressive, asset-reducing image to Wall Street. Several levels down the ladder, however, a new vice president for a particular business found himself saddled with exorbitant operating costs when, during a reorganization, those plants purchasing gas from Brown at inflated prices came under his purview. The high costs helped to undercut the vice president's division earnings and thus to erode his position in the hierarchy. The origin of the situation did not matter. All that counted was that the vice president's division was steadily losing big money. In the end, he resigned to "pursue new opportunities."

One might ask why top management does not institute codes or systems for tracking responsibility. This example provides the clue. An explicit system of accountability for subordinates would probably have to apply to top executives as well and would restrict their freedom. Bureaucracy expands the freedom of those on top by giving them the power to restrict the freedom of those beneath.

On the Fast Track

Managers see what happened to the vice president as completely capricious, but completely understandable. They take for granted the absence of any tracking of responsibility. If anything, they blame the vice president for not recognizing soon enough the dangers of the situation into which he was being drawn and for not preparing a defense—even perhaps finding a substitute scapegoat. At the same time, they realize that this sort of thing could easily happen to them. They see few defenses against being caught in the wrong place at the wrong time except constant wariness, the diffusion of responsibility, and perhaps being shrewd enough to declare the ineptitude of one's predecessor on first taking a job.

What about avoiding the consequences of their own errors? Here they enjoy more control. They can "outrun" their mistakes so that when blame time arrives, the burden will fall on someone else. The ideal situation, of course, is to be in a position to fire one's successors for one's own previous mistakes.

Some managers, in fact, argue that outrunning mistakes is the real key to managerial success. One way to do this is by manipulating the numbers. Both the chemical and the textile companies place a great premium on a division's or a subsidiary's return on assets. A good way for business managers to increase their ROA is to reduce their assets while maintaining sales. Usually they will do everything they can to hold down expenditures in order to decrease the asset base, particularly at the end of the fiscal year. The most common way of doing this is by deferring capital expenditures, from maintenance to innovative investments, as long as possible. Done for a short time, this is called "starving" a plant; done over a longer period, it is called "milking" a plant.

Some managers become very adept at milking businesses and showing a consistent record of high returns. They move from one job to another in a company, always upward, rarely staying more than two years in any post. They may leave behind them deteriorating plants and unsafe working conditions, but they know that if they move quickly enough, the blame will fall on others. In this sense, bureaucracies may be thought of as vast systems of organized irresponsibility.

FLEXIBILITY & DEXTERITY WITH SYMBOLS

The intense competition among managers takes place not only behind the agreeable public faces I have described but within an extraordinarily indirect and ambiguous linguistic framework. Except at blame time, managers do not publicly criticize or disagree with one another or with company policy. The sanction against such criticism or disagreement is so strong that it constitutes, in managers' view, a suppression of professional debate. The sanction seems to be rooted principally in their acute sense of organizational contingency; the person one criticizes or argues with today could be one's boss tomorrow.

This leads to the use of an elaborate linguistic code marked by emotional neutrality, especially in group settings. The code communicates the meaning one might wish to convey to other managers, but since it is devoid of any significant emotional sentiment, it can be reinterpreted should social relationships or attitudes change. Here, for example, are some typical phrases describing performance appraisals followed by their probable intended meanings:

Stock phrase	Probable intended meaning
Exceptionally well qualified	Has committed no major blunders to date
Tactful in dealing with superiors	Knows when to keep his mouth shut
Quick thinking	Offers plausible excuses for errors
Meticulous attention to detail	A nitpicker
Slightly below average	Stupid
Unusually loyal	Wanted by no one else

For the most part, such neutered language is not used with the intent to deceive; rather, its purpose is to communicate certain meanings within specific contexts with the implicit understanding that, should the context change, a new, more appropriate meaning can be attached to the language already used. In effect, the corporation is a setting where people are not held to their word because it is generally understood that their word is always provisional.

The higher one goes in the corporate world, the more this seems to be the case; in fact, advancement beyond the upper middle level depends greatly on one's ability to manipulate a variety of symbols without becoming tied to or identified with any of them. For example, an amazing variety of organizational improvement programs marks practically every corporation. I am referring here to the myriad ideas generated by corporate staff, business consultants, academics, and a host of others to improve corporate stucture; sharpen decision making; raise morale; create a more humanistic workplace; adopt Theory X, Theory Y, or, more recently, Theory Z of management; and so on. These programs become important when they are pushed from the top.

The watchword in the large conglomerate at the moment is productivity and, since this is a pet project of the CEO himself, it is said that no one goes into his presence without wearing a blue *Productivity!* button and talking about "quality circles" and "feedback sessions." The president of another company pushes a series of managerial seminars that endlessly repeats the basic functions of management: (1) planning, (2) organizing, (3) motivating, and (4) controlling. Aspiring young managers attend these sessions and with a seemingly dutiful eagerness learn to repeat the formulas under the watchful eyes of senior officials.

Privately, managers characterize such programs as the "CEO's incantations over the assembled multitude," as "elaborate rituals with no practical effect," or as "waving a magic wand to make things wonderful again." Publicly, of course, managers on the way up adopt the programs with great ethusiasm, participate in or run them very effectively, and then quietly drop them when the time is right.

Playing the Game
Such flexibility, as it is called, can be confusing even to those in the inner circles. I was told the following by a highly placed staff member whose work requires him to interact daily with the top figures of his company:

"I get faked out all the time and I'm part of the system. I come from a very different culture. Where I come from, if you give someone your *word*, no one ever questions it. It's the old hard-work-will-lead-to-success ideology. Small community, Protestant, agrarian, small business, merchant-type values. I'm disadvantaged in a system like this."

He goes on to characterize the system more fully and what it takes to succeed within it:

"It's the ability to play this system that determines whether you will rise. . . . And part of the adeptness [required] is determined by how much it bothers people. One thing you have to be able to do is to play the game, but you can't be disturbed by the game. What's the game? It's bringing troops home from Vietnam and declaring peace with honor. It's saying one thing and meaning another.

"It's characterizing the reality of a situation with *any* description that is necessary to make that situation more palatable to some group that matters. It means that you have to come up with a culturally accepted verbalization to explain why you are *not* doing what you are doing. . . . [Or] you say that we had to do what we did because it was inevitable; or because the guys at the [regulatory] agencies were dumb; [you] say we won when we really lost; [you] say we saved money when we squandered it; [you] say something's safe when it's potentially or actually dangerous. . . . Everyone knows it's bullshit, but it's *accepted*. This is the game."

In addition, then, to the other characteristics that I have described, it seems that a prerequisite for big success in the corporation is a certain adeptness at inconsistency. This premium on inconsistency is particularly evident in the many areas of public controversy that face top-ranking managers. Two things come together to produce this situation. The first is managers' sense of beleaguerment from a wide array of adversaries who, it is thought, want to disrupt or impede management's attempts to further the economic interests of their companies. In every company that I studied, managers see themselves and their traditional prerogatives as being under siege, and they respond with a set of caricatures of their perceived principal adversaries.

For example, government regulators are brash, young, unkempt hippies in blue jeans who know nothing about the businesses for which they make rules; environmental activists—the bird and bunny people—are softheaded idealists who want everybody to live in tents, burn candles, ride horses, and eat berries; workers'compensation lawyers are out-and-out crooks who prey on corporations to appropriate exorbitant fees from unwary clients; labor activists are radical troublemakers who want to disrupt harmonious industrial communities; and the news media consist of rabble-rousers who propagate sensational antibusiness stories to sell papers or advertising time on shows like "60 Minutes."

Second, within this context of perceived harassment, managers must address a multiplicity of audiences, some of whom are considered adversaries. These audiences are the internal corporate hierarchy with its intricate and shifting power and status cliques, key regulators, key local and federal legislators, special publics that vary according to the issues, and the public at large, whose goodwill and favorable opinion are considered essential for a company's free operation.

Managerial adeptness at inconsistency becomes evident in the widely discrepant perspectives, reasons for action, and presentations of fact that explain, excuse, or justify corporate behavior to these diverse audiences.

Adeptness at Inconsistency

The cotton dust issue in the textile industry provides a fine illustration of what I mean. Prolonged exposure to cotton dust produces in many textile workers a chronic and eventually disabling pulmonary disease called byssinosis or, colloquially, brown lung. In the early 1970s, the Occupational Safety and Health Administration proposed a ruling to cut workers' exposure to cotton dust sharply by requiring textile companies to invest large amounts of money in cleaning up their plants. The industry fought the regulation fiercely but a final OSHA ruling was made in 1978 requiring full compliance by 1984.

The industry took the case to court. Despite an attempt by Reagan appointees in OSHA to have the case removed from judicial consideration and remanded to the agency they controlled for further cost/benefit analysis, the Supreme Court ruled in 1981 that the 1978 OSHA ruling was fully within the agency's mandate, namely, to protect workers' health and safety as the primary benefit exceeding all cost considerations.

During these proceedings, the textile company was engaged on a variety of fronts and was pursuing a number of actions. For instance, it intensively lobbied regulators and legislators and it prepared court materials for the industry's defense, arguing that the proposed standard would crush the industry and that the problem, if it existed, should be met by increasing workers' use of respirators.

The company also aimed a public relations barrage at special-interest groups as well as at the general public. It argued that there is probably no such thing as byssinosis; workers suffering from pulmonary problems are all heavy smokers and the real culprit is the government-subsidized tobacco industry. How can cotton cause brown lung when cotton is white? Further, if there is a problem, only some workers are afflicted, and therefore the solution is more careful screening of the work force to detect susceptible people and prevent them from ever reaching the workplace. Finally, the company claimed that if the regulation were imposed, most of the textile industry would move overseas where regulations are less harsh.[5]

In the meantime, the company was actually addressing the problem but in a characteristically indirect way. It invested $20 million in a few plants where it knew such an investment would make money; this investment automated the early stages of handling cotton, traditionally a very slow procedure, and greatly increased productivity. The investment had the side benefit of reducing cotton dust levels to the new standard in precisely those areas of the work process where the dust problem is greatest. Publicly, of course, the company claims that the money was spent entirely to eliminate dust, evidence of its corporate good citizenship. (Privately, executives admit that, without the productive return, they would not have spent the money and they have not done so in several other plants.)

Indeed, the productive return is the only rationale that carries weight within the corporate hierarchy. Executives also admit, somewhat ruefully and only when their office doors are closed, that OSHA's regulation on cotton dust has been the main factor in forcing technological innovation in a centuries-old and somewhat stagnant industry.

Such adeptness at inconsistency, without moral uneasiness, is essential for executive success. It means being able to say, as a very high-ranking official of the textile company said to me without batting an eye, that the industry has never caused the slightest problem in any worker's breathing capacity. It means, in the chemical company, propagating an elaborate hazard/benefit calculus for appraisal of dangerous chemicals while internally conceptualizing "hazards" as business risks. It means publicly extolling the carefulness of testing procedures on toxic chemicals while privately ridiculing animal tests as inapplicable to humans.

It means lobbying intensively in the present to shape government regulations to one's immediate advantage and, ten years later, in the event of a catastrophe, arguing that the company acted strictly in accordance with the standards of the time. It means claiming that the real problem of our society is its unwillingness to take risks, while in the thickets of one's bureaucracy avoiding risks at every turn; it means as well making every effort to socialize the risks of industrial activity while privatizing the benefits.

THE BUREAUCRATIC ETHIC

The bureaucratic ethic contrasts sharply with the original Protestant Ethic. The Protestant Ethic was the ideology of a self-confident and independent propertied social class. It was an ideology that extolled the virtues of accumulating wealth in a society organized around property and that accepted the stewardship responsibilities entailed by property. It was an ideology where a person's word was his bond and where the integrity of the handshake was seen as crucial to the maintenance of good business relationships. Perhaps most important, it was connected to a predictable economy of salvation—that is, hard work will lead to success, which is a sign of one's election by God—a notion also containing its own theodicy to explain the misery of those who do not make it in this world.

Bureaucracy, however, breaks apart substance from appearances, action from responsibility, and language from meaning. Most important, it breaks apart the older connection between the meaning of work and salvation. In the bureaucratic world, one's success, one's sign of election, no longer depends on one's own efforts and on an inscrutable God but on the capriciousness of one's superiors and the market; and one achieves economic salvation to the extent that one pleases and submits to one's employer and meets the exigencies of an impersonal market.

In this way, because moral choices are inextricably tied to personal fates, bureaucracy erodes internal and even external standards of morality, not only in matters of individual success and failure but also in all the issues that managers face in their daily work. Bureaucracy makes its own internal rules and social context the principal moral gauges for action. Men and women in bureaucracies turn to each other for moral cues for behavior and come to fashion specific situational moralities for specific significant people in their worlds.

As it happens, the guidance they receive from each other is profoundly ambiguous because what matters in the bureaucratic world is not what a person is but how closely his many personae mesh with the organizational ideal; not his willingness to stand by his actions but his agility in avoiding blame; not what he believes or says but how well he has mastered the ideologies that serve his corporation; not what he stands for but whom he stands with in the labyrinths of his organization.

In short, bureaucracy structures for managers an intricate series of moral mazes. Even the inviting paths out of the puzzle often turn out to be invitations to jeopardy.

REFERENCES

1. There is a long sociological tradition of work on managers and I am, of course, indebted to that literature. I am particularly indebted to the work, both joint and separate, of Joseph Bensman and Arthur J. Vidich, two of the keenest observers of the new middle class. See especially their *The New American Society: The Revolution of the Middle Class* (Chicago: Quadrangle Books, 1971).

2. See Max Weber, *The Protestant Ethic and the Spirit of Capitalism,* translated by Talcott Parsons (New York: Charles Scribner's Sons, 1958), p. 172.

3. See William H. Whyte, *The Organization Man* (New York: Simon & Schuster, 1956), and David Riesman, in collaboration with Reuel Denney and Nathan Glazer, *The Lonely Crowd: A Study of the Changing American Character* (New Haven: Yale University Press, 1950).

4. Karl Mannheim, *Man and Society in an Age of Reconstruction* [London: Paul (Kegan), Trench, Trubner Ltd. 1940], p.55.

5. On February 9, 1982, the Occupational Safety and Health Administration issued a notice that it was once again reviewing its 1978 standard on cotton dust for "cost-effectiveness." See *Federal Register,* vol. 47, p. 5906. As of this writing (May 1983), this review has still not been officially completed.

How to Snoop on Your Competitors

Gathering intelligence on the opposition has become a lot more common of late. Most of it is legal, some is even ethical. Herewith a guide that sorts the utterly sleazy from the merely hardball.

Steven Flax

How would you like to know your competitors' sales plans, key elements of their corporate strategies, the capacity of their plants and the technology used in them, who their principal suppliers and customers are, and a good bit about new products your rivals have under development? No, you don't have to break any laws to get this information. While illegal corporate espionage makes headlines occasionally, it probably accounts for only a small fraction of corporate intelligence-gathering. There are many other ways you can find out what your competitors are up to that are completely legal, if sometimes ethically questionable.

The legal use of intelligence-gathering techniques has increased dramatically as more and more companies learn how cheap and effective it is. U.S. corporations known to collect intelligence on competitors include Ford Motor Co., Westinghouse Electric, General Electric, Emerson Electric, Rockwell International, Celanese, Union Carbide, and Gillette. Digital Equipment Corp. and Wang Laboratories both have batteries of competitor analysts. Nor is snooping limited to companies that make highly engineered hardware. Enterprises such as Chemical Bank, the USV Laboratories subsidiary of Revlon, the specialty grocery products group of Del Monte, General Foods, Kraft, and J. C. Penney are all busy monitoring what the other guy is doing.

How much is what they learn worth? Consider the example of Cordis Corp., a Miami-based manufacturer of heart pacemakers. In 1980 Cordis came up with a new line of pacemakers whose technology was better than anything else on the market. Oddly, though, sales didn't improve; indeed, in some territories they worsened. Puzzled, Cordis asked its sales representatives to investigate the tactics being used against them.

The salesmen learned that competitors were plying physicians with cars, boats, and lavish junkets. While Cordis claims it was suprised to find that such promotions could sway cardiologists, sales were in fact deteriorating most where its competitors' giveaways were most aggressive. Cordis increased its educational support for doctors, began fielding many more service representatives, and, yes, matched some of the giveaways—not boats, but equipment related to pacemakers and their use. The effort helped make sales soar.

Companies have always needed to know what competitors were doing—so why more so now? The answer, in a word, is competition. Businessmen believe competition has intensified and become global. In industries where growth has slowed, executives realize that most of the increased business they need will have to come out of the hides of their competitors. In addition, the corporate strategy vogue of the 1970s—remember all those matrices and market share calculations?—has left as a legacy the thought that competitive intelligence is a necessary ingredient in executing strategic plans. Henry P. Allessio, a founding partner of Easton Consultants of Stamford, Connecticut, says flatly, "You can't get there from here without it." Companies realize that, without taking the behavior of competitors into account, their strategic plans don't work. Says Harvard Business School Professor Michael Porter, a guru of strategy, "If your competitors respond the wrong way to your 'right move,' they can make the right move wrong."

The heightened interest in snooping has given rise to an industry that offers textbooks, seminars, and consultation on how to do it, together with a raft of companies that provide the service for a fee. FIND/SVP, a research firm in New York City, has had such an increase in requests for monitoring clients' competitors that it recently created a special service to handle the requests. Attendance at competitive intelligence seminars put on by outfits such as Information Data Search of Cambridge, Massachusetts, has shot up over the last couple of years. Businessmen are still snapping up copies of Porter's three-year-old book *Competitive Strategy*, which offers advice on how to gather corporate G2.

Obtaining competitive information is getting easier these days. Electronic data bases, which store information to be retrieved by computer, are proliferating. Some 2,000 are now available. One, called Economic Information Systems, published by a subsidiary of Control Data Corp., lists the names and locations of industrial facilities along with estimates of each plant's dollar volume of output, number of employees, and the share of market that its production represents. Another data base, called Investext, published by Business Research Corp. of Brighton, Massachusetts, gives subscribers the full text of research reports on companies by security analysts and investment bankers.

There are now even services that monitor such data bases for you. Selective Dissemination of Information (or SDI), offered by data base distributors such as Dialog Information Services, provides subscribers with surveillance and periodic reports on competitors' appearances in data bases. Unfortunately, some of the information in these data bases is inaccurate, irrelevant, or stale. But nuggets can be found—and competitive intelligence is a bits-and-pieces business. Says Michael Porter, "Once you have 80% of the puzzle, you begin to see things in what people say that you didn't see when you had 20%."

Competition in the competitive intelligence business is getting as rugged as in the industries the snoopers monitor. Leonard Fuld, managing director of Information Date Search, discovered, for example, that a competitor had enrolled in one of his seminars under an assumed name. During another seminar his lecture notes and source book were stolen.

Stealing is not a technique the experts recommend—it's against the law. But no unequivocal test of legality exists for many other intelligence-gathering activities. Deciding whether a particular practice is ethical is even more difficult. A manager can apply simple rules of thumb—would you want the fact that your company is doing this disclosed in the press? But even these tests are subject to shifting opinions about what is immoral vs. what is tough but blameless competitiveness.

The techniques fall into four broad categories. The first covers ways of getting information from competitors' employees, past or present:

Milking Potential Recruits   When they interview students for jobs, some companies pay special attention to those who have worked for competitors, even temporarily. Job seekers are eager to impress and often have not been warned about divulging what is proprietary. They sometimes volunteer valuable information.

For example, this February a university student in California who had been employed for a summer by a computer company was interviewed by another corporation for a regular job. The prospective employer asked about her summer work. She said that she had evaluated all of the commercially available software packages capable of performing a certain function. Had she stopped talking there, she would have answered the recruiter's question. In her eagerness, however, she went on to say that she had found them all inferior to her summer employer's internally developed package and that the company was going to go with its own. To creators of this kind of software—the interviewing company was not one—such a revelation would have been of immense importance. Several companies now send teams of highly trained technicians instead of personnel executives to recruit on campus.

Picking Brains at Conferences   Companies send engineers to conferences and trade shows to question competitors' technical people. Often conversations start innocently—just a few fellow technicians discussing processes and problems that seemingly do not relate to trade secrets. Yet even though they are aware of the value of proprietary information, engineers and scientists often brag about surmounting technical challenges, in the process divulging sensitive information. Like the student, they hunger for recognition, even from an interlocutor wearing a badge that identifies him as the employee of a competitor.

If you are thinking of trying this, be aware that it's important that your employees be honest about their corporate affiliations. If they misrepresent whom they work for, ask specifically for proprietary information, or coax competitors with money or various entertainments, you could be charged with attempting to steal secrets.

Conducting Phony Job Interviews   Companies sometimes advertise and hold interviews for jobs that don't exist in order to entice competitors' employees to spill the beans. The practice is legal, provided the interviewer doesn't explicitly ask for trade secrets. Often applicants have toiled in obscurity or feel that their careers have stalled. They're dying to impress somebody. Says Stanley H. Lieberstein, an attorney and a recognized authority on trade secrets, "The candidate is not deliberately revealing secrets and is not being bribed to do so. But secret information—or tiny portions of it—leaks out." If a company interviews enough people, it can often obtain an accurate picture of a competitor. It is also, of course, lying about what it's up to and manipulating the people it interviews.

Hiring People Away from Competitors   In probably the hoariest tactic in corporate intelligence-gathering, companies hire key executives from competitors to find out what they know. Within the last two years, though, Avis Inc. and Coca-Cola Co. have been sued for hiring top executives from Hertz Corp. and PepsiCo. respectively. The key legal distinction in such cases is between "unintentional but inevitable" use and "intentional" use of the information the newly hired employee brings with him. However antagonized your competitor may be if you recruit one of its top executives, courts recognize that he will inevitably use some of the knowledge he developed in his last job, and they uphold his right to do so. To legally challenge the hiring, competitors must prove that your company hired him intentionally to get specific trade secrets. A flurry of information-gathering by him immediately prior to resignation is circumstantial evidence of this intention.

Interviewing Competitors   Companies don't usually ask competitors what they're doing directly—they hire management consultants to find out. These consultants, often the biggest names in the business, will ask their client's competitors for information, saying that they are doing a study of the industry and that they will share with all respondents the data they develop. They do give something back, but it's often in-nocuous. The good stuff is Client's Eyes Only.

Debriefing Design Consultants   In certain industries—computers, for example—competitors frequently use the same design consultants. While conferring with a consultant it has hired to help it with a new product, a company can sometimes learn confidential information about products competitors are developing.

Debriefing Competitors' Former Employees   They will often supply damaging information about the company they used to work for, especially if they left on bad terms. If they are leaving the industry and have remained friendly with salespeople they competed against, they just might reveal how they were able to, say, crack an account.

The second general category consists of techniques to get information from people who do business with competitors:

Encouraging Key Customers to Talk   In every industry companies show new products to certain key customers because their willingness to buy the product is considered indispensable for success. These customers are sometimes loyal to a competitor, however, and will get on the phone to it as soon as a competing salesman has left the office.

For example, a while back Gillette told a large Canadian account the date on which it planned to begin selling its Good News disposable razor in the U.S. The date was six months before Bic Corp. was scheduled to introduce its own disposable razor in America. The Canadian distributor promptly called Bic and told it about the impending product launch. Bic put on a crash program and was able to start selling its razor shortly after Gillette did.

Getting Customers to Put Out Phony Bid Requests   A company will sometimes ask a loyal customer to put out a request for proposal (RFP) to the supplier's competitors, soliciting the competitors' bids on pro-viding parts so technically advanced that they could not be obtained from the industry's current stock of products. When the proposals come in, they are loaded with descriptions of technical capabilities or ad-vanced products that the suppliers had been keeping confidential.

Why would any company cooperate with a supplier in such a scheme, thereby betraying other suppliers? It depends on how important the sup-plier who asks is to that customer. In cases where suppliers are of vital importance, customers have capitulated and participated in what is, after all, a lie.

Press Release   Classified want ads can offer a wealth of information on your competitors' intentions, strategies, and planned products. This ad, which appeared on April 1 in the *Dallas Morning News*, gives advance notice of a "nationwide telemarketing effort" by the Embassy Suites hotel chain.

Grilling Suppliers   Say a company wants to find out how much its competitors are manufacturing, or are planning to manufacture. Its purchasing department might ask suppliers how much they are producing in total or what they plan in the way of new capacity or advanced processes. Since the company knows the capacity and capabilities it needs from the supplier, investments in sophisticated technology not required by the company may shed light on its competitors' needs and plans.

If you do not know who the suppliers are, take a look at the box your competitor packs his product in. On the bottom or a flap, you will find the stamp of the box manufacturer. From him you can sometimes find out how many boxes a competitor has bought and estimate how many units a competitor has been shipping lately.

What would make a box maker reveal information about a customer? You might tell him you're thinking about using him as a supplier, if he can prove he has the capacity to handle both accounts. Typically, in his desire to land you as a customer, the box maker will divulge his total capacity and how much your competitor uses to show he can handle the business.

Infiltrating Customers' Business Operations   Companies may provide their engineers free of charge to customers in the hope that the collaboration will lead the customer to design their components into its product. The close, cooperative relationship that the engineers on loan cultivate with the customers' design staff often enables them to learn what new products competitors are pitching.

In 1979 Intel Corp. heard that Motorola Corp. was developing its 68000 microprocessor chip. Intel, which was developing a competing chip, promptly deployed some of its applications engineers to the engineering organizations of customers to whom it assumed Motorola would try to sell the new chip. Through these contacts, Intel's applications engineers confirmed the rumors and figured out the design details of Motorola's chip. Intel then launched Operation Crush, an all-out sales campaign to get customers to specify its chip in their products. Salesmen's commissions were restructured to produce extraordinary rewards if they scored with large customers. The result: Intel got most of the high-volume design contracts, including those with Xerox and IBM.

Pumping Buyers   Salesmen can learn plenty about a competitor's sales from their customers. Let's say that a ballpoint pen salesman has persuaded a retailer to agree to run his first two-for-one special on the salesman's pens. A clever salesman will ask the retailer for his competitor's normal sales volume and two-for-one sales volume, saying that he hasn't used this sort of promotion in this chain of stores before and he wants to make sure that his local warehouse stocks enough inventory to make the sale a hit. The buyer also wants to avoid running out of stock if the sale is a hit, so he coughs up the information. The same ploy can be used by companies moving products into sales territories new to them.

The third general category consists of ways to find out what a competitor is up to from published material and documents often available from public sources:

Analyzing Help-wanted Ads   Help-wanted ads are in effect press releases. Months before MCI Communications Corp. announced its electronic mail service, it ran ads recruiting technicians and engineers trained in the kind of data communications used in such a service. A competitor following these ads could have figured out months in advance that MCI might be planning to offer electronic mail. MarkeTrack Inc. of Bloomfield, New Jersey, provides want ad monitoring of clients' competitors on a regular basis.

Analyzing Labor Contracts   Emerson Electric and other companies obtain labor contracts that have been negotiated by their competitors. From these they can compute the competitors' average labor costs for different sorts of manufacturing.

Studying Aerial Photographs   Although it is often illegal for a company to photograph a competitor's plant from the air—it's a form of trespassing—there are legitimate ways to get the photos. If a competitor's plant is near a waterway or was the subject of an environmental impact study, aerial photos often are on file with the U.S. Geological Survey or Environmental Protection Agency. These are public documents, available for a nominal charge. Obtaining these photos from time to time will reveal plant expansions, the layout of a competitor's manufacturing facility (often a clue to the processes being used), and inventory buildups (a tip-off to upcoming sales drives).

Obtaining Freedom of Information Act Filings   Thank you, Big Brother. Companies can get information about competitors from government agencies by asking for it under the Freedom of Information Act. But such requests are themselves public documents and could be obtained by the competitor by using the FOIA. This could tip him off about your hopes to, say, copy his new product. If you wish to make your inquiry discreetly, a company dedicated exclusively to that task, FOI Services Inc. of Rockville, Maryland, will make the request for you.

Reading Uniform Commercial Code Filings   In most states, when a secured loan is made, the lender files with the state data about the company to which it lent the money. From these filings, which are public documents, one may draw inferences about the finances of the borrower and what the loan was to be used for, as well as other valuable information.

The fourth category embraces techniques for directly observing competitors or analyzing physical evidence of their activities:

Measuring Rust on the Rails   In the absence of better information on market share and the volume of a product competitors are shipping, companies have measured the rust on the rails of railroad sidings leading to their competitors' plants or have counted the tractor-trailers leaving loading bays there. By noting the length of the trailers and the dimensions of the cartons carrying the competitor's product, the snooper can estimate how much is being shipped in each truckload.

Taking Plant Tours Companies often have executives take tours of competitors' plants to get details of their manufacturing processes and output. If tours are not given to the public and if the people requesting the tour are not honest about their identity, this is probably illegal.

Under a chief executive who has since died, Avalon Industries Inc., a crayon and toy manufacturer in Brooklyn, New York, encouraged its salespeople to make tours of competitors' plants under assumed identities. Posing as potential distributors or potential customers who had just invented a game that required crayons easily got Avalon's salespeople inside plants where they obtained sensitive information about the competitors' manufacturing processes. To make sure they could do this, Avalon trained its salespeople in the different types of machinery used in the industry. Color me dirty.

Doing Reverse-engineering Companies increasingly buy competitors' products and take them apart to examine their components. From such analysis they can determine costs of production and sometimes even manufacturing methods.

Advanced Energy Technology Inc. of Boulder, Colorado, learned firsthand of such tactics. No sooner had it announced a patented new product, a type of speed-reduction gear, than it received 50 orders. About half of the requests were from competitors asking for only one or two of the gears.

Buying Competitors' Garbage While it is illegal for a company's personnel or its agents to enter a competitor's premises to collect his leavings, it is legitimate to obtain them from a trash hauler. Once it has left the competitor's premises, refuse is legally considered abandoned property. While some companies now shred the paper coming out of their design labs, they often neglect to do this for almost-as-revealing refuse from the marketing or public relations departments.

A final observation about ethics. Some of these practices seem unassailable. In fact, an executive who fails to take advantage of information that is publicly available may be neglecting his fiduciary duty to shareholders. But many more questionable practices seem to fit one of two unsavory patterns. In the first, the snooper deals directly with the competitor, its employees, or its former employees. He often misleads the person he's dealing with or at least trades on his or her credulity. In the second pattern the snooper goes to somebody else—a supplier, say, or a customer—and deceives or pressures him. As part of the bargain, usually this person in turn betrays the confidence of someone who trusted him, a betrayal the snooper has helped bring on.

Is this kind of behavior worth it? The answer to that separates honorable managers from the other kind.

Mum's the Word

Susan Chace and James A. White

The signs that used to warn sailors not to tell their sweethearts where they were bound sometimes show up on the walls at International Business Machines plants. "Loose lips sink ships," they say.

IBM has spent $7.9 billion on research in the past six years. The effort has generated thousands of bits of information that would be valuable to rivals in its highly competitive and technologically fast-moving computer business. IBM has long prided itself on beating those rivals to the market with new equipment while also keeping them off balance through pricing and product-timing strategies.

But IBM has a world-wide system of computerized communications networks, with hundreds of plants, laboratories, branch offices and administrative buildings. There are in all more than 350,000 IBM employees. The combination of having countless important trade secrets, a huge and farflung staff and a powerful sense of corporate self-interest gives IBM the incentive for a mighty effort at confidentiality, and it makes that effort. As a spokesman for the company observes, "We take extraordinary measures to protect our assets."

THE STING

The public got an idea of those measures recently when charges were brought against 22 Japanese, American and Iranian businessmen for allegedly conspiring to steal IBM computer information. IBM cooperated with the Federal Bureau of Investigation in a "sting" operation to nab officials of Hitachi Ltd. and Mitsubishi Electric Corp. who allegedly paid more than $600,000 in an attempt to get IBM product manuals, code books and computer parts.

IBM's security effort has had lapses as well as successes. But on the whole it has been remarkably effective, especially in view of the company's size. Says Jack Bologna, the president of a computer-security consulting firm, "Anyone in that position is going to get clipped once in a while, but IBM does a better job than anyone else making commercial computer equipment of protecting its assets."

The perils to a computer company's "assets" are numerous. The most obvious is theft. A complete computer memory device was once stolen from an IBM factory in San Jose, California.

But IBM also has to worry about "theft" of people, the people who know its secrets. This is obviously hard to prove, but the company sometimes tries. IBM sued one small computer firm because 66 of its 150 employees were former IBMers supposedly hired for their knowledge of IBM methods, and it complained that Memorex Corp. was doing the same thing. Both suits were settled out of court.

PROJECT KGB

But while the company makes a great effort to imbue the staff with a sense of confidentiality, it doesn't just rely on that conscience. IBM makes frequent security checks on employees, keeps careful track of all classified documents and makes copious use of code names. When Peachtree Software Inc. of Atlanta developed materials for the IBM personal computer, IBM even took over the trash-disposal system at Peachtree's cordoned-off work rooms. Security was so tight that Peachtree dubbed the operation "Project KGB."

One big worry is the departing employee who is going to work for a rival company. Of the 2,500 former employees listed in the IBM Alumni Directory, "well over 2,000" are still working in computer-related fields, says Robert McGrath, the directory's publisher. Many hold high positions at their new firms.

A recent issue of Think, IBM's internal magazine, told of an engineer who quit to join a competitor, only to return the next day. He explained that the competitor just wanted to milk his IBM knowledge, and he said he had indignantly refused to cooperate. He got his old job back—then quit again a few months later, joining the same competitor but this time carrying lots of confidential information with him. IBM says its lawyers met with officials of the other company and the man was fired.

Those who leave IBM are expected to sign certificates saying they have returned all classified documents. The force of this certificate is such that many former employees say that if they later find classified papers that may have slipped into other material, they immediately shred them.

The affidavits also say the departing employee won't ever discuss confidential IBM information. One former employee, George McQuilken, says that at his signing he was also presented with an attached list of confidential items to which IBM said he had been exposed. Mr. McQuilken, now the president of Spartacus Computers Inc. of Lexington, Mass., protested that he hadn't even heard of some of the documents, and on his lawyer's advice he refused to sign the list.

Documents at IBM come in four different levels of confidentiality. The lowest, "for IBM internal use only," applies to such matters as a bare-bones telephone directory without titles. "IBM confidential" covers such things as maintenance manuals and was the classification of some documents allegedly sought by Hitachi. The third layer, "restricted confidential," covers routine business analysis, while the super-secret "registered confidential" applies to sensitive product designs and plans.

NEED TO KNOW

At each major facility, a registrar of classified documents keeps the most confidential material. This official also maintains a "need to know" list, telling which employees can see what. Special couriers move documents between buildings, and most copier machines print codes on each page duplicated to help trace any later leaks. Security officers check to be sure people who have signed out secret documents still have them.

The officers also make random night checks to be sure that confidential information isn't left on desks and that every desk that has a lock *is* locked. Glen Myers, a former IBMer now at Intel Corp., says he once was cited for neglecting to lock a file cabinet that was empty.

Heaven help the employee who loses a document. "Nobody would dare ask for a second copy of a sales plan after signing for it," says Dik Vink, a former IBM marketing manager, because doing so "would arouse suspicion that it was given away."

IBM employees may also find their electronic files subject to scrutiny. Former IBMers say the company audited electronic files randomly and without warning, telling employees that it was checking to make sure no one was playing computer games, moonlighting or otherwise misusing computer equipment or information. IBM defends such checks as necessary to protect shareholders' assets.

Finally, IBM is a devotee of the code name, a device widely used in the computer industry to throw nosy competitors off the scent. Code names tend to be changed frequently, confusing outsiders—and even some uninformed employees—by making it unclear whether a project has been scrapped or just rechristened.

So it was that a group of IBM office products were named after champion horses; there was a Secretariat, for instance, and there was a Whirlaway. Telecommunications products tend to take on the aroma of flowers: IBM has used carnation, rosebud and primrose. Small mainframe computers of the 4300 series were named after tribes such as the Inca, the Aztec and the Maya. And when IBM approached the FBI last October, setting in motion the recent sting operation, it said Hitachi had obtained secret knowledge about the Adirondacks—not the mountains but the 3081 family of computers.

A General Strategy for Getting Out of Traps

Samuel A. Culbert

THE MODEL

The model portrays a strategy for gaining greater control of our organization life, a strategy that entails a process of consciousness-raising and self-directed resocialization. In theory, this process can be broken down into five sequential stages, each of which involves a separate consciousness-raising activity. In practice, of course, these five stages can be intermingled and used out of sequence. Where possible, however, the stages should be followed in sequence because the insights developed at one stage provide the beginning points for consciousness-raising at the next stage. Learning at each stage depends on our developing skills and receiving peer group support.

Consciousness-raising can best be accomplished by focusing on a single area of organization concerns and working our way through each of the five stages of the model. Maintaining focus on a single area at a time requires discipline because insights in one area inevitably spark insights in others. Overall, the consciousness-raising process can be likened to eating an artichoke. One starts with the less meaty leaves on the periphery and progressively spirals in toward the more meaty leaves closer to the heart. Unlike eating an artichoke, however, we don't reach the heart, that is, gain control over our organization life; we merely get closer. Each insight paves the way for a meatier realization.

Experience in using this model has shown that a preliminary overview of all five stages facilitates a deeper understanding of each stage. That is the purpose of this chapter. . . .

STAGE 1: RECOGNIZING WHAT'S "OFF"

Consciousness-raising begins with a gut experience. We develop a vague awareness that something in our organization life is "off," although we can't quite put our fingers on exactly what it is. Such feelings of incoherence are frequent occurrences in our organization life, but usually we try to forget about them. However, if we want our consciousness raised,

---

we've got to be ready to pay attention to what seems minor. Closer scrutiny will usually show much more beneath the surface than we saw originally.

Our vague feelings of incoherence serve as clues to identifying discrepancies between our nature and the expectations of the organization system. Such discrepancies usually fall into one of two categories. The first is when the organization seems to expect something that is unnatural for us or inconsistent with our best interests. The second is when we do what comes naturally and learn afterward that it was deemed inappropriate by the system.

Transforming feelings of incoherence into a more precise statement of discrepancies requires some concepts and some emotional support. The concepts will help us pinpoint where we and the organization are in conflict, and the support will help us resist our tendency to shoulder all the blame for these conflicts.

STAGE 2: UNDERSTANDING OURSELVES AND THE ORGANIZATION

Being able to specify discrepancies may make us feel that we can now proceed to solve our problems with the organization and put our minds at ease. Usually, this proves to be a short-sighted strategy. We need to treat discrepancies for what they are, symptoms rather than problems. In practice, taking our conflicts with the organization at face value and "resolving" them can be the surest way to keep from seeing the fundamental ills of the system as we currently live it.

Treating discrepancies as symptoms, on the other hand, helps us to understand aspects of ourselves and the organization that we had not previously recognized. We have a chance to probe beneath the discrepancy by asking ourselves what human qualities and what organization attributes can produce the conflicts we're experiencing.

Transforming discrepancies into new understanding requires skills to think divergently and support to resist our inclinations to think convergently. Divergent thinking keeps us focused on the fact that a discrepancy is a symptom of some lack in basic understanding. The support we get will help us resist our impulses to converge on a solution that prematurely puts our anxieties to rest.

STAGE 3: UNDERSTANDING OUR RELATIONSHIP WITH THE ORGANIZATION

Greater understanding of ourselves and of the organization system helps us to recognize alternatives that suit our interests and to resist external attempts to control us. We sense a new personal freedom. However, getting carried away by this "freedom" proves to be another short-term strategy for gaining control. It puts us underground, "working" the system. But eventually, those who however unwittingly influence and control us will discover that we've eluded them, and we'll be back playing cat and dog again.

In order to really improve things, we'll need, at some point, to focus directly on our relationship with the organization. The new understanding we developed in Stage 2, about ourselves and the organization, can now be transformed into a more thorough understanding of the assumptions that link us to the organization system. This requires that we learn about our conditioning in the organization and that we get assistance in doing this from people we trust. Some of our biases are so ingrained we will require tough-minded challenging to break through to them.

STAGE 4: MOVING TOWARD A MORE NATURAL LIFE IN THE ORGANIZATION

Increased understanding of ourselves, the organization, and our relationship with the organization will give us a new sense of power; we can now formulate the types of relationships that will give us greater control over our organization life. But while we can envision more optimal relationships, we do not yet know all that we need to know in order to see whether we can formulate alternatives that express our self-interests and yet appear practical from the standpoint of organization goals.

Transforming understanding of ourselves, the organization, and the assumptions that link us to the organization into practical alternatives also requires new skills and support. We need skills in identifying tensions between assumptions the organization makes about us and the person we're discovering ourselves to be. We need support to help us reflect on personal priorities before getting caught up in our attempts to renegotiate our relationship with the organization.

STAGE 5: AFFECTING THE ORGANIZATION LIVES OF OTHERS

Being able to envision practical alternatives gives us a great deal of control over our organization life. We derive a new sense of independence from knowing that our options are no longer limited to the best ideas that others have for us. However, as long as others in the organization are still out of control, their spontaneous actions will set off forces that oppose the mutually beneficial directions we may try to take.

Making suggestions that change and improve the organization system requires that we be mindful of the personal realities of all the people affected. To adopt a strategy where we impose our improvements on others runs counter to our reasons for wanting change in the first place. We need to think about change as if we were statesmen concerned with the well-being of all the people. We need support from a peer group that recognizes what we're trying to accomplish and that can help us maintain our focus at times when its difficult for us to observe the effects our efforts are having.

REFLECTION

This model is applicable to most nontechnical aspects of organization life. It is one attempt to reverse the machinery of a runaway system that influences us without our knowing it.

Gaining control eventually means probing all critical areas of organization life. However, the best place to start is with the area that is currently causing the greatest discomfort. This is where you've got the energy to maintain your focus. Of course, the first area will require the greatest concentration because you'll not only be learning specific things about your organization life but you'll also be acquiring the analytic skills necessary for consciousness-raising. Thus, you can expect a cumulative effect that enables gains made in one area to shorten the work needed in another. Nevertheless, consciousness-raising is a continuing process that requires returning over and over again to the same areas. . . . We're now at a point where we can develop more confidence in our grasp of this model by following an example through each stage of consciousness-raising.

Example

The following experiment was carried out by a group of European engineers and their wives. It grew out of their distress and sense of helplessness over the personnel practices that governed relocations to company headquarters in the United States. At the end of the experiment, they were asserting themselves and suggesting improvements of a quality seldom expressed at their company level.

Each of the thirteen engineers involved was beginning a one-and-a-half to two-year training assignment in the United States, spoke English, and were men. Most had first- or second-level supervisory experience. All were married. Their ages ranged from thirty to forty-five, and they had between three and twenty-five years experience with the company. The typical person was about thirty-three, had been with the company five years, and had two children. Initially, these engineers met to discuss adjustment problems created by their recent transfer. But when they became familiar with the consciousness-raising process, they decided to expand the scope of their discussions. They began meeting regularly, one entire day a month, and went on meeting for a year and a half.

As we have learned, the first stage of consciousness-raising uses feelings of incoherence to identify discrepancies, and this requires support and time for catharsis. In this instance, the engineers needed to overcome a feeling that "If I were just a little more adequate, I wouldn't have all these adjustment problems." They also needed time to release pent-up feelings of anger and frustration over the specific problems they'd been experiencing.

There was resentment with the company in general, and early discussions revealed problems and discrepancies in nearly every aspect of their work life. Some engineers complained that they had not been consulted when the transfer was planned for them, and some felt that not knowing the career consequences of turning it down forced them to move at inconvenient times for their family. Some resented that their wives were expected to leave good jobs without permits to work in the United States.

There was also resentment with the personnel department, which was charged with helping families relocate. The engineers complained that the neighborhoods chosen for their relocation suited the company's image rather than their own styles and preferences; that unfair policies dictated what they were allowed to ship at company expense; and that they had lost money as a result of the compensation formula that was supposed to provide them with a standard of living comparable with what they had left in Europe and commensurate with what people in the United States earn for performing similar jobs.

There was resentment against the departments to which they had been reassigned. Some complained of bosses who were only understanding of relocation pressures as long as they put in a productive eight-hour day. Some complained that their expertise was disregarded because U.S. engineering practices were considered the best in the world.

The engineers resented their families because they were expected to make friends for their wives and were held accountable for problems that their children encountered at school. Some complained that their families treated the U.S. assignment as if it were a long vacation and were putting pressures on them to sightsee on weekends, when they needed time to rest and recoup from the pressures of the week.

The engineers resented the managers who made the decisions for international relocations. They didn't like the idea that they were considered a part of a mobile work force that could be picked up and moved every few years. Some felt misled by the promises of rapid advancement that had been made when they were hired.

Overall, each of the engineers seemed to be suffering the pains of culture shock, because even the smallest problems seemed to be causing them high levels of concern and anxiety. Moreover, although each engineer complained of something different, listening to one another's complaints caused them to realize that various problems had similar causes.

The engineers soon realized that for their support group to be complete their wives would have to be included. Not only were the women deeply affected by relocation pressures but they were an essential part of the family's resources for coping with adjustment problems. At the end of the second meeting, the men decided to expand their group to include their wives. This type of unprecedented involvement in company matters, however, seemed to present additional adjustment pressures for two wives, and they declined to participate.

Once a list of discrepancies was identified, the group could turn their attention to the second stage of the consciousness-raising model. A period of divergent analysis produced many insights and clarifications about the actual workings of the organization system. The engineers' insights included discovering that they believed that the company knew what's best for them; that they were afraid to turn down a transfer; that they were excessively dependent on the advice they get from higher level managers; that they felt the technical expertise they had developed in Europe was damn good and often superior to the methods used in the United States; that the longer they work for the company, becoming more technically specialized, the less desirable they become on the open job market; that being transferred caused them to feel insecure and marginal, like a guest who should follow the customs of his host; and that, in general, they didn't have the information they needed to manage their organization life intelligently.

Divergent analysis clarified their view of the organization system. The engineers discovered that policies regarding transfer allowances and compensation were not open for discussion, despite the image the personnel department tried to create; that people were controlled by never being sure of the consequences of saying no to a managerial request; that while people were encouraged to explore differences openly, they had better not be caught differing with their bosses in public; that a fail-safe system was emphasized, where the rewards for being right were seldom high enough to offset the punishments for being wrong; that they couldn't count on self-perspectives being solicited or considered when decisions were made about them; that families were treated as if they were mere appendages to the husband; and that the company's desire to put forth a conservative image often invaded their personal lives.

Strengthened by the divergent analysis of discrepancies, the engineers and their wives decided to collect some additional information about the actual way the system works and the assumptions made about them. They focused on the transfer process, because it was the primary source of their current anxieties, and on the personnel department that administered these transfers. They decided to interview a representative sampling of those involved in transfer decisions. In order to cover themselves organizationally, they advised the personnel director of their plan. Because they were not asking for his permission, it would have taken more energy than it was worth for him to object.

The engineers and their wives were surprised at the results of their interviews. They discovered that despite the reassurances that management gave them about the transfer process, their feelings of uneasiness were well founded. Before a transfer was offered, the proposed move was passed up the line, level by level, to a vice-president. If blessed by him, the word went out to the personnel department, which asked the man about his interests. By this time, all managers concerned with the man's career are convinced that the transfer is a good idea. If the man refuses, the reasons for his refusal go back up the line to "a very disappointed" vice-president. The engineers concluded that it's misleading to assume that an immediate supervisor, representative of the personnel department, or any other company manager can present them with even-handed advice. They realized that each person in this chain had to answer many questions if a proposed transfer was refused.

Most families felt that they were not advised about all the benefits that were due them. The interviews determined, contrary to some of their suspicions, that the personnel department was not getting cost-effectiveness credit for saving money on unused transfer allowances. While personnel representatives didn't tell people about all the benefits to which they were entitled, they did this out of fear that a superior might come down hard on them if the company were exploited by a transferring family. As the personnel director frankly admitted, "Most line managers, as well as myself, have a tendency to formulate policies that protect against the two percent who are inclined to test the rules. I guess we sometimes overprotect the company."

Many other realizations crystallized as group members discussed what they had learned from their interviews. However, the main point was established: the engineers and their wives obtained perspectives that added to what they were able to induce from their own experience. Combined with what they had formerly realized, they were able to construct a better picture of the assumptions made about them and the actual way the organization worked. The fact that they chose to investigate transfers is secondary to the fact that they investigated an organization process.

Combining the information received from facing feelings of incoherence, identifying discrepancies, using divergent analysis, and interviewing others gave the engineers and their wives a more realistic picture of their relationships to the organization. At this point, they were involved in the third stage of consciousness-raising, and they began to comprehend more fully the vulnerabilities and costs involved in paternalistic liaisons like the ones they had formed with the company. They had traded understanding themselves and the organization for promises of protection and security. They discovered that company terms like career track, maturing process, and professional development were cover-ups for moving people around to meet corporate needs. Recognizing that transfers were motivated at least as much by company needs as by their own needs for training and development, they learned what they needed to know to make demands and direct company resources toward their own personal and professional objectives. If a so-called training assignment was not teaching them much, they realized it was their responsibility to make the trade-off more equitable. Consciousness-raising was exposing assumptions that blocked the self-management of their lives.

The engineers and their wives were also surprised to discover that the more they learned about how the system worked, and the assumptions made about the people who comprise the system, the fewer villains they found. Increased knowledge led them to realize that no one was doing them in intentionally. For example, they could no longer reason that the personnel department was simply trying to make their own jobs easier at the expense of transferring families. If anything, the personnel department was in a worse box, for they were expected to have an answer for every question, and their answers were supposed to be consistent with any number of company policies built on erroneous and inconsistent assumptions about the human qualities of the people involved.

While each stage of consciousness-raising had its own immediate effects, providing the engineers and wives with increasingly accurate pictures of reality, there was a bigger payoff. This came in the fourth stage of consciousness-raising, when they used what they had learned to envision alternatives. Among the specific problems that transferring families had with personnel procedures was the almost inconsequential one in which a family of music buffs was refused an allowance to ship some records to the United States. The family reasoned that because they had not used two of their three-crate allowance for books, they were entitled to ship at least two crates of records. The personnel representative handling this request reasoned that this was not possible, because if he granted them permission to do this, others would demand the right to ship records in addition to books.

At first glance, it seemed like this couple was making a big deal out of nothing. Someone else might reason, "The hell with personnel. I'll ship the records at my own expense and tack on an extra twenty-dollar cab fare to my moving expenses." But to this couple, their problem seemed to hold symbolic importance, although they couldn't initially figure out why. In fact, when I first asked them why it was so important, they looked sheepish and self-doubting.

But as the consciousness-raising progressed, their problem became the group's rallying point, and when its meaning and solution became evident, the group's sign of success. Wrapped up in this problem were all the assumptions an organization system makes when treating workers like children. Only if you assume you are a child, can you, as a matter of course, think of asking permission for something as inconsequential as substituting records for books. When the group discovered that the company leaders and the personnel director really intended to make transfers as easy as possible without much concern for costs, they were able to see numerous problems stemming from the same kind of discrepancy.

As the engineers and their wives discovered more about themselves, they learned that they often chided and complained like kids who don't get their way or when they felt trapped by a seemingly irrational company policy. The consciousness-raising process eventually led them to see that the entire transfer process was built on assumptions that they were children who must be monitored and closely supervised. The incident about the records would never have taken place if the existing procedure did not begin by telling people what they were entitled to take.

Envisioning alternatives became a relatively easy task once the group spotted inconsistencies between the organization's assumptions and expectations and what they believed to be their true nature. Until they discovered this difference in assumptions, each of their counterproposals merely perpetuated their dependence. Once they were able to articulate that they'd like to be treated like adults, it was relatively easy for them to envision alternatives. If prior to consciousness-raising someone had asked the engineers whether or not they were being treated and acted like adults, I'd guess only a few would have noticed that they were not. The tendency to believe that we are like our ideals is one of the most troublesome barriers to envisioning alternatives to current practices.

Reflection

In contrast to the pictures of reality acquired during socialization, the process of envisioning alternatives is mainly conscious, compatible with self-interests, and based on the lessons of our own experience. This time around, we shape our own reality, and if we get in trouble with the system, we'll have to take our lumps. But the lumps we take replace the lumps we've been taking all along without knowing it.

Newly envisioned alternatives stimulate an inner need either to change the organization system or to renegotiate our relationship with it. If the system fails to change or is intolerant of the changes we want to make, then we have a decision to make. At the extremes, we can either leave or live in discontent. Ultimately, no system is ideal for all the people who live in it. Some adaptation is always necessary; that's the nature of man's social contract. We'll have to reach our decision to stay or leave by weighing our priorities for change against our alternatives outside the organization. But we also must realize there is no Camelot; certain compromises are always necessary, and explicating our compromises allows us to take responsibility for our organization life.

Deciding whether or not there's a match between the alternatives we formulate and the goals of the system is a crucial step. We must not waste time deluding ourselves that we can make irreconcilables fit. We must know when we can modify our proposal in a way that makes no appreciable difference to us. This relies on our developing a thorough knowledge of the actual system. And, of course, we must also see when there's a ready fit. For example, the engineers and their wives formally proposed that personnel change their policies to treat them like responsible adults. They suggested that personnel ask transferring families what they need to take and what assistance they might like to have in making their transfer comfortable. Then if a request seemed excessive, the personnel representative could inquire further. A task force set up to consider their suggestion recommended that it be embodied in an experiment. Management expects this experiment to save the company money by people no longer shipping things they're entitled to, but don't particularly need, by reduced managerial aggravation, and by quicker adjustments to a new culture for the families involved. And the families are getting what they want: more control and autonomy in their relocation.

Even in instances such as the above, where benefits to the organization are readily apparent, there may be resistance. This is due to people with power assuming that each small step we take toward greater freedom and self-management means less control for them. They may not fear the particular step being negotiated as much as the step we'll want to take next. . . .

CONCLUSION: THE IMPORTANCE OF BEING OURSELVES

Why would a Ph.D. chemist spend years trying to invent a new toothpaste flavor? Why would an administrator spend his work life putting other people's plans into action? Why would a manager put in long hours away from home to earn money for stockholders he's never met? These people are not that different from us; in fact, they are us. Our commitment to the goals of the organizations for which we work exceeds the money we receive for our efforts. We are committed to our jobs because of the opportunities that they provide us with to do something personally meaningful with our lives. We seek work that allows us to develop and expand our capabilities, and form associations that give a deep human dimension to our lives. Working to invent a new toothpaste flavor, to put the ideas of others into action, to earn money for stockholders are all vehicles for accomplishing something more important. Yet it's so easy to lose perspective and think these are our goals.

We have lived too long with the assumption that organizations are accountable only to their owners. They also should be accountable to us, the people who comprise organizations. We have staked our lives on their ability to provide us with meaningful and challenging work. We must not be unduly intimidated by the numbers of people who are worrying exclusively about rates of return on invested capital, performance effectiveness, or whatever, as if these constituted all there was to evaluating the organization's output. We can't afford to put our fates exclusively in the hands of people who don't relate to the greater meaning our work holds for us.

If we can't count on them, then we've got to count on ourselves! Each of us needs a personal frame of reference that gives focus and commitment to our projects and helps us see when our activities are out of sync with personal priorities. We know organization life is a compromise; we don't need to hear that one again. But we want to lead our lives with our compromises explicit. We want to know when we're in danger of sacrificing something that must not be compromised or when we're sacrificing more than we're receiving in exchange.

When we approach the organization with our own frame of reference, we run the risk of having such a narrow focus that all we get is what we expect. Creating an open-ended focus that still allows us to extract personal relevance from the infinitude of what's taking place depends on the types of questions we ask ourselves. When our questions are convergent, then our organization world becomes a closed system. But when our questions are phrased divergently, then we open ourselves to surprises, new meaning, and learning.

Asking the right kinds of questions, developing a frame of reference that allows us to be our own organization man, gets us to the point where we can declare ourselves and make our own special peace with the organization world, if only to revise it at another time. Making peace is not the same as copping out or retiring on the job. It means developing our own focus and pursuing it as long as it makes sense to us. During a candid discussion on career development, I heard a fifty-year-old manager with a solid record of organization service say to the big boss, "I don't want to be president. I don't even want to be a division head or an associate head. I'm no longer all that concerned with status. I don't have all the money that I could use, but I have all I need. I just want to be challenged." Then he turned down a promotion to manage a very large operation in a technical area in which he had years of experience, and volunteered to manage a small and little-understood aspect of the company's business. It was an impressive moment.

But learning how to live with the divergent questions necessary for developing this kind of perspective is not all that easy. In the divergent thinking sessions I've led with management groups, I've never seen one go by without somebody becoming quite upset with the process. In a typical instance, a normally rational advertising manager stood up, red in the face, shouting, "I can't see where all this is going to get us," as if he was sure it was going to sweep us right down the tubes. And this was only ten minutes into an all-day meeting. A few minutes of gentle inquiry were all that was necessary to set him straight. It turned out that he wasn't even angry; he was anxious. Because he couldn't identify anything that could be making him anxious, he assumed he was angry, and seized upon a reason to explode. He had the right event, just the wrong emotion. In focusing divergently, we were violating a thought structure from which he normally derived security. As this became explicit, others admitted to their own uneasiness, and normal color returned to his face. The advertising manager then settled back and became a keen contributor.

Meeting organization life with a divergent focus requires support. Throughout this book I've emphasized the role a support group plays in helping us do this. Everyone I've ever seen make substantial progress has had the support of a group. People who lack understanding of how to get group support, or who excercise extreme discipline and aren't able to blow their cool, like the advertising manager blew his, do not get the support they need to aggressively seek out greater consciousness.

Perhaps the biggest obstacle to making organization life more consistent with our needs and interests lies in the difficulty people have in being themselves and holding candid discussions about the human elements in their work life. Even so-called human development experts are reluctant to approach human concerns directly. We have learned that it's easier to get an audience when we begin talking about new ways to improve productivity or increase work group effectiveness. We've taken this tack as a foot-in-the-door to getting people to talk about the personal and social qualities of their life in the organization. We reason that planners cannot think too long about productivity goals without thinking about the people involved. We reason that work groups can't talk too long about decision making and communications without discussing personal and interpersonal needs. But while our reasoning is logical enough, we often lose out in practice. We consistently underestimate the resistance people marshal when it comes time to exhibit and talk about the human and personal issues of their organization life. Too often our tactics wind up merely supporting the status quo!

Thus, I have my doubts about any strategy for organization change that indirectly approaches the human elements of organization life. I also have my doubts about any strategy that allows people at the top to plan for people on the bottom, or any strategy that features people at any level critiquing others, but not themselves.

More than anything else, I believe the quality of our organization life depends on the level of humanity and naturalness we're personally willing to discover and exhibit. We can't reasonably expect to exhibit more candor to others than we are willing to accept in ourselves. Self-candor begins with self-acceptance. We need to accept who we discover ourselves to be, and open-endedly inquire whether or not there's more. No doubt we'll uncover some crucial gaps between our ideals and our reality. Acknowledging these gaps and divergently reflecting on their meaning take us to the next frontier of self-understanding and expression.

Of Boxes, Bubbles, and Effective Management

David K. Hurst

Harvard Business Review
Soldiers Field Road
Boston, Massachusetts 02163

Dear Editors:

We are writing to tell you how events from 1979 on have forced us, a team of four general managers indistinguishable from thousands of others, to change our view of what managers should do. In 1979 we were working for Hugh Russel Inc., the fiftieth largest public company in Canada. Hugh Russel was an industrial distributor with some $535 million in sales and a net income of $14 milllion. The organization structure was conventional: 16 divisions in four groups, each with a group president reporting to the corporate office. Three volumes of corporate policy manuals spelled out detailed aspects of corporate life, including our corporate philosophy. In short, in 1979 our corporation was like thousands of other businesses in North America.

During 1980, however, through a series of unlikely turns, that situation changed drastically. Hugh Russel found itself acquired in a 100% leveraged buyout and then merged with a large, unprofitable (that's being kind!) steel fabricator, York Steel Construction, Ltd. The resulting entity was York Russel Inc., a privately held company except for the existence of some publicly owned preferred stock which obliged us to report to the public.

As members of the acquired company's corporate office, we waited nervously for the ax to fall. Nothing happened. Finally, after six weeks, Wayne (now our president) asked the new owner if we could do anything

---

Editor's note: All references are listed at the end of the article.

to help the deal along. The new chairman was delighted and gave us complete access to information about the acquirer.

It soon became apparent that the acquiring organization had little management strength. The business had been run in an entrepreneurial style with hundreds of people reporting to a single autocrat. The business had, therefore, no comprehensive plan and, worse still, no money. The deal had been desperately conceived to shelter our profits from taxes and use the resulting cash flow to fund the excessive debt of the steel fabrication business.

Our first job was to hastily assemble a task force to put together a $300 million bank loan application and a credible turnaround plan. Our four-member management team (plus six others who formed a task force) did it in only six weeks. The merged business, York Russel, ended up with $10 million of equity and $275 million of debt on the eve of a recession that turned out to be the worst Canada had experienced since the Great Depression. It was our job then to save the new company, somehow.

Conceptual frameworks are important aids to managers' perceptions, and every team should have a member who can build them. Before the acquisition, the framework implicit in our organization was a "hard," rational model rather like those Thomas Peters and Robert Waterman describe.[1] Jay Galbraith's elaborate model is one of the purest examples of the structure-follows-strategy school.[2] The model clearly defines all elements and their relationships to each other, presumably so that they can be measured (see the *Exhibit*).

Because circumstances changed after the acquisition, our framework fell apart almost immediately. Overnight we went from working for a growth company to working for one whose only objective was survival. Our old decentralized organization was cumbersome and expensive; our new organization needed cash, not profits. Bankers and suppliers swarmed all over us, and the quiet life of a management-controlled public company was gone.

Compounding our difficulties, the recession quickly revealed all sorts of problems in businesses that up to that time had given us no trouble. Even the core nuggets offered up only meager profits, while interest rates of up to 25% quickly destroyed what was left of the balance sheet.

In the heat of the crisis, the management team jelled quickly. At first each member muddled in his own way, but as time went by, we started to gain a new understanding of how to be effective. Even now we do not completely understand the conceptual framework that has evolved, and maybe we never will. What follows is our best attempt to describe to you and your readers what guides us today.

Yours truly,

The management team

TWO MODELS ARE BETTER THAN ONE

The hard, rational model isn't wrong; it just isn't enough. There is something more. As it turns out, there is a great deal more.

At York Russel we have had to develop a "soft," intuitive framework that offers a counterpart to every element in the hard, rational framework. As the exhibit shows and the following sections discuss, in the soft model, roles are the counterparts of tasks, groups replace structure, networks operate instead of information systems, the rewards are soft as opposed to hard, and people are viewed as social animals rather than as rational beings.

That may not sound very new. But we found that the key to effective management of not only our crisis but also the routine is to know whether we are in a hard "box" or a soft "bubble" context. By recognizing the dichotomy between the two, we can choose the appropriate framework.

- ■ **Tasks** ...&...
- ■ Static
- ■ Clarity
- ■ Content
- ■ Fact
- ■ Science

- ● **Roles**
- ● Fluid
- ● Ambiguity
- ● Process
- ● Perception
- ● Art

These are some of our favorite words for contrasting these two aspects of management. Here's how we discovered them.

The merger changed our agenda completely. We had new shareholders, a new bank, a new business (the steel fabrication operations consisted of nine divisions), and a new relationship with the managers of our subsidiaries, who were used to being left alone to grow. The recession and high interest rates rendered the corporation insolvent. Bankruptcy loomed large. Further, our previously static way of operating became very fluid.

In general, few of us had clear tasks, and for the most part we saw the future as ambiguous and fearful. We found ourselves describing what we had to do as roles rather than as tasks. At first our descriptions were crude. We talked of having an "inside man" who deals with administration, lawyers, and bankers versus an "outside man" who deals with operations, customers, and suppliers. Some of us were "readers," others "writers," some "talkers," and others "listeners." As the readers studied the work of behavioral science researchers and talked to the listeners, we found some more useful classifications. Henry Mintzberg's description of managers' work in terms of three roles—interpersonal (figurehead, leader, liaison), informational (monitor, disseminator, spokesperson), and decisional—helped us see the variety of the job.[3] Edgar Schein's analysis of group roles helped us concentrate on the process of communication as well as on what was communicated.[4]

The most useful framework we used was the one Ichak Adize developed for decision-making roles.[5] In his view, a successful management team needs to play four distinct parts. The first is that of producer of results. A *producer* is action oriented and knowledgeable in his or her field; he or she helps compile plans with an eye to their implementability. The *administrator* supervises the system and manages the detail. The *entrepreneur* is a creative risk taker who initiates action, comes up with new ideas, and challenges existing policies. And the *integrator* brings people together socially and their ideas intellectually, and interprets the significance of events. The integrator gives the team a sense of direction and shared experience.

According to Adize, each member must have some appreciation of the others' roles (by having some facility in those areas), and it is essential that they get along socially. At York Russel the producers (who typically come out of operations) and administrators (usually accountants) tend to be hard box players, while the entrepreneurs tend to live in the soft bubble. Integrators (friendly, unusually humble MBAs) move between the hard and the soft, and we've found a sense of humor is essential to being able to do that well.

The key to a functioning harmonious group, however, has been for members to understand that they might disagree with each other because they are in two different contexts. Different conceptual frameworks may lead people to different conclusions based on the same facts. Of the words describing tasks and roles, our favorite pair is "fact" versus "perception." People in different boxes will argue with each other over facts, for facts in boxes are compelling—they seem so tangible. Only from a bubble can one see them for what they are: abstractions based on the logical frameworks, or boxes, being used.

■ Structure ...&...	● Groups
■ Cool	● Warm
■ Formal	● Informal
■ Closed	● Open
■ Obedience	● Trust
■ Independence	● Autonomy

Our premerger corporation was a pretty cold place to work. Senior management kept control in a tight inner circle and then played hardball (in a hard box, of course) with the group presidents. Managers negotiated budgets and plans on a win-lose basis; action plans almost exclusively controlled what was done in the organization. Top managers kept a lot of information to themselves. People didn't trust each other very much.

The crises that struck the corporation in 1980 were so serious that we could not have concealed them even if we had wanted to. We were forced to put together a multitude of task forces consisting of people from all parts of the organization to address these urgent issues, and in the process, we had to reveal everything we knew, whether it was confidential or not.

We were amazed at the task forces' responses: instead of resigning en masse (the hard box players had said that people would leave the company when they found out that it was insolvent), the teams tackled their projects with passion. Warmth, a sense of belonging, and trust characterized the groups; the more we let them know what was going on, the more we received from them. Confidentiality is the enemy of trust. In the old days strategic plans were stamped "confidential." Now we know that paper plans mean nothing if they are not in the minds of the managers.

Division managers at first resented our intrusion into their formal, closed world. "What happened to independence?" they demanded. We described the soft counterpart—autonomy—to them. Unlike independence, autonomy cannot be granted once and for all. In our earlier life, division personnel told the corporate office what they thought it wanted to hear. "You've got to keep those guys at arm's length" was a typical division belief. An autonomous relationship depends on trust for its nourishment. "The more you level with us," we said, "the more we'll leave you alone." That took some getting used to.

But in the end autonomy worked. We gave division managers confidential information, shared our hopes and fears, and incorporated their views in our bubble. They needed to be helped out of their boxes, not to abandon them altogether but to gain a deeper appreciation of and insight into how they were running their businesses. Few could resist when we walked around showing a genuine interest in their views. Because easy access to each other and opportunities for communication determine how groups form and work together, we encouraged managers to keep their doors open. We called this creation of opportunities for communication by making senior management accessible "management by walking around." Chance encounters should not be left to chance.

Although the primary objective of all this communication is to produce trust among group members, an important by-product is that the integrators among us have started to "see" the communication process.[6] In other words, they are beginning to understand why people say what they say. This ability to "see" communication is elusive at times, but when it is present, it enables us to "jump out of the box"—that is, to talk about the frameworks' supporting conclusions rather than the conclusions themselves. We have defused many potential confrontations and struck many deals by changing the context of the debate rather than the debate itself.[7]

Perhaps the best example of this process was our changing relationship with our lead banker. As the corporation's financial position deteriorated, our relationship with the bank became increasingly adversarial. The responsibility for our account rose steadily up the bank's hierarchy (we had eight different account managers in 18 months), and we received tougher and tougher "banker's speeches" from successively more senior executives. Although we worried a great deal that the bank might call the loan, the real risk was that our good businesses would be choked by overzealous efforts on the part of individual bankers to "hold the line."

Key to our ability to change the relationship was to understand why individuals were taking the positions they were. To achieve that understanding, we had to rely on a network of contacts both inside and outside the bank. We found that the bank had as many views as there were people we talked to. Fortunately, the severity of the recession and the proliferation of corporate loan problems had already blown everyone out of the old policy "boxes." It remained for us to gain the confidence of our contacts, exchange candid views of our positions, and present options that addressed the corporation's problems in the bank's context and dealt with the bank's interests.

The "hard" vehicle for this was the renegotiation of our main financing agreement. During the more than six months negotiating process, our relationship with the bank swung 180 degrees from confrontation to collaboration. The corporation's problem became a joint bank-corporation problem. We had used the bubble to find a new box in which both the corporation and the bank could live.

■ Information processes ...&...	● Networks
■ Hard	● Soft
■ Written	● Oral
■ Know	● Feel
■ Control	● Influence
■ Decision	● Implementation

Over the years our corporation has developed some excellent information systems. Our EDP facility is second to none in our industry. Before the acquisition and merger, when people talked about or requested information, they meant hard, quantitative data and written reports that would be used for control and decision making. The crisis required that we make significant changes to these systems. Because, for example, we became more interested in cash flow than earnings per share, data had to be aggregated and presented in a new way.

The pivotal change, however, was our need to communicate with a slew of new audiences over which we had little control. For instance, although we still have preferred stock quoted in the public market, our principal new shareholders were family members with little experience in professional management of public companies. Our new bankers were in organizational turmoil themselves and took 18 months to realize the horror of what they had financed. Our suppliers, hitherto benign, faced a stream of bad financial news about us and other members of the industry. The rumor mill had us in receivership on a weekly basis.

Our plant closures and cutbacks across North America brought us into a new relationship with government, unions, and the press. And we had a new internal audience: our employees, who were understandably nervous about the "imminent" bankruptcy.

We had always had some relationship with these audiences, but now we saw what important sources of information they were and expanded these networks vastly.[8] Just as we had informed the division managers at the outset, we decided not to conceal from these other groups the fact that the corporation was insolvent but worthy of support. We made oral presentations supported by formal written material to cover the most important bases.

To our surprise, this candid approach totally disarmed potential antagonists. For instance, major suppliers could not understand why we had told them we were in trouble before the numbers revealed the fact. By the time the entire war story was news, there was no doubt that our suppliers' top managers, who tended not to live in the hard accounting box, were on our side. When their financial specialists concluded that we were insolvent, top management blithely responded, "We've known that for six months."

Sharing our view of the world with constituencies external to the corporation led to other unexpected benefits, such as working in each other's interests. Our reassurance to customers that we would be around to deliver on contracts strengthened the relationship. Adversity truly is opportunity!

Management by walking around was the key to communicating with employees in all parts of the company. As a result of the continual open communication, all the employees appreciated the corporation's position. Their support has been most gratifying. One of our best talker-listeners (our president) tells of a meeting with a very nervous group of employees at one facility. After he had spent several hours explaining the company's situation, one blue-collar worker who had been with the company for years took him aside and told him that a group of employees would be prepared to take heavy pay cuts if it would save the business. It turns out that when others hear this story it reinforces *their* belief in the organization.

We have found that sharing our views and incorporating the views of others as appropriate has a curious effect on the making and the implementing of decisions. As we've said, in our previous existence the decisions we made were always backed up by hard information; management was decisive, and that was good. Unfortunately, too few of these "good" decisions ever got implemented. The simple process of making the decision the way we did often set up resistance down the line. As the decision was handed down to consecutive organizational levels, it lost impetus until eventually it was unclear whether the decision was right in the first place.

Now we worry a good deal less about making decisions; they arise as fairly obvious conclusions drawn from a mass of shared assumptions. It's the assumptions that we spend our time working on. One of our "producers" (an executive vice president) calls it "conditioning," and indeed it is. Of course, making decisions this way requires that senior management build networks with people many layers down in the organization. This kind of communication is directly at odds with the communication policy laid down in the premerger corporation, which emphasized direct-line reporting.

A consequence of this network information process is that we often have to wait for the right time to make a decision. We call the wait a "creative stall." In the old organization it would have been called procrastination, but what we're doing is waiting for some important players to come "on-side" before making an announcement.[9] In our terms, you "prepare the box and wait in the bubble."

Once the time is right, however, implementation is rapid. Everyone is totally involved and has given thought to what has to be done. Not only is the time it takes for the decision to be made and implemented shorter than in the past but also the whole process strengthens the organization rather than weakening it through bitterness about how the decision was made.

■ People ...&...	● People
■ Rational	● Social
■ Produce	● Create
■ Think	● Imagine
■ Tell	● Inspire
■ Work	● Play

In the old, premerger days, it was convenient to regard employees as rational, welfare-maximizing beings; it made motivating them so much easier and planning less messy.

But because the crisis made it necessary to close many operations and terminate thousands of employees, we had to deal with people's social nature. We could prepare people intellectually by sharing our opinions and, to some extent, protect them physically with severance packages, but we struggled with how to handle the emotional aspects. Especially for long-service employees, severing the bond with the company was the emotional equivalent of death.

Exhibit The hard and soft model and how they work together

The hard, rational model

The two models working together

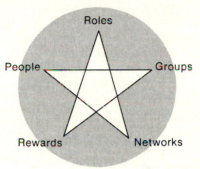

A soft, intuitive model
and how it works

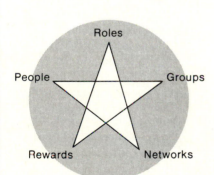

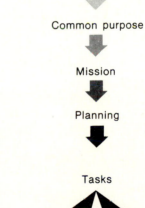

Jay Galbraith, *Organizational Design*, © 1977, Addison - Wesley, Reading, Massachusetts. Pg. 30, Fig. 2.9
(adapted material). Reprinted with permission.

Humor is what rescued us. Laughter allows people to jump out of their emotional boxes, or rigid belief structures. None of us can remember having laughed as much as we have over the past three years. Although much of the humor has inevitably been of the gallows variety, it has been an important ingredient in releasing tension and building trust.

Now everyone knows that people are social as well as rational animals. Indeed, we knew it back in the premerger days, but somehow back then we never came to grips with the social aspect, maybe because the rational view of people has an appealing simplicity and clarity. Lombard's Law applied to us—routine, structured tasks drove out nonroutine, unstructured activities.[10]

■ Compensation systems ...&...	● Rewards
■ Direct	● Indirect
■ Objective	● Subjective
■ Profit	● Fun
■ Failure	● Mistake
■ Hygiene	● Motivator
■ Managing	● Caring

In our premerger organization, the "total compensation policy" meant you could take your money any way you liked—salary, loans, fringes, and so forth. Management thought this policy catered to individual needs and was, therefore, motivating. Similarly, the "Personnel Development Program" required managers to make formal annual reviews of their employees' performances. For some reason, management thought that this also had something to do with motivation. The annual reviews, however, had become meaningless routine, with managers constrained to be nice to the review subject because they had to work with him or her the next day.

The 1981 recession put a stop to all this by spurring us to freeze all direct compensation. Profit-based compensation disappeared; morale went up.

The management team discussed this decision for hours. As the savings from the freeze would pay for a few weeks' interest only, the numbers made no sense at all. Some of us prophesied doom. "We will lose the best people," we argued. Instead, the symbolic freeze brought the crisis home to everyone. We had all made a sacrifice, a contribution that senior management could recognize at a future time.

Even though the academics say they aren't scientifically valid, we still like Fredrick Herzberg's definition of motivators (our interpretations of them are in parentheses).[11]

- Achievement (what you believe you did).
- Recognition (what others think you did).
- Work itself (what you really do).

- Responsibility (what you help others do).
- Advancement (what you think you can do).
- Growth (what you believe you might do).

THE NEW FRAMEWORK AT WORK

The diagram of the soft model in the exhibit shows our view of how our management process seems to work. When the motivating rewards are applied to people playing the necessary roles and working together in groups that are characterized by open communication and are linked to networks throughout the organization, the immediate product is a high degree of mutual trust. This trust allows groups to develop a shared vision that in turn enhances a sense of common purpose. From this process people develop a feeling of having a mission of their own. The mission is spiritual in the sense of being an important effort much larger than oneself. This kind of involvement is highly motivating. Mission is the soft counterpart of strategy.

■ **Strategy ...&...**	● **Mission**
■ Objectives	● Values
■ Policies	● Norms
■ Forecast	● Vision
■ Clockworks	● Frameworks
■ Right	● Useful
■ Target	● Direction
■ Precise	● Vague
■ Necessary	● Sufficient

Listed are some of our favorite words for contrasting these two polarities. We find them useful for understanding why clear definition of objectives is not essential for motivating people. Hard box planners advocate the hard box elements and tend to be overinvested in using their various models, or "clockworks" as we call them. Whether it's a Boston Consulting Group matrix or an Arthur D. Little life-cycle curve, too often planners wind them up and managers act according to what they dictate without looking at the asumptions, many of which may be invalid, implicit in the frameworks.

We use the models only as take-off points for discussion. They do not have to be right, only useful. If they don't yield genuine insights we put them aside. The hard box cannot be dispensed with. On the contrary, it is essential—but not sufficient.

The key element in developing a shared purpose is mutual trust. Without trust, people will engage in all kinds of self-centered behavior to assert their own identities and influence coworkers to their own ends.

Under these circumstances, they just won't hear others, and efforts to develop a shared vision are doomed. Nothing destroys trust faster than hard box attitudes toward problems that don't require such treatment.

Trust is self-reproductive. When trust is present in a situation, chain reactions occur as people share frameworks and exchange unshielded views. The closer and more tightly knit the group is, the more likely it is that these reactions will spread, generating a shared vision and common purpose.

Once the sense of common purpose and mission is established, the managing group is ready to enter the hard box of strategy (see the right-hand side of the exhibit). Now the specifics of task, structure, information, and decision processes are no longer likely to be controversial or threatening. Implementation becomes astonishingly simple. Action plans are necessary to control hard box implementation, but once the participants in the soft bubble share the picture, things seem to happen by themselves as team members play their roles and fill the gaps as they see them. Since efforts to seize control of bubble activity are likely to prove disastrous, it is most fortunate that people act spontaneously without being "organized." Paradoxically, one can achieve control in the bubble only by letting go—which gets right back to trust.

In the hard box, the leadership model is that of the general who gives crisp, precise instructions as to who is to do what and when. In the soft bubble, the leadership model is that of the shepherd, who follows his flock watchfully as it meanders along the natural contours of the land. He carries the weak and collects the strays, for they all have a contribution to make. This style may be inefficient, but it is effective. The whole flock reaches its destination at more or less the same time.[12]

■ Boxes ...&...	● Bubbles
■ Solve	● Dissolve
■ Sequential	● Lateral
■ Left brain	● Right brain
■ Serious	● Humorous
■ Explain	● Explore
■ Rational	● Intuitive
■ Conscious	● Unconscious
■ Learn	● Remember
■ Knowledge	● Wisdom
■ Lens	● Mirror
■ Full	● Empty
■ Words	● Pictures
■ Objects	● Symbols
■ Description	● Parable

Thought and language are keys to changing perceptions. Boxes and bubbles describe the hard and soft thought structures, respectively.

Boxes have rigid, opaque sides; walls have to be broken down to join boxes, although if the lid is off one can jump out. Bubbles have flexible, transparent sides that can easily expand and join with other bubbles. Bubbles float but can easily burst. In boxes problems are to be solved; in bubbles they are dissolved. The trick is to change the context of the problem, that is, to jump out of the box. This technique has many applications.

We have noticed a number of articles in your publication that concern values and ethics in business, and some people have suggested that business students be required to attend classes in ethics. From our view of the world, sending students to specific courses is a hard box solution and would be ineffective. Ethical behavior is absent from some businesses not because the managers have no ethics (or have the wrong ones) but because the hard "strategy box" does not emphasize them as being valuable. The hard box deals in objectives, and anyone who raises value issues in that context will not survive long.

In contrast, in the "mission bubble" people feel free to talk about values and ethics because there is trust. The problem of the lack of ethical behavior is dissolved.

We have found bubble thinking to be the intellectual equivalent of judo; a person does not resist an attacker but goes with the flow, thereby adding his strength to the other's momentum. Thus when suppliers demanded that their financial exposure to our lack of creditworthiness be reduced, we agreed and suggested that they protect themselves by supplying goods to us on consignment. After all, their own financial analysis showed we couldn't pay them any money! In some cases we actually got consignment deals, and where we didn't the scheme failed because of nervous lawyers (also hard box players) rather than reluctance on the part of the supplier.

Bubble thought structures are characterized by what Edward de Bono calls lateral thinking.[13] The sequential or vertical thought structure is logical and rational; it proceeds through logical stages and depends on a yes-no test at each step. De Bono suggests that in lateral thinking the yes-no test must be suspended, for the purpose is to explore not explain, to test assumptions not conclusions.

We do the same kind of questioning when we do what we call "humming a lot." When confronted with what initially appears to be an unpalatable idea, an effective manager will say "hmm" and wait until the idea has been developed and its implications considered. Quite often, even when an initial idea is out of the question, the fact that we have considered it seriously will lead to a different, innovative solution.

We have found it useful to think of the action opposite to the one we intend taking. When selling businesses we found it helpful to think about acquiring purchasers. This led to deeper research into purchasers' backgrounds and motives and to a more effective packaging and presentation of the businesses to be sold. This approach encourages novel ideas and makes the people who generate them (the entrepreneurs) feel that their ideas, however "dumb," will not be rejected out of hand.

In hard box thought structures, one tends to use conceptual frameworks as lenses, to sit on one side and examine an object on the other. In bubble structures, the frameworks are mirrors reflecting one's own nature and its effect on one's perceptions; object and subject are on the same side. In the hard box, knowledge is facts, from learning; in the bubble, knowledge is wisdom, from experience.

Bubble thought structures are not easily described in words. Language itself is a box reflecting our cultural heritage and emphasizing some features of reality at the expense of others. Part of our struggle during the past three years has been to unlearn many scientific management concepts and develop a new vocabulary. We have come up with some new phrases and words: management by walking around, creative stall, asking dumb questions, jumping out of the box, creating a crisis, humming a lot, and muddling. We have also attached new meanings to old words such as fact and perception, independence and autonomy, hard and soft, solve and dissolve, and so forth.

THREE YEARS LATER

What we have told you about works in a crisis. And we can well understand your asking whether this approach can work when the business is stable and people lapse back into boxes. We have developed two methods of preventing this lapse.

1. If there isn't a crisis, we create one. One way to stir things up is familiar to anyone who has ever worked in a hard box organization. Intimidation, terror, and the use of raw power will produce all the stress you need. But eventually people run out of adrenalin and the organization is drained, not invigorated.

In a bubble organization, managers dig for opportunities in a much more relaxed manner. During the last three years, for instance, many of our divisions that were profitable and liquid were still in need of strategic overhaul. During the course of walking around, we unearthed many important issues by asking dumb questions.

The more important of the issues that surface this way offer an opportunity to put a champion (someone who believes in the importance of the issue) in charge of a team of people who can play all the roles required to handle the issue. The champion then sets out with his or her group to go through the incremental development process—developing trust, building both a hard box picture and a shared vision, and, finally, establishing strategy. By the time the strategy is arrived at, the task force disciples have such zeal and sense of mission that they are ready to take the issue to larger groups, using the same process.

Two by-products of asking dumb questions deserve mention. First, when senior management talks to people at all levels, people at all levels start talking to each other. Second, things tend to get fixed before they break. In answering a senior manager's casual question, a welder on the shop floor of a steel fabrication plant revealed that some critical welds had failed quality tests and the customer's inspector was threatening to reject an entire bridge. A small ad hoc task force, which included the inspector (with the customer's permission), got everyone off the hook and alerted top management to a potential weakness of the quality control function.

Applying the principles in other areas takes years to bear fruit. We are now using the process to listen to customers and suppliers. We never knew how to do this before. Now it is clear that it is necessary to create an excuse (crisis) for going to see them, share "secrets," build trust, share a vision, and capture them in your bubble. It's very simple, and early results have been excellent. We call it a soft revolution.

2. Infuse activities that some might think prosaic with real significance. The focus should be on people first, and always on caring rather than managing. The following approach works in good times as well as bad:

- Use a graphic vocabulary that describes what you do.
- Share confidential information, personal hopes and fears to create a common vision and promote trust.
- Seize every opportunity (open doors, management by walking around, networks) to make a point, emphasize a value, disseminate information, share an experience, express interest, and show you care.
- Recognize performance and contribution of as many people as possible. Rituals and ceremonies—retirements, promotions, birthdays—present great opportunities.
- Use incentive programs whose main objective is not compensation but recognition.

We have tried to approach things this way, and for us the results have been significant. Now, three years after the crisis first struck our corporation, we are a very different organization. Of our 25 divisions, we have closed 7 and sold 16. Five of the latter were bought by Federal Industries, Ltd. of Winnipeg. Some 860 employees including us, the four members of the management team, have gone to Federal. These divisions are healthy and raring to go. Two divisions remain at York Russel, which has changed its name to YRI-YORK, Ltd.

Now we face a new question, such as how one recruits into a management team. We know that we have to help people grow into the team, and fortunately we find that they flourish in our warm climate. But trust takes time to develop, and the bubble is fragile. The risk is greatest when we have to transplant a senior person from outside, because time pressures may not allow us to be sure we are compatible. The danger is not only to the team itself but also to the person joining it.

Our new framework has given us a much deeper appreciation of the management process and the roles effective general managers play. For example, it is clear that while managers can delegate tasks in the hard box rather easily—perhaps because they can define them—it's impossible to delegate soft bubble activities. The latter are difficult to isolate from each other because their integration takes place in one brain.

Similarly, the hard box general management roles of producer and administrator can be formally taught, and business schools do a fine job of it. The soft roles of entrepreneur and integrator can probably not be taught formally. Instead, managers must learn from mentors. Over time they will adopt behavior patterns that allow them to play the required roles. It would seem, however, that natural ability and an individual's upbringing probably play a much larger part in determining effectiveness in the soft roles than in the hard roles; it is easier to teach a soft bubble player the hard box roles than it is to teach the soft roles to a hard box player.

In the three-year period when we had to do things so differently, we created our own culture, with its own language, symbols, norms, and customs. As with other groups, the acculturation process began when people got together in groups and trusted and cared about each other.[14]

In contrast with our premerger culture, the new culture is much more sympathetic toward and supportive of the use of teams and consensus decision making. In this respect, it would seem to be similar to oriental ways of thinking that place a premium on the same processes. Taoists, for instance, would have no trouble recognizing the polarities of the hard box and the soft bubble and the need to keep a balance between the two.[15]

■ Heaven ...&...	● Earth
■ Yang	● Yin
■ Father	● Mother
■ Man	● Woman

These symbols are instructive. After all, most of us grew up with two bosses: father usually played the hard box parts, while mother played the soft, intuitive, and entrepreneurial roles. The family is the original team, formed to handle the most complex management task ever faced. Of late, we seem to have fired too many of its members—a mistake we can learn from.

TOWARD A MANAGERIAL THEORY OF RELATIVITY

The traditional hard box view of management, like the traditional orientation of physics, is valid (and very useful) only within a narrow range of phenomena. Once one gets outside the range, one needs new principles. In physics, cosmologists at the macro level as well as students of subatomic particles at the micro level use Einstein's theory of relativity as an explanatory principle and set Newton's physics aside.[16] For us, the theory in the bubble is our managerial theory of relativity. At the macro level it reminds us that how management phenomena appear depends on one's perspective and biases. At the micro level we remember that all jobs have both hard and soft components.

This latter point is of particular importance to people like us in the service industry. The steel we distribute is indistinguishable from anyone else's. We insist on rigid standards regarding how steel is handled, what reporting systems are used, and so forth. But hard box standards alone wouldn't be enough to set us apart from our competitors. That takes service, a soft concept. And everyone has to be involved. Switchboard operators are in the front line; every contact is an opportunity to share the bubble. Truck drivers and warehouse workers make their own special contribution—by taking pride in the cleanliness of their equipment or by keeping the inventory neat and accessible.

With the box and bubble concept, managers can unlock many of the paradoxes of management and handle the inherent ambiguities. You don't do one or the other absolutely; you do what is appropriate. For instance, the other day in one of our operations the biweekly payroll run deducted what appeared to be random amounts from the sales representatives' pay packets. The branch affected was in an uproar. After taking some hard box steps to remedy the situation, our vice president of human resources seized the opportunity to go out to the branch and talk to the sales team. He was delighted with the response. The sales force saw that he understood the situation and cared about them, and he got to meet them all, which will make future contacts easier. But neither the hard box nor soft bubble approach on its own would have been appropriate. We need both. As one team member put it, "You have to find the bubble in the box and put the box in the bubble." Exactly.

The amazing thing is that the process works so well. The spirit of cooperation among senior managers is intense, and we seem to be getting "luckier" as we go along. When a "magic" event takes place it means that somehow we got the timing just right.[17] And there is great joy in that.

REFERENCES

1. Thomas J. Peters and Robert H. Waterman, *In Search of Excellence* (New York: Harper and Row, 1982), p. 29.

2. For the best of the hard box models we have come across, see Jay R. Galbraith, *Organization Design* (Reading, Mass.: Addison-Wesley, 1977).

3. Henry Mintzberg, "The Manager's Job: Folklore and Fact," HBR July-August 1975, p. 49.

4. Edgar H. Schein, *Process Consultation: Its Role in Organization Development* (Reading, Mass.: Addison-Wesley, 1969).

5. Ichak Adize, *How to Solve the Mismanagement Crisis* (Los Angeles: MDOR Institute, 1979).

6. Edgar H. Schein's *Process Consultation,* p. 10, was very helpful in showing us how the process differs from the content.

7. Getting consensus among a group of managers poses the same challenge as negotiating a deal. *Getting to Yes* by Robert Fisher and William Ury (Boston: Houghton Mifflin, 1981) is a most helpful book for understanding the process.

8. For discussion of the importance of networks, see John P. Kotter, "What Effective General Managers Really Do," HBR November-December 1982, p. 156.

9. For discussion of a "creative stall" being applied in practice, see Stratford P. Sherman, "Muddling to Victory at Geico," *Fortune,* September 5, 1983, p. 66.

10. Louis B. Barnes, "Managing the Paradox of Organizational Trust," HBR March-April 1981, p. 107.

11. In "One More Time: How Do You Motivate Employees?" HBR January-February 1968, p. 53.

12. For another view of the shepherd role, see the poem by Nancy Esposito, "The Good Shepherd," HBR July-August 1983, p. 121.

13. See Edward de Bono, *The Use of Lateral Thinking* (London: Jonathan Cape, 1967), and *PO: Beyond Yes and No* (New York: Simon and Schuster, 1972).

14. To explore the current concern with creating strong organizational cultures in North American corporations, see Terrence E. Deal and Alan A. Kennedy *Corporate Cultures* (Reading, Mass.: Addison-Wesley, 1982).

15. For discussion of Tao and some applications, we highly recommend Benjamin Hoff, *The Tao of Pooh* (New York: E. P. Hutton, 1982), p.67; also Allen Watts, *Tao: The Watercourse Way* (New York: Pantheon Books, 1975).

16. Fritjof Capra, *The Tao of Physics* (London: Fontana Paperbacks, 1983).

17. Carl Jung developed the concept of synchronicity to explain such events. See, for example, Ira Progoff, *Jung, Synchronicity and Human Destiny—Non-Causal Dimensions of Human Experience* (New York: Julian Press, 1973). For an excellent discussion of Jung's work and its relevance to our times, see Laurens van de Post, *Jung and the Story of Our Time* (New York: Random House, 1975).

Boardroom Politics at Wall Street and Vine

The Columbia Pictures scandal was a lesson in what happens when big business meets show business, when corporate self-interest challenges personal ethics, and when a decision maker is unable to decide

David McClintick

Despite the higher visibility of the Los Angeles film colony, a handful of skyscrapers within a half-mile radius of the corner of Fifty-seventh Street and Fifth Avenue in New York house a group of corporations that wield, in the aggregate, considerably more power over the motion picture, television, and record industries in America than is wielded by their West Coast counterparts. This neighborhood is sometimes called Hollywood East. Columbia Pictures is at 711 Fifth. Warner Communications is four blocks south at Fifty-first, and Paramount is just across Central Park. The headquarters of ABC, CBS, NBC, and Home Box Office are within five blocks of one another on Sixth Avenue in the Fifties. The world headquarters of International Creative Management, the largest of the talent and literary agencies, is on Fifty-seventh, and its principal rival, the William Morris Agency, is just around the corner. Most of the big law firms serving these companies are nearby, too, as are dozens of producers, film financiers, smaller agencies, and individual entertainment entrepreneurs of all stripes.

The show-biz ambience of Hollywood East is hard to miss. On a Thursday at the Russian Tea Room, or at the bar of the Sherry Netherland Hotel, or in the corridors of Warner Communications, one often sees the same faces and hears the same talk that one encountered on Tuesday at the Beverly Hills Hotel or Chasen's or the Fox commissary, or that one ran into on Wednesday in the first-class cabin of American 32 or

---

This account is based on hundreds of hours of interviews, many of them tape-recorded, which the author conducted with the principals of the story and with others who had firsthand knowledge of the events described; the author has also made extensive use of the complete transcripts of sworn testimony gathered by the SEC. He has generally reconstructed conversations when two or more sources could verify the content; the sources were usually the speaker and his audience, but in a few instances included people who did not participate in the conversation but were reliably informed on it.

United 6 or TWA 8. The two Hollywoods, in fact, sometimes seem not so much like separate communities as like a single, homogeneous community that has been divided arbitrarily into two parts and placed at opposite ends of a three-thousand-mile air corridor through which the residents regularly shuttle.

Such appearences are deceiving, however. One has more perspective in New York. Even though a great deal of power over the entertainment industry is concentrated in a few blocks, one cannot stroll those streets without realizing that Exxon and Revlon and dozens of other giant corporations in other industries make their homes not only in the same city but in the same neighborhood. In Los Angeles, the film studios and television production facilities are physically and psychologically so imposing, and other institutions so lacking in a sense of presence, that one can live and work for days without once being reminded that there is any business in the world except show business. The insularity of Los Angeles, after a while, begins to distort the vision and jostle the equilibrium of all but the very strong and the very independent.

Which is where New York comes in. When Hollywood needs an injection of reality, when it needs to be brought up short, it is New York, the true seat of power, that does the job.

New York is the enforcer. New York is where the heads roll.

This time—September 1977—the head in jeopardy was David Begelman's.

Begelman, the flamboyant and charming former talent agent who ran the Burbank-based movie and television operations of Columbia Pictures Industries, had been instrumental in bringing Columbia from the edge of bankruptcy to robust prosperity in less than four years. With the corporation more than $200 million in debt, one of its most worried creditors, veteran producer Ray Stark, fifty-nine, had turned for help to a close friend, Herbert Allen Jr., the serious, even-tempered, thirty-three-year-old scion of the maverick Wall Street investment house of Allen & Company. Convinced that Columbia could be saved, Allen had gained the confidence of its largest stockholder, Geritol tycoon Matthew Rosenhaus, and had effectively taken control of the company by buying a block of stock roughly equal to Rosenhaus's. Allen had then installed his long-time associate Alan Hirschfield, thirty-seven, as Columbia's president, and the two, with Ray Stark's help, had recruited fifty-two-year-old David Begelman, a friend of Stark's and a leading agent for more than two decades, to head the ailing studio. While Hirschfield, who had had previous experience on the corporate side of the entertainment business, wrestled adroitly with the corporation's financial structure, Begelman presided over a string of successful movies—*Funny Lady, Shampoo, Tommy, Taxi Driver,* and *The Deep.* By late summer 1977, Columbia was preparing to open a film it was ballyhooing as "the most beautiful, frightening and significant motion picture adventure of all time," *Close Encounters of the Third Kind.*

Just then, without warning, a strange and ominous event jolted the company's inner councils. On Wednesday, September 14, a Beverly Hills police detective telephoned chief executive Hirschfield with a report that David Begelman apparently had forged a ten-thousand-dollar Columbia Pictures check drawn to Oscar-winning actor Cliff Robertson and had pocketed the money. A dumbfounded Hirschfield sent Columbia's chief financial officer, Joseph Fischer, to Los Angeles the next morning to investigate. Fischer not only confirmed the Robertson forgery but also found evidence that Begelman had stolen an additional thirty-five thousand dollars by means of a bogus contract. Later it would be discovered that he had forged other Columbia checks in the names of film director Martin Ritt and Los Angeles restaurateur Pierre Groleau.

A welter of perplexing questions engulfed Alan Hirschfield, a droll, playful man with little aptitude for facing acute crises involving other human beings. Why would David Begelman steal? Were these thefts just a few among many? Should he be fired summarily? Should Columbia suspend him and conduct a private investigation? Should the matter be turned over to the law-enforcement authorities? Quick answers were not forthcoming, and the questions soon prompted other, more complex and ambiguous questions involving the power dynamics of the corporation itself and the relationships among the people who ran it and would handle the David Begelman problem—relationships that had deep roots and involved a tangle of mixed motives.

Groping for a proper approach to the embezzlements, Hirschfield gave Herbert Allen the bad news, and they decided to summon Ray Stark to New York for advice on what to do. Told that Begelman might be suspended pending a private inquiry, Stark offered to run the studio in Begelman's absence. Hirschfield, who believed that Stark's sway at the studio was already too powerful, rejected the offer. Stark took the rejection as evidence that Hirschfield wanted to exploit the Begelman problem in order to acquire more power for himself. Following Stark's lead, Herbert Allen also grew suspicious of Hirschfield's motives.

Hirschfield, for his part, was indeed worried about his station within the company. But he had no interest in crowding David Begelman. Hirschfield's main worry was Herbert Allen, Columbia's ultimate boss. The Hirschfield-Allen relationship was well into its second generation. Herbert Allen's uncle, Charles Allen, the patriarch of Allen & Company, and Alan Hirschfield's father, Norman Hirschfield, had been close friends since the 1920s in Wall Street, where they had met as would-be tycoons barely out of their teens. Alan Hirschfield had gone to work for Allen & Company directly from Harvard Business School in 1959 and in effect had been its employee ever since, whether on the firm's payroll as an investment banker or representing its interests as an officer of corporations the Allens controlled. By 1977, however, riding the crest of the recovery he had orchestrated for Columbia, Hirschfield yearned for recognition in his own right and for independence of the Allens. He particularly resented the dominion over his life of Herbert Allen, who Hirschfield felt was a less able businessman than he and held his position not because he had earned it but because he had been born to it.

Hirschfield had never stated his frustrations in Allen's presence. However, of all the personal relationships that bore on the handling of the Begelman issue, and the future of Columbia Pictures in general, none held more potential for trouble in 1977 than that between Alan Hirschfield and Herbert Allen.

The nine men who gathered in Hirschfield's office at eleven-thirty on the morning of Friday, September 23, did not leave for six and a half hours, except to use Hirschfield's private bathroom. Lunch was brought in. The nine, constituting a quorum of the board of directors of Columbia Pictures Industries, included four people who had not been part of the early deliberations on the Begelman problem. They were Matty Rosenhaus, the bombastic Geritol magnate; Leo Jaffe, the shy, aging board chairman who was a holdover from the old Columbia management; Irwin Kramer, who was Charlie Allen's son-in-law, chairman of Columbia's audit committee and executive vice-president of Allen & Company; and Robert Werbel, an attorney for Allen & Company who had been asked to attend the meeting by Kramer and Herbert Allen. Also there, in addition to Hirschfield and Allen, were Joe Fischer, the chief financial officer; Robert Todd Lang of the law firm of Weil, Gotshal & Manges, Columbia's chief legal counsel; and Victor Kaufman, who was the company's staff lawyer.

In a thickening cloud of cigar smoke, the group reviewed every aspect of the Begelman matter.

"We've got to figure out a way to help David," Rosenhaus insisted.

"He ought to be fired and thrown in jail," said Irwin Kramer.

The discussion of what action to take against Begelman was protracted, but by the end, much of the spirit had ebbed from the argument that he had to be fired immediately. Although it was decided to brief the Securities and Exchange Commission privately, the majority of the group felt that they did not yet have sufficient information about the embezzlements on which to base more-definitive action. Thus, they chose to postpone a decision on Begelman's ultimate fate until after an internal Columbia investigation and instead carve out an interim status for him. He was to resign from the board of directors of the corporation and from his corporate title of senior executive vice-president. But he would remain in his most visible position as president of the studio. And he would continue to draw his full $4,500-a-week salary plus benefits.

There was little disagreement about the need for an investigation. The group decided that the inquiry appropriately fell under the aegis of audit committee chairman Irwin Kramer and should be conducted by Weil, Gotshal & Manges, with the assistance of Price Waterhouse & Company, the CPA firm that handled Columbia's regular annual audits.

David Begelman had flown to New York to await the results of the board meeting. He sat alone down the hall in an office he used when visiting New York. After the meeting was over, the only Columbia person Begelman saw was Matty Rosenhaus, who gave him a tearful recital of what had been decided. Begelman was aboard the seven-fifteen TWA flight to Los Angeles that night and managed to have a pleasant weekend. On Saturday evening he and his wife, Gladyce, attended a VIP screening of *Bobby Deerfield*. As *Newsweek* would later report, somewhat snidely, Begelman looked that night as if he "owned the town—which in many ways, he did. He was riding high, universally respected, trim and handsome, a real doer."

A few days later, Columbia discovered one of the additional forgeries (in which Begelman had employed the name of the Los Angeles restaurateur) and decided that David could not stay in his studio post after all; he would have to take a "leave of absence" in addition to resigning his corporate positions, and it was suggested that he seek psychiatric care. Still, he was retained by the board as a "consultant" and continued to receive his presidential salary.

Over lunch on Tuesday, October 11, with Herbert Allen and Matty Rosenhaus, Alan Hirschfield suggested that it might be wise if he began at least an exploratory survey of potential candidates for the studio jobs Begelman had vacated. (Though Begelman presided over both the motion picture and the television divisions, the presidencies historically had been held by two people.) Allen, recalling that Hirschfield had rejected Stark's offer to run the studio, recommended that they await the investigators' findings. The three men then joined the other Columbia directors and top executives to hear a report from Peter Gruenberger, a Weil, Gotshal & Manges attorney designated to conduct the investigation, on the initial stages of the inquiry and his plans for carrying it on.

At the Hirschfield home in Scarsdale the following Saturday evening, the dinner guest was one of Alan's newer friends, David Geffen. Geffen had been the most spectacular impresario in the record business until he grew weary of the grind and sold his company to Warner's.

Geffen and Hirschfield had first met at Ray Stark's home and became fast friends. Geffen was something of a *kochleffl* in the Hollywood community—a pot stirrer, an energizer. Wired snugly into the important power grids and grapevines, which tended to intertwine, he usually knew the difference between truth and idle rumor. And on this October evening in Scarsdale, Geffen warned Hirschfield to be careful of Ray Stark. Although Geffen and Stark were friendly, they disagreed on the significance of the Begelman issue. Geffen claimed that Stark was beginning to work against Hirschfield, that Stark was impugning Hirschfield's "moral" stance and claiming that Alan was in fact exploiting Begelman's problems to inflate his own power at the studio. Ray, said Geffen, could be a powerful foe.

Hirschfield thanked Geffen and told him to keep his ears open. But he failed to see how Ray Stark's comments to friends on the Hollywood social circuit could have any effect.

Among Alan Hirschfield's most important achievements in 1976 and 1977 was the establishment of new business relationships between Columbia Pictures Industries and prestigious corporations outside the movie-production industry. In addition to opening up new financial opportunities for Columbia, these relationships helped to build its reputation as a company that was no longer a second-echelon film studio but was moving toward the front ranks of respected mutinational entertainment conglomerates like Warner Communications and MCA. One such relationship was with Time Inc., which had agreed to invest several million dollars in Columbia's motion pictures. Another was with IBM, which was considering making Columbia its partner in the development of a laser video system. Still another was with General Cinema Corporation, a large Boston-based concern that made half its money from soft-drink bottling and the other half from its original business, the nation's largest chain of movie theaters. The two companies had been negotiating a plan by which General Cinema would invest upwards of $26 million in Columbia's motion picture program.

Hirschfield had made special efforts to reassure Time and IBM that the Begelman problem was isolated and under control, and on Monday morning, October 24, he and Dan Melnick, the head of production and acting studio president, flew to Boston for a visit with the chief executive officer of General Cinema, Richard A. Smith. Hirschfield wanted to show off Melnick, one of the brightest people in Hollywood, as a way of assuring Smith that Columbia's film program was in good hands even without Begelman. Before introducing Melnick, however, Hirschfield spent a few minutes alone with Smith. Hirschfield was ready with his usual cautiously worded explanation of how Columbia was handling the Begelman problem, why it was investigating carefully, and why it had suspended Begelman rather than dismiss him. Dick Smith, it turned out, already knew the pertinent facts and had formed strong opinions about them.

"Let me make one thing very clear to you," Smith told Hirschfield. "As far as I am concerned, we're investing in Alan Hirschfield and his management team. We want to meet Melnick and make sure he has his head screwed on straight, but basically we're looking to a relationship with Columbia as represented by you. If Begelman comes back into the company, there will be no deal with General Cinema. We can't afford those kinds of relationships. That's not the way we run our business. I assume your board will come to the same conclusion. I don't know what's taking so long."

Having been warned about Ray Stark's hostility, Hirschfield scheduled a lunch in Los Angeles with Stark for the next day, Tuesday. They ate at Stark's favorite restaurant near the Burbank studios, Chow's Kosherama Deli.

Hirschfield was more surprised than he should have been that Stark was lobbying for Begelman's reinstatement as president of the studio. He knew that the investigative team was finding evidence that the relationship between Stark and Begelman was closer than Hirschfield had thought. But he had not grasped the ramifications of these signals and thus was unprepared for a sophisticated encounter with Stark, who not only sketched a rationale for Begelman's restoration but also hinted that the continuation of his multipicture contract with Columbia might depend on Begelman's return. The Stark contract, which Columbia valued very highly, was in the midst of renegotiation.

"I really can't sign any deal until I know who's going to be running the studio," Stark told Hirschfield. "Maybe you'll bring in somebody I don't like or who doesn't like me." Hirschfield dismissed that notion. Stark then said he understood that Begelman was making excellent progress in his psychotherapy with Dr. Judd Marmor, a former president of the American Psychiatric Association, who was known as "psychiatrist to the stars."

"At best," Hirschfield dissented, "David has severe psychological problems that will take a lot of time to treat. At worst, he's nothing but a crook. In any event, he has lied up and down."

"Alan, you've got to have a more flexible attitude," Stark replied. "He's coming along well. Besides, he's the best in the business at what he does, and you two have been a great team. It would be a tragedy to break it up."

Alan Hirschfield met Herbert Allen for lunch on Tuesday, November 1, at the same La Côte Basque table where he had given Allen the initial news about Begelman precisely six weeks earlier. As they had several times since then, the two men discussed the Begelman issue without total candor. Hirschfield recited the arguments against reinstating Begelman, but he stopped short of asserting the unequivocal opposition he really felt. Allen recited the arguments for reinstatement—Begelman is responding well to psychotherapy; he is owed another chance because of his contributions to the company; and replacing him with someone as talented will be very difficult—but he stopped short of unequivocal support for reinstatement. Allen stressed, in fact, that Hirschfield, as the chief executive officer, would be expected to make the final decision and that the board of directors would support whatever he decided.

Hirschfield outlined his conversation with Richard Smith of General Cinema in Boston the previous week.

"Baloney," Herbert Allen said. "Smith's just bluffing. He'll be with us with or without Begelman. He needs us more than we need him."

"Herbert, you don't understand this guy. You're dealing with a real straight shooter who is very sensitive to public image. You mark my

words, there will be no General Cinema. In addition to which, there will
be no IBM."

"We shouldn't be deciding this issue based on what some other company thinks. It's none of their business."

"We're living in the world, Herbert, not in a vacuum. We've got to
think about how this looks."

Two weeks later, on Tuesday, November 15, Columbia Pictures
staged the world premiere of *Close Encounters of the Third Kind.* It was
a night when Alan Hirschfield, sitting in the audience watching the film,
finally knew with absolute certainty that the corporation he had led from
the brink of bankruptcy to modest prosperity would shortly become
very rich and take its place as a truly important purveyor of entertainment to the world.

But that Tuesday night was also a night of menace. It was a night
when Alan Hirschfield received a signal that the smoldering dispute over
David Begelman—a dispute over one man's misdeeds, a dispute that had
grown so gradually from the chance discovery of a single forged check—
was about to explode into something much more ominous. Hirschfield
learned that night that the board of dirctors of Columbia Pictures Industries was prepared to go so far as to launch a serious attack on his
own personal integrity, and on the personal integrity of his wife, Berte.

Just before seven-thirty, as the crowd was filing into the Ziegfeld
Theater, attorney Todd Lang took Hirschfield aside. Lang had talked to
Peter Gruenberger, the chief investigator, who had gotten a phone call
from Allen in-law Irwin Kramer. It seemed that Kramer's audit committee was going to broaden the investigation. In addition to investigating
Begelman, it was going to investigate Alan and Berte Hirschfield. More
precisely, it was going to investigate a possible conflict of interest in the
employment of Berte Hirschfield by a company that conducted market
research for Columbia Pictures.

Alan was stunned. "That's absurd," he said to Lang. "We cleared that
with the board two years ago. It was as clean as a whistle. You said so
yourself."

"I know," Lang replied, "but they're determined to bring it up again.
They claim they never got to the bottom of it."

"This is nothing but a lever to get me to cave on Begelman,"
Hirschfield asserted. "It's out-and-out blackmail!"

Even though Berte's employment had been entirely legitimate, Alan
could imagine the headline if a distorted version were leaked to the press:
HIRSCHFIELD, TRYING TO CENSURE BEGELMAN, HAS SKELETON IN OWN CLOSET.
The facts never quite catch up with such headlines.

The morning after the premiere, the board of directors gathered at
711 Fifth to hear the investigator's report on Begelman's thievery. Containing his rage at the news that Irwin Kramer was planning to make an
issue of Berte's employment (Kramer had loyally reversed his initial view

that David Begelman should be banished and prosecuted), Hirschfield listened to a detailed recitation of how Begelman had stolen more than sixty thousand dollars in four separate acts of forgery and embezzlement and had misappropriated an additional twenty-three thousand dollars by manipulating his expense account.

After several questions, David Begelman was invited in to the meeting to defend himself, having been summoned to New York by Herbert Allen and Matty Rosenhaus over Hirschfield's objections. Dressed in a conservative dark suit and carrying a large manila folder, he shook hands around the table and then sat down, his voice quavering slightly as he spoke.

"When I came to this company, it was a shambles. You took a gamble that I could help rescue it. Along with others, I worked long and hard to make it work, and we succeeded. But somehow, just when I was at my peak, I began to self-destruct. I committed grievous transgressions, vile acts, against Columbia and against you, my friends. I must face the fact that I did these things, even though, emotionally, it is still impossible for me to believe it. But over the past six weeks, with the help of one of the finest doctors in the country, I have learned a great deal about the roots of my misdeeds. The roots go deep, all the way back to my childhood and my relationship with my parents and my siblings. In sum, the problem amounts to an unnaturally low self-esteem, a feeling of unworthiness, and an inability to accommodate success. The tangible results were a series of highly neurotic acts by which I tried to punish and injure myself. There is no logical, rational excuse for what I did, no justification. But in the therapy which I sought immediately upon the revelation of these acts six weeks ago, it quickly became clear to me that there were valid—not justifiable, but understandable in retrospect—reasons for these highly neurotic acts, which were not directed at Columbia or against any individual but against myself.

"Now I appear before you with the acts revealed. If you can summon up the mercy to grant me another chance, you will find that I will work day and night and do everything humanly possible to justify your faith in me. I will rededicate my life to the success of Columbia Pictures."

Begelman paused as tears streamed down Matty Rosenhaus's face. In fact, the only people not visibly moved by Begelman's words were Alan Hirschfield, Herbert Allen, and the lawyers.

With hands trembling slightly, Begelman picked up a stack of letters and telegrams and held them aloft.

"In case any of you are concerned about my standing in the Hollywood community as a result of my difficulties, I want to share with you a number of expressions which I have received in recent weeks." He proceeded to read messages from Paul Newman, Mel Brooks, Sue Mengers, George Segal, Barbra Streisand, and many other big names in Hollywood. Although few if any of these people knew what Begelman had done to cause his suspension from the company, they all declared him to be an outstanding executive with whom they would be delighted to work in the future.

Then Begelman shifted his chair and looked straight at Hirschfield. "Now, Alan, I'd like to talk directly to you. You have been a friend to me, you took a chance with me by hiring me, and you have stood by me through some very difficult times. I've betrayed you. I've given you every reason not to trust me. I know that the only way you will ever trust me again is if I actively win back your trust, win back your faith, win back your admiration. I want you to know that I will work with every breath in my body to accomplish this if you will just give me a chance. I promise you, you will have no more loyal servant than me. I beg of you to give me that chance."

With that, Begelman rose, picked up his notes, and again circled the table shaking hands. Matty Rosenhaus, still dabbing at his eyes with a handkerchief, escorted Begelman from the room.

As Rosenhaus was returning to his seat Hirschfield said, "That was quite an act, trembling hands and all."

Rosenhaus shouted, "I deeply resent that comment! For God's sake, the man bares his heart and soul and you say something like that. It's despicable!"

"I didn't forge the checks, Matty," Hirschfield retorted.

Everyone in the room who was not a member of the board was asked to leave so that the board could deliberate in private. Each of the seven men expressed himself in turn. Kramer and Allen voiced the familiar arguments in favor of reinstating Begelman. Then Matty Rosenhaus, never content simply to register assent in such a situation, delivered a sermon.

"I don't know when I've ever been more moved than I was by David here this morning. This clearly is a reformed man. Not only does David deserve another chance, he *needs* another chance. He needs our approval in order to recover. God knows what will happen to him if we don't give it to him. He was in such a state. Couldn't you see the way his hands were shaking? It's up to you, Alan. You have to look into your heart, and then open your heart to David."

It was Leo Jaffe's turn.

"I understand the pleas you're making. I, too, was touched by David's talk. But there are certain things you can forgive a man for doing as a human being but that have no place in a publicly owned company. We are a public company. We have to think about the public, the share-holders, and our employees."

Finally the floor was Hirschfield's. After seven difficult weeks, during which he had decided he had to oppose Begelman's return to the company, the time for confrontation was at hand.

"First of all," he began, "the question of David's qualifications was never an issue. His value to the corporation has never been doubted by me. But I think it's highly questionable that we're dealing with temporary aberrational behavior. And the issue of the double standard worries me. If we bring him back, we're in effect condoning this kind of behavior for other employees. We can't have a double standard.

"As to outside appearances, I think they're vital in this day and age. I challenge any person sitting in this room to tell me one, just one, company in the Fortune 500, or even the Fortune 1,000 that, faced with this same problem, would take a person like this back. Then, also, on a personal moral basis, taking him back goes against everything I stand for. I have great sympathy for David. I don't want to see him prosecuted. I'm happy to consider giving him a production deal if the lawyers say that won't cause us trouble. But we cannot have a forger and an embezzler in this company, whatever the extenuating circumstances."

After a few seconds of silence, Matty Rosenhaus spoke: "Alan, we have committed ourselves to support whatever decision you make as the chief executive officer, and we are prepared to honor that commitment. But I implore you, I beg you, I ask you as strongly as I possibly can, to reconsider your position and try to find a way to work with David. The decision doesn't have to be made today. Think it over for a few days."

"I'm ninety percent sure," Hirschfield said.

"With ten percent, there's always hope," Rosenhaus replied.

Hirschfield reluctantly agreed. He promised to render a tentative decision by Friday and to give a final decision the following week. The issue of his wife's employment had not been mentioned during the meeting.

As he had annually for several years, Alan Hirschfield took his family to Los Angeles for Thanksgiving week. His heart wasn't in the holiday, however. Thoroughly mystified by the board's insistence on restoring Begelman to the presidency of the studio, and still furious at the threat to investigate Berte's entirely proper employment record, he steeled himself for the scheduled confrontation at which he was obliged to render his final decision.

The board meeting was scheduled for four o'clock (New York time) on Tuesday, November 22. Herbert Allen, Irwin Kramer, and other key executives gathered around a speaker telephone in Leo Jaffe's office. Matty Rosenhaus was on a telephone in his office three blocks away.

Alan Hirschfield sat alone at a large desk in Columbia's visiting executives suite in Burbank. Before him were five sheets of yellow legal-size paper on which he had made notes with a felt-tipped pen.

"Is everybody there?" he asked.

"Yes, we're all listening, Alan. Go ahead."

"I stated my basic position on this matter last Wednesday. I accept your decision that in the end I have to decide what's best for the company. I am also mindful of the board's promise to support my decision. For all of the reasons I stated last Wednesday, I have decided not to reinstate David in any kind of management position."

There was hostile muttering at the New York end of the line.

"Let him go on," Jaffe said.

Hirschfield then unleashed the rage that had been building for weeks and had been close to exploding since "the Berte issue" had been raised several days earlier.

"I feel I've been treated shabbily," Hirschfield said. "I feel that after four and a half years of a good record, good decisions, and having given everything I've got, after four and a half years where every man on this board has benefited, the board walked away, allowed an adversary relationship to develop, acted behind my back, and is now attempting to blackmail me and my family. I won't stand for it.

"Instead of supporting me, it's obvious that the board has let Ray Stark become the final word and authority where Columbia is concerned. Suddenly I am a power-hungry megalomaniac who would 'go Hollywood' at the first opportunity. There's not a shred of evidence in this accusation. What I am now asking for is support and confidence, at least the same support and confidence given to David Begelman. If the board isn't willing to do this, it will have a fight on its hands."

By the time he finished his speech, the board was stunned. Herbert Allen spoke: "Ninety percent of what you've said, Alan, is incorrect, offensive to this board, and irrelevant to the issue."

"I think what I've said is right on target."

"Well, at least you've finally made a decision, even if it's a bad one, and even if it's from behind a telephone three thousand miles away."

"What difference does it make? The decision is made. It was you who asked me to reconsider."

Rosenhaus trembled with anger. "This is a terrible day for this company. You've got to learn how to forgive people, give them another chance."

"This has nothing to do with forgiveness, Matty. Besides, David will be better off in the long run. I'm willing to give him a production deal, a generous deal within the limits of the law."

"Who's going to tell David?" Herbert asked. "You've made yourself conveniently unavailable, Alan, unless you want to call him. He's here in town at the apartment, waiting."

"I can't help the fact that I'm in California, Herbert. I come out here for Thanksgiving every year."

"There are some of us who feel you owed the board the courtesy of delivering this decision in person."

"It's irrelevant where the decision is delivered. It's made and that's it."

It was decided that Allen and Rosenhaus would go to the apartment Columbia maintained in Manhattan for visiting executives and inform Begelman of Hirschfield's decision, and that the company would issue a press release by the next day.

Hirschfield hung up the phone elated.

He had actually fired David Begelman. They had expected him to cave in and take David back, and he had surprised them.

Alan and Berte dined that evening at Ma Maison and toasted the firing of Begelman. But their elation and relief lasted less than twenty-four hours. Early the next afternoon, the day before Thanksgiving, senior vice-president Joe Fischer telephoned Hirschfield from New York with two pieces of very ominous news. First, the press release about Begelman's permanent departure from the presidency of the studio had been canceled after Begelman complained that it did not mention his future relationship with the company as a producer and a consultant —a relationship whose terms had not yet been formulated. Second, and more serious, the board members, still furious at Hirschfield's decision to banish Begelman, had again stated their determination to make an issue of Berte's job.

Dumbfounded, Alan sank into a black mood that lasted through the weekend.

Berte and the children returned to New York on Sunday, and Alan began his week's business that very afternoon with the most sensitive meeting of all, a session with David Begelman to discuss Begelman's new arrangements with Columbia Pictures as a producer and a consultant.

Hirschfield dreaded the meeting. He hated giving people bad news or dealing with people who had just received bad news for which he was responsible. And he had been forced to assume a very uncomfortable negotiating posture. On the one hand, Rosenhaus and Allen had ordered that Begelman be "made whole" financially. On the other hand, they were taking no responsibility for the actual terms of the deal. Hirschfield therefore had to follow their orders and at the same time shoulder the potentially contradictory problem of having the deal scrutinized by the SEC, the press, and other outsiders. The deal had to be rich, but not too rich.

Begelman looked wan and discouraged when he arrived at Hirschfield's bungalow at the Beverly Hills Hotel. Hirschfield tried to couch the conversation in positive terms. He was terribly sorry, he said. Nothing personal, of course. But he knew that Begelman would be pleased with the "terrific" production deal he was going to get. To Hirschfield's chagrin, Begelman's fatigue and depression had not dulled his negotiating skills. He was far from pleased with the general terms Hirschfield outlined. The two weren't even close.

Then Hirschfield surprised Begelman. Recalling that Columbia was considering acquiring the motion picture rights to *Annie,* Hirschfield asked if Begelman would be interested in producing the film version.

It was a display of carelessness by Hirschfield. Just a month earlier, at dinner with Leonard Goldberg, a prominent Hollywood producer, Hirschfield asked Goldberg if *he* would be interested in producing *Annie.* Hirschfield had not considered the overture formal, but Goldberg had taken it at the very least to be an informal offer and had told David Begelman, one of his closest friends, about it. Was Hirschfield naive enough to think that Leonard would not have relayed this major piece of news to his friend?

"Well, Alan," Begelman said, "it's going to be a little crowded on the set of *Annie* when I arrive to produce it and Len Goldberg is standing there."

"I didn't offer it to Len."

"He says you did."

"Well, it came up in conversation. I certainly didn't offer it to him. But maybe you and Len could produce it together."

Begelman looked skeptical. "Well, that's a different issue. That's possible. That might work."

The conversation withered. Instead of attracting Begelman, Hirschfield's raising of the *Annie* issue had heightened the awkwardness they had felt at the beginning of the meeting. Begelman agreed to meet again in a few days and obtained Hirschfield's assurance that no press release about his leaving the Columbia studio presidency would be issued until the terms of his future affiliation were settled.

Ray Stark, meanwhile, had been very busy calling his friends at Columbia on Begelman's behalf. Apart from the influence implicit in his close friendship with Herbert Allen, Stark's pictures had generated in excess of $200 million for the corporation—far more than those of any other producer—and on that basis alone the board of directors was prone to listen to him. And while Ray Stark concentrated on the Columbia board, others in Hollywood had been lobbying indirectly, through the "creative community." Sue Mengers, Begelman's close friend, who had become one of the two most powerful agents on the Coast after starting as his protégée, urged her clients, friends, and acquaintances to send telegrams. Mengers dispatched some of them from her office, even sending a wire on behalf of an actor whom she had not consulted, Jack Nicholson. He was not pleased.

Although Hirschfield had planned to spend the full week after Thanksgiving conducting business at the studio, it became impossible by the middle of the week to function normally. The phone calls from New York were unrelenting. It was clear that a severe crisis was brewing at 711 Fifth Avenue, that his decision to fire Begelman was not adhering, and that indeed Hirschfield was now facing a problem much more sinister and volatile than a dispute over one man. He was facing a broad crisis of corporate governance at Columbia Pictures Industries, including a threat to blacken his own and his wife's reputation. On Wednesday evening, November 30, he flew back and, to his horror, began getting signals in his office the next morning that his own job might be in jeopardy.

The first indication came in a telephone conversation with William Thompson of the First National Bank of Boston, Columbia's principal banker, with whom Herbert Allen had spoken within the previous twenty-four hours. According to Thompson, Allen had said of Hirschfield:

"We're going to get him for the way he's handled this situation."

"How can you get rid of Hirschfield at the same time you get rid of Begelman?" Thompson claimed to have asked Allen.

"If we don't get him now, we'll get him in six months. He can be replaced in three days," Allen reportedly replied. (Recalling this conversation later, Herbert Allen said that his remarks did not constitute an explicit threat to fire Hirschfield but rather were part of an attempt to convince Thompson that Hirschfield had behaved badly and was naive if he thought he could win a fight with the board of directors.)

No sooner had Hirschfield spoken with Thompson than Irwin Kramer called. "Look, I just thought you ought to know that you're in trouble," Kramer said. "Herbert and Matty are really pissed. It won't go away. If you don't come around, there are going to be problems."

"I can't believe this!" said Hirschfield. "What kind of people are you! A week ago, and the week before that, you committed yourselves to support my decision, like it or not. Now it's like those promises were never made. You're not only going back on your word, you're using the dirtiest kind of blackmail tactics. How dare you drag my wife into this thing!"

"We have every right and responsibility to examine the outside business connections of key executives," Kramer said.

Hirschfield hung up the phone, incredulous.

Herbert Allen strode into Hirschfield's office and closed the door.

"Have you reconsidered your decision, Alan?"

"No, my decision stands."

"I feel compelled to restate," Herbert said, "that I think you're making a very serious mistake that is threatening this company. From what I hear, the studio is on the verge of collapse."

"That's certainly news to me. I just came from there, and as of the day before yesterday, it wasn't on the verge of collapse."

"Melnick appears to be a horror as a stand-in for Begelman. The most important producers on the lot are threatening to leave."

"That's ridiculous."

"You're wrong!" Allen declared, in a voice higher, louder, and more agitated than Hirschfield had ever heard come from him. "The studio *is* going to collapse! The studio can't make deals with anybody. There's no one there who can make deals. Melnick can't do it. The only one who can do it is Begelman, and we've got to bring him back!"

"If you and the board would only give me your support," Hirschfield shouted, "there are plenty of people we can get! What happened to all the support I was going to get, that you pledged to give me? What happened to that scenario?"

"That was then, and this is now, and you've got to bring David back."

"No way."

Neither man spoke for several seconds.

"Look, Alan," Herbert said, his voice quieter, "do it for me. I've never put anything on a personal basis before, but we do have a long personal relationship that means a lot to me. Leaving aside everything else, how about doing it for me, because of who I am, because of who you are, because of who *we* are."

"This is not a personal matter, Herbert."

"I'm making it a personal matter. I want you to do it for me."

"Well, I won't do it for you."

It was time to join Matty Rosenhaus, Irwin Kramer, and Leo Jaffe for an informal meeting of the principal directors. Rosenhaus had demanded the meeting once he learned that Hirschfield had returned early from Los Angeles.

Old arguments were repeated, and Allen stated his new argument that "the studio is on the verge of collapse."

"We may lose Ray," Rosenhaus added.

"If we lose Ray Stark, we lose Ray Stark," Hirschfield replied.

"Ray's the most important asset this company has," Allen said.

"This company has a lot of important assets," Hirschfield retorted. "Ray is one, but there are others. Furthermore, I must reemphasize that if David Begelman comes back, nobody respectable will have anything to do with us."

One board member said, "If Begelman is brought back, the board must show its support for Alan with a new contract, so that people will know that Alan is running the company. Not David, not the board, but Alan."

"Absolutely," Rosenhaus said. "Alan should have the best deal in the industry."

"I feel," said Hirschfield, "that it is somewhat inappropriate to be discussing my contract in connection with whether I bring Begelman back. In less-polite circles it might be called a payoff."

"Alan, please don't be unreasonable," Rosenhaus replied. "It would be the most appropriate thing in the world for us to show the world and you how much we value you by giving you a new contract."

"I really don't think we should be discussing this," Hirschfield said.

"Well, be that as it may," Rosenhaus said, "we're asking you to once again reconsider your decision, to look at this thing with a fresh eye. You and David have done so much together. You're a winning team. I remain convinced that it would be a tragedy for the company if the team were to break up."

Hirschfield sighed. "All right. I'll do this: In an effort not to appear to be just a totally stubborn human being, I'll think the whole thing through again. I'll reconsider in good faith. And I'll let you know Monday."

On Saturday morning, Todd Lang and Peter Gruenberger, the two principal lawyers, sipped coffee and munched pastry in the Hirschfields' sunny, art-adorned living room in Scarsdale. "What would the consequences be if I decided to bring him back?" Alan asked.

The question was not a total surprise to Lang and Gruenberger, who had sensed that the pressure on Hirschfield was growing torturous. Although their legal work for the corporation was scrupulously objective, Lang and Gruenberger personally were sympathetic to Hirschfield's plight. The resolution of the Begelman problem, as it had evolved, turned less on strictly legal issues than on issues of morality, philosophy, public relations, and business judgment. The core of Lang's advice, in fact, had been that *legally* the corporation could either reinstate Begelman or fire him, as long as it could show that its decision was rooted in "prudent business judgment," a well-established legal principle.

"Essentially, I have my choice of disasters," Hirschfield told the lawyers. "If I fire him, the board will be so down on me that my own days at the company will be numbered. They won't let me accomplish anything. If I bring him back, all the bad things we've talked about will probably happen—the publicity, the image, and so on and so forth. So let's suppose for the moment that I brought him back. How can we minimize the bad things?"

Lang began by reiterating the ramifications of the business-judgment rule. To protect itself against allegations of imprudence if it reinstated Begelman, Columbia among other things would probably have to deny him direct access to corporate funds. If Columbia were willing to take such a step, Lang said, there was a chance that it could reinstate Begelman without inordinate risk of acute public embarrassment and problems from the SEC.

Hirschfield told Lang and Gruenberger that he had to give the board his final decision by Monday and would let them know if there was any change in his stated anti-Begelman position.

It was noon. Hirschfield went upstairs to the privacy of his study and telephoned Herbert Allen at the Carlyle Hotel.

"I'm seriously considering taking David back into the company."

"That's great news, Alan."

"I haven't yet made up my mind for sure," Hirschfield said, "but I wanted you to know I'm reconsidering it and will let you know my final decision on Monday."

At home on Linden Drive in Beverly Hills, Begelman took a call from

David Geffen, who had remained close to both sides of the Begelman dispute.

"Are you happy?" Geffen asked.

"Happy about what?"

"Alan's going to reinstate you. Haven't you heard?"

"I've heard no such thing."

"It's not definite, but he's leaning heavily in that direction. The board essentially has given him no choice. They've got him by the throat."

"I thought everything was final," Begelman said. "I was just getting used to the idea of being an independent producer."

"Well, you can think again. You're probably going to be offered your job back. I suppose I should congratulate you, but in reality, David, I must tell you that I think it would be very unwise for you to return to this job. If you go back, you'll only succeed in drawing a great deal of attention to this situation, which thus far it hasn't attracted. Besides, if Alan does this number under extreme duress, and really doesn't want you, the job may not be worth having. The situation could get even worse than it is now."

Afterward, Begelman dialed the Hirschfield home. "Alan, I just got a call from David Geffen, who tells me that he understands that you are seriously considering reinstating me, that you've been under unbearable pressure from the board, and that in effect I'm being shoved down your throat. I just wanted you to know, first, that I've had nothing to do with any pressure on you, I've literally just found out about it within the last few minutes; and second, that I am fully prepared to go ahead and make that production arrangement. I feel it's probably the best thing for me, for you, and for everybody else under the circumstances."

"Well, David, I'm glad to hear you say these things. The fact is, I am reconsidering, and I don't know where I'm going to come out. It's a tough decision. It's become impossible for me to run the company the way things have been, and I'm really down to groping for a way to salvage the company itself at this point. But you've made it much easier by what you've said, and I appreciate it."

Hirschfield was flabbergasted. Could it be that, after more than two months of fighting tenaciously for his job, Begelman was giving up?

Later, the phone rang again. It was Herbert. Begelman had called him, too, and told him that he wanted to proceed with his independent production arrangement.

"I just wanted you to know, Alan, that if this is what David wants, then it's what I'll support. All I've ever wanted was what was good for David, and to make sure that he was treated fairly. If he's happy, then I'm happy."

"Wait a minute, Herbert. Too much has gone on here for this just to be sloughed off this easily. I think you should call David back and go over it with him again, and make sure that he's thought it through and is sure of his position."

Herbert called back in the late afternoon. Begelman had assured him that he meant what he had said.

"Look, Alan," Herbert said, "I know I've put pressure on you, but as far as I'm concerned it's all off if David wants to be an independent producer."

"I can't believe this is happening, Herbert. What about Matty and Ray? I've seen how hysterical Matty is. You've told me my relationship with him is irreparable. You've told me Ray isn't going to sign his new contract."

"I'll call Matty and Ray. They'll be all right once they know the circumstances."

"Would you mind calling Leo, too? I think he should hear this, and I think it would be appropriate if he heard it from you."

Hirschfield, production chief Dan Melnick, and financial officer Joe Fischer were seated around the coffee table in Hirschfield's office on Monday morning discussing candidates for the presidency of the studio when Leo Jaffe walked in. Jaffe looked stunned.

"Matty just called. He wants to know when the meeting is."

Hirschfield looked at Jaffe incredulously.

"What's he talking about? Didn't he hear from Herbert?"

"No. No one's contacted him."

"But the meeting's off. There is no meeting."

"That's what I told him—that everything is settled and there is no meeting to discuss it. He didn't know what I was talking about. He wants a meeting."

Hirschfield called Herbert Allen.

"We just heard from Matty. He wants to know when the meeting is. Didn't you speak to him?"

"No, I didn't speak to him."

"You said you were going to call him and tell him the meeting is off."

"Well, what's your decision?"

"What do you mean, what's my decision?"

"What's your decision on Begelman?"

"Herbert, you told me on Saturday that as far as you were concerned everything was settled. You were going to call Matty and Ray and there would be nothing to meet about."

"Well, I don't remember saying all that. If Matty wants to have a meeting, then there should be a meeting, and you really have to give your decision."

"Herbert, this isn't what we discussed! If you're changing your mind, tell me you're changing your mind. Or if something else has happened, tell me! Has Begelman had a change of heart?"

"I haven't spoken to him."

Furious and dumbfounded, Hirschfield slammed down the phone.

"Am I going crazy? This is the most bizarre conversation I've ever had with any human being. These people are determined to hold my feet to the fire. They're determined to make this thing as horrendous as they possibly can. Leo, thank God Herbert called you on Saturday so I've got a witness. Otherwise, it would be like I dreamed the whole weekend."

They were silent for a few moments. Then Melnick said, "You know what probably happened? Somebody must have gotten to David and Herbie and turned them around. Either Matty or Ray must have said something like, 'We've been fighting to get you back in. We've got Hirschfield on the ropes. He's reconsidering. And now you say you don't have the stomach for it. Well, screw you!' They won't let him stop at this point. And David is probably saying, 'Hey, I'm the one who may go to jail for this.'" (Stark later denied pressuring Begelman as Melnick speculated.)

Hirschfield finally telephoned both Allen and Rosenhaus and told them that his original decision stood.

"This is a tragedy for the company," Rosenhaus declared. "You're making a very serious mistake."

At one o'clock on Thursday, December 8, the board of directors of Columbia Pictures Industries assembled at 711 Fifth Avenue for its regular monthly meeting. Although the most important directors —Hirschfield, Rosenhaus, Allen, and Kramer—had conferred several times informally, the entire board had not been together in one room since November 16, when David Begelman had made his dramatic plea for mercy. Even though it had appeared briefly over the previous weekend that Hirschfield had won, Herbert Allen's position had hardened again by Monday, and by Thursday it was clear not only that the Begelman issue remained unresolved but that the authority crisis had deepened still further. The hatred in the boardroom was palpable.

Matty Rosenhaus proclaimed that if Begelman were not to return to the presidency of the studio, he must have producing and consulting arrangements that would "make him whole and happy" financially. "He has saved this company, and it's not his fault that he's not coming back," Rosenhaus declared.

Alan Hirschfield said: "I have an obligation to this board to tell you that it makes no sense to get into more trouble for giving away the store to Begelman than we would get into for bringing him back into the company. There are people out in the woods who would love to get their hands on this, and if it appears that we are rewarding him for his transgressions, we're all going to look like a bunch of fools."

"You're making too much out of this," Herbert Allen asserted. "Just go ahead and make a deal with him."

"It's not just another production deal, Herbert," Hirschfield responded.

"What do you mean, 'production deal'?" Rosenhaus shouted. "It's a production *and consulting* deal! Are you trying to make just a production deal?"

"No, Matty, I misspoke," Hirschfield retorted contemptuously. "It's obviously a production and consulting deal."

Rosenhaus proposed that Columbia Pictures purchase full-page advertisements in trade publications "thanking David Begelman for his enormous contributions to the company." Leo Jaffe suggested that if that were done, ads should also be run "thanking Alan Hirschfield for his leadership and contributions to the company." Herbert Allen responded: "Alan's still here. We don't need to take any ads for Alan right now." (No ads were taken for either man.)

Later in the meeting, Leo Jaffe presented for board approval a television production arrangement between Columbia's television company and two Hollywood producers. The deal had been approved by the top officers of the television company, as well as by Hirschfield and Jaffe, but it was standard procedure to clear such deals with the full board.

Matty Rosenhaus insisted that David Begelman's approval be sought before the board voted.

"But Matty," Hirschfield said, "this already has been approved by all the appropriate people."

"Are you afraid to let David express his opinion?" Rosenhaus asked.

"Matty, David's no longer with the company."

"Well, he's a consultant, isn't he?" Rosenhaus said. "We just authorized him to be a consultant. In that capacity, he should approve deals like this."

"Matty's right," Allen said. "That's a great suggestion. That's what we've got David as a consultant for. We'll really get our money's worth."

Leo Jaffe was instructed to go to his office and telephone Begelman in Los Angeles. Begelman blessed the TV deal.

Toward the end of the board meeting Herbert Allen reiterated his opinion that Dan Melnick was not capable of running the studio. Hirschfield reaffirmed his confidence in him.

"You'd better get the next Streisand movie," Allen said to Hirschfield.

"What do you mean, I'd better get it? Is that some sort of threat?"

"Never mind," Allen said. "Just be sure you get it."

The meeting ended after the board ordered Hirschfield to summon Begelman to New York immediately and conclude a production and consulting deal with him by the beginning of the following week.

"There no longer is a right answer and a wrong answer," Hirschfield said to his wife two days later—on Saturday evening, December 10. "There are only wrong answers. There are only bad decisions. As compelling as the arguments are against reinstating him, they lose a lot of their compelling quality when I see that if those arguments are followed it will be impossible for me to run the company. The board made it abundantly clear at the meeting on Thursday that it is willing to systematically undermine my ability to run the company, and that it is going to treat

Begelman as the president of the studio whether his title is president or only consultant. So what options do I have left? I can't and won't resign. It would be total surrender, and I'm not going to leave without a lot more of a fight than I've put up so far."

He paused.

"So it's quite possible that the only thing to do under the circumstances is to take him back. It's a short-term solution, like a shot of morphine to relieve the pain overnight; but if I don't take it, I may be dead by next week."

Begelman arrived at Alan Hirschfield's home at noon the next day. They shut themselves in the living room and, except for a bathroom break, did not leave for six hours. They talked about the production deal and the consulting Begelman would do, apart from producing films.

"If it was up to the board," Hirschfield said, "you're the de facto president of the company, so I guess you'll be a full-time consultant."

"Well, in my opinion, I have a large contribution to make. I can be very helpful."

"I'm sure that's the case. There's never been any question about your talents. But we can't run a company where someone else is president in title and someone else is the president in fact. We can't have the board running to you to second-guess every deal that the president of the studio or the president of TV wants to make."

Hirschfield recounted the board meeting of the previous Thursday. "There have been all kinds of threats and mandates laid down by the board," Hirschfield continued, "about how the company is to be run—the role you have to play, the role I have to play. I am in deep trouble with the board, and quite frankly, David, you are really no longer the issue here. I assume you've heard about Herbert's threats, and I assume you've heard about Ray's threats, and I assume you know about Berte and the threats that have been made against her."

Begelman professed ignorance of the details of the pressure on Hirschfield.

"Well, all of that has been a way of life here for the past couple of months," Hirschfield said. "Whether you come back or you don't come back, this is a contest of wills between me and Herbert Allen, and me and Matty Rosenhaus, but essentially Herbert, who feels that he has the right to call the shots as to who's going to run this company."

"Alan, perhaps I could be of help in repairing that damage. I'd be happy to do anything I can."

"I don't think there's anything you can do. You're simply a pawn at this point. But I must say that faced with the prospect of having you become a consultant and in effect run the company in that capacity without my direction, it might be better if you came back into the company and we tried to use that as a mechanism whereby perhaps we could put this whole thing to rest and get on with our lives. David, I cannot run this company this way. It's clear that I no longer have the backing."

"Look, I'll do anything you want. Obviously, more than anything else in the world I would like to come back. I'll give up everything I've asked for in terms of the independent arrangement. I know I can't have a new contract. I know I'll have to abide by my old contract. You just name the terms, and I'll sign the piece of paper."

At six o'clock, Hirschfield went across to the den and asked a bewildered Joe Fischer, who had been waiting there all afternoon, to summon lawyers Lang and Gruenberger, who had been on call nearby at Lang's home. With the five men assembled in the living room, Hirschfield asked the lawyers to reiterate the likely consequences of Begelman's return. They listed the well known risks. If Hirschfield wanted to change his mind, they would inform the staff of the Securities and Exchange Commission the next day.

"I want to think about it some more," Hirschfield said.

"Alan, please," Begelman pleaded, "I'll do whatever you want, but I must know for sure before I leave here. The uncertainty is tearing me apart."

Hirschfield stood by a window staring up into the cold starlit sky.

"Okay, I'll take him back."

David Begelman stood and embraced Hirschfield. "I won't let you down," he said.

Hirschfield telephoned Allen later that evening: "You've made him the de facto president of the company anyway. He might as well have the title. This is what you've always wanted. Maybe it'll give us an opportunity to repair some of the damage. He's coming back, unless I have a change of heart in the next few days."

Without responding to Hirschfield's anger, Allen said simply and gently: "I think that's terrific. That's the right decision. You two will work it out."

"It may not work out so well, Herbert. There's going to be a storm of publicity."

"It'll all blow over in a week."

"I hope so. I'm going to call Matty."

To Hirschfield's horror, Rosenhaus was angry.

"How could you do this? I thought you were going to negotiate a deal."

"Matty, we couldn't negotiate a deal. It was the wrong deal. It was an outrageous deal."

"There's nothing wrong with the deal. We can give him whatever we want. If you don't want him, you shouldn't bring him back."

"Look, Matty, this is what you wanted and you've got it! For better or worse, you've got it, Matty! I'm going to bring him back!"

A month later, Hirschfield, Begelman, and Fischer met at the studio to talk about a number of projects, among them *California Suite,* which Neil Simon had adapted from his play and which Ray Stark was producing for Columbia. Despite the potential appeal of the film's cast, which included Jane Fonda, Walter Matthau, and Richard Pryor, Hirschfield questioned whether the film stood much chance of making a profit, and posed the idea of selling a half interest in it to another studio. But Begelman, who had considerable faith in the project, staunchly opposed dividing it. They argued until nearly eight o'clock and decided to continue over dinner.

Bored with *California Suite*, Hirschfield began complaining about his fight with the board and with Matty Rosenhaus in particular.

"Matty says he doesn't trust me. He said to me, 'I never trusted you, Alan, from the day you came to this company.' How could Matty say a thing like that to me?"

"Alan, I don't know what passed between you two," Begelman said, "but I know what must pass in order to resolve this. You've got to make a speech to Matty that goes something like this: 'This has been a time for which no textbook has ever been written. Perhaps no one has acted as well as one would have liked, given the circumstances, but we must forget the events of the recent past. We must wipe the slate clean.' If you make that speech, I can't imagine a reasonable man in the world who won't say, 'Amen, okay, done!'"

"Matty's not a reasonable man."

"He's not so unreasonable that he wouldn't respond to a plea such as that," Begelman said.

"I think you're really underestimating the depths of their feelings," Hirschfield replied.

"No, I know their feelings are deep. They feel you misled them all the way through the investigation, and you did. People had reason to believe by the things you said or implied that you were going to be open-minded. If you were going to be open-minded, then they felt that, as a reasonable man, you were available for persuasion. But it turned out that your mind was made up all along. And yet you never let on that it was made up."

"It wasn't made up until all the evidence was in," Hirschfield said.

Warming to his subject, Begelman continued with his own speech, which he had been waiting for months to make.

"The one thing you were never able to say to me, Alan, man to man, was 'David, I don't want you back. Period.' Nicer than that, but clearly, in words that were unmistakable. They might have been sympathetic or commiserating words, but unequivocal. You never said that to me on the day I was placed on leave of absence. You never said that after the board meeting in November. We had breakfast the next morning, and you gave me reason to hope there was a chance. If you had said, on the advent of my leave of absence, 'We're going to go through this investigation because we have an obligation to our shareholders and to the Securities and Exchange Commission. If it's this and no more, then, in consideration of your seeking psychiatric assistance, in consideration of your past service to this company, in consideration of your ability to render further service to this company, we will make an arrangement that will see you self-employed as an independent producer making pictures for Columbia so that your talents and abilities will not be lost to us. But under no circumstances are you coming back to Columbia.' If you had said that, it would have been a *clear signal* to everyone—to me, but more important, to your associates, to Herbert, and to Matty. And none of this brouhaha would have gotten started. Since you did not make your position clear, the board, in the end, felt you had led them on a merry chase. They felt betrayed."

Hirschfield shrugged, sighed, and rolled his eyes. Chief executive officers had fired line officers for comments far less blunt and critical than those Begelman had just uttered.

Depressed, Hirschfield flew back to New York.

Six months later—after a media onslaught that finally forced David Begelman out of the company for good; after Hirschfield plotted secretly but vainly with several outsiders in an attempt to buy control of Columbia and overthrow Herbert Allen; after Begelman was sentenced to probation and a fine for his crime; after the revelation of another major embezzlement at the studio, this time by the eccentric chief accountant of Columbia's television-commercials company; after Begelman was named to produce the screen version of *Annie*, to the consternation of its Broadway creators; after Irwin Kramer infuriated Hirschfield by again raising the Berte issue, and was again assured by the lawyers that she was innocent; after Hirschfield accused the board in a formal letter of trying to discredit and harass him, improperly challenging his authority in breach of his contract; after the heads of Columbia's divisions assembled overnight in New York from two continents to confront the board of directors on his behalf—Alan Hirschfield was fired.

He spent several months at Warner Communications as a consultant, then moved to 20th Century-Fox, where, after another power struggle, he was named chairman and chief executive officer by Fox's new owner, oil baron Marvin Davis. He held that position at press time.

To replace Hirschfield at Columbia, Herbert Allen hired Francis T. "Fay" Vincent Jr., a Washington lawyer. Allen and Vincent retained Frank Price, whom Hirschfield and Melnick had hired, as head of the studio (Melnick followed Hirschfield to Fox) and withstood a determined effort by MGM owner Kirk Kerkorian to take control of Columbia. By early 1982, Allen, Vincent, and Price still had not equaled the record profits posted by the company in Hirschfield's last year. However, the Coca-Cola Company found Columbia attractive enough to buy it and left the incumbent management in place.

After less than a year as a producer, and his release from probation and the criminal charges against him, David Begelman was hired to head a rejuvenated film-making effort at MGM, which later bought United

Artists. Few of his films made money, however, and on July 12 of this year Begelman was removed from his job.

Ray Stark, his power underscored by the firing of Hirschfield, took over the *Annie* project. The film stands as the most expensive in Columbia's history.

The Securities and Exchange Commission's investigation of Columbia Pictures withered and died. Intense and brutal psychological warfare, involving gross displays of power and arrogance, does not necessarily violate the corporate and securities laws of the United States.

Vancouver Sun, February 25, 1984.

'King' Henry Fuels Iacocca's Rage

DETROIT (UPI)—Chrysler chairman Lee Iacocca says he will never forgive Henry Ford II for firing him and considers the Ford family wealthy snobs who "practiced the divine right of kings."

NBC will air Sunday the hour-long documentary Iacocca: An American Profile. In it, Iacocca takes on the Ford family and its aristocratic values.

Of his firing five years ago by Ford, Iacocca, over his dinner table, vows: "That's something I won't forgive the bastard for. I told my kids, 'Don't get mad, get even' . . . I did it in the marketplace. I wounded him badly. It took five years. I could have spilled my guts and maybe felt good inside if I'd done it in five minutes but then what have I proved?"

Earlier, Iacocca, the son of Italian immigrants, expresses bitterness toward the Ford family and its wealth and snobbery. "I knew how to make money for the company," Iacocca says of his lengthy career at Ford. "The Ford family practised the divine right of kings. They were a cut above even WASPs. I mean, they wouldn't even socialize with you, that's for sure. You could produce money for 'em but you weren't about to hobnob with 'em."

Ford, then chairman of the company his grandfather founded, abruptly fired Iacocca as Ford president in 1978. He is widely quoted as telling Iacocca at the time he simply didn't like him. Iacocca is credited with pulling Chrysler back from the brink of bankruptcy.

EPILOGUE

We call this an epilogue only because it comes at the end of the book. We intend it, however, as a prologue to the reader's own independent consideration of what we called in the introduction, the shadow side of organizations. After all, even though we introduced this book by noting its value for visitors from a foreign planet, our purpose was to affect Earthlings.

It seems to us, in retrospect, that the origins of this book and our decisions about what to include in it were guided by an underlying perspective or an unconscious spirit that the three of us shared initially and developed as we worked. This perspective or spirit continues to shape how we deal with organizations—both personally and professionally. Before concluding, we want to make this perspective or spirit explicit and invite our readers to make it an active part of the way they approach organizations.

Behavioral scientists view organizations as open social systems. Some emphasize that organizations are different from other social systems because they are deliberately constructed to achieve some purpose(s). Our perspective stresses an additional descriptor—organizations are *human* systems.

While seemingly trite, the emphasis added by the label *human* is important because it stimulates us to expect and to take seriously the full range of human motives and experiences that exist in organizations. Recognition that organizations contain and express all aspects of humanness has several consequences.

First, we see how incomplete any one intellectual perspective will be as a guide to understanding organizations.

Second, we come to see the importance of the trivial. The contemporary state of any human system is the product of many small events—the failure to tell Sally Quinn what the red light on the TV camera meant and Alan Hirschfield's announcing a decision by phone instead of face-to-face are but two examples that we saw in this book of how important the seemingly trivial can be. Exactly how to be sensitive to and manage the trivial without becoming obsessed and dominated by it, is a major issue for managers that seldom is accorded the attention it deserves either in business schools or elsewhere.

Third, the emphasis on fully human systems sensitizes us to the continuity between life in organizations and life. Just as life contains tragedy and comedy, love and hate, war and peace, and reason and emotion, so do and so must organizations. An adequate understanding of organizations must recognize this complexity.

Finally, and most important, recognition of the fully human nature of organizations makes learning about them a continuous process built on the data that are the substance of our daily being. In this light many movies, plays, and other artistic expressions; most newspapers and magazine articles; a large percentage of our contacts with other people; and of course the daily experiences that all of us have as members of organizations, become additional chapters of *Organizational Reality*.